TRAVELLERS
AUSTRALIA &
NEW ZEALAND
SURVIVAL KIT

SUSAN GRIFFITH
and
SIMON CALDER

Published by Vacation Work, 9 Park End Street, Oxford

TRAVELLERS SURVIVAL KIT —
AUSTRALIA & NEW ZEALAND
by Susan Griffith & Simon Calder

Copyright © Vacation Work 1988

ISBN 0 907638 88 0 (softback)
ISBN 0 907638 89 9 (hardback)

Cover Design
Mel Calman

Miller Craig & Cocking Design Partnership

Chapter headings, logos and maps by William Swan

Cartoons by Patrick Ayoub

Distributed in New Zealand by David Bateman Ltd.,
PO Box 65062, Auckland 10, New Zealand

Printed by **Gibbons Barford Print**, Wolverhampton, England

Contents

AUSTRALIA

NEW ZEALAND

Maps

Preface

In both Australia and New Zealand you can eat the same food, drink the same beers and speak roughly the same language as in Britain and North America. Yet both are delightfully alien and unpredictably unique in so many ways that more and more people are deciding that a trip is well worth the investment. The America's Cup in 1987 and the Australian Bicentenary of 1988, with all the attendant publicity, have been partly responsible for boosting the number of travellers to Australia, to the point that for the first time visitors going as tourists to see the country now outnumber those going to see their relations. Not to be outdone, New Zealand has just announced that it expects over a million visitors a year (equivalent to a third of its population) by 1990. The word is getting around: with far more than their fair share of natural wonders and colourful characters, these surprisingly undiscovered countries can offer a uniquely enjoyable and satisfying holiday.

The urban areas have all the familiar trappings of modern life, yet the cosmopolitan charm of Sydney or Auckland and the easy pace of Cairns or Christchurch have a refreshing and irresistible appeal. Travelling beyond cosy suburbia soon brings you to some fascinating places, since both Australia and New Zealand encompass extraordinary landscapes and distinctive flora and fauna. Though you may doubt the repeated claims that Antipodeans are among the most friendly and hospitable people in the world, your doubts are likely to be dispelled after a few encounters, if only with a bank clerk who is curious about your travel plans or a bus driver who cracks a joke.

Whether you intend merely to dip a toe in the Indian Ocean or to immerse yourself in the culture by finding a job (perhaps with a view to starting a new life down under), the *Travellers Survival Kit: Australia and New Zealand* will help you to find real bargains in travel, accommodation and entertainment, and the best ways to explore the Great Outdoors. This book also provides the survival information promised in the title, which will help you to cope with a multiplicity of nasties: from spiders to crocodiles, flash floods to bush fires — no worries.

Simon Calder and Susan Griffith
January, 1988

Acknowledgments

Many individuals and organizations have co-operated with the writing of this book. In particular, the assistance of Dr Deirdre Coleman and Steve Rout has been invaluable. Alison Baker, Sandra Gray and Simon Whalley each made a substantial contribution to the chapters on *Melbourne & Victoria, Tasmania* and *Perth & Western Australia,* respectively. Bill Best reported on his experiences cycling around Australia, while Anne Hogan helped with work on northern Australia. We are also especially grateful for the comments and criticisms of the following Australian and New Zealand residents who, besides supplying insights and information about their countries, often gave generously of their hospitality during our visits to Australasia:

Armin Birrer, Lee Coleman, Liz Conlon, Stephen Collocott, Michael De Hamel, Rob and Hilary Fraser, Ron and Rene Harris, Fran Hattam, Alyson Holcroft, Graham Ley, Corinne Lloyd, Cynthia Millar, Graham Palmer, the Railton family, Teresa Rodrigues, Alan Tucker, Sue Uniacke, Jenny Vanderlelie, Pat and Lindsay Watson and Hugh and Jane White.

In addition we wish to thank the host of travellers to Australia and New Zealand who willingly shared their discoveries and impressions with us, among them:

William Barnett, David Bishop, Stuart Britton, Ian Fleming, Alexandra Green, Stephen Hardy, Fiona Hattersley-Smith, Mary Kostin, Andy Smith, Martin Spiers, Gordon Turnbull, Leah Whittaker and Mel Wills.

We have made every effort to ensure that the information contained in this book was accurate at the time of going to press, but some details are bound to change within the lifetime of this edition. In particular, inflation is substantial in both Australia (nearly 10%) and New Zealand (over 15%), and so prices quoted should therefore be adjusted upwards accordingly as time passes.

We intend to revise and update the *Travellers Survival Kit: Australia and New Zealand* regularly, and are very keen to hear comments, criticisms and suggestions from both natives and travellers. Please write to Susan Griffith and Simon Calder at Vacation Work, 9 Park End St, Oxford OX1 1HJ. Those whose contributions are used will be sent a complimentary copy of the next edition.

BEFORE YOU GO

RED TAPE

Passports. A full ten-year passport is required for travel to both Australia and New Zealand. Application forms are available from post offices and should be sent with the appropriate fee, photographs and supporting documents to your regional passport office. Allow at least one month for processing by mail. If you're in a tearing hurry or realize your existing passport is soon to expire, you can usually obtain one more quickly in person if you're prepared to queue all day at a passport office.

For visits to Australia, your passport should have a minimum of three months to run, and have two blank facing pages for the visa and entry/departure stamps. If you intend to visit New Zealand, the expiry date of the passport should be at least three months beyond your intended date of *departure* from that country. This rule is not rigidly enforced but nonetheless could be used as a reason to deny you entry.

If your passport is lost or stolen while travelling, contact first the police then your nearest Consulate. Obtaining replacement travel documents is easier if you have a record of the passport number and its date and place of issue.

Visas for Australia. New Zealanders, diplomats and members of the British Royal Family apart, all visitors to Australia require a visa which must be obtained in advance from a High Commission or Consulate. No charge is made for tourist or business visas. To get one, you need an application form (M48) available from many travel agents or from any Australian diplomatic mission, including:

United Kingdom: Visa Section, Australian High Commission, Strand, London WC2B 4LA (01-379 4334); Australian Consulate, Chatsworth House, Lever St, Manchester M1 2DL (061-228 1344); Australian Consulate, 80 Hanover St, Edinburgh EH2 2DL (031-226 6271).

Irish Republic: Australian Embassy, Wilton Terrace, Dublin 2 (tel: 761517).

United States: Australian Embassy, 1601 Massachusetts Ave, Washington DC 20036; or Consulates in Chicago, Honolulu, Houston, Los Angeles, New York and San Francisco.

Canada: Australian High Commission, National Building, 130 Slater St, Ottawa K1P 5H6.

New Zealand: Australian High Commission, 72-78 Hobson St, Thorndon (PO Box 12145), Wellington.

You are strongly advised to complete the visa application truthfully (including the questions on criminal convictions and contagious diseases), since the Australian authorities have been known to go to extreme lengths to check the veracity of your replies. They may, for example, phone your employer or run your name through a computer.

The completed application form must be submitted to a High Commission or Consulate together with your passport and two photographs. If you apply for a visa through a travel agent or by post you can expect to wait up to four weeks, assuming your documents are in order; if there is any problem, the time scale increases substantially. Personal application is time-consuming and tedious, but essential if you are short of time; apart from the peace of mind granted by having your visa safely inside your passport, any problems with your application can be sorted out on the spot. If you submit a visa application to the High Commission in London before 3pm, you can normally pick it up between 4pm and 5pm on the same day or any subsequent working day. The queues are longest from September to December. If you can't get to an Australian mission yourself, there are visa agencies such as the Visa Shop (44 Chandos Place, London WC2; tel: 01-379 0419) and Rapid Visa Service (15 Hogarth Road, London SW15; tel: 01-373 3026) which charge around £9 to do the leg work for you and can obtain a visa in a few days.

As of January 1988, a visitors' visa will allow you to enter Australia as often as you like, at any time during the life of your passport. Most foreigners (including North Americans) are permitted to stay up to three months, but British passport holders usually get six months. Travellers intending to work during their stay should see page 41 for information about the working holiday visa.

Note that an Australian visa is no more than a permit to apply for entry to the country. For details of entry procedures when you get there, see *Red Tape* at the start of the Australian section. In particular your prospects of a smooth passage through Immigration are enhanced if the details you provide on the landing card match those you supplied when applying for a visa.

Visas for New Zealand. Holders of British, Irish, Canadian or US passports do not require a visa for short visits, providing they carry proof of onward or return travel. British passport holders are generally allowed to stay six months, other nationalities three months. If you lack the required proof of a ticket out of the country (perhaps you intend to find a yacht to crew across the Pacific) you can buy a suitable ticket in advance with a credit card, then — once New Zealand immigration has been successfully cleared — return it to the issuing airline for a full refund to your account.

Travellers intending to stay longer than three or six months, or to work should consult a New Zealand High Commission or Consulate such as:

United Kingdom: New Zealand House, Haymarket, London SW1Y 4TQ (tel: 01-930 8422).

United States: New Zealand Embassy, 37 Observatory Circle, NW, Washington DC 20008 (tel: 202-320-4800).

Canada: New Zealand High Commission, Metropolitan House, 99 Bank St, Ottawa K1P 6G3 (tel: 613-238-5991).

Australia: New Zealand High Commission, Commonwealth Ave, Canberra, ACT 2600 (tel: 062-73 3611).

Migration. If you enter either country as a tourist (or Australia on a working holiday visa), you will not be able to apply for permanent residence unless you get married to a citizen of the country you choose, and furthermore can prove to the satisfaction of the authorities that it is not a marriage of convenience. Failing that, if you wish to migrate you must approach the authorities well in advance of your intended departure from home.

For nearly 200 years, almost any British subject could obtain the right of residence in Australia and New Zealand. Many enjoyed free or cheap travel to Australia whether as convicts or as beneficiaries of the "assisted passage" scheme under which you could buy a one-way ticket for just £10. Now things are much tougher. Only 120,000 carefully selected immigrants were allowed into Australia in 1987, and considerably fewer make the grade in New Zealand.

To be chosen from the million-plus who apply to live in Australia each year, you need to score a high number of points gained by such attributes as age, higher education and a skill such as computer programming or refrigerator repairs. It is also of considerable benefit if you have family in Australia willing to sponsor you. If you want to apply for permanent residence, you must complete a migration form (available from High Commissions and Consulates) and submit it with an initial fee of A$60. If you meet the strict criteria for admission, there is a further fee of A$165 for final processing of the application and an immigration charge of $5 when you arrive in Australia. The Australian immigration authorities are discussing the possibility of compulsory screening of prospective migrants for HIV, the virus which causes the disease AIDS.

Similarly, people hoping to migrate to New Zealand must jump through a number of hoops before they are accepted. Assuming you do not have close family in New Zealand, you will have to qualify on occupational grounds, as well as being of good character and sound health. A copy of the current Occupational Priority List, which includes such professions as boatbuilding and psychiatric nursing, can be obtained from the Migration Branch of New Zealand's diplomatic missions, along with leaflet L71-*Permanent Residence in New Zealand*.

There are signs, however, that controls and quotas may soon be eased: in the light of falling birth rates in each country, the governments have been gradually increasing quotas to avoid the threat of a diminishing and ageing population.

Vaccinations. If you have visited an area where Yellow Fever is endemic (parts of Africa and Latin America) within the six days before you arrive in Australia or New Zealand, you are required to produce a valid certificate of inoculation against the disease. There is a possibility that Australia may soon follow the lead of some other countries and insist upon all visitors (not just migrants) carrying a certificate showing them to be free of the AIDS virus. A recent survey in the Melbourne *Age* showed that three in five Australians were in favour of such compulsory tests.

INSURANCE

It is quite possible to survive a trip to Australia and New Zealand without insurance. The most important reason for travel insurance elsewhere in the world is for emergency health care. But emergency treatment in Australia is free for all visitors, and both countries have a reciprocal agreement with the UK whereby free hospital treatment is provided for British citizens. Some literature put out by the New Zealand tourist authority appears to contradict this by suggesting that all visitors should be covered by insurance, but the DHSS leaflet SA30 *Medical Costs Abroad* clearly states that in-patient treatment is free to British visitors. Further details on medical treatment may be found under *Health* in the introductions to both countries.

Crime levels in both countries are relatively low, so insurance against theft might be regarded as an expensive luxury. And if you have the misfortune to be involved in an accident in New Zealand, you can benefit from the government scheme which compensates every victim, regardless of the cause and their nationality. All in all, it is unlikely that travelling uninsured will bring about financial ruin. Even so, insuring yourself and your possessions can prove beneficial, since only a minimum of care and compensation is provided free of charge. For visitors from North America, who do not benefit from the reciprocal medical agreements, insurance is strongly recommended.

The cover provided by most policies is fairly standard: delay and cancellation insurance of up to £2,500; around £250,000 for medical expenses and emergency repatriation; the same amount for personal liability; £20,000 for permanent disablement cover; lost or stolen baggage up to £1,000 (sometimes valuable single items are excluded); and cash to a maximum of £250. Every airline, tour operator and travel agent is delighted to sell you insurance because of the high level of commission (sometimes over 40%) it earns them. Shopping around can save money or get you better cover for the same premium. In particular, Endsleigh Insurance (Cheltenham Spa, Glos GL50 3NR) offer good rates for their worldwide ISIS scheme. In 1987, for example, one month of cover from most travel agents cost around £40, but Endsleigh charged only £25.50 for a similar policy. The ISIS policy is available in the USA from the Student Travel Network, Suite 507, 2500 Wilshire Boulevard, Los Angeles, CA 90057 (tel: 213-380-2184), SOFA, 17 East 45th St, New York, NY 10017 (tel: 212-986-9470) or campus offices of the Council on International Educational Exchange. In Canada, the ISIS policy may be bought from offices of the Canadian Universities Travel Service, whose head office is at 187 College St, Toronto, Ontario M5T 1P7.

If you stay longer than expected, you can buy a new policy from any insurance broker in Australia or New Zealand, but note that these policies do not cover the cost of flying you home for medical treatment. You can also insure yourself as required for risky activities such as skiing or scuba diving, for which a more expensive policy covering dangerous sports is required.

Three groups of travellers are automatically insured. Clients of some travel agents receive several weeks' insurance with full-price air tickets, effectively giving a discount on the air fare. Holders of Diners Club cards (annual subscription £20) who use the card to pay for travel or accommodation expenses receive full cover; note that this is substantially better than the travel accident insurance provided by most credit card companies which merely gives compensation for accidents while in transit. Members of the British Airways Executive Club receive travel insurance as a free benefit of membership; there is no requirement to travel on BA. The annual subscription of £55 compares well with the cost of two months' cover, and provides insurance for an unlimited number of trips.

If you are unfortunate enough to have to claim on your insurance, the golden rule is to amass as much documentation as possible to support your application. In particular, compensation is unlikely to be paid for lost baggage or cash unless your claim is accompanied by a police report of the loss.

GETTING THERE ... AND BACK

For most people, the cost of reaching Australia or New Zealand is the biggest obstacle to going there. Certainly a full-fare return ticket from London to Australia (costing £2,120 in economy, £4,196 for first class) is beyond the budget of most. But fares per mile to the Antipodes can be among the lowest in the world. Many British travellers opt for the excursion fares offered on British Airways, Qantas and Air New Zealand, which range from £747 for a low-season round trip from London to Perth to £1,295 for a high-season return ticket from

Manchester to Auckland. These tickets can be bought from any High Street travel agent, and the only condition is that you stay away for at least two weeks. There are no advance booking requirements, and you can change flight timings (but not your route) at will; the ticket is valid for a year and if you decide to cancel before setting off you can get a full refund. You can fly in to one city and back from another, and take advantage of free stopovers in Asia or North America.

People in the USA and Canada do not yet benefit from the cheap tickets available to the British, and may begrudge paying almost as much to fly to Australasia as a Londoner who has flown twice as far. To make matters worse, the cheapest tickets from North America to Australia and New Zealand are hedged with restrictions such as advance booking requirements and heavy cancellation penalties. But competition is increasing, so fares may soon fall below their current levels.

From Britain. London is the cheap fare capital of the world. The economics of international air travel throw up all sorts of anomalies, many of them to the advantage of those who want to include other destinations as well as Australia and New Zealand. For example it is not significantly more expensive to fly from London to Brisbane, Sydney or Melbourne with a stopover in Tokyo than it is to fly only to the Japanese capital. Round-the-world tickets are also worth investigating; see below for sample fares.

The price of a ticket is determined by the date of your outbound flight. Not surprisingly, everyone seems to want to escape from the Northern Hemisphere to Australasia as soon as temperatures start falling. The peak season for outward travel is September plus the two weeks before Christmas. For the lowest price, you should travel out between March and June, the season classed as "basic". The next cheapest is off-peak, comprising February, July and the week from Christmas Eve to New Year's Eve. The remaining times are "shoulder" season, costing a little less than peak. At times you may find it difficult getting a seat: the worst periods are peak season (when it seems everyone wants to travel, regardless of cost) and the first few days after a drop in fares, e.g. early March and October. It is wise to book a seat as early as possible, bearing in mind that you can usually change the date without penalty.

There is a score of airlines which will fly you from London to Australasia. The various companies clamouring for your custom include the obvious ones like British Airways, Air New Zealand and Qantas, plus less well-known carriers such as Garuda Indonesia and Philippine Airlines. Your choice of airline will determine the stopovers you may take, from Dallas to Delhi and Bangkok to Bali; furthermore, the fares on Third World and North American carriers are often substantially cheaper than on European and Australasian airlines.

The rock-bottom basic return fare from London to Melbourne or Sydney being offered by discount travel agencies (bucket shops) at the time of going to press was £650 on Garuda. (One-way fares on most airlines are usually about 60% of the return fare.) Good deals are also available on other Asian airlines such as Air India, Thai International and Malaysian Air Systems (MAS), and on the American airline Continental. Most of these services take 28 hours or more from London and require a change of aircraft en route, although they also allow some interesting stopovers. You might also find a bargain on a combination flight via Singapore, e.g. Royal Jordanian then MAS to Sydney or Melbourne, or Aeroflot then British Airways to Adelaide or Perth. There is often a sweetener such as a night or two in a Singapore hotel thrown in. Possibly the best deal for those who live far from London or Manchester is to travel on Canadian Airlines International via Toronto or Vancouver. This airline has no flights into Britain, so instead the carrier will throw in a flight from any airport in the UK which has direct flights to Amsterdam. These can be as far away as Aberdeen, Belfast or Teesside.

In order to come to grips with the many permutations of season, route and airline, you should find a travel agency which specializes in long-haul flights to Australia and New Zealand. Consult the advertisements in the quality press or magazines such as *Time Out, LAM, New Australasian Express, TNT* and *New Zealand News UK*. The following agencies are particularly recommended:

> STA Travel, 74 Old Brompton Road, London SW7 3LQ (01-581 1022); STA has offices all over Australia, plus a couple in New Zealand, which can be useful if your travel plans change.
> REHO Travel, 15-17 New Oxford St, London WC1A 1BH (01-242 5555); REHO also has offices in Melbourne and Sydney.
> Trailfinders, 42-48 Earls Court Road, London W8 6EJ (01-603 1515). Trailfinders is the largest independent retail agent in Europe, and has a hi-tech computer system linked with over 600 airlines worldwide. The company specializes in tailor-made itineraries for independent travellers, and can offer a very wide range of routes and destinations for every class of travel. As well as low-cost air fares, backed by all the necessary licences and bonds, Trailfinders has its own travel insurance (underwritten at Lloyds) and a range of other in-house services for the traveller. For those planning stopovers in exotic locations en route to Australia or New Zealand, there is a free medical advisory service (linked by computer to the database of the London School of Hygiene and Tropical Medicine) and an on-site Immunization Centre. The Trailfinders travellers' library and information service is free to clients and includes up-to-date material on everything from climate and visa information to timetables of local buses and trains at a wide range of destinations around the world. There are two dedicated library staff, and you can also seek advice from any of the consultants who between them have visited almost every corner of the globe. Finally, clients booking long-haul flights are entitled to the free Trailfinders Travel Pass, which gives discounts of up to 50% on ground arrangements booked before or during your trip: the pass can be used to save money on hotels, local buses, car hire, etc. in Australia, New Zealand and many places along the way.

Don't be alarmed when your discount ticket shows a fare which bears little relation to the amount it cost you; typically, it might show the official excursion fare of £995 for a ticket for which you have actually paid only £750. This is an administrative convenience designed to circumvent international air regulations. You won't be asked to pay the difference, but your ticket will be endorsed to prevent you cashing it in at face value.

Despite the extremely competitive fares offered by other airlines, there are several advantages in flying on the more reputable international airlines. At the time of writing, the fastest way to get to Sydney from London is on British Airways or Qantas flights which stop only once, at Bangkok, and take under 22 hours for the whole journey. During 1988/89 it should become possible to fly non-stop from London to Perth aboard the new Boeing 747-400 (the one with the wing tips bent upwards). Thus a journey which once took 15 months will become a 15-hour hop, and Australia will be only two in-flight meals and a couple of movies away. Singapore International Airlines (SIA) are next fastest at present, and offer a one-stop service to other Australian cities. SIA currently has the quickest services to Auckland and Christchurch in New Zealand.

These three carriers, plus Air New Zealand, have a good range of cheap stopover packages from Tahiti to Thailand. These are often subsidized to attract passengers; for example you can sometimes arrange to stay one night in a top Singapore hotel for £12. Qantas has the advantage of being the safest airline in the world, and offers its passengers a free "Qantas Connections" card. This card is available to anyone who books a return journey to Australia with over half the travel on Qantas. It is valid for one year from your departure date and offers savings on a wide range of goods and services within Australia and in the stopover destinations served by Qantas. Full details can be obtained in Britain by calling the Qantas Connections Hotline (toll-free) on 0800-444114.

Passengers on both Qantas and British Airways qualify for the Circle Australia fare, an add-on to excursion tickets which allows you four flights between Australian cities for only £100 more than the fare from London. Each flies on certain routes within Australia, but you are restricted to the services of the airline on which you fly in to Australia. This may not prove as good a deal as it sounds, since neither airline has a comprehensive network around Australia (there are no Qantas flights between Adelaide and Melbourne, for example), so you would need to study their schedules before selecting this option. In 1987, Air New Zealand and British Airways offered a similar deal in New Zealand, where for £845 return from London, you could fly to Auckland or Christchurch and back, with four domestic flights thrown in. This offer proved popular and so may well be repeated.

If you intend to travel via the USA on any service other than Air New Zealand's direct London-Auckland flights via Dallas or Los Angeles, you *must* hold a valid US visa (and, incidentally, pay a US$8 Customs User fee). There are no transit facilities for passengers connecting from one international flight to another, which means you must clear American customs and immigration before checking in for the connecting flight.

A very good way to visit both Australia and New Zealand is on a round-the-world (RTW) ticket. The lowest fares from discount travel agents (such as the three listed above) at the time of going to press were around £800, in contrast to the £1,250-plus RTW fares sold direct by airlines. For about £900, for example, you can get a RTW discount ticket combining the services of Thai International and Canadian Airlines International, visiting Bangkok and Vancouver as well as Australia and New Zealand.

The idea of becoming a casual air courier might appeal to those who are prepared to travel with only hand luggage and to put up with a few inconveniences. Unfortunately free or heavily subsidized flights are no longer available, though IML Air Services (Astronaut House, Hounslow Road, Feltham, Middlesex; tel: 01-890 8888) were recently recruiting one-off couriers to fly Qantas to Sydney for between £500 and £600 return.

From North America. Cities with direct air services to Australia and New Zealand include Vancouver, San Francisco, Los Angeles, San Diego, Dallas and Honolulu. The main gateways are Auckland, Christchurch, Cairns, Brisbane, Sydney and Melbourne. Most services are operated by Air New Zealand, Canadian Airlines, Continental, Qantas and United Airlines. The cheapest way to reach Australia or New Zealand is with an advance purchase ticket, which must be bought three weeks before travel and has heavy cancellation penalties. From North America, peak season operates during May, August and September, with the lowest fares in March, October and November. Not surprisingly, the cheapest ticket is from Honolulu (about US$500 low season,

$750 peak to Auckland); for a return flight between Los Angeles and Sydney, expect to pay at least US$1,100.

Between Australia and New Zealand. If you can, buy a ticket from your home country which includes travel to both Australia and New Zealand rather than buy a ticket locally. The lowest return fare between the two countries is about A$375 or NZ$450, whereas the trans-Tasman journey can usually be added to an international ticket for less.

Getting Back. Australia has a lively discount air travel market, and fares to Europe and back can be even cheaper than tickets bought in Europe (partly helped by the favourable exchange rate at the time of writing). Therefore if you intend to travel twice in a year, buy a return ticket in Australia for the middle flights. Prices quoted for low season travel in 1988 included A$1,299 (less than £600) return to London from Sydney or Melbourne or NZ$1,699 to London and back from New Zealand. Round-trip fares to the west coast of North America started at A$950 from eastern Australia or NZ$999 from Auckland. To get the best deal, consult one of the discount travel agencies listed under *Arrival and Departure* in each regional chapter or keep a close eye on newspaper advertisements. Don't be tempted to buy an unused ticket from another traveller, since the details on your passport will be checked against the name on the ticket or boarding pass and you will be prevented from travelling if there is a discrepancy.

Sea. CTC Lines sells tickets for occasional sailings from Southampton to Sydney via Singapore aboard Soviet cruise ships. The journey takes five weeks, and the fare of £1,750 includes a free air ticket back to London. The London office of CTC is at 1 Regent St, SW1Y 4NN (tel: 01-930 5833). To reduce the cost and the time taken, you can fly out as far as Hong Kong or Singapore and start your cruise to Australia from there: the Far East Travel Centre (3 Lower John St, London W1A 4XE; tel: 01-734 7050) will get you to Perth, Melbourne or Sydney for as little as £605 one-way from London. If you fancy taking a slow boat home from Australia, contact Cunard Travel, 447 Kent St, Sydney, NSW 2000 (tel: 267 6945).

Crewing on yachts is a slow but pleasurable way to travel to or from Australasia. Skippers of private yachts often need casual crew for voyages between Singapore or Bali and the north and west of Australia, notably Darwin and Fremantle. There are also plenty of boats sailing between South Pacific islands and New Zealand. Be prepared to share expenses unless you are an experienced sailor.

MONEY

It helps if you take your funds in a mixture of cash, travellers cheques and credit or charge cards, since each has its advantages and drawbacks. Australian or New Zealand currency can be ordered through your bank, or you can wait until you arrive at the destination airport where exchange facilities are open for every flight arriving from abroad. Foreign currency (including Australian dollars in New Zealand and vice-versa) will need to be changed at a bank or *bureau de change* before you can spend anything. While this is no problem in big cities or in tourist towns such as Cairns and Rotorua, it might be difficult to persuade a small country bank to change foreign notes or travellers cheques. In such circumstances, a credit card can be a flexible friend. If you anticipate having to have money sent to you from home, see page 50.

Travellers Cheques. Australian dollar travellers cheques can be obtained through banks and travel agencies (particularly American Express and Thomas Cook) and are changed for face value by banks in Australia. Most visitors, however, buy their travellers cheques in sterling or US dollars and exchange them as their supply of cash dwindles.

The most easily negotiable travellers cheques are American Express, Thomas Cook and Visa. Using American Express travellers cheques has the added advantage of entitling you to use their customer mail service (the addresses for mail collection are given in the regional chapters). They are sold by Lloyd's Bank and the Royal Bank of Scotland in Britain, and by many North American banks. Account holders of the Leeds Permanent Building Society are entitled to commission-free American Express cheques; if you don't have an account, you are at liberty to open one with, say, £500 in cash then withdraw it immediately in the form of travellers cheques, saving the normal £5 commission on the cheques. Visa cheques are issued by Barclay's, the Co-op, Yorkshire and the Trustee Savings Bank in the UK, and by Deak Perera in the USA. Thomas Cook cheques can be bought at branches of the Midland Bank as well as at Thomas Cook travel agencies and *bureaux de change.*

Carry your passport as ID when changing travellers cheques, although you might not always be asked to show it if the bank has the appropriate computer information on lost or stolen cheques. Keep a separate record of the cheques you have, and where and when the last was cashed. Note the emergency phone numbers provided with the cheques so that if you lose the cheques you can claim a refund quickly and easily. American Express normally issue replacements for their travellers cheques as soon as you have completed a form at one of their offices. But if you don't have the numbers of the cheques (or you have an obscure brand), it can take several days. There is no charge for replacing lost or stolen travellers cheques.

Cheques. Unless you have a charge card which allows you to cash cheques against it (see below), or you think you might be able to persuade an Australasian branch of your own bank to cash a cheque, a foreign cheque book is virtually useless. Details of how to open a bank account in Australasia are given under *Money* in the Australia and New Zealand sections.

Credit and Charge Cards. Credit cards are very popular in Australasia and many enterprises — from Australian taxi drivers to New Zealand youth hostels — accept them. A card is also an accepted guarantee of your financial reliability when hiring cars, booking hotel rooms or possibly even clearing immigration. Since plastic cards can prove so useful, it would be unfortunate to run up against your credit limit or to fail to pay the sum required each month. Therefore if you're going to be away from home for more than a few weeks, you should make arrangements with a friend or relation at home to make the appropriate payments, or send in regular cheques by post yourself. Keep a separate record of the numbers of your cards and the emergency telephone line to call in case of loss or theft. Report any loss to the local police and call the card company collect.

When you use a card at establishments in Australasia, don't be alarmed if you have to wait while the number is cleared with the issuing company; checks for stolen or abused cards are more frequent than in Britain. Increasingly many enterprises have terminals linked to bank computers which make this check automatically and also print out an instant sales voucher. Foreign Access/MasterCard and Visa cards are accepted in most places which take the Australasian credit card *Bankcard*. You can also use these cards to draw cash at banks displaying the appropriate Visa or Access/MasterCard symbol, though cash advances incur a service charge or interest immediately. Fewer establishments accept American Express and Diners Club cards, and you can't use charge cards to withdraw cash as you can with credit cards. However, American Express offices will cash cheques for their cardholders, and Diners Club members can cash cheques at branches of Citibank.

PLANNING AHEAD

This book should give you some good ideas about where to go, how to travel and so on. But you can supplement this with information on specific interests — from Aboriginal culture to zoology — by contacting Australian or New Zealand tourist offices before you go. They can also help with comprehensive lists of accommodation, details of available tours, etc., allowing you to plan some or all of your itinerary. In addition, members of motoring organizations should ask for free information on driving and services provided by affiliated organizations in Australasia. And even if the idea of staying in a Youth Hostel is anathema to you, you are strongly advised to join your local Youth Hostels Association. Many enterprises in Australia and New Zealand, from bus companies to cafés, give good discounts to YHA members, which makes the price of membership well worthwhile.

Some of the best unlimited travel deals by air and bus are available only to people who book and pay for them abroad. Look under *Getting Around* for each country to see the offers available and details of how to book. In particular, if you intend to fly around New Zealand you should buy the tickets you require in advance to avoid the 10% tax on tickets bought in New Zealand.

Australia. For a country of just over 16 million inhabitants, Australia produces a remarkable range of information for tourists. Its international publicity organization Tourism Australia produces an annual *Travellers Guide* with different versions aimed at travellers from the UK and Ireland, the USA and Canada, etc. The British edition can be obtained by post from the Tourism Australia Distribution Department, Park Farm Road, Folkestone, Kent CT19 5DZ, or ordered by telephone on 01-434 4371. North Americans can obtain their edition from the Tourism Australia addresses below. As well as the statutory glossy pictures and glowing text, the *Travellers Guide* contains a great deal of hard information: from the telephone numbers of major National Parks to long-distance railway timetables. It also has coupons for requesting specific information from tourist offices or tour operators. Other information can be obtained from one of Tourism Australia's offices around the world, including the following:

United Kingdom: Fourth Floor, Heathcoat House, 20 Savile Row, London W1X 1AE (01-434 4371).
United States: 31st Floor, 489 Fifth Avenue, New York, NY 10117 (212-687-6300); Suite 1200, 2121 Avenue of the Stars, Los Angeles, CA 90067 (213-552-1988).
Canada: 120 Eglinton Avenue, Toronto, Ontario M4P 1E2 (416-487-2126).

In addition, each of the mainland states has a government office in London whose primary task is to increase trade rather than to promote tourism, but they also have tourism departments and are worth contacting. It helps if you can be as specific as possible about the information you need, otherwise you can expect only a glossy brochure full of pictures. The offices are close to the Australian High Commission in central London:

New South Wales: 66 Strand, London WC2N 5LZ (01-839 6631).
Queensland: 392 Strand, London WC2R 0LZ (01-836 3224).
South Australia: 50 Strand, London WC2N 5LW (01-930 7471).
Victoria: Melbourne Place, Aldwych, London WC2B 4LA (01-836 2656).
Western Australia: 115 Strand, London WC2R 0AJ (01-240 2881).

Information on the Australian Capital Territory, the Northern Territory and Tasmania is available from Tourism Australia. If you have access to Prestel (or can persuade a friendly travel agent to use it for you), you can call up the Australian Information Service on 2529 or order brochures on 2901116.

Tourism Australia and state representatives abroad hold only a small selection of the available travel literature. Most travel promotion is done at state level, so if you know in advance which states you'll be visiting, contact the headquarters of the tourist organizations in Australia:

Australian Capital Territory: Canberra Tourist Bureau, Joliment Centre, Northbourne Avenue, Canberra City, ACT 2601 (062-45 6464).
New South Wales: Travel Centre of NSW, 16 Spring Street, Sydney, NSW 2000 (02-231 4444).
South Australia: Government Travel Centre, 18 King William Street, Adelaide, SA 5001 (08-212 1644).
Northern Territory: Government Tourist Bureau, 31 Smith St Mall, Darwin, NT 5794 (089-81 6611).
Queensland: Government Travel Centre, 196 Adelaide St, Brisbane, Qld 4001 (07-226 5337).
Tasmania: Tasbureau, PO Box 1469, Launceston, Tas 7250 (002-30 0211).
Victoria: Victour, 230 Collins St, Melbourne, Vic 3000 (03-619 9444).
Western Australia: Tourist Office, 772 Hay St, Perth, WA 6000 (09-322 2999).

New Zealand. Publicity is handled nationally by New Zealand Government Tourist Offices in various countries around the world, including:

United Kingdom: New Zealand House, Haymarket, London SW1Y 4TQ (01-930 8422).
United States: 630 Fifth Avenue, New York, NY 10111 (212-586-0060); plus offices in Los Angeles and San Francisco.
Canada: 2 Bloor St East, Toronto, Ontario M4W 1A8 (416-961-1137).

If you want more specific information on a particular area, you can write to the various local tourist offices listed under *Help and Information* for each region of New Zealand.

Phoning Ahead. You can find most numbers in Australia and New Zealand from Britain by dialling international directory enquiries on 153. To call a number in Australasia from Britain, dial the international access code (010) followed by the country code for Australia (61) or New Zealand (64) and the area code without the initial zero (for Sydney dial 2, for Auckland 9, etc.) and then the number. So to call the British High Commission in Canberra (area code 062) from the UK, dial 010-61-62-73 0422. From the USA and Canada the international access code is 011, and so to call the US Embassy in Wellington (code 04) you should dial 011-64-4-722-068. If you wish to make a collect (reverse-charge) call to Australia, you can dial straight through from the UK to the Australian operator on 0800-890061, a call which (for you) is free.

Before ringing relations to announce your arrival, or calling a hotel to make a booking, estimate what the time is at your destination; see *Time,* below. Also bear in mind that your conversation will cost 80p per minute between 2.30pm-7.30pm and from midnight to 7am, and £1 per minute at other times. Some tourism-related organizations in Australia, however, have special lines which allow people abroad to call Australia for the price of a local call; for example if you dial the Qantas linkline number in the UK (0345-747767) after office hours, your call will automatically be switched through to the airline in Sydney.

Travellers' Clubs. If you lack friends and relations in Australasia, you might consider joining an organization which arranges hospitality exchanges. For example members of the Globetrotters Club (BCM/Roving, London WC1 3XX) can request a list of members in Australia, New Zealand and other countries who have expressed a willingness to provide hospitality to other globetrotters. Membership costs £7 and the list of members costs £1.

Servas International is an organization begun by an American Quaker which runs a worldwide programme of free hospitality exchanges for travellers, to help the cause of peace and international understanding. To become a Servas traveller, it is necessary to be vetted by a member (to weed out freeloaders) and to pay a joining fee of about £10/US$15. If you are interested, contact Servas at PO Box 885, London W13 9TH (tel: 01-352 0303) or, in the USA, at Room 406, 11 John St, New York, NY 10038.

A new non-profit organization called Students International Lodging Exchange (STILE) is worth investigating. A membership fee of US$29 entitles you to have an entry in two directories (published in May and November) of student members willing to swap accommodation, whereupon you contact your fellow members in the places you wish to visit (and in turn are contacted by them). STILE may be contacted in Europe at 9 rue Charcot, 92200 Neuilly-sur-Seine, Paris, France (tel: 1-47 47 28 82) or in the USA at 210 Fifth Avenue, New York, NY 10010.

Handicapped Travellers. Before your flight to Australia you may wish to consult *Care in the Air,* a free booklet published by the Civil Aviation Authority, 129 Kingsway, London WC2B 6NN; and a guide to London and Scottish airports obtainable free from the British Airports Authority, 130 Wilton Road, London SW1V 1LQ (tel: 01-834 9449). Every airline gives free assistance to handicapped travellers, and will provide a wheelchair at 24 hours notice. Some airlines, including British Airways, Qantas and Air New Zealand, require a medical certificate of fitness to travel.

The Royal Society for Disability and Rehabilitation have a holidays officer who can provide specialist advice. Write to RADAR at 25 Mortimer Street, London W1N 8AB, or call 01-637 5400. Mobility International exists to promote international travel for the disabled; their UK office is at 62 Union St, London SE1 1TD (tel: 01-403 5688). North Americans can consult the Society for the Advancement of Travel for the Handicapped (SATH) at 26 Court St, Brooklyn, NY 11242 (tel: 718-858-5483). See *Help and Information* in the introduction to Australia for details of similar organizations at your destination.

WHAT TO TAKE

Maps. Free maps are issued by the national and state tourist offices listed above. Most visitors are satisfied with these hand-outs, but if you want a more detailed map for specialist purposes, you might want to purchase a government topographical map, for example a map of the Coromandel State Forest at a scale of 1:50,000. To see what is available before you set off, write to The Map Shop, 15 High Street, Upton-upon-Severn, Worcestershire WR8 0HJ (tel: 068 46 3146) and ask for their Australia/New Zealand list. In addition, Roger Lascelles (47 York Road, Brentford, Middlesex TW8 0QR; tel: 01-847 0935) distributes leading series of Australian and New Zealand maps.

Electrical Items. Australia and New Zealand have power supplied at the same voltage (240) and frequency (50Hz) as the UK and most of Europe. But if you're taking a travel iron, hair dryer or anything else electrical you'll need an adaptor. The standard Australasian mains plug has three pins but is unlike other plugs elsewhere in the world. Since convertors which accept British three-pin plugs are difficult to find in Australia and New Zealand, buy a suitable adaptor before leaving or simply buy a new plug locally. Equipment made for use in North America may also need a voltage transformer if the appliance does not have a voltage selector, and electro-mechanical equipment will run at the wrong speed due to the difference in frequency.

Medications. Any prescribed drugs (except contraceptives) which you intend to take with you should be accompanied by a doctor's letter explaining why you need them. Do not carry any non-prescribed drug stronger than aspirin or Alka-Seltzer, and then only in the original packs. Customs officers are highly sensitive about drugs of all kinds, and can be suspicious of some which can be bought over the counter in Britain but which are available only on prescription in Australia and New Zealand.

If you are planning a long trip, it is better to take a prescription from your doctor — which can be endorsed by a doctor in Australasia and used to obtain drugs — than to try to import large quantities of medication.

Gifts. There is something of an art in choosing what to take to impress friends or relations, or to ingratiate yourself with friends-of-friends on whom you wish to impose. If your beneficiaries are British migrants, then virtually anything British — from newspapers to Scotch whisky — will be appreciated. Otherwise, take the kinds of things which are more expensive in Australasia, such as foreign books or (in the case of New Zealand) electrical goods.

What Not to Take. Because of the stringent quarantine laws in both Australia and New Zealand, don't bother taking any sort of food even if your Australian friends are Stilton-lovers. And don't splash out on a new wardrobe of clothes for your trip; you can find equally fashionable garments more cheaply in Australasia, or you can pick them up cheaply in Asian countries you may visit en route. Finally, unless you intend to stay longer than three months in Australia or a year in New Zealand, don't waste money on an International Driving Permit. Although plenty of sources (especially the motoring organizations which sell them) recommend an IDP, your national licence is sufficient for short stays in both Australia and New Zealand.

TIME

Travelling to and around Australia and New Zealand can be chronologically confusing. Australasia straddles several time zones, which means that at noon in Western Australia it is already 4 or 5pm in Christchurch and Auckland (depending on whether Daylight Saving Time is in operation in New Zealand). While New Zealand is covered by a single time zone, Australia is divided into three during the winter and six in summer, when some states implement Daylight Saving Time but Western Australia, the Northern Territory and Queensland do not. The time in each state is indicated in the table below compared to 9am Greenwich Mean Time (4am Eastern Standard Time):

	WA	NT	SA	NSW	ACT	Vic	Tas	Qld	NZ
Winter (Oct-Mar)	5pm	6.30pm	6.30pm	7pm	7pm	7pm	7pm	7pm	9pm
Summer (Mar-Oct)	5pm	6.30pm	7.30pm	8pm	8pm	8pm	8pm	7pm	10pm

Australasian Daylight Saving Time usually begins on the last Sunday in October and ends on the first Sunday in March which is contrary to Daylight Saving Time in the Northern Hemisphere. As a rough guide, you can assume that Western Australia is eight hours ahead of British time and 13 hours ahead of Eastern Time in North America, and the other Australian states are about 10 hours ahead of Britain, 18 ahead of eastern North America. Converting "am" to "pm" or vice-versa will give you a rough idea of the time in New Zealand compared with Britain.

Australasia has not fully adjusted to the 24-hour clock. In most timetables times are given in local time using the 12-hour clock. The convention is that times printed in light type are before noon, those in **bold** after noon.

On business cards, classified advertisements and so on, you'll sometimes see "AH" and "BH", meaning "after (working) hours" and "business hours".

USEFUL CONVERSIONS

Australia and New Zealand have gone metric with a vengeance. Although you may still hear people talking about "gallons", "miles" and "ounces", everything from speed limit signs to packs of butter are in metric units. Some of the trickier conversions are given below.

Capacity and Volume. The standard unit for liquids is the litre (l), approximately $1\frac{3}{4}$ Imperial pints or 2.2 US pints. There are about $4\frac{1}{2}$ litres to an Imperial gallon, $5\frac{1}{2}$ to a US gallon. In a pub, most measures are in millilitres: 585ml is an Imperial pint (20fl oz). See *Drinking* for the most common measures.

Fuel Consumption. Australasians reckon in terms of the number of litres they use to travel 100 kilometres (litres/100km). To convert fuel consumption between miles per gallon (mpg) and litres used per 100km (litres/100km):

mpg (UK)	20	25	30	35	40	45	50
mpg (US)	16	20	24	28	32	36	40
litres/100km	14	$11\frac{1}{2}$	$9\frac{1}{2}$	8	7	6	$5\frac{1}{2}$

Tyre Pressure. The unit used in Australia and New Zealand is kilograms per square centimetres (kg/cm^2), sometimes known as the *kilopascal*. To convert from pounds per square inch (psi):

psi	16	18	20	22	24	26	28
kg/cm^2	1.1	1.3	1.4	1.5	1.7	1.8	2.0

AUSTRALIA

CLIMATE

Although most people are aware that the seasons in the Southern Hemisphere are opposite to those north of the equator, it can be very difficult getting used to the fact that schools adjourn for their summer holidays around Christmas and the ski season begins in June. The terminology can become quite confusing when you are making plans to meet up with an Australian friend on a future occasion: "See you next summer" always has to be clarified by naming the months intended. But while you are in Australia, spring means September to November, summer is December to February, autumn is March to early June and winter is the rest.

The Australian sun needs no elaboration. Even the capital of Tasmania gets over five hours of sunshine a day on average, while Perth gets nearly eight. Many visitors ascribe the success of their visit to the generous quantities of sunshine they experience. People say that even when you have no money in Australia, the weather presents you from becoming low-spirited. Furthermore the water temperatures are wonderfully warm in most places, and Poms trained at Scarborough and Southend will have no trouble diving into the sea. (Meanwhile the more mollycoddled Aussies close down their open-air swimming pools when the water temperature falls below about 20°C.)

To judge from the weight of media coverage, Australians have an obsession for information about the weather. Many newspapers devote a full colour page to forecasts, and news programmes on radio and television are usually followed by several minutes of extremely detailed weather analysis and forecasts. Since the weather patterns in Australia are usually more stable than they are in Britain, the meteorologists have a higher success rate, though they are often over-confidently precise.

Australia's vastness means that there are tremendous variations from zone to zone, encompassing Alpine regions (like Tasmania) and sub-Equatorial Monsoonal regions (like Darwin). July in Canberra is decidedly cold, with minimum temperatures approaching 0°C, while Cairns is 15-20°C warmer. The main coastal cities of Sydney, Brisbane, Melbourne, Adelaide and Perth all have temperate winters and hot summers. Naturally the direction you must travel to reach warmer climes is opposite to the one to which Europeans and North Americans are accustomed, which gives rise to such expressions as the "Deep North" usually applied to northern Queensland. For the really scorching heat

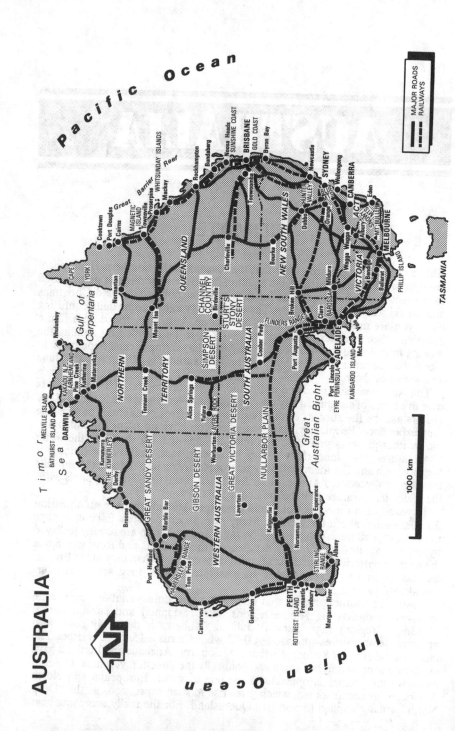

which can make railway lines buckle and lakes evaporate you will have to penetrate into the interior of the country, where you often get a series of "snorters" (i.e. exceedingly hot days).

Darwin and Cairns are true tropical cities, and are therefore subject to rainy and dry seasons, invariably referred to in Australia as the Wet and the Dry. These areas are best avoided in the wet season, which lasts from about December to April, not only because it is less enjoyable travelling in rain but because the downpours are so severe that roads become flooded or impassably muddy, possessions go mouldy and, even when it isn't raining, it is unbearably humid. Travellers in the dry Outback should beware of the flash floods which can follow rainstorms. In particular, you should never pitch a tent on the bed of a dried-up river or stream in case an overnight flood washes you away.

Sydney and Brisbane can become unpleasantly humid in summer, though refreshing sea breezes and the occasional "cool change" bring relief. On the other hand, the heat of the west coast, though intense, is very dry, and Perth's wet season falls in winter.

If you are in Australia for a long period, it is possible to follow the seasons around, ideally seeing Queensland and the interior deserts between June and September, before arriving in Western Australia in time to see the wild flowers bloom in spring, and crossing back to the southeast for the long balmy evenings and sunny days of summer. Each regional chapter provides a more detailed description of the kind of weather you can expect at the time of your visit.

THE PEOPLE

back of Bourke	remote place, like "the back of beyond"
banana bender (or banana eater)	person from Queensland
bitumen blonde	an Aboriginal girl or woman
blow-in	a newcomer to any place; a person who has not yet been accepted by local inhabitants as one of themselves
bumjumper	male homosexual
corroboree	Aboriginal ceremonial dance; or any social gathering especially if rowdy
croweater	person from South Australia
Dad and Dave	two fictional characters from the 1890s who typify outback humour and tenacity
de facto (noun)	a commonlaw partner
derro	a tramp or derelict person
drongo	a stupid person
fringe-dweller	Aboriginal who sets up camp near a white owned property and lives on handouts
gin	Aboriginal woman
God-botherer	one who touts religion
hoon	lout, stupid youth, layabout
inland	any part of the Australian mainland not on the coast, specifically the Outback
Koories	name Aboriginals call themselves
larrikin (or lair)	unruly youth, rogue, someone who doesn't take things too seriously
lezzo	lesbian; or any woman who rebuffs an advance

Mexican	person from Victoria (due to location south of the New South Wales border)
Ocker	a typical yobbo-like Australian
poon	lonely, somewhat crazy, outback dweller; also a simpleton or fool
ratbag	rude or eccentric person
root	sexual intercourse
sandgroper	person from Western Australia
septic (or seppo)	an American (from rhyming slang tank/Yank)
sticky beak	nosey person
Taswegian (or Tazzie/Tassie)	person from Tasmania
Topender	person from the far north, especially the Northern Territory
woodheap	a white man who has been ostracized by white Australians for associating with Aboriginal women
wowser	straight-laced killjoy (origin unknown)

At last count there were 15,973,900 Australians, about half of them less than 30 years old. You may be disappointed to learn that not many of them spend their time wrestling with crocodiles, mesmerizing savage beasts by outstaring them or attending Aboriginal corroborees, and that mythical heroes like Crocodile Dundee are few and far between. Another manifestation of the myth is the swagman who wandered the country living on his wits and precious little else, rejecting all forms of authority, a law unto himself, living from one day to the next. He too is a dying breed.

In fact Australia is an overwhelmingly urban culture, though it treasures its bush lore as can be seen in its choice of principal bicentennial events including camel races, enormous cattle musters, "Spirit of Australia Endurance Horse Ride," and so on. While the people cling to the edges of their vast island continent — 80% live within 20 miles of the sea — they glorify their untamed interior. They will regale you with stories of the dangers or rewards that lurk in the Outback, but they are most unlikely to have eaten a kangaroo steak themselves, seen a crocodile except in a zoo or met an Aboriginal.

Even if your average Australians would not know where to begin to shear a sheep or fight a bushfire, they have some unique characteristics which set them apart from their North American and European counterparts. One of their most endearing qualities is that they place a higher value on leisure than on work, on relaxation than on money. People visiting on business are often taken aback by the seemingly slack hours kept by their Australian colleagues. At weekends, everyone, including shop employees, are at the beach or a barbecue or a sporting event, and therefore downtown areas are empty, like a shearing shed during a bush dance as the locals might say.

Of course all these generalizations need to be qualified and in Sydney and Melbourne and maybe even Darwin there are executives suffering from stress, while in Perth and Adelaide you will find a few individuals who are more intent on making money than on having fun. But the majority maintain their traditional priorities; perhaps as a remnant of their convict past, they value their freedom from external constraints above most other things.

Australia's trading partners, especially Japan and the US, find these laissez-faire attitudes quite staggering and are exerting pressure on Australian managers to increase productivity. These pressures are apparently having some impact judging from reports that American motivation schemes have started to catch on. The recession which hit Australia in the early 80s has caused genuine alarm (though no significant hardship) and there is a suspicion growing in some quarters that the "no worries" attitude which has always prevailed is no longer sufficient. "She'll be right" may yet turn out to be an over-optimistic forecast. But such habits of mind and expectations are (fortunately) slow to change in a workforce, especially one which is as heavily unionized as Australia's. Australians are by nature dismissive of authority which sometimes verges on contempt and makes it all the more difficult for bosses to try to alter traditional loyalty to leisure.

If the world is divided between debunkers and dreamers, Australians would almost without exception fall into the first category. Since the Great Aussie Dream has often been identified as owning a house and since the vast majority of working Australians already own a home, there is little point in being a dreamer. At their best, Australians can be gifted and colourful when they decide to take the mickey, and as long as you do not find yourself on the receiving end, their conversation is often very amusing.

Although the word Ocker is sometimes translated as down-to-earth basic Aussie, it carries with it in most circles pejorative connotations. The image of the beer-swilling, gambling Ocker has been glorified as constituting the Australian identity, which is now lamented as having been lost. This process is described in a recently published book called *Ocker Chic* by Michael Thomas, which maintains that the beer-swillers now drink Australian Chablis in streetside cafés, the slobs now wear designer T-shirts, and instead of playing the "pokies" (slot machines) or watching the footy (football) on TV, they now catch the latest Australian film or go jogging. The satiric force of Barry Humphries' Cultural Attaché Sir Les Patterson is now somewhat diminished since Australia is fast losing its boorishness. The ever-increasing numbers of Aussies coming to Europe for extended stays have contributed to the de-Ockerization of Australia.

A sociological analysis might claim that this transformation is inevitable when a predominantly working class culture becomes middle class — due to increased affluence and improved education — and not everyone bemoans this shift. This school of thought expresses unmitigated relief that Australiana is no longer considered synonymous with hard-drinking philistinism and rampant male chauvinism. The visitor will have to decide for him or herself just how far real Australians have left that image behind. If you do get away from the cities you are quite likely to meet the so-called "dinkum" (i.e. authentic) Aussies who wear old pairs of stubbies (shorts) and seem to be happy as long as they have a good supply of the other kind of stubbies (bottles of beer) and a few mates with whom to discuss the coming football match.

ETHNIC BACKGROUND

Three-quarters of the Australian population have British origins, and one million (out of less than 16 million) were born in the United Kingdom. Furthermore Britons continue to flock to the land of opportunity and the UK continues as the largest source of migrants, about 15%, just ahead of New Zealand. This makes it all the more remarkable that Australia has such a separate identity. But it also accounts for the large number of similarities with Britain, from driving on the left side of the road to the prevalence of fish and chip shops.

The word "Pom" or "Pommie" is in widespread use to refer to English people. Although it is often used neutrally, it can also convey a hint of disdain. Poms are caricatured as stuffy and snobbish, complaining and inflexible. The myth endures of Pommy trade unionists who are all work-shy troublemakers and (along with America) responsible for any economic problems Australia has. The origin of the word is not certain, but it has been suggested that it was an abbreviation for "Prisoners of Motherland" used of the early convicts. A more pleasing derivation is given by D. H. Lawrence in his (otherwise unpleasing) novel set in Australia called *Kangaroo* in which he claims Pommie is short for pomegranate which is rhyming slang for immigrant, and furthermore recently-arrived Brits turn red in the sun like pomegranates. Apparently the word Pom has begun to be replaced with "pongo" which in a nation addicted to rhyming slang seems to be an uncomfortable amalgam of drongo and Pom.

Despite this recent unflattering coinage, hostility towards Poms appears to be fading, as Australians grow more secure in their independence from the mother country. There are some indications that Americans may be taking over the role of most-resented foreigners. After the post-war generation in Australia embraced everything American from junk food to foreign policy, there are now signs of rebellion. The blows that have been dealt by the USA to Australia in international trade (such as on the wheat market) are bitterly resented. The power of American-owned multinationals, not to mention American military involvement in nuclear defence stations like Pine Gap near Alice Springs, has soured Australian feeling towards the United States and bred distrust, at least at the level of pub politics. But most Australians have had little contact with Americans except through television and the movies — only one in 500 of the Australian population is American in origin — and on an individual basis, Americans do not generally arouse animosity.

The cultural diversity of Australia is one of the country's most appealing features. To take just two examples, the Germans who settled the Barossa Valley near Adelaide in the 19th century and the descendants of Chinese pearl divers who live in Broome, Western Australia have maintained cultural traditions which add immeasurably to the colour and variety of the social spectrum. More significant has been the influx of Europeans since the Second World War, especially from Greece and Italy. These waves of immigration were encouraged by the government to provide manpower for expanding industries, but had the fringe benefits of introducing many aspects of Mediterranean civilization such as good food and (possibly) a Latin temperament.

Although Southern Europeans continue to arrive, the most recent waves of "new Australians" (as migrants are known) are coming from Asia, particularly Vietnam, the Philippines and Malaysia. In fact a third of the annual intake is now from Southeast Asia. These newcomers are having the same beneficial effect on the economy and on the cultural-cum-culinary life of Australia as their European predecessors did.

Most new arrivals encounter difficulties in adjustment, though they are given free accommodation in migrant hostels and, if necessary, free English lessons for three months. But Anglo-Saxon Australians are not known for their broad-minded tolerance of different cultures, and new Australians have certainly suffered and continue to suffer discrimination, the least harmful being a range of derogatory names used to describe them, such as reffos (refugees), dagos, wogs, ikeys, ities, balts, spags, slopeheads, choongs, etc. A nation whose first Minister for Immigration was capable of saying, "Two Wongs don't make a white" is bound to make life difficult for newcomers. Understandably national groups cling together and as a result many immigrants never adapt to Australian life, in fact some never learn English. The suburbs of many cities, especially Sydney, are delineated along ethnic lines, and the newest migrants tend to occupy the poorer areas. Despite all this, patriotic feeling runs high among migrants, just as it does in the USA, and most new Australians will claim to be Australian rather than Italian, Yugoslav or Malaysian.

ABORIGINAL PEOPLE

Many visitors who arrive in Australia are almost as eager to see Aboriginal culture as they are to see the Sydney Opera House, the Great Barrier Reef or Ayers Rock. Many are disappointed. Not only do they fail to see Aboriginals playing the didjeridu, hunting with boomerangs or feasting on witchetty grubs, but they see hardly any at all. The estimated total population of Aboriginal people (including many of mixed race who are now more inclined to claim their Aboriginal ancestry than previously) is between 200,000 and 300,000 which is less than 2% of the Australian population and only double the number of migrants which Australia accepts in any one year.

Overall their numbers are sadly depleted. It is conjectured that about a quarter of a million were wiped out in the first couple of generations after European settlement. Just as in North America white man's diseases, to which the indigenous people had no immunity, were at least as destructive to the Aborigines as the great plague was to 14th-century Europe. Furthermore there was wholesale slaughter of the natives who were considered troublesome by the settlers, though on the whole the Aborigines were far more pacific than their North American Indian counterparts.

People often contrast the appalling conditions of Aboriginal life now to the much happier situation of the Maori in New Zealand. But Aboriginal culture, especially in the desert, was less advanced than the seafaring Pacific Island Maori culture and had correspondingly greater problems of adjustment to the alien invaders. Anthropologists studying some of the remote tribes in the Great Australian Desert who had had very little contact with whites until the 1950s, maintain that these were the last living stone age people on earth, with the possible exception of the Bushmen of the Kalahari Desert in Africa. Their social organization and means of survival were incomprehensible to Europeans and vice versa.

In earliest British legal documents, Australia is described as "Terra Nullius", that is, uninhabited land. This was not because the first arrivals did not encounter the native people — Captain Cook describes his meeting with them in 1770 — but because they seem to have been considered sub-human. This is a cause of bitter grievance today. Aboriginals had been in Australia, having crossed from Southeast Asia, for at least 40,000 years and possibly much longer by the time the first fleet sailed into Sydney Harbour in 1788 carrying its cargo of convicts. The whole razzmatazz of the Australian Bicentenary is resented by many Aborigines and other Australians sympathetic to their cause, since it celebrates something which is seen to have brought nothing but misery to them. Aboriginal activists have been completely unmoved by the Bicentennial Committee's attempts to placate them with well-meaning rhetoric about diversity within unity. Among the most radical Aboriginals, there is a feeling that the whites should return to the places from whence they came.

Aboriginal people have suffered enormous spiritual losses and terrible damage to their self esteem. Their religion revolves around the Dreamtime, an oral tradition relating to an ancient time when spirits roamed over the land creating all animate and inanimate objects, tree and stone, rivers and people. According to some interpretations, the land itself is sacred, not just specific features. So white man with his fences and animals and railway lines inevitably interfered with this network of significance, as the indigenous people watched helplessly and without comprehending. (For an unsentimental but fascinating account of this see Bruce Chatwin's book *Songlines*).

This attitude to the land, which is completely at odds with European notions of ownership, is at the root of the land claims which dominate discussion of Aboriginal affairs nowadays. Large chunks of Australia were set aside as reserves from the beginning of this century. But just like the so-called homelands of South Africa, they were usually established on barren and remote land, and the occupants were not allowed to govern themselves. They were administered by missionaries, police or government officials, and many communities still rely on white leadership. Furthermore, their rights to the land were overridden if a mining company found some new source of wealth on a reserve. Although this is now changing to some extent, as in the highly controversial decision to return Ayers Rock to the Pitjantjatjara tribe to whom it is sacred, there are still bitter disputes to be fought. Anyone interested in learning more about land rights in Australia before setting off should contact Survival International (310 Edgware Road, London W2) or the Aboriginal Land Rights Support Group (19c Lancaster Road, London W11 1QL).

This subject is a very delicate one for any government. Unlike the Maori people or the Canadian Indians, Aboriginals signed no treaties with the colonizers and so have no legal basis from which to start proceedings. It would be very difficult to draft a document to which both sides could agree, though a treaty of some kind might prevent the native peoples from being at the whim and mercy of changing political opinion. Prime Minister Hawke claims to be working towards some kind of constitutional change, partly in an attempt to legitimize the Bicentenary for the Aboriginal population, but this may have little effect. At last report, Aboriginal groups had come together to press for 7% of the gross national product as part of a negotiated treaty.

Few Aboriginals are to be seen in the capital cities. They do congregate in certain suburbs (such as Redfern in Sydney) but these are usually well away from tourist areas. Most live in or near country towns, mostly in Queensland and the Northern Territory. In the Territory, Aborigines represent a quarter of the total population and have won rights to over a third of the state. It is illegal to visit most Aboriginal reserves without permission from the community and these are given sparingly. If you do have some special reason for wishing to visit a reserve you must write to the relevant Land Council four to six weeks in advance. Addresses are given in the appropriate chapters of this book and further advice is available from Aboriginal support groups in all the major cities.

After regretting the scarcity of Aborigines, it can be distressing when you do eventually see these people whose mystique has been widely publicized. Travelling on a train to Alice Springs, you may notice a group of Aborigines (or "black fellows" as they sometimes refer to themselves) sitting next to the track at a small Northern Territory station. As you get closer and as other tourists on the train are reaching for their cameras, you notice that they are staring straight ahead with seemingly unseeing eyes, oblivious to trains and cameras and dust. They seem utterly demoralized, though there is no way of knowing whether this is an accurate assessment.

Not all exposure to Aborigines is so depressing. Many who have adopted European attitudes display the same friendliness as white Australians and hitchers, particularly in the north of the country, frequently get lifts with them. Conversely, you might encounter some on a bus through the Outback and attempt to strike up a conversation as you have done with so many other Australians, only to find that your conversational gambits fall flat, leaving you feeling rebuffed. Pure Aboriginal culture does not have much place for small talk with strangers. Again a typical exposure might be a group sitting in a park in northern Queensland, sharing a few bottles of wine and listening to Country music on a cheap radio, until a policeman comes along and the Aboriginals meekly disperse.

The sad fact is that the Aboriginal "problem" is very complex and difficult, and namby-pamby liberal criticisms of past atrocities do not achieve very much. It is crucial for white Australia to acknowledge that the 200 years of their occupation has resulted in the extermination, slavery and economic oppression of Aboriginals, who weren't even given full citizenship until the 1960s. Although a handful of Australians with Aboriginal blood have gained positions of authority, the majority remain silent and powerless. Even when Aboriginals seem to have adapted to the modern age, they are subject to the old ways such as "going walkabout", which Europeans find inexplicable. Even the few blacks who have achieved fame as painters or actors, are depressingly liable to fall foul of the law.

The statistics for alcoholism and crime among Aborigines are horrific. Their life expectancy is 20 years less than for white Australians, and their health and housing are abysmal in comparison to whites. Their plight is often compared to the plight of South African blacks and indeed there are some similarities. But the comparison is not a fair one: the essential difference is that racial discrimination is not now legislated in Australia. Aboriginals have had full rights of citizenship since 1967, and have equal (and some special) rights. Belatedly and fuelled by guilt, the government gives generous handouts (over 70% of Aboriginal income derives from the nation) and funds a multiplicity of worthy projects such as setting up an Aboriginal television station, recording Aboriginal music (look for the Larrikin label), making a computerized dictionary of Aboriginal languages (of which there were about 500), etc. Many white support groups are struggling to improve the standards of health, housing and education, and specifically trying to teach them how to assume control of their lives.

But reforms of the law can accomplish only so much. Racial discrimination is still very widespread among the white population, especially in the south. Many were taught at school that Aboriginals are savages who refuse to adapt to the higher culture introduced by Europeans. In otherwise reasonable urban white settings, derogatory words like "boong", "coon" and "Abo" are used quite unselfconsciously. Even more disconcerting for the visitor is the way city folk (who have probably never talked to an Aboriginal in their lives) advise foreigners not to talk to blacks, not park by the roadside in Outback areas and to carry a shotgun for self-defence. This is nonsense. There have been virtually no unprovoked attacks or molesting of whites; if there had been it would have made unforgettable headlines. What is making headlines is the ill-treatment of Aboriginals by whites especially police in remote areas. In 1987 there was a scandalous series of prison suicides committed mostly by very young Aboriginals. In another publicized case, an Aboriginal was sent to jail for three months for stealing two loaves of bread, which is an ironic reminder of the harsh sentences meted out by British justice to the early convict settlers for trivial offences. There are also occasional reports of barbaric behaviour such as making Aboriginal women sterile without their permission.

Of course it is not an unmitigated tale of woe. Aspects of Aboriginal art and culture are on display in many museums around the country with one of the best collections of artefacts in Adelaide's South Australia Museum. The Australian Museum in Sydney publishes a useful leaflet called *Aboriginal Australia* (for 50¢) which provides a brief introduction to concepts like the Dreamtime, but concentrates on tribes which inhabited New South Wales. The Tourist Commission of the Northern Territory publishes some literature which might also be of interest; ask for their booklet *People of Two Times* which understandably glosses over many of the problems. Plenty of books have been written about Aboriginals, many of them with names like *The Passing of the Aboriginals* or *The Aborigines the Way they Were*. One book which has become quite a standard work is A. P. Elkin's *The Australian Aborigines* (Angus & Robertson, $14.95) which has been revised many times since it was written in 1938. Very little has been written by Aboriginals themselves. One book caused a stir but later turned out to have been written by a Yugoslav anthropologist impersonating an Aborigine and writing under the name of B. Wongar. But despite its fraudulent authorship, *Walg* presents a very sympathetic picture of Aboriginal life, to the point of idealization.

You may be lucky enough to get some first hand taste of contemporary Aboriginal culture. Look out for Aboriginal bands such as Coloured Stone which has a large following in the central part of the country but receives scant attention from the disc jockeys and club owners on the east coast. Occasionally Aboriginal festivals of dance are held, for example at the annual women's festival in Adelaide or by the Bararroga Mimi Dancers from Arnhemland. Inevitably you will also find some commercialization of Aboriginal culture, particularly the handicrafts in tourist shops. But at least now some of the profits are finding their way to the communities which make the souvenirs.

MAKING FRIENDS

Australians are no-nonsense folk who do not suffer fools gladly. Just as Eskimos have a large vocabulary for the concept of snow, so Australians have an impressive range of descriptions for a fool: nong, dill, drongo, galah, dickhead, peanut, boofhead, someone with kangaroos in his top paddock, three bangers short of a barbie, a shingle short, like a stunned mullet, silly as a cut snake, off his kadoova, silly as a two-bob watch, mad as a goanna, and so on. Despite this flair for abuse, you are unlikely to be victimized (unless of course you happen to be a dill, a drongo, etc.). In any case their disrespect is almost always good-natured and is underpinned by a strong sense of fair play.

Australians are the first to poke fun at pomposity, and are themselves the most unpretentious of people. This leads to the frequent characterization of openness, i.e. they will tell you their opinions straight. This in turn can result in a certain insensitivity. For example visitors may be shocked to hear racist sentiments or political views expressed, before any attempt has been made to discover the likelihood of a favourable hearing.

Their openness falls well short of unburdening their hearts, as Americans are prone to do. Analysis of the emotions is not a very popular pastime. (Woody Allen would probably not make friends very quickly if he were to emigrate.) Even when people are good mates, in this land where "mateship" is venerated, they are liable to demonstrate their attachment not through words but actions (archetypally risking their lives in a crisis). In keeping with their penchant for irony and lack of sentimentality, an exchange of verbal abuse can be one way of expressing affection. It might also explain why the family dog in Australia is more often than not referred to as "the mutt," which in other countries would be a pejorative expression.

They may take a similar line on their country and be reluctant (compared to Americans at any rate) to throw themselves behind nationalistic schemes like the Bicentenary. Nevertheless most natives harbour few doubts that Australia is the best country in the world, the "lucky country", and the level of patriotism sometimes rivals that encountered in the USA. Just as in the States, it is unwise (not to mention discourteous) to speak critically of Australian habits and assumptions. The romantic view of the convict heritage, of bushrangers (i.e. bandits), explorers and outback characters has taken on the mythic quality of America's Wild West, sometimes with as much papering over of the truth. But it is not your role as guest to disillusion them.

Outside the cities and especially in the Outback, the natives are very eager to help a visitor. Advice and offers of assistance are often most welcome in areas prone to drought, flood and widely scattered fuel supplies. Your fellow travellers are also a valuable source of information and company. A surprisingly large proportion of people travelling in campervans in remote areas are older Australian couples who undertake major expeditions as soon as they retire. In a spirit of camaraderie, they are always willing to share information about road conditions, etc; along some routes, such as the Great Northern Highway on the coast of Western Australia, it is customary to prepare lists of recommended campsites and attractions which you then exchange with people travelling in the opposite direction.

The Australian love of leisure is a boon to visitors who often find that new acquaintances are generous with their time. And of course it is much easier to meet people if they are frolicking on a beach or drinking in a pub rather than buried away in an office block.

An attempt to identify "typically Australian" characteristics and pin down the national character as generous, gregarious, egalitarian and so on, must always be frustrated by the enormous differences between city and country, recent and long established migrant, European and Asian, not to mention the differences from state to state. A pub encounter in Tasmania is bound to be very different from one in Queensland, and the citizens of Melbourne are more difficult to get to know than the people of Alice Springs.

But given the native open-heartedness of the majority and the common language (with occasional exceptions), you will find it so easy to make new friends that you may even need to buy a new address book.

Visiting Friends and Relations. Eight million Britons have relations, near or distant, living in Australia. Even if you are not in this category, you are quite likely to have some addresses pressed upon you by friends, neighbours, colleagues or bank managers. Do not refuse these. Even if you feel inhibited about making contact with strangers, give it a chance. After all, Australians visiting Britain have been doing this in good conscience for years.

The two main situations to which you might give some thought are visiting your own relations (whom you may or may not have met previously) and looking up distant contacts who will feel no particular obligation towards you. Always make it clear that you are a traveller on the move, rather than a freeloader (known as "bludger" in Australia). Unless you are very obtuse (a dill, a drongo. . .) you should be able to tell whether it is appropriate to visit. When you unfold your plans for the rest of your stay in Australia, you may well find that your current host immediately calls his or her mate on the other side of the country, tells them what a "ripper" person you are and insists that they pick you up from the airport or bus station and look after you.

Sex. The Australian male is the source of much discontent on the part of the Australian female. Many theories, such as the dire shortage of women in the early days of the colony, have been put forward to account for the unshakeable male chauvinism of so many Australian men. Although equal opportunities legislation is now in force in most of the states (with the notable exception of Queensland), there are still gross discrepancies between men and women in earnings and promotions, and sexism is rampant in many quarters.

Women may notice that travelling in Australia, especially in country areas, is a little like travelling in a Moslem country, where men either treat you as though you do not exist (swapping dubious jokes over your head with their mates) or else paying unwanted attention. Most advances can be repelled with a straightforward rebuff, which means you revert to being treated as though invisible. Obviously there are countless exceptions to this and the women's movement is making it more difficult for this kind of passé behaviour to go unnoticed or unchallenged. But it may still take a long time before men and women can strike up friendships as equals.

In spite of the prevailing image of the Australian male as aggressor, many people are struck by the frankness of overtures made by Australian women towards men. Foreign men may find themselves approached at parties or on beaches (but not usually in pubs). If the opportunity for casual sex presents itself, you should be aware that the whole range of venereal diseases flourishes in this land of sexual freedom. AIDS is a serious problem, especially in Sydney which has Australia's largest gay community. The macho elements of Australian society are intolerant of gayness, and in the state of Queensland male homosexuality is actually illegal (though prosecutions are rare).

Language. Snobs and purists tend to think that Australians subject the English language to some hideous indignities. Not content merely with abbreviating words, Australians insist on adding the suffix "o" to the result, as in "garbo" (dustman), "derro" (down-and-out, from derelict) and male names such as Geoffo, Robbo, etc. Such formations inevitably strike the visitor's ear as childish.

Australian slang at its best is full of humour and vitality. An expression like "ankle-biters" or "rug rats" is much more vivid that "kids" or "infants", and "flat out like a lizard drinking" is infinitely preferable to "very busy". Another favourite way of giving emphasis is to use absurd comparisons as in "busier than a brickie in Beirut" or suggesting that a car is so economical that it "runs on the smell of an oily rag" or "he felt as inconspicuous as Liberace at a wharfies' (i.e. dockworkers') picnic" or describing someone who is so undynamic that "he couldn't organize a piss-up in a brewery".

Pronunciation (or lack of enunciation) can present problems for the visitor. The excuse often given for the Australian habit of barely moving the lips while talking is that it keeps out the flies and conserves energy in the heat. Predictably accents are broadest in isolated rural areas whereas they are weaker among people representing "Old Money" who have tended, until the present rise of nationalism, to pride themselves on their "Britishness". Just remember that a long "a" becomes a long "i" (and so Australia becomes (Au)strilya and mate becomes mite) and "i" becomes "oi" (so pie-eyed meaning drunk becomes poy-oyed). Meanwhile other vowel sounds, like "ai" and "ou", are pronounced so as to turn fairy tales into "furry tiles" and down south into "den seth". Furthermore Australians have adopted an unusual interrogative inflection, so that statements sound like questions. Try to avoid the temptation of supplying answers to these non-questions.

Most British speakers of English will encounter few real problems of misunderstanding, though there are some borrowings from Aboriginal languages which may be unfamiliar such as "corroboree" for social gathering and "bombara" for submerged reef. Americans can expect the same problems which they would encounter in Britain with words like "boot" and "bonnet", and expressions like "Would you like to be knocked up in the morning?" A habit more familiar to Americans than to Poms is to transmute nouns into verbs such as "to suicide" and "to headquarter".

The term "bastard" is widely used when addressing males and is often a sign of familiarity and affection. Foreigners should probably avoid aping this expression since they might get the nuance wrong.

Literature. Marcus Clarke's novel *For The Term of his Natural Life* (1874), a sensational tale of convict life, documenting all the horrors of the penal system, is a good starting point. Another 19th century writer who should not be missed is Henry Lawson, whose short stories about life in the Australian bush and male "mateship" are most entertaining.

Miles Franklin rocketed to fame in 1901 with *My Brilliant Career*, a novel of pioneering life which has become familiar through the recent film version. Whereas Lawson's focus is on the poor bush battlers, Franklin describes the well-off lives of established landowners (the "squattocracy"). Katherine Susannah Prichard did something new by venturing into the harsh and arid outback in her novel about an Aboriginal woman, *Coonardoo* (1929); if this kind of subject matter appeals to you, then you will also enjoy Xavier Herbert's massive *Capricornia* (1938), a story of race conflict set in the Northern Territory.

Contemporary Australian literature is very much alive, with such internationally acclaimed writers as Christina Stead and the Nobel prize winner, Patrick White. Olga Masters, writes seemingly simple tales of narrow-minded rural towns in the 20s and 30s revealing unpalatable truths about domestic and family life. Helen Garner is another well-known author whose novel about drug-addiction, *Monkey Grip*, has also been made into a film. The fiction of Peter Carey is sometimes harrowingly surrealistic (e.g. "War Crimes" in his collection of short stories entitled *Exotic Pleasures*), while David Malouf will appeal to those who like poetic prose (try *Imaginary Life*). Thomas Keneally is a prolific novelist whose *Schindler's Ark* won the Booker Prize in 1982. In recent years a number of fine Aboriginal poets have emerged, such as Kath Walker, Kevin Gilbert and Colin Johnson, and Jack Davis is an Aboriginal playwright who wrote *Barungin*. Amongst white Australian playwrights, David Williamson is probably the best known for *Don's Party*, a bitingly satiric look at middle-class Australian life.

The vast majority of travellers to Australia arrive by air and, after a flight which may have lasted 24 hours or more, are subject to a bewildering series of official controls. Most flights from abroad land at the major gateways early in the morning, and the queues for immigration and customs can add a couple of hours to your ordeal. It is easy to develop an instantly unfavourable (and undeserved) image of Australian society.

Before you touch down, you will be handed an *Incoming Passenger Card* and a *Customs, Quarantine and Wildlife Statement* to complete. As well as the predictable questions about name, age, length of stay, the Card asks you about how you intend to spend your visit. The authorities are quick to point out that this is not a sinister erosion of civil liberties but merely a means of identifying tourism trends. The Statement asks yes/no questions about the goods you are carrying and whether you have visited a farm or abattoir in the last three months.

About ten minutes after the cabin has been sprayed, the insecticide is deemed to have done its work, the doors are opened and the passengers may then leave the aircraft. If you are continuing on an international flight to another Australian city, you will reboard the aircraft (or, on many Qantas flights, a replacement aircraft) and clear immigration and customs at your final destination. (If you face a long wait for the onward flight, you should be able to take a free hot shower which can be found at most Australian airports.) All other passengers, including those transferring to domestic flights, should head for the immigration desks. On the way you can pause to buy duty-free drinks and cigarettes at the airport shops.

IMMIGRATION

Don't expect an easy ride from Australian immigration officials; if you anticipate an unfriendly welcome and close questioning then at least you may be pleasantly surprised if your encounter with them turns out to be less than stressful. There are estimated to be 50,000 illegal immigrants in Australia (nearly a quarter of them British) and the authorities are not keen for this number to increase. So you can expect to be quizzed about your motives for visiting the country, and how you intend to support yourself during your stay.

Your visa will probably contain a machine-readable strip which will be read by computer. You should bear in mind that your visa merely confers permission to apply for entry into Australia rather than the right of automatic admittance; "subject to entry permit on arrival" is the wording used. To pass this hurdle successfully, you should ensure that you have as much in your favour as possible. In particular, you have agreed when signing your visa application form to have an onward or return ticket, which you will probably be asked to produce. You have also promised that you have "sufficient funds" to support yourself during your stay, and the immigration officer may ask you to verify this with a display of your wealth. Although travellers on working visas carrying as little as $35 have been allowed in, you should try to have at least a couple of hundred dollars in cash or travellers cheques backed up by a credit card or two. This is particularly important if you are travelling on a visitor's visa, which specifically prohibits taking up employment during your stay. If you are not flush with funds, the authorities will be keen to see the address of a person (preferably a relation) who you claim will look after you during your stay.

Assuming you satisfy the officer that you are a suitable candidate for entry into Australia, he or she will stamp your passport and write in the maximum length of stay. If all is in order, this should be six months for British citizens and three months for North American visitors.

If you are coming to the end of your permitted stay, you can apply for an extension from the Immigration Department, but will have to have a convincing story and plenty of money. Otherwise it will be necessary to fly out to New Zealand or Indonesia and reapply. You can never change a visitor's visa to a working visa, so don't try.

Overstaying. Many people stay beyond the maximum permitted duration and by no means all are caught before leaving. You will certainly be found out upon departure, as the normal passport check will reveal your offence, which may result in your being blacklisted for a year.

Occasionally overstayers are detected before they reach the airport. Prosecution and subsequent deportation are not automatic if you are caught overstaying. Although the maximum penalty is $1,000 plus six months imprisonment, most illegal immigrants are simply asked to leave. If they are discovered by the Immigration Service but leave of their own accord, they are barred for three years. Those who are actually deported are prohibited for five years, or longer if they still owe their fare to the government.

QUARANTINE

The officer who deals with your immigration will also carry out a preliminary quarantine check. The zeal with which the authorities try to keep out plants and animals and their derivatives may seem excessive. However, the nation's agriculture is free of most of the world's serious diseases and the Australians intend to keep it that way. On your Statement you will have been asked if you are carrying any plants or animals (alive or dead) or items derived from them: from dogs to dairy products, and salami to snakes. Even the straw hat you might have picked up in Singapore is prohibited.

Be prepared for the official to look you straight in the eye and ask you to verify your claims verbally. To avoid this grilling, there are bins placed strategically in which you can dump suspect items. This is also where you should throw away the biscuits which you forgetfully lifted from the airline meal tray. As well as these prohibited items, you are supposed to declare all wooden articles (including matches), flower seeds and baby food. The immigration officer will ask a customs official to inspect them (so don't wrap the teak salad bowl you've brought as a gift for Cousin Sheila), but you will normally be allowed to take them through. If you admit to visiting a farm in the last three months, you may be asked whether you have with you the shoes you were wearing at the time.

Avoid any temptation to evade the quarantine laws. In keeping with the authorities' concern for keeping out alien diseases, the penalties for failing to declare all dubious items can be stiff; the maximum is a $50,000 fine and ten years imprisonment. Frequent travellers to Australia report that by declaring a harmless little item or saying you have recently visited a farm, your honesty rating is considerably enhanced and you may get through the customs formalities more quickly.

CUSTOMS

The last thing the immigration officer will do is to mark your *Customs Quarantine and Wildlife Statement* with a single letter. The meaning of these is mystifying to outsiders, but it is a code which indicates whether your belongings should be checked by customs. You pick up your (freshly sprayed) luggage from the baggage carousel and proceed to the customs area. At the entrance, an official will direct you either to the least crowded customs desk or — if you have the right letter — straight through the exit to the outside world. In any event you'll be handed a Health Warning Card which you are supposed to keep for six weeks and show to a doctor if you fall ill.

Alcohol and Tobacco. Australian duty-free allowances are not overgenerous. Travellers aged 18 or over may import only one litre of alcoholic liquor (beer, wine or spirits) plus 250 cigarettes or 250 grams of tobacco. As mentioned above, you can buy your allowance upon arrival. This useful facility means you need not lug drink and tobacco from one side of the world to the other, but note that the prices are much higher than at Middle Eastern duty-free shops such as Abu Dhabi, Bahrain and Dubai.

Prohibited and Restricted Goods. In addition to the articles forbidden under the quarantine laws, there is a wide range of other goods which it is illegal to import or for which you need a permit. For specific information, contact the Australian Customs Service, Blackall St, Barton, Canberra, ACT 2600 (tel: 062-73 3922).

The restrictions may be divided into two categories: animal products which do not carry a health risk but which are derived from endangered species, including ivory and rare furs; and items which are thought likely to endanger Australian society such as weapons, obscene publications and non-prescription drugs. As in many countries, the Australian authorities make stringent checks to keep out illegal narcotics. The penalties for trying to import even a small amount of cannabis, cocaine or opiate are severe, and anyone caught bringing in a "commercial" quantity of any illegal drug may be locked up for life.

Despite Australia's stringent quarantine regulations you can bring in a cat or dog from the UK or Ireland subject to getting the required certificates and leaving Rover or Tiddles in quarantine kennels for three months after arrival. You can get the relevant forms from the Commonwealth Veterinary Officer, Australia House, London WC2B 4LA (tel: 01-379 4334).

Other Goods. You are allowed to import a "reasonable amount" of personal effects free of duty, plus gifts up to a value of $400 ($200 for travellers under 18). The next $160-worth is taxed at a concessionary rate of 20%, and duty on higher amounts can be much steeper. In addition, television sets and fur products do not qualify for exemption.

Currency. There is no limit to the amount of money which you can take out of Britain or into Australia, but you may not re-export more than $5,000 in Australian notes and coins. Americans wishing to import or export sums of US$10,000 or more must declare the fact to US Customs.

DEPARTURE

For a country which is otherwise generally civilized, Australia imposes an improperly high charge on anyone who wants to leave the country. Departure tax of $20 is payable by almost every international traveller aged 12 or over. This is not purely an airport tax (such as the Airport Development Tax levied by New Zealand) but a revenue-raising device by the federal government. As such, you have the option of paying it to any office of the Department of Immigration and Ethnic Affairs in advance. While this is worthwhile for people who can't trust themselves to preserve $20 to pay the tax upon departure, most travellers simply pay at the airport.

After checking in for your flight, you must go to a special counter to hand over your $20 and have a stamp affixed to your ticket. The tax can no longer be paid by credit card; only Australian dollars in travellers cheques or cash will do. If you are utterly penniless, you will be permitted to leave the country after filling out a form explaining your plight (but not readmitted until you have paid the Australian government their money).

Two classes of travellers are exempt from departure tax. The first group is those who have been in Australia for less than two calendar days: i.e. if you arrive on one day and depart at any time the next day, you are exempt. Note that you are allowed to leave the airport (for example to stay in a hotel overnight before an onward flight to New Zealand), so long as you have a valid Australian visa. The other exception is for those who take a side trip overseas during their visit to Australia. If you visit New Zealand, Indonesia or anywhere else during the course of your stay, exemption is granted after you have paid the tax once, until you return to your "point of origin" (your home country); this is to avoid the iniquity of having to pay the departure tax more than once. The process of claiming exemption is easier if you can produce a return ticket for the side trip, but this is not always necessary. Indeed, some travellers who have made successive trips to Australia from their home country over a space of a few months have claimed to have spent the intervening time in Bali and thereby earned exemption. If you qualify for either of these exceptions, it is still necessary to go to the departure tax counter to get an "exempt" stamp.

Customs and Migration. You have to pass through customs and migration checks on your way out of Australia, which is where they discover if you've overstayed. You are required to fill out an *Outgoing Passenger Card* explaining when you arrived and where you're heading. In addition, your luggage may be searched, and any goods made from endangered species will be confiscated. In view of the large number of crocodiles and goannas which appear to be thriving in Australia, you may be surprised to learn that they are on the list of threatened animals, and any items made from their skins will be seized. You need a permit to export "items of heritage significance to Australia", such as Aboriginal relics and ancient fossils; contact the Cultural Heritage Unit, PO Box 1252, Canberra, ACT 2601 (tel: 062-46 7211) if you think you might require a permit.

Duty-free Goods. As well as the usual airport duty-free shops, many Australian cities have downtown shops where you can buy goods free of duty within the 72 hours before you leave the country. Prices at these city centre places are lower than at the airport duty-free shops, and you can take the goods out of the shop (rather than just ordering them and then picking them up at the airport as in most countries). A label indicating the fact that you have bought duty-free goods will be firmly attached to your flight ticket and is inspected at the airport of departure. The contents of your bags will be checked against the paperwork, so don't consume any of your purchases beforehand.

Returning to Britain. Apart from the culture shock induced by returning from, say, the coast of Queensland to a wet Monday morning at Heathrow Airport, your biggest problem is likely to be bringing in expensive purchases (some of which you may have picked up en route at bargain prices in the Far East). You are allowed only £28-worth of goods free of duty; on the remainder, you have to pay Value Added Tax of 15% plus additional duty on some items.

The duty-free allowance for alcohol is one litre of spirits or sparkling wine plus two litres of still wine. The standard size for wine bottles in Australia is 750ml, so if you bring in three bottles you'll be marginally over the limit but are unlikely to be charged duty on the excess. You may also bring in 200 cigarettes or 50 cigars or 250g of tobacco.

Returning to (or through) the USA. American customs laws apply equally to returning US residents and other travellers passing through the States en route to Canada, Europe or elsewhere. The alcohol and tobacco limits of one quart plus 200 cigarettes or equivalent are available only to travellers above the minimum drinking age of the state you first arrive in; in the case of California, this is 21 years. Gifts to the value of US$100 are allowed duty-free. The booklet *Know Before You Go* (free from the US Customs Service, PO Box 7407, Washington, DC 20044) contains full details of duty rates and restricted goods.

TRAVEL RESTRICTIONS WITHIN AUSTRALIA

There are numerous quarantine regulations governing the movement of agricultural produce across state borders to prevent the spread of pests such as the aphid phylloxera (which attacks vines), Queensland fruit fly and boil smut (which affects corn). The rules are enforced by occasional agricultural checkpoints. The best advice is not to take fruit and vegetables across any state border. There are also some local restrictions within states, such as the rule which prohibits bananas being taken into an area within 40km of the post office at Carnarvon, Western Australia.

It is illegal to visit certain areas of Australia without first obtaining a permit to do so. Most restricted areas are those on Aboriginal land or around Aboriginal communities. Information is given in the relevant state chapters concerning how to apply for a permit. There are also restrictions on visiting military zones, such as the areas of South Australia around Woomera rocket station, and Maralinga where the British tested atomic bombs in the 1950s.

award rate	union-negotiated wage in certain fields of employment
blockie	vegetable or fruit farmer
CES	Commonwealth Employment Service (job centres)

compo	workers' compensation
dole bludger	one who lives off social security
jackaroo	station hand (female version is a jillaroo)
penalty	extra pay for working unsocial hours
sickie	a day off due to sickness (normally feigned)
smoko	coffee break
yakka	hard work

Despite the grumbling of the natives about high unemployment (which stands at about 8%), there are still lots of opportunities for casual work even in those states (i.e. Queensland and Tasmania) where unemployment is above the national average. Furthermore, if you are the right age, there is a good chance that you will be able to satisfy the requirements for a working holiday visa to make it all perfectly legal. Travellers who have a working holiday visa in their passports will be allowed into the country even if their funds have been depleted by a long trans-Asia trip, and many have found it possible to save enough in a couple of months to fund a major voyage around Australia and perhaps on to New Zealand. This is not so surprising in a country where the average adult wage is over $450 per week. The trades unions are strong in Australia and in many fields of employment have negotiated high wages and some interesting benefits. Weekend work is usually paid at "penalty" rates, often twice the hourly wage. The building unions have considerable clout: among other perks, all workers on buildings over eight storeys high earn a height allowance, even if their work keeps them firmly on the ground. There are many other such perks, such as holiday pay at a level $17\frac{1}{2}$% above the basic wage, but these are unlikely to benefit temporary employees.

Working Holiday Visas. British, Irish, Canadian and Dutch people between the ages of 18 and 25 are eligible to apply for a working holiday visa. (New Zealanders can work in Australia without any formalities.) American students can participate in the SWAP programme whereby students qualify for working visas lasting six months. Details are available from the Council on International Educational Exchange, 205 East 42nd St, New York, NY 10017.

UK citizens over 25 and under 30 are occasionally given a visa if they plead their case especially well at an interview. The visa is meant for people intending to use any money they earn in Australia to supplement their holiday funds. Working full-time for more than three months is considered contrary to the spirit of the visa.

In 1987 over 16,000 working holiday visas were issued in Britain, a 72% increase over the previous year, disproving the rumour that the Australian government is trying to phase out the scheme. The first step is to get the working holiday application information sheet MIG 25/SA and application form from any Australian consular office (e.g. Australia House, Strand, London WC2B 4LA; Hobart House, 80 Hanover St, Edinburgh EH2 2DL; or Chatsworth House, Lever St, Manchester M1 2DL). Travellers have reported that it is easier and faster to get visas outside London: Edinburgh, San Francisco, Bangkok and Kuala Lumpur have all been praised for their speed and efficiency.

The second step is to get as much money in the bank as possible. Each application is assessed on its own merits, but the most important requirement is a healthy bank balance. The amount recommended at present is £1,500 for six months or £2,000 for 12 months. Exceptions are often made if you can supplement your meagre £500 or £600 with an official letter of guarantee from a bank manager who has been persuaded a large sum will be coming your way. The more money you can scrape together the better, especially if you can't supply the authorities with a list of friends and relatives in Australia willing to bail you out financially if necessary. If you have borrowed a large sum to bump up your balance, rather than saved steadily over a period of time, be prepared to provide a plausible explanation for this. Sometimes the visa will be processed by return of post, but at other times of the year (particularly autumn) it can take weeks, so don't make a firm flight booking until your visa comes through.

Once you are in Australia, you may want to apply for a visa extension. These are given at the discretion of the Immigration & Ethnic Affairs Department, the addresses of which are given for the major cities. Rumour has it that Sydney and Melbourne are the most stringent, insisting on scheduled interviews, while Hobart and Darwin are more lenient. If you haven't broken the terms of the visa, if you can show financial assets to cover the return flight (e.g. $800) and about $300 for each month of the proposed extension, and confidently present a travel itinerary, you have a good chance of getting an extension. But you can't count on it.

Official Work Schemes. STA Travel are setting up a working holiday package for British young people who hope to work in Australia. This will include flights to Australia, advice on working visas, orientation on arrival and a back-up service from STA offices throughout Australia or from the allied organization SSA (Student Services Australia, PO Box 399, Carlton South, Victoria 3053). For details of the new programme, contact STA Travel, 74 Old Brompton Road, London SW7 3LQ (tel: 01-581 1022).

The Careers Research & Advisory Centre (Bateman St, Cambridge CB2 1LZ; tel: 0223 354551) administers the Britain Australia Vocational Exchange scheme which matches about 100 undergraduates with employers in their field of study, principally engineering and science. Student participants work during July and August and spend September travelling around Australia. Application forms are available in November and should be submitted as far in advance of the deadline (February 28th) as possible.

The organization GAP Activity Projects (7 King's Road, Reading, Berkshire RG1 3AA: tel: 0734 594914/5), which arranges work overseas for school-leavers during their "gap" year before starting college, has several projects in Australia starting at various times of the year. They last between four and nine months and usually involve working on farms or helping in schools.

Red Tape. Working holidaymakers were entitled to claim the dole of about $100 a week, until this "lurk" (Australian term for "dodge" or trick) was removed in a 1986 budget. Another privilege which in theory was removed was the right to apply for a tax rebate after a relatively short stint of work. In the early 1980s, the Commissioner of Taxation withdrew the tax-free threshold (now $5,100 or about $100 a week) from non-residents. This means that you should be taxed at the full rate of 30.67% from the moment you start earning and cannot get any of it back. It seems however that almost all employers (including accountancy firms which specialize in tax) routinely give out exemption forms to all their employees, including foreigners on working holiday visas, which means that you may well be taxed at the residents' rate of 24% and be able to apply for a rebate at the end of your stay, assuming that you have earned less than $5,100 in any one tax year (July to June).

The position on tax rebates is very confusing. Some working holidaymakers who have filed tax claims have received cheques for hundreds of dollars either before or after they have left Australia, whereas others have not only been refused a rebate but have been asked for further tax payments. Different tax offices tell different stories. One tax official is quoted as having replied to a foreign worker's enquiry, "Why not have a go mate?"

Many visitors to Australia do not have a working holiday visa, and yet still find it easy to get casual work. Your chances of doing this are highest in industries where cash-in-hand payments are made, such as agriculture and catering. There have been a few reports of immigration crackdowns resulting in deportations but these are uncommon.

In the face of massive opposition, the Hawke Government's proposed Australia Card identity scheme was killed off in 1987. The sting in the tail, however, was a promise to tighten up on taxation files. If this move succeeds, foreigners would find it more difficult to bend the rules than they do at present, making Australia more like the US in this respect.

THE JOB HUNT

Many British travellers have been greeted very positively by prospective employers, despite the Australian propensity for "Pommy-bashing" (as illustrated in a popular joke quoted in *G'Day!*: "Q: What is the difference between a Pongo (i.e. Pom) and a computer? A: You have to punch information into both of them, but with a computer you only have to do it once". Naturally employers do not want to hire a mere tourist who might take off on a whim, so it is a good idea at interviews to say that you are in Australia for an "indefinite period". A little experience goes a long way with Australian employers, so it may also be wise to exaggerate your experience.

Most people agree that the best way to find work is to walk-in-and-ask, especially at bars, restaurants and stores in the cities and at farms in the country. In fact this is the method used by about one third of all successful job-seekers in Australia. Otherwise there are four main ways of finding work: the Commonwealth Employment Service, private employment agencies, newspaper advertisements and notice boards.

The CES. Despite its name, the Commonwealth Employment Service is not solely for the benefit of Commonwealth visitors; it happens to be the name for Australian job centres. Like job centres anywhere the CES posts details of vacancies which have been registered with them. The card should give the name and address of the employer, the number of helpers required, the approximate duration of employment, accommodation (if any), pay and conditions. In some offices free phones are provided for contacting prospective employers and, if you are short of money, they might even supply a bus ticket to your work destination.

Some CES offices have separate departments which specialize in casual work or in jobs in the hospitality industry; look for branches called Temp-Line or CasHire. Often the work is for only a few hours, perhaps unloading a ship or moving office furniture. Competition for short-term jobs varies from place to place, but there will always be a hard core of travellers attracted by the prospect of instant cash (usually $40-$80 a day). To be in the running for such day jobs, you usually have to turn up very early (between 5 and 6am) and even then you might have to put in an appearance on two or three consecutive mornings before you get sent to a building site, factory, restaurant, warehouse, etc.

Reports vary about how useful the CES is. Obviously it depends on the individual office and time of year. Some users have said that smaller suburban offices tend to be more helpful than big city branches, though they probably have less choice of work. The addresses of the main offices in the state capitals are given in the regional chapters, together with other suggestions for finding work. Further addresses can be found in any Australian telephone directory; look under "Employment Agencies" in the *Yellow Pages*. In smaller towns, the CES may be represented by an agent in a post office or shop, and it may be open only for a limited season, for example for the duration of a local harvest or busy resort season.

Private Employment Agencies. Although not as widespread as in Britain, private agencies are a good potential source of jobs for travellers, especially those who have some office experience. Some have even been known to advertise on Youth Hostel notice boards (e.g. Drake Overload in Melbourne). The major agencies include Centacom, the Staffing Centre and Western Personnel Services. It is worth comparing terms and wages among these agencies; some pay your wages directly and these can be higher than those paid by individual firms for similar work. Some agencies specialize in rural, station and farm placements or in offshore tourist resort placements. It may take some time before you are sufficiently established with an agency to get continuous assignments. It is worth sticking with a good agency for a reasonable length of time, since placements will become more frequent and more interesting once they realize you are reliable and hardworking.

Newspaper Advertisements. The "Casual Work Available" columns of the daily press carry a tempting-looking range of opportunities from "promoting art" (=selling prints) to work as a film extra (where you will be required to pay a registration fee with little immediate prospect of work). Although you may occasionally find worthwhile employment this way, many travellers find more fruitful opportunities under specific headings such as "Positions Vacant — Hospitality Industry". If you think you might make a successful door-to-door salesman, the newspaper is the place to look, and some Poms have said that their accents went over surprisingly well on Australian doorsteps.

You should buy local suburban papers as well as the main dailies. There is so much competition for the jobs listed in papers like the *Sydney Morning Herald,* Melbourne *Age* and Perth *West Australian* that you should try to buy the paper the preceding evening (anytime after 9.30pm from the newspaper offices) so you can start your job search first thing in the morning. Sometimes labouring jobs are advertised and usually the first person to arrive at the site (usually by 8am) gets the job. Specialist magazines might also be worth checking such as *Queensland Country Life* for station work.

Notice Boards. Always check notice boards at Youth Hostels, at popular private hostels or at universities, especially as summer approaches (October/ November). If you are settled in one place and are looking for work, ask the landlord for permission to put up a notice in the window of the hotel.

WORKING IN THE COUNTRY

To discover the more exotic features of Australia, it is necessary to leave the comforts of city life behind, and one of the best ways is to get a job as a seasonal farm worker on a fruit farm or in the Outback. You may well make good money, but even if you don't you can save most of what you earn, while working in uninterrupted sunshine. But bear in mind that the hours will be long, the work hard, the flies infuriating and the spiders and snakes a constant worry.

Fruit Picking. The country CES offices should be able to help, if only by giving you the *Harvest Table* which they publish; this is a good starting place, though it is by no means comprehensive. Asking in local pubs and hostels is also liable to turn up a lead. Also try the local fruit-growers' association (if there is one), some of which are so eager to attract foreign pickers that they distribute a leaflet through Australian diplomatic missions abroad (see *Melbourne and Victoria: Work*).

Harvest seasons vary from state to state: crops ripen first in Queensland and finish in Tasmania as you move further away from the equator. Even the two major grape harvests of New South Wales and South Australia do not necessarily take place simultaneously during the harvest months of February, March and April. Mechanization has reduced opportunities for itinerant grape-pickers but there is a growing trend to market "hand picked" wines which guarantees a certain amount of work.

Just as in Europe and North America, there are professional pickers who follow the harvests around the continent, so if you find yourself falling behind your fellow-workers during the first few days of the harvest, you should console yourself with the knowledge that you are competing with years of experience. The standard hours for a fruit picker working in hot conditions are 6am-6pm with two or three hours off in the middle of the day. Most picking is paid at piece rates though in some cases you will be paid an hourly wage of approximately $8. Not many fruit farmers can supply accommodation, so serious fruit-pickers carry a tent. It also helps to have your own transport, first to find a vacancy and then for shopping, banking, socializing, etc. Failing that, you will have to rely on hitch-hiking. Details of various fruit and other harvests (including tobacco in Queensland and Victoria, hops in Tasmania, etc.) are given in each of the regional chapters.

Conservation Volunteers. Several organizations give visitors a chance to experience the Australian countryside or bush. The Australian Trust for Conservation Volunteers (PO Box 423, Ballarat, Victoria 3350; tel: 053-32 7490) welcomes overseas participants on their projects, which are mostly in the state of Victoria but also in New South Wales and Western Australia.

After joining ATCV for $10, volunteers can join either a short-term task (one day, weekend or week) in which a contribution towards expenses of $6 a day is expected, or a more expensive and elaborate long-term package expressly designed for overseas volunteers over the age of 17 (e.g. $700 for 13 weeks which includes all living expenses and transport including airport pick-up, and a one-week recreation excursion canoeing, rafting, surf kayaking, climbing, ski touring or bushwalking). The work may include fencing off areas where the soil has been eroded or where birds and flowers need to be protected, controlling noxious weeds and vermin, planting trees, restoring historic buildings, constructing trails or bird hides in National Parks, etc. Accommodation might be in shearers' cottages, village halls, ski lodges or under canvas.

There is also a relatively new but active organization called Willing Workers on Organic Farms (WWOOF) in Australia, whose headquarters are at Mount Murrindal Reserve, West Tree, Via Buchan, Victoria 3885 (tel: 051-55 0235). Their 100 or so member farms grow food organically and are keen to have volunteer helpers to whom they can show off their home region.

The Outback. Working on a station or ranch is one of the most authentic experiences of Australia you can have. Some properties are so big and so remote that flying is the only practical means of access. Despite the vast areas and enormous flocks, it is usually possible for one or two experienced stockmen to look after the property, though they may need an assistant (a jackaroo or jillaroo) at busy times, which vary between states and specialization of the property. If you can't ride, you might get taken on as a cook or home help to amuse and teach the children. Station work is easiest to find in the Northern Territory, Western Queensland and northern Western Australia, especially in February/March when station managers tend to do their seasonal hiring.

Since more and more working stations are also being opened to tourists, you may also find work as a Jack (or Sheila)-of-all-trades on a ranch, looking after the guests. There is no special season for this, so check newspaper adverts. Before answering such an advert, you should remind yourself of all the hazards and drawbacks of outback life (see *Great Outdoors*) and bear in mind that it is often a rough male-dominated world, so not for fragile types of either sex.

TOURISM AND CATERING

As in the hospitality industry anywhere, most employment demands in Australian tourism are seasonal and therefore ideally suited to the traveller. Working for a few months at any of the hundreds of coastal resorts, particularly in Queensland, can be one of the most enjoyable ways of saving money. In remote areas, the employee turn-over is often brisk and there is a good demand for waitresses and barmaids (though be sure to distinguish between these and "hostess" jobs which require altogether less savoury skills). Australian bars and hotels are not renowned for their sexist-free attitudes though in 1987 the South Australian Equal Opportunities Tribunal won a victory for sexual equality by insisting that an Adelaide restaurant advertising for topless staff must take on shirtless men as well as women.

Casual catering wages are high compared to the equivalent British wage: typically $8.50-$9 an hour, time and a half for Saturday work and weekday overtime (anything over eight hours) and double time on Sundays and public holidays. Since many pubs and restaurants are shut on Sundays jobs which require you to work on Sundays are rare and, because of the high pay, much in demand. Remember that you can't expect to earn much extra in tips.

In addition to the multitude of resorts along the Great Barrier Reef (see *Queensland: Work*), another holiday area to consider is the Australian Alps where ski resorts are expanding and gaining in popularity. Mount Buller, Falls Creek and Mount Hotham on the Victorian side and Thredbo and Perisher on the New South Wales side are relatively developed ski centres where you might find work.

Fishing. It should be possible to get work on prawn fishing vessels out of Darwin, Cairns, Townsville, Broome or Karumba on the Gulf of Carpentaria, work which can be idyllic outside the rush periods when there is spare time for snorkelling, island-hopping, etc. The standard procedure is for the skipper to pay deckhands between 3% and 7% of the overall profits; although the catch may sometimes be poor and earn you only $300 for a three-week voyage, many travellers report earning twice or three times as much for a good haul. Bear in mind also that you don't (and can't) spend your wages on food, accommodation and entertainment while on board.

The main jobs assigned to male deckhands are net-mending and prawn-sorting. Work is especially demanding during the "banana prawn" season of March/April, since banana prawns travel in huge schools which are caught in one fell swoop, requiring immediate attention. Women are taken on as cooks. They should make it quite clear before leaving harbour whether or not they wish to be counted among the recreational facilities of the boat, since numerous stories are told of the unfair pressures placed on women crew members at sea. There are even worse potential dangers; a few years ago a prawn trawler was capsized by a whale and the two deckhands were dismembered and eaten by sharks.

Naturally, skippers prefer to recruit experienced deckhands. If after enquiring at all the fishing offices and after making yourself a familiar sight at the wharfs you still have had no luck, you might consider going along to a net shed and volunteering to work unpaid for a few days, learning how to mend nets. Then if an opening on a boat does crop up, you will be the first to be considered for the job.

The CES harvesting booklet includes prawning and scalloping on the coast of Western Australia around Carnarvon. The season lasts from March to October and accommodation is available in caravan parks. Sometimes you see advertisements for "oyster openers", a skill worth cultivating if only for your own consumption. Scallop-splitting is another favourite among casual workers, e.g. around Bicheno on the east coast of Tasmania, though the 1987 season was a complete fiasco.

Australia represents extremely good value for British and American visitors. Since the Australian dollar was allowed to float freely against other currencies in December 1983 it has sunk in value considerably, falling by about 40% against the US dollar and the British pound. At times it has been so shaky that some natives grumble that it has become the "peso of the Pacific". It has settled recently to about $2.50=£1 and $1.40=US$1.

Exchange rates are listed in the Australian daily press, but are quoted in terms of what the local dollar is worth (typically £0.40 or US$0.70); to convert to what your £ or US$ will buy, you'll need to divide one by the rate quoted.

Coins. 1¢, 2¢, 5¢, 10¢, 50¢, $1; a $2 coin celebrating the Bicentenary is to be introduced in April 1988, and the 1¢ coin may soon disappear. British visitors will be familiar with the 10¢ and 20¢ coins (identical in size and weight to 5p and 10p pieces respectively) but should remember that the Australian versions are double the units of their British counterparts. Most visitors quickly learn to hoard 20¢ and 50¢ coins for use in all sorts of machines from parking meters to chocolate bar dispensers.

In addition to these coins in general circulation, there are gold "Australian Nuggets" whose face value is between $15 and $100 but whose actual value is many times this. Watch out for New Zealand coins in your change; they are worth less than their Australian counterparts.

Notes. $2 (yellow/green), $5 (orange/mauve), $10 (turquoise/yellow), $20 (red/khaki), $50 (gold/green), $100 (blue/grey). The lowest denomination note will disappear once the $2 coin is established. As with high-value notes anywhere, $50 and $100 bills may be treated with some suspicion and are unlikely to be welcomed by taxi drivers.

BANKS

There are four big nationwide banks in Australia: ANZ, National Australia Bank, Westpac and the government-owned Commonwealth Bank. In addition there are numerous smaller banks (notably the new Challenge Bank and the State Banks of Victoria and New South Wales), plus many savings institutions such as building societies and credit unions. Since financial deregulation in Australia, a number of foreign banks such as Barclays and Citibank are appearing.

Foreign travellers cheques are changed free of charge by most banks, but the Commonwealth and the National charge a few dollars for each transaction. Banking hours are usually 9.30am to 3.30 or 4pm, Monday-Thursday, with late opening until 5pm on Fridays. Some city-centre branches open 8am to 6pm, Monday-Thursday and to 8pm on Fridays. In rural areas, you may find that the only bank for miles around opens on only one or two days each week.

Except at international airports, you will find it difficult to change foreign currency or travellers cheques outside banking hours. Travel agencies and luxury hotels are worth trying, but you will probably get a less favourable rate. If you are desperate, consider if you can get out to the airport; exchange facilities are open to meet all incoming flights from overseas. You may experience difficulty changing money in out-of-the-way towns, so to be on the safe side conduct your financial business in the cities. If a small town bank won't change your cash, try to draw funds on Visa or Access/MasterCard. Better still, organize a bank account in Australia.

Opening a Bank Account. It is surprisingly quick and easy to open an account in Australia. Although you need to have a mailing address in Australia, you are unlikely to be asked for references and can open an account with just a few dollars. Cheques are used less frequently in Australia than in Britain (partly because automatic banking is so efficient) and cheque guarantee cards are only just catching on, so a cheque account is likely to be of little use. It is more profitable to open an interest-bearing savings account with a passbook or an automatic banking card. Another advantage of an Australian account is that you can lodge important papers with your branch, either free or for a nominal fee.

Since the Commonwealth Bank has more branches than the others, and has links with most post offices allowing withdrawals to be made by passbook holders, you would be advised to open an account with them. If you intend to travel in rural areas, a passbook account is best since you can then withdraw cash at most post offices; but if you want rapid access to your money in cities at any time, opt for the Keycard account. One irritating feature of Australian bank accounts is that state and federal taxes are levied on transactions; they amount to only a few cents, but make it difficult to keep precise track of your finances; it is worth allowing 10¢ or 20¢ for taxes on each transaction.

If you wish to open a bank account before you go, forms are available from the Commonwealth Bank of Australia, 8 Old Jewry, London EC2 (tel: 01-600 0822), or Westpac, 23 Walbrook, London EC4N 8LD (tel: 01-626 4500). If you are travelling only to Western Australia, you could try the London branch of the state's Rural and Industries Bank at 16 Finsbury Circus, EC2M 7DJ (tel: 01-256 5600). Customers of the Clydesdale Bank in Scotland and Ireland's Northern Bank may find it easiest to open an account with the National Australia Bank, which now owns them both. Americans can open an account through Westpac, 200 Park Avenue, New York, NY 10166 (tel: 212-551-2700).

You pay in funds in sterling or US dollars and nominate the branch in Australia where you wish your account to be. This branch will open an account for you and have a passbook, cheque book or automatic banking card ready for your collection on arrival. You are unlikely to be granted an overdraft facility unless you are (according to Westpac) "a resident customer with a stable, long-term job", but there's no harm in trying. You could also apply in Australia for a credit card, although again evidence of secure employment will probably be necessary.

Automatic Banking Machines. Australian banks are well ahead in terms of the flexibility of their "hole-in-the-wall" money machines. If you get an automatic banking card, you will also be given a four-digit code number enabling you to use the automatic teller machines outside almost every bank. These are considerably more versatile than mere cash dispensers. This valuable function is, of course, catered for, and you can even specify the denominations of notes you'd like. But you can also shift funds from one account to another, check your balance and even pay the electricity bill. The four main banks have brand names for their money machines: ANZ — Night & Day; Commonwealth — Autobank; National Australia — Flexiteller; Westpac — Handybank. They are gradually becoming linked together, so that any customer can use the machine of any bank. You can also use your card to pay for goods and services through retailers equipped with electronic shopping facilities.

Credit Cards. Australians, it seems, like nothing better than to use a credit card. At the time of writing they collectively owe $2,500 million to the Australasian credit card *Bankcard,* equivalent to over $150 for each Australian woman, man and child. While many shops are unwilling to accept cheques, they gladly take credit cards. In general, any establishment which accepts Bankcard also takes Access/MasterCard and Visa. In keeping with the electronic revolution in Australian finance, an increasing number of establishments wipe your card through a machine to check its validity and solvency. This also means that the amount is charged to your account much more quickly than used to be the case.

You can also draw money on a foreign credit card when the banks are open. They will advance cash up to your credit limit without undue formality, and may not even want to see your passport.

TIPPING

You are probably unlikely to find yourself in a situation where you feel obliged to tip. Restaurant staff in particular are paid (by law) a fair hourly wage and good overtime, and casual staff earn "penalty rates" for weekend work. But even in occupations like taxi-driving where there is no guaranteed wage, tips are not expected. While a number of tourist guides recommend a 10% gratuity for restaurants, hotels, etc., in reality this is practised in only the more upmarket establishments favoured by American and Japanese customers. And since these places are also frequented by some Australians who would rather die than leave a tip, you can cheerfully fail to tip without giving offence. You might feel inclined to round up a $4.75 taxi fare to $5, but you're also likely to find a driver rounding down a fare of $10.25.

EMERGENCY CASH

You may find yourself "boracic" (short of money) for a number of reasons: the banks being closed, non-arrival of promised funds from abroad or dropping your wallet into the South Pacific. If you have just a little, there is virtually no limit to the ways in which you can gamble your last $5 to make $1,000, but the odds are stacked against you. When this strategy fails to pay off, being penniless need not spell total disaster. If you have a refundable airline ticket you could try to cash it in to sustain yourself until help arrives, and then buy another. British Consulates can cash a personal cheque drawn on a British bank and backed with a cheque card for up to £50 in an emergency, though they do so reluctantly. You can do this only once.

Alternatively, you can get a relative or friend to send you an International Money Order in sterling or dollars. After paying a commission of around £3, your benefactor then sends the Order through the post. If you have money in your own bank account, you can cable the bank to telegraph funds to a specified Australian bank. It helps to nominate a bank linked with your own bank at home, such as the National Australia Bank (which owns the Clydesdale and Northern Banks in the UK). Even so you should allow at least 48 hours for your funds to reach a branch in major cities and longer in the depths of the Northern Territory or Tasmania. Should weekends or public holidays intrude, you may have to wait up to a week.

Provided you have an interesting story to tell about the cause of your financial embarrassment, you might approach the local (small town) newspaper. If they publish your tale, they may slant it in the form of a request for assistance, and with luck soft-hearted Antipodeans will respond with cash and offers of help. The information given under *Work* could suggest a more reliable solution to a cashflow crisis. But, as a last resort, your government will get you home. Once their efforts to find someone to pay your fare have failed, then they will reluctantly put you on a plane. Your passport will be removed upon your arrival in your home country and will not be returned until you have paid the government for the flight plus a "handling charge".

TELEPHONE

Australia's efficient national telephone system is operated by Telecom. In common with networks in Europe and North America, it is taking new innovations on board at a feverish rate while retaining long-established features such as manual exchanges and radio telephones in outlying areas, and antiquated payphones. One great benefit of the system is that you can, at present, make local calls of unlimited duration for the price of a single unit (20¢ from private telephones, 30¢ from payphones). And considering the distances involved, charges for trunk calls are very reasonable (e.g. across the country for 32¢ per minute at night). A feature which you may enjoy less is the propensity of many businesses to play schmaltzy music while you hang on.

Tones. The tones you will hear are the same as in Britain, which may be a little confusing for visitors from other countries. The dial tone is a constant buzz or continuous note. The ringing tone is two short rings in quick succession, followed by a longish pause. The engaged tone — a single repeated note — sounds similar to the American ringing tone. Dial 1100 (a free call) to hear the entire repertoire.

Numbers. Every Australian number has a two or three digit area code. The codes for the capital cities are:

Adelaide 08	Hobart 002
Brisbane 07	Melbourne 03
Canberra 062	Perth 09
Darwin 089	Sydney 02

Calls within the same area code are by no means all classed (and charged) as local calls: for example the Northern Territory is counted as all one area (code 089) but calls from Alice Springs to Darwin are charged at long-distance rates.

Directories. You may be pleasantly surprised to find that most phone booths in Australia have intact directories. The introductory pages of the phone book contain a wealth of useful information, from what to do in the event of a cyclone (Darwin) to a map of the suburban railway network (Melbourne). Directories are made up of "white pages" (the regular alphabetical listing, sometimes divided into separate areas), the classified "yellow pages" listing everything from abattoirs to zoos, and "blue pages" containing community information and government organizations. In large cities, directories are split into separate volumes, and there may be a separate commercial directory such as the Melbourne BIG (Business Information Guide).

Numbers for directory enquiries (information) vary from place to place, but in most cities you should dial 013 for local numbers, 0175 for other destinations within Australia and 0013 for international assistance. A "silent" telephone number is an ex-directory private line.

Dial-a-Service. Every city has a wide range of numbers to call for various types of information or advice, many of which are shown at the beginning of the telephone directory (a list which invariably includes a number for the latest cricket scores). Unlike many of the similar services offered by British Telecom, all these calls are charged at local rates. For an alarm call (price $1), dial 0173.

Payphones. You should not need to go far to find a public telephone in Australian cities, though many of the street booths are vandalized or otherwise out-of-order. But a great many pubs, restaurants, shops, etc. have a different version of the payphone called "Red" or "Gold" phones (differentiated below) which are only slightly larger than domestic phones and usually in working order. As mentioned above, another advantage of public telephones in Australia is that a local call can last as long as you like for 30¢. You may find it difficult to adjust to the idea that you can talk for as long as you wish for a single payment, rather than having to rush breathlessly through your conversation before the pips sound, but once you acquire the habit don't ignore the queue forming to use the phone (some payphones bear a sign saying "three minutes maximum, please").

The telephone found in most street booths, and at post offices, airports, bus and rail stations, is the "Green" phone. It is a large, metallic instrument which looks fairly archaic. All green phones accept 10¢ and 20¢ coins, some also take 50¢ and a few $1. Those which take only low-value coins are known as *STD* (Subscriber Trunk Dialling) phones and can be used to call anywhere in Australia plus New Zealand and some South Pacific islands. For long-distance calls, you may insert up to seven coins initially, then replenish supplies gradually as the money drops through. To call elsewhere in the world from an STD phone, you must go through the operator (for charges see *International Calls,* below). Green phones which also take 50¢ or $1 coins are marked *ISD* (International Subscriber Dialling) and permit direct dialling worldwide. A notice tells you how many coins can be inserted at any one time. The warning for time expiry is both audible (a short burst of pips) and visible (a flashing red light). If you don't insert more coins, you have about 10 seconds from when the warning starts until you are cut off. Any unused coins are returned at the end of the call. Note that this does not mean you will get change from a $1 coin if you make only a 30¢ call. Only wholly unused coins can be refunded, so it is better to insert plenty of 10¢ and 20¢ pieces rather than 50¢ or $1 coins.

A variant of the green phone is the "hands-free" type, a frightening machine on which you press a button to disconnect the handset and activate a loudspeaker and microphone arrangement. To stand any chance of being heard, you have to yell into the microphone and even then you're unlikely to be understood. Avoid them if possible.

Red phones, commonly found in shops, restaurants and bars, etc., are very handy for local calls but are unable to handle anything more ambitious. They take only 10 and 20¢ coins. Gold phones are a modern derivative (located in similar establishments) which can cope with the full range of telephonic possibilities, from local calls to international direct dialling. These push-button phones take 10¢, 20¢ and 50¢ coins (some also take $1) and give a display showing how much money you have left. As with green phones, any unused coins are returned at the end of the call.

For those without pocketsful of loose change, there is an increasing number of "credit card phones" which are ideal for long-distance and international calls. They accept only American Express and some Australian cards at present, but are being adapted to take most international credit cards. You "wipe" the magnetic stripe on your card through the slot, key in your personal identification number, then dial and talk. There is a fairly high minimum charge of 70¢, so try not to use them for local calls.

Long Distance Calls. There are five separate rates increasing according to distance, combined with the different charges depending on the time of day. The cheapest calls can be made at the "economy" rate from 10pm to 8am daily and all day on Sundays. Next up is the "night" rate from 6pm to 10pm, Monday-Saturday. The "intermediate" rate covers weekday lunchtimes (12.30pm to 1.30pm). At all other times you pay the peak "day" rate. For a call from a private phone in Sydney to Perth this costs $0.63 per minute, from Adelaide to

Melbourne $0.42 per minute. Savings at other times are 10% (intermediate), 33% (night) and 50% (economy). Payphone tariffs are 50-100% higher. Dial 012 (a free call) for further information on charges.

International Calls. The international service is operated by Overseas Telecommunications (OTC), a separate organization from Telecom. By no means all telephones in Australia are connected to the international network. Payphones which have this facility are clearly marked "ISD", and include all gold phones. To determine if a telephone is equipped for ISD, dial 00 11 00 (a free call). If it is, you'll hear a message of confirmation ("congratulations: you're connected to ISD..."); if not, there will be no answer. Once you find a suitable phone, dial the international access code (0011), the country code (1 for North America, 44 for the UK, etc.), the area code without the initial zero, and finally the number. So, to call Vacation Work Publications in Oxford from Australia, dial:

International Access Code	Country Code	Area Code	Number
0011	44	865	241978

For calls to New Zealand and the South Pacific, the access code is 0014.

The following are the standard rates per minute from private telephones. Charges from payphones are approximately double.

New Zealand and the South Pacific:	$1.40
UK, Asia, North America, Western Europe:	$1.80

To make an international call in areas where direct dialling is impossible, you must go through the international operator on 0101. You will be asked whether you want a particular person (called, accurately, the "Particular Person" service) or merely a number ("Call-A-Number"). Charges for the latter are roughly half those for personal calls. On all operator-assisted calls, the minimum you pay for is three minutes. To call a number in the UK or USA, the minimum cost is $12.30.

For reverse-charge (collect) calls from private phones, dial 0101; from STD payphones, 0176; and from ISD payphones, 0107. For international reverse-charge calls to three countries, there is an alternative system called Country Direct. You can dial straight through to an operator in the UK (0014 881 440), the USA (0014 881 011) or Japan (0014 881 810). The overseas operator will place the call for you but the recipient will be charged the current international reverse-charge rate in any event, so it makes no difference to the cost. For international directory enquiries, dial 0103 in state capitals; elsewhere, check the local directory.

Hotels. Free phones for local calls can often be found in the lobbies of the most expensive hotels. The instructions will tell you to dial the access digit (usually 9 or 0) followed by the local number. Your chances of using these phones undisturbed are enhanced if you look like you could be a guest, or at least as if you could be visiting a guest. Beware of making non-local calls from a hotel room: rates for long-distance and international calls are high.

Manual Exchanges. A surprising number of rural areas still have a manual telephone exchange. To get through, you should call the appropriate operator (listed under "area codes" at the start of the *White Pages*).

Radio Telephones. Some outlying settlements (particularly in Western Australia and the Northern Territory) are served only by radio telephone; numbers are shown as, for example, "Alice Springs R/T 1234". It is possible to make calls between the national network and these places via the Radio Telephone Exchanges, but charges are at trunk rates plus 10¢ for each three minutes (the minimum call time). Only one person can speak at a time. It helps if you say "over" when you finish speaking, and don't try to interrupt the other person.

POST

Australia Post does a reasonable job considering the vastness of its territory. Even in areas a thousand kilometres from the nearest city, mail is flown in once a week. Although there is no mail delivery at weekends, service is fairly quick and reliable; ordinary letters are despatched by air mail to distant destinations within Australia, for which there is no extra charge. Prices are not excessive: to send a letter from coast-to-coast (or from one side of Melbourne to the other) costs 37¢. Writing abroad is not an overly expensive occupation either; the air mail price for postcards is currently 63¢, and an aerogramme costs only 53¢, which is a bargain compared to the $1 postage for an air mail letter. (If you want to be a real cheapskate and will be stopping off in Singapore on your journey, buy your stamps and post your cards at the airport there, to take advantage of probably the lowest air mail rates anywhere.) Surface mail from Australia can take months to reach Europe or America, and the savings are not enormous; a postcard sent surface costs only 16¢ less than by air.

Mail boxes are red with a white stripe. The modern ones resemble litter bins, but there are still some elegant Victorian "receiving pillars" dotted around if you prefer a more classy version.

Post Offices. Every town and village has a post office, although in outlying areas it may double as a petrol station, restaurant and general store. The range of services is impressive: as well as buying stamps or collecting poste restante mail (see below) you can make telephone calls, send telegrams, pick up application forms for driving licences or naturalization, etc. At main offices, credit cards can be used to pay for purchases totalling $10 or more; but when the office is crowded you won't be popular if you use your Visa card to buy 20 postcard stamps. Opening hours are normally 9am to 5pm, Monday-Friday. However, the main office in each state capital has extended hours for a restricted range of services. In addition, there are sub-post offices attached to shops (and sometimes even restaurants) which often open on Saturday mornings and late on some evenings.

Outside post office hours, stamps can be bought from some postcard retailers and newsagents, or from machines. Most issue stamps of fixed values but the more sophisticated electronic machines print out gummed "postage labels" of the denominations you require.

Addresses. Australian addresses have a couple of quirks: "care of" is written c/- rather than c/o; and for small settlements, you should write "Amoonguna *via* Alice Springs" rather than *near*. The phrase "locked bag" in an address means roughly the same as a Post Office box number. In cities, don't expect always to see a street number; if an address is given as "cnr. George and Oxford Streets", copy it out faithfully and your letter will get to the appropriate street corner.

Because of the tendency of towns to have the same name (there are no less than five settlements called Woodstock), all addresses should contain the name of the state (which is normally abbreviated to ACT, NSW, NT, Qld, SA, Tas, Vic or WA). To further speed your mail (and to distinguish between towns with the same name such as the two Breakfast Creeks in New South Wales, 200km apart), use the four-digit post code. These codes are listed at the back of any Australian *White Pages* and follow a fairly logical system, with the first digit indicating the state: 2=New South Wales and the Australian Capital Territory; 3=Victoria; 4=Queensland; 5=South Australia and the Northern Territory; 6=Western Australia; 7=Tasmania. The post code for the central area of each state capital ends -000, so the code for downtown Adelaide is 5000. (For Canberra, the code is 2600 and for Darwin 5790.)

One infuriating feature of Australian addresses is that they give no clue if a locality is close to, or part of, a larger city. For example, it is not obvious that Highgate WA is a small area a few hundred metres from the centre of Perth; postal addresses bear only the name of the suburb without indicating that it is part of the state capital. You can to some extent deduce the proximity to the main city from the last three digits of the postcode; numbers close to -000 tend to be near the city centre.

Poste Restante. It is easy for people to write to you in Australia if you have an approximate idea of where you will be going and when. They should address mail to you "c/- Poste Restante, Chief Post Office" at a city you plan to visit, and should include the state and postcode (2000 for Sydney, 3000 for Melbourne, etc.) You then take your passport to the main post office in the city and collect your mail. There is no charge for this service. At popular places such as Cairns, the scramble around the Poste Restante desk can be chaotic (although some travellers report these queues to be an excellent place to meet people). If you prefer to avoid the queues and are an American Express customer (by virtue of carrying their travellers cheques, for example), you can have mail (but not parcels) sent to their offices in Australia; addresses are given under *Help and Information* for each city.

Overseas Mail. Air mail service to countries with direct flights can be impressively fast, taking only three or four days between Australia and the UK or USA. To minimize delivery time, try to catch the latest posting times for international mail which are displayed at post offices and printed in the daily press. A cheaper and slower alternative to air mail, yet one which is much faster than surface, is "Surface Air Lifted." Your despatch travels overland to an airport, whereupon it is consigned by air cargo. Typical time to the UK or North America is two weeks. If, on the other hand, you are desperate for fast delivery of your letter, you can send it *International Priority Paid:* if you take a document to the main post office in Sydney by 10am, it is guaranteed delivery in central London the next day. Such speed, however, costs $20.05, and you cannot use the service for anything other than paper.

Parcels. All parcels must be securely wrapped and clearly addressed. The counter clerk at the post office will not hesitate to send you away to re-wrap a parcel if he or she considers it not to meet Australia Post regulations. Charges increase according to distance: parcels to neighbouring towns or cities cost less than those of the same weight being sent across the country. All parcels are sent overland unless you pay an extra amount for air mail. When sending parcels abroad you must complete a customs declaration form, available at all post offices. Take note of Australian postal and customs regulations before you send a parcel: in 1985 two West Germans were given six months' imprisonment for attempting to post 135 live reptiles out of the country.

TELEGRAMS

You can send a telegram (cable) within Australia from telephones (dial 015) or post offices. They can either be delivered to an address or, more cheaply, read over the telephone to the recipient. The cost for delivery is $6.50 for the minimum of 15 words, $4.50 for the telephone service; each additional word costs 20¢. This normally guarantees delivery within four hours. If your message needs to be delivered even more quickly (usually within an hour to city destinations), you can pay double for the "urgent" rate. Ordinary telegrams to Britain or the USA cost 50¢ per word with a minimum of seven words (hardly enough for an address).

A cheaper alternative for urgent messages within Australia is Australia Post's *Lettergram* service which works like a *Telemessage* in Britain or *Mailgram* in the USA. You go to a post office or phone in your message which can contain up to 100 words. It is relayed electronically to an office near its destination where it is printed out and delivered. Express delivery of your lettergram is available to most cities in under two hours. The cost is $9 for the express service, or $4 if you are content with next-day delivery. To send a message from a private phone, dial 008-337 466 in South Australia, Western Australia and the Northern Territory, or 008-112 422 in other states (for the price of a local call).

Yet another variation is the *Imagegram,* where your own handwriting can be sent by facsimile transfer across Australia. You take an A4-sized message to a major post office, where it can be "faxed" to most cities and delivered within four hours for $6. A similar facility is offered by a number of rapid print shops. You can also send fax messages abroad from major post offices.

blow	cyclone
blowie	blowfly
bung-eye	a painful eye inflammation caused by flies
crook	ill (when used about a person)
fall pregnant	become pregnant
going for a sixer	stumbling/falling over
mozzie	mosquito
Noah	shark (rhyming slang with ark)
optometrist	optician
podiatrist	chiropodist
quack	any doctor
troppo	affected by the heat
wetcheck	condom (Durex is a brand of adhesive tape)
wog	illness, particularly flu or diarrhoea

Health care in Australia is sophisticated and reaches the remotest parts of the nation. Food and drink are normally prepared and served in hygienic conditions. Tap water, despite often being unpleasant in taste and colour, is safe to drink everywhere. But there is more to Australian wildlife than cuddly koalas, kangaroos and wallabies, and the range of lethal species in Australia — both in the water and on dry land — is extraordinary. And there is a host of other natural phenomena which threaten both natives and visitors. But to keep the risks in perspective, bear in mind that statistically the biggest threat to your health in Australia is a road accident.

CLIMATIC HAZARDS

Heatstroke and Sunburn. Most visitors from the cooler reaches of the Northern Hemisphere are unused to the high temperatures encountered in Australia, particularly in the central deserts and tropical north. To avoid "going troppo" and collapsing from heat exhaustion, you should wear suitable clothing and a hat to keep as much of the sun off as possible. Drink plenty of non-alcoholic fluid, and avoid over-exertion until you acclimatize.

Of course many people visit Australia to bask in the sun, a practice shared by the natives. Perhaps because of their Pommie origins, many Australians are careless about protecting themselves, and as a result Australia has the highest incidence of skin cancer in the world. Although a temporary visitor is unlikely to succumb to a melanoma, it is very easy to become badly burnt. As a reaction to the cold European winter (or summer) they have just left, many British visitors ignore their better judgment and spend a whole day on the beach resulting in severe sunburn. The advice adopted by cancer campaigners sounds childish, but bears repeating for temporary visitors: "Slip, Slop, Slap". The idea is to *slip* on a shirt, *slop* on some sun lotion and *slap* on a hat. The sun's rays are at their most severe between 10am and 3pm. Start off with a lotion of a high protection factor (at least 6 or 7, or even 15 is not too high for sensitive skin), and re-apply the cream at frequent intervals, particularly after swimming. Try to ration your sunbathing (known by Australians as "sun-baking") so you don't literally become sun-baked.

One notable sunscreen favoured by Australians is zinc cream. This mixture of zinc, lanolin and oil is sold in various lurid colours (e.g. fluorescent green) and is usually applied to the nose and surrounding exposed flesh to prevent burning. Its effectiveness in preventing sunburn over long periods gives rise to the cricketing joke "What's the definition of an optimist? A Pommie batsman wearing zinc cream." Other precautions used include Arab-style neck flaps attached to sun hats.

If you ignore these precautions and become severely burnt, seek medical advice. Treat a mild dose of sunburn with a lotion such as Caladryl (calamine lotion — cheaper in Britain than Australia). Coconut oil is widely available but has recently been found to cause blotches on the skin after persistent use. Try natural yoghourt instead.

Acts of God. Australia is not nearly so seismologically active as New Zealand, and you are most unlikely to encounter one of the infrequent earth tremors which are usually confined to the south of Victoria. But to keep you on your toes, particularly in the far north, there are plenty of meteorological threats. The worst are cyclones ("blows"), one of which devastated Darwin in 1974. During the risk season from November to April you may hear news of one or more degrees of alert for cyclones from blue (little risk) to red (severe danger). The standard advice is to take shelter in the nearest secure building, fill the bath (to ensure a supply of water if the mains supply is cut off) and keep tuned to the radio. If you are out of doors and the winds pick up (they can reach over 250km/h), try to find a ditch to lie in and keep well away from anything which might be blown on top of you.

Fire. The long, hot, dry summers which much of Australia enjoys create just the right conditions for bush fires to start, whether naturally or triggered by man. Bush fires can affect any area of Australia with forest (especially eucalyptus), scrubland or the desert weed spinifex. By reading the local press and (particularly) listening to the radio, you can learn which are danger areas and try to avoid them.

During "total fire bans" when trees and scrub are tinder-dry, no fires may be lit in the open and you should not throw cigarette butts from your vehicle; the penalties for transgression are severe. It is sensible to avoid such areas, but if you do go into them you should look for places such as pools and clearings where you could take refuge. If you find yourself in an area where a fire has broken out, there are several steps you should take to maximize the chance of survival. In buildings, you should close all doors and windows, clear the gutters of leaves then block them and fill them with water and stay inside until the fire passes. If you are driving, but unable to get away from the fire, park as far away from vegetation as possible. Close all the windows and air vents, turn your headlights on (so rescuers can find you), lie on the floor and wait for the fire to pass. Don't attempt to empty your petrol tank, since this would merely fuel the fire around you, and if the temperature gets high enough to ignite the tank it is likely you would perish anyway. Walkers should try to find an open space and clear combustible material away from it. Water is better still, but don't try to take refuge in a raised water tank since you may be boiled alive.

PERILS OF THE DEEP

One of the more staggering facets of Australia is the number of aquatic nasties which will not hesitate to deliver a fatal sting, bite or snap. The chief menaces are sharks, crocodiles and an unpleasant little creature known as a marine stinger. One beast can even kill you when it's dead: the ugly-looking toad fish has deadly poisonous flesh.

Sharks. Man-eating sharks can be found at many places around the coast of Australia, in the south during the southern summer and mainly in the north from May to October. Some Australians may try to unnerve you with grisly stories, but it is most unusual for sharks to attack near the shoreline. In addition, most popular bathing spots (particularly around Sydney) are protected by netting, and the incidence of attacks by sharks is very low. These nets do not provide a continuous barrier against sharks, but manipulate their migration patterns sufficiently well to keep them away from beaches.

If you find yourself in shark-infested waters, it is better to do the breast-stroke, which creates an impression of calm strength, than the crawl, which can make it look as though you are flailing helplessly. It also helps if you are wearing a wet suit, so that if you are bumped by a shark you will not lose blood into the water. If you are feeling confident, a sharp tap on the shark's nose is sometimes sufficient to send it packing.

Marine Stingers. These potentially lethal creatures are also known as sea wasps and box jellyfish, and are common on the coast of Queensland and the Northern Territory from October to May. Don't rely upon seeing them before they see you, since they are almost transparent. They have tentacles over a metre long which attach themselves to you and inject a sometimes-fatal sting. The venom is contained in stinging capsules, and can cause violent shivering, nausea, a fall in blood pressure and paralysis of breathing muscles. Apart from these symptoms, the pain can sometimes be so excruciating that victims die of shock. If you are stung, applying vinegar to the affected area within a minute or two counteracts the sting. A tight tourniquet should be applied and you must get to hospital as quickly as possible for a dose of antivenom. The only sensible way to escape the threat is to stay out of the sea during the marine stinger season. If, despite the constant warnings, you insist on swimming, wear long-sleeved clothing, women's tights or a wet suit.

Crocodiles. Saltwater crocodiles ("salties") are the world's largest living reptile. In recent years they have killed far more people than have sharks, due partly to their newly acquired status as a protected species. They are found on or near the coast of the northern half of Australia. Despite their name, they can and do live in fresh water as numerous unfortunate victims have discovered. You should *never* swim in an area that you're not sure about: if there are no warning notices, check with locals anyway as many of the signs are vandalized or taken home as souvenirs. It is likely that swimming in an area inhabited by crocodiles will soon become an offence. Don't camp next to a river bank in the Outback, and don't leave food or remains around from your fishing expedition.

Freshwater or Johnston's crocodiles are smaller and unlikely to attack you, although nesting females can get a bit upset. The accepted wisdom about what to do if confronted by a crocodile is to run in a zigzag direction, since although they are the speediest reptiles on land, they find it difficult to change direction. The favourite foolproof method described by tour guides is to go bushwalking in crocodile areas only with someone who runs slower than you.

If you are caught, don't give up all hope. There are survivors of attacks by crocodiles who have escaped when the animal has momentarily opened its jaws to get a better grip. If this doesn't work and you are well and truly caught, don't expect to be eaten immediately. Most crocodiles prefer to drown their prey first, using the notorious "death-roll" technique where victims can expect to be brought up for air several times before drowning. Then the body is usually hidden away on an underground ledge for future consumption.

A good introduction to the beasts is *Crocodiles — A Few Simple Facts*, a pamphlet published by the Conservation Commission of the Northern Territory, PO Box 1460, Alice Springs, NT 5750 (tel: 089-50 8211).

Reefs and Rockpools. It is not a good idea to go walking barefoot on a coral reef, or to investigate a rockpool too closely. Various types of coral can inject a nasty poison if you tread on them in bare feet, and the crown of thorns starfish (which is currently attacking the Great Barrier Reef) has a painful sting. Stonefish like nothing better than to imitate a rock in shallow water, waiting for an unfortunate victim to step on them and be mortally stung. They are indistinguishable from ordinary small, grey rocks until their jaws open, revealing a vile yellow mouth complete with poison glands. Similarly, the tiny and pretty blue-ringed octopus which lives in shallow rockpools can give you a fatal venomous bite if you poke around too much. (The blue rings appear only when the creature is angry.) As with marine stingers, you should apply a tight tourniquet and get to hospital as quickly as possible.

Other marine hazards include venomous sea-snakes (found in the same places at the same times as marine stingers), and catfish which can sting so savagely that you die of shock caused by the pain.

INSECTS

You will have to contend with the danger, not to mention the annoyance, of Australia's famous insect life. An anonymous poem called *The Bushman's Farewell to Queensland* could just as easily have been written about the other states:

> Queensland thou art a land of pests,
> For flies and fleas one never rests
> E'en now mosquitoes round me revel —
> In fact they are the very devil.
> Sandflies and hornets, just as bad,
> They nearly drive a fellow mad;
> With scorpion and centipede
> And stinging ants of every breed...
> To stay in thee, O land of mutton,
> I wouldn't give a single button,
> But bid thee now a long farewell,
> Thou scorching, sunburnt land of hell!

The standard advice offered by the natives regarding insect bites is "don't scratch." People from parts of the world where being devoured by all manner of insect life is not a normal daily occurrence will find this difficult advice to follow. Always carry a powerful repellent and, if camping, be careful not to turn on a light inside your tent or van before making sure the door is tightly closed.

Spiders. Arachnids in Australia can be alarmingly large: most have a body length of 25mm or over. The majority are relatively harmless, such as the enormous Huntsman spider which commonly lurks behind picture frames, only to emerge in the evening. Another favourite haunt of spiders is on top of sun visors in cars; try to check this before setting off since there can be few more disconcerting surprises than to have a huge spider land on your lap on the freeway. Although a bite from a spider can be painful or induce nausea, it is not usually dangerous.

However, there are two species which are potentially lethal. One is the Funnel Web (*Atrax robustus*), found mainly in gardens in the Sydney region. This vicious creature is much more aggressive than most insects, and rears up on its hind legs to attack. The male version (very dark and shiny, with a spur on each of its second front legs) is the most deadly, although an antivenom has recently been found. The bite of the Redback (*Latrodectus hasselti*; black or brown with sometimes — but not always — a red flash) can also prove fatal, but there have been no deaths from its bite since an antivenom was discovered in 1959. The Redback, known elsewhere as the Black Widow, is infamous for its habit of lurking under toilet seats and biting the bottoms of the unwary. One other particularly nasty creature is the Wolf Spider (found mainly in Victoria), whose bites can cause gangrene and paralysis.

You should seek medical attention for all spider bites, and if you have any reason to suspect the offending beast of being lethal, immediately apply a tourniquet between the bite and the rest of the body, and wash the affected area. Try to kill the spider and take it to the hospital or doctor, so they can give you appropriate treatment. The Flick Pest Control company produces a useful guide to identifying spiders, which can be picked up from any of the company's offices in Australia. However, if you're close enough to distinguish between a male Funnel Web and the painful but non-lethal male Trapdoor, you're probably too close.

Mosquitoes. These creatures are a pest anywhere in the world. Those found in Australia are not malarial, but mosquitoes in the southern half of the country can spread two serious, though rare, diseases. The more common is epidemic polyarthritis, a virus whose effect is similar to influenza but causes considerable pain in wrist and ankle joints. It can last for several weeks, but after you have suffered once from the disease you should be immune for life. A more serious (but very rare) threat is a bite from a mosquito carrying Australian encephalitis, a virus which attacks the brain and can cause brain damage or death. To protect yourself against mosquitoes keep the screens on doors and windows closed, wear long sleeves and trousers (particularly in the evenings) and use a repellent. The best repellents contain diethyl toluamide (DET, commonly known as "deet") and should be applied to your skin every few hours or, for longer effectiveness, used to impregnate cotton clothes. The most widely used repellent is "Aerogard".

Flies. The corks around the stereotyped Australian hat are not there for decoration. They serve a useful purpose in keeping away flies, of which Australia has far more than it has rabbits, sheep or kangaroos. Buffalo flies are found mainly in the northern half of Australia. They are huge blue-green flying insects (reputedly growing as big as matchboxes) with a long sucker which is plunged into your skin. The resulting bite is more painful and itchy than a mosquito bite. You are much more likely to encounter the sandfly, a small but vicious brute which can cause painful and itchy bites. Sandflies usually live in sand near fresh water, and respond to the same repellents as do mosquitoes. If you are sleeping outside, try if possible to find somewhere raised above ground (e.g. on a roof), since sandflies are land-based and cannot jump more than 60cm.

Ticks, Fleas and Lice. The bites from these irritants can, in northern Australia, pass on typhus, whose early stages are like flu and which can develop into nausea, skin rashes and even pneumonia.

OTHER HAZARDS

Snakes. Australia has more than its fair share of poisonous snakes, most of them unknown in the rest of the world. They include the Yellow Whip, the Taipan, the Tiger Snake and the Death Adder, plus (most lethal of all), the unassumingly named Brown Snake. You will only be bitten if you provoke a snake (by treading on it, or rolling over it in your sleep), and since snakes' jaws are not designed to bite humans many people survive attacks by venomous reptiles. When walking in the Outback you should wear sturdy footwear and keep an eye out for them, but the old adage "for every snake you see, a hundred see you and slide away" is quite true. If you are unlucky enough to get bitten, try to fix in your mind a description of the offending snake (or, better still, kill it and take it with you). All hospitals carry serums against the venom of local species, so get help as quickly as possible.

Malevolent Mammals. Australia has no man-eating mammals, nor any cases of rabies, but there are plenty of beasts which can cause you damage. The native wild dog — the dingo — may or may not devour babies, but does on occasion bite tourists. Bites from dingoes or domestic dogs, whether "bitsers" (mongrels) or pedigree breeds, should be cleaned and dressed and you should get a jab against tetanus if you haven't had a recent booster. In more remote areas, you may find water buffaloes and wild pigs: leave them well alone.

MEDICAL TREATMENT

The Australian version of a National Health Service is the *Medicare* system. UK residents on short-term visits are entitled to treatment under the same terms as Australians for any "episode of ill-health which occurs during the visit". This specifically excludes treatment for pre-existing conditions. In order to qualify for Medicare you need to register with any Medicare office, producing your passport and visa. This can be done retrospectively, so if you need treatment urgently go direct to a hospital or doctor. If you prefer to be well-prepared, obtain a Medicare card shortly after arrival. There are Medicare offices in all the main towns, or you can apply by post to PO Box 9822 in any capital city. In either case you will need a mailing address in Australia. The card takes about two weeks to come through, and will be valid for the length of stay you indicate on the form. People staying longer than six months must pay contributions towards Medicare.

Under Medicare, all in- and out-patient treatment at a public hospital is free, apart from drugs and dressings for which a nominal charge is made. Ambulance charges, however, are not covered and must be paid for in full. The cost of a visit to a doctor is less predictable. Medicare refunds at least 85% of the scheduled cost of treatment by a GP and you make up the difference (to a maximum cost to you of $10). These costs are worked out according to a table of charges, notably $16.40 for a visit to a GP. But although Medicare's contribution is fixed according to this schedule, doctors may charge whatever fees they like. Some philanthropic GPs do not charge the patient at all, but merely send the bill for 85% of the schedule fee direct to Medicare. Most others, however, charge $18-$25 for a consultation, leaving you to pay the excess above the $13.94 (85% of $16.40) refunded by Medicare. If you are covered by travel insurance, you can claim back any shortfall from your insurer.

Visitors from North America receive free health care only for emergency treatment; for subsequent convalescence or non-urgent treatment they must pay in full. Insurance is therefore a wise investment for US and Canadian citizens.

The major hospital in each state capital is listed under *Help and Information* in the regional chapters; elsewhere, ask the police or any local for the nearest hospital.

Royal Flying Doctor Service. The scheme to fly doctors to patients in the Outback, and patients to hospitals was set up in 1927 by the Reverend John Flynn. Nowadays the flying ambulances are more likely to be controlled by satellite links than crackling radio-telephones, but the principle of providing rapid medical attention in outlying areas remains the same. If you are unfortunate enough to require their services, anyone in the Outback will know the fastest way to summon help.

Dental Treatment. Dentistry is not covered by Medicare and must be paid for in full. It can be very expensive (typically $40-$50 for a simple filling), so ensure that your teeth are in good order before travelling to Australia or take out insurance which covers emergency dental treatment. To ease the pain a little, most dentists accept credit cards. If you are uninsured, dental teaching hospitals can treat you for less than the usual cost of a private dentist.

Blood. There are no opportunities for selling blood, but you may donate it through Red Cross centres in return for a hot drink and a Mars bar. All donors are screened for antibodies to HIV (the virus which causes AIDS), but this test is not 100% effective.

AIDS. According to a BBC report in 1987, the Acquired Immune Deficiency Syndrome was spreading faster in Australia than in any other country except the United States. There are estimated to be nearly 50,000 carriers of the HIV virus. The number of cases of full-blown AIDS is doubling every eight months, and at this rate there will be 3,000 victims of the disease by 1990. Most cases at present are confined to New South Wales (which has 69% of known victims), attributed to the large numbers of homosexuals and drug abusers in Sydney. Significant numbers of cases of the disease have also been reported in Victoria, Queensland and Western Australia. The Federal Government instituted a massive health education campaign based upon a television commercial featuring the Grim Reaper knocking down victims like skittles in a bowling alley. Apart from infuriating owners of ten-pin bowling alleys, the campaign has had little obvious effect. This is perhaps unsurprising in Queensland, since one of Sir Joh Bjelke Petersen's last acts was to ban condom vending machines in an attempt to reduce promiscuity.

Getting Around

Never underestimate the size of Australia when planning your itinerary. It is a massive country, as big as the USA or Europe. It is also a continent where the harshness of the terrain has made it difficult for land links to be built or maintained. For example, the last stretch of the road from Adelaide to Alice Springs was paved only in 1987, a few months after Highway 1 around the circumference of Australia was completed. Away from the state capitals, the volume of traffic using both road and rail is so low that little investment has been made in modernizing links to allow for higher speeds.

Time is not a problem if you fly across the vast empty interior, but finding the cash for highly expensive air tickets may well be. To make the most of your stay, allow plenty of time or money for your travels, and try to take advantage of the many special deals available to foreign visitors to Australia. Hitch-hiking is fine for short or medium-length trips, but can be slow and problematic over long distances. Cycling is not always pleasurable in the largest cities, but is perfect for touring a particular country area or — if you have the time and stamina — even tackling a trans-Australian trip.

AIR

Easily the fastest way to travel around Australia is by air. But you pay a high price for the luxury of travelling hundreds or thousands of miles in a few hours. Until October 1990, the federal government is continuing its policy of permitting only two major airlines to operate comprehensive domestic services: Ansett Airlines of Australia, and the government-owned carrier Australian Airlines (formerly TAA, and still sometimes referred to as such). They charge the same fares and operate near-identical services: often the only direct flights of the day from one city to another will depart at exactly the same time, offering no flexibility to the traveller. There are flights at least daily between the major cities (although some, like Melbourne to Darwin, require several stops) but demand is insufficient on many other routes to justify more than one or two services each week.

East-West Airlines — now owned by Ansett, but operated as a separate company — offers a "no-frills" service and has fares about 15% lower than the two main domestic airlines. Its route network is restricted to the east coast and Tasmania, plus a couple of flights from Cairns and Sydney to Perth via Ayers Rock. Because of East-West's low fares (reduced still further by the various discounts described below) its services are very popular and booking well ahead is recommended. Good local services are operated within each state by local carriers, but most use small aircraft which are often booked up well in advance.

From July 1988, foreign visitors can travel on the internal sectors of international flights by Qantas, if these tickets are booked in conjunction with an international ticket to Australia on Qantas or any other airline. Fares will be lower than on Ansett and Australian Airlines. Note, however, that Qantas does not have a comprehensive network around Australia and that flights are prone to depart at unsocial hours.

Fares. With little competition for air travellers' dollars, fares are generally higher than in the USA and Europe. The short hop from Melbourne to Adelaide costs $161 one-way, and a coast-to-coast return flight from Perth to Sydney or Brisbane is nearly $1,000. Full-fare economy class tickets, although expensive, allow considerable flexibility: dates, times and airlines can be changed at will, and if you decide not to travel you can obtain a full refund. A good trick with these tickets is to include a stopover free-of-charge: for example, if you're travelling from Brisbane to Cairns, take the first flight out as far as Townsville, spend the day there and continue your journey to Cairns on the last flight of the day. As long as you make the journey in one day, you pay only the through fare.

If you're feeling flush, you can pay an extra 10% to travel business class (on Australian Airlines only) or an extra 50% for first. This buys separate, more comfortable seating, better food and free drinks. The following special deals, which start with the cheapest, are available only in economy.

Flexi Fares. These tickets, which give a 45% discount on return fares, are marketed under different names by Ansett (Flexi Fare), Australian (Excursion 45) and East-West (Super Savers). They are considerably more flexible from the airline's point of view than from yours. The main catch is that the time of your flight cannot be guaranteed. The usual conditions are that you must book between four and 14 days in advance and stay away at least overnight but for no more than three weeks. Having booked for the day you wish to travel, you must call the airline after noon the day before. On routes served daily, you will be told the time of the flight you have been assigned; you have no choice in this assignation, which will often be inconveniently early or late. For the many routes which have no more than one flight daily, you will be told whether you are on this flight or on the next one — which could be up to a week later! A cancellation fee of 50% is charged if you are unable or unwilling to travel on your assigned flight.

Go Australia Airpass. This is not an unlimited-travel deal, but a relatively cheap way of travelling long distances by air in Australia which saves around 40% on normal fares. It is available on both Ansett and Australian, and costs $600 for up to 6,000km of air travel (profits compared to normal fares start at around 3,700km), or $950 for 10,000km (profits after 6,000km). The Airpass is sold abroad and within Australia. Foreign visitors with excursion air tickets to Australia who buy it abroad or within 30 days of arrival in Australia are entitled to more stopovers (a maximum of five on the 6,000km pass, eight on the 10,000km ticket) and less restrictive conditions than the ordinary version sold in Australia. Two routings which maximize travel are, respectively:

Melbourne — Canberra — Sydney — Alice Springs — Adelaide — Hobart — Melbourne (which comes out at 5919 air kilometres).
Perth — Hobart — Melbourne — Canberra — Sydney — Gold Coast — Mackay — Alice Springs — Perth (a total of 9977km).

To help you to calculate your own itinerary, flight distances are included in the *Travellers Guide* brochure published by Tourism Australia.

East-West Airlines offers three interesting air passes. Each costs $570; the "Coastal" pass allows travel up or down the east coast of Australia, from Cairns to Hobart via the major cities en route. The "Transcontinental" pass permits one-way travel from Perth via Ayers Rock and Sydney to Cairns or vice-versa. The "East-Side" pass allows 14 days of unlimited travel within the area bounded by Ayers Rock, the Sunshine Coast, Sydney and Hobart.

If your plans include only those cities served by British Airways and Qantas, the Circle Australia fare (which offers five domestic flights on international services) will work out much cheaper; see page 15 for details.

Advance Purchase (Apex) Fares. To save 35% on round trips with guaranteed flights, you need to book and pay 30 days in advance. You must stay away for a minimum of a week and a maximum of a year. If you cancel within the 30 days before your flight, you get a refund of half the cost of the ticket.

See Australia Fares. These tickets can be of great benefit to visitors to Australia; not only do they offer a better discount — 30% — and considerably less stress than flying standby, they are also almost as flexible as full-fare tickets. See Australia fares are available only to visitors from overseas, though they need not be bought outside Australia. There is a misconception that these fares can be used only to connect with an international flight (e.g. for a Perth-Adelaide sector immediately after you've arrived from overseas in Perth). In fact these tickets can be used at any time within 45 days of your arrival in Australia, and do not have to bear any relation to your international flight (for example, if you arrive and depart from Sydney, you can still buy a See Australia ticket from Brisbane to Darwin).

To qualify, you must book no more than 30 days after your arrival in Australia, and the itinerary must be more than 1,000km (625 miles). Therefore it is important to know which air journeys do not exceed 1,000km. These include Sydney to Brisbane, Melbourne or Canberra; Canberra to Brisbane, Adelaide or Melbourne; and Melbourne to Adelaide or Hobart. But if you combine these trips to make an itinerary of over 1,000km (e.g. Brisbane — Sydney — Melbourne), the whole journey qualifies for the 30% discount. Another crucial condition is that you must present a round-trip *excursion* ticket from your home country. This is designed to exclude business travellers from getting the discount, but it may also preclude those who have bought from bucket shops. If you intend to buy a bucket shop ticket to get to Australia, it's worth checking with the bucket shop that your ticket will qualify for the See Australia discount. To make doubly sure, buy your domestic ticket in advance from a travel agent or Qantas office outside Australia.

Once you have your ticket, it is as flexible as any full-fare economy ticket: bookings and airlines can be changed or full refunds obtained.

Student Discounts. Overseas students under 26 years can claim a 25% discount on normal economy fares by producing an ISIC card or, alternatively, an international airline ticket issued at a student discount.

Standby. As anywhere, standby travel (giving 20% off normal fares) is fraught with anxiety. You should get to the airport as early as possible before the flight, to buy your ticket and register at the standby desk. If the flight is lightly booked, you may be issued with a boarding pass immediately. More likely, however, you will be told to report back ten minutes before the flight departs. After giving full-fare passengers every possible chance to turn up, the staff will eventually call out the names of the lucky standby passengers. If you are not among them, you can try for the next flight or obtain a full refund. Standby tickets on Ansett and Australian are interchangeable, so if the staff of one airline tell you there's no chance of a seat, try the other. Note, however, that once you begin your journey you must stick to the same airline.

For any standby flight it is well worth calling the airlines in advance and asking how heavily loaded they are. This is particularly recommended for multi-sector flights such as Brisbane — Sydney — Melbourne, on which you must standby for each individual sector. If you don't succeed in getting back on the same flight, any costs for overnight accommodation and meals must be paid for yourself.

If you're travelling alone, don't leave the standby desk until the aircraft has left. It is not unknown for one partner in a couple who'd hoped to travel together to get halfway up the steps and change his or her mind about travelling, leaving the flight with an empty seat unless you are close at hand.

Airports. Travellers who are used to busy European or North American airports may be surprised when arriving at Australian airports. For most of the time they are deadly quiet, bursting into life only for a few hours each day when a number of flights arrive and depart in a flurry.

In most cases the international terminal is quite separate from the domestic building, ranging from next door (e.g. Hobart) to 10km apart (Perth). Consult the *Arrival and Departure* section of each regional chapter for details of links from the airport to the city and between terminals. International terminals at smaller airports are locked up and deserted for most of the time. They open two hours before arrivals or departures and close shortly after the last flight has arrived or left.

Domestic Sectors of International Flights. Travelling on these services is a radically different proposition to regular domestic flights. The first difference is that you should go to the international terminal. Check-in will be considerably earlier, due to the formalities you will have to undergo. The authorities are paranoid about the opportunities for smuggling afforded by the intermingling of passengers and their belongings, so you are subject to the same controls as international passengers. The boarding pass you receive will bear a "D" sticker to indicate you are a domestic passenger. You must queue up for the passport and customs check; your boarding pass will be stamped and must be retained for collection upon arrival at your destination. You will, of course, arrive at the international terminal. Follow the signs for "Aircrew and Domestic Pass Holders" to make a quick getaway through Customs.

Smoking. Smoking is banned on all scheduled domestic flights, with a maximum $500 fine for offenders. This ban does not apply to charter flights, nor to the Prime Minister's private jet. So at the time of writing, a smokers' rights group planned to set up a new charter airline flying between Sydney and Melbourne, where passengers will be given complimentary cigars; with little respect for the Prime Minister, the airline is to be called Hawkair.

Safety. Australian carriers are fastidious about safety. This can be irritating (e.g. you might be instructed to move your handbag from behind your feet to in front of them) but their attitude is to be commended and has made Australia the safest place in the world to fly. Be careful of what you consume beforehand; an Air Navigation Order makes it illegal to "board an aircraft whilst intoxicated."

Baggage. In keeping with this concern for safety, carry-on luggage rules are enforced very strictly. These allow a small bag — which must fit inside the metal frames dotted around each airport — plus a suit bag, and, for women, a handbag. The total weight of these items must not exceed 4kg. As you'll be warned repeatedly, if you try to conceal the true extent of your luggage and try to take it all aboard as hand baggage, it may be confiscated at the aircraft door and travel on a later flight. Economy class travellers are allowed one piece of checked baggage whose weight must not exceed 30kg.

Left Luggage. Most airports have lockers where you can leave your belongings. After the 24 hours that your 20¢ buys, the locks may be closed to force you to pay the excess due. To save the small change, it's worth asking the airline baggage enquiry office if you can leave your bags. Ansett permits this for up to 24 hours if you are travelling with them.

Gift Vouchers. Australian Airlines sells air travel gift vouchers which can be used to pay for tickets and associated services. If somebody gives you one, you can convert it to cash by buying a full-fare ticket then claiming a refund.

BUS

Buses cover almost every stretch of tarmacked highway in Australia, and with increasing competition there are some real bargains to be found. Bus Australia, Deluxe Coachlines, Greyhound and Ansett Pioneer are the four main companies, each with a countrywide network. It is also worth checking out smaller companies like Intertour and Border Coaches; although they lack a comprehensive network, they provide competitive fares on some major routes.

Despite the relative luxury of Australian coaches (many of which are equipped with air-conditioning, loos, reclining seats and even video screens), bus travel is not everyone's idea of fun: journeys can be long and arduous, lacking the freedom of movement offered on trains. Away from the main inter-city routes, services tend to be infrequent and fares high. But for those unwilling to risk the vagaries of hitch-hiking and unable to meet the cost of flying or buying their own vehicle, it provides a reasonable means of seeing a great deal of the country.

Reservations. Like any other form of transport, the earlier you book the more likely you are to be able to travel on your chosen service. Although it is possible to book through travel agents or airline offices abroad, it is best to book direct with the operator concerned either before or after your arrival in Australia. You can make reservations in advance in the UK for Bus Australia through branches of YHA Travel (such as 14 Southampton St, London WC2E 7HY; 01-240 5236); the other three main operators have the following offices:

Ansett Pioneer, c/o Traveland South Pacific, 10 Maddox St, London W1R 9PN (01-439 1849).

Deluxe, c/o Australian Travel Marketing, 70 Brewer St, London W1R 3PJ (01-434 9734).

Greyhound Lines International Sales, 14-16 Cockspur St, London SW1Y 5BL (01-839 5591).

Deluxe also have an office in California, at Suite 820, 9841 Airport Boulevard, Los Angeles (213-410-9734).

Within Australia, you can book either in person or by telephone. Greyhound have a nationwide number (008-077 014) which enables you to make reservations after hours (i.e. between 8pm and 8am) for the price of a local call.

The ticket you receive bears more than a passing resemblance to an airline ticket. Each destination has a three-letter code like an airport code, and indeed cities which have an airport use the same code: thus ADL=Adelaide, BNE=Brisbane, CNB=Canberra, etc. These codes are quoted in timetables; if checking baggage, ensure that the code on the luggage tag matches that of your destination.

Fares. Bus prices are typically one-third of the corresponding air fare and two-thirds of the rail fare (although for some journeys trains are about the same or marginally cheaper). Ansett Pioneer, Deluxe and Greyhound charge around the same fares, with Bus Australia and smaller operators a little cheaper. Some approximate examples: Sydney-Melbourne $40, Melbourne-Adelaide $38, Adelaide-Perth $99 and Sydney-Perth $160. In general, the more popular the route among travellers, the greater the competition and the lower the fares. Few travel agencies command a total understanding of the services on offer, so to get the best deal possible you should do some leg-work or some extensive telephoning, since the rival companies do not usually share a single bus terminal. (Addresses and phone numbers of depots in the major cities are given under *Arrival and Departure* in the regional chapters.) Most operators charge cancellation fees of $5 or $10 providing you cancel at least 24 hours before the journey (thereafter you lose the lot).

Stopovers. As you may deduce from the sample prices above, it is much cheaper to buy one ticket for a long trip rather than separate ones for shorter journeys. You can normally stop off en route at state capitals for no extra charge.

Discounts. Pensioners and children usually qualify for a 20% discount. Many operators offer a discount of 10% to students, and some extend this to YHA members as well. For example, Bus Australia gives a 10% discount to YHA members for inter-city routes and Deluxe a 10% discount for all trips. To qualify for the YHA discount, you must in most cases book through YHA offices in Australia. A more substantial discount of 40% on their (already low) fares is offered by Bus Australia; known as "Flexi-Fare", it is bookable two to 14 days ahead with the condition that the actual departure time may be moved up to 48 hours later; you must phone them 12 hours before your intended departure to find out your assigned service. One little-known deal is offered by Greyhound to anyone leaving Australia on Continental Airlines: upon production of your ticket, you can get a 25% discount on a one-way ticket from wherever you find yourself to your airport of departure.

Unlimited Travel Passes. Each of the major companies has a selection of bus passes, which are cheaper when bought abroad than in Australia. The one you choose depends largely upon your itinerary. For example, Greyhound covers the south and east very efficiently (through its tie-up with Stateliner in South Australia, which accepts the Greyhound BusPass) and has a good network in Western Australia, while Ansett Pioneer, in association with Tasmanian Redline, allows free travel around Tasmania.

Greyhound's *Overseas BusPass* costs $182 for seven days, $231 for ten days, $286 for 14 days, $380 for 21 days, $523 for 30 days and $781 for 60 days. The same pass is obtainable within Australia at slightly higher prices. YHA members can get a 10% discount on all these prices. Greyhound also has a deal called *Aussie Explorer*. This offers a choice of popular routes, costing from $160 to $690, which you may cover at your leisure within 12 months.

The Ansett Pioneer *Aussiepass* allows unlimited travel for periods of seven ($195), 15 ($260), 30 ($465) or 60 days ($690). YHA members qualify for a 10% discount, and holders of Qantas Connections Cards get 15% off. As well as bus travel the *Aussiepass* entitles you to free or half-price Ansett Pioneer city sightseeing tours. Another interesting innovation from Ansett is the *Adventure Passport*. This card gives a one-third discount on standard fares on the express coach network and 20% off Ansett sightseeing tours, and is available to all foreign visitors (at a price in the UK of £25). It is particularly useful for visitors who wish to travel long distances over a long period of time.

Prices for Deluxe Coachlines' *Koala Pass* go from $176 for seven days to $1,095 for 90 days. They also have a *Space Pass* which saves 30% on these prices but is usable only if space is available. This is not usually a problem, but you do take the risk of being stuck for 24 hours or more. Prices range from $123 for seven days to $766 for 90 days. Deluxe have a selection of *Wanderer Passes* covering specific itineraries, each valid for 12 months: a Sydney — Brisbane — Adelaide — Melbourne — Sydney trip costs $233, while a round-Australia trek with a detour to Alice Springs and Ayers Rock costs $747.

The *Bus Australia Pass* can, like the company's tickets, be purchased through YHA offices abroad. Prices range from $238 for 16 days to $895 for 90 days, lower than the other companies but with the disadvantage that services are less frequent and the network less comprehensive.

Surcharges. A supplement on the basic fare is payable for luxury or high-speed services such as Deluxe *Super Deckers,* Greyhound's *5-Star* and Ansett Pioneer's *Silver Service.* Holders of unlimited travel passes are permitted to use these services, but only upon payment of the difference between the basic fare and the higher charge. Examples of the supplement: Brisbane-Cairns $6; Sydney-Melbourne $5; Perth-Adelaide $11.

Rules. There are a surprising number of regulations affecting bus travellers. On some services, travel between two points in the same state is prohibited by licensing regulations. And travellers' behaviour is carefully controlled. For example, on Deluxe buses you will be instructed not to drink from cartons, not to put rubbish in the ashtray and told of the precise location of the flushing mechanism in the toilet. On Ansett Pioneer, eating is confined to odourless foods and drinking to non-spill cartons. You may also get a stern lecture about alcohol and non-prescription drugs; these must be deposited with the driver (no questions asked). If you are caught drinking alcohol on a bus, you will be put off at the nearest police station (maximum fine $500) and your ticket will be ripped up.

Smoking is permitted only on certain services, and then only in the last few rows of seats. It is prohibited throughout Queensland and on all coaches run by Bus Australia and Executive Express.

TRAIN

Rail travellers have far less choice of routes and services than bus passengers. The network is sparse, consisting basically of a route across the south from Perth to Sydney (the *Indian-Pacific*), a spur from this line up to Alice Springs, a loop from Adelaide through Melbourne to Sydney, and the line north along the east coast as far as Cairns. High-speed links between major cities are rare; instead there are long, slow runs on creaking tracks at speeds around 50km/h, with a few high-speed trains in the southeast and networks of suburban services around the main cities. For some alarming stories about rail travel in Australia — such as the passenger obliged to wait five days for a connection — consult *Great Rail Non-Journeys of Australia* by Colin Taylor (Queensland Press, $22.95).

Despite its imperfections, a train journey can be a fascinating way to see the country with a fair degree of comfort. If you are able to get a standby ticket or use a rail pass, it can also be a cheap way to get around. Another great benefit is that you can usually break your journey as often as you wish with little formality.

Railways still form an essential part of rural Australian life: great expresses draw to a halt in the middle of nowhere to deliver passengers and sustenance to an outback cattle station. Train treks across the country appeal to many, although the romance (and scenery) may begin to pall a little after the 480km arrow-straight run across the Nullarbor — the longest straight stretch of railway in the world — which forms part of the 40-hour journey from Perth to Adelaide. Your fellow travellers may not all be entirely to your taste, since long-distance trains seem to attract a fair amount of heavy-drinking lowlife.

Each state has its own railway company, but there are also some interstate trains operated by the state enterprise Railways of Australia. Long-distance trains have glamorous names which the rolling stock sometimes finds it difficult to live up to. The carriages of suburban trains are often equally decrepit, but provide a useful mode of rapid transit around the major cities. Genuinely fast trains are confined to the *Prospector* from Perth to Kalgoorlie, and a few lines radiating from Sydney to other New South Wales cities and Canberra; these services are operated by "Intercity XPT" (based on British high-speed trains).

There is talk, however, of building a 350km/h "VFT" (Very Fast Train) link between Sydney and Melbourne.

Reservations. Local services do not require reservations — you just buy a ticket and board the train. Long-distance trains are a different matter; on some routes there are only one or two services each week, so advance reservations are essential. These can be made at stations or city ticket offices. The latter is usually quicker, since computerization has not yet reached many country stations. Some operate a quota system, and if their allotment is used up you won't be given a place even if the train has empty seats. If you're unable to call in personally, you can make or change reservations by telephone:

Adelaide 217 4111	Melbourne 62 0771
Brisbane 225 0211	(elsewhere in Victoria: 008-136 109)
Canberra 49 8159	Perth 326 2222
Launceston (Tasmania) 34 6911	Sydney 217 8812

If you wish to book from abroad, you may do so through Compass Travel, 46 Albemarle St, London W1X 4EP (01-408 4141); the Australian Travel Service, 1101 East Broadway, Glendale, CA 91205 (1-800-626-6665); or Private Label Travel, 3080 Yonge St, Toronto, Ontario M4N 3N1 (1-800-387-8480).

Timetables. As with other forms of transport, Australian railway schedules do not use the 24-hour clock. Times before noon are shown in ordinary type, those after noon in **bold**. All times quoted are local times, so be sure to set your watch correctly after crossing state borders. It's also worth checking that you know the right date; with journeys from west to east sometimes spreading over four days, schedules can be confusing.

Fares. Basic economy class fares on shorter journeys (e.g. Sydney-Canberra) work out at about $7 for 100km, but can be considerably less for very long journeys. Sample one-way prices include Sydney — Melbourne $67, Melbourne — Adelaide $53, Adelaide — Perth $125 and Brisbane — Cairns $95. First class fares are about 40% higher. With ordinary tickets, you may break your journey anywhere en route providing you have onward reservations. Children aged 4-15 years and Australian pensioners are entitled to half-price travel.

Supplements. Sleeper berths cost extra, but you may think the added expense worthwhile for long journeys. The overnight rate is as little as $15 in economy services in Queensland, but up to $35 on other routes. Sleeping accommodation on some services is confined to first class; on others, such as the *Prospector* between Perth and Kalgoorlie, a meal is included in the fare.

Cheap Deals. Standby fares between the major cities in southeast Australia are real bargains. If there is space after 4pm the day before you wish to travel, you can get from Sydney to Melbourne for $30 (saving 55%) or from Melbourne to Adelaide for the same price.

"CAPER" (Customer Advance Purchase Excursion Rail) fares are available on all main routes and guarantee you a seat. They offer a 20-30% discount on inter-city journeys, reducing the cost of an Adelaide — Perth trip, for example, to $100. Booking must be made and paid for at least seven days in advance of travel, and no refunds are made for cancellations within a week of travelling.

Holders of Qantas Connections Cards get a discount of 15% on all long-distance trains; this reduction also applies to supplements. The Railways of

Australia student concession card reducing fares by up to 50% is intended primarily for Australian students, although some foreign students have managed to obtain the card by taking an ISIC card to a student travel office. Season tickets for regular travel on suburban routes yield a reasonable discount and, in some cities, take the form of an unlimited travel pass for the whole suburban network.

Unlimited Travel Passes. The *Austrailpass* is sold only outside Australia to foreign passport holders. It allows unlimited travel on all rail services except Adelaide suburban services and special excursion trains. Prices for the Budget Austrailpass (economy class) are $320 for 14 days, $410 for 21 days, $500 for one month, and $710 or $820 for two or three months respectively. A one-week extension to the 14-day pass can be bought in Australia for $160. Supplements for meals and sleeper berths are not included. To ensure maximum benefit from the Austrailpass, reservations should be made as far in advance as possible; these can be changed subsequently at no charge if your plans change.

Some states offer rail passes covering their network; details are given in the appropriate regional chapters.

Baggage. The free allowance is 80kg per passenger. If your luggage is bulky, you may be obliged to check it into the guard's van, and you should arrive at the station early enough to do so.

Special Trains. Railway buffs may be interested in a couple of tastefully refurbished excursion trains. Australia's answer to Europe's Orient Express is the *Southern Cross,* a train made up of 1920s Pullman cars which this steam-hauled train operates once weekly between Sydney and Melbourne for a fare of over $400. The *Silver City Limited* is more modern: an exotic 1950s-style train which runs three times each week between Adelaide and Broken Hill. The seven-hour journey can be whiled away listening to five channels of audio entertainment on stereo headphones.

DRIVING

bowser	petrol pump
brown bomber	traffic warden in some cities
canary	yellow sticker attached by traffic police to parked vehicles which they wish to inspect for mechanical soundness
clicks	kilometres
drop or *chuck a U-ey*	make a U-turn
Imperial ton	100 mph (160km/h)
late model	new (ish) car
long paddock	the open road
Moke	small open-topped jeep available for hire in seaside resorts
muffler	silencer
nature strip	grass verge in suburban street
prime mover	tractor unit of articulated lorry
rego	(pronounced "redgo") registration (road tax)
RWC	Certificate of Road-Worthiness
run-out	new car made obsolete by new stock, hence sold off cheaply

semi	articulated lorry
traffic area	zone with parking restrictions
traffic officer	traffic warden
ute	utility vehicle, i.e. pick-up truck

If your first journey is by car from Sydney Airport to the city centre, you may quickly become convinced that driving in Australia is a battle fought on inadequate roads by badly behaved motorists. If your driving is confined to the metropolitan areas, you might not find any cause to alter this opinion.

Apart from the more heavily used routes, Australian roads are generally poor. The low density of cars (only nine million in a country the size of the USA) makes it uneconomic to maintain roads to the standards found in Europe and North America. Only one-third of the total of 850,000km is sealed, and you can't rely upon finding a properly tarmacked road. Even main highways, such as the Queensland coastal road, often consist of one paved lane with broad dirt shoulders. This means you must drop your nearside wheels into the dirt or gravel whenever you meet oncoming traffic. Freeways are few and far between, usually restricted to short stretches out of the major cities. Some highways have an unnerving habit of degenerating from a fast dual carriageway into the main street of a small town, complete with badly parked cars, traffic signals and battle-hardened jaywalkers.

Even when a real freeway is built around a town, the locals steadfastly refuse to acknowledge it as such. Don't be surprised to find people and animals crossing a freeway as though it were an ordinary road. Most regular highways have only two lanes, though there is sometimes one paved shoulder on to which slower moving vehicles move when they notice a vehicle coming up behind. Quite a few rural roads and tracks can be negotiated only by four-wheel drive vehicles (often written *4WD* or *4×4*). Because of the wide variation in road conditions, making deadlines for completing a long trip in Australia is a risky business.

The Australians have imported the British habit of driving on the left, at least in theory. This qualification is added advisedly, because you're unlikely to meet such bad drivers anywhere else in the western world. Despite its stringent anti-drink/drive laws, Australia is still one of the most dangerous countries in which to drive. Around 3,000 people are killed on the roads each year, twice the rate in terms of population as Britain. Most daily newspapers publish a Road Toll Chart, showing harrowing statistics for the city or state, such as "total deaths this month" and "best death-free run" (i.e. the most consecutive days without a fatal accident — often a distressingly low figure).

Of course, driving in Australia can have its compensations. Motoring in a country where most road users regard a queue of five cars as a traffic jam can't be all bad. Outside the cities, traffic is light and driving is often a real pleasure.

Licences. You must carry your licence at all times while driving. Your national driving licence is valid for three months, an International Driving Permit (issued by a motoring organization in your home country) for a year. If you stay longer or take up residence, you must apply for a state licence. Holders of full British or North American licences need not take a driving test to obtain one, but must undergo a physical examination and an oral or written test based on the appropriate state traffic code.

Fuel. Petrol costs 60¢-70¢ per litre in cities, about 15% more in rural areas. This corresponds to about £1.25 per Imperial gallon, US$1.75 per US gallon. Visitors from densely populated nations may be perturbed to discover that most service stations keep limited opening hours, typically 7am-6pm Monday to Friday and 7am-noon on Saturday. Details of fuel outlets which keep longer hours are given in the local press, or you can ask at a police station. In rural areas there is normally a rota, while in the cities one or two stations on main routes out of town open 24 hours. Some which advertise "24-hour petrol" merely provide an automatic dispenser which takes $2, $5 or $10 bills, so ensure you have a good selection of notes. Ordinary petrol stations normally accept credit cards.

Australia is rapidly converting to unleaded petrol ("ULP"), which can cause some confusion on the forecourt to those unused to this fuel. Petrol is sold in one leaded grade (super — around 97 octane), and two grades of unleaded. The nozzles of unleaded fuel pumps are smaller, to prevent drivers of unleaded-only vehicles filling up with leaded fuel. However, it is quite possible to fill up a vehicle intended to use leaded fuel with unleaded petrol. This won't necessarily be a disaster since many cars can run happily for a time on unleaded fuel, but you should top up with the leaded variety as soon as possible. For further advice, consult one of the motoring organizations in Australia.

Fuel consumption is measured in litres used per 100km. Confusingly for visitors, this means that the higher the figure the less economical the vehicle. To convert to miles per gallon, see page 22.

Motoring Organizations. Each state has its own organization, under the umbrella of the Australian Automobile Association (AAA — 212 Northbourne Avenue, Canberra, ACT 2601). If you are a member of a foreign motoring organization, you can ask for a free copy of their *Motoring in Australia* booklet. The state motoring organizations have reciprocal arrangements with each other and with British and North American associations, so foreign members can take advantage of their free route information and breakdown services. Their acronyms are not always obvious: for example, New South Wales' NRMA stands for National Roads & Motorists Association. Details are given under *Getting Around* for each regional chapter.

Routes and Maps. Before embarking on any long distance jaunt, you should acquire a good map. The motoring organizations produce good ones (free or at cut rates to members of overseas associations), or you can buy the excellent George Philip *Australian Road Atlas* (published also in London and Boston by Faber & Faber).

When choosing a route or asking directions, remember that road numbers are rarely used: highways are known by names instead, such as the Princes Highway along the southeast coast from Adelaide via Melbourne to Sydney, and the Great Northern Highway in Western Australia which links Perth with Broome.

Road Signs. The quality of direction signposting varies from good to less-than-adequate, and on unfamiliar territory you should keep your eyes peeled for signposts concealed behind trees. On main roads, there are small shields every five kilometres bearing the initial letter of the last or next major town above the distance in kilometres: thus $\frac{S}{25}$ indicates 25km to or from, say, Sydney. Direction signs for tourist drives (popular around the cities) can be identified by their brown five-sided signs. City streets are full of "road furniture", and identifying direction signs among the plethora of instructions, warnings and hoardings can be a problem.

Australia is gradually moving towards the use of internationally recognized symbols on warning signs, and most of those used will be familiar (or obvious) to European and North American motorists. When artistic inspiration fails the signwriters, instructions are spelt out in clear English, such as "Wrong Way — Go Back". Signs are often reinforced by painted warnings on the road surface. Until you get used to it, this can be confusing, since from the driver's point of view they are written in reverse; thus you will see CLEAR first followed by KEEP.

At junctions controlled by traffic signals, you will often see a sign saying "turn left at any time with care", which means there is a filter lane to allow turning traffic to avoid the lights. Don't however, ignore pedestrians crossing the filter lane nor traffic on the road you wish to join. School crossings are clearly indicated by flashing yellow lights, often indicating a reduced speed limit for that stretch of road.

RULES OF THE ROAD

Motoring regulations vary from one state to another, and quirks are pointed out under *Getting Around* in the appropriate chapter. On the open road, the usual rules apply; on freeways stopping is prohibited except in an emergency, U-turns are not permitted and cyclists and pedestrians (including hitch-hikers) are banned. Australian drivers do not scrupulously stay in the nearside lane unless overtaking, and so be wary of cars passing on the inside. City driving is more problematic, with a number of rules which seem designed to confound the uncertain visitor. It is almost invariably illegal to make a U-turn at traffic signals, or anywhere in a "Central Business District" (i.e. town centre); you are expected to drive around the block instead. At some crossroads, particularly deep in suburbia where priority is not given, the rule is to give way to traffic from the right. This often means that cars travelling along a main thoroughfare must slow down or stop for vehicles turning out of minor side streets.

At some sets of traffic lights there are curved dotted lines to indicate the route a vehicle should take when turning right, which can be confusing to the uninitiated; you should turn keeping your offside wheels inside the appropriate dotted line. Visiting drivers often find it difficult to decide which is the correct line to follow, and prefer to steer a sensible course without reference to the line.

It is compulsory to wear seat belts if they are fitted, as they certainly will be (to both front and back seats) on modern vehicles.

Speed Limits. The maximum permitted speed varies from one state to another, but is generally 100 or 110km/h; the exact limit is shown inside standard red circular signs. Lower limits are posted as appropriate; on city and town streets the maximum is usually 60km/h. A double arrow above a speed limit sign indicates that the limit is a continuation of one imposed earlier on the road. As is the case almost anywhere, limits are widely flouted, particularly on highways through open country.

Alcohol. In the wake of appalling accident statistics — many attributed to drink — the police have built up a considerable repertoire of deterrents. Breath tests are not so much random as mandatory, since traffic police regularly set up road blocks and test every driver who comes along. In some cities, "booze buses" fitted with testing equipment are on hand to give an instant and definitive reading. The blood/alcohol limit varies between states and sometimes depends on age (with those under 21 subject to a lower limit). The legal maximum in New South

Wales, Queensland, Tasmania and Victoria is 0.05, while in Western Australia and the Northern Territory it is 0.08 (the same as in Britain). South Australia is planning to reduce its limit of 0.08 to 0.05.

Some pubs have breath testing machines on hand, on which you can check your approximate blood/alcohol level. Be warned, however, that these machines are not foolproof; and even if you are below the legal limit, the police can still charge you with "driving under the influence" if they believe your driving to be impaired.

Drugs. It is an offence to drive while under the influence of drugs, legal or otherwise. A new breath-testing machine which detects cannabis has been developed at the University of Tasmania and is likely soon to be used by the police.

Penalties. Traffic police in Australia are more vigilant than their counterparts in Europe, and the fines for motoring offences are stiff. Illegal manoeuvres of the kind which might earn a caution abroad are treated more seriously: a safely executed U-turn at an otherwise deserted set of traffic lights could cost you $100, and a fine of $250 for jumping a red light is commonplace. (Don't assume you're safe if you run a red light at an otherwise deserted junction: some traffic signals are equipped with cameras which photograph vehicles which jump the lights.) Fines for speeding tend to increase exponentially: exceeding the limit by 10km/h typically costs $20; by 20km/h, $80; and by 30km/h, $150. The fines for these misdemeanours are accompanied by the award of "demerit points", which can result in your being banned from driving if you accumulate too many. Penalties for exceeding the alcohol limit are very severe, usually comprising a ban (notified to your home country), a large fine and possible confiscation of the vehicle.

HIGHWAY HAZARDS

Animals. Even in the crowded southeast the number of creatures roving across and along the roads at night is alarming. Kangaroos are the worst "offenders"; a collision with one at speed can cause considerable damage, not to mention the harm done to the animal. "Roo bars" are fitted to the fronts of many vehicles used for long-distance journeys. Buffaloes are a menace in the northern part of the country. Try to drive slowly enough, especially at dusk, to avoid any wildlife or farm animals which cross your path, and pay particular heed to signs warning of animals in the vicinity.

Outback Driving. Some motorists choose to ignore the warnings put out by the road authorities and set out ill-equipped for journeys across inhospitable terrain; modern folklore is laced with stories of skeletons being discovered still inside their broken-down cars. The first essential when planning a journey off the beaten track is to ensure your vehicle is fit for the task. It should be mechanically sound, and suitable for the roads you intend to use. Always seek advice from a motoring organization, the police or locals on whether your vehicle is fit for the journey you plan to make. (On some roads through the Outback, you are required to fill in a destination card for the police, giving your expected time of arrival in the next town.) Secondly, at least two spare wheels are advisable; the heat on desert roads can melt the bitumen, which then sticks to tyres. Petrol stations can be very thin on the ground and cannot always be relied upon, since fuel deliveries are occasionally held up. Substantial supplies of fuel and water should be carried, not least in case you need to help out a less well prepared motorist. A selection of spare parts such as a fan belt and electrical fittings is also advisable. Should you break down, stay with your vehicle until help arrives.

Many roads and tracks in the Outback are deeply rutted. There is said to be a certain skill in "riding the ruts", which involves travelling at the appropriate speed to match your vehicle's suspension rhythm to the undulations. In northern Australia, roads can be washed out by flash floods, and can remain impassible for days or weeks.

One of the hazards on unsealed (or newly surfaced) roads is of flying stones hitting the windscreen. Some drivers take the precaution of placing their fingers on the windscreen whenever they meet an oncoming vehicle, which absorbs the shock of the impact and reduces the risk of shattering. If the windscreen breaks, however, use gloves or a cloth to punch out a hole to see through. It is a good idea to carry a plastic windscreen for emergency use. Otherwise, drive to a service station with the other windows closed, to reduce the strain on what remains of the windscreen. Note that most rental agreements for hired vehicles specify that windscreen replacement is not covered by the insurance.

Road Trains. These fearsome beasts terrify other motorists, hitch-hikers and kangaroos alike. A road train consists of a powerful tractor unit pulling three or four full-sized trailers and weighing over 100 tonnes. This massive brute can attain high speeds, making its momentum such that stopping or swerving is a tortuous process. Therefore other road users are obliged to yield to road trains, even if this means driving off the main carriageway. Although their use is restricted to certain roads (notably across the Nullarbor, and up the Stuart Highway through Alice Springs to Darwin), they have to leave and arrive somewhere. So think twice before attempting to overtake one on the suburban approaches to, say, Darwin.

CAR HIRE

The minimum age for hiring a car is usually 21, and drivers under 25 may have to pay extra for insurance or accept a $200 excess on any insurance claim. Most rental agreements apply only to a single state, and many restrict you to a radius of 150km from the rental outlet or to sealed roads. To breach these regulations invalidates the insurance cover. Among the major companies it is usual for different rates to be quoted in cities, "country areas" and "remote areas" (Alice Springs and Darwin count as "remote"). If the basic daily rate in, say, Sydney or Perth is $40 per day unlimited distance, you might be charged 25¢ per kilometre after 200km in country areas, and the same in remote areas plus a surcharge of $10 per day. Most companies add a collision damage waiver (about $10 per day) and state government stamp duty of 1% or 1.5% onto the daily rate. Some smaller operators boast fully inclusive rates (often with a full tank of petrol), which are worth considering if you want to be certain of the final cost.

The major multinational car rental corporations — notably Avis, Budget, Hertz and Thrifty — have various special deals (such as the "Super Savers" offered by Avis) which can bring prices down to around those charged by smaller operators. Rates for one-way rentals, however, are very high, comprising the full daily rate plus a distance charge plus a fee for dropping off the vehicle elsewhere (known as "repositioning"). When you see the final bill, you'd be forgiven for believing you've bought the car. The major operators have reservation numbers enabling you to call from anywhere in the country for the price of a local call:

Avis: 008-22 5533   Budget: 008-33 1331
Hertz: 008-33 3377   Thrifty: 008-22 6434

If you arrive at an airport and need a car in a hurry, ask the Budget desk to see if they have any "standby" cars available, giving a 25% reduction on normal prices. YHA members are entitled to $5 per day off regular Budget rates.

Cheaper deals are available from local operators or from cut-rate nationwide chains such as Half Price (tel: 008-22 1888). Companies with names like "Rent a Rocket" and "Hire a Heap" are usually cheapest of all (about $20 per day, unlimited distance), but their vehicles are not the fastest, quietest or most economical on fuel.

Campervans. Renting a campervan for the family holiday is less popular in Australia than New Zealand. Nevertheless it may be attractive to visitors looking for a fairly economical way to travel and sleep. Rates range from around $100 to $200 per day depending on size, season and location. You will be told which roads are closed to you because of their poor surface; for example, rented campervans may not be used north of Mossman, Queensland or north of Geraldton in Western Australia. Most companies impose a minimum hire period of at least three days (but check for surcharges at weekends) or, more commonly, one week.

Hertz and Avis (numbers above) rent out campervans; so too does Newmans Rentals, 10th Floor, Network House, 84 Pitt St, Sydney 2000 (tel: 02-231 6511). UK bookings can be made through Newmans Tours Ltd, 42 Harrow View, London W5 1LZ (tel: 01-998 4612). If you plan to undertake a major tour of the country, you may want to consider buying a van (see below).

Car Delivery. Partly because of the hassles involved in re-registering vehicles in another state (see below), car delivery is rare in Australia. In addition, rental cars which need to be returned to base are few and far between.

BUYING A CAR

For longer stays it can be worthwhile to buy a cheap secondhand vehicle and sell it (quite possibly for the price you paid for it) at the end of your stay. Most of the cars on Australian roads will be familiar to visitors. There are many Japanese models (some assembled in Australia) and plenty of locally produced Fords: the Falcon is equivalent to a Granada, and the Telstar broadly similar to an Orion. But the leading marque is the Australian manufacturer Holden. This company is now part of General Motors, and its products similar to GM models elsewhere in the world; the Holden Camira is the same as a Cavalier, while the Gemini approximates to a Chevette. The Holden Barina is a small hatchback. However, if you have only $1,000 to spend, you can forget about owning one of these models. You might find a 1972 Holden Premier or a 1966 Volkswagen Beetle instead. The amount you will need to spend on maintaining your vehicle is more difficult to predict, but if you intend to cover long distances you may find that your tyres wear out at a fearsome rate; you can replace them most cheaply by buying retreads.

The best source for buying or selling a vehicle is the notice board at hostels, where travellers about to leave Australia advertise their cars. At present it is a seller's market, with vehicles snapped up almost as soon as an advertisement is posted. Otherwise, try the classified columns or, if you are mechanically-minded, the car auctions which are held regularly in the cities. Vehicles bought from secondhand car dealers tend to be more expensive. Note that some dealers use private classified advertisements, so when you phone ask if this is the case.

Once you buy a vehicle you take on the responsibility for the annual "rego check", the compulsory mechanical check required to permit a vehicle to be registered each year. If you wish to re-register the vehicle in a different state (as you will need to if you plan to sell it outside the state in which it was originally registered) you must submit it for a new mechanical check. Even if you have a valid "rego", the police may still take an interest in the health of your car. In most states the police can attach a yellow sticker (known as a "canary") which tells you they wish to inspect the vehicle; if they attach a red sticker, it means you may not move it because they consider it unroadworthy.

The fee for registration usually includes the cost of compulsory third-party insurance cover. Charges for a typical four-cylinder car vary considerably, from around $200 in Western Australia to $320 in New South Wales and Queensland. Surcharges, "recording fees" and charges for processing registrations can add a further $10 or $20 to the total cost.

Insurance. As mentioned above, cover for personal injuries to third parties is compulsory and is usually charged for with state registration fees. This is the minimum required by law. If you have motor insurance with a no-claims bonus in the UK, the discount may well be transferable to your Australian insurance. Take a letter from your insurers.

Campervans. The advice above on buying a car applies equally to campervans. One of the most popular vehicles is a Volkswagen Kombi van, and there is normally a fairly active secondhand market among travellers in Australia. With a little bargaining, you should be able to pick one up for around $2,000.

HITCH-HIKING

British visitors will find hitching around Australia comfortably familiar. While the proportion of drivers prepared to pick you up is lower than in the UK or New Zealand (partly because of the bad experiences some motorists have had after picking up hitch-hikers), there are enough friendly drivers to make most journeys pleasantly straightforward. Considering the length of most trips, it is surprising how many drivers are willing to gamble on your acceptability. The risk of attacks from malevolent drivers is low, but single women should think carefully before accepting a long-distance ride through the Outback.

One major difference compared with hitching elsewhere is that Australians tend to hitch with a finger pointing down at the road, since an upraised thumb can be construed as an offensive gesture. You should be prepared for a surprisingly large number of knockbacks and yelled insults, perhaps due to the national contempt for "bludgers", i.e. spongers.

The key to fast travel is, as anywhere, a question of picking the time and place. There are plenty of areas where you certainly don't want to get stuck. These include homesteads on the road across the Nullarbor, Coober Pedy in the South Australian desert and Three Ways in the Northern Territory (where the roads from Townsville, Darwin and Alice Springs meet). At places like these it is not uncommon to spend a couple of days standing fruitlessly by the roadside. Many visitors find hitching fine for short- and medium-distance travel, but for long distances you may prefer the predictability of the bus or train. Hitching on Australian freeways is not so much life in the fast lane, more life on the hard shoulder. The access roads are the only places where hitching is legal, but are mostly lightly travelled. You are much better off on an ordinary highway where all the traffic is channelled past your waiting thumb.

Advice for hitching out of the state capitals is given in the appropriate *Arrival and Departure* section. A destination sign, with "please" added, is a useful adjunct. You might wish to draw attention to your foreignness by composing a jokey sign, such as "London to Wagga Wagga" or "Canada to Canberra". Alternatively, fasten your national flag to your backpack. It is useful to be able to recognize the number plates of each state at a distance:

ACT: blue on white	Queensland: green on yellow
New South Wales: black on yellow	South Australia: black on white
Northern Territory: red on white	Tasmania: black on white
Victoria: green on white (new); white on black (old)	
Western Australia: black on yellow (new); black on white (old)	

You will see many other varieties in addition to those listed above; these are for commercial, official or diplomatic vehicles, or personalized registrations.

Lift Sharing. The sharing of driving and fuel costs on long trips is very popular among young travellers in Australia. Advertisements for lifts offered and wanted are posted on notice boards at Youth Hostels and University Students' Unions. A variant of lift-sharing is to visit the depots of long-distance trucking firms on the outskirts of the major cities; you can always ring the despatcher ahead of time, but a personal visit is usually more successful. A surprising number of lorry drivers are willing to take passengers, especially foreign visitors to whom they can point out the sights.

The notion of hitching a ride on a light aircraft or helicopter is not too far-fetched in outback areas. Many people in the Outback use helicopters like cars, and even fly them like cars, dropping down to read road signs. Light aircraft do not have quite this versatility, but are still a popular means of getting around. If you spend any time in an isolated community, you will get to hear about who flies where, and need feel no embarrassment in asking for a ride.

MOTORCYCLING

There is a buoyant market in Japanese bikes, and again Youth Hostel notice boards are a good source. You might pick up a five-year-old Honda or Yamaha 250cc machine for around $500. Buyers who choose carefully should have no trouble reselling at the end of their stay. The information above regarding buying and registering a car is true also for motorcycles. You can hire motorcycles from around $25 per day from dealers in most cities. For further information, contact the local branch of the Motorcycle Riders' Association (MRA), listed in the *Yellow Pages* under the heading "Clubs: Motorcycle".

Bikers should take great care in the big cities, where motorcycle couriers are as unpopular as elsewhere, and car drivers react accordingly. Because of the custom among bank robbers of using motorcycling helmets as a form of disguise and protection, most banks now have signs directed at motorcyclists asking "Please remove your helmet before entering this bank."

The largest operator of motorcycle tours in Australia is Outback Motorbike Safaris, 1080 Stud Road, Rowville, Victoria 3178 (tel: 03-763 7907).

CYCLING

The Australian climate — and much of its terrain — lends itself to cycling. Only the keenest cyclists will attempt to cover the long distances between major centres, but there are many interesting areas ideally suited for bicycle touring. For example, a bike is a very pleasant way to explore the South Australian wineries, the Snowy Mountains of New South Wales and the East Coast of Tasmania. Cycling enables you to take a much closer look at Australian wildlife. Due to your speed and relative quietness you have a much better chance than other road users of seeing animals and birds. Don't be surprised if a kangaroo hops along beside you. See *The Great Outdoors* for more information about cycling. If outback cycling appeals, you could try the Simpson Desert Cycle Challenge. This is an event only for mountain bikes, crossing 1,200 sand dunes. It takes place each Easter and over a 370km course from Alka Seltzer Bore, South Australia to Birdsville, Queensland.

You can hire a bicycle by the hour for $2 upwards, with a day's rental costing $10-$20. Most outfits require a deposit of around $25, or a passport as security. It soon becomes worthwhile to buy a secondhand bike which you can sell at the end of your stay. Good secondhand bikes are advertised weekly in the *Trading Post* and shouldn't cost more than about $100. Brand new, good quality bikes will cost $200 and upwards from one of the numerous bike shops in the capital cities. Bike thefts are common in cities, so buy a good lock and try to insure your bike. One way to do this is to enrol with Australian Bikefile, a nationwide bicycle registration and insurance scheme for which you pay an annual fee of $10 plus $2 for every $100 that your bike is worth; you can get details of the scheme from cycle dealers, or contact Bikefile direct at 23 Turner St, Maroochydore, Queensland (tel: 008-07 2201 for the price of a local call).

It is possible to transport your bicycle on buses and trains, although some suburban trains impose restrictions. The cost varies, but is usually lower if the bike is dismantled and boxed. One drawback using bus services is that the operators do not guarantee that the bicycle travels with you, so you may have to wait around for it at your destination. You can also take your bike by air, so long as you box it and deflate the tyres to avoid high-altitude explosions.

CITY TRANSPORT

For details see appropriate chapters.

Public Transport. One of the more pleasing features of city transport networks in Australia is the flexibility of tickets. In most areas, tickets for buses, trams and suburban trains are valid for free transfers to any other mode of transport within a certain time limit (usually two hours).

Taxis. Cabs are usually large, brightly coloured saloon cars. They can be hailed in the street or found at ranks in busy locations. Availability is indicated by a light on the roof. Some cabs announce themselves to be "Share Ride" taxis, so it is always worth hailing cabs which are already occupied.

Even if you're on your own, taxis are not prohibitively expensive. There are generally two rates: one for weekdays, and a higher rate for night and weekend use. The standing charge is fixed at between $1.25 and $2, covering the first kilometre, and costs for each subsequent kilometre are about 60¢ (80¢ at the higher rate). Supplements are payable for extra passengers, large amounts of luggage and journeys outside the city limits.

It is customary (for males, at least) to sit in the front seat. Don't neglect the chance to chat to the driver, as they are invariably good sources of information and opinion. Visitors are often pleasantly surprised by the apparent absence of avarice among Australian taxi drivers. While few reject a tip, none will expect one and some will switch off the meter while tracking down a precise location.

Finding Your Way. Basic city street maps are available from tourist offices, but you may have to pay. To save the cents, pick up a free copy which can usually be found in the lobbies of more expensive hotels. Every state capital has a *Gregory's Street Directory,* sold in bookshops and kiosks for about $15. These are fairly thick volumes due to the sprawling nature of Australian cities. To help you find houses in suburban streets, numbers are sometimes painted on the kerb of the road outside.

Pedestrians. Illuminated instructions to pedestrians are supplemented aurally to help those with sight impairments. In fact, many crossings sound like crazed computer games; most emit a regular subdued pulse until it is safe to cross, whereupon they burst into activity, buzzing or beeping to startle the uninitiated pedestrian. But be warned that some automatic banking machines emit noises which sound very similar to those of traffic signals, so check whether you're standing near a cash machine before starting to cross.

demountable	portable prefabricated motel units
dunny	outdoor loo (of which there are not many left these days)
flatting	sharing an apartment
garbo	dustman/refuse collector
humpy	crude hut shelter
on-site	common abbreviation for on-site caravan
private hotel	unlicensed accommodation
pub	any hotel
Salvos	Salvation Army
snib	door latch
unit	flat/apartment/condominium

In the places where travellers tend to go (or pass through), there is generally a good selection of reasonably priced accommodation. Hostelling is popular among a broader spectrum and age group than it is in Europe or North America and, for many, hostels are the key to their entire holiday. Not only do they provide an affordable place to sleep (usually less than $10) but they provide access to a valuable range of information about what to see, how to get there and who to go with.

If you venture off the beaten track in Australia — and until fairly recently even Ayers Rock would have qualified — the low density of population, both resident and visiting, means that accommodation is fairly sparse, and what there is has a captive market so can charge almost what it likes. It is better under such circumstances to be self-sufficient for accommodation (see *Camping* below).

If you arrive in a big city and, need a place to stay, you could do worse than check advertisements in the *Yellow Pages;* look up the headings "Homes and Hostels", "Hotels — Private" or "Guest Houses".

Youth Hostels. The hostelling movement is thriving in Australia, from ski huts to beach retreats (one of which, at Mission Beach Queensland, is in a tree-house), from Tasmanian rainforest to Northern Territory desert. There are 124 year-round hostels throughout the country, offering beds costing between $4.50 and $12. Anyone hoping to travel extensively on a low budget should consider joining their national Association, which automatically gives membership of the International Youth Hostels Federation (IYHF). There is nothing to stop you from joining the Australian Association, but it may well be cheaper to join before your arrival: new members over 18 pay £6.50 in Britain as against $27 in Australia. You can purchase an international guest card in Sydney for $20 but then you forfeit the magazine *Hostel Yarn* which fully-fledged members receive six times a year.

The Australian hostelling handbook is an invaluable source of accommodation and travel information. Not only does it describe in detail all the hostels and affiliated hostels, with instructions on how to find them, lists of available facilities (such as laundry, bicycle hire, barbecues, etc.) but also includes other accommodation such as campsites and alpine club huts in the hostellers' price range. Unfortunately the handbook is not stocked by the YHA Store in London, and so you will either have to write ahead for a copy to the National Office, 60 Mary St, Surry Hills, NSW 2010 (tel: 02-212 1151) enclosing $2, or else rely on the much sketchier information given in Volume II of the IYHF *International Handbook* which includes Australia and is widely available in all hostelling countries.

The main drawback to hostelling, especially in the major cities, is its popularity, and the resulting scarcity of available beds. You might want to pre-book your first couple of nights in Australia by following the instructions provided in the *International Handbook*. It is slightly complicated since in some states, viz. Tasmania and Queensland, the state headquarters handles bookings for all (or some) of the hostels, whereas in the rest of the country you must book directly with the hostel. After arrival at your first Youth Hostel the manager or warden is usually willing to book you a bed at the next hostel on your itinerary for the price of the phone call.

The notice boards in popular hostels are a priceless source of information especially if you are looking for some people with whom to share expenses on a long car journey. Another advantage of joining the Youth Hostels Association is that your card entitles you to an impressive range of discounts from travel books and maps at a Sydney bookstore to ferries to Kangaroo Island.

For further information about hostels in a specific state, you might want to contact the regional offices whose addresses are as follows:

New South Wales: 355 Kent St, Sydney 2000 (02-29 1295)
Queensland: 462 Queen St, Brisbane 4000 (07-831 2022).
Victoria: 205 King St, Melbourne 3000 (03-670 7991).
South Australia: 1st Floor, Recreation & Sports Centre, corner King William and Sturt Streets, Adelaide 5000 (08-51 5583).
Tasmania: 1st Floor, 28 Criterion St, Hobart 7000 (002-34 9617).

Western Australia: 1st Floor, 257 Adelaide Terrace, Perth 6000 (09-325 5844).

Northern Territory: Darwin Hostel Complex, Beaton Road via Hidden Valley Road, Berrimah 5789 (089-84 3902).

Private Hostels. Some people find the compulsory morning duties and the restrictions (especially the no-alcohol rule) at Youth Hostels irksome, and so there is a growing demand for cheap accommodation without the rules. A further advantage is that many non-YHA hostels offer single and double rooms as well as dormitory beds. A few complaints have been heard that privately-run hostels are more nakedly commercial and that their managers show less concern for the welfare of travellers than is the case at Youth Hostels, but most are excellent. Backpackers Resorts of Australia is one group which has been especially successful and provides stiff competition for Youth Hostels, especially in Queensland and New South Wales. Their headquarters are at 3 Newman St, Nambucca Heads, NSW (tel: 065-68 6360) from where you can get an up-to-date booklet listing their 25 hostels. Their prices rival those of official Youth Hostels, starting at $6.50 a night in the dorm and $14 for a double.

Several city YMCAs and YWCAs ("Ys") offer casual accommodation to both men and women, though their prices are well above Youth Hostel levels. These and other places offering budget accommodation are listed in the regional chapters.

At some of the cheaper places you may find that a key deposit of $5-$30 will be charged (assuming you have a private room rather than a dormitory bed). If this is likely to cause a cash flow crisis, you can offer your camera or passport instead; just take extra care not to lose the key.

Student Residences. Out of term-time (mid-November to mid-February), University halls of residence (known as colleges) are let out to travellers, with priority and lower rates given to those who can produce student identification. A student might pay $12-$15 per night for a single room, while the cost for others is typically 50% higher. Often part of the college will be taken over by a convention, so you could find yourself sharing a corridor with ophthalmologists, jugglers or born-again Christians.

Some suggestions of colleges worth trying are given in the regional chapters; for others, call the Accommodation Officer whose number should be listed in the *White Pages* under the main University heading.

Even during term-time it is worth checking out the local University, particularly if you are looking for longer-term accommodation. Although many Australian students live at home during their University careers, there are still plenty of flat-sharing advertisements.

Camping. The cheapest accommodation of all is a tent, which is always an attractive option in a hot country (though bear in mind that when it rains, it rains hard, and when insects bite, they do so in earnest). Camping is popular among holidaying Australians, and so there are plenty of campgrounds, though the communal washing and cooking arrangements are usually not as sophisticated as they are in New Zealand. Note that some caravan parks do not accept tents. The standard fee is $8-$10 for pitching a two-man tent in commercial campsites, a little less in national park sites. Motoring organizations such as the NRMA publish caravan and camping directories. The best deal of all is staying at a council-run campsite with which a few towns are blessed; here it shouldn't cost more than $2 or $3 to pitch a tent.

Australia is such an empty country that it is usually possible to find a free place to pitch a tent. Camping by the side of the road and in rest areas can be done, though discretion is recommended. The roadsigns are often peppered with bulletholes and so it is advisable to camp in a place hidden from the highway. Most rest areas offer water, toilets, tables and barbecue stands. Away from rest areas, finding a supply of water may then present problems. Never be tempted to camp in a dried-up river bed, since a flash flood can wash you away. If you are travelling by car, an axe can be a useful addition to your boot, for building campfires (though if you stay at campsites, you can usually borrow one), provided there is not a fire ban in force.

Caravanning is extremely popular both among locals and overseas holidaymakers, especially in campervans (see *Getting Around: Driving*). These permit a degree of luxury unknown in tents, especially if you stop at campgrounds where you can plug into a power supply (usually at a cost of $12 a night) to run a fridge and/or a TV.

Even travellers who do not have a tent or campervan should not discount the possibility of staying at campsites. On-site caravans can be found on the majority of campgrounds around Australia, and are especially worthwhile if you are travelling with a group of friends (or if you are a tent-camper who has hit a patch of bad weather). The price will be in the neighbourhood of $25 for two people or $35 for four people, which includes the use of all cooking equipment, but not bedding.

Furthermore there are companies which hire out pre-erected tents, a form of accommodation which has gained recent popularity among British holidaymakers on the Continent. The scope is fairly limited (e.g. mainly seaside resorts) but the prices are as low as $5 per night or $30 a week. Campus Holidays (26th Floor, St Martins Tower, 44 St George's Terrace, Perth, WA 6000) arrange this mostly in Western Australia, but also in the Northern Territory. Their brochure is available in the UK from Exchange Travel, Parker Road, Hastings, Sussex TN34 3UB.

Hotels. At first you may be a little puzzled to hear how often the word "hotel" crops up in the conversation of the locals, and not in the context of where to house their mothers-in-law on their annual visits. Usually they are referring to the local pub, since the licensing laws of Australia (as in New Zealand) require drinking establishments to offer accommodation as well. Although some pubs do have rooms available for travellers — and it is always worth asking, especially in country areas — the majority of pubs are not set up to offer overnight accommodation. Some hotels emphasize their ability to provide accommodation by calling themselves "hotel/motels."

To distinguish hotels which have accommodation but no bar, the term "private hotel" is used. These are a little thin on the ground though you can find them in the cities with prices starting at $20 for a single. But in many places there is an uncomfortable gap between hostels and campsites on the one hand and pricey motels on the other. The equivalent of the British bed and breakfast or the European one-star hotel is missing on a large scale.

Licensed hotels in the country are more likely than city ones to have accommodation. All settlements, however remote, have a pub and therefore a hotel, often called the "Commercial" since its main customers were travelling sales reps. Some are classics, with crumbling verandahs, chatty proprietors and colourful histories. They tend to have more character, less luxury and lower prices than the purpose-built tourist hotels which are being built in resort areas to cope with the sudden increase in visitor numbers especially from the USA and Japan. Ask any tourist office for recommendations on country hotels. Sometimes the breweries issue details of their tied houses which offer accommodation as in the case of the Tooth Brewery's list of country inns in New South Wales. Prices vary greatly, from say $75 single for one week to $75 double for one night.

Motels. Just as in North America, motels are the favourite style of accommodation for Australian families. And like their American counterparts, motels in Australia are usually comfortable but indistinguishable from one another and unlicensed. Predictably they are to be found on the approach roads to cities and towns. Look for the major chains like Flag Inns, Homestead Motor Inns, and Quality Inns or the slightly cheaper ones like A1. A full colour directory of all 450 motels in the Flag Inn chain is widely available, and 24 hour booking is available by ringing 008-335 005. The premier class of motel charges about $70 single and $80 double, moderate motels charge approximately $45/$60 and budget motels charge $30/$35. The various state motoring organizations sell or issue their own lists of accommodation.

Airlines and tour operators in your home country will be keen to sell you vouchers for use at motels in the major chains, each of which entitles you to a night's accommodation at a reduced rate compared to normal tariffs. If you intend to stay in motels anyway, this is a good deal, but you may tire of identical decor in indistinguishable buildings away from the centre of town.

If you are travelling by car in remote areas, you will probably travel between road stations, which normally comprise a petrol pump, snack bar, pub and perhaps a few motel type units, sometimes in prefabricated portable constructions called "demountables". They may also provide a shady place for campers as well as showers which will either be free or cost 50¢ or $1.

In contrast to the outback, resort areas offer an abundance of accommodation in all price brackets. Often motels in these popular areas will offer self-contained fully-equipped "units" for people who want to cater for themselves. However these are not nearly as widespread as they are in New Zealand.

Homestays and Farmstays. With the recent tourism boom, more and more Australians are opening their houses to overseas visitors, and the tourism authorities are only too delighted to encourage this trend and to exploit the Australian reputation for friendliness and hospitality. Home-hosted holidays are clearly becoming a part of mainstream tourism since the Qantas-owned British tour operator Jetabout launched a homestay programme for the Bicentenary with advertised rates starting at £11. Although the system is not developed to the same extent as it is in New Zealand, it is gaining popularity, especially the farm stays which are taking advantage of the growing interest in outback tourism.

A typical listing for a station offering hospitality would include a resumé of the hosts' hobbies, such as "ex-grazier interested in horses; wife interested in spinning and weaving". Most farmstays include all meals and activities. Prices start at about $70.

Several organizations act as agents for a number of city homes or farms and ranches. Although it is not necessary to book before you arrive in Australia, you might like to request the literature from one or more of the following:

Farm Holidays: PO Box 384, Woollahra, NSW 2025 (02-387 6681). Contact them for information about the newly formed National Association of Host Farms.
Host Farms Association: 7 Abbott St, North Balwyn, Victoria 3104 (03-857 6767).
Australian Home Accommodation: Suite 4, 209 Toorak Road, South Yarra, Melbourne, Victoria 3141 (03-241 3694).
Bed & Breakfast Australia: PO Box Q184, 396 Kent St, Sydney, NSW 2000 (02-264 3155).

The 1988 prices quoted by Bed & Breakfast Australia range from $28/$34 per person in a double for bed and breakfast in a private home to $60/$85 per person for full board on a ranch. Their brochure describes everything from a homestay in central Sydney run by a ballet-loving Hungarian-speaking retired couple to a Queensland cattle station with Arab horses and peacocks.

Travellers who belong to certain clubs may be able to stay in Australian homes, but not on a commercial basis. For example the Bicycle Institute in Sydney (802 George St) and in Melbourne (285 Little Lonsdale St) can give out lists of their members who are willing to put up touring cyclists.

Longer Term Accommodation. If you are planning to stay put for three months or more, possibly in order to work, check hostel notice boards for possible flat shares, which is less hassle than relying on newspaper adverts. Unfortunately demand for rented accommodation outstrips supply in all the main cities (except Brisbane) and so bargains are few and far between. Modest one-bedroom flats vary from about $60 per week in Adelaide to $120 in Sydney. Most flats are let on term leases and these are most commonly for 6 or 12 months. Usually one month's rent is payable in advance and another month's rent is deposited with the agent as security. If possible bring written references from previous landlords. For traditional "digs" where the landlady will provide meals and do your laundry, look under "Board Vacant" in the classified columns.

If you are a member of the home-owning classes, you might consider the possibilities of home exchange, though the fees charged by agencies which arrange this are very steep (e.g. $350). But if you do own a home (preferably in London or Boston rather than Doncaster or Pittsburgh) it can be worth considering if you want to be based in one place in Australia for several months. An Australian agency which claims to have a strong demand for home exchanges between Australia and the south of England is International Travel and Home Exchange, 234 Stoneville Road, Stoneville, WA 6554 (tel: 09-295 1185).

brekkies	breakfast
bug	small crab tasting rather like crayfish or prawn
Cherry Ripe	chocolate-covered bar of coconut and cherry jelly
Chiko rolls (pronounced chicko)	Australian fast food faintly resembling a spring roll

chook (pronounced as in book)	chicken
Coon	brand of Australian cheddar cheese
counter meal	food served at a pub
cut lunch	sandwiches
damper	unleavened bush bread, often sold at country fairs
dead horse	tomato sauce
dim sims	Australasian corruption of Chinese Dim Sum, consisting of bland meat and vegetables wrapped in pastry then steamed or fried
dog's eye	meat pie
entree	starter or hors d'oeuvre
flake	shark meat
hoggett	sheep killed at between one and two years old
hot bread shop	baker's shop
jaffle	toasted sandwich
jatz	cracker/biscuit especially popular in Queensland
lamingtons (lammies)	classic Australian cakes: cubes of sponge covered with chocolate and coconut
lollies	sweets/candies
milk bar	small (and usually dowdy) snack bar
pavlova (pav)	classic Australasian meringue, cream and fruit dessert
Pavlova Magic	freeze-dried egg whites, sold in a plastic egg and used to make inferior versions of the above
paw-paw	papaya (tropical fruit)
sammie	sandwich
savouries	canapés, finger food
show bag	bags of sweets and other items sold at country fairs for $3-$5
snags or *snaggers* (aka *mystery bags*)	sausages
spicy tucker	food at an ethnic restaurant
Twisties	cheesy corn snack to which most Australians are extremely attached
witchetty grubs	Aboriginal delicacy: the white larvae of certain beetles
Vegemite	yeast spread, which Australians claim to be far superior to Marmite
veggies (or *veges*)	universally used abbreviation for vegetables
Violet Crumble bars	chocolate-covered honeycomb bars (like Crunchies) in purple wrappers
yabbies	freshwater crayfish
yiros (pronounced year-oss)	doner kebabs
zucchini	courgette

Eating is one of the great pleasures in Australia. Whether you dine at the fanciest restaurant, grab lunch at a pub or buy the ingredients for a picnic from market stalls, you can usually rely upon good, fresh food at reasonable prices. It is easy to put on weight in Australia due to the great abundance of cheap and tasty food; but it is also easy to eat very healthily and (in cities, at least) diversely. After having been notorious meat eaters, Australians are now consuming 20% less red meat than they were five years ago, and are eating more poultry and fish.

Most of the raw ingredients will be familiar to the visitor: Australians enjoy good beef, pork, lamb and poultry, but are conservative in their tastes for meat and eat little offal or rabbit. There is plentiful seafood and fresh fish, and a marvellous range of tropical and temperate fruit and vegetables, sold at prices which seem very cheap to British visitors (e.g. 10¢ for a lemon or 50¢ for a paw paw). Corn flakes will never hold the same appeal again once you have enjoyed fresh mango, guava and pineapple for breakfast.

Of the indigenous produce, you are more likely to encounter unusual crustaceans like bugs and yabbies than crocodile steaks (very expensive, and resembling a chewy cross between pork and chicken) or the Aboriginal delicacy of witchetty grubs (when crushed, said to taste like peanut butter). Whereas American cuisine has arguably been homogenized into one huge hamburger, Australian food is still developing and assimilating a vast number of influences. Successive waves of immigrants from different ethnic backgrounds have adapted their native cuisine to the plentiful and excellent produce of Australia. And your meal can be washed down with some of the best beers and wines in the world.

Mealtimes. One unfortunate habit which Australia has retained from its British colonial past is inflexible eating times. Although there are a growing number of 24-hour restaurants, most places keep limited hours and you may well have to adjust your evening eating pattern to fit in. "Tea" is not a late afternoon snack, but the main evening meal which is ideally taken no later than 6 or 7pm. By 10pm most diners will have left the average restaurant and the staff will be clearing up around the stragglers. In small towns, you may find it difficult to find anywhere except the local fast-food outlet prepared to serve you after 7.30 or 8pm. The fancier restaurants in cities stay open until late (incidentally allowing diners to circumvent licensing laws).

The Barbecue. In keeping with their love of the outdoors, Australians are great ones for barbecues. Whether in the back garden, in the grounds of a Youth Hostel, on the beach or in a National Park, steaks, chops, "snags" and vegetables wrapped in foil can be grilled over glowing charcoal or firewood, electric bars or gas (with adjacent meters taking 20¢ coins). The resulting feast is served with bread, salad and copious quantities of beer. If you are invited along to one, take some meat and drink. To avoid looking out of place at these gatherings, you should first apply an insect repellent, to save you from scratching your way through the evening. Men should join in with ministering to the fire and turning the meat, while women are generally permitted only to assist with preparing the side dishes, yelling advice and clearing up afterwards. Barbecues are an essential ingredient of Australiana and you should attend or initiate at least one during your stay.

Picnicking. It is easy to prepare a tasty picnic very cheaply. Bread costs a dollar a loaf, cheeses and cold meats are only $2-$5 per kilogram and fruit from market stalls is very cheap. If you have the use of a car, you might want to invest in an "Esky" (cold box) to keep your food fresh.

Pub Food. Many pubs, especially those with large courtyards or gardens, operate a splendid system whereby you select a piece of meat and cook it over the pub's barbecue yourself. The price (usually around $10) in most cases includes unlimited bread and salads to which you help yourself.

The standard pub meal is known as a "counter meal", which is always a reliable and reasonably priced option, if a little repetitive. You can be sure of finding a good steak or chop with potato and salad for $5-$10 at many pubs, in large cities as well as smaller towns (where the pub may be the only place to eat out). The hours during which food is served are if anything more restrictive than those of restaurants: unless you order between 12.30-1.30pm and 5.30-7pm, there is no guarantee you'll be served. Nevertheless, many pubs are becoming increasingly like restaurants and at some you can eat at any time during licensing hours.

Cheap Deals. The Scandinavian term *Smorgasbord* can refer to any buffet, and if you're hungry, a lunchtime eat-what-you-like deal can fill you up for the day. A surprising number of employees' canteens, particularly of public service organizations, are open to the public and can be relied upon for cheap and filling (if not necessarily tasty) food.

Free Food. There is no need to take a course in Aboriginal eating techniques to eat for free, especially in the tropical north where fish can be caught, oysters collected and fruit picked. If you're desperate to eat in the cities, take advantage of the Australian insistence on freshness and try to pick up unsold bread or fruit from round the back of supermarkets. Some unscrupulous types have also been known to help themselves to the salad bar at "cook-your-own-steak" pubs without buying the steak.

RESTAURANTS

It is difficult to make many useful generalizations about Australian restaurants, since the range of style and ethnic cuisine is remarkable: from small Greek, Italian and Vietnamese cafés where the proprietor is likely to cook, serve, wash up and take the money, to impeccable French restaurants with elaborate hierarchies of waiting staff.

Prices are lower than you would pay for similar food and surroundings in Britain or North America. For as little as $5 you can gorge yourself at a cheap café, while a good evening out in a mid-range restaurant with three courses and coffee will probably cost $15-$20 per person. Even if you splash out at the most expensive restaurant in town, you'll pay less than in similar establishments in Europe or North America. The bill should arrive without any additions for tax and service, although at weekends you may have to pay an extra dollar or two per person to meet the higher cost of staff. In cheaper places, few people leave a tip, while at mid-range restaurants the habit is growing to leave 5-10%. But you won't be badly treated or verbally abused if you fail to tip. If the restaurant is busy, it is common practice to leave the correct money (rounded up plus a tip if you wish) in the saucer and walk out.

In the state capitals you can choose from dozens of price brackets and cuisines. Outside the big cities, however, the choice of places to eat narrows dramatically, and often the only alternatives will be the local pub, a branch of a fast-food chain and possibly a chip shop. But there are always surprises to be found; one of the finest French restaurants in New South Wales — La Petite Malice — is hidden in a shopping arcade in Thirroul, an anonymous suburb of Wollongong.

At any restaurant more fancy than a cheap café, you may well encounter rules governing dress. Despite the highly casual attire to be found on the streets of Australia, many pubs and restaurants — including those which could hardly be described as the ultimate in sophistication — have strict rules about their clients' clothing. In particular, thongs are unpopular, which usually means shorts are banned (unless you are prepared to abandon all sartorial pride and wear shorts with shoes and socks).

Foreign Cuisines. Melbourne and Sydney, the premier eating cities, each has at least as wide a range of cuisines as London or New York. You could eat three meals a day for a month before coming close to exhausting all the possibilities. While most visitors are familiar with French, Greek and Italian food, there are plenty of more exotic options. In particular, every Asian country from Turkey to Japan is represented and you may well try your first Kampuchean or Burmese meal in Australia. It is well worth being adventurous, since you are unlikely to have a bad experience: spicy dishes are usually taken down a step or two in hotness, and alarming dishes such as roast dog from Korea, raw monkey brain from Singapore or pickled jellyfish from Japan have not survived the transition to Australia.

The Southeast Asian concept of "food markets" has been imported into some of the cities. The idea is that a central eating area of tables and chairs (sometimes out of doors, sometimes incorporated into a shopping arcade) is surrounded by kiosks offering all manner of interesting foods. Thus you can buy a Lebanese starter from one vendor, a Japanese main course from another and an Italian ice cream and *cappuccino* from a third.

Fast Food. The predictable multinational chains such as Kentucky Fried Chicken and McDonalds (where a Big Mac costs $2 and large fries $1) crop up repeatedly, but there are some chains displaying more flair and imagination. For example, the Mmmunchies group sells muffins in such flavours as cheese and Vegemite, chocolate chip and wholemeal banana, and the Hungry Jack chain sells excellent hamburgers (not called beefburgers in Australia). Despite recent scandals about Australia selling kangaroo meat to American fast food chains, burgers are usually of reliably good quality in Australia. The authentic Australian fast food is the pie and pastie (pronounced *par*-stie); these and other traditional takeaways such as fish'n'chips are good solid fuel.

Milk Bars. These establishments serve the closest that Australia has to a national cuisine, which does a great deal to explain why foreign food is so popular. Their staple is the meat pie (usually costing $1), topped with tomato ketchup. Australians munch their way through two million pies each day.

Licensing. Only a small proportion of Australia's restaurants is licensed, which is a great advantage to those on a tight budget. Most restaurants are "BYO", allowing you to Bring Your Own beer, wine or stronger liquor. Usually corkage of around $2 per bottle or $1 per person will be charged, but some places advertise "no corkage." Many licensed restaurants also allow customers to bring their own wines, but most charge a stiffer corkage fee. Even so, you can usually reckon on saving considerably by bringing your own wine, thereby avoiding paying $8 or more for a bottle of house wine. The exceptions to this rule are restaurants which advertise "wine at bottle shop prices"; in fact the prices are likely to be more expensive than the Liquorland store down the road, but still lower than in most licensed restaurants. In wine-growing areas, the restaurant wine list is supplanted by a wine selection room where you choose from the wines made on the property.

It has been known for diners to get a drink from unlicensed restaurants. The trick is to ask in a naïve tone about where you can get a beer: sometimes the patron will produce one and charge you at cost. This transaction should, of course, be handled discreetly.

DRINKING

amber nectar	beer
billy	a tin can on which water is boiled for tea
bombo	cheap wine
bottle shop	liquor store/off-licence
Bundy	rum from Bundaberg, Queensland
chunder	vomit, usually after excessive drinking (also *technicolour yawn, pavement pizza* and many other expressions)
DD	drunk driving
echo	returnable bottle, found mostly in South Australia and Victoria
Esky	insulated cold box to keep food or (more usually) drink cool; also *chilly-bin*
grog	any drink containing alcohol
grog on	to keep on drinking
heart starter	first drink of the day
hotel	pub
jamberoo	a party at which excessive drinking is the norm
LA	low-alcohol beer
lunatic soup	cheap wine
neck oil	alcohol
nobbler	small measure of spirits, a nip
package beer	beer sold in bottles or cans, rather than on draught
session	a long spell of afternoon drinking at a pub, usually on Sundays and with free entertainment.
shout	round of drinks (it is said about stingy types that they "wouldn't shout if a shark bit them")
sly grog	after-hours drink; the act of obtaining sly grog is known as "running the rabbit"
steam	cheap wine
stubby	bottle of beer
throat charmer	beer
tinny	can of beer
two-pot screamer	one who gets drunk easily
waterbag	teetotaller
yankee shout	paying only for one's own drinks in a pub

In addition, there are numerous expressions for being drunk, including *drunk as Chloe, drunk as a fowl, full as a tick, full as a goog, inked, on the slops, on the tiger, schicked* and *stinko.*

A great deal of time, money and energy is spent on drinking in Australia, not merely as a social activity but — by some — for its own sake, trying to get as legless as possible. A common expression for "would you like a drink?" is "could you hold one down?", and a large proportion of the male population seems determined to reinforce the stereotype of Australians as a nation of heavy-drinking slobs. Many more, however, enjoy the excellent local drinks in moderation, and demand for wine is rising (up 12% in five years) at the same rate as consumption of beer is falling.

Pubs. In Australia, all pubs are known officially as "hotels". However, the main function of most of these places is to supply drink. In many hotels, such rooms as there are exist only to satisfy licensing regulations. If you ask for a room at most city hotels, you probably won't get one (although in country areas you often can). Many hotels also sell drink for consumption off the premises; see *Bottle Shops,* below.

While an Australian town does not have the same range of pubs as a British one would have, there are places to suit most tastes: raucous, barn-like drinking palaces, lazy tropical bars in northern Australia, and country hotels with spacious verandahs, ornamented with fretwork. The interior furnishings are determined by the clientele (or vice-versa). The public bar of the very roughest dives will certainly not be carpeted (except possibly by sawdust or a plastic sheet on the floor to make cleaning up easier) and many are the venue for regular fights. Women, while not actively prohibited from such places, will be made to feel most unwelcome and might receive unwarranted attention from the drunker customers; most feel more comfortable in the lounge bar. It is relatively easy to avoid this type of pub in cities (where they tend to be in deprived inner-city areas) but in the Outback they may constitute the only social centre for 100km in any direction.

Most city and town pubs, however, are pleasant and friendly. They tend to be larger than pubs or bars in Europe or North America, and are often equipped with noisy juke boxes but friendly staff. You should always go to the bar to order and pay, before taking your drinks (almost always beer) to a table (often outside). The most popular pubs are those with built-in breweries (see *Real Ale,* below); while not typical of Australian pubs, they are probably the busiest, trendiest and most enjoyable for a good night out. Australia has few wine bars at present, although their numbers may grow as the taste for wine increases.

Returned Services League (RSL) clubs and other private clubs for certain trades or ethnic groups are popular drinking places, particularly in southeastern Australia. As the number of returned servicemen dwindles, clubs are being increasingly opened up to all-comers. In many country towns they constitute the main social centre (with "pokies" for gambling and satellite TV transmissions of sporting events), while the city clubs are often venues for rock bands. Admittance is officially only for "members and bona-fide guests in the company of a member", but in practice most admit strangers who are signed in by anyone who happens to be around.

Licensing Laws. Hours vary from state to state, pub to pub and even season to season. As a rough guide, weekday opening is 10am-10pm or 11am-11pm; on Sundays between noon and 10pm. There are numerous exceptions: some pubs serving the market trade open at 6am, and the landlord of any pub is not obliged to open for the maximum hours permitted by law. Needless to say, a great deal of drinking takes place after 10 or 11pm: at pubs with late licences, in nightclubs and discos (some of which remain open until 6am) and at restaurants. To drink legally after hours at a restaurant, you must have an "intention to dine"; in one or two places this rule is satisfied at closing time by every customer being given an unsolicited plate of spaghetti. If you want to find out where to get "sly grog", ask a taxi driver.

The minimum drinking age is 18. No one younger than this is allowed into bars. Anyone who appears under age is likely to be asked to produce ID with evidence of age before being served.

Prohibition. Partly as a response to increasing alcoholism amongst Aboriginals, the government has restricted alcohol in and around some Aboriginal settlements. Notices on the approaches to these areas warn that "possession or consumption of liquor without a permit can lead to a $1,000 fine or six months, plus the confiscation of your vehicle".

Bottle Shops. You can save money by buying liquor from bottle shops, which can be found in any town centre or suburban mall. Many are part of hotels, and some are drive-in shops, sometimes with two lanes marked "browse" and "express" (for those who just want the regular 24-can case of Foster's). Prices are often extremely competitive, with the lowest to be found at branches of chains such as Liquorland and Liquor Mart. The maximum permitted hours are the same as for pubs (except that in some states bottle shops are closed on Sundays), but most close at 10pm or earlier.

BEER

Beer is a fact of life in Australia, the third most hard-drinking country in the world (after Belgium and West Germany), and 115 litres per head is consumed every year (having peaked in 1975 at a remarkable 141 litres per capita). Knock off work? Crack a couple of stubbies. Going to a barbecue? Bring a carton. Going fishing? Fill up the Esky.

From the widespread advertising of certain Australian beers abroad, you'd be forgiven for thinking that the natives drink only Foster's or Castlemaine XXXX. This is not true. South Australians swear by West End, Western Australians by Swan, Tasmanians by Boag's or Cascade, and Territorians by NT Bitter. One of the most popular beers in the southeast is VB (Victoria Bitter), and smaller regional varieties such as Coopers in South Australia and Emu in Western Australia have devoted followings. There are also some excellent beers produced by the new "boutique breweries" which will certainly be to the taste of English real ale buffs.

Most beer, however, is a fairly strong (5% alcohol), sweet and bland lager-style brew, nine-tenths of which is produced by two beer combines: Carlton & United products include Foster's and VB, while Bond Brewing makes Swan and Castlemaine XXXX among others. Not only is most beer sold almost ice-cold (usually 2°C), but the glasses are often chilled in a cold cabinet and bottles and cans insulated in a "stubby holder" made of polystyrene. Fresh glasses are always given.

Measures. Apart from the 2.25 litre Darwin stubby, most beer is sold in small measures in Australia. This does not signify any restraint on the part of native drinkers, but is due to the fear of beer warming up to anything approaching room temperature. Even without a drink or two, it is easy to get confused by the variety of measures, especially when one name can mean different sizes in different states. To muddle things further, some of the new "real ale" pubs have reverted to the Imperial measures of half-pint (285ml/10fl oz), and pints (575ml/20fl oz). This table shows the most common quantities and names used in each state:

ml	NSW & ACT	NT	Queensland	SA	Tasmania	Victoria	WA
115					small beer		
140			small beer				
170					beer	six	small beer
200	seven	seven		butcher			glass
225	glass	glass	glass	glass	glass	glass	
285	middy	handle	pot	schooner		pot	middy
425	schooner	schooner		kite			schooner
575	pint						pint

Prices. In view of how cheap food and wine are in Australia, you may be surprised to find that beer in pubs is no cheaper than in Europe or North America. Prices for 285ml start at around $1.10 in an ordinary pub, and increase dramatically in more plush surroundings. Posher places, indeed, may not sell draught beer at all. Bottled beer is usually sold in 375 or 750ml bottles. It is a little cheaper to buy beer in a jug and a lot cheaper to drink it at home after buying in bulk (unchilled) from a bottle shop. The cost of a dozen 750ml bottles varies from about $17 to $23 ($1.40-$1.90 per bottle), while a single chilled bottle from a bottle shop will cost around $2 and the same quantity of beer drunk in a pub at least $2.90. A new 500ml bottle called a "midi" has recently been introduced, as has a 345ml "stubb-ette" aimed at women drinkers. The standard 375ml can at a bottle shop works out at around $1.25 for single cans, reducing to $20 for a case of 24 (84¢ per can). As part of the "Keep Australia Beautiful Campaign", you can get a 1¢ refund on some empty steel drink cans. There are now some "generic" (i.e. unbranded) beers on the market which have names like "No Name". They do not taste significantly different from branded varieties and cost about 20% less, since they do not bear the cost of advertising, sponsoring cricket matches, etc.

Light Beer. The trends towards health consciousness and away from drunk driving have led to the introduction of various brands of light or low-alcohol (LA) beer, such as Swan Light and Foster's LA. The strength of these varies from 0.9% alcohol to 3.3%, and the taste does not suffer greatly in comparison with regular beer. The brewers, however, do not pass on the savings in excise duties on these weaker beers, and so you can expect to pay the same prices as for ordinary beer.

Real Ale. For years it has been difficult to find cask-conditioned beer in Australia, but now afficionados can taste dozens of "real" ales. Coopers, a South Australian brewery, has always made beer traditionally, and is still the largest purveyor of real beers in the form of its naturally-conditioned bottled ale and stout, which can be found throughout Australia. But each of the southern mainland capitals has a number of "boutique breweries", usually built into pubs and making a range of beers which are as enjoyable as their names are imaginative: Brass Monkey Stout, Yellow Mongrel and Thunder Ale. They are served warmer than other Australian beers, but still much cooler than in English pubs. As well as drinking at the pubs, you can take away bottles and casks of the beer. Prices for these premium brews are higher than for other beers, typically $3 or $4 per pint. The best real ale houses are listed under *Eating and Drinking* in the regional chapters.

There are a number of foreign beers available in Australia (including Guinness, brewed under licence in Melbourne), but the increasingly diverse range of native brews should be enough to keep your thirst pleasantly quenched and to save you paying premium prices for imported beers.

WINE

Australian wine is a bargain, both in its own country of origin and around the world. For many years the industry had a reputation abroad for producing large quantities of poor wine. In the last decade or two, however, wine-making techniques have improved greatly. Nowadays most cheap Australian wine is good in comparison with the *vin ordinaire* of Europe and America, and a good

Australian wine is excellent by any standards. The three largest producers are Penfolds, Lindemans and Orlando (known collectively as "PLO"), but there are over 400 other wineries making as diverse a range of wines as any country could wish for. Many of these wineries produce only small quantities of wine for local consumption, and are well worth seeking out.

Making sense of labels can be difficult for the uninitiated, since many at first sight appear to be a jumble of English, Aboriginal and French or German names. A South Australian bottle described as Watervale/Coonawarra — Shiraz/Cabernet Sauvignon contains a blend of Shiraz grapes (known in Europe as Syrah and used for Côtes du Rhône) from Watervale in the Clare Valley, and Cabernet Sauvignon grapes from Coonawarra near the Victorian border. Similar unlikely combinations of names occur frequently. Most labels on casks and bottles admit to the addition of preservatives such as sulphur dioxide. Don't be unduly alarmed: such additives are present in most wines worldwide, but Australia is among the few nations that insist that their presence is recorded. One additive — ascorbic acid — is positively beneficial, being better known as vitamin C. Due to the imaginative attitudes to blending wines, there is no national wine appellation and quality control scheme, despite several attempts at state level.

The cheapest wine comes in four or five-litre boxes, costing as little as $4.99, enabling you to consume wine at less than 50p a litre. Slightly better blends in two-litre casks cost from about $4. Although sophisticated Australians turn their noses up at them, these "cask" wines account for two-thirds of sales and anyone used to French or Italian table wines will find them perfectly acceptable. They are also subjected to discriminating assessment by experts and some are pronounced decidedly good.

The cost of a 750ml bottle of wine starts at about $2 but you would need to spend twice that to get anything better than just adequate. A good bottle such as Penfold's Coonawarra Bin 128 might cost $6.75 (compared to £4.50 for the same bottle in Britain), and this is the sort of price you should aim for when selecting a wine to take for dinner. The highest price is more difficult to estimate, although connoisseurs think nothing of paying $30 or more for the rarest vintages. Australian "Champagne" costs as little as $2.99, but for this price the drink has very little in common with its illustrious French namesake. However, for less than $5 you can get an excellent Methode Champenoise wine, fermented in the bottle like proper Champagne. European (particularly French) wines are available but are very expensive.

Free Wine. Every Australian state grows grapes (even the Northern Territory has Chateau Hornsby, near Alice Springs) and the associated wineries almost always welcome visitors. In the most important wine-making areas — around Adelaide, on the Margaret River in Western Australia and in the Hunter Valley of New South Wales — wine-tasting is a major industry and it is possible to drive, cycle or even travel by balloon or camel around neighbouring wineries. The most popular areas are described in the regional chapters.

Every winery encourages "cellar door" sales of their product. Prices, however, are not always as low as you might expect: you might find the same bottle sold a little more cheaply at a liquor store hundreds of kilometres away.

Coolers. These are blends of cheap white wine with sugar and fruit juice or fruit flavour, and have names like Island Cooler, Capricorn Cooler and Bliss. Their alcoholic strength is around 5% (about the same as beer) although the taste is misleadingly similar to drinking a non-alcoholic punch. Indeed, the packaging may also be almost indistinguishable from fruit drink containers. In a tasting for this book, West Coast Cooler was rated least bad (described as "not unpleasantly tart"). Beware of the effects of coolers (particularly if you plan to drive) and be warned that some people suffer an almighty hangover after drinking the stuff which they attribute to excessive amounts of sugar and flavouring, and the poor quality of the wine used to make them. To quench your thirst, an ice-cold light beer is far more effective.

Stronger Liquor. Consumption of whisky and other hard liquor is fairly low (only one litre per person per year on average), but this is not because of prohibitively high prices. For a litre of imported Scotch you could expect to pay $16, while home-produced spirits such as brandy and Bundaberg rum are a few dollars cheaper. A 30ml nip in a pub costs $1.50-$2. The usual range of liqueurs is available, but the most popular after dinner drink is port. Australia produces some excellent varieties, and even at the cheapest end of the market you are unlikely to be disappointed by a $5 bottle of the stuff.

For a long period in Australia's recent history the arts stagnated as a result of the Cultural Cringe. The Cultural Cringe was a massive inferiority complex which led Australians to believe that Australia was in fact the cultural desert depicted by Monty Python, Dame Edna and Sir Les Patterson. Talented Australians fled to Europe leaving a cultural vacuum which made everybody back home cringe the more. There is a strong streak of anti-intellectualism in Australian society which has made it very difficult for writers and thinkers to find an appreciative audience: perhaps it is no accident, as the noted Melbourne journalist Phillip Adams has observed, that the coat-of-arms comprises two of the smallest-brained beings around, the kangaroo and the emu.

Things started improving in the early 70s partly as a result of the investment in the arts made by the Labor Government under Gough Whitlam. Not only were more plays written and films made, but they began receiving international recognition. And, as appreciation of Australian artists, musicians, film-makers and writers has sky-rocketed, both at home and abroad, the arts have continued to flourish. In an average week one in 40 Australians attends a live theatrical or musical performance, and cinema attendance is now about a third higher than it was in 1980.

As well as the so-called high culture which Australia has to offer, there are many other popular indigenous entertainments to satisfy the deeply felt Australian need for a good time. These include the spectacle of Surf Carnivals (see *Sport* below) and a whole range of bizarre contests such as dwarf-tossing (a practice recently condemned by the European Parliament), melon-seed spitting and throwing-a-Barbara Cartland-novel (for female competitors only).

Tickets. You can buy a ticket for most of the major entertainment events anywhere in the country from BASS. This is a national chain of ticket agencies linked by computer with downtown and suburban branches. The BASS Australia-wide credit card booking service on 008-33 8998 is open Monday to Saturday 9am-9pm, allowing you to reserve tickets for events anywhere in Australia for the price of a local call. Tickets to the big name performances (e.g. Cleo Laine, a Broadway musical, a touring ballet, etc.) range from $18 to $30 with about a third off for students and pensioners. If an event is sold out, you'll have to try your luck with the touts (called "scalpers" as in the US).

MUSIC

Rock Music. You may be relieved to learn that the pinnacle of Australian popular music is *not* represented by Rolf Harris, Olivia Newton-John and the Bee Gees. On the other hand, not many Australian musicians ("musos") have become household names. When the band Men At Work reached the top of the British charts in 1981 with *Down Under* (a song laced with Australian motifs such as "Vegemite sandwiches"), many pundits claimed that the band was the vanguard for a wider appreciation of Australian music. But despite the successes abroad of the groups AC/DC, Air Supply, Mental As Anything and singer John Farnham, "Oz Rock" has yet to make much of a global impact.

There is, of course, a bright side to music in Australia. Mainstream rock artists such as Ice House, Crowded House and the Hoodoo Gurus have considerable local followings, and more innovative bands such as INXS (pronounced in-excess) have achieved cult status both on their home territory and abroad. Midnight Oil, Australia's politically-aware answer to U2, are immensely popular for their radical stance and predominantly heavy metal music. See *Juke* and *RAM* for information on gigs.

Aboriginal Music. To the Western ear, the music of Australia's original inhabitants can sound monotonous and inharmonious, but the more you hear the more you are likely to appreciate the constantly changing rhythms. Ancient instruments such as the didjeridu (a tube of wood producing a strange, haunting sound) are used to accompany ceremonial dances. The biggest problem is hearing an authentic performance; while many places in northern Australia stage "corroborees" (like Papua New Guinean "sing-sings"), these are normally diluted and sanitized for easy consumption. Short of getting the necessary permit to visit an Aboriginal reserve, your chances of catching an authentic performance are highest around Alice Springs and Darwin, or at special cultural festivals in the big cities; keep an eye on the local press for interesting events.

There have been many attempts to draw Aboriginal music into mainstream western music, including "Koori Music", an unusual cross between traditional Aboriginal and Country music. Some Aboriginal musicians have moved towards electric instruments and have combined traditional with modern elements; in particular, the Aboriginal rock band Coloured Stone are worth a listen. A new recording company for Aboriginal musicians has recently been established in Alice Springs, which should increase the accessibility of Aboriginal music. You may also hear of "gumleaf bands" which are usually (but not exclusively) composed of Aboriginals who create music by blowing on gum leaves.

Folk Music. The music which derives from the early European settlers consists largely of songs of the Outback, of which *Waltzing Matilda* is by far the best known. As in Britain and North America there is a loyal following, and you can find folk clubs in every city. Folk/rock is making advances, especially through the successful group Redgum and through "bush bands" such as Bloodwood (who were well received in Britain in 1987), while bands like the Bushwackers are famous throughout Australia. A popular percussion instrument among such bands is the "lagerphone" (also known as a zob stick), a wooden cross covered in metal bottle tops and alternately hit with a stick or thumped on the ground.

Australia's closest equivalent to Nashville is Tamworth, New South Wales. Every January, the town is invaded by around 30,000 Country music enthusiasts who drink, sing and listen to simple songs of the hazards of love.

CINEMA

Australian cinema has a noble history. Long before the renaissance of the 70s and 80s, Australians were making copious and impressive newsreels, an era of film-making captured very well in the film *Newsfront*. The Australian Film Commission has been funding and supporting film-makers since 1972, much to the envy of struggling film industries in other countries. Most state capitals host film festivals. Films like *Picnic at Hanging Rock, Breaker Morant, Gallipoli* and *My Brilliant Career* are not just movies in themselves, but they also illuminate aspects of the Australian character and situation, so are especially worth trying to see if you have a chance. The current generation of film-makers are moving beyond the pretty costume dramas which have been so successful abroad.

Crocodile Dundee, while caricaturing certain Australian traits very effectively, is in a separate category for having been made in Hollywood. When Australian-made films go to America, they almost always end up in art cinemas specializing in foreign films, and therefore never have a chance to break box office records the way *Crocodile Dundee* has done.

One of the largest cinema chains is Hoyts which offers discounts to ISIC-card holders. Movies standardly cost $7 no matter how posh or flea-bitten the surroundings. In most places, you can see a film for half-price on Tuesdays. Most cinema seats are bookable in advance. Smoking is generally banned.

The censorship classifications are as follows: G (general release), PG (parental guidance for children under 15; not recommended for children under 12); M (approved for mature audiences over 15) and R (restricted to those who are not between 2 and 18).

The great American tradition of the drive-in movie ("drives") has flourished in the benevolent Australian climate and Saturday evenings spent watching the big screen from a motor car are favourite social occasions.

MUSEUMS AND GALLERIES

Australians are especially keen on the visual arts, and in a recent 12-month period, six million people visited a public art gallery. (Exhibitions are sometimes referred to as "ekkas".) Although Australia's famous painters such as Arthur Streeton, Tom Roberts and, more recently, Sidney Nolan are perhaps not as widely known outside Australia as her writers, they are well worth investigating. One of the most interesting contemporary schools of art is the Brushmen of the Bush which, appropriately enough, is not found in Perth or Sydney but in the remote mining town of Broken Hill. Here painters like Jack Absalom, Pro Hart and John Pickup display their *naif* paintings of shearing scenes and other outback subjects, and give art classes (in case you want to learn how to capture the essence of a gum tree).

Canberra is the place which houses the national collection of paintings, but there are interesting galleries and many worthwhile museums in all the state capitals. The Bicentenary has provoked an enormous amount of interest in Australia's past with a nationwide appeal for any old documents and artefacts of interest. It is likely that the number of small local museums and historical exhibitions will increase dramatically as a result of this campaign. Each state has its own National Trust which cooperates with the federal Heritage Commission to preserve and open to the public many buildings of historic interest.

Admission to the majority of Australia's museums is free.

SPORT

Most Australians are sports mad. The climate is ideal for almost every outdoor sport, facilities for watching and participating are excellent and the leading sports are given massive coverage by the media. This is unfortunate for people who do not have a great interest in sport, but visitors have no choice but to accept its high profile and resign themselves to sport as a constant topic of conversation.

Australian nationalism manifests itself more visibly in sport than in any other activity. If their chauvinism becomes unbearable, try mentioning the time an Australian cricketer bowled underarm at New Zealand in order to prevent the opposing team from hitting a six and winning the game.

The main team games are cricket in summer (October-March) and "footy" in winter (March-October). "Footy" is used to refer to Australian Rules football and the two codes of Rugby football (League and Union).

Australian Rules Football. To form an accurate picture of Australian society, you should try to see at least one game of this extraordinarily aggressive sport. The game originated among Irish gold miners in Victoria as a loose interpretation of Gaelic football, where any part of the body can be used to propel the ball. Today Rules footy is a kind of organized mayhem remarkable for its lack of obvious rules. There are 18 players on each side (plus two substitutes), and large amounts of violent bodily contact as each team strives to get the oval ball past the opposition's back line for a "behind" (which scores one point) or to kick a goal between the uprights (six points). The game requires a much larger playing area than most other ball games, and is usually played at cricket grounds ("ovals").

There are four quarters of 25 minutes each, but the overall length of the game can be extended to three hours or more with the addition of intervals between quarters and "time on" added for stoppages due to treatment of injured players, disputes with the "field umpire" (referee), etc. The score is given for each quarter with goals and behinds listed separately followed by the final score, in the style:

| Fitzroy | 4.2 | 4.4 | 6.8 | 8.10 | (58) |
| Carlton | 2.1 | 4.3 | 7.5 | 8.9 | (57) |

Match reports include lurid details of injuries suffered, and players reported by the field umpires for foul play which usually verges on grievous bodily harm.

For a good history of the game, read *Up Where, Cazaly? The Story of Australian Rules Football* by Leonie Sandercock and Ian Turner (Granada Books). You can see Australian Rules on television most weekend afternoons in winter, and usually hear commentator Lou "The Lip" Richards giving his outspoken interpretation of events on the field.

Rugby League. Compared to Australian Rules, Rugby League football seems almost genteel. The standard of Rugby League clubs in New South Wales and Queensland is comparable to that of the north of England, and the national team — the Kangaroos — is currently the best in the world. (If you tire of hearing this assertion, remind the teller that the British champions Wigan beat Australia's best — Manly — in a challenge match in 1987.) The State of Origin series is a competition between teams representing each of the states, and is almost invariably won by New South Wales or Queensland.

Rugby Union. This 15-a-side variant is still largely an amateur game, played by "gentlemen" rather than professionals. Interestingly, Rugby Union is notable as the sport in which Aboriginal players excel.

Soccer. Given the high profile that Australian soccer has in Britain (where the results are used for summer pools coupons), it may come as a shock to see how primitive are the standards of some of the grounds and skills of the players. The Australian national team (the Socceroos) were knocked out of the qualifying stages for the 1986 World Cup by a weak Scotland side. The standard of play in the best State Leagues compares with Fourth Division teams in England, and crowds are similar (typically 1,000-5,000). The best players are attracted to European teams (such as Craig Johnston, now of Liverpool), further diminishing the domestic game. The leading teams are those with a strong ethnic base, such as Sydney Olympic (predominantly Greek) and the Italian-led teams of Melbourne.

Cricket. In 1977, cricket traditionalists were appalled when media mogul Kerry Packer introduced innovations such as coloured clothing, black pads and evening matches played under floodlights (to make the game more telegenic), but these one-day matches are usually fast-moving and exciting. Each state fields a team for the national championship, the Sheffield Shield, in which matches lasting three or four days are played at fortnightly intervals. Once you acquire a taste for the game, you may wish to see a full five-day Test match between Australia and a visiting side from overseas, which take place at intervals from the beginning of November until the end of January.

Horseracing. The Turf creates a fervour which rivals that of "footy" or cricket, and most of the state capitals have several race courses ("tracks"). While few Australian horses are in the same class as the top thoroughbreds from the USA or Britain, the best Australian jockeys (such as the former champion Scobie Breasley) are outstanding. Major events can attract crowds of tens of thousands. One big attraction is the chance to gamble, and if you are prepared to lose a few dollars it can be great fun to embroil yourself in the excitement of a big race meeting. The biggest annual event is the Melbourne Cup, held each November at the Flemington track; the whole of Australia grinds to a halt to watch the race. All races are listed in the press, together with a guide to form which is impenetrably complicated for the uninitiated. See *Gambling,* below, for off-track opportunities for betting on the nags.

In small country towns you might find a picnic race meeting, usually the biggest annual get-together and well worth attending. Farmers from hundreds of miles around plus a few city slickers join the local population on a monumental betting spree fuelled by huge quantities of liquor. A certain amount of audience participation is encouraged, and not merely in the form of gambling. Prizes may be awarded to the best-dressed couple, to the winner of an egg-tossing competition and so on. The event often ends with a bush dance. The most notable such race meeting is held each year at Birdsville in remotest Queensland; see page 355.

Two other meetings well worth attending are the two-week picnic races at Grafton (500km up the coast from Sydney), which coincides with the Jacaranda Festival, and the Bong Bong Cup weekend held each February at Mittagong (100km southwest of Sydney); this event was suspended for two years after excessive drinking and outrageous behaviour, but is set to return in 1988.

Trotting. Most race courses have days or evenings set aside for "the trots", where jockeys (known as reinsmen) drive around the track in a cart attached to a horse. Recently the sport has been trying to improve its image by changing the name to "harness-racing", the name used in North America. The day's races are shown under this title in newspapers, but the sport is still widely known as trotting.

Motor Sport. You may gather from their sometimes overexuberant style of driving that Australians enjoy motor racing. Indeed, two of the best Formula One drivers ever — Jack Brabham and Alan Jones — are Australian. The main attraction is the Australian Grand Prix (held in Adelaide in early November), which began only in 1985 but attracts a massive following. It is the last and often decisive race in the Formula One calendar and therefore usually very exciting. There are many smaller races held each year, including rally driving, speedway and moto-cross. The Bathurst 1000 is the leading domestic event, an endurance race for production cars held each year at the town of Bathurst, 150km inland from Sydney.

Participation. When the federal government became concerned at the number of Australians watching (usually with a beer to hand) rather than joining in with sport, it instigated a campaign to persuade all unfit armchair sportsmen to become active. The result is "Life — Be In It", in which a cartoon character

"*WINNERS TEND TO BE FARMERS WHO HAVE TRAINED IN WELLIES.*"

exhorts Australians to take full advantage of the country's many sporting facilities. Whatever your chosen sport, you will be able to practise it in Australia (with the possible exception of dog-sledding). Tennis, golf and competitive cycling are popular and well provided for, and the climate usually cooperates. Jogging has many devotees, and many city parks and riversides have suitable tracks. There are plenty of events for amateurs to join, whether a 5km fun-run or a full Marathon. If you want to take part in the world's longest point-to-point athletic race, join the Ultrathon run from Melbourne to Sydney which is held each spring. The 1987 winner took a shade over $5\frac{1}{2}$ days to run the 1,060km course. Winners of this event tend to be farmers who have trained by running around their properties in Wellington boots.

A popular event amongst obese males in the Outback is "whammying", in which two pot-bellied contestants attempt to knock each other down using only their stomachs. Other less demanding activities include bowls (which enjoys surprisingly strong support) and kite-flying; Launceston, Tasmania is the site for the 1988 World Kiting Festival.

Since most of the population lives close to the sea, it is understandable that watersports attract the greatest participation. Swimmers and surfers argue constantly about the best beaches, anglers about the finest reaches and sub-aqua divers about the most beautiful coral. Windsurfing (also known as boardsailing) is becoming more popular; beginners will make much faster progress on inland water than on the ocean.

Surf Carnivals. There are 55,000 volunteer lifesavers who patrol the beaches of Australia every weekend. Surf lifesaving is a combination of a sport and a service. Each summer Lifesaving Clubs organize surf carnivals which make a very colourful spectator sport. When the surf is up, it is unlikely that you can find as exciting a sporting competition anywhere. The carnivals begin with a precision march of hundreds of be-hatted lifesavers who proceed to demonstrate their team skills in surfboat races and their individual skills in endurance swimming and surfski riding in their bid to win the highest accolade of "iron man".

GAMBLING

Australians are inveterate gamblers and will bet on virtually anything, so it will come as no surprise to find that there are limitless ways to make a fortune or lose your shirt. The non-specialist masses are entertained by poker machines or "pokies" (slot machines/one-armed bandits), housie (bingo), state lotteries and football pools, while on- and off-course betting and casinos cater for those who prefer to put a little study into the art of winning or losing money.

You should certainly try to observe Australians as they gamble away a fortune: about three times the annual defence budget. The easiest way is probably to go to a social club where dozens of "pokies" are in constant use. Many advertise that they can be played for small change (i.e. 20¢) or boast of massive jackpots (e.g. the largest payout to date of $21,000, won in 1984). You might also visit a betting shop or casino, or stumble upon the national game of chance known as "two-up". If you intend to indulge in a little risk-taking yourself, do so where the odds are least stacked against you: casino games like roulette and blackjack are a better bet than lotteries or poker machines. Try to set aside a certain amount which you can afford to lose.

Casinos. To satisfy some of this phenomenal appetite for gambling, most states have a casino or two. Although Las Vegas has nothing to fear, Australian casinos are big and ritzy, and enforce strict dress rules: no T-shirts, running shoes, thongs or shorts. In 1987 the Australian Minister for Tourism turned up at the Casino in Alice Springs only to be told that his $150 Reebok training shoes were unsuitable footwear; when he revealed his identity, the manager told him "in that case you can afford a better pair of shoes". If you can get in, casinos are great places to see the sleazy side of society, where gamblers become frighteningly involved with the business of winning or losing money. As anywhere the odds are against the punter: the casino has the edge by 2.7% in roulette (with one zero), 5.8% in blackjack (played mathematically correctly) and up to 25% for Keno. If you decide to take part, you can maximize the length of time it takes to lose your money by betting small amounts on red/black or odd/even chances at roulette.

At most casinos visitors are encouraged to play "keno". This game is related to bingo in that numbers are drawn, but the difference is that you mark your own card. The keno ticket carries 80 numbers. You cross between one and 15 numbers, and if your numbers are among the 20 that are drawn, you win. If you mark more than three, then you win even if some of your numbers fail to come up. The usual minimum stake is $1, and payouts generally correspond to three-quarters of the mathematical odds; in the simplest case, if you mark only one number, the chances of it coming up are four to one, and if it does you win.

Two-up. This game, sometimes known as "swy" is the purest form of gambling in Australia, and yet it is illegal outside casinos. Bets are placed on two coins which are tossed together. If one is heads and the other tails, there is no result. If both show the same, you win or lose depending on whether you bet on two heads or two tails. There are further sophistications such as betting on a run of heads or tails. If one coin fails to spin when tossed, it is known as a "butterfly" or "floater" and the spin is usually declared void by the "boxer", a person who arbitrates tosses and bets. Casinos take their cut of around 3% by keeping the stakes on a sequence of five identical events (unless you also bet on this possibility).

"EVEN MINISTERS ARE NOT EXEMPT FROM THE CASINO'S DRESS REQUIREMENTS."

Lotto. This game is basically large scale bingo where the participants select six or more numbers from 1 to 40. Six numbers are drawn once or twice each week, and anyone selecting three or more correct numbers wins a prize. The average payout is around 60% of the total money staked. The minimum stake is $1, and the maximum win decided by the number of participants but is likely to be in the thousands. Results are published in the press (even by the conservative *Australian*) and may be heard on special "hotline" telephone numbers.

Soccer Pools. British visitors will be familiar with the idea of picking games to end in draws, and will also know the names of Australian teams whose fixtures are used when British clubs are not playing. In fact the coupons used by Australian Soccerpools (the national organization) do not even mention teams, but just use numbers which can be correlated with the matches by looking in the daily press. The minimum stake is about $1 and if you use any of the many complex permutation systems the cost of your entry goes up at the same rate as your chances of winning.

Horses and Dogs. You can bet on horse races, harness-races and greyhounds either at the track, or at betting shops run by State Totalisator Agency Boards (TABs). State governments take a cut of around 15% on bets placed, i.e. about 85% of stakes are returned in winnings. The times that TAB outlets operate are given in daily newspapers. In general, the hours are around 10am to 8pm on Saturdays, with later opening and earlier closing on other days.

To place a simple bet on a horse, write the beast's number and that of the race on one of the slips provided and hand it in with your payment. If the horse wins, you can usually collect your payout soon after the race so long as no enquiry is announced. (To create an impression of familiarity with the sport if it loses, mutter about the animal having "run like a hairy goat".) Bets are totalled and payouts made according to the proportion staked on the winner, thus not necessarily providing the same keen starting prices to be found at racecourse bookmakers. There is an illegal betting fraternity which quotes starting prices off-course and also operates on events not covered by the TABs, dealing only in large amounts. Although you may get better odds from these characters, you have no recourse to the law if you are cheated.

MEDIA

Australians support an extraordinary range of newspapers, radio and television. Collectively they buy 27 million newspapers each week, making them among the world's most prolific readers (twice as many as Canada and France, for example). They can tune into radio broadcasts in 52 different languages, and — in the bigger cities — watch five regular television stations plus two major satellite TV networks. Equally surprising is the way that ownership of much of the media is concentrated in the hands of a few proprietors, notably Rupert Murdoch (publisher of the London *Times* and *Sun,* and many American newspapers), Robert Holmes a'Court (known as "Hacca") and John Fairfax. Interference in editorial decisions is not unknown; one former television tycoon was known for his habit of ringing up to order movies to be cancelled so that races featuring his horses could be screened. The federal government has strong links with these media barons, and also effectively controls two national TV networks. Some pundits argue that Australia has the least independent media in the world. Nevertheless, the reader, viewer or listener has a great deal of choice.

Newspapers. Standards of journalism in the Australian press are variable. The leading quality dailies are excellent newspapers (although some may find them a little conservative), while some popular tabloids are supremely tasteless examples of junk journalism, purveying smut and sensation. One criticism among British visitors and migrants is that newspapers in Australia are too parochial with foreign news being poorly covered, and that only bad news from the UK is published.

The recommended retail price of most newspapers is around 40¢ (but up to $1 for the bulky weekend editions, generally published on Saturdays). This cover price applies only within the area close to where it is printed; in isolated locations newspapers cost 10¢-20¢ more than the cover price, and prices are higher still in other states or distant cities. So you can buy the Perth-based *West Australian* in Adelaide, but it will cost $1.70 rather than the cover price of 40¢.

There are two national dailies: *The Australian* and the (less popular) *Australian Financial Review*. The national Sunday paper (and one of the few newspapers to be published at all on Sundays) is the excellent *Times on Sunday*. The best Australian dailies, however, are regional publications. The *Sydney Morning Herald* and Melbourne *Age* are among the finest papers in the English-speaking world. These and other leading broadsheets (such as Adelaide's *Advertiser* and the Brisbane *Courier-Mail*) manage to maintain high circulations (and decent standards) despite the efforts of the rival tabloids to capture readers. Newspaper bingo originated in Australia, and proprietors are constantly looking for ways to increase sales of downmarket tabloids. In 1987 these ploys included a competition in the Alice Springs *Centralian Advocate* where readers were invited to smear margarine on a square of the newspaper. If a message appeared, you won $1,000. Most towns of any size support a weekly paper, although in the smallest settlements the only print medium may be a notice board.

Weekly journals enjoy more independence than much of the daily press. Recently a disillusioned journalist began publishing *The Eye,* a monthly journal featuring satire, comment and "the stories the Big Boys won't print" (price $2.50). The weekly *Bulletin* (which incorporates part of *Newsweek* magazine) has good coverage of international events.

As in North America, newspapers carry a great deal of advertising, and you may soon tire of wading through endless advertisements in search of real news. On the other hand, you may find the classified sections useful when looking for work or a secondhand car. When confronted by this mass of advertising, don't overlook the highly useful entertainment sections that most quality newspapers include once a week.

If you wish to consult Australian newspapers abroad, visit the Library at any High Commission or Consulate. The London offices of individual states always carry a selection of the local state press. To keep in touch with life at home while in Australia, a good but slightly outdated selection of foreign newspapers is available from city-centre kiosks, and in the Library of High Commissions and Consulates. Daily newspapers from Europe and North America cost around $5 (Sunday editions $9), and the lightweight *Guardian Weekly* only $1.75. *USA Today* is widely available for $2, the same price as *Pravda* in English. There are also a number of specialist publications produced in Australia for homesick Poms, such as *British Soccer Week*.

Radio. A sweep along the tuning dial of your radio in any Australian city will reveal a surprisingly large number of radio stations. The nationwide network is operated by the Australian Broadcasting Corporation (ABC), widely known as "Aunty". Licence fees were abolished in 1974, and ABC radio and television are now funded entirely by the government. The equivalent of BBC Radio 4's *Today* programme is broadcast on the ABC AM network each morning, inelegantly entitled *National Radio Breakfast*. It includes regional slots for local news, *World Round-Up* (international news sent by satellite from the BBC in London) and plenty of soothing classical music to fill in the gaps.

Few Australians wake up to ABC, however. Most tune in to one of the many local commercial stations, a far cry from the well-modulated tones and high technical standards of the ABC network. There seems an insatiable appetite for pop music blended with constant news updates, traffic and weather reports. In the cities, this is catered for by sometimes dozens of competing stations, many operating on a shoestring. (It is not unknown for a city station to play a recording of helicopter sound effects behind an announcer who pretends to be flying above the city's traffic while instead he or she is sitting in a studio reading reports from the highway police.) The location of a radio station can be deduced from its call sign, the first number of which corresponds with the first digit of the state's postal code: thus 2UE is a Sydney station, 3CR a Melbourne one, etc.

As well as mainstream pop and rock, there are stations to cater for almost every taste in music. A number of AM music stations broadcast in stereo (using a new American transmission system) but the quality is inferior to FM stereo. There are also a large number of "talkback" stations which fill transmissions largely with phone-ins. Many have star presenters who try to outdo each other in their outrageous behaviour, rudeness to listeners who phone in, etc. Community radio stations are considerably more restrained, but often make interesting listening with a varied diet of ethnic programmes, broadcasts for women and local information. At the other extreme, you should try to hear a sports programme or two, since their entertainment rating can be high even if you know nothing about the sport at issue. The major stations (such as 2GB in Sydney) employ over-the-top commentators who don't mince their words, and are appallingly rude about players' performances.

In each chapter you will find some indication of the format of local stations in the area, but this should be taken as a guide only. Australian commercial radio is notoriously volatile, and adverse audience figures can change the format of a station from middle-brow talk to rock music overnight.

To become acquainted with Australian radio before you go, you can listen to Radio Australia (the overseas service of the ABC). Their short-wave English-language broadcasts can be heard in Britain from 7 to 10am (GMT) on 9655kHz, and from 3.30 to 8.40pm on 7205kHz. For details of progammes like *Aboriginal Australia Today* and *Jazz Australia,* write to Radio Australia, PO Box 428G, Melbourne, Victoria 3001 (tel: 03-235 2222).

Television. Although the larger cities have a wide choice of viewing, the programmes on offer are mostly unimaginative: soap operas ("soapies"), chat shows, sensationalized news coverage and large doses of sport are the norm. The government-financed ABC goes after high ratings as ruthlessly as any of the privately-owned networks. It is often known as ABN 2 (Australian Broadcasting Network 2) or simply as "Two" from its usual place on the dial. The other networks call themselves "Seven", "Nine", "Ten", etc.

SBS (Special Broadcasting Service) is another government-sponsored station catering especially for minority groups and interests. It is broadcast on UHF and is not available in all areas of Australia. The standard fare of SBS is similar to Channel 4 in Britain or PBS in the USA. In *Okker Chic,* which contains

Michael Thomas's irreverent study of Australian life, it is unkindly described as "Egyptian soap operas, Iraqi sit-coms and wacky zero-rating Herzegovinian folk-dancing shows". This is, of course, a ludicrous exaggeration: SBS shows many English-language programmes and has the best international news coverage. But its audience figures are so low (1-2%), that despite loud protests from some sections of the community, it may be subsumed into ABC and become the national broadcaster's second channel.

All stations except ABC and SBS carry large amounts of advertising. The number and frequency of commercials exceeds even American television. They take up more than one-fifth of airtime and include continual self-promotions of the stations (and sometimes their proprietors). Many pubs and clubs subscribe to one of the satellite stations on offer. *Superstation* and *Skychannel* broadcast a mix of major sporting events and rock music videos. Schedules for these channels are normally published in the daily press along with terrestrial TV network information. The magazine *TV Week* (price $1) contains details of all programmes, with separate editions for each state. Note that time differences between the states means that nationwide programmes are transmitted earlier in the western half of the country.

Visitors from the UK may be delighted to learn that British soap operas including *EastEnders* and *Brookside* are shown on Australian television. You should be warned, however, that they are many episodes behind the transmission schedules in the UK. These imports are complemented by home-grown soaps, of which a disproportionate number have medical settings: *A Country Practice* and *The Young Doctors* are typical of the genre. Some tabloid newspapers — such as the Sydney *Sun* — carry daily synopses of soap opera plots. American viewers will feel at home watching Channel Seven: the network regularly transmits the *Today* show from NBC and news from the Cable News Network in Atlanta, complete with inappropriate data such as US time checks and weather reports.

Amid this diet of imports there are some good original Australian programmes. *Sunday* on Channel Nine (9am-11am) is a good mix of news, current affairs and arts. If you want to acquire an understanding of the intricacies of Australian politics, watch a few editions of *Four Corners*. Sadly, one of the most innovative programmes in years — ABC's *The Dingo Principle*, which made the British show *Spitting Image* look tame by its extremely hard-hitting satire — was axed after successive editions generated outrage from, among others, the Iranian government, the Soviet Embassy and the Bishop of Melbourne.

Films on TV are rated just as they are for cinema performances. Although the networks are less paranoid about nudity than in America, you're unlikely to see anything terribly explicit on Australian television. Serious current affairs programmes and documentaries are most likely to be found on ABC, while the best international news is on SBS at 6.30pm (eastern time), with *Worldwide* at 9pm.

Although sport features heavily on all the networks, purists would regard the coverage it receives as contemptible. Cricket is probably worst affected: commercials are shown after every over or dismissal (i.e. every three minutes or less), and sometimes advertisements are shown at the foot of the screen during play. The networks are even prepared to replace crucial points in the game with commercial breaks in order to maintain their maximum allowance of 13 minutes of advertising per hour.

daks	trousers
dancing shorts	men's baggy shorts ("plenty of ballroom")
deli	corner store
durex	brand of sticky tape
lay by	putting a deposit of about 20% on an article to be paid for and collected at a later date
rollies	roll-up cigarettes
shonky	dubious, fake
strides	trousers
stubbies	shorts (also beer measure)
thongs	rubber flip-flops

Australian society is not yet as consumer-oriented as American society, though you shouldn't have any trouble buying whatever you need. One indication that Australian consumerism has not got out of control is the relatively restricted shopping hours. In small-town Australia, do not expect anything to be open except from 9am to 5 or (sometimes) 5.30pm Monday to Friday, and from 9am to noon on Saturdays. In the cities, the same basic hours are followed by most stores with an added bonus of late-night shopping until 8 or 9pm one night a week, usually Thursday or Friday. In well-populated areas, you can always find a corner shop ("deli") open later. There are strong moves to extend shopping hours in Victoria and Queensland to make Saturday afternoon trading legal. Twenty-four hour convenience store chains like 7-11 and Food Plus, often with a petrol station attached, are increasing in number at the expense of neighbourhood businesses and "strip shops", i.e. the suburban rows of shops which traditionally supplied essentials to the local community.

Outside the major city centres, shops are surprisingly shabby and old-fashioned looking, though the service is usually excellent without being obtrusive. (The garish signs on the other hand are anything but unobtrusive.) The main department stores are David Jones, Coles and Myers while the discount chain K-Mart is also widespread. Many Australian shops carry notices to the effect that by entering you consent to having your bags searched upon leaving. In addition, in many supermarkets you are obliged to take a trolley even if you only want to buy a carton of milk.

Students who are in possession of an ISIC card should obtain a free copy of the Australian Studentsaver Guide which lists over 2,000 outlets which give ISIC holders a discount. Enquire at Students Services Australia (PO Box 399, Carlton South, Melbourne, Victoria 3053; tel: 08-348 1777) or pick up a copy at any office of STA Travel.

Duty Free. As mentioned under *Red Tape,* each capital city has a tempting range of duty-free shops downtown. Their range of cameras, liquor, opals, etc. is often significantly cheaper than at the airport duty-free shops, and competitive with any duty-free shop in the world. Upon presentation of a valid international air ticket, you can buy these things and take them away, though the fact that you have them will be indelibly marked on your ticket and the bag itself will be sealed with a large red sticker saying "Important — duty-free goods in possession".

Although there is no general government sales tax on most goods, some items, especially luxury goods like jewellery, are taxed at a rate of up to 30%. Foreign visitors should be allowed exemption on these if they produce their air ticket and passport, though many retailers are reluctant to go through the necessary paperwork.

Tobacco. Cigarettes are sold in a bewildering range of quantities: 10, 15, 20, 25, 30 or 35 cigarettes to a pack. The price for 25 or 30 is usually around $2.50 or $3 except in Queensland where taxes are lower and prices about 50¢ less. You can save money on bulk purchases of 200, typically $12 in Queensland or $16 elsewhere. At the time of writing the two states of South Australia and Victoria were proposing an increase of 50¢ on a pack of cigarettes, which makes it all the more worthwhile buying your smokes in Queensland. Hand-rolling and pipe tobacco costs $6 for 50grams (2oz).

Photography. The cost of developing and printing your holiday snaps is high in Australia. The lowest price for printing 24 colour pictures is about $9, although the cost of film (about $5 for a roll of 24) is about the same as in Britain and North America. Another good reason for waiting until you get home to get your pictures developed is the extra weight and bulk of prints or slides. Beware of the adverse effects which dust and extreme heat can have on film. Keep your films in their plastic or foil containers and, if necessary, inside a plastic bag for protection.

Books. While Americans are used to the idea of discount book stores, British visitors may be pleased to learn that a number of Australian bookshops routinely sell their stock at 10% less than the recommended price.

The Australian appetite for the printed word is voracious and their publishing industry is thriving. Bibliophiles will be delighted by the prevalence of seven-day-a-week (and sometimes night) bookshops in the cities. One of the best gifts or souvenirs you can buy is a well-produced book on Australia of which there are a great many, from collections of realistic photographs of modern Aboriginal life to cartoon books. Try to confine youself to books published in Australia since there is a 25%-50% mark-up on imported books.

GIFTS AND SOUVENIRS

A number of Australian items from Akubra hats (the bush hat worn by Crocodile Dundee) to Vegemite have almost become cultural artefacts and might make suitable presents for your loved ones. There is an astonishing number of shops specializing in Australiana where you should be able to find something to take home which is suitably kitsch, such as a wind-up koala which plays Waltzing Matilda, a set of pink koala salt and pepper shakers, a koala tea cosy (so life-like that guests will think there is a marsupial sitting on your table) or a triple life-size sew-it-yourself kookaburra. There are a few tasteful gifts too such as opals and sheepskin products. If you have a taste for the bizarre, look out for goanna oil, said to be good for arthritic pains. One of the more unusual items in the *Australian Bicentennial Official Merchandising Catalogue 1988* is a tin of dehydrated convict sweat, the perfect accompaniment for an iron ball and chain also for sale in the catalogue.

Clothing. T-shirts can be high fashion in Australia (as a result of the climate) and shops stock an amazing range, from hand-printed designer numbers to ones with mildly obscene cartoons demonstrating the Australian sense of humour.

One of the most famous names in Australian clothing is R. M. Williams, a firm which started in Adelaide as a mail-order supplier of riding apparel for agricultural workers mainly elasticated leather boots (like English jodphur boots) and "strides" made from moleskin, a superior quality cotton twill. R. M. Williams has now achieved boutique status and has spread to all the big cities.

Aboriginal Artefacts. It is very easy to tell from the price, and usually from the appearance, which are the fakes made in Taiwan and which are the real thing. Boomerangs are the most obvious choice and will appeal to the kite-flying and frisbee-playing set. Most come with a leaflet explaining how they should be thrown. Although most boomerangs used by Aboriginals are weapons which are not designed to return, those sold by gift shops usually come back when thrown expertly. Didjeridus, an Aboriginal wind instrument, might appeal to those who play the bag-pipes; other people find their lungs are not equal to the task of producing a sound. Woomeras (spears) and bark paintings are also tempting, though prices for all authentic Aboriginal artefacts are high. Aboriginal Arts Australia Ltd. was established by the government to market Aboriginal and Torres Strait Islander arts and crafts, there are artists' galleries in all the major cities (addresses in regional chapters).

billabong	waterhole left by retreating river
bogey hole	any swimmable water hole
bombora	submerged rocks or reef which creates disturbed water dangerous to swimmers
bore	a well in the Outback, sometimes containing brackish water
brumby	wild horse
bush (to go)	to go into the country
bushwalking	hiking, like New Zealand tramping
cossie (also bathers, togs)	swimming costume
dumper	large wave which breaks unexpectedly and scrapes swimmers and surfers along the bottom
free beach	nude beach
iceberg	dedicated surfer who surfs in all weathers
langlauf	cross country skiing
rip	strong undersea current
spinifex	outback grass with sharp spikes which have an irritant chemical
sun-baking	sun-bathing

Attractive as the cities are, few people cross oceans to see only the buildings, restaurants and cultural entertainments in Australia. The endless beaches, primeval deserts, hills and reefs with their unique and abundant wildlife are a tremendous attraction to most tourists, as are the activities which can be enjoyed such as diving, ballooning, hiking and rafting. The event which marked a giant increase in tourist interest was the America's Cup in Perth when Australia's sea, surf and sunshine were brought to the world's attention. And as part of the burgeoning interest in the Australian outdoors, is a growing desire on the part of both Australian and foreign city-dwellers to visit the Outback.

THE OUTBACK

Merely seeing the Outback from a bus or train window can be a disappointment; it is far better to experience it, canoe on its rivers, walk amidst its ancient geological formations, meet the people who live there, etc. For all the glamour that attaches itself to windswept sand dunes and the *frisson* of excitement associated with crocodile-infested waters, it must never be forgotten that outback landscapes can be unimaginably dull. Although there are points of interest such as Aboriginal rock drawings and opal mines, there can be a lot of nothingness between them. Dreaming of endless horizons where, some say, you can actually see the curvature of the earth, is quite different from the reality of a marathon train or coach journey across the Nullarbor where the only variation in scenery is determined by the intensity of the heat haze. In the Kimberleys of northern Western Australia, cattle properties are limited by law to one million acres, larger than Suffolk or Shropshire.

Outback Australia is among the most hostile environments in the world. It has been a place of suffering and tragedy from the time of the hunter-gatherer Aboriginal tribes who had to devote every waking moment to the business of wresting a living from the desert, to the present day when the newspapers carry reports every year of people who have become lost and have died of dehydration or from contact with the wildlife.

The early explorers and settlers were often defeated by the land, as a quick perusal of a map of Sturt's Stony Desert will convey: "Cadelga Station (uninhabited)", "Miranda (ruins)", "Coongie (abandoned)" and so on. Other places marked on the road atlas in the same area include the Ephemeral Lakes, Lake Yamma Yamma ("full only twice this century") and nearby a vast area of outback Queensland labelled "subject to inundation". When there isn't a drought there's a flood, and the rainy season, which usually lasts from January to March in northern Australia, can cut homesteads off for weeks.

All of this can sound more than a little daunting to visitors. Any trip into the remote Outback cannot be undertaken lightly: four wheel drive vehicles fitted out with spare parts, water tanks and extra fuel are essential for any trips off the principal long distance routes. Secondary tracks often peter out and it is easy to become lost in the featureless scrub and spinifex (spiky grass). The earth can get so hot that it burns through rubber-soled shoes.

A large water bottle and sun hat are essential pieces of equipment. Water is a precious commodity in places where the time between rainfalls is measured in years rather than days, and it should never be squandered. On drought-stricken properties, it is not unusual for bath water to be recycled for laundry and for showers to be rationed. One of the worst crimes that city slickers commit is to pollute bores of drinking water with soap powder. The red dust of northern Australia seems to get everywhere necessitating daily dousing of vehicles (including the interiors) and of clothes, though the dust never seems to disappear completely. Visitors to the Outback must be prepared for a certain amount of discomfort from the heat and dust if nothing else.

To reach remote attractions, it is worth considering an outback adventure tour. The provision of these is a rapidly growing industry. It is best to choose one operated by an established organization, such as those offered by the Youth Hostels Association (60 Mary St, Surry Hills, Sydney, NSW 2010), which range from two-day trips into the Kakadu National Park for $170 to 21-day camping safaris to the Gulf of Carpentaria for $1,450. Rob's Outback Tours are also run in conjunction with the YHA, and details of his "passenger-involved tours" to the northern tip of Queensland or the deserts of Western Australia, which cost about $25 a day, are obtainable from the New South Wales YHA office (355 Kent St, Sydney 2000). More upmarket outback adventures, which claim to "visit new frontiers", are organized by two long-established companies both based in Melbourne: Centralian (1 James Clay St; tel: 03-544 8644) and AAT King's (108 Ireland St; tel: 03-329 8022; also in the UK at 15 Adam St, London WC2N 6AH). If you want to hire a four-wheel drive vehicle and drive it yourself you can join a convoy of six to ten vehicles led by Centralian. If you are contemplating a big trip, you might want to browse in *The Outback on a Budget* by Brian Sheedy (Roadwrite, $16.95) and *Safe Outback Travel* by the well known painter of the Outback Jack Absalom (Five Mile Press, $6.95).

THE WILDLIFE

No matter how slim your grasp of Australian geography may be, everyone knows something of its wildlife. Because the continent of Australia became an island eons ago, animals developed in forms quite different from anywhere else in the world; in fact marsupials (mammals whose partially-developed young are carried in pouches) are peculiar to Australia, with one minor exception in South America. Koalas, kangaroos, possums, wallabies and wombats are all marsupials, and these can be seen at various wildlife parks throughout the country.

Provided you get far enough from the cities, you are very likely to see kangaroos, especially at dusk or dawn, grazing in paddocks or woods or trying to cross the road. Sadly you will also see a number lying dead by the roadside. Despite the threat from motor vehicles, they are so numerous that they are constantly being culled (about 1.3 million a year in Queensland alone) by farmers who view them as competing with sheep and cattle for a share of the sparse grazing.

You are less likely to see koalas in the wild, since their numbers have been severely depleted first by man (two million koala skins were exported in a single year in the first half of this century) and more recently by a sexually transmitted disease, which is seriously disrupting their reproduction patterns. It has even been suggested that the species is headed for extinction though this seems unduly pessimistic. To be sure of seeing a koala, head for a zoo or wildlife reserve where you may be encouraged to cuddle one. When the Minister of Tourism referred to koalas a few years ago as smelly little creatures (after one had reportedly relieved itself on him) there was a huge public outcry and the number of people eager to cuddle-a-koala did not seem to be affected. Apparently in the US, koalas are sometimes referred to as Qantas bears, which might please the airline ad man who chose the symbol but would distress all those who object to hearing koalas inaccurately referred to as bears. The word koala is thought to come from an Aboriginal word meaning "does not drink water", which accurately describes them. The average koala is quite happy to spend his or her life in the branches of a single eucalyptus tree, munching on gum leaves (which are mildly intoxicating) and spending most of the time asleep. To learn more, consult *The Official Koala Handbook* by Simon Hunter (Chatto & Windus, £6.95).

The kookaburra's distinctive laugh (and its mirth, unlike the koala's disease, can be contagious for humans) is heard in urban areas as well as in the bush where it fulfils the same function as the rooster and so is sometimes called the "bushman's clock". There are many other memorable birds such as galahs, parrots and the pink and grey rosellas which enliven dry, brown landscapes wonderfully. You may be struck by the preponderance of screeching or calling birds instead of songbirds. The Royal Australian Ornithologists Union (tel: 03-370 1272) operates bird identification courses.

But not all Australian wildlife is so charming. Dingoes are wild dogs whose howling at nightfall can be alarming to the uninitiated. They also pose a real threat to stock animals. The Dingo Fence which roughly follows the borders of Queensland and New South Wales, stretches an astonishing distance of 7,725km (more than from London to Bombay) and must be constantly maintained to protect the sheep on the eastern side from the dingoes on the other.

Crocodiles are a serious menace. Although they very occasionally turn up in town drains or culverts, you can be fairly confident of avoiding an encounter by refraining from swimming in crocodile habitats, which are usually signposted. Of the 24 deaths from crocodile attacks in the past 100 years, a third have been in the past two years, which probably just illustrates that more tourists are entering crocodile territory rather than that the crocodiles are becoming more fierce. For more information about crocodiles and other dangerous wildlife, see *Health: Creatures to Avoid.*

NATIONAL PARKS

Over the past century, 488 areas of land have been set aside by the government, covering every possible habitat from bleak desert to mangrove swamp. It is now being realized that some of Australia's deserts and scrubland are in fact very fragile and need to be protected; the Nullarbor Plain is being considered as a possible addition to the World Heritage list of unique and significant features worthy of world recognition and protection.

Information boards and park rangers will help you to enjoy the Australian wilds and to avoid coming to grief. National park rules prohibit the lighting of

"THE LONGEST FENCE IN THE WORLD SEPARATES THE SHEEP FROM THE DINGOES"

fires during fire ban periods, taking in pets, leaving rubbish, desecrating Aboriginal sites and tampering with the flora and fauna (including crocodiles, since park representatives have proposed that people who enter crocodile areas of national parks be heavily fined). With cuts in government funding, some have started to charge a modest entrance fee. It is usually possible to camp in national parks and there is often a supply of chopped firewood to which you are welcome to help yourself assuming there is no fire ban in force.

ACTIVITIES

Most of the states are readily associated with some activity: in Queensland it's scuba diving, in Tasmania it's bushwalking, in Western Australia it's sailing, in Victoria it's skiing. But you can find most sports and outdoor activities being taught, practised and enjoyed in every state. Having a go in Australia is more important than mastering an activity. If for example you decide to go riding on an outback property there is unlikely to be much preamble before setting off. Similarly in the ski resorts, there isn't much emphasis on formal instruction. Beginners learn by doing and by watching others. Remember that you may need special insurance if you undertake dangerous activities

Bushwalking. You can of course come undone by being ill-prepared for certain activities including bushwalking. For example long distance walks in Tasmania require careful provisioning and waterproof equipment. If you intend to do a lot of hiking in one state look for the series of books *100 Walks in Tasmania, 120 Walks in Victoria,* and so on, published by Hill of Content in Melbourne. High achievers might be interested to learn that a 5,000km National Trail will open for the benefit of hikers and riders in the year of the Bicentenary. It will stretch from Cooktown (north of Cairns) to Melbourne, following the old stock routes, bush tracks and fire trails, and will have campsites at appropriate intervals.

Cycling. Cycling too can become a serious undertaking in a land where food and water supplies can be hundreds of kilometres apart. (At least cyclists don't have to worry about the next petrol station.) In such conditions you should inform the local police of your intentions. Only the most enthusiastic cyclists will undertake one of the trans-continental routes which are apparently popular with Japanese cyclists who appreciate the contrast with cramped living conditions in Japanese cities.

The condition of the roads in Australia varies and your route will determine the type of bicycle you use. A mountain bike is recommended if you want to get off the beaten track to some otherwise inaccessible but very worthwhile places. Beware of plank bridges in the country; the gaps are sometimes wide enough to trap a wheel and cause a nasty accident. Beware also of dogs, especially unleashed blue cattle dogs, a common and vicious breed. A couple of thwacks around the nose with a bicycle pump is enough to deter most brutes. The sealed roads are generally quite good, though even a modest amount of traffic can interfere with your pleasure due to the aggressive driving techniques favoured by the locals (much more dangerous than dogs, country bridges and venomous snakes put together).

Climbing over the Great Dividing Range, which separates the coast between Melbourne and Sydney from the interior, is an exhilarating experience, though it can be a gruelling one. Due to the way the continental shelves are formed it is easier to cycle from west to east; in the opposite direction one is faced with almost a brick wall, though with a 10 or 12 speed touring bike with a mountain block it is possible. Mountains in Australia like the Snowy Mountains are no more difficult than their North American or European alpine counterparts. Some roads will be blocked by snow in the winter, so check weather forecasts with police and tourist organizations before setting off. Being stranded in cold, wet conditions can be just as dangerous as being stranded in the desert.

Cycling up the Queensland coast is less strenuous, principally due to the helpful tailwind which will blow you all the way to Cairns, Daintree and beyond (though the bitumen stops at Daintree).

Detailed information on cycle routes and touring can be obtained from the following organizations:

Bicycle Australia: PO Box K499, Haymarket, NSW 2000. (They publish an excellent booklet *Pacific Bicycle Route* detailing the cycle route from Brisbane to Sydney; cost $15 plus postage.)
Bicycle Institute of New South Wales: GPO Box 272, Sydney 2001.
Bicycle Victoria: GPO Box 1961R, Melbourne 3001.
Tailwinds Bicycle Touring: PO Box 32, Canberra, ACT.

The Australian cycling magazine *Freewheeling* also provides good information on cycle touring and can be contacted through Bicycle Australia, the national bicycle touring association, which is not a commercial company. It organizes several guided bicycle tours in New South Wales and Victoria, starting at about $120 including food and accommodation for a long weekend. Also Trochos Publications (16 Kellaway St, Maidstone, Victoria 3012) publish articles of interest to touring cyclists.

Water Sports. Frolicking in ocean waves seems harmless enough sport until a freak wave or rip current occurs. Anyone who decides to have a go on a surfboard should, after attaining a certain level of confidence in the waves, be accompanied by an experienced surfer. Body surfing is universally enjoyed and requires only a modicum of skill. There are numerous variations on the surfboard which do not require the skill and balance, such as the surf mat, surfoplane and boogie board. This latter is a lightweight body mat with wrist strap which costs about $150, but can sometimes be hired from surf shops. Another way of enjoying the balmy ocean is to go "boom-netting" as described in *Queensland*. The risks of which swimmers should be aware are set out in the chapter *Health,* but bear in mind that swimmers who go out beyond the line of breakers are known as "sharkbait".

Skiing. Snow-skiing is not a sport which one normally associates with Australia. However there are two alpine regions — one in the Snowy Mountains on the New South Wales/Victoria border, the other in Tasmania — whose ski resorts are attracting increasing numbers of beginners and experts between June and September. The former region boasts a larger area of ski mountains than Switzerland. The relatively high altitude of the Snowy Mountains means that the snow is more reliable than in Tasmania, though it tends to become slushy more readily than in the Alps of Europe or New Zealand. Cross-country skiing is particularly popular (and is usually referred to in Australia by its German name *langlauf*), though the main resorts are equipped with plenty of lifts and pistes for downhill skiers.

Australian travel companies have realized for a long time that many visitors want to be introduced to the water, air or earth in a gentle and supervised way. So you will be soon faced with a plethora of choice, from small local firms which will take you ballooning, camel riding, snorkelling or river rafting to national organizations like the Youth Hostels Association or the Australian Adventure Centre in Queensland (PO Box 109, Stafford, Brisbane 4053; tel: 07-359 6651) which arrange all these and others. Each regional chapter includes a section *Sport* and, at the end of the chapter, *The Great Outdoors*.

barrow	Black Maria
bashed	beaten up
blue	fight
bong	opium pipe with bowl, often used for smoking marijuana
bongover	the morning-after effect of smoking too much marijuana
crim	criminal (noun)
demon	policeman, detective
dob in	to turn someone in, grass on them
donnybrook	bar fight
early release licence	parole
ginger	a prostitute who works with an accomplice to rob a client
hop	policeman
hop-head	heavy smoker of marijuana

Most Australians are refreshingly trusting and trustworthy. This does not mean that they are all law-abiding: there is less personal crime than in most parts of the western world, but conversely Australia has plenty of scandals involving corrupt politicians and crooked police, and there are vast underground networks of criminals. The visitor is unlikely to be affected by this except as a topic of discussion in pubs. Indeed you may feel so safe that you could be lulled into a sense of false security. Sneak thieves do, of course, exist, and relaxed tourists rank among their favourite targets. Don't leave your possessions on full view in a car. Pickpocketing is a threat in crowded areas, especially at major sporting events. Although some tourist literature maintains that "mugging is a crime that does not exist in Australia, either by day or by night", it is a growing danger in the cities. A more likely threat, however, is that you will be the victim of thefts by other travellers, particularly in hostels in popular areas.

Violent Crime. Gun laws are formulated and enforced by individual states which leads to some worrying discrepancies. While most states have strict controls, weapons are on open sale in Queensland and Tasmania. The result is that any Australian can buy a gun by mail order from a dealer in Brisbane or Hobart. There are over 3,500,000 privately-owned guns, around one for every four inhabitants. While many are used for sport or farming, others find their way into the hands of criminals and the mentally unstable. In recent years there have been several massacres where psychopaths have indulged in random murder. Bear in mind that the free availability of weapons means that their use cannot be ruled out in mugging attempts.

Most women visitors feel much safer in Australian cities than in, say, London or New York although walking alone late at night in badly lit areas is not advisable. A particular hazard for both women and men is the fighting which can break out in and around the rougher sort of pubs at closing time.

THE LAW

Most Australian police are armed but not necessarily dangerous. You are most likely to encounter them if driving around late at night, and are required to provide a sample of breath or blood if they suspect you of drinking.

Australia has its own version of MI5 or the CIA, known as ASIO (the Australian Security and Intelligence Organization), which is popularly thought of as incompetent in the extreme.

Arrests and Charges. The police in Australia have wide powers of arrest, and may arrest you if they have "reasonable grounds" for suspecting you of having committed an offence. If you are arrested, you are obliged only to give your name and address and are entitled to contact a friend or lawyer before answering any other questions. (The police will be able to supply a duty lawyer.) In several states, your interrogation will be recorded on video. If you are subsequently charged with an offence, you may be remanded in custody or released on a surety. Foreign visitors are likely to have their passports confiscated so that they don't attempt to leave the country.

Before a court appearance, legal advice should be sought. Each state has a Legal Aid Commission who should fund the cost of a lawyer to represent you. These are admirably even-handed bodies, and can be relied upon to do their best to get you off the hook. Most prosecutions are made by the Crown (technically representing the Queen but in reality a branch of law enforcement). If your sentence is considered too lenient, the Crown may appeal for a tougher one just as you can ask for clemency if you feel you have been too harshly treated.

Drugs. Marijuana grows extremely well in most parts of Australia, including a large number of back yards. Among young middle-class Australians smoking marijuana at a private gathering is considered as natural as drinking beer (and almost as cheap), and joints are offered around as casually as cigarettes. But the laws on drugs are complicated and can be harsh. Each state fixes its own penalties which are generally more severe than in Britain or liberal states of the USA. However, the possession of a small amount of cannabis for personal use has been virtually decriminalized in South Australia; it earns only a small on-the-spot fine like a parking ticket. But in Queensland, it is a serious crime punishable by a large fine and (if you are unlucky or a large quantity is involved) a prison sentence. Penalties for possessing harder drugs, including the increasingly popular cocaine, are severe as are those for dealing of any kind.

Other Laws. One vestige of Australia's convict past is the number of seemingly trivial rules and regulations which each state concocts. Controls on drinking alcohol have already been mentioned; some may seem ludicrous — like the time restrictions on drinking on the *Sunlander* train between Brisbane and Cairns — but are taken very seriously by the authorities. Taking alcohol onto

Aboriginal lands is also a serious offence. Queensland has perhaps the oddest law in all Australia: it is an offence to serve alcohol to anyone who displays "deviant" tendencies, a law designed to make life difficult for gay people. Homosexual practices are an offence only in Queensland, and then only among men.

In amongst these anachronistic laws are a number of progressive pieces of legislation, in particular those outlawing discrimination on grounds of race or gender. If you feel you have been unfairly discriminated against, you should get in touch with the state's Equal Opportunity office, or contact the Human Rights Commission, PO Box 629, Canberra, ACT 2601 (tel: 008-026 110 toll-free).

As the laws on marijuana become more liberal, controls on smoking tobacco increase. Smoking is banned on almost all city buses and trains, in cinemas and theatres, in lifts, museums and galleries, in public buildings such as post offices and all federal government offices. Melbourne has gone one stage further and is banning smoking even in some outdoor areas. Finally, you should note that every state, city, town and national park has strict laws against littering, with stiff fines for transgressions.

Sources of Help. If you do get into trouble with the law, inform your nearest Consulate. Although they will not be able to secure your release, they can help to ensure that you are treated in accordance with Australian law and can supply a list of local lawyers. In the case of longer-term incarceration, British residents should contact the National Council for the Welfare of Prisoners Abroad, 82 Rosebery Avenue, London EC1 (tel: 01-833 3467). American citizens should get in touch with the International Legal Defense Council, Suite 315, 14320 Walnut Avenue, Philadelphia, PA 19102 (tel: 215-545-2428).

TOURIST INFORMATION

You may be surprised by the sheer range and quantity of information that Australia produces for tourists. This is partly because most tourism promotion is carried out at state level, and each state spends a great deal on extolling its virtues to other Australians as well as to foreign tourists. See *Before You Go* for sources of information which you can obtain from abroad. But when you arrive in Australia it's well worth calling in at the travel bureaux of the states you intend to visit. You can get information about a particular state from its tourist office in the capital of other states: thus there is a Western Australian Tourist Office in Melbourne, a Queensland Government Tourist Bureau in Adelaide, etc. A couple of hours spent touring the tourist offices for each state in, say, Sydney can equip you with more than enough information for a nationwide tour. The addresses of each state's tourist bureaux are listed under *Help and Information* in the regional chapters. These organizations act both as information sources and as travel agencies, so that Tasbureau for example can tell you about accommodation on the island and book a ferry crossing to Tasmania.

When you call or write to a state tourist office, mention any special interests such as theatre, cycling or ornithology, since the offices have leaflets on all sorts of subjects. But don't expect a very discriminating tone in the bumph; be prepared for the hard sell. It is a worthwhile exercise for the free maps and the list of forthcoming events.

As well as these official organizations you will encounter a number of other "information bureaux". These fall broadly into two categories: the first type are local or regional tourist offices, such as those run by City Councils or Regional Tourism Associations, which supplement the state's promotional activities with a stronger emphasis on local attractions; the second are privately-run enterprises which make money by charging organizations for the privilege of recommending them to tourists. You are unlikely to be given a full picture of possibilities from these offices, which are most often found at airports and in city centres.

Each city or region has at least one free magazine or newspaper. The giveaways *This Week In. . .* and *What's On In. . .* can be found in all major cities, at hotel and hostel receptions, transport terminals and information bureaux. They are good sources of information on coming events and normally have a map or two.

Emergencies. In state capitals and larger towns, dial 000 for the police, fire or ambulance service. Different numbers may apply elsewhere, but will be shown in the front of directories and in telephone booths. If you need emergency medical assistance see the chapter *Health* and the hospitals/health centres listed under *Help and Information* for each city. For dealing with a financial crisis see *Money*. You can find the addresses of the post office, American Express and Thomas Cook under *Help and Information* for each of the major cities.

There are British diplomatic representatives in Brisbane, Canberra, Melbourne, Perth and Sydney; addresses are given in the relevant chapters in the *Help and Information* sections. Unless you lose your passport, get arrested, become destitute and want to be repatriated or war breaks out in the South Pacific, you won't need to consult these addresses. (If you lose your money, try to have the consulate cash a cheque for up to £50 as mentioned under *Money*). If your passport is lost or stolen, notify the police immediately, and go to the nearest consulate where you will be issued with travel documents which will allow you to complete your stay and return to Britain. It is also worth notifying the local office of the Department of Immigration and Ethnic Affairs of the loss, to avoid suspicion of overstaying.

The Australian equivalent of the Samaritans is known as Life Line (not to be confused with the government's Life be in it — Line, a recorded message giving advice on healthier living). The number of the nearest branch can be found at the front of the telephone directory. Note that in smaller towns, the line may operate only at night. For more specific crises (such as those experienced by women, alcoholics, drug abusers and gay people) most big cities have additional agencies, listed under *Helplines* in each chapter.

Handicapped Travellers. In general, provision for travellers with disabilities is good. All new building projects provide special facilities, with the gradient and length of ramps shown on signs. The book *Accommodation for Disabled Travellers in Australia* is one of the many available from the Australian Council for Rehabilitation of the Disabled (ACROD), PO Box 60, Curtin, ACT 2605 (tel: 062-82 4333). The Australian travel industry is highly aware of the problem facing handicapped travellers and makes careful provision for ease of access. Accommodation presents few problems as long as you book well in advance.

Facilities for the visually handicapped are good, in particular to help cope with city traffic. The audible signals from pedestrian crossings are helpful, and some cities even provide ridged pavements to indicate crossing points. Further information from the Australian National Council for the Blind, PO Box 162, Kew, Victoria 3101 (tel: 03-860 4444).

PUBLIC HOLIDAYS

As well as the eight days noted below, each state has two or more extra holidays which are listed in the *Calendar of Events* at the end of each chapter.

January 1	New Year
January 26	Australia Day
March/April	Good Friday
March/April	Easter Monday
April 25	Anzac Day
June (second Monday)	Queen's Birthday (except in WA where it is celebrated on the first Monday of October)
December 25	Christmas Day
December 26	Boxing Day (except in SA which instead celebrates Proclamation Day on December 28)

There is growing pressure for National Aborigines Day (celebrated on the second Friday in September) to be declared a full public holiday nationwide.

If a fixed Bank Holiday falls on a weekend, it is normally taken on the following Monday. The one exception is Anzac Day, which is moved only when it falls on a Sunday.

Finally, you should be aware of school holidays in Australia: accommodation can be in short supply, and trains, buses and aircraft fully booked. There are three main holiday periods each year; dates vary radically from one state to another. School children have two weeks off in the autumn/winter starting anywhere between early May and early July, two weeks off in the spring, starting in late August or late September and finally a long summer break from mid-December to early February.

Sydney and New South Wales

Population of Sydney: 3,390,000 **Population of NSW: 5,500,000**

In the imaginations of many, Sydney has overtaken Paris, Rome and San Francisco as the city of style and romance. According to a recent survey, one quarter of young Londoners would choose Sydney as the next best place to live after London. Nearly all tourists to Australia include Sydney on their itineraries and find that the reality of the city comes close to matching the dream. Few visitors can fail to be impressed with the rich variety of the city from Opera House to Kings Cross and from Harbour Bridge to golden beaches.

Morale is especially high at present. Public spending on projects to improve the city — mostly prompted by the excuse of the Bicentenary — is at such a pitch that complaints about the unhealthy national economy ring false. After partially restoring the area known as the Rocks, where the original settlement was built, the authorities have now turned their attention and resources to the Darling Harbour Project which, will transform an area of tumble-down warehouses, derelict docks and a railway goods yard into a showpiece of boutiques, restaurants and the inescapable viewpoints. Meanwhile Circular Quay, where the many harbour ferries dock, is also the subject of an expensive and worthy "uptarting" process which will include ambitious glassed-in arcades, more chic shops and restaurants and a two-kilometre promenade along the waterfront past the Opera House.

Much of Sydney's life is focused on its infinitely praiseworthy harbour and coastline. Each little indentation in the coast has its own name and atmosphere from famous Bondi Beach to the bizarrely named Dee Why Beach north of the harbour. Outdoor theatre venues, restaurants, towers and a zoo have all been placed so as to maximize exposure to the magnificent harbour. The Sydney Harbour Bridge which, even when it opened in April 1932, some found more impressive than beautiful, provides an important landmark; as long as it is visible you can orient yourself. The harbour's beauty is not best captured in a static photograph, since much of its interest and charm exist in the activity it generates: private speed boat taxis, dinghies, ferries and hydrofoils, supertankers and 18-foot skiffs. These fast little sailboats race at weekends between September and April, and it is possible to join spectator ferries which depart at 2pm. But most of the harbour spectacle can be appreciated free of charge from any number of vantage points on or beside or above the harbour . If you happen to be in Sydney on Australia Day (January 26th), try to take in the "ferrython", when Sydney's ferries race around the harbour.

Added to all these physical delights are the social and cultural pleasures of a city whose level of sophistication has catapulted in the past decade or so. And there is as much diversity in the suburbs of Sydney as there is in the boroughs of London or the *arrondisements* of Paris. There is yuppy-cum-gay Paddington, slum-turned-alternative Darlinghurst, radical Glebe, conservative moneyed Vaucluse, trendy Balmain and sleazy Kings Cross. All have their own bookshops, art galleries, cafés and nightlife which would take years to exhaust. You may (rightly) feel that all these areas are a million miles from kangaroos and the Outback, but in Sydney the bush is just beyond the city limits, much of it in its virgin state.

First there was New South Wales then there was Australia. What the early sailors saw of the coast reminded them of the green and jagged southern edge of Wales. It was only later that the name Australia, meaning "south" in Latin, was coined. With over 60% of the state's population concentrated in the capital, it is easy to deduce that the rest of the state (which is six times the size of England) is very sparsely populated. Few foreigners can name other cities in New South Wales such as Wagga Wagga, Wollongong and Dubbo. Although the interior of the state is not altogether devoid of interest — there are for example over 30 national parks in New South Wales — the most rewarding parts of the state are the coastal resorts stretching both north and south from Sydney, the Blue Mountains near Sydney, Mount Kosciusko National Park where Australia's highest peak may be found and the famed vineyards of the Hunter Valley, about 170km northwest of the state capital.

CLIMATE

In an area so vast there are great differences in climate from the drought-prone Outback to the bushfire-prone forests all around Sydney, from the balmy coasts near the Queensland border to the winter snows in the Snowy Mountains. Snow and ice are unknown in Sydney itself but inland roads through the Blue Mountains occasionally become impassible in winter.

But it is Sydney's climate about which most prospective visitors to Australia are curious. Sydney's renowned climate clinches the impression of beauty set up by the intricate patterns of land and water along the harbour and by the picturesque waterborne transport. Of course there are grey and wet days when the city is not at its best; surprisingly some rain falls on an average of 150 days of the year, so you should be prepared for some very heavy downpours at any

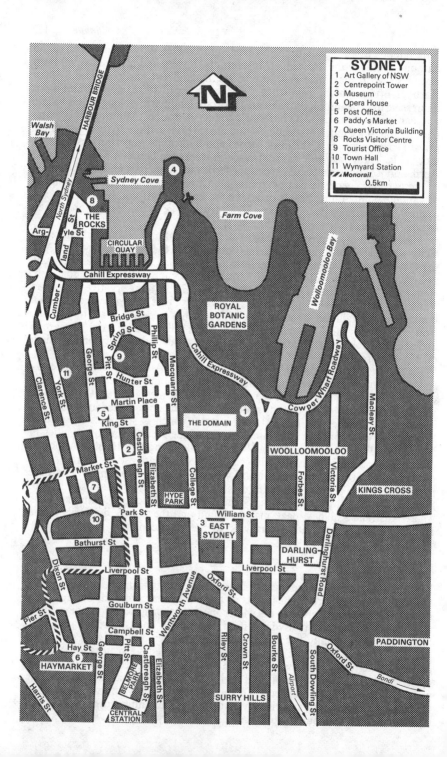

time of the year. But most visitors are treated to the sparkling sunshine and opaque blue skies which make the harbour and outdoor activities around it so memorable, and which account for Sydneysiders' smug assumption of superiority over Melbourne.

There is no season one needs to avoid. The summers are whole-hearted summers when the heat and humidity sometimes become intense. But, unlike other cities in a heat wave, tempers in Sydney do not seem to soar. Sydneysiders simply flock to their favourite city beach, where the water and breezes of the Pacific Ocean deflect any bad temper. One famous breeze is known as the "Southerly Buster" a wind which blows at the end of a scorching day bringing the temperature down as much as 15°C and upsetting dinghies. Much more common are the cooling breezes called north-easters and the gusty southerlies which accompany a cool change. This latter phenomenon takes place frequently and results in fairly dramatic drops of temperature for a few days.

The most humid time is January to March while the wettest months are April to June. The driest months are September to November with less than two centimetres of rain falling in September. The air in winter is crisp though the temperatures remain mild, usually averaging about 13°C/55°F in July and August.

THE LOCALS

Sydneysiders, as the natives are known, share with New Yorkers the easy confidence that their city is the "Big Smoke". One rhyming slang name for it — Steak and Kidney — is a term of affection not a slur, though the same could not be said of Melbourne's favourite nickname for its rival, "Sinney", which successfully conveys something of the sensuous enjoyment and ostentation which the natives go in for. The inhabitants, like the tourists, seem to have fallen under the spell of their city and the great Australian pastime of belittling one's circumstances is less in evidence in Sydney than in other cities.

But they do demonstrate many other Australian characteristics to perfection, such as a penchant for shrugging off anxiety. The fact that their city is invariably linked with political and financial scandal does not worry them unduly. Sydneysiders are even less prudish and puritanical than their fellow Australians. They are on the whole tolerant, worldly and pleasure-loving. This is a society which is descended from petty criminals rather than one (like North America) which is largely derived from people escaping religious persecution.

The spectrum of races and nationalities which have congregated in Sydney contributes to the interest and complexity of this great city. According to the recent census, one in five New South Wales residents have at least one parent born in a non-English-speaking country. And this is not only a recent phenomenon; in the 1880s 15% of the population of New South Wales was Chinese. From the New Zealanders who favour Bondi to the Aboriginals, of whom there are a total of 11,000 in Sydney, in the inner city suburb of Redfern, from the Greeks in South Sydney to the Italians in the inner west, Sydney is a city which has a place (though not necessarily a job) for everyone. There is a small-but-flourishing Chinatown on one side of the Central Station and a pronounced Middle Eastern influence in Surry Hills on the other side. There are mosques and Japanese grocers, Highland gatherings and German folk festivals, and over 10,000 citizens who were born in the Soviet Union. Among the sprawling suburbs, many of them unfashionable, there are unexpected and remarkable concentrations of different nationalities. For example Lebanese people dominate Bankstown while Cabramatta is largely (and very recently) Vietnamese. Before the Vietnamese refugees began arriving in such numbers, Cabramatta was predominantly Hungarian. But as the older immigrants have improved their economic status they have moved to more desirable parts of town, closer to the city centre. Spanking new neon signs in Asian characters for textile importers and Vietnamese restaurants are being erected alongside the fading obsolete signs of Middle European watch repairers, demonstrating the state of flux to which many residential areas of Sydney are subject and the degree of social mobility which still exists in Australia.

While the new migrants join in the scramble towards affluence, Sydneysiders downtown lead relatively indulged lives, spending a lot of time and money eating out, drinking, surfing and listening to music whether pricey productions inside the Opera House or free jazz outside on the terrace. By outback Australian standards, Sydney is full of posers. But despite being compared frequently to California, Sydney is no Los Angeles. Apart from the sprinkling of picturesque weirdos, trendies and snobs (who practise what Harpers & Queen calls "Kangasnoot"), Sydneysiders are sane, happy-go-lucky people with whom you can share a drink and a joke without much ado.

Making Friends. So much of Sydney's life is lived outdoors that it is easy to meet people, whether families swimming at Manly Beach, office workers eating lunch in Martin Place while listening to free entertainment or odd bods promenading around Kings Cross late at night.

Despite its sleazy aspect, Kings Cross has a thriving and eccentric nightlife, where it is easy to meet both young locals and travellers. Establishments like Barons "up the Cross" are open until 6 or 7am and women may find that they are treated to drinks by men whose intentions are not necessarily suspect. Darlinghurst, near Kings Cross, is also full of friendly trendies; try Rogues at 10 Oxford Square or the Cauldron at 207 Darlinghurst Road.

But you don't have to be in Kings Cross to meet people. The pubs and restaurants in Newtown and Glebe are favoured by students from the nearby "uni" (Sydney University). There are two other universities in Sydney, the University of New South Wales next to the Randwick Racecourse and Macquarie University in the northern suburbs, though the density of student haunts is lighter than around Sydney University. In Randwick try the Royal Hotel (corner of Perouse Road and Cuthill St) which is a popular singles meeting place especially on Thursdays.

There is such a high concentration of travellers in Sydney, that you can't help but run across them. The Sydney Regional YHA holds regular get-togethers on Monday evenings at 275C Pitt St. Many choose to work in Sydney, often in bars and restaurants, where it is easy to make a few friends among the staff or regular customers.

If you feel really homesick, contact the Britannia Club of Australia at 33 Dagmar Crescent, Blacktown (tel: 621 2381). They have just opened a club for expatriate and visiting Poms, and hold sing-songs around the piano and serve British beer. If you are more interested in meeting the "local talent," read (or write in to) the regular "To Meet" column in the *Sydney Morning Herald*. Scanning the forthcoming events in the same newspaper is bound to introduce you to some form of social entertainment, whether guided walks around Aboriginal cave drawings in North Sydney's bushland or the weekly vegetarian dinner ($3) held at the anarchist Blackrose Bookshop at 36 Botany Road in Alexandria (south of Redfern).

ARRIVAL AND DEPARTURE

Air. Sydney's only airport is called Kingsford-Smith, after a famous aviator, but is more commonly referred to as "Mascot" after the suburb in which it is located. It juts out into Botany Bay only 12km south of the city centre. But the price to be paid for this proximity is dreadful overcrowding and the resultant delays and confusion. The problems are worst in the early morning when numerous international flights arrive at once (due to the restriction on night landings to placate Mascot's residents). Altogether it is dismally equipped to be Australia's leading gateway. A $20 million expansion to be completed in 1989 will alleviate some of the problems. Meanwhile a new airport about 50km west of the city at Badgery's Creek has been much discussed. Until either of these plans materializes, jaded travellers must expect long queues. To freshen up, use the free shower adjacent to gate 6 in the international terminal or, for men only, on the ground floor of the Australian Airlines domestic terminal.

The international and domestic terminals are 2km and a $1.50 bus ride apart. It is not possible to walk from one to the other due to the no-pedestrian rule on the link roads.

Do not be discouraged by your first impressions formed on the drive from the airport; things quickly improve. For travel to the city, take the yellow Airport Express 300 bus service which stops outside both terminals. It charges a flat fare of $2.20 into town and is scheduled to take 15 minutes to get to Central Station, then stops several times on George St before arriving at Circular Quay another 15 minutes later. In heavy traffic these times can be nearly doubled, so allow for this if travelling to the airport during a rush hour. The 300 service begins from downtown at 6am and from the airport at 6.25am, and runs every 20 minutes during the day and then every 30 minutes after 6.30pm. The last bus leaves Circular Quay at 9pm and the airport at 10.15pm.

The Kingsford Smith Airport Service is a private bus which runs every half hour and costs $3 to downtown. This is the service which Qantas recommends to arriving passengers, although the chief advantage of the extra fare is that it also serves Kings Cross. If you want to use this service when you are departing, dial 667 3221 to reserve a seat and a pick-up from your hotel or hostel. If you are waiting at one of the Airport Express stops, and are running late for your flight, passing Kingsford Smith minibuses might stop for you if hailed.

The cheapest journey into town is on city bus 302 which departs from outside the Ansett building of the Domestic Terminal and runs to Circular Quay via a suburban route. The most expensive is by taxi, which costs $12-$15.

There are several daily minibus services direct to Wollongong (the third largest city in New South Wales) for $11 one way.

If you are in the market for an air ticket out of Australia, check the *Travel Review* in the Saturday *Sydney Morning Herald* where a large selection of Sydney's hundreds of discount travel agencies advertise cheap flights to anywhere. Ringing round will not guarantee the cheapest flight, since some refuse to discuss fares over the telephone for fear of giving away information to competitors; you may have to call in personally. The Sydney Flight Centre is recommended for offering consistently low prices and efficient service. The agency is in the underground Shopping Circle at Martin Place between Castlereagh and Elizabeth Streets (tel: 221 2666). Reho Travel are at Tower

Square, 155 Miller St, North Sydney (tel: 957 6969), while STA are at 1A Lee Street, Railway Square (tel: 212 1255).

Qantas passengers may want to take advantage of the new facility for checking their luggage in downtown between two and 12 hours before departure at the Regent Hotel on George St. This facility operates only between 8am and 5pm. There are mail boxes after the Customs and Immigration controls, which are handy for last-minute post-cards.

Air N.S.W. (8-18 Bent St; tel: 268 1894) have a comprehensive network within the state, and offer the same range of discounts as Ansett who owns them. Their "Network 30" discount is available only to overseas visitors who buy in advance. Air N.S.W. offers mystery flights starting at $28; dial 268 1242 for details.

Coach. At present there is no central station for long distance buses in Sydney. When you arrive, you will be dropped at the Central Railway Station or, if you prefer, at the company offices, all of which are centrally located. When you want to buy a ticket out of Sydney, you will have to do some systematic comparisons, preferably by telephone (numbers below). As described in the introductory section *Getting Around: Bus* there is a great deal of competition on the interstate routes, for example there are at least 13 companies vying for your business to Brisbane by offering more leg room, air-conditioning, faster services, lower prices, etc. Sample prices from Sydney are: to Canberra $18, to Adelaide $75 and to both Brisbane and Melbourne $40, though these can be undercut; in particular try Bus Australia for low prices, especially if you are prepared to leave at short notice.

Here is a selection of the principal operators:

Ansett Pioneer: Oxford Square, corner of Oxford and Riley Streets (268 1881).
Aussie Express: Shop 13, 221 Elizabeth St (261 1622; toll-free: 008-08 8112).
Bus Australia: McKell Building, corner of George St and Rawson Place (281 2266).
Deluxe: corner of Castlereagh and Hay Streets (212 4888).
Executive Express: Bus Booking Centre, 22 Wesley Arcade, 210 Pitt St (264 3273).
Greyhound: Oxford Square, corner of Oxford and Riley Streets (268 1414).
Intertour EET: 869 George St, Broadway (212 5600).
Kirklands: Corner Riley and Oxford Streets (267 5030).
McCafferty's: 179 Darlinghurst Road, Kings Cross (33 0919).
Newell Express: 7th Floor, 10 Martin Place (231 5600).

Several of these long distance services stop at one of the bus stops on Eddy Avenue between Central Station and Belmore Park, a stretch of road which often becomes chaotic and congested. A plan is under discussion to use the "air space" over Central Station to build a private coach terminal, a heliport and tourist hotel, but this is some years off.

If you want to travel between Sydney and another nearby New South Wales city such as Wollongong or Katoomba in the Blue Mountains, you must take the train, since in order to protect State Rail, the government imposes restrictions on coach companies, for example passengers are prohibited from making a coach journey of less than 160km within the state.

Train. New South Wales State Rail is efficiently run and has cheap and frequent services to, from and around Sydney. Second class one-way fares on long distance services are generally about 7¢ per kilometre, with first class costing about 40% more. Both commuter and long-distance ("country") trains are run by the same authority and share Central Station which is referred to as "Sydney Terminal" on country train timetables. While country trains use platforms 1 to 15, suburban trains leave from platforms 16 to 25.

Anyone who intends to make more than one long train journey within the state should consider the 14-day Nurail pass. It is available in first class only, and costs $110 compared to $75 one way first class Sydney to Broken Hill and $65 to Murwillumbah near the Queensland border. The *Western Mail* which connects the country towns of Bathurst and Dubbo with Sydney is threatened with closure, since the new XPT expresses were introduced.

State Rail are very proud of the services by XPT (express passenger trains) which are replicas of British Rail's Intercity 125 trains. They run north to Grafton City, inland to Armidale and Dubbo and south to Canberra and Albury on the border with Victoria. The fastest overland route between Sydney and Adelaide is known as "Speedlink" which uses the XPT train to Albury (departing Sydney at midday) than a connecting coach service on V/Line Luxury Coaches to Adelaide taking a total of less than 20 hours. There are two services daily to Melbourne: the *Intercapital Daylight Express* and the overnight *Melbourne Express*. A third alternative is the privately-run *Southern Cross Express* consisting of a dozen refurbished pullmans which leaves each Friday at 7.10am and costs $400 one way or more if you take the optional one-night stopover in Canberra. Call 03-615 0040 for details.

If you want to go for a Sunday outing in New South Wales, enquire about the Up and Away Ticket which allows half price travel on Sundays only. This discount is even available on some XPT services. There are discounts of up to 20% on off-peak journeys, i.e. ones commencing after 9.30am on weekdays and anytime at weekends. For further discount information see *City Transport*.

The helpful information office in Central Station publishes a series of free pocket timetables which detail the times of all state services, but do not include fares. All rail enquiries by telephone should be made to 2 0942. Country and interstate bookings may be made by telephone on 817 8812. The Rail Travel Centre is at 11 York St (at one end of the New South Wales Urban Transit Authority offices).

The pleasant and spacious Central Station has other useful facilities such as a luggage checking office at one end of the concourse. Luggage lockers cost 50¢ a day and articles must be removed by 11pm. The checking counter or "cloak room" is a better deal: it is open from 6am to 11pm and a payment of 30¢ entitles you to deposit your bag for the rest of the day plus the following day. One of the things you might want to leave behind is your packet of cigarettes since smoking is banned on all metropolitan services; it would still be prohibited on all inter-city journeys lasting less than three hours except outbreaks of violence between smokers and non-smokers caused the rule to be dropped.

Driving. The main approaches to Sydney are via the scenic (and usually empty) Princes Highway along the south coast and the busier Pacific Highway from the north which seems to get held up at every suburban junction until expanding into a glorious six lanes. Otherwise you may be on the Hume Highway from Canberra or the Great Western Highway from the Blue Mountains and beyond (Lithgow and Bathurst). Whichever route you choose be prepared for what seems like a never-ending sea of suburbs, which stretch 55km east-west and 90km north-south. Central Sydney is fairly well signposted from all directions though drivers should try to arrange to have a passenger with a good road atlas, since it will take all their concentration to dodge Sydney's aggressive drivers.

The rules of the road do not differ very much from other states. If you are planning to drive extensively around the state you might like to acquire the Traffic Authority of New South Wales's free *Motor Traffic Handbook* (PO Box 110, Rosebery, NSW 2018). The alcohol limit is a stiff .05 and there are frequent random checks carried out by "booze buses" in towns throughout the state. The speed limit is generally 100km/h on the open road but 60km/h where there are street lights. It is an offence to pass on the inside or to drive slowly in the passing lane, so Poms may find driving around the state more familiar than in some of the other states.

As usual, car hire firms impose restrictions on your destinations, or impose surcharges if you want to visit remote parts. Try Letz Rent-a-Car (116 Darlinghurst Road; tel: 331 3099) or Thrifty Rent-a-Car (85 William St; tel: 360 4055). For cut-price firms, keep your eyes open in Kings Cross for bargains and branches of Rent-a-Wreck. Betta Rent-a-Car at 199a Darlinghurst Road (tel: 331 5333), Kings Cross Rent-a-Car at 169 William St (tel: 33 0637) and Half-Price Rent-a-Car at 29a Oxford St (tel: 267 7177) all offer good deals, for example Betta have cars on offer for $15 a day unlimited kilometres. The catch is that insurance is charged at $10 a day. Don't forget all the usual extras which will be added, including 1.5% New South Wales stamp duty.

If you want to buy a second-hand vehicle, Kings Cross is the best area to check noticeboards and adverts.

The National Roads and Motorists Association (NRMA) in Sydney is at 151 Clarence St (corner of Barrack St); tel: 260 9222/236 9211. They will supply information on road conditions if you ring 1521.

Hitch-hiking. In a city of 3.4 million inhabitants, the majority of whom seem to be on the roads at any one time, you must get past the suburbs before attempting to hitch any distance. The best plan for heading north is to take the train to Gosford; if going south, get a train to Waterfall, a small station on the edge of the Royal National Park where the freeway which runs parallel to the Princes Highway begins (either route will suit you if you are heading along the coast). For the Hume Highway to Canberra, you should take the train to Mittagong ($1\frac{1}{2}$ hours from Central Station) which is well clear of both suburbia and the freeway stretch of the Hume Highway where hitching is illegal.

CITY TRANSPORT

City Layout. You will hear the locals constantly referring to neighbourhoods such as Glebe, Woolloomooloo, Mosman and so on, which can be difficult for the new arrival to follow, especially if he or she hears references to Darling Harbour, Darlinghurst, Darlington and Darling Point in a short period of time. Things get even more complicated when nicknames are used, for example taxi drivers invariably refer to Double Bay as Double Pay, due to the extortionate prices in the shops. Also confusing is a designation such as "East Sydney" which refers to a small area east of Hyde Park. The "Eastern Suburbs" is the correct way to refer to the city spreading east of downtown. Similarly the North Shore refers to the salubrious suburbs which line the harbour on the other side of the Sydney Harbour Bridge and the Western Suburbs describe the hundreds of less sought-after areas which are a long way from the ocean, such as Parramatta,

Bankstown, etc. (Surfers call anyone who is not within sight of the surf a "westie").

A good map is essential. The *Sydney Visitors Map* which is distributed free by New South Wales tourist offices is recommended for being clear and detailed, provided you don't mind seeing the Shell company's logo all over it. If you plan to travel hither and yon in Sydney, the $1 *Travelmap* published by the Urban Transit Authority and available in most newsagents is a wise investment.

Walking. For the first day or so, you will probably confine yourself to the downtown area, many of whose attractions are within easy and pleasant walking distance of one another. It is not much more than one kilometre from the heart of the historic area of the Rocks to the Opera House via Circular Quay, where the ferries dock. At the time of writing this was not a very enjoyable stroll, since the Circular Quay development project had littered the area with construction cranes and piles of bricks, four million of which will eventually be laid to create a new promenade, some of it glassed-in and featuring parkland, an information centre, restaurants and boutiques. When it is completed it will be possible to walk along the waterfront for two kilometres from Wolloomooloo (on the other side of the Botanic Gardens) past the Opera House and under the Bridge to Walsh Bay.

But even without this ready-made scenic route along the waterfront, it is possible to enjoy walking around the city. For example you can walk from the railway station to the Opera House (a distance of about three kilometres) almost entirely through parks. This route will not appeal to shoppers who will prefer to walk along George St, a busy shopping thoroughfare, which is so crowded with pedestrians that in a few places the authorities have painted lanes on the pavements.

If you would prefer to join an organized walking tour try Sydney Footnotes, otherwise known as North Shore Walking Tours (tel: 646 3119) for their Saturday morning and weekday walks around interesting neighbourhoods like Balmain and Kirribilli. These cost between $5 and $10. Another possibility is Maureen Fry's Walking Tours of Historic Sydney (tel: 660 7157). The Australian Museum Society also conducts walking tours; ring 339 8225 for details.

Public Transport. The Urban Transit Authority (UTA) of New South Wales runs an integrated service which includes suburban trains, buses and ferries. There is even some discussion of resurrecting the trams which once ran in the city though this would merely be a tourist ploy. Although

"PEDESTRIAN LANES HAVE BEEN INTRODUCED IN PARTS OF SYDNEY"

Sydney's public transport is more expensive than that of any other Australian city, it is still quite reasonable, for example $1.60 pays for a 16km journey by bus or train. Combination tickets on bus and train are sold, so state your final destination when boarding either bus or train. All times and prices are available by ringing "Metro Trips" on 29 2622 between 7am and 10pm any day of the week. Or call in at the UTA in Transport House at 11-31 York St, adjoining Wynyard Station (pronounced Winy'd). If you are staying in Sydney for some time and intend to do a lot of travelling, you should investigate the range of travelpasses available. One of the most attractive is the weekly ticket (Monday to Sunday) which covers travel on trains, buses and ferries in the central zone, a large area on both sides of the harbour; this costs $10.30. Further details of travelpasses are available by phoning 219 1694/5. If you want to see a lot of Sydney quickly, enquire about the Day Rover, valid on bus, train and ferry.

Bus. Sydney is well served by buses, from free downtown shuttles to long suburban runs. There is a bus information kiosk opposite Circular Quay (on Loftus St) which distributes timetables for individual routes and will direct you to the appropriate stop. The telephone number specifically for bus enquiries is 2 0543 (7am-7pm). There are 14 different terminal points, most of them within walking distance of Circular Quay. Bus stops are painted yellow.

Suburban routes are usually served every half hour between early morning and early evening but there are severe curtailments at weekends. One of the few all-night services is route 150 which runs at infrequent intervals through the night between Wynyard Station and Manly Wharf. The daytime bus service to Manly (which operates only at weekends and on public holidays) is called the Bendy Bus; one way by bus plus one way by ferry costs $3.30. Another unusual run is route 190 to Palm Beach (a flash suburb well north of the city). Antique double deckers are used since the union rejected the new articulated buses.

Fares are calculated according to the number of zones crossed starting at 60¢ for one zone, $1.10 for two zones and increasing to $2.20 for the bus trip to Manly. Tickets may be purchased on the bus (exact fares not required). Remember that smoking is banned on all buses.

There are two free bus services. The first is route 666 which runs between Wynyard Station and the Art Gallery of New South Wales in the Domain Park, making several stops on its outgoing route along Macquarie St and back via Market St. This runs every half hour daily from 10.10am until 4.40pm (except Sunday mornings).

The other UTA free bus covers roughly the same ground. Route 777 is principally meant as a park-and-ride service across town between the Domain Parking Station and Wynyard Station. It runs only on weekdays between 9.30am and 4pm.

Visitors are urged on all sides to take the Sydney Explorer bus, which costs $10 for the day. It runs continuously around 20 points of interest, and you can get off and on as often as you like. But many of the attractions on its route are clumped together around the Rocks or Kings Cross and are more efficiently explored on foot than by bus. By the time you locate the bus stop and wait a potential 16 minutes for the next bus, you could have walked to the next attraction. A further disadvantage is that it stops running about 5pm and few people want to visit Kings Cross in the daytime.

Train. The State Rail network provides what amounts to an underground system for the city centre as well as serving the suburbs. The principal downtown stations are Central, Town Hall, Wynyard, St James, Museum and Circular Quay. Fares range according to distance from 60¢ upwards with small reductions for day returns outside the weekday morning peak (called "Minifares"). Often the ticket you buy bears the name of a different destination from the one you asked for, but trust the booking clerk: the frequency of fare increases means that ticket stocks are often out-of-date and are used up by selling to the "wrong" destination at the correct price.

The trains themselves consist mainly of double decker carriages on which the doors are rarely closed during warm weather, so hold on tight if you are standing near an entrance. Many have the nifty feature of seats which can be reversed so that passengers may face forwards, or face their friends if they are in a group. Some trains are composed of four rather than eight cars; the signs on each platform bear a red and yellow stripe, with the yellow section indicating the end of the platform at which these half-length trains will stop.

Family weekend tickets cost $6.60 for unlimited travel for a day for up to two adults and two children available Saturday, Sunday and on public holidays. Even if you are not travelling as part of a family, it is worth obtaining the State Rail brochure with the less-than-snappy title, *How To Show Your Kids Sydney Systematically*. It includes 101 places of interest from the waxworks museum in Kings Cross to the Marineland at Manly, and tells you the nearest railway station for each attraction.

Monorail. The privately-owned TNT Monorail, due to open April 1988, will run in a loop from Market and Pitt Streets in the city centre, along Liverpool St and around the Sydney Entertainment Centre and Darling Harbour complex, returning over Pyrmont Bridge to the Casino. It is widely hated, and was condemned by conservationists since the mirror-clad pylons fail abysmally to blend in with the surroundings, but the monorail is easily the best way to reach Darling Harbour. It operates from 6am to midnight and is predicted to move 5,000 people per hour. Call 29 3294 for details of fares.

Car. Driving in Sydney is not very relaxing at the best of times and quite terrifying at rush hours. Although the locals complain loudly about the number of traffic lights, some of which they swear stay red for as much as three minutes, these provide a much needed respite for harassed drivers from out-of-town.

The toll on the Sydney Harbour Bridge is charged heading south only, at the booths on the north side of the Bridge. Some of the booths have automatic coin-collecting baskets into which you hurl your $1 coin, but there is always at least one manned booth for those without change. Tolls leapt 400% in 1987 and are set to rise again soon by 50¢. The increased revenue is being used to finance the building of a cross-harbour tunnel due to open in September 1992. The tunnel will connect the Cahill and Warringah Expressways and should alleviate the severe congestion on the Bridge. If you consider the toll too steep, you may wish to join the many Sydney drivers who have switched to the western routes over Gladesville or Ryde bridges, where no tolls are charged, though the traffic problems have increased accordingly.

The "tidal flow" system of traffic management where lanes are switched between inbound and outbound traffic according to the hour of day has reached an art form on the Bridge and its approach roads, so keep your eye on the lane markers.

Parking downtown can be a serious problem especially in the vicinity of Circular Quay. There are several privately run "parking stations" as they are called but their charges are astronomical ($2.50 for half an hour is typical). Metered parking is more reasonable; before 8am and after 6.30pm street parking is free. In prime locations, however, there may be a maximum of one hour or even less. The council-run Domain Parking Station (entrance on Cathedral Road) is one of the most useful since free bus 777 runs nearby, as does a park and ride bus to the Opera House in the evenings (5.30pm to midnight).

The *Sun* publishes a regular list of discount petrol stations, compiled by their very own "Petrol Pete".

Taxis. With a standing charge of $1.25 plus 75¢ per kilometre, Sydney taxis are the most expensive in Australia. An extra 70¢ is charged for a telephone summons and an extra $1 is charged if a bridge toll is involved in your journey. At least there is no surcharge late at night. A large proportion of cabs accept credit cards for fares of over $5. An even larger proportion of cabs are driven by Greek migrants, so you might ask your driver for advice on restaurants. The main ranks are at Central Station, Circular Quay and St James Station. To request a cab in the Sydney area by telephone, dial Legion (2 0918), RSL (699 0144), TCS (332 8888) or Western District (622 2200). It is virtually impossible to get a taxi late at night, since demand always outstrips supply.

Ferry. A ferry ride in the harbour, especially the trip to Manly, is among Sydney's foremost delights and is even more enjoyable than the famous trip to Staten Island. Even if you are not particularly interested in what's on the other side of the harbour, it is worth going out to admire the view of downtown Sydney from the water.

Fortunately the opening of the Harbour Bridge in 1932 did not entirely remove the ferry trade and there is a network of ferries running between Circular Quay (which is in fact square) and numerous points around the harbour. The principal destinations are Balmain, Taronga Zoo, Kirribilli, Neutral Bay, Mosman, Cremorne and Manly. The 30-minute trip to Manly is a bargain at $1.20 when the scant ten-minute trip to the Darling St Wharf in Balmain costs $1, though this shorter trip has the advantage of taking passengers under the Bridge. Services operate frequently during rush hours but are reduced to as little as one an hour during the day and at evenings and weekends. Tickets are sold at Circular Quay to both departing and arriving passengers, which can mean long queues when a crowded ferry arrives. UTA publish a comprehensive timetable of all ferry services and connecting buses. Most services run between about 5.30am and midnight. For information by phone on the Manly ferry, ring 27 9251 and on inner harbour services 27 5276.

In addition to UTA ferries there are a few privately run services such as N. D. Hegarty & Sons which go to the amusement fair Luna Park as well as to the standard destinations. These are generally more expensive than the city ferries. There are two big new hydrofoils with a capacity of 240 passengers and a speed of 32 knots (compared to the 14 knot ferries); the Manly Hydrofoil costs $1.40. There are plenty of cruises and waterborne tours from which to choose, such as the Hegarty cruise to the Hawkesbury River (ring 455 1566 for details) or the range of Captain Cook Cruises incorporating morning coffee, luncheon or a candlelit dinner (tel: 27 4416). Even the UTA run scenic cruises for a modest $7.50 or $10 depending on whether you choose the 90 minute evening "Harbour Lights Cruise" or the $2\frac{1}{2}$ hour daytime cruise.

Cycling. Anyone used to cycling in London will be able to cope with Sydney; others may come to the conclusion that it isn't worthwhile. Although there is a cycle path across the Harbour Bridge, it is difficult to find when approaching from the east.

Bicycles including tandems may be hired from Centennial Park Bicycle Hire, 50 Clovelly Road, Randwick (tel: 398 5027). For advice on cycle touring or equipment, visit Cranks Bike Shop, 92 Pacific Highway, Roseville (tel: 411 5116). The Bicycle Institute of New South Wales is at 802 George St.

Since most people spend more than a few days in Sydney, it is worth being more particular about your lodgings than usual. There is a great deal of choice, though the ones that are both cheap and pleasant, including the YHA hostels, tend to be full much of the time. Contact the new Hotel Hotline (231 4441) for information on all kinds of accommodation from ranches to hostels in Sydney and the rest of the state.

Youth Hostels. There are three Youth Hostels in Sydney. The closest to the city centre is Forest Lodge near Sydney University; but with only 30 beds, it is very often fully booked. The address is 28 Ross St (tel: 692 0747) just off the busy Parramatta Road, along which many buses (for example 412, 438, 440 and 461) frequently ply. Not far away is a relatively new hostel at Glebe Point (262 Glebe Point Road; tel: 692 8418) which is larger and also more expensive at $12 instead of $8. Further away but with more capacity (it is the largest hostel in Australia) is the Dulwich Hill Hostel at 407 Marrickville Road (tel: 569 0272) which is about a seven-minute walk from the Dulwich Hill Station. Stays are limited to five nights at all these hostels.

If you want to be within range of Sydney but in a rural setting, the Youth Hostel at Pittwater (26km north of Sydney) is an excellent place to stay (tel: 99 2196). It has the further charm of being on the edge of the Ku-ring-gai Chase National Park and is accessible only by ferry, which make commuting into Sydney tricky. (The whole trip takes about two and a half hours.) You may unwind here for as long as three weeks.

You can join the YHA at any of the above hostels or at the Association's New South Wales headquarters at 355 Kent St (tel: 29 5068).

Other Hostels. The majority of budget accommodation is located in the lively, unconventional area of Kings Cross, which can be reached on foot from Central Station in about 45 minutes or by train on the frequent Eastern Suburbs service. Although there are no reports yet of touts patrolling Sydney Station as they do in Amsterdam and Athens, competition is fierce at this end of the market, and so prices don't seem to have been affected by Sydney's recent tourist boom which has made luxury hotels increase their prices dramatically. In budget hostels, you should be able to find a bed in a dormitory for $8 a night or $50 a week, and most of these will offer a range of facilities such as kitchen, lounge, TV room, etc.

Among the most popular Kings Cross hostels are the Downunder Hostel at 25 Hughes St (tel: 358 1143) which is part of the Backpackers chain and charges $9 for a dorm bed and $24 for a double, and Travellers Rest at 156 Victoria St (tel: 358 4606). Another place to consider is the Kings Cross "Cotel", part of the California-based network which offer private and shared rooms with 24-hour access for about twice the price of a dormitory room. The Cotel is at 170 Victoria St (tel: 356 3844).

Outside Kings Cross it is also possible to find affordable hostels, such as Rucksack Rest at 9 McDonald St, Potts Point (tel: 358 2348) which is not far from Kings Cross. In the other direction from the Cross is Surry Hills, where you can find what is reputed to be Sydney's cheapest traveller's hostel, Beethoven Lodge at 661 South Dowling St (tel: 698 4203), which is a good place for finding out about casual work. West of the city is the Wattle House Hotel at 44 Hereford St, Glebe (tel: 692 0879). Coogee Beach Backpackers Hostel is in the pleasant beach suburb of Coogee (south of Bondi) at 94 Beach St (tel: 666 7735), which will collect you from the airport if you give them a call.

Women travellers on a tight budget might want to investigate the Women's Hostel at 47 Bedford St, Newtown (tel: 516 4420) which charges $4 for a bed; breakfasts cost $1 and children are free. They will also help any women in distress for whatever reason.

Hotels and Guest Houses. If dormitory accommodation does not suit, try the Sydney Tourist Hotel downtown on Pitt St (at number 400; tel: 211 5777) where singles cost $22 and doubles are $32. If you don't object to the noise of disco music late at night, you can get rooms at the Rex Hotel next to the attractive Alamein Fountain in Kings Cross for about $18. A more sedate address is Neutral Bay on the North Shore near Kirribilli. The Neutral Bay Lodge (45 Kurraba Road; tel: 90 4199) charges $35 for a double room. The Leichhardt Bed and Breakfast in Italian-dominated Leichhardt (tel: 810 8906) charges $20 per person in a double room and $30 single. Another recommended guest house is the Alfred Park Lodge in Redfern (207 Cleveland St; tel: 699 4031) run by an elderly couple from Kent. Doubles are available from $30 plus a few dollars extra for breakfast.

If you can wait until 1990 to visit Sydney, the Darling Harbour project is going to incorporate a new 900-room hotel which they claim will cater for "budget-minded tourists" though this is likely to be true only in comparison to the Hilton or the Regent.

Longer Term. Although less extreme than rents in London or Manhattan, flats in Sydney do not come cheap. A small unfurnished apartment in an unfashionable area is likely to cost over $100 a week, while two-bedroom units won't be much under $150. Furthermore demand for rental accommodation drastically outstrips supply, so you must move quickly after reading the adverts in the *Sydney Morning Herald* (especially Wednesdays and Saturdays) or noticing a card posted on a hostel notice board. Agencies such as Dial-a-Home (tel: 264 1133) are permitted to charge a fee, typically $50-$100, and often give out scant details about houses advertised in the newspaper anyway.

Rooms or bed-sits in divided houses are usually a little cheaper and you can usually find space in a house by reading the notices posted by other travellers at budget hostels or by Sydney students on university notice boards. Seedy Kings Cross is once again your best bet for cheap flats. The atmosphere in rooming houses is often less pleasant than in hostels, with permanent rather than casual residents. You may also be able to rent a room above a pub for about $75 a week.

Eating and Drinking

Recommending places to eat in "Steak & Kidney" is both fraught with difficulties and perhaps superfluous, since there are so many good places scattered all over the city. Even an unpromising suburban row of shops is quite likely to contain a good Thai restaurant, Italian pizzeria or vegetarian café. Sydney has the ideal combination of access to superb ingredients (including tropical fruit from Queensland, fresh fish and shell fish and regional cheeses) and a cosmopolitan population to prepare them in interesting ways. To admire the high quality of produce visit Paddy's Saturday market (see *Shopping* below) or the new fish markets at Blackwattle Bay at Pyrmont.

Anyone who intends to eat out more than a handful of times should buy *Cheap Eats in Sydney,* a discerning and yet comprehensive guide to about 650 restaurants almost all of which are described in such loving detail that you are prompted to add each one to your list of possibilities; the book costs $4.95 and is on sale everywhere. Where to eat is just as popular a topic of conversation among Sydneysiders as defending their favourite beach, so you'll soon be directed to a few undiscovered hideaways.

RESTAURANTS

Neighbourhoods with the highest concentration of good eating establishments are Kings Cross, Surry Hills, Paddington, Glebe, Balmain and Bondi, as well as downtown. Crown St stretching from Surry Hills to the large downtown park known as The Domain has scores of interesting restaurants and cafés. If you haven't chosen a place by the time you reach Oxford St, turn east towards Paddington and you will soon pass dozens of other possibilities. *Cheap Eats* includes a convenient index by surburb as well as by type of cuisine from Cajun to crepes, Vietnamese to vegetarian.

As usual Bring-Your-Own restaurants are usually cheaper than licensed ones, especially those which charge nothing for corkage. There is an increasing trend for restaurants to have both a licence and to allow you to bring your own liquor, which is useful if you have not remembered to stock up.

Before venturing into Sydney's many ethnic cuisines, you might find yourself in the Rocks looking for lunch. Try the Gumnut Tea Gardens (where despite the name you can drink wine as long as you have remembered to bring some) at 28 Harrington St. Bypassing the touristy Spaghetti Factory and the Rocks Café, try the generous hamburgers with salad and chips at the Cove Café for about $7 or the Park Royal for $6.

Other bargains worth investigating are the daily specials from $6.50 at BJ's Eatery (99 Glebe Point Road) open every evening, the all-you-can-eat-for-$10 specials on Sunday evenings at Chasers Restaurant (252 Pitt St), the wholefood main dishes costing about $5 at Doc Dinkums Natural Cafe on the North Shore (566 Willoughby Road, Willoughby) and the Hare Krishna café at 112 Darlinghurst Road where a good meal costs $5 and free meals can be picked up on the takeaway side if you don't mind discussing life, the universe, etc. Elsewhere try the pancakes at Pancakes on the Rocks (10 Hickson Road, The Rocks), or the Magic Mortuary Station just south-west of Central Station, both of which are open 24 hours a day. BYO creperies are usually excellent value and can be found all over Sydney.

At the expensive end, you might want to join the queue of tourists (sometimes willing to wait as long as an hour) at the famous Doyles Restaurant at Watsons Bay which specializes in serving unadorned fresh fish; you can travel there by water taxi from Circular Quay. Another favourite among tourists is the Centrepoint Tower where the self-service buffet on Level Two will cost about $25 (they impose a minimum of $17.50), which is considerably less than Level One's restaurant though it is a few metres higher (see description of building below). The prices are more down-to-earth at the self-service restaurant at the Opera House while the view is equally enjoyable. Try not to let your attention wander too far, however in view of the management's policy as stated on their sign: "No refunds will be given to customers whose meals are taken by seagulls".

Finally, Rowntrees Australian Restaurant (188 Pacific Highway, Hornsby; tel: 476 5150) serves Aboriginal food.

Pub Food. Pub eating in Sydney is more sophisticated than anywhere in Australia, so that you are just as likely to find spiced fish (at the Albury Hotel in Paddington) or deep-fried Camembert (at the Woolahra Hotel at 116 Queen St, Woollahra near Bondi) as steak and chips. Most hotels which serve meals tend to separate the two functions, so you will hardly be aware of being in a pub, for example the hamburger specialist Cove Café mentioned above is part of the Sydney Park Royal Hotel in the Rocks, and the nearby Sorrento's Seafood at Circular Quay is part of the Paragon Hotel. Even the deluxe hotels may be worth a visit: the Old Sydney Bar of the Sheraton-Wentworth (61 Phillip St) serves filled bagels at lunchtime for about $8, while the 5-star Regent at 199 Regent St near the Rocks (Australia's premier "pub") was at last report serving *tapas,* tasty Spanish snacks ranging from garlic bread for 85¢ to a small portion of paella for $4.25.

Of course there are plenty of places serving standard pub fare, such as the East Sydney Hotel at 111 Cathedral St or the Dolphin Hotel at 412 Crown St in Surry Hills. To cook your own steak, go to Phillip's Foote in the Rocks (101 George St) which has an outdoor dining area open seven days a week, the Royal George Hotel at 115a Sussex St in the City or the Bondi Junction Hotel not far from the station of the same name.

Ethnic Restaurants. If you have been travelling around Australia long enough to have grown tired of steaks, the range of authentic ethnic cuisines at which Sydney excels may hold more appeal than the pubs.

Although Sydney's Chinatown might lack the colour and bustle of Hong Kong or even San Francisco, the streets around Dixon and Hay are lined with good Chinese restaurants where many Chinese people gather to shop and dine. You can choose between the proletarian style of Chinese canteens (such as the China Wok at 201 Hay St) where main dishes cost only $4, and the more expensive establishment such as Buck Goong on Harbour St which specializes in seafood, or anything in between. On average a main dish will cost $7.50 — with fish dishes costing a little more — and a bowl of soup $2.50.

"*NO REFUNDS TO CUSTOMERS WHOSE MEALS ARE EATEN BY SEAGULLS*"

Other Asian cuisines are also superbly represented in Sydney including Indian which is a more recent arrival in Australia. If you are homesick for a good curry, visit the licensed Bombay at 33 Elizabeth Bay Road, Kings Cross or the informal Curry Bazaar across the Bridge in the unlikely suburb of Crows Nest (334 Pacific Highway). If you want to have a choice of a dozen or so Vietnamese restaurants in one area, you will have to take the train to the distant suburb of Cabramatta. Otherwise try Chu Bay (312A Bourke St, Darlinghurst), Tien (95 Glebe Point Road, Glebe) or the Saigon Beach Restaurant at 710 George St on the edge of Chinatown which is a good BYO place though its background music can be intrusive.

The choice of other East Asian cuisines is also bountiful. Still near the station try the Kampuchean Mekong Restaurant at 711 George St, highly recommended for cheap yet exotic food: a choice of three dishes costs $3.50 with extra dishes costing an extra $1 each. Indonesian and Thai cuisine are both at the forefront of Sydney trends so try Effa's Indonesian at 148 King St in Newtown (with very good satay) or the Thai Silverspoon at 203 Oxford St in Darlinghurst.

Lebanese food is less trendy and in many places the prices are rock bottom. The best plan is to go to the corner of Elizabeth and Cleveland Streets in Surry Hills, a comparatively unprepossessing area were it not for the choice of excellent value Lebanese restaurants within 50m of the junction. These include Emads at 298 Cleveland St and Abdul's at 563a Elizabeth St, where a set meal of six main dishes plus a few side dishes will cost about $12. These are great places to go with a group of friends.

European cuisines are just as well represented as Eastern ones and are almost as cheap. Even good Italian restaurants in prime downtown locations such as Al Parco on the edge of Hyde Park will serve you a delicious bowl of pasta and a glass of wine for $8. Other recommended Italian restaurants are the Mixing Pot (178 St Johns Road, Glebe), Forbe's (155 Forbes St, Woolloomooloo), which is understandably crowded since it offers three-course meals for $12, La Boheme (312 Crown St, Surry Hills), Nido (7 Stanley Lane, East Sydney) and Sorrentino (266 Darling St, Balmain). Youth hostellers might take note of Ebbs at 127 Booth St in Annandale (a short walk from the Forest Lodge Hostel) and Lorenzo's in Canterbury (114 Canterbury Road) just two stops past the Dulwich Hill Hostel. Both are licensed and have interesting Italian menus. For pizzas try Eli's at Taylor Square in Darlinghurst (open until 2am) or Papa Giovanni's at 128 Campbell Parade, Bondi Beach.

The selection of Greek restaurants in Sydney is not as great as it is in Melbourne, however Diethnes at 336 Pitt St in the City has an inexpensive range of Greek dishes as well as Retsina. According to a Greek informant, it serves better food than anything to be had in Greece.

Snacks. Since your finances are unlikely to allow constant eating out, you will have to rely on snacks, fast food and picnics to some extent. Still on the ethnic theme you could try the Chinatown Centre on Dixon St where you can choose a $4 dish from one of the dozen or so stalls representing Japan, Malaysia and Vietnam as well as China. The basement of the MLC Building offers a variety of ethnic stalls plus superb fruit salads, all served in convenient take-away containers for outdoor consumption. Similarly in Australia Square downtown and at Tower Square just off Miller St in North Sydney, you can choose a different dish from neighbouring kiosks before sitting at communal tables. Downtown there are numerous sandwich bars and doner kebab stalls where you should be able to find something appetizing to munch during the lunchtime concert in Martin Place. Snack bars on the ground floor of Centrepoint offer plenty of choice. If you find yourself rebelling against all the *nouveau* and imaginative food around you, buy a meat pie and sachet of tomato sauce down at one of the milkbars at Circular Quay and watch the ferries and the buskers come and go.

Sydney must have some of the most elegant branches of McDonalds anywhere, for example the tasteful Victorian conversion in North Sydney or the hi-tech branch built into the Entertainment Centre. Less predictable fast food may be found in the form of burgers with a hot sauce at HB's Prime Rib at the corner of George and Goulburn Streets.

Pastry and coffee shops abound, many of which will be open when you emerge after a play or film. Try the cappuccinos and ice cream at Café Troppo on Glebe Point Road and on the same road (at number 144a) the wonderful sweets at the Pudding Shop, which despite its name also serves savoury snacks as well. Vienna Gold (121a King St, Newton) serves equally well-recommended cakes and has the added attraction of a range of German beer. Finally don't miss out on the best frozen yoghurt and "smoothies" in Sydney at the Pure and Natural Food Company on Liverpool St or at any of the company's other outlets.

The beach suburbs are well supplied with takeaway places; try the excellent fish and chips for sale at Manly or Bondi.

DRINKING

Despite claims that Sydneysiders are becoming less enthusiastic drinkers as a result of the new health-consciousness and the "booze buses", few could complain about the density of hotels in Sydney. Furthermore many of these hotels have character, such as the comfortable old hotels in the beach suburbs and the attractively renovated Victorian pubs especially in Paddington. A great many hotels have live music (see *Entertainment*) and some have happy hours as well, usually from 5pm; try the ornately fitted-out Marble Bar in the Hilton at 25 Pitt St or Nachos in the northern beach suburb of Collaroy (1066 Pittwater Road) which serves Mexican food to accompany your half-price drinks between 5 and 7pm. Most hotels are licensed from 11am to 11pm in summer and 10am-10pm in winter, with a few staying open until midnight or beyond on Fridays and Saturdays especially in tourist areas, and a few others having a 6.30am-6.30pm licence to serve the market trade. Hours are restricted on Sundays to noon to 10pm.

The most popular sizes of beer glass in New South Wales are the 10oz/285ml "middy" and the 15oz/425ml "schooner". Otherwise you may ask for a "pint" (20oz/575ml) or a "seven" (200ml) or even a "lady's waist" which is (or was) New South Wales slang for a 5oz glass. The two New South Wales breweries which traditionally vied for Sydney's custom had very similar names — Tooth's and Tooheys. Although these have both been taken over by huge conglomerates (Carlton and Swan respectively) they continue to use the same names for the same brews such as KB lager (which stands for Kent Brewery) and the highly recommended Toohey's Old (called Hunter Old when packaged). The most popular take-home beers in Sydney are probably Toohey's Draught and the ubiquitous Fosters. Try Reschs (in cans or on tap) which is slightly more bitter than the average Australian drop. If you call the Carlton Brewery on Broadway (tel: 20941), they may be able to arrange a conducted tour including some free samples.

A few pubs serve speciality beers such as Guinness which is available at the Orient Hotel in the Rocks and the Clock Tower at 470 Crown St in Darlinghurst. The Brewer on Bourke St also in Darlinghurst serves four different beers brewed on the premises plus 50 imported beers.

If you are particular about the architecture when you go drinking, try the National Trust-listed Rag and Famish (at 199 Miller Road, North Sydney), the Royal Hotel in Randwick (corner of Cuthill St and Perouse Road) and the Bellevue in Paddington (at 159 Hargrave St), all of which serve excellent food as well as being in attractive buildings. One of Sydney's most famous gay pubs, the Albury Hotel at 6 Oxford St Paddington, also serves good food (in huge quantities) in its upstairs restaurant called Hog Heaven. There is no shortage of atmosphere at the many old hotels in the Rocks, such as the Hero of Waterloo, the Mercantile or the Fortune of War, all of which tend to fill up inside but you can usually find a spot on the pavement or in the beer garden if they have one. One of the several candidates for "oldest pub in Sydney" is the Lord Nelson which was recently taken over by a boutique brewery from Adelaide and prices (as well as turnover) have shot up accordingly.

If the gardens in the Rocks are too cramped for you, the trendy Golden Sheaf in Double Bay (New South Head Road) has a more spacious one and is a good place to meet people especially at the end of the weekend. Also Watsons Bay Hotel next door to Doyles Restaurant (1 Military Road) has a picturesque outdoor drinking area. Away from the Rocks, there are few decent pubs in the city centre. Two busy friendly and reasonably priced places are Jacksons on George St opposite the Regent Hotel and the George Street Bar. If you are looking for a typical and unpretentious drink, cross the Bridge to Milsons Point and look for the Rest Hotel opposite the station. Their resident entertainer performs on Fridays.

If you develop an academic interest in pubs and beer, the brewing exhibition due to open at the Powerhouse Museum in 1988 might prove interesting.

Cocktail bars and discos of course stay open much later than hotels, and Kings Cross is full of them. If you like self-consciously stylish places try JoJo's at 40 Macleay St in Potts Point whose bar is attached to a pricy Cajun restaurant which stays open until 3am and features a life-sized mannequin of a black piano player. The cocktails are first-rate.

For stocking up before eating at a BYO restaurant, visit one of the discount wine stores such as Liquorland which can be found downtown as well as in suburban shopping plazas. The wines are usually organized according to state of origin, so if you want to sample the local wines, head for the Hunter Valley shelves. Wine tastings at the Australian Wine Centre in the Rocks are widely publicized but don't seem to be readily available to visitors who are not in the market for cases of premium Australian wines.

If you just fancy a restful drink to accompany the harbour view, invest in an only slightly over-priced glass of wine or can of Fosters on the Opera House terrace. These are guaranteed not to interest the seagulls.

There is never a dull moment in Sydney. Whether it is one of the surf carnivals outdoors or a jazz concert indoors, whether a trip up the 305m Centrepoint Tower or down below the harbour waters in a scuba diving class, there is always something to watch or listen to in Sydney at any time of the year. There is plenty of free entertainment, from the buskers in Circular Quay to the Council-sponsored concerts in Martin Place on weekdays at lunchtimes.

One of the best times to visit Sydney is during the Festival of Sydney which starts on New Year's Eve and continues through January (and, in 1988, through February). In some ways it resembles the Edinburgh Festival, including a range of fringe events called "Umbrella Events". But Sydney's Festival has a stronger emphasis on free events such as Opera in the Park and also outdoors in Parramatta, and lots of other jazz, folk, rock and classical concerts in the Domain. Arrive early with a picnic and an esky. Although sultry summer evenings are the norm, an alternative "rain date" usually a day or two later is sometimes provided. There is a pronounced carnival atmosphere, especially in Hyde Park where rides, puppets, minstrels and various stalls and street theatre amuse visitors.

A free festival magazine is widely distributed or you can ring the Festival Hotline on 264 1212 which offers recorded information. A Festival Information Centre is set up near the Archibald Fountain in Hyde Park North and the *Sydney Morning Herald* publishes a daily Festival diary.

Even if you miss the Festival, there is usually plenty of free entertainment. There is a small open-air amphitheatre in Martin Place outside the MLC Centre skyscraper where free concerts are held at 12 and 1pm. Some downtown churches like St Andrews Cathedral put on lunchtime organ recitals. On Sundays you can choose between the jazz outside the Opera House, the word-spinners holding forth at Sydney's version of "Speaker's Corner" in The Domain and the bands which accompany "Art in the Gardens" at the Botanic Gardens.

The *Herald* is a good source of information on entertainment at any time of the year. The "Metro" Supplement appears (on blue newsprint) each Friday and is essential reading.

Also check with the Visitor Information Centre for details of special events, some of which are listed at the end of this chapter. One which is not normally promoted in the official "Coming Events" list is the Gay Mardi Gras held each February. As befits the world's second gay capital (after San Francisco), a spectacular fancy dress parade is followed by a party in Sydney Showground where champagne is served and cabaret entertainment is put on (entrance fee $23).

Most mainstream cultural events can be booked through the BASS ticket agency, either over the phone with a credit card (266 4800) or by visiting one of their many outlets, for example in Wynyard Station, the Entertainment Centre next to Chinatown or GB's Store on Market St. BASS's general purpose cultural information number is 11688 and is partially sponsored by the radio station 2Day FM.

Buildings and Venues. Sydney's arts centre is the famous Opera House, where far more than operatic productions are mounted. The ingenious and beautiful building — only churls could deny this — is often described as a symbol of modern Australia, although it was designed by a Dane (just as the Harbour Bridge of which Sydney is so proud, was built by a firm from Newcastle in England). The Opera House, sometimes referred to locally as the Nun's Scrum, contains five theatres for drama, opera, concerts, ballet and films, as well as two restaurants (the fancy Bennelong and the cafeteria-style Harbour). Guided tours are available for $2.50 daily between 9am and 4pm from the Exhibition Hall; special $5 tours take place on Sundays and include backstage. Although it will cost you a lot more (tickets range from $12 to $60 with surcharges on some Saturday performances), it is more rewarding to attend a performance than take a tour, though you should be prepared to mingle with Sydney's "Kangaglam" (the glitterati). The box office number is 20525. Tickets may be booked in advance from abroad through any Qantas office or by post to PO Box 4274, Sydney, NSW 2001 (tel: 250 7197).

A less elitist venue is the new Sydney Entertainment Centre in Haymarket, which seats up to 12,500 people for concerts (the big rock acts usually perform here), sporting events (such as wrestling and tennis) and various other spectacles. The telephone number is 1 1581/211 2222.

Some lament the tearing down of old corner pubs and old-fashioned stores to make way for Sydney's "skyline". It is hard to believe that in the early 70s, Sydney's tallest building was only 15 storeys high and even that created a sensation. But now the appetite for tall and yet taller buildings seems insatiable. After proudly opening the 305m Centrepoint Tower in 1981 (sometimes called, for no apparent reason, the Tupperware Tower), the Bond group is now planning to build Sky Tower 76m higher near the Town Hall, while in the Rocks another syndicate is rumoured to be planning a 445m tower code-named CBD to become the highest building in the world (tied with Centre Place in Brisbane).

Especially on a clear day, few visitors can resist joining the queues at Centrepoint and paying $3.50 to take in the view, which is indisputably excellent, though the development has a self-congratulatory American-style big-business atmosphere which does not perhaps show Sydney at its most original. Although Centrepoint can be easily spotted from a distance, it is possible to lose track of it at close range among the other skyscrapers, so head for the corner of Market and Pitt Streets, enter the shopping centre and follow signs to the lifts. The Observation level is open 9.30am to 9.30pm (except Sundays 10.30am-6.30pm).

There are other eminences from which to enjoy a view. For example you can pay 50¢ to climb the 200 steps inside the pylon at the south side of the Harbour Bridge (Saturday to Monday only). This is at the furthest extremity of the Rocks, an area full of buildings of historic interest. The best plan for exploring the area is to find the Rocks Visitor Centre, housed in the old courthouse at 104 George St (tel: 27 4972) and pick up the leaflet on walking tours which will direct you to one of Sydney's oldest buildings, Cadman's Cottage built in 1816, the old Police Station (now a craft centre), some old restored pubs, and so on. This area is of special interest to shoppers (see *Shopping* below).

The National Trust has its headquarters on Observatory Hill in the Rocks, housed in an early 19th century military hospital. They publish a selection of leaflets on Sydney's historic buildings. If you are interested in old Sydney buildings, Vaucluse House is arguably the oldest (built in 1803) and one of the most interesting; admission is $2 (tel: 337 1957). The first owner built a moat and filled it with soil from his native Ireland to keep out snakes, on the assumption that St. Patrick's protection was portable. Take bus 325 from Circular Quay.

For something really architecturally unusual, go to Kings Cross to see their bicentennial offering, a giant echidna, which is a hedgehog-like Australian mammal with a spiny back, a long snout and a toothless mouth.

Museums and Galleries. The newest and most modern building in Sydney is the Powerhouse Museum which opens in March 1988 as part of the ambitious Darling Harbour development which will offer everything from a simulated rainforest to the largest casino in the world. The Powerhouse combines a science centre with plenty of participatory gadgets, and displays of decorative arts and social history.

The Australian Museum on College St near Hyde Park is among Australia's best museums and specializes in natural history. The Aboriginal displays are especially recommended. The Museum is open Tuesday to Sunday 10am-5pm, with free admission. There are free guided tours daily at 12, 2 and 3.30pm from the College St foyer (tel: 339 8111). There are also some Aboriginal exhibits at the Art Gallery of New South Wales in the Domain, along with representative paintings of some of Australia's foremost artists including some unfashionable but interesting academic painters.

There are plenty of specialist museums and exhibitions, from the small collection of ancient artefacts in the Nicholson Museum at Sydney University to the Environment Centre at 176 Cumberland St in the Rocks, from the National Maritime Museum in Darling Harbour (opening October 1988) to the Geological and Mining Museum in the Rocks, which is especially recommended for people planning to visit New Zealand, since a new exhibit is planned which will simulate an earthquake and a volcanic eruption.

Theatre. The "Halftix" Kiosk in Martin Place sells half price theatre tickets on the day of performance from 12-6pm (plus service charge). All tickets must be bought in person and with cash.

Metro includes a full-page theatre directory which will point you to half-price previews, pub theatres, outdoor performances and experimental plays as well as the mainstream theatre venues like the Opera House, the Belvoir St Theatre in Surry Hills (tel: 699 3257) and the York Theatre in the Seymour Centre on the corner of Cleveland St and City Road (tel: 692 3511). The Sydney Theatre Co can be seen at their home in the Rocks, the picturesque Wharf Theatre on Pier 4, Hickson Road, Walsh Bay (tel: 250 1777). The Bondi Pavilion is an unusual and attractive venue where plays as well as art exhibitions are put on (tel: 30 7211). The Griffin Theatre at 10 Nimrod St, Kings Cross (tel: 33 3817) occasionally puts on free shows for students, pensioners and the unemployed. Tickets for most productions in the city cost $12-$25 while fringe theatres charge $5-$15. Some late-night coffee shops in Darlinghurst double as alternative theatres. For comedy try the Gap (in the Trade Union Club of Surry Hills) or the Monday night sessions in Glebe's Harold Park Hotel.

For impromptu theatre you can sit in the gallery of the New South Wales Parliament when it is in session (tel: 230 2111 for details).

Cinema. The highest concentration of cinemas is along George St near Town Hall. The Academy Twin Cinema in Paddington (3a Oxford St; tel: 33 4453) and the Valhalla in Glebe Point Road usually have interesting programmes. The once-famous experimental cinema called the New Mandarin on Elizabeth St closed in 1987 and now shows only Chinese films. In cinemas owned by the main chains — Hoyts, Village and Dendy — tickets are half price on Tuesdays.

Films are shown free of charge at the "theatrette" in the Government Information Centre at 55 Hunter St at 12.30pm Tuesday to Thursday. These are generally Australian travelogues or movies which sing the praises of various government projects.

Music. The established venues for serious music are the Opera House, the Town Hall (where tickets usually cost $22, $18 for students) and the Pitt Street Uniting Church at 264 Pitt St. The University puts on concerts in the Old Darlington

School (tel: 818 1329) which are generally much cheaper, while the Conservatorium of Music in the Botanic Gardens puts on free lunchtime concerts at 1pm on Wednesdays.

The principal rock venue is the Sydney Entertainment Centre though other big concerts are held elsewhere such as at Cronulla's Endeavour Field, otherwise known as Ronson Park. A shuttle bus usually operates from Woolooware station whenever there's a concert. There is a no-alcohol rule at most events and bags will be inspected as you enter.

Sydney has a very lively pub and club circuit, especially in Kings Cross (try the Manzil Rooms and Kardomah Café), Paddington (for instance at the Hip Hop Club open until 3am and Incognitos), and Balmain (try the Unity Hall Hotel and the Cat and Fiddle Hotel). The Tivoli in George St and Sheila's Tavern at 77 Berry St in North Sydney can also usually be relied on to feature good bands. Some of these charge admission of up to $6.

Jazz and folk are also well represented at pubs scattered throughout the city. If you want to find out what folk events are forthcoming, contact Folkways Music at 282 Oxford St, Paddington (tel: 33 3980) where you can also buy tickets for some events. If you don't mind the touristy trappings, the Argyle Tavern in the Rocks often has folk bands. Dick's Hotel in Balmain is another popular folk venue, often featuring the well known electrified folk band Hat Trick, especially on Saturday afternoons. Also popular is the Rose, Shamrock and Thistle (known as "The Three Weeds") in nearby Rozelle.

For jazz, try the Cafe Zambesi at 182 King St, Newtown, the Orient Hotel in the Rocks, the Basement at 29 Reibry Place at Circular Quay, Soup Plus Restaurant at 383 George St in the City or the Blue Moon Café in Kings Cross, and watch for some of Sydney's finest such as the Morrison Brothers and Galapagos Duck. Call the Jazz Hotline on 818 5177 and check the Friday *Metro* supplement to the *Sydney Morning Herald* which provides exhaustive listings. A surprising number of gigs in Sydney take place in RSL clubs, which will usually admit non-members, especially those from overseas. It is best to ring ahead to check.

At the Covent Garden Hotel on the corner of Hay and Dixon Streets, there is a free Country-and-Western sing-along most nights.

Nightlife. Again the back page of the *Metro* tells you the line-ups at Sydney's nightspots. Among the most popular are Selina's in the Coogee Bay Hotel and the Cauldron at 207 Darlinghurst Road. Many such establishments are open until at least 3am and charge an entrance fee of $6. A few hotels advertise "bop till you drop" evenings which can mean a closing time of anything from midnight onwards.

Kings Cross, which can be depressing by day, is the place to go at night, and is full of lively places. The tourist copywriter's description of Kings Cross as "bohemian" is somewhat euphemistic. It is repeatedly at the centre of scandals involving sex and drugs and police corruption, though if you stroll through of an evening, you are more likely to be jostled by other curious onlookers rather than heroin dealers, and the sleazy side need not affect you. Prostitutes may be seen along William St, usually recognizable by their favourite apparel, swimming costumes. But you should be prepared to see plenty of peep shows and massage parlours, at least one of which has adopted a high moral tone with a sign "Underpants are compulsory. No sex. No extras. No relief."

Darlinghurst which is adjacent to Kings Cross has some good discos: try Spago at 238 Crown St and Via Mexico at 217 Oxford Square. Famous dinner theatres include the Comedy Store on Margaret Lane in the City and Les Girls at 2c Roslyn St in Kings Cross. Women travellers may wish to invest in the recently published *Single Girl's Guide to Sydney* (Angus & Robertson, £3.95) to find the places worth visiting and the dives to avoid.

Gambling. Until the casino opens in Darling Harbour, billed as the largest in the world, gamblers will have to make do with poker machines and horse races. Residents of New South Wales are among the heaviest gamblers in the world; they spend over $1½ million each day on lotteries alone. The TAB agency has nearly 1,000 outlets in the state. Their betting shops are usually open from 11am to 6pm.

SPORT

Spectator Sports. As elsewhere, horse racing is a major preoccupation in Sydney. There are four courses, viz. Randwick, Rosehill, Canterbury and Warwick Farm. Flat racing usually takes place on Wednesdays and Saturdays, while harness racing events are held at Harold Park, Glebe on Tuesdays and Thursdays and sometimes Friday evenings. Also in Glebe, the Wentworth Park Trots is not a left-wing political group but another trotting venue.

Anyone who is keen (or merely lukewarm) about cricket should try to visit the Sydney Cricket Ground (SCG) during the season (October to March). The "Hill", where the riff-raff recline on the grass, is a famous Sydney landmark. The atmosphere is reputed to be a lot tamer since they banned eskies and limited spectators to buying their beer in small, easily spilled styrofoam cups. Beware of the stampede when the giant video screen above the Hill shows replays. Admission is usually about $10 to the Hill, $20 plus to the stands. Take bus 378 from Railway Square or 380 from Circular Quay to Centennial Park.

Rugby League is the favoured version of football in Sydney and is played at various venues including the newly renovated Sydney Sports Ground adjacent to the SCG. There are matches on most Saturdays between April and September. The home of Rugby Union is the Concord Oval near the Parramatta Road in the suburb of Concord. It is here that the Grand Final is held in late September. The best place to see soccer is at the new Sydney Football Stadium, home of the predominantly Greek side Sydney Olympic who are hoping to sign up England's Bryan Robson.

Motor racing takes place at the Amaroo Park track in the far western suburbs. Look out for the unusual event of the Shell Mileage Marathon, when the object of the exercise is to go as far as possible on a single gallon of fuel; the record is 5,691 miles to the gallon.

There is no shortage of media coverage of sporting events, but important results can always be heard on Sportsline (telephone 1630 or 1187) sponsored by Radio 2GB. If you are a genuine sports fan you may want to visit the Hall of Champions at 157 Gloucester St in the Rocks, open afternoons only.

Although most visitors go to Sydney's beaches not to observe but to participate, you might try to take in one of the Saturday surf carnivals held at various beaches in the summer, for example the *Sun* Pentathlon at Fresh Water Beach or the rough water swim in early February at Bondi Beach. Further information is available from the State Centre of the Surf (tel: 663 4298) or the Surf Lifesaving Association (tel: 199 1126). Locations of surfing competitions are apt to be chosen at the last minute to take advantage of the best surf conditions.

Participation. If you are intent on keeping fit, visit the Sydney City Squash Centre at 152 Riley St (ring 331 4621 to book a court) while the Rushcutters Bay Tennis Centre on Waratah Street (beyond Kings Cross) is open to the public (tel: 357 1675). The downtown Fitness-to-Perfection Centre in the Westpac Plaza in George St, charges a modest $5 for an initial visit where you can join a class and take a sauna.

If you are in Sydney in August, you might be tempted to join the 25,000 runners who participate in the 14km City to Surf marathon between Hyde Park and Bondi Beach. For more leisurely exercise there are plenty of bushwalks within easy range of the city (see *Great Outdoors* below). A newly opened 30km walking trail from Manly to Palm Beach is yet another Bicentennial project due to open in 1988.

Parks and Zoos. The harbourfront of the Botanic Gardens and also Hyde Park are pleasant and popular jogging venues. The free *Welcome Visitor* guide to Sydney includes a map of the city showing five jogging routes from .75km to 2.25km long.

You don't have to be a jogger of course to enjoy the Royal Botanic Gardens (tel: 231 8123) which feature palm groves, a cactus collection, huge Moreton Bay fig trees and temporary exhibits on topics as various as Japanese grasses and rainforest flora. (Another place you might see a rainforest habitat is in the Darling Harbour area where the ingenious designers hope to create rainforest conditions in the shade of the overhead freeway.) Free tours of the Botanic Gardens are held on Wednesdays and Fridays, starting from the Visitor Centre at 10am. On Sunday artists display their work and a band performs.

The highlight of a visit to Observatory Park in the Rocks is the chance to view the southern sky by telescopes which are open six nights a week; you must book in advance on 241 2478.

Taronga Zoo (tel: 969 2295) is a good place to be introduced to some of Australia's native wildlife. There is a koala park (where the koalas seem to be a little more lively than at other zoos), kangaroos and so on, as well as gorillas, tigers and elephants whose pen is said to be on one of the most valuable pieces of real estate in the city. Colourful native parrots and kookaburras fly overhead wild. Admission is $7.50 or $9.50 including the return ferry from Circular Quay and shuttle bus to the entrance (a very short distance). Maps are not distributed at the gate and it is difficult to cover the large area systematically while relying on the sparsely distributed signboard maps. The zoo authorities seem to prefer putting up corny signs ("Sidnee Village — The Natives are Friendly") and "talking toadstools" where for 20¢ you can hear a short lecture on a specific animal.

Manly Marineland on the Esplanade at Manly features sharks, among other ocean creatures. Shark feeding times vary so ring 949 2319 for details. Admission is $6.

Beaches. The ocean swimming in Sydney's many bays is superb, and there is enough choice of beach (in fact 70 in total) that it is even possible to swim in virtual solitude, for example at some of the northern beaches. At the main beaches there is no need to worry about sharks, since the marine authorities have strung an underwater net which stretches 80km along the coast to prevent sharks from coming in to shore. Unfortunately harmless creatures such as sea turtles become entangled, and so the nets are patrolled daily and rescues carried out where necessary. But never swim in harbour estuaries since sharks are prevalent in these waters.

But nets cannot protect swimmers from other dangers such as rips; there is a particularly dangerous one at Bilgola, 36km north of the city. Always be sure to swim between the flags. Furthermore these beaches are not free of pollution. Call the Water Board's Surf-line on 269 5450 for information on the state of the beaches, or read "WaterWatch" in the *Sydney Morning Herald,* where a typical bulletin might be, "Sewage grease at Bondi and Curl Curl; stormwater rubbish at North Bondi. Algal froth around most beaches but should clear". If the report is too discouraging, head for the open-air Iceland swimming pool on Chalmers St, on the way to the airport.

Fame has not spoiled Bondi Beach, though council developers are threatening to do so. Its pleasing curve of perfect sand with a backdrop of painted wooden houses covering the surrounding green hillsides is scenically at its best on a clear winter's day. Dodging all the body-surfers can be tiresome on a summer weekend, but that is when it is fun to watch the surfies and their female admirers. (If you want to admire females, the south end only is topless.) There are plenty of cafés, gelaterias and pubs to choose from for your post-beach refreshments. There seems to be a perpetual carnival atmosphere. To get there by public transport take the train to Bondi Junction and then bus 380 to the beach.

The next beach along is Tamarama (usually called Glamarama) which is also pleasant, but Coogee Beach a kilometre or so further south is extremely congenial, despite its unpromising Aboriginal meaning of "stinking fish". Take bus 372/3/4.

After Bondi, the most famous beach is Manly, whose motto is "Seven Miles from Sydney and a Thousand Miles from Care". Riding the ferry is far more carefree than taking the long road round, though this will mean you'll miss the sign directing you to the "Manly Women's Rowing Club". Manly Beach is a classic city beach, crowded with sun lovers, surfers, families and life-savers. It is lined with Norfolk pines and excellent fish and chip shops (as well as plenty of more ambitious eateries).

There are several nude beaches though the city fathers have chosen ones which are difficult to get at. Try Reef Beach, Obelisk Bay and Lady Jane on Watsons Bay, which require walks of varying lengths and ladder descents.

Water Sports. If you would like to take up scuba diving contact the Fun Dive Centre (225 Stanmore Road, Petersham; tel: 569 5284) who may be repeating their "Discover Scuba" programme, which involved a free trial session in a pool. If you take to the sport, the fee for an introductory course in the sea is $25. Alternatively, contact Pro-Diving Services (tel: 665 6333).

The Department of Sport and Recreation runs activities in January, for example snorkelling and trawler fishing; contact their regional office at 45 Forest Road, Hurstville (tel: 588 5055).

Sail Australia (tel: 957 2577) offers a free introductory sail, and runs courses and charters. No experience is needed.

SHOPPING

Shopping hours in Sydney are usually 9am to 5.30pm Monday-Friday, and till 9pm on Thursdays. Many of the arcades downtown are open until noon or 4pm on Saturday and a few of the 80 speciality shops in the tourist-frequented Rocks stay open seven days a week. Late night shopping is available on Thursday and/ or Friday until 9pm.

Downtown Sydney is packed full of swanky shopping centres, such as the

Strand Arcade between George and Pitt Streets which is decorated with wrought-iron balconies and catwalks, the Centrepoint Shopping Complex and Pier One on the harbour just past the Rocks. But the prize for elegant downtown shopping must go to the recently restored Queen Victoria Building at the corner of Market and George Streets. It looks like a giant department store from the outside but inside are several levels of shops and cafés linked by ornate staircases and footbridges, all of which bear an uncanny resemblance to the famous GUM store in Moscow. As you'd expect, the Sydney emporium is considerably more appealing and a lot more expensive than its Soviet counterpart, and many shops will be familiar to English visitors such as the Body Shop and Monsoon. The largest department stores in Sydney are Grace Brothers and David Jones both connected to the Centrepoint Complex by underground passages. If you want to shop in ultra-glamorous surroundings, go out to Double Bay, Sydney's equivalent of Fifth Avenue or Bond Street.

At the other extreme you have the jumble sales on Thursday and Friday mornings at the Hornsby Salvation Army Centre (corner of Hunter and Burdett Streets). There are plenty of discount stores along the unfashionable parts of George St between the pinball arcades and the taco joints. For a good range of cheap clothes try Seconds Galore at 334 George St opposite Wynyard Station. Smokers with a craving for a particular brand of cigarettes or tobacco should try Sol Levy ("Tobacconist Extraordinaire") at 713 George St not far from the Central Station.

Serious shoppers might like to browse in (though not necessarily purchase) *The Bargain Shopper's Guide to Sydney* (published by the same publisher as *Cheap Eats in Sydney*) at $5.95. Also check the "Browsing and Buying" section of the *Sydney Morning Herald's* Friday *Metro* section for information on sales of everything from roses to antiques.

A few shops offer discounts to members of the International Youth Hostels Federation such as Fleets Sportsworld at 154 Parramatta Road (tel: 799 7888).

Duty Free. Duty-free stores proliferate in downtown Sydney, all offering a similar range of goods (cameras, opals, etc.) at similar prices, which are among the cheapest duty-free prices in the world. Anyone with an outgoing ticket can buy duty free goods, preferably at the downtown shops which are much cheaper than the airport shop; for some items such as film, the difference can be as much as 30%.

If you are in the market for opals and are planning to travel in an opal mining area (such as Lightning Ridge in northern New South Wales — see *Further Afield*) then it is better to buy on location, and cut out the middlemen. But if you aren't, you may want to visit the Opal Skymine on the sixth floor of the Australia Square Tower.

Souvenirs. In Sydney there is no escaping the full range of Australiana gifts and souvenirs, and after a morning of browsing in the Rocks, you may never want to see another stuffed koala or plastic boomerang again. The former police station at 127 George St is now a Crafts Centre and is worth visiting more in the spirit of a museum than a shop since prices are high. At the Sidewalk Gallery in the Rocks you can see craftsmen and women at work on Sundays. Most downtown shopping complexes have at least one shop specializing in Australian-made handicrafts, everything from designer mohair jumpers to handprinted greeting cards. Typical of the genre are the five branches of Everything Australian including one in the Mid City Centre near the Strand Arcade (tel:

212 3844). Away from the town try Manly Arts & Crafts near the Corso in Manly on weekends.

Aboriginal handicrafts may be viewed (and purchased) at a number of outlets, including:

Dreamtime Aboriginal Art Centre: Level One, Argyle Centre, Playfair St, The Rocks. (Also on Walker Lane, Paddington).

Bush Church Aid Society: 135 Bathurst St.

Aboriginal Artists Gallery: 477 Kent St, behind Town Hall (261 2929). This one is government-funded and has a better and more reasonably priced collection of authentic arts and crafts.

Paintings from Arnhemland are also on sale at 614 Darling St, Rozelle. The Aboriginal Cultural Centre can be found in the unlikely setting of Pier One, which is yet another glamorous renovated shopping centre, under the Bridge. Admission to the Cultural Centre is $4, where you can see a somewhat idealized view of Aboriginal customs and life. The adjacent handicraft shop does not charge admission.

Books. If Pitjanjatjara bark paintings, hand-printed silk shirts and hand-turned Tasmanian pine bowls are out of your price range, you might prefer to shop for souvenirs in one of Sydney's hundreds of bookshops. One of the most interesting and accessible is the Heritage Bookshop at $81\frac{1}{2}$ George St in the Rocks, where they carry a full range of second-hand and new guides, books and maps of Australia. They also have a good selection of post cards and greeting cards.

Dymocks at 424 George St is the largest bookstore in Sydney and has an excellent travel section. The specialist Travel Bookshop can be found in the Old Scots Church (dating from 1824) at 1 Jamison St on the corner of York St (tel: 29 1666); it offers discounts to Youth Hostel members. Ariel at 42 Oxford St, Paddington opens 10am-midnight daily; you might find a 10% discount voucher in the giveaway magazine *This Week in Sydney*.

Other interesting places to browse are the Mary Martin Bookshop at 47 York St which claims to specialize in "ethnographica and ratbaggery", the anarchist Blackrose Bookshop at 36 Botany Road in Alexandria and the New Edition Tea Rooms at 328a Oxford St, Paddington. One of the best sources of second-hand books is Glebe Point Road, especially Gleebooks at numbers 191, which sells cards and calendars too as well as being a good source of information about what's going on in the neighbourhood. Many other second-hand book and record shops are clustered around the junction of Goulburn and Pitt Streets. One of the most popular is Ashwoods (376 Pitt St) with books from 10¢ and records from 30¢. Folkways at 282 Oxford St, Paddington offer discounts to Youth Hostel members on records and Australiana.

Markets. Among the excellent markets in Sydney, the two you should try not to miss are the Paddington Church Market on Saturdays and Paddy's Market in Haymarket on the edge of Chinatown on weekends. Paddington Market, which is held in the grounds of the Uniting Village Church on the corner of Newcombe and Oxford Streets, is a colourful affair where Sydney's counter culture tends to congregate. Like the Camden Market in London you can buy old jewellery, rag rugs, hand screen-printed clothes and leather goods.

Most tourists find their way to Paddy's Market as well as thousands of locals; it is located on the corner of Thomas and Hay Streets and has over 1,000 stalls selling fruit and vegetables, clothes and household goods, toys and everything else. In addition to its Haymarket location (which is just a stone's throw from Central Station) it reappears in Flemington (near Flemington train station) on Fridays and Sundays. It is worth walking around the area of the Haymarket even when Paddy's is closed; once an area of derelict warehouses and goods yards, a noble attempt has been made to preserve old facades, including fading hoardings advertising such importers as the "Modern Banana Company".

The Kirribilli Market in the lovely harbourside suburb of the same name (five minutes by ferry from Circular Quay) is held on the last Saturday of the month from 7am. Over 160 stalls offer toys, clothes, handicrafts, exotic foods, homemade chocolates, stained glass and many other interesting items. It is held in the gardens of the Kirribilli Neighbourhood Centre at 16 Fitzroy St.

The best bargains are probably to be found well away from the city, such as the Menangles Park Markets (over 50km away on the train line to Moss Vale) or the Penrith Arts, Crafts and Collectables Bazaar in the High St Mall, Penrith; both are held on Sundays.

THE MEDIA

If you are staying in Sydney long enough to want an occasional evening indoors, buy the Monday *Sydney Morning Herald* which has a media supplement called *The Guide,* carrying complete listings for radio and television for the coming week with previews, reviews and recommendations.

Newspapers. The *Sydney Morning Herald,* which has been recommended throughout this chapter, is an excellent newspaper and leaves the other New South Wales competition far behind. The other morning papers are the *Australian* and the *Daily Telegraph,* while the evening papers are the sensationalist *Sun* and *Daily Mirror.*

Some cafés and brasseries stock newspapers for the benefit of customers, for example the New Edition Tea Rooms in Paddington (328a Oxford St), though you'll have to arrive early to beat Sydney's celebrities who favour this café-cum-bookstore.

Radio. The choice of many listeners is determined by the character of the anchormen who become prima donnas in Sydney. For example John Laws who hosts the morning programme on Sydney's leading talk-back station 2GB (873AM) commands a salary of $12 million over five years. John Singleton, the former announcer on 2KY (the racing station on 1017AM), became a household name during his controversial association with the station which is owned by the New South Wales Union Movement. The second most popular talk station is 2UE on 954AM. The leading adult-oriented rock station is 2DAY on 104FM. One station which disdains the rivalry and has announcers in the Radio 3 mould is 2MBS on 101.5FM, specializing in classical music and run by enthusiastic amateurs.

ABC National Radio broadcasts on 576AM and 92.9FM. For solid stereo middle-of-the-road music, try 2CH on 1170AM. At the other extreme 2MMM (105FM) offers nothing but heavy metal all day and 2CBA (103FM) offers only religious devotions. The foreign language station 2EA on 1386 offers programmes in everything from Macedonian to Mandarin.

Television. Sydney viewers have a choice of five channels, including three commercial stations ATN7, TCN9 and Ten. ABN on Channel 2 (which is the government-run ABC station) and SBS (on channel 28 on the UHF band requiring a special aerial) have the most adventurous programming, but even these offer an overdose of sport at weekends. You can telephone 11660 for television programmes. If you would like to become part of the audience of a television programme, contact Channel 9's *Midday Show* with Ray Martin (tel: 958 9999) which is recorded live weekdays at the Channel 9 Studios in Willoughby on the North Shore.

Sydney has been described as a "wholesome Manhattan", a huge and energetic metropolis without much crime. This is perhaps a result of the relative absence of poverty and deprivation compared to New York. The inner suburb of Redfern is a slum by Australian standards but would barely qualify as such in Europe or the US. Furthermore New South Wales has a lower crime rate even than the other states of Australia, possibly because it has a higher police-to-population ratio. So there are few areas in which the visitor needs to feel at all anxious. If you are out late at night it is likely to be in a place like Kings Cross where there will be plenty of other pedestrians into the small hours, though you probably wouldn't want to be there by yourself much after 3am. Kings Cross is not of course free of illegal activities, however these are unlikely to affect the visitor unless he or she chooses to get involved. Whereas massage parlours are illegal, brothels aren't. Men will probably want to avoid the gay prostitutes of Oxford St. Also try to avoid entering an empty train compartment late at night since muggings are not unknown, especially if you look the part of an out-of-town "high roller".

Drugs are used as widely in Sydney as elsewhere in Australia, but possession is against the law. Rules forbidding liquor at sporting or musical events are also enforced with rigour.

Sydney has its share of yobbos and vandals who have, for example, vandalized a high percentage of public telephones. Driving at high speed under the influence, especially in the Bondi Beach area, is less popular among "larrikins" (unruly youths) than it was before police began their crackdown on drinking and driving. It takes just three middies of beer in a short time to put someone over the limit of .05% and, if caught, the fine is $1,000.

Police headquarters are at 14 College St (tel: 20966).

Safety. As has been explained already, the chances of being eaten by a shark are fairly remote, and the blue-ringed octopus is rare. However, funnel web spiders which are commonly found throughout Sydney and environs, are a genuine cause for concern, even if the statistics are not overly alarming (13 deaths in 60 years). These spiders usually live underground, but can occasionally be seen appearing from suburban drain pipes or even in swimming pools. The funnel web has an ugly brown body and evil-looking mandibles. Do not stick your hand into piles of rotting leaves, and be sure to shake out shoes which have been left outside before putting them on. They have just developed an anti-venom so if you are bitten seek medical help instantly.

A confrontation with New South Wales' version of the Abominable Snowman, the eight foot tall Yowie, is far less likely, though as recently as the winter of 1987, police were following up reports of sightings near the Woronora Dam in Sydney's southern suburbs.

Help and Information *i*

The area code for Sydney is 02. For emergency fire, police and ambulance dial 000.

Travel Centre of New South Wales: 16 Spring St, corner of Pitt St (231 4444). Open Monday-Friday 9am-5pm. Other branches in New South Wales in Albury and Tweed Head, and in only three Australian cities outside the state:
Adelaide: 7th Floor, 144 North Terrace (08-51 3167).
Brisbane: Corner of Queen & Edward Streets (07-229 8833).
Melbourne: 353 Little Collins St (03-67 7461).
Sydney Visitors Bureau: Martin Place (235 2424). Same hours as the Travel Centre.
Tourist Information Service: 669 5111. Tourist information by telephone available 8am-6pm every day.
Rocks Visitors Centre: 104 George St (27 4972). Open seven days a week.
Tourist Newsfront: 22 Playfair St (27 7197). Non-government information centre which holds large number of brochures, and offers advice only about participating tour operators, etc.
Travellers' Aid Society: Assembly Platform, Central Station (211 2275). Open 7am-5pm Monday-Friday and 7am-noon on Saturdays. A charitable organization which aims to help the travelling public, especially the handicapped or others with special needs.
NRMA: 151 Clarence St (260 9222).
British Consulate-General: Gold Fields House, 1 Alfred St, Circular Quay (27 7521).
US Consulate: T & G Tower, Corner Elizabeth and Park Streets (264 7044).
American Express: 388 George St (239 0666).
Thomas Cook: 175 Pitt St (234 4000). Currency Exchange Centre in Shop 509, Hyatt Kingsgate Shopping Centre, Corner of Darlinghurst and Kings Cross Roads (356 2211).
Hospitals: Sydney Hospital — 230 0111.
Medical Attention: Dr J. E. Kendall, 21st Floor, National Mutual Building, corner of York and Market Streets (29 1709 or 959 3468 after hours). There are now lots of 24-hour emergency medical centres.
Dental Emergency Service: 267 5919.
Chemist: 438 3333.
General Post Office/Overseas Telecommunications Commission: 32-36 Martin Place. Open 8.15am-5.30pm Monday to Friday, 8.30am-noon on Saturdays. Telegraph Counter is open 24 hours and can supply stamps and arrange phone calls and telegrams.
Helplines: Weather 1196; Rape Crisis 819 6565; Drug & Alcohol Counselling 331 2111; Lifeline 264 2222; Wayside Chapel Crisis Centre in Kings Cross 358 6577; Poisons Information Centre 519 0466.

Work

Sydney seems to be able to absorb a great many working travellers into its employment scene. Plenty of jobs are advertised in the daily papers, especially the Monday "Job Market" in the *Sydney Morning Herald,* which has a "Casual Work" column and a "Hospitality Industry — Positions Vacant" section. To improve your chances try to get hold of the morning paper the previous evening and plan an early start. The jobs advertised can be discouraging since they often have farflung suburban locations which are difficult to find, let alone find ahead of the competition.

There always seem to be classified advertisements for "art" salespersons, which involves trying to sell uninspiring prints door-to-door (tel: 356 3500 or 389 2699). Another favourite is selling pens. If you turn up at the Australian Quadraplegic Association office (800 George St; tel: 212 3922) at 8.30am with some form of identification, they will supply you with cheap ball point pens on a sale-or-return basis. You get to keep one third of your total sales.

The main budget hostels in Sydney like the Downunder and the Beethoven are accustomed to helping overseas travellers find casual jobs. Check all noticeboards regularly. They may even need you themselves to clean or help man the office. Another good notice board for casual work can be found at the University of New South Wales Student Union on Anzac Parade, Kensington; it is on the second floor of the Blockhouse.

Most job-seekers join the crush at the Casuals Department of the Central Sydney Commonwealth Employment Service at 818 George St in Railway Square (tel: 219 7200). By getting there at 5am, women can usually pick up a day's work in a kitchen, waitressing or cleaning while men are sent out on demolition, removal or printing work. Women usually earn $40-$60 a day while men earn up to $80. The CES sometimes checks for working visas, which is not always the case elsewhere. The Readers Digest (26 Waterloo St, Surry Hills) sometimes offer lucrative night shifts to casuals. People with office experience should contact the Staffing Centre (Australia Square; tel: 27 8472) or Prime Appointments (34 Hunter St; tel: 221 3955), for temporary work. Private agencies are often good sources of work for those with visas. Try Drake Industrial at 50 York St (6th Floor; tel: 29 3101/2).

The most productive method of finding work in Sydney is the direct approach. In a city with literally thousands of restaurants, hotels and stores, vacancies are constantly occurring which are filled before the procedures of advertising or registration at the CES need to be set in motion. Few new arrivals in Sydney have to wait more than ten days before their speculative visiting of restaurants and pubs pays off. Try Myer's Department Store which often needs casual sales staff, and pays about $10 an hour.

There are plenty of opportunities outside the big city, some of which you may find out about in Sydney, for example the *Sydney Morning Herald* sometimes carries advertisements for job openings in remote parts of New South Wales and the Downunder Hostel may be able to put you in touch with farmers in the Sydney area who need assistance.

The main fruit-growing areas are the Hunter Valley (famous for wine-making), around Orange which despite its name is not a citrus town but a soft fruit and apple growing centre, near the Murray River in the south-west corner of the state (around Wentworth) and around the towns of Griffith and Leeton in the very successful Murrumbidgee Irrigation Area where peaches and apples are picked in the late summer and autumn while onions are picked throughout the summer. Even if the local CES office (see introductory chapter *Work*) is discouraging, talk to farmers and publicans about possibilities. Other harvests take place nearer Sydney such as the strawberry harvest in Campbelltown and Glenorie September to December and the apricot harvest in Kurrajong (on the northern edge of the Blue Mountains) in November. If you get taken on for the peak of the harvest you should be able to save over $500 in a fortnight.

Further Afield

No other state is so dominated by its capital as New South Wales. Whereas no one goes to Queensland specifically to visit Brisbane or to the Northern Territory to see Darwin, the situation is reversed in New South Wales.

And yet there are good arguments for exploring further in the state before heading elsewhere. Anyone travelling by rail or coach to another capital city can easily arrange a stopover or two, not only to break those interminable journeys, but to see some of the remarkable scenery and equally remarkable animal and human life which is so different from anything Sydney can offer.

DAY TRIPS FROM SYDNEY

If you have your own transport and need a map, the *Weekend Sydney Map,* available from petrol stations, etc. for a couple of dollars, shows various routes and points of interest and covers the following suggested day trips.

The Blue Mountains. Apart from the enjoyable day excursions which can be made to either of the national parks just north and south of Sydney (see *Great Outdoors*), the best day trip is probably to the Blue Mountains, about two hours by road or rail from the city. This destination has the advantage of being easily accessible by a delightful railway service to Katoomba and beyond, which operates very frequently from Central Station. Otherwise, you can join a tour for $30 from Sydney: contact Sydney Pathfinder Tours, 448 Bourke St (tel: 360 1665) for details. The Blue Mountain Information Hotline number is 047-39 1177.

Although the Blue Mountains are really just hills, they presented an impenetrable barrier to the early settlers, many of whom believed China was on the other side. Summer temperatures in the Blue Mountains are at least five degrees cooler than in Sydney and so in summer the towns have a bustling yet quaint hill station atmosphere. The main centre for tourists is Katoomba, famed for its viewpoints over the mountains and valleys of eucalyptus trees which emit an oil which gives the area its bluish haze when the sun shines. It is possible to descend to the valley floor either by foot on the 1,000 step Giant Stairway or by the funicular which is not recommended for the fainthearted; just watching the bright yellow train descending the seemingly vertical wall and disappearing into the dense bush before arriving at the bottom is sufficient excitement for some. An alternative heart-stopper is the scenic skyway which costs $2.

There is a well-appointed Visitor Information Centre at Echo Point in Katoomba (tel: 047-82 1833) open every day, complete with bird feeders which attract some of the colourful parrots and other tropical birds which favour this mountain habitat. At the Centre you can find out more about the various walking tracks, some of which have been designed around certain themes such as vegetation, geology or the history of mining in the area, with points of interest well signposted. Riding and cycling are also popular and there are plenty of local outfits willing to hire you the vehicle of your choice.

Other Blue Mountain towns along the rail line such as Leura and Mount Victoria are also pleasant and picturesque. The region abounds in tea rooms, craft shops and graciously restored hotels such as the delightful Victoria and Albert Guest House in Mount Victoria. Some are less expensive than they look, especially if you take advantage of off-season mid-week packages. There is a

Youth Hostel in Katoomba (tel: 047-82 1416) and another on the edge of the Blue Mountains National Park at Hawkesbury Heights (tel: 047-54 1213).

The Hawkesbury River. Unlike so many of Australia's rivers, the Hawkesbury runs abundantly year round, debouching into the sea north of Sydney between the Ku-ring-gai Chase National Park to the south and the Brisbane Waters National Park to the north. The Pacific Highway provides ready access (though with frequent traffic delays) to these parks. If you want to avoid paying a toll, leave the highway before it turns into a tollway at Berowra (which incidentally is the turn-off to the Berowra Waters Inn, widely regarded as the best restaurant in the country).

The Hawkesbury River is both scenic and ideal for water sports of all kinds. Cruisers may be hired from the bustling little marina at Akuna Bay, though they are very expensive. A more affordable option is to join a cruise such as the one on the old wooden ferry-cum-mail boat which departs Monday to Friday at 9.30am from Brooklyn near the freeway (tel: 455 1566) or on the *MV Bataan*, an ex-World War II navy launch. It is even cheaper to hire a canoe and paddle yourself from Bobbin Head, where the park headquarters are situated. The nearby Youth Hostel at Pittwater (see *Sydney: Accommodation*) hires out boats and will direct you to the Aboriginal engravings in the park. One of the highlights of any visit to this area is dining on the fresh fish, especially the oysters from the dozens of oyster leases on the river. One final possibility is the Waratah Park Wildlife Reserve; if you were ever a fan of *Skippy the Kangaroo,* this is his home.

NORTH OF SYDNEY

The Hunter Valley. The Hunter Valley is Australia's oldest wine-making region and today makes some very distinctive wines as well as a range of quaffable table wines. One of the centres is Cessnock, also a mining town, 170km north of Sydney. Most of the wineries which spread up the valley to Muswellbrook (94km from Cessnock) are open to the public for tastings and buying. Visit the information centre on Wollombi Road in Cessnock to pick up a leaflet on the "Wine Trail". One of the most venerable and attractive wineries is Tyrrells near the village of Pokolbin (tel: 98 7509) which has tried to retain their old wooden presses and picturesque vats while keeping the new-fangled stainless steel machinery out of view as much as possible. Another good one is Rothbury Estate, Pokolbin (tel: 98 7555) which has the advantage of being open on Sunday afternoons. Without your own car, you will have to join a tour or hire a bicycle; for example from the Trading Post, Broke Road, Pokolbin (tel: 98 7670). The nearest Youth Hostel is at Scone (famed as a centre for horse-breeding), 26km beyond Muswellbrook. It is worth asking here and at local pubs for farmers looking for grape-pickers if you are interested in earning some money in February/March.

The North Coast. Travelling along the Pacific Highway is not as enjoyable as it may sound, since the road is often very busy and rarely goes along the coast. Many prefer the inland New England Highway which passes through rich agricultural country, and the town of Tamworth, the self-proclaimed Country & Western capital of Australia. But despite the advantages of the New England route, many will not want to miss the coast, since some of the coastal resorts such as Byron Bay, Lennox Head, Nambucca Heads and the Myall Lakes near Forster are real gems and preferable in many ways to the more brassy resorts

urther north over the Queensland border. There are a few stretches of coast
n northern New South Wales which have been over-developed (such as Port
Macquarie) but it is not difficult to find solitude on perfect beaches. Since this
s a favourite area for backpackers, there are lots of hostels competing for your
business, by offering the free use of bicycles or canoes, heated swimming pools,
tc. One of the best is the "Piggery" in Byron Bay which has a jacuzzi and
egular barbecues cooked by the manager for $3.50; as well as dorms at $7 there
re "on-site tents" for $4.50. The 30km round trip by bicycle from Byron Bay
which is the most easterly point in Australia) along Seven Mile Beach to Lennox
Head is highly recommended, as is drinking cappuccino by the seashore after
njoying a pizza at the Earth & Sea Pizzeria opposite the Byron Bay station.

About 75km inland is the interesting community of Nimbin, which you may
ave heard referred to in Sydney in the sneering expression, "gone to grow
nuesli in Nimbin". From the early 70s, hippies and their successors have settled
n this lush area to grow organic vegetables and to practise handicrafts which
nay be admired and purchased at any number of shops and at the weekend craft
narkets. The largest commune in Australia at Turntable Falls may be visited.
There is a Youth Hostel with the charming address Granny's Farm on the Creek
tel: 066-89 1333).

THE SOUTH COAST

Unlike the Pacific Highway north of Sydney the Princes Highway allows
frequent and spectacular views of the south coast. The seaside towns south of
Sydney have a less glamorous reputation than those further north. There are
so many fine beaches all along the Pacific coast of Australia that it is inevitable
that many will be known only to the locals. Places like Austinmer, Bombo and
Ulladulla are hardly household names, even in Sydney; and yet these little towns
have splendid beaches which in less generously endowed nations would have
been turned into prize resorts long ago. Although Bombo's railway station has
the distinction of being as close to the sea as it is possible to be, comparatively
few people get off the train here. Only the occasional caravan park indicates
that holidaymakers have discovered this coast.

Any visitors considering exploring this part of New South Wales should not
allow themselves to be put off by the surprise tinged with contempt which
Sydneysiders who have never visited properly are bound to express at the idea.
Wollongong, the major city on this coast is invariably described as ugly, since
it is associated with the enormous steel works at Port Kembla a few kilometres
further south. Yet it is an attractive city in a lovely setting between excellent safe
surf beaches and the dramatic Illawarra Escarpment. The region is full of
surprises, such as the unexceptional little town of Thirroul just north of
Wollongong which turns out to have an extremely good restaurant called La
Petite Malice (tel: 042-47 4774) and a beachside house where D. H. Lawrence
lived for most of his stay in Australia in 1923. The restaurant is in an
unprepossessing side street while the Lawrence house gets no mention in the
tourist literature let alone a blue plaque (or Australian equivalent thereof). It is
this understated quality which makes the whole region so attractive to those who
may have tired of following a prescribed tourist trail. There are of course a few
well-known attractions such as the blowhole at Kiama (just beyond the Blowhole
Caravan Park and a shop with what must be the biggest display of souvenir
teaspoons in the world) which blows to a spectacular height in rough seas (but
not otherwise).

Further south, historic places like Eden and big game fishing ports like Bermagui are better known, but are still unspoiled. Eden's whaling past is particularly colourful if somewhat improbable even by Moby Dick standards: the local museum proudly displays the skeleton of a killer whale which is said to have cooperatively towed the whalers' boats out to the herds of lesser whales where it attacked them and then shared the spoils with the fishermen. Bermagui also has its share of legends, mostly on the theme of giant marlin being caught from the shore. Game fishing here is more like its counterpart in New Zealand than, say, some ritzy Queensland resorts, i.e. it is not just the preserve of the wealthy. It is possible to join a boat party for about $60 or hire small tackle for $15. In some pools you can collect prawns without any equipment at all.

INLAND

Like the other states, New South Wales covers a vast area traversed by several routes. Except for the recently improved Hume Highway between Sydney and Melbourne, driving any of the highways is a major undertaking, especially the route to Adelaide via Broken Hill, on which you have to be sure to carry emergency supplies of petrol. Although in the same state as Sydney, Broken Hill is 1,161km from the capital and for most purposes behaves as part of South Australia; most importantly the city observes South Australian time (30 minutes behind the rest of New South Wales). The huge deposits of zinc, lead and silver which spawned Australia's most powerful corporation, Broken Hill Proprietary (BHP), guarantee a high standard of prosperity not normally associated with the Outback. But despite its financial and industrial importance it clings to its outback culture and is an interesting place to stop over if you have a chance.

But there are plenty of places of interest before you get to Broken Hill and other remote places in New South Wales, such as Cameron's Corner where three states meet in an empty land, or picturesquely-named places like Wilson's Downfall and the Risk, or even Bourke where the railway ends (from whence derives the expression "Back o' Bourke" to refer to any godforsaken place) or Wagga Wagga whose name (pronounced "Wogga") is probably more memorable than its attractions. The Willandra Lakes Region is a World Heritage listed area because of its Aboriginal remains. There are many small wayside towns like Berrima and Carcoar which were settled early and have retained their colonial atmosphere. (The Surveyor-General Hotel in Berrima is said to be the oldest continually licensed pub in Australia.) Bathurst, 200km from Sydney, is worth visiting. There are the inevitable large follies such as the ridiculous turd-like potato in Robertson, the centre of a potato-growing area near the scenic Kangaroo Valley and Fitzroy Falls, inland from Wollongong. There are the opal mines at farflung Lightning Ridge in the central-north part of the state and in White Cliffs which is even further from civilization where it is possible, with a permit, to do some fossicking for opals. One of the opal miners is hoping to open his underground mansion as a guest house in due course.

Local tourist offices will eagerly supply you with plenty of literature on any of these country attractions. They will also be able to tell you about forthcoming special events — such as the Festival of the Falling Leaves each May in Tumut, the Great Goat Race in Lightning Ridge in April, or the balloon races in Canowindra — which are always worth trying to take in. The Tourism Commission of New South Wales publishes a comprehensive listing *Coming Events*. Another worthwhile experience is a farmstay. For example ten farms

cattered over a fairly large area northwest of Sydney belong to the Quirindi
Iost Farms Group (PO Box 293, Quirindi, NSW 2343; tel: 46 1545) where
angaroo-spottings are virtually guaranteed and you can pay as little as $50 for
inner, bed and breakfast.

The Great Outdoors

New South Wales offers great
environmental contrasts from the highest
snow-capped peaks in Australia to the
unrelenting desert which covers the whole of
the country's interior and therefore much of
New South Wales. Furthermore water-based activities of all kinds can be
njoyed along the 1,120km coastline.

The state boasts nearly 40 national parks which come in all shapes and sizes,
ome massive like Kosciusko (pronounced cozy-*oss*-co), incorporating part of
he Snowy Mountain range, others tiny with just one feature, such as Cathedral
Rock National Park near the university town of Armidale; some within easy
ange of Sydney (see below), others extremely remote like the Mallee Cliffs
National Park near the Victorian border to which there is no road access; some
are coastal such as the lovely Ben Boyd National Park around Eden, others are
n desert locations like the Sturt National Park in the north-western corner of
he state 360km north of Broken Hill. The National Parks and Wildlife Service
n Sydney (189 Kent St, Sydney 2000) can provide further information if you
have a specific interest in certain habitats, wildlife, zoology, etc. Most National
Parks charge admission of about $3 per car. If you want to join an active tour,
contact Off The Edge Expeditions (tel: 02-977 6209) who organize five-day
walking or rafting trips to areas of scenic beauty. The Australian School of
Bushcraft and Survival in Nowra (165km south of Sydney) runs one-day and
weekend activities in a range of sports (ring 044-22 1379 to find out their very
reasonable prices). If you want to make yourself useful while enjoying the great
outdoors, you might join the keen conservationists who organize tree-planting
excursions in New South Wales (tel: 02-560 2973).

Near Sydney. Many Sydney-based organizations can help you explore the
bushland near the city. For example the Australian Museum organizes weekends
away for (non-serious) bushwalkers and the Three Peaks Outdoor Society in
North Sydney can take you canyoning, hiking, abseiling, rock-climbing, cycling
and canoeing (tel: 02-648 2118). Those who prefer the gentle art of birdwatching
might like to join Geoff Sainty's Nature Excursions (tel: 02-358 4788) which
depart at 6am in order to take advantage of the dawn activities of the birds.

Bush Experiences (tel: 047-84 2361) organize guided bushwalks in the Blue
Mountains lasting from half a day ($20) to three days with two nights camping
($160 inclusive). They also organize fully-catered cycling holidays with a similar
choice of duration, starting at a half day which costs $25. Riding is another
popular way of seeing the Blue Mountains. If interested contact the Pack
Saddlers (tel: 047-87 9150) or Werri Berri Trail Rides (tel: 047-87 9171) both
in the Megalong Valley not far west of Katoomba. The Katoomba Outdoor
Centre at 285 Main runs climbing and abseiling courses and takes guided trips
into the hills and canyons; enquire about discounts for Youth Hostel members.

The Royal National Park (tel: 02-521 2230) which is a short train ride south
of Sydney has the distinction of being Australia's oldest (and the second oldest
in the world after Yellowstone in the United States). The highlight here is the
chance to walk along sea cliffs. The hardier breed of youth hosteller will be

interested in the primitive hostel at Garie Beach which is accessible only on foot either a kilometre from the car park, 12km from the railway station at Waterfall or 15km along the coastal track from Bundeena where the ferry from the Sydney suburb of Cronulla docks. This Hostel is unmanned so you must pre-pay at the Dulwich Hill Hostel in Sydney before you can obtain the key. Stanwell Park just south of the Royal National Park is a favourite spot for hang-gliders.

The two National Parks which straddle the Hawkesbury River north of Sydney are not so well suited to bushwalkers since much of their area is covered by mangrove swamp. Ku-ring-gai Chase National Park is especially attractive in spring when the wild flowers bloom in profusion. The park rangers organize activities during the school holidays, for example tours of Aboriginal drawings and nocturnal nature walks; ring 02-457 9322 for details. Similarly in the summer you can join a walk for $1 with a park guide to the rock engravings at Kamaregal and to the now defunct quarantine station at North Head (tel: 02-977 3292/337 5511 for details). It is possible to cross Broken Bay at the mouth of the Hawkesbury by ferry, from the exclusive suburb of Palm Beach to Ettalong; cyclists are also allowed to use this service.

At all these ocean-side parks, there is good surfing, canoeing, fishing and also bush camping if you have permission from the park authorities.

Bushwalking. There are opportunities for good walking throughout the state from the Kangaroo Valley (inland from Wollongong) to the memorably named Warrumbungle National Park, where you are more likely to see a field of kangaroos than in the Kangaroo Valley since it is so much further from the big cities. (If you do get as far as the Warrumbungle Range north of Dubbo try to visit the Siding Spring Observatory, a NASA space centre with powerful star-gazing telescopes.)

The 6,200 square kilometre area of Kosciusko National Park, which is so well known to skiers, is also a fine walking area in the summer. A superb view of the Snowy Mountains can be had from any of the peaks in the park; the walk up Mount Stilwell from the Chalet at Charlotte's Pass on the eastern slopes of Mount Kosciusko is especially recommended. Mount Kosciusko itself (2,230m) is a rounded hill which can also be climbed without difficulty in summer.

If walking in the rainforests in the northern part of the state, beware of giant leeches.

Skiing. Kosciusko National Park which contains a large area of the Snowy Mountains and is 450km from Sydney is the place everyone heads to in winter, since the Blue Mountains are not high enough to be skiable. There are six ski areas in the state, all of them in the Snowy Mountains. Although there is a large choice of downhill runs, cross-country skiing or "langlauf" is especially popular in this area. The ski season lasts from July to September, though the snow stays on the upper slopes until November or even December.

The main resorts like Thredbo (which specializes in teaching beginners), Guthega (mainly for families), Perisher, etc. are not cheap. For example the Thredbo Youth Hostel charges $20 in the ski season instead of the summer price of $8. If you want to economize stay in one of the sub-alpine towns such as Berridale or Jindabyne and commute to the slopes on one of the regular buses. The Jindabyne Accommodation Reservation Centre has a toll-free number: 008-02 6331. A new addition is the Skitube, an underground railway which covers 3km between the Thredbo Road and Perisher. A further 3km to the new Blue Cow Ski Area opens in 1988 (and has been dubbed the "Moo Choo-Choo").

Watersports. There is year-round surfing off the north coast of the state at places like Ballina and Byron Bay. Other well known places are Port Macquarie and Redhead Beach near Newcastle. But the sport is equally popular on the south coast. Watch for aquatic carnivals throughout the summer, for example the Australia Day celebrations held near Taree about half way up the coast. You don't have to be on the coast to enjoy water sports: Menindee Lake is a huge man-made sea over 1,000km from the ocean, where there is even a nude beach.

Windsurfing, diving and snorkelling are widely available. Hostels can usually advise or even hire out equipment themselves as at the Backpackers Hostel at Lennox Heads, while the dive shop attached to the Arts Factory in Byron Bay arranges scuba and snorkelling trips. Although the south coast is not quite so balmy, contact the South Coast Promotion Committee (PO Box 475, Nowra 2541; tel: 004-21 0778) for their excellent booklet about adventure holidays.

Other Activities. Many species of wildlife thrive in corners of the state. The Tollgate Islands, offshore from Batemans Bay, are a penguin reserve. Birdwatching is a rewarding pastime at any of the vast coastal lakes north of Sydney such as Lake Macquarie and the Myall lakes (part of a National Park of the same name). If you are travelling the Hume Highway, stop at the Mount Gibraltar Reserve near Bowral and listen for lyre birds, the amazing bird which can imitate sounds it hears frequently, and not just the sounds of other species but man-made sound such as that of a chainsaw. Koalas can also be seen there in the wild, though the largest numbers inhabit a few North Coast localities. Closer to Sydney, you might want to visit the koalas and kangaroos at Koala Park, Castle Hill Road, West Pennant Hills.

Those who prefer the pursuit of inanimate Australiana, i.e. minerals and fossils, might try their hand at fossicking, which originally referred to hunting for gold but is used more generally now to cover opals and other minerals. Contact the Department of Mineral Resources in the State Office Block in Sydney for further details and also for a fossicking licence.

Calendar of Events

January 1st	Highland Gathering
January (all month)	Festival of Sydney
January 26th (Australia Day)	Celebrity Thong-throwing Contest at Dee Why Beach
January/February	Chinese New Year (Chinatown festivities)
March/April (Easter Tuesday)	Show Day
June (second Monday)	**Queen's Birthday**
June	Sydney Film Festival
August (first Monday)	**Bank Holiday**
August	City to Surf Race
August	August Moon Festival (Chinatown)
October (first Monday)	**Labour Day**
early October	Manly Jazz Carnival
October	Kings Cross Carnival
November	Queen St Fair, Woollahra
December 26	Sydney to Hobart Yacht Race begins

Public holidays are shown in **bold**

Canberra

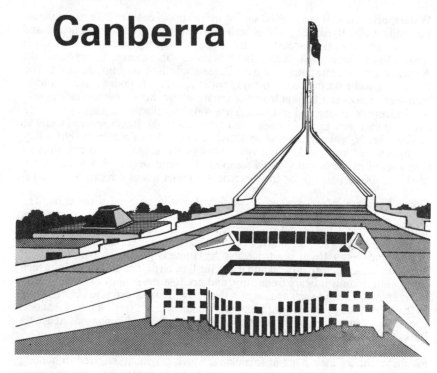

Population of Canberra: 255,000   **Population of the ACT: 264,400**

Canberra is one of those places which evokes an instant and often hostile response. Jokes comparing the nation's capital to a cemetery with lights on are commonplace. Many Australians will tell you that it's a soulless city though they all admit it's in a lovely setting. It certainly is a city whose surface invites easy generalizations, unlike large complex cosmopolitan cities like Sydney or Melbourne. But in view of Canberra's extreme youth and small size, comparisons are unfair. Of *course* the nightlife is not as varied as in Sydney nor the choice of restaurants as great as in Melbourne. But people who live there seem to like it and someone has suggested that the old cliché should be revised in the case of Canberra to read "nice place to live, but you wouldn't want to visit."

Anyone remotely interested in town planning should make an effort to visit, since Canberra is one of the most pleasing examples of planning in the world, especially when compared to such places as Brasilia, Milton Keynes, or Chandigargh, the bleak city in Northern India which Le Corbusier designed. If you are the kind of person who revels in the noise and chaos of Old Delhi and is bored by the orderly quadrants of New Delhi, or who laments the changes brought about when the Baron Haussmann imposed his grand boulevards in 19th-century Paris, you may find yourself in the ranks of those who dislike Canberra.

But there is no denying it is an attractive and congenial city. The large man-made lake at the city's centre is named after the American architect Walter

Burley Griffin whose progressive thinking won him the chance to plan Australia's capital in 1911. In fact it has taken his successors many decades to implement (and adapt) the original plans, and the process continues.

Canberra's *raison d'être* is as the seat of federal government. A site was chosen in the middle of nowhere from a long list of contenders as a way of placating Sydney and Melbourne which were bitterly opposed to their rival being chosen. Canberra is often thought to be roughly half way between Sydney and Melbourne, though this is a convenient fiction, since it is $3\frac{1}{2}$ hours from Sydney and 8 hours from Melbourne. Another little fabrication favoured by the city fathers is that Canberra means "meeting place" in an Aboriginal language; however some experts contend that it means "a woman's breast". The city lies within the Australian Capital Territory (ACT), a 60km by 95km island of land in the south-eastern part of New South Wales. One very peculiar quirk of the ACT is that its charter stipulates that it must have access to the sea. So it has an ocean annexe at Jervis Bay also in New South Wales 230km due east, a naval base as well as recreation area.

Canberra is a strange and artificial place, self-consciously a showpiece. To maintain high aesthetic standards in this planned environment, residents must comply with a number of restrictions such as not being allowed to have outside TV aerials or to use motor boats on the lake. Not only does the municipality lovingly tend its gardens and streetside floral displays, but it gives away trees to new residents who are expected to do their part for local beautification. Flowering trees, including some exotic species, transform the streets in spring, and deciduous trees do likewise in autumn. Canberra deserves to call itself a garden city, which it prefers to another commonly heard sobriquet the "bush capital". But Canberrans like to have it both ways; they are proud of their city's sophistication but equally proud of the bushland which impinges on the urban setting sufficiently to make the occasional sighting of a kangaroo within the city limits a possibility.

CLIMATE

Canberra experiences four distinct seasons, with baking dry summers (complete with an invasion of flies), crisp cold winters and proper transitions between them. Although temperatures in winter drop below freezing, it rarely snows in the city. To experience snow, you will have to drive 200km to the Snowy Mountains. The Canberra Tourist Bureau posts two telexes a day on mountain snow conditions or you can ring 11544 for the snow report. Winter days are not unpleasant since they are usually bright and sunny. In fact Canberra receives an average of seven hours of sunshine around the calendar. There is almost no industry in or near the city, so the air is always pristine. Rainfall is very low (an average of 64cm per year) and is fairly evenly distributed.

THE LOCALS

It is perhaps more difficult to meet the locals in Canberra than elsewhere. Some would say that the place is crowded out with fat cats not worth meeting anyway and of course Canberra has its share of besuited career bureaucrats with whom the average traveller would have little in common. But there is also a large and important university, the Australian National University (ANU), which attracts a large proportion of overseas students as well as Australians from all over the country.

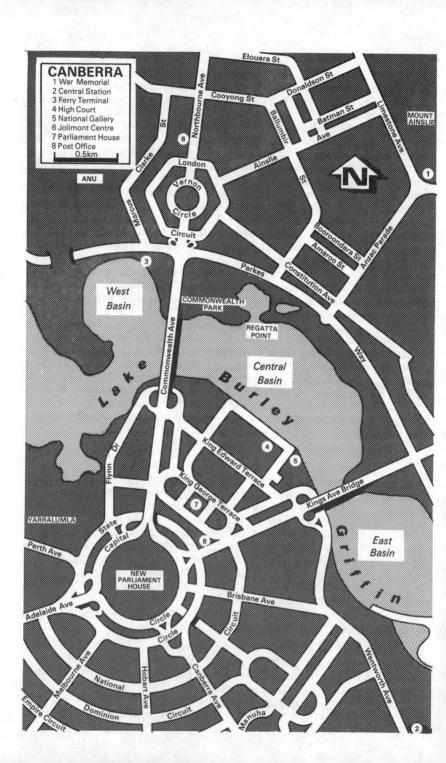

Although a high proportion of Canberrans are involved with government in some way, this does not mean that it is a dull place. There are Aboriginal activists, lobbyists, journalists and also people from many different ethnic backgrounds. The range of clubs is enormous, from Lithuanian to Croatian, Dutch to Welsh. Locals who are involved in government often have a sharp eye for both the positive and negative aspects of Australian culture and politics, and are well worth meeting. Like the city itself, the population is comparatively young — there are no grandparents in Canberra and so it is said there is a huge demand for childminders — and the vast majority of residents were not born in Canberra.

The average Canberran spends a lot of time in the great outdoors, partly because populations with a high proportion of yuppies tend to be concerned about fitness and partly because Canberra offers more to the sportsman and sportswoman than to those with disco mania. The Youth Hostel arranges regular outings, weekend trips and social events; so check their notice board even if you are staying elsewhere.

If you are arranging to meet someone, a good meeting place is the old merry-go-round in the city centre at the corner of City Walk and Petrie Plaza.

It is surprising that a national capital does not have an international airport, and that it is about 70km off the major train routes and the main Hume Highway.

ARRIVAL AND DEPARTURE

Air. Flying from Sydney or Melbourne is easy, since there are dozens of flights a day on the two main domestic carriers Ansett (tel: 45 1111) and Australian Airlines (tel: 68 3333). Standard fares are as follows: $95 to Sydney, $208 to Adelaide or Brisbane and $134 to Melbourne. East West Airlines (Shop 3/4, Cinema Centre, Bunda St, Civic; tel: 57 2411) also serves Canberra and their fares are sometimes cheaper. Cheapest of all is Air New South Wales (like East-West, a subsidiary of Ansett) which flies propeller aircraft between Sydney and Melbourne calling at Canberra. Price for a ticket on these "no frills" services are $67 to Sydney and $85 to Melbourne.

The airport is 10km southeast of the city centre. Although there is an airport bus service costing $2.50, it runs only twice a day, and there is no public bus service. The taxi fare will be about $7.

Coach. Coach services between Sydney and Canberra are frequent: Deluxe Coachlines, Greyhound and Ansett Pioneer run five or six services each throughout the day with Greyhound starting from Sydney at 6.45am and Ansett Pioneer providing the last service at 11.30pm (on most days). The local company Murrays runs three services daily. The trip takes between four and five hours, and the cost is a very reasonable $18. The Coach Station is in the Jolimont Centre on Northbourne Avenue, as are the offices of Deluxe and Greyhound:

Deluxe: 47 0588
Greyhound: 57 2659
Ansett Pioneer: 150 Northbourne Avenue, corner of Ipima St (45 6624).
Murrays Coaches: 1 Mugga Lane, Red Hill (95 3677).

There are direct services to other cities in New South Wales, for example to

Wollongong and Eden on the coast south of Sydney and to Cooma and the Snowy Mountains. The New South Wales licence restrictions mean that only travellers coming from or going to another state can travel between Canberra and certain towns in New South Wales such as Newcastle and Lismore by coach. Because competition is less intense on non-Sydney routes, prices are higher, for example the fare for the three-hour journey to Wollongong is $24 with Canberra Cruises (Mundaring Drive, Kingston; tel: 95 3544), and the trip to Perisher Ski Resort in the Snowy Mountains (also three hours) is $42 on Ansett Pioneer. Unfortunately the mountain coach services are timed to suit Sydney skiers and hikers rather than Canberra ones, so you might have to depart Canberra at 4am or arrive in Perisher or Thredbo at 1.45am. The only reasonable time is the 12.30pm departure from Canberra. The Youth Hostel arranges its own excursions to the Snowy Mountains which you might prefer to join.

Canberra is also connected with the other eastern capitals: the 16-hour trip to Adelaide costs $75 and the nine-hour trip to Melbourne costs $35. The new V-line coach/rail service takes just over eight hours and costs $39 (tel: 47 6355). All Queensland services go via Sydney.

Train. The main Sydney-Melbourne line passes through the nondescript little town of Yass, 67km north of Canberra, where you must disembark if you are trying to get from Melbourne to Canberra. A local bus service between Yass Junction and Canberra connects with only one train a day from Melbourne, so unless you take the Intercapital Daylight Express (which departs Melbourne at 8.40am) then you will have to wait around in Yass or hitch along the Barton Highway into Canberra. There is no Yass-Canberra bus service on Sundays.

Services to Sydney are much more convenient. There is an XPT service which departs Sydney every day at 6.35pm arriving in Canberra about four hours later. The XPT departs Canberra at 7.13am. The cost is $23 economy, $32.60 in first class. There are three other services on the Monaro Express in both directions most days. For timetable and fare information contact State Rail in Canberra on 95 1555. The Station is about six kilometres south of the city centre just off Wentworth Avenue.

Driving. Four highways converge on Canberra: the Monaro Highway from Cooma and the south, the Kings Highway from the New South Wales coast, and the Federal and Barton Highways which both join the Hume Highway north of Canberra. The approach roads to the city are so wide that there is never any traffic congestion.

The majority of car hire firms in Canberra are not of the rent-a-heap ilk since rusting Volkswagens are not the preferred vehicle of visiting delegates and dignitaries. Many car hire firms are located along Lonsdale St in Braddon, for example Discount (tel: 49 6551), Actcar (tel: 47 5400), Budget (tel: 48 9788) and Thrifty (tel: 47 7422). You may be able to get a better deal away from the city centre; try Rumbles at the corner of Kembla and Wollongong Streets, Fyshwick (tel: 80 7444) or Rick's, 162 Melrose Drive, Phillip (tel: 85 1053).

The National Roads and Motorists Association (NRMA) is on Northbourne Avenue at the corner of Elouera St (tel: 43 3777).

Hitch-hiking. You tend to get a better class of lift when hitching out of Canberra. One of the authors was picked up by a Canberran (a former Australian trade commissioner to Bahrain) who carried in his car taped lectures on Australian history for the edification of hitch-hikers on long journeys.

If you want to get on to the Monaro or Kings Highway, take a bus or train 12km to the New South Wales town of Queanbeyan (not pronounced Queen-bean, but *Queen*-bee-un). To join the Hume Highway take any of the buses heading north: for the Barton Highway take bus 906 to Hall; for the Federal Highway take bus 383 (or on weekends 362).

CITY TRANSPORT

The main commercial centre is around London Circuit, north of the lake. The area south is largely devoted to administrative and diplomatic life. Try to obtain a copy of the tourist office free map *Canberra and District,* though for a street and suburbs index, you'll need the excellent UBD Tourist Map which has insets of the city, the university and the whole ACT.

Bus. The public transport system of Canberra is confined to buses called ACTION (ACT Internal Omnibus Network) which serves all suburbs though at infrequent intervals and has a series of sightseeing routes. Timetable and fare information is available from the Bus Interchange office at the top of City Walk (tel: 51 6566) open 6am to 11.30pm except Sundays when it opens 8.30am to 6.30pm.

Like Sydney and Melbourne, Canberra has an Explorer bus operated by Murrays (tel: 95 3677); tickets are available at the Tourist Office for $7. This is an unnecessary extravagance, since ACTION buses can take you most places, though some of the routes operate only at weekends. Ask for timetables 904-907 and 909. Prices vary from $3-$4.50 on these special sightseeing routes. A further disadvantage of the Explorer bus is that there are only six a day departing from the Visitor Information Centre at hourly intervals between 9.40am and 3.40pm whereas ordinary buses run between 6am and midnight. ACTION day passes may be purchased from the Youth Hostel as well as from the ACTION office.

Car. Many newcomers to Canberra encounter difficulties in navigation, partly because the planners wanted to avoid a boring grid system and partly because they seem to have been very sparing in their use of street signs. Careful study of a good map is essential before trying to get from A to B.

A further difficulty is the seeming invisibility of petrol stations. Ugly as the approach roads to most cities are, lined with garages, motels, etc., at least you can easily find petrol. Not so in Canberra, where you must look for the discreet blue signs pointing you towards a fuel supply. There is a 24-hour petrol station on Lonsdale St in Braddon.

One problem you won't encounter is heavy traffic: The main thoroughfare Northbourne Avenue is usually empty and you could wheel a television across it at midday with no difficulty. Avoid using bus lanes and watch out for cycleways across streets. Red lines on the kerb mean that you can't park. Just as in New South Wales, random breath testing is commonplace, though in the ACT a limit of .08% applies rather than .05% as in New South Wales.

As befits a city planned with the motor car in mind, there are few parking problems. Vast car parks surround the city centre both inside London Circuit and west of Ballumbir St. In Civic Centre there is some metered street parking.

If you do have a car, you might like to follow one or more of the five tourist drives, all of which start at the City Hill Lookout on Vernon Circle and radiate in various directions towards various attractions.

Taxi. Flagging a taxi on the streets of Canberra is an almost impossible task, principally because there are very few taxi firms. Ring Aerial Taxis (tel: 46 0444) for a cab.

Boat. Although there is a designated ferry terminal on Lake Burley Griffin, there are in fact no ferries. However you can get good views of the civic buildings from the lake, so you might want to join a two-hour cruise at 1pm ($10) or an economy one-hour tour at noon ($6.50) from the Acton Ferry Terminal. Otherwise you can paddle yourself out into the lake (see *Sport* below).

Cycling. Canberra is very proud of its cycleways, many of which cut through parks and across open spaces rather than go alongside the roads. There are over 100km of cycle paths, which are marked on most maps, as well as on the tourist office's free brochure called "Canberra Cycleways". The term cycleways is a partial misnomer since the paths are also used by pedestrians; this is only fair since cyclists may legally ride on the footpaths of Canberra.

Bicycles may be hired from the Youth Hostel, from Mr Spokes Bike Hire (Acton Ferry Terminal) at weekends only or from Canberra Bicycle Hire, (Woolley St, Dickson, near the corner of Northbourne Avenue and Antill St) any day. Canberra Bike Rental (tel: 41 2216) will deliver hire mountain bikes to your door for $35 a day. For group cycle tours, contact Tailwinds, 9 Sargood St, O'Connor (tel: 49 6634).

A complete list of Canberra's 40 or so motels, five caravan parks and few hostels and guest houses may be found in the tourist office leaflet *The Inns and Outs of Where to Stay.* The Tourist Bureau also keeps a register showing price, type and availability of accommodation.

The Youth Hostel is on Dryandra St in O'Connor (tel: 48 9759), 5km from the centre of town near bus routes 360, 380 and 390. Although not many overseas travellers go to Canberra, the Hostel is often booked out with groups of Australian school children, so it might be an idea to book ahead for one of the 40 beds (postal bookings only; the nightly fee is $10).

Canberra has plenty of anonymous motels and hotels which are outside the price range of budget travellers. Some of these are registered at the Canberra Accommodation Centre at 30 National Circuit, Forrest (tel: 95 34333 or 008-02 6129 from anywhere in Australia) where reservations can be made. The Tall Trees Lodge Motel at 21 Stephen St in Ainslie (tel: 47 9200) charges $29 for a double in their lodge.

Many Australian families on holiday stay at one of the camping and caravanning parks which are signposted on the approach roads. The Motor Village (tel: 47 5466) is the most central, just a stone's throw from the Youth Hostel and north of the Black Mountain Nature Reserve. It has on-site caravans at the standard rates but no tent sites. The South Side Motor Park in Fyshwick (tel: 80 6176) is further from town but larger, with nearly 5,000 sites including some for tents.

Out of term you can try the university residences, though their rooms are not really a bargain. For example, University House on Balmain Crescent (across from the ANU Information Centre) charges $65 a day for a small single room.

If you are planning to be in Canberra for an extended period, a one-bedroom flat will cost at least $100 a week.

Eating and Drinking

Seeking local advice on eating places is always a good idea, but in Canberra it is especially worthwhile, since many good restaurants are not in obvious locations. Authentic Sri Lankan, Chinese and Turkish restaurants or unpretentious seafood restaurants are often concealed in suburban shopping malls or are inauspiciously attached to motels and clubs. (The Olive Branch in the Kythera Motel at 100 Northbourne Avenue claims to raise its own kid for authentic Greek stews.) But it is also possible to find worthwhile places on spec by walking around the Civic Centre, comparing menus and prices. Northbourne Avenue, East Row and nearby Garema Place are worth strolling along. A few spots have entertainment such as Dorette's Bistro upstairs at 17 Garema Place which offers live jazz and classical music on alternate nights. Classical music buffs might also appreciate the background music at the Honeydew Wholemeal Restaurant (55 Northbourne Avenue) which is a gourmet vegetarian BYO restaurant open 6-9pm only.

Many of Canberra's restaurants do special businessmen's lunches at reasonable prices (compared to similar meals served in the evening). The majority of restaurants open Monday to Saturday. If you are hungry on a Sunday, ethnic restaurants are most likely to be open, such as the Vietnamese restaurants at 21 and 27 East Row. Next door is Sinbad's a licensed Lebanese restaurant which is open seven nights a week. The Pancake Parlour on the corner of Alinga St and East Row is open 24 hours a day every day, and provides a good late-night alternative to the mobile food vans which appear each night, especially near the university campus. The crepes served at the French Kitchen in the Boulevard Centre on Akuna St are less mass-produced, and are popular after the theatres and cinemas in the area adjourn.

If you want to sample a specific ethnic cuisine you might contact the relevant club, most of which allow visitors to dine in their restaurant but not to use the bars. Try the Trevi Restaurant in the Italo-Australian Club (78 Franklin St, Forrest; tel: 95 2037) or the dining room at the Austrian-Australian Club (Southlands, Mawson; tel: 86 5793). One of the best known club restaurants is the Tramway Eatery at the Tradesmen's Union Club in Dickson (Badham St) where seating is in one of four old city trams from Sydney, Melbourne, Brisbane and Adelaide.

There are plenty of conveniently located cafés and take-aways for quick snacks, such as the cafeteria-style café in the High Court and the Bistro in the Jolimont Centre. You might also investigate the university canteens; sometimes ploughman's lunches are available when lunchtime concerts are being performed.

Picnics are also highly recommended at any of the 60 parks and lakeside reserves, many of which have coin-operated barbecue facilities. You can buy a picnic hamper at the new restaurant at Regatta Point, which is also a pleasant place to dine indoors or out for less than $20. Surprisingly, food is substantially cheaper in Canberra than in other Australian cities; in fact the cost of living is one of the lowest for capital cities in the developed world.

DRINKING

There are no licensing restrictions in Canberra so hotels can stay open as long as they like, and the occasional nightspot like the Private Bin at 50 Northbourne

Avenue stays open for drinking and dancing until dawn. Even if you are not feeling particularly homesick for British beer, you might enjoy an evening at the Boot and Flogger near the station (Green Square, Jardine St) since they have nightly rock music (except Fridays when they have jazz). The beer is imported from Britain but the menu is Australian (mostly steaks). Although you will probably want to leave the miniature English village at Cockington to the "wrinklies" (a common Australian expression for old people), you might like to visit the George Harcourt Inn nearby which serves draught beer in Imperial measures. Unfortunately it is a long way out of town to go for a pint (take bus 906). You may or may not want to visit on Friday/Saturday evenings or Sunday afternoons when there are sing-alongs.

A larger proportion of Canberra restaurants are licensed compared to other Australian cities, though there are some BYO establishments. If you want to try a fancy wine, visit the Private Cellar in the Dickson Shopping Centre. Although Canberra is hardly famous for its wines, there are a couple of wineries within range of the ACT. Advertisements urging Canberrans to support their local wine industry were recently used to promote a wine called Lake George costing $8 (an excessive sum in Australian terms) which tasted much inferior to the wines of the Hunter Valley, where growing conditions are obviously more congenial (and economic). But vineyards in Australia can change character and improve rapidly, so you might like to make an expedition to the Murrumbateman Winery, 30 minutes by car along the Barton Highway. The winery is set in pleasant grounds with picnic facilities and wine tastings seven days a week.

Not far away is the village of Gundaroo, where tourist-oriented entertainments are held at the Old Gundaroo Pub, involving traditional Australian "tucker", unlimited drink and a bush band. If you think that you can eat, drink and enjoy $40 worth (which includes Murrays coach transport there and back), enquire at the tourist office.

You can eat and drink just as much for a lot less if you happen to be around for the Canberra Festival in March. The Food and Wine Frolic (sponsored by American Express) attracts thousands of people who either buy sampling tickets ahead of time or on the spot, and then trade them for a selection of the many snacks prepared by some of Canberra's 200 restaurants and for tastes of wine representing wineries from all over the country. The annual event is held in Commonwealth Park.

For a city of its size, Canberra has plenty going on, and not just for the benefit of diplomats and plutocrats. Canberra's entertainment weekly is called *Pulse* which may be picked up free of charge at the tourist office or various pubs and entertainment centres around town. Most gigs are listed in *Pulse* with articles about local and visiting bands, theatre companies, etc. This supplements the more conventional listings published daily on the "I Page" of the *Canberra Times,* which is a guide to events, tours, exhibitions and performances. The student newspaper, called *Woroni,* will keep you informed of events on the campus.

Canberra can be seen at its most lively during the Canberra Festival which lasts ten days each March. Many of the events take place outdoors and are free, such as the Birdman Rally (in which contestants attempt to propel themselves 50m through the air without motorized aids), lunchtime jazz and other outdoor concerts, flower and art shows, raft races and processions. To get a complete calendar of festival events, contact the tourist office or ring the Festival Information service on 49 1277.

All cities are changing all the time but in Canberra the process is more in evidence and more self-consciously promoted as entertainment in itself. The new Parliament Building, the new museum and the new science centre all have an exhibition centre with sophisticated models, detailed plans and films pitched at the general public. Anyone with a glimmer of interest in modern architecture or town planning will enjoy these displays, which are free since they are part of the government's public relations. The one which gives the best general picture of Canberra and its development is the Canberra Planning Exhibition at Regatta Point (tel: 46 8797).

Before you strike off to see specific buildings or to search for Canberra's nightlife, you should admire the city as a whole. Since the site of Canberra was chosen partly for its pleasing situation, there are several hills from which to admire the city's lake and buildings. Mount Ainslie is the highest hill at 842m, though the highest viewpoint is from the top of the Telecom Tower (195m) on the top of Black Mountain (812m). Admission to the viewing platforms is from 9am to 10pm and the cost is $2.

Buildings and Venues. Until the new Parliament House opens on May 9, 1988, the National Gallery (which opened in 1982) together with the adjacent High Court are Canberra's most striking examples of modern architecture. Not everyone likes them and some even think that they clash with each other; others find them splendid buildings, especially when considered in their lakeside setting. In any case they are worth a visit.

These buildings form part of the Parliamentary Triangle, an area south of the lake and enclosed by Commonwealth Avenue and Kings Avenue. At the apex of the triangle is Capital Hill site of the unusual and lavish new Federal Parliament House. Its uniqueness derives from the fact that its low profile in the shape of two back-to-back boomerangs follows the contours of the hill rather than towers above it. If you do happen to be in Canberra for the grand opening, you should swell the numbers a little with your presence, to help them avoid the debacle of 1927 when far fewer people than expected showed up for the opening of Parliament House and 14,000 meat pies had to be ignominiously buried. There is some suggestion that the old building will meet a similarly inglorious conclusion in being converted into a casino, though it is more likely to become the government archives or a museum.

The new Parliament House is being billed as the "building of the century" or (more prophetically) a "building for the 21st century". These publicists continue their campaign seemingly oblivious to rumours that the New York architects may have underestimated the amount of space the Australian government needs, though it is to be hoped that the Prime Minister's office will never require an extension since it is the size of six family homes and nearly four times the size of the opposition leader's office.

Whether or not the government has moved to Capital Hill by the time you visit, you may want to attend a debate. Ask about tickets as soon as you arrive in Canberra since many Australians making a pilgrimage to their capital will have pre-booked tickets by post (to the Principal Attendant, House of Representatives, ACT 2600) or by telephone to the King's Hall enquiry staff (72 6606). Just as in London the House of Lords is much less appealing to tourists than the House of Commons, so the Senate of Australia (the upper house) is less popular than the House of Representatives, so you should be able to visit the former without any problem. Question time in both Houses usually starts at 2pm.

The campus of the Australian National University (ANU) is north of the lake between the city centre and Black Mountain. In addition to attending concerts and plays at the Arts Centre, you may want to visit some of the university institutes which have specialist exhibitions open to the public. Enquire at the ANU Information Centre (tel: 49 2229) on Balmain Crescent (a street which is confusingly in two sections).

Another area of Canberra worth exploring on foot or bicycle, whether or not you need any visas, is the Embassy belt. Most of the more exotic embassies (of the 70 in Canberra) are located in Yarralumla just west of Capital Hill along Empire Circuit, Arkana St and Turrana St. Elements of the vernacular architecture are reflected in some of the buildings, such as those of Thailand and Papua New Guinea, though not in sufficient measure to permit you to imagine yourself in Bangkok or Wewak rather than Canberra suburbia. The Papua New Guinean High Commission and Indonesian Embassy both have exhibitions of art and artefacts open to the public. If you want to see inside any of the others, you will have to wait for one of their occasional "open house" days, which usually take place in January, June and October.

The Australian Capital Territory incorporates some old colonial mansions and farmhouses, some of which are still in use as in the case of Duntroon House built in 1833 which is now part of the Royal Military College, while most others have been restored as tourist attractions with tea shops, gardens, and craft centres, such as the Ginnenderra School House off the Barton Highway. The Lanyon Homestead and the nearby Cuppacumbalong Homestead, both set on the Murrumbidgee River less than an hour south of Canberra, are in delightful settings and their grounds are occasionally used for outdoor concerts.

Museums and Galleries. The Australian War Memorial claims to be the second most heavily visited attraction in all of Australia after the Sydney Opera House. This museum of war is housed in a suitably dignified building at the top of Anzac Parade and was the largest war memorial in the world when it was built in 1941 (at a time when the Australian population was just four million). Most Australians take great pride in their country's military history, particularly the heroism of Gallipoli, and all of the theatres of war in which they were involved including Vietnam, are dealt with in the museum displays, which are open every day from 9am-4.45pm (tel: 43 4211; admission is free). Voluntary guides conduct free tours at 10.30am and 1.30pm on weekdays.

The Australian National Gallery (tel: 71 2501) has 11 spacious galleries in which to show off its excellent permanent collection of Australian painting and its other holdings. The National is also the Australian gallery which is most likely to attract major international touring exhibitions from Europe or America, and mounts an impressive array of supporting events such as films, lectures and concerts. The normal admission fee of $2 is usually increased to $5 for one of these prestigious visiting exhibitions.

The work of one of Australia's most important contemporary artists, Sidney Nolan, is on display at Lanyon Historic Homestead (tel: 37 5136; admission $1.50). Closer to the city centre you might prefer to inspect the collection of unusual and antique bicycles at the Canberra Tradesmen's Club on Badham St in Dickson (tel: 48 0999; free admission). The National Film and Sound Archive on the university campus (McCoy Circuit; tel: 67 1711) chronicles the development of the Australian media with interesting visual and audio exhibits.

Theatre and Music. The BASS ticket agency sells tickets to most Canberra events; phone 47 2844 or visit their downtown outlet in the Jolimont Centre.

Canberra has its own symphony orchestra and opera company, as well as a choice of local theatre companies including several fringe groups such as Black Inc. and the Ensemble Theatre Project. The Canberra Theatre Centre in Civic Square (tel: 57 0177) has several auditoria of varying size and is the principal venue. The Repertory Society (tel: 43 5711) is based at the University in the School of Art on Ellery Crescent. Canberra also has more cinemas than most cities with a similar population. The main cinemas downtown are the Electric Shadows off Akuna St (tel: 47 5060) which has late night films at weekends, and the Civic Twin Cinemas on Mort St (tel: 47 5522). There are also a couple of drive-in cinemas on the outskirts of Canberra.

The main rock venue is the Canberra National Indoor Stadium in Bruce. Most other popular music can be heard in pubs or clubs with which Canberra is generously supplied. Clubs of all kinds — for working men, for school teachers, for Finns, etc. — all have regular evenings of entertainment; check for details in *Pulse*. Among the pubs which have music are the Leather Bottle Tavern in Belconnen (tel: 51 3765), the Ainslie Hotel in Braddon (tel: 48 5511) which has free jazz on Sunday afternoons, and the Eureka Stockade at 17 Lonsdale St (tel: 47 0848) which organizes the sort of evening where men pay an admission fee of $3 while "ladies" are admitted free.

If you want to hear music free of charge, and are not entitled to free admission to the Eureka Stockade, loiter in the vicinity of Kings Park (on the north side of Kings Avenue Bridge) on Wednesday or Sunday afternoons and listen to the recital of the carillon (set of bells) which was a gift to Canberra from Britain in 1963. Otherwise tune in to Canberra's newest FM station KIX 106.

If all the world's a stage then the universe must surely supply plenty of drama. The Tidbinbilla Deep Space Tracking Station (38km south-west of Canberra) is open to the public from 9am-5pm daily (tel: 49 0818) and has photographs and models of the galaxy. If you don't have your own transport, either take ACTION bus 907 or join a Murray's coach tour; the half day trip to the Station on Wednesdays (cost $24) is just one of many which Murrays offer.

Visitors with a scientific bent will want to visit the new National Science and Technology Centre scheduled to open in the Parliamentary Triangle in 1988. It is intended to incorporate many of the hands-on exhibits currently on display in the University's Questacon Centre at the old Ainslie Public School in Elouera St, Braddon.

Parks and Zoos. Canberra is famed as a garden city and green spaces virtually surround the lake. Furthermore the streets have been carefully planted with many species of flowering tree, so that September is especially lovely when the Japanese apricots flower followed by the cherry plums and wattles. High summer is probably the worst time to visit, since the lack of rain turns the city drab and brown, especially the central strip of Anzac Parade.

The National Botanic Gardens are interesting at any time of the year. They are unique in that they contain primarily native Australian flora. The gardens occupy the eastern slopes of Black Mountain, itself a very large nature reserve. Guided tours leave from the Visitor Information Centre (tel: 67 1811) every Sunday at 10am and 2pm, though it is not necessary to have a guide to enjoy the trails, such as the one-kilometre Aboriginal Trail (where labels indicate the uses to which the Aboriginal people put the species available to them) and the simulated rainforest in a normally parched gully. There is also a selection of eucalpytus species which might persuade you that gum trees are not as boring as most people think. You should note that cycling is not permitted in the Gardens. There is a branch of the Botanic Gardens at the ACT's outpost on the coast, Jervis Bay.

Instead of tracking stars at Tidbinbilla, you might prefer to track kangaroos and emus through the Tidbinbilla Fauna Reserve, or hope to meet one walking along the track up Mount Ainslie at nightfall. The range of habitats near Canberra includes wetlands at the eastern end of Lake Burley Griffin which attract many exotic birds especially pelicans. Only 6km south of the lake you can visit the Mugga Lane Zoo (admission $2) where it is claimed that 100 species of animals and birds live.

SPORT

Lake Burley Griffin is very handy for lovers of water sports who find themselves in Canberra. Its landscaped foreshores include several sandy beaches where swimming is popular in summer. Others head to one of the city's many sports complexes and swimming pools or else to a recreation area out of town such as the Cotter Reserve 22km west of the city where swimming is popular.

If you have driven in from Sydney, you might have noticed inviting-looking Lake George, 40km northeast of Canberra. However, don't bother to plan a swim here, since its vast surface is never more than a few inches deep, and in dry summers the water disappears completely.

Windsurfers, canoes and rowboats may be hired from Dobell's Boat Hire at the Acton Ferry Terminal for frolicking on Lake Burley Griffin. You might even catch a fish from the lake; no fishing licences are required in the ACT. The lake hosts special events such as the raft race held during the Canberra Festival or the difficult-to-imagine surf carnival to be held as a special bicentennial event on 25th November 1988.

As in any city with a high concentration of yuppies, jogging is popular especially at lunchtimes when the two main bridges over the lake can become clogged with joggers heading for their favourite lakeside route. There is an annual fun run in October sponsored by the *Canberra Times*. Plenty of executive-types also ride bicycles though usually not for recreation. The 35km circumference of the lake can easily be cycled in three hours.

Skiers and bushwalkers will probably head for the Kosciusko National Park about three hours drive south of Canberra (see *New South Wales: Great Outdoors*) though some people head for the artificial snow slopes much nearer town at Corin Forest just past Tidbinbilla, 30 minutes drive from the city.

Spectator Sports. Just because Canberra is full of bureaucrats and intellectuals does not mean that there isn't much interest in sport. There are a great many sports clubs and the Sports Results telephone number (1187) is dialled just as frequently as elsewhere in Australia.

The Canberra Rugby League team is up with the best in the New South Wales league, and can be seen in action at the Seiffert Oval (which also stages cricket in summer). Soccer is played at the National Stadium in Bruce.

The premier horse race of the year is the Black Opal Stakes which take place at the Canberra Race Course during the Festival. The course, which is located where the Barton Highway meets Northbourne Avenue, has the distinction of having introduced Sunday racing to the nation. Harness-racing takes place at the National Exhibition Centre.

SHOPPING

Most shops are open the usual Australian hours with late night shopping on Fridays and morning-only shopping on Saturdays. Outside these hours you can go to the Eight Till Late Supermarket at 10 Lonsdale St, Braddon, where food and drink can be purchased until midnight every day of the week.

Buying something at the corner store is not usually a simple matter in Canberra, and automobiles are usually involved in the simplest shopping expedition. Although most suburbs have their own shopping centres, these are not always easy to find since they are tucked out of sight and away from the main thoroughfares. A proper map of Canberra, such as the UBD map, will highlight shopping centres in colour. The main city centre shopping mall is the Monaro Mall though the suburban Belconnen Westfield Shopping Town and Woden Plaza are much larger. The Belconnen Mall has all the main stores such as Grace Brothers and Woolworths and offers free parking, babysitting services, etc. For more unusual items, visit the 14 stalls of the Fyshwick Antique Centre in the unlikely suburb of Fyshwick, an industrial estate.

Fyshwick is where a weekend fruit and vegetable market is held and also where several of Canberra's many bookshops are located, such as Academic Remainders at 28 Kembla St (open 7 days a week) and Winchbooks (secondhand and rare books) at 68 Wollongong St. The Alternative Bookshop is at 46 Northbourne Avenue, City (not a very alternative address), while Dalton's Bookshop is in Marcus Clarke St, with Mary Martins just around the corner in Alinga St in the city.

Canberra at night is as safe and peaceful as it looks during the day (unlike, say, Washington DC). Poverty and crime are virtually non-existent and the daily newspapers are hard-pressed to find any sensational local news (outside the arena of politics). Even with the large political and diplomatic contingents, security is very low-key. You probably don't need to worry about anything worse than being hit by an inattentive cyclist on a footpath.

The area code for Canberra is 062. For emergency fire, police and ambulance, dial 000.

Canberra Tourist Bureau (CTB): Jolimont Centre, Northbourne Avenue, Canberra City 2601 (49 6464). Also office on Northbourne Avenue between Wakefield and Antill Streets. Both open 7 days a week.

CTB branches also in Sydney: 64 Castlereagh St, just above Martin Place (02-233 3666), and in Melbourne: 247 Collins St (03-654 5088).

British High Commission: Commonwealth Avenue (73 0422).

US Embassy: Moonah Place, Yarralumla (73 3711).
American Express: corner of City Walk & Petrie Plaza (47 2333).
Thomas Cook: 21 London Circuit (57 2222).
Hospitals: Royal Canberra, Acton Peninsula (43 2111); Woden Valley, Yamba Drive, Garran (84 2222).
Emergency Chemist: City Health Promotion Centre, Marcus Clarke St (49 1919)
General Post Office: Jolimont Centre, corner of Moore and Alinga Streets (48 5211). Open Monday to Friday 9am-5pm.
Police: London Circuit, corner of Knowles Place (49 7444).
Helplines: Weather — 1196; Babysitting — 41 3882; Rape Crisis — 47 2525.

Calendar of Events

January	Sports Carnival (10 days)
February	Royal Canberra Show
March (third Monday)	**Canberra Day**
March (starts second Saturday)	Canberra Festival (10 days)
March	Black Opal Stakes
March/April	National Sheepdog Trials
March/April	National Rally Sprint
April	Nike Marathon
April-June	National Eisteddfod
June (second Monday)	**Queen's Birthday**
June	Festival of Australian Drama
August (first Monday)	**Bank Holiday**
October (first Monday)	**Labour Day**
October	*Canberra Times* Fun Run
November	National Wine Show

Public holidays are shown in **bold**

Melbourne and Victoria

Population of Melbourne: 2,900,000　　**Population of Victoria: 4,200,000**

Approximately the same size as Great Britain (with an area of 227,000km²). Victoria is easily Australia's smallest mainland state. Yet it contains as great a variety of terrain as any other state, encapsulating almost the entire range of Australian landscape and climate in microcosm: from the Little Desert to the Grampians and Snowy Mountains, rich pastures to rainforest, and tumbling vineyards to dramatic coastline. It comprises big-city style and small-town country life, laced with a fascinating colonial history. Victoria is the most densely populated state in Australia, and mightier than New South Wales in its economic power: mineral reserves and fertile farmland, commerce and hi-tech industries. Underpinning its financial strength is the sprawling city of Melbourne, the only rival to Sydney for sophistication.

Melbourne has received a relatively bad press as a destination for travellers, not least from other Australians; for a start, its climate is noticeably cooler than elsewhere on the mainland. And compared to the spectacular setting of Sydney, Victoria's capital can strike the newcomer as a trifle drab. Set around the muddy Yarra River, Melbourne has little appeal to the eye and the solid Victorian buildings convey an air of dourness. But Melbourne is even more cosmopolitan than other Australian cities, and boasts the best sport, the liveliest arts and indisputably the finest food. If you stick to the city centre of Melbourne you'll be disappointed as it is an ungraceful business and shopping area. Like London or Manhattan, there are picturesque neighbourhoods dotted around the heart of Melbourne which are far more interesting and satisfying than the commercial centre: St Kilda, once a seaside resort for the wealthy, now a down-at-heel yet attractive beachside suburb; Port Melbourne, a refurbished waterfront area; Carlton, Fitzroy and Richmond, paradise for cut-price gourmets.

You cannot miss the rivalry between Sydney and Melbourne, vying to be the most dynamic and exciting state capital (even Melburnians will admit that Sydney is more beautiful). Sydneysiders abuse Melbourne for its weather, its staidness and its social competitiveness, most prominent among those with "old money" inherited from the pioneering days. The people of Melbourne roundly condemn Sydney for what they see as a lack of real values and concern, and an insatiable quest for wealth. Melbourne itself is comfortably rich, with sturdy Victorian banks and is the largest financial centre in Australia: it is sometimes described as the economic engine room of the nation.

The state had inauspicious origins, since the colonial powers in Sydney had little interest in exploiting far-flung regions. The first attempted settlement in 1803 on Port Phillip Bay (on which Melbourne now stands) was abandoned in May 1804, and the settlers moved to Van Diemen's Land (now Tasmania). The first overland crossing to the Great Southern Ocean was made in 1836 by Surveyor-General Thomas Mitchell, who travelled past Port Phillip Bay as far west as the present-day town of Portland. Since permission had not been granted for any settlement of the southern regions, he was startled to discover a European family, the Hentys, who — disgruntled with life in Tasmania — had sailed across the Bass Strait in 1834. Edward Henty had been followed in May 1835 by John Batman, who bought a million acres of land around Port Phillip Bay from the Aboriginals. Melbourne was founded three months later by John Fawkner, who built a house on the banks of the Yarra River. Two hundred more "squatters" had arrived before the area was officially declared open for settlement in 1836.

The settlers resented being governed at a distance by Sydney, and after mounting protests the new state of Victoria was established in 1851. In the same year, gold was discovered inland in the region around Ballarat and Bendigo. In the gold rush which followed, the population of Victoria increased seven-fold. Melbourne grew into a real city, since a nearby port was needed to service the miners and their production. The government of Victoria was keen to take a share, and made licences compulsory for prospectors (enforced by the Red Coats, a harsh militia). Resistance against the increasing demands of the state and poor treatment of "diggers" culminating in the storming by troops of a makeshift stockade at the Eureka claim near Ballarat. Twenty-two miners were killed, and the public outcry that followed forced the government to capitulate to many of the demands for social reform.

No other state is so much a part of the development of an Australian consciousness, of the struggle for independence and individuality. The most significant figure was Edward "Ned" Kelly: he came from a typically poor rural family and, through a series of skirmishes with the police, became an outlawed bushranger. Although eventually captured, convicted and hanged in Melbourne Gaol, Ned Kelly was regarded as a folk hero who epitomized the fight of the impoverished against injustices perpetuated by the authorities.

CLIMATE

If you stay in Melbourne for any length of time you are sure to be told that the city experiences all four seasons in a single day, or to be asked "Don't like the

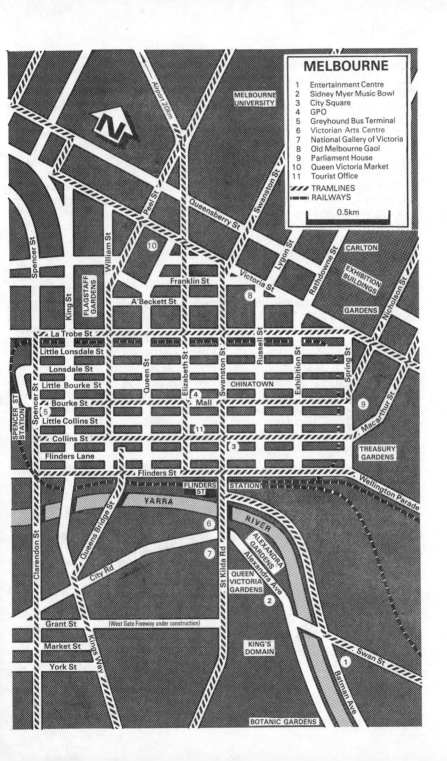

weather? Don't worry, it'll change in a minute". While it is true that the weather rarely takes a grip for weeks on end as it does in other parts of Australia, the climate of Victoria is certainly more benign than that of Tasmania, Scotland or New England. The weather is quite English: there can be unremitting cloud, cold and rain in winter and long, hot spells in summer, but mostly it is blustery and changeable.

Melbourne lies in a climatic region classified as "warm temperate". The average maximum during the hottest months (January and February) is 25°C/78°F, with occasional summer heatwaves touching 40°C and (because of Melbourne's southerly location) long, balmy summer evenings. The mean midwinter maximum in June and July is 14°C/57°F. While temperatures in the city rarely fall below 4°C/40°F, the mountainous areas of Victoria can be below freezing point for long stretches in winter. Rainfall averages 66cm annually, slightly less than in London and New York. Although it is highest in June and July, there are showers throughout the year: even the driest month, January, has only 15% less rain than the average.

THE LOCALS

In the past 150 years, two million people have migrated to Victoria, three-quarters of them since 1945. The 1981 census revealed that 23% of Victorians were born overseas, with immigrants from over 100 different countries. Melbourne has the largest Greek population (115,000) of any city outside Greece, plus large Italian, Vietnamese, Lebanese, Chinese, German and Maltese communities.

In view of this rich, multicultural mix, it is perhaps surprising that most Melburians are fairly conservative. The first settlers were pioneering "squatters", opening up the land and rapidly becoming rich and powerful. The influence of the "squattocracy" is still pervasive. Melbourne is the home of old money: while these establishment families have been financially dwarfed by the new tycoons, their conservative influence prevails.

Making Friends. A good way to remove the social barriers is to find work in hospitality industry, since you are sure to meet some of Melbourne's more colourful characters. If time does not permit getting a job, or if your funds don't require topping up, you could visit some of the livelier pubs in the city: HJ's in Chapel St, South Yarra, the Red Eagle in Albert Park or the Flower in Port Melbourne. The city has a large student population, and it is easy to meet people on the University of Melbourne campus in Carlton; in particular, try Milligan's café on the ground floor of the Union building, or the nearby Albion Arms on Lygon St.

Getting Around

ARRIVAL AND DEPARTURE

Air. Melbourne's main airport is Tullamarine, 20km northwest of the city centre and the only airport in Australia to be open 24 hours a day. The international and domestic terminals are adjacent, making transfers easy. The airport coach into Melbourne is the *Skybus* (tel: 663 1400) which runs every half-hour (from 6.30am to 11.30pm) to the depot at 58 Franklin Street in the north of the city centre. The one-way fare is $6. If you have time to spare, you can travel between the airport and the city by public transport for $2.10; this involves taking the bus to the suburb of Essendon (which also has an airport) where you change to a train or tram. There are also privately-run airport buses from Tullamarine to various suburbs of Melbourne including Dandenong (tel: 791 2848), Frankston (tel: 781 3325) and Knoxton (tel: 793 3325); and to the town of Ballarat (tel: 053-31 2655). If you land at a quiet time for arrivals (particularly in the evenings), you may find that the supply of taxis far outweighs demand. A driver may offer to take you into town at a cut-price rate (which should be no more per person than the normal airport bus fare). At other times the fare is about $20.

Melbourne's second airport is at Essendon, between the city and Tullamarine. Its airport code is MEB, distinguishing it from the international airport (MEL). The only services from Essendon are local flights to other Victorian towns and to Tasmania on Staywood Airlines, Flinders Island Airways, Airlines of Tasmania and others. There are also flights to Tasmania from the airport at Moorabbin (southeast of Melbourne) and from Cowes on Phillip Island.

Melbourne does not have quite the range of cheap fares abroad that Sydney has, but there are still many bargains to be found using Garuda Indonesia, Lufthansa or the Yugoslav airline JAT to Europe, or United and Air New Zealand to the USA. The main STA office is at 220 Faraday St, Carlton (347 6911); there are seven other branches dotted around. The Melbourne Flight Centre (no relation to the Sydney Flight Centre) is at 317 Swanston St (200 metres from Museum Station; 663 1304) and the associated Flight Shop is nearby at 287 Elizabeth St (67 5565). REHO Travel has an office at 21 Toorak Road, South Yarra (267 7822), and another at 563 Nicholson St in Carlton (387 0544).

Passengers flying from Melbourne on Qantas can check in at the Hyatt Hotel on Collins St between two and 12 hours before their flight; this facility is available 8am-5pm daily, and saves you lugging your bags out to the airport.

Coach. All country and interstate coachlines have terminals in the city centre, with easy access to trams, buses and taxis. The major companies are:
  Ansett Pioneer: 465 Swanston St (662 2422)
  Bus Australia: 122 Flinders St (653 5311)
  Deluxe: 422 Elizabeth St (663 6144)
  Dysons: 134 Flinders Street (467 6111)
  Executive Express: 14 Spencer St (614 5255)
  Greyhound: corner of Franklin and Swanston Streets (668 2566)
  Dysons is the main operator for country services within Victoria. Almost all inter-city bus services to or from Melbourne offer free connecting bus links to some of the city's suburbs.

Competition is fiercest between Melbourne and Sydney, and fares are only $30-$40. The trip to Sydney takes about 12 hours. The fastest land link between Melbourne and Adelaide is Greyhound's *Statesman* service, which takes $9\frac{1}{4}$ hours and costs $55. This includes a half-hour stop for a meal at their expense. Fares to Adelaide on other services start at $38.

Train. The Victorian State Railway network V-Line operates daily rail services to Sydney and Adelaide plus routes to many Victorian country towns and cities. Country and interstate trains use Spencer Street railway station, at the west of the city centre. For rail information call 619 1500, or 008-13 6109 from outside Melbourne for the cost of a local call.

The overnight *Sydney Express* departs daily from Spencer Street at 8pm. (The corresponding train from Sydney is the *Melbourne Express,* which departs at the same time.) It is normally for both first and second class passengers (although there are sleeping berths only for first class), but at busy times a relief service leaves at 9.35pm (8.30pm from Sydney) and the *Sydney Express* is then restricted to first class. Tickets for the 13-hour trip cost $67 for economy, $94 for first class and $129 for a private sleeping cabin. There is a bargain standby fare of $30 on the corresponding daytime service, the *Intercapital Daylight Express*. The service leaves Melbourne at 8.40am every day except Sunday, arriving at 9.50pm.

The *Overland* bound for Adelaide costs $53 for economy or $30 standby. Departures are at 8.35pm daily, and the journey takes 12 hours. Fares are the same on the daytime *Daylink* service which leaves Spencer St each morning at 7.55am: you take the train as far as Dimboola, then change to a connecting bus service. In the reverse direction, you leave Keswick rail station in Adelaide at 7.15am, arriving in Melbourne at 6.38pm.

The fastest surface link to Canberra is the daily *Canberra Link,* involving a train from Melbourne to Wodonga and a bus connection from there to Canberra. The journey time is just over eight hours and the one-way fare $39.

V-Line produces a booklet of *Day Away Tours* by train from Melbourne, ranging from a Rutherglen Winery Cycleabout Weekend ($179 including bicycle hire, meals and accommodation) to a $26.50 day trip across the New South Wales border to "Albury and the Pokies" (the Pokies are not a geographical area, but fruit machines which are outlawed in Victoria). For longer trips, you could buy the Victoria Pass, which costs $99 for 14 days' unlimited travel throughout the state in first class.

Ferry. Station Pier in Port Melbourne (4km southwest of the city centre) is the terminal for the *Abel Tasman,* a three-times-weekly ferry to Devonport, Tasmania. See *Tasmania: Arrival and Departure* for times and fares. There are also frequent services to Phillip and French Islands.

Driving. The roads of Victoria are more crowded than those of other states. The overall maximum speed limit is 110km/h, reduced on some highways to 100km/h and with the usual 60km/h limit in towns. The maximum allowable blood/alcohol level is .05%, and there are many random breath test stations. Those who are caught are fined heavily and banned from driving for usually not less than two years.

Tolls are charged on some stretches of freeway around Melbourne, typically costing 40¢ for 20km. The most popular and shortest route from Sydney to Melbourne is via the Hume Highway (number 31). However, if you have some time to spare, the Princes Highway (number 1) will take you along the southern New South Wales coast and through some interesting beachside towns. There are a few highways you can take from Adelaide to Melbourne: the most direct is the Western Highway (number 8), but the Princes Highway is more picturesque.

The state motoring organization is the Royal Automobile Club of Victoria (RACV), whose head office is at the corner of Bourke and Queen Streets. Call 540 2211 for their emergency road service. The RACV publishes a good road map of the state which is sold to members of foreign motoring organizations for 40¢. The Victorian Tourist Commission produces a useful brochure called *Your Motoring Holiday Planner,* available from Victour offices and many travel agents.

Hitch-hiking. Melbourne's sprawling suburbs make hitching difficult, but fortunately good hitching spots on the main routes to Sydney and Adelaide are fairly easy to reach. For the Hume Highway north to Canberra and Sydney, take a train on the Broadmeadows line to Craigieburn and walk a few hundred metres north to the junction with Craigieburn Road. To hitch northwest to Ballarat and Adelaide, get the Melton line train to Deer Park and walk northwest to the start of the Western Freeway.

CITY TRANSPORT

City Layout. Metropolitan Melbourne covers an area spanning 80km from east to west and 100km from north to south, making it larger by half than greater New York and three times the size of greater London. The central business district lies alongside the Yarra River, which forms one of its boundaries. The other boundaries are Spencer, Victoria and Spring Streets. Within this area the roads form a grid pattern, making navigation fairly straightforward. If you're trying to find an address within the central area, remember that the low numbers are at the southern ends of north-south streets, and at the eastern ends of east-west streets. A possible source of confusion with main east-west streets is that most have another street a block north prefixed "Little", e.g. Little Bourke St runs a block north of Bourke St.

The *Melbourne Tourist Map* (free from tourist offices) is adequate for short stays, but if you intend to stay awhile you should invest $20 in the *Melway Street Directory*. About the size of a telephone book, the *Melway* is an essential part of living in Melbourne: locations given on advertisements often quote the map reference for the directory. As well as street maps of the whole area, it lists almost everything you could possibly want to locate, from bicycle tracks, bus and tram depots, cinemas, libraries and markets to squash courts, swimming pools, parks and gardens, tennis courts and skating rinks. The *Melway* also includes detailed information on train and tram travel, with helpful diagrams of the various types of tickets available, and even has a double page map of the Victorian Arts Centre complex.

Public Transport. Melbourne's transport system is both cheap and efficient. The best complement to the *Melway* guide is the excellent *Get around on The Met* public transport map, price $2. It is a comprehensive guide to the tram, bus and rail services which are known collectively as "The Met". Before embarking on the Met, buy the map from any railway station or the Met information kiosk in Royal Arcade (off Bourke St Mall). For information by telephone call 617 0900.

Once you have mastered the basics of the zonal pricing system, it is easy to calculate how much your journey will cost. The "Inner Neighbourhood" covers the city centre and a large area around it. There are nine other zones outside, each of them fairly big. Tickets are fully interchangeable from one mode of transport to another. A basic "Inner Neighbourhood" ticket ($1.30) allows two hours travel within the central area. The "Inner Plus One Neighbourhood" ticket ($2.20) permits two hours travel in the central area and one of the nearby suburbs; this is the ticket you need to get to Tullamarine Airport from the city centre by public transport. For $2.40 you can buy an "Inner Neighbourhood Travelcard" which gives unlimited travel on trains, trams and buses for a full day within the "Inner Neighbourhood" area; an "Inner Plus One Travelcard" is $4.20; and a day's travel anywhere on the network costs $5.

For short journeys within the city centre you pay 75¢, or you can buy the ten-trip "City Saver" ticket for $5.30 (a saving of 30%).

Trams. The best way to get around the city and inner suburbs is on Melbourne's efficient tram system, which has 700 trams on 325 kilometres of track. *How to track it down by tram on The Met* is a free guide to the system, available at railway stations and tourist offices. If you don't already have a ticket when getting on a tram you should buy one from the conductor on board. On the older trams, he or she will approach you; on new ones you must enter at the front and pay the ticket collector. On Sundays some trams are replaced by bus services.

The "Tourist Tram" charges $2 for a short tour around the city centre. This is poor value compared to an "Inner Neighbourhood" ticket costing $1.30 which permits you to take as many regular trams as you wish within two hours.

Suburban Trains. Areas beyond the reach of the tram system are served by electric trains; call 619 8888 for information. The city-centre part of this network forms an underground railway around the centre, known as the "City Loop". The stations on the Loop are Spencer Street, Parliament, Museum, Flagstaff and Flinders Street, the latter being the main station for the suburban network. All suburban lines converge on the city loop, which means you can get out to any destination from one of these stations. Frequent trains run from Monday to Friday, but at weekends some services are reduced to one an hour. Timetables and tickets are available at the usual Met outlets.

Bus. Many Melbourne bus services are privately owned, but all operate within the Met system, charging standard fares and accepting Met transfer tickets. There are very few routes in the central area; most run in the inner and outer suburbs, connecting with tram and train services.

The double decker "City Explorer" bus operates every day except Monday from 10am to 4pm, departing on the hour from Flinders Street Station. Tickets cost $8 for adults, $4 for children, $6 for pensioners and $18 for a family of four, and you can board and reboard as often as you like in a single day.

Taxis. Partly because of the tough drink-driving laws, taxis can be in short supply after the pubs close. At other times you should have little trouble hailing one in the street or picking up a cab at one of the many ranks in the city suburbs. To summon a taxi by telephone (for an extra fee of 30¢), call one of the following companies:

Arrow — 417 1111	Embassy — 320 0320
Astoria — 347 5511	Regal Combined — 810 0222
Black Cabs — 567 3333	Silver Top — 345 3455

On top of the standing charge of $1.10 there is a 10¢ supplement for up to two items of luggage or 20¢ for three or more. The lower tariff of 55¢ per km applies from 6am to 9pm Monday-Friday and on Saturdays from 6am to 1pm. At other times you pay 68¢ per km.

Car. The most confusing thing about driving in Melbourne is the peculiar form of turning right at city-centre junctions which are crossed by a tram line. Drivers intending to turn right indicate so, then pull into the *left* lane, go across the lights and come to a halt in front of the cars waiting to go straight ahead. When the lights change they make their turn. These "hook turns" are something of an acquired skill, so try to watch the natives in action before attempting the manoeuvre.

Trams must always be passed on the inside, never on the outside. Also, you must never pass a stationary tram unless directed by a tram driver, conductor or policeman. Passengers getting on or off have the right of way until they are safely on the footpath.

Parking anywhere in the centre during business hours is difficult, and illegal parking earns a $25 fine. The City Parking Information service based at the Town Hall (tel: 658 9800) can offer advice, but they will usually recommend that you leave your vehicle on the city fringes. Their free *City Parker's Guide* shows all off-street car parks in the city centre. On-street parking in the evenings is fairly easy, but you should by law leave a gap of 1.2 metres between your vehicle and the next.

Outside the city, the grid system for roads disappears, so a good map is recommended. Suburban Melbourne is covered by a huge network of arterial roads and an efficient freeway system, except during peak hours when holdups are commonplace.

There are numerous car hire outfits and rates are highly competitive. Worth a try are Half-Price (267 2177), Rent a Bomb (429 4033), Ugly Duckling (534 8078) and Dam Cheap Hire (428 3487).

Pedicabs and Horse Power. A novel addition to the streets of Melbourne is the pedicab, a three-wheel pedal-powered vehicle fitted with stereo loudspeakers. They are licensed to carry the driver plus two passengers and depart from outside the Arts Centre on St Kilda Road and from the corner of Bourke and Swanston Streets. Short hops cost $4, or you can hire the cab for 30 minutes ($12.50) or an hour ($20). For more information call 890 2991. On the opposite corner of Bourke and Swanston Streets, Cobb & Co (tel: 338 7050) offer 15-minute horse-drawn rides for $3.

Cycling. With its boulevards, parks and gardens, and the absence of steep gradients, Melbourne is a good city to cycle around. Furthermore Victoria has a positive attitude to cycling, and there are over 100km of cycle tracks around the capital. The State Bicycle Committee produces a guide called *Melbourne's Bikepath Book* which is available at most bike shops, or by post from the Committee at PO Box 4910, Melbourne 3001 (tel: 619 6686). It has detailed maps of the tracks and surrounding areas, and covers such topics as train crossings and other danger areas, track surfaces and places of interest slightly off the track. The most central and popular bikepath is the Yarra Path. Starting beneath the Victorian Arts Centre, it follows the Yarra River along parkland, past the Botanical Gardens, on through the wealthy suburb of Toorak, finishing at Hawthorn. You can take your bicycle on off-peak suburban trains by buying a ticket for it, or get a *Bikepass* for unlimited trips.

To cope with the difficulty of turning right in city-centre traffic, most cyclists practise the box turn (like the hook turn described in *Car* above), where you cross in the left-hand lane to the corner of the street, wait for the lights to change and go across with the flow of traffic. Because of the high number of accidents involving bikes, helmets for cyclists are likely soon to be made compulsory in Victoria.

You can rent a bike from several outlets in the city. In particular, Hire a Bicycle (288 5177) operates in several locations: during school holidays and at weekends, their trailer is parked on Jeffreys Parade immediately southeast of

Princes Bridge. Rates range from $3 per hour to $15 for a full day (double for tandems). A $5 deposit is required. The Melbourne Bicycle Centres at 179 High St, Prahran (tel: 529 3752) and 37 Queens Parade, Clifton Hill (tel: 489 5569) will hire you a secondhand bike for $10 per day; if you subsequently decide to buy, the rental paid is deducted from the cost.

Ferry. The MV *John Batman* sails between the World Trade Centre and Williamstown via St Kilda on Sundays and public holidays; call 397 225 for details.

Hostels. The YHA of Victoria is based at 205 King St (670 7991). Of the 21 hostels in the state, two are in North Melbourne. Although some way from the city centre, they are close to interesting areas for eating, drinking and socializing, and like other Youth Hostels are excellent places to exchange information. One is at 76 Chapman St (328 3595), which has 100 dormitory beds and costs $10 per night, while the other Melbourne Youth Hostel is 200 m around the corner at 500 Abbotsford St (328 2880), and has 42 beds costing $9.50 per person per night. To reach them, take tram 50, 54 or 57 north along Elizabeth St and Flemington Road, and get off at stop 19 (Abbotsford St); on Sundays, buses 450 and 457 substitute for the trams. If you are travelling in from the airport, ask the Skybus driver to drop you off at Abbotsford St.

The YWCA hostel and headquarters is in the city centre at 489 Elizabeth Street (329 5188), close to the Skybus, Ansett and Greyhound terminals. Rates are $15 for a single, decreasing to $7.50 per person for four people sharing. Weekly rates are about five times the corresponding daily rate. There is another YWCA hostel, Doery House, at 353 Church Street, Richmond (428 6349) and another at 58 Springvale Road, Nunawading, about 25km from the city (not an ideal location).

The Backpackers City Inn and Carlton Hotel is one and the same establishment: it is located at 197 Bourke Street near the junction with Russell St, right in the city centre (650 4379). The nightly rate is $9, but as there are only 28 dormitory beds it fills up quickly. The Melbourne Travellers Inn & Backpackers Centre at 2 Enfield St, St Kilda (534 8159) charges between $9 and $22. Call the same number for bookings at the Backpackers Centre at 28 Grey St, which charges the same rates. Both can be reached by tram 15 or 16 from Swanston St to stop 29 on Fitzroy St, or by train to St Kilda; there is also a courtesy pick-up service from bus, train and Skybus terminals.

Hotels and Motels. Avoid the motels and private hotels opposite Spencer Street station unless you're completely stuck. Whilst these places are cheap they are also home to a weird selection of local transients. The motels and private hotels of St Kilda, the closest Melbourne has to a red light district, aren't a great deal better, but the better quality motels in the area (e.g. the Diplomat at 12 Acland Street; 534 0422) are clean and safe enough. Cheap private hotels include the Hollywood at 348 Beaconsfield Parade (534 3402; $18 for a double including breakfast) and the Hampton House at 24 Grey St (534 5283; $12 for a single). Many decades ago, St Kilda was the seaside holiday destination for Melbourne's wealthy. It still has the grand old homes and hotels, wide streets and other once beautiful buildings, though now they are a little the worse for wear. However, its central location and newly restored beach make it a good place to stay if you don't mind rubbing shoulders with the occasional prostitute.

Student Residences. The University of Melbourne has several colleges which are open to visitors during student vacations. Although more expensive than the cheapest hostels, the University is very well situated north of the city centre and the quality of accommodation and breakfast is good. Rates are around $28 for bed and breakfast (students may get a reduction) or $38 for full board, although this option is unimaginative considering the range of inexpensive food nearby. Try Ormond College (347 2014 or 347 4784), Queens College (347 4837) or St Hilda's College (347 2258 or 347 1171).

Longer Term Accommodation. There are plenty of apartments to choose from in Melbourne, but they can be expensive. The notice boards at the Union building in the University always have advertisements for flat-sharers, and the *Age* has a good selection on Saturdays and Wednesdays. If there are several of you together you might prefer to try for an apartment in the suburb of St Kilda (see above), such as Ace Serviced Apartments at 35 Nicholson Street (266 8016) where the daily tariff is $45, reducing to $37 per night on a weekly basis; or Aston Apartments, 42 Powell Street (266 2953) which charges $60 daily, $47 per night on a weekly basis.

Camping. There are no sites close to the city centre. The Half Moon site (tel: 314 5148), at the corner of Geelong Road (Princes Highway) and Millers Road in North Altona, is about 10km west of the city and on the Met network (bus 411, 412 and 414 from West Footscray station). The Melbourne Caravan Park/Motel also takes tents, and is 10km north in Coburg at 265 Elizabeth St (tel: 354 3533), reached by train from the city centre.

The Camping Association of Victoria (589 Malvern Road, Toorak, Victoria 3142; tel: 240 0832) publishes a list of over 300 campsites in Victoria and Tasmania, called *Where To*. The Association also offers a free booking service.

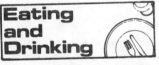

Eating and Drinking

In terms of value and variety, Melbourne is arguably the best city in the world for eating out. Melbourne has over 2,000 restaurants, four-fifths of them BYO. The *Yellow Pages* devotes 31 pages to restaurants. Such is the quality, range and cheapness of most, that you can indulge yourself in some excellent eating. Dining out is one of the most popular forms of entertainment for Melburnians, and is taken very seriously.

To assist with your choice of restaurant, the Melbourne *Age* produces an annual called *Cheap Eats in Melbourne* ($8.95) which is a bible for budget gastronomes. It covers the Melbourne metropolitan area, country, hills and Yarra Valley areas. Other sources include the free newspaper *After Dark* which features numerous restaurants, and the free Restaurant Advisory Service on 328 4442 or 328 3800 (although this service is sponsored by certain restaurants and is not, therefore, altogether objective). The following selection is just the tip of the iceberg, but all are strongly recommended as providing good value.

One of the best places for breakfast is Mittons (10 Murphy Street, South Yarra, just around the corner from Toorak Road). Mittons is very popular on Sunday mornings (it opens at 7am) and is famous for its home-cooked eggs benedict, brains and kidneys, at reasonable prices, with newspapers provided.

Melbourne's Chinatown is at the Spring Street end of the city and extends three blocks into the city. The area has many Asian cuisines besides the basic Chinese varieties of Cantonese, Szechuan and Mandarin. The cheapest tend to be the Malaysian restaurants, for example Little Elephant (at 11-12 Liverpool Street, just off Little Bourke Street) which offers cheap Malaysian meals in bright, clean surroundings. The curry laksa ($4 for a huge bowl) is great value and a meal in itself, but you have to like your food hot. Little Malaysia (662 1678), on the corner of Little Bourke Street and Liverpool Street, is slightly more expensive but serves good food and is still cheap if you stick to the many dishes that don't contain crab, prawns or lobster. Unless you book, be prepared to wait for a while during peak times; Sunday nights are particularly busy. "Little Saigon" is the Vietnamese quarter on Victoria St in North Richmond. Most of the places are cheap and basic with formica-topped tables, but serve excellent Vietnamese food for next to nothing. There is also a Vietnamese community, and hence restaurants, in the suburb of Footscray.

There are several good Thai restaurants which cost about $20 for a filling meal; try Ruan Thai, 91 Johnston St, Collingwood (419 4814) or Thai 505 at 505 Chapel St, South Yarra (241 8682), both of which are BYO; Sawasdee is more central at 139 Little Bourke St (663 4052), but is licensed and hence a little more expensive.

Most University of Melbourne students eat at the cafés and restaurants on Lygon St, though the canteen on the ground floor of the Union building (which outsiders are welcome to use) has filling daily specials for about $3. Lygon St probably has more pizza restaurants per kilometre than any street in Italy, and the smell of garlic and baking dough assails your nostrils as you walk along it. Signs in café windows say "never mind if you don't speak Italian — we speak a good broken English". You can buy pizza by the metre from Da Salvatore at number 132. Toto's at 101 claims to be the first pizzeria in Australia, and its speciality is the "Aussie" consisting of cheese, tomato, bacon and egg. Toto's also does a "spaghetti" ice cream, a brilliant creation which looks like spaghetti bolognese; piped banana ice cream is topped with strawberry sauce and grated white chocolate. At 141 Lygon St is Casa di Lorio (347 2670), which is notable for the large proportion of Italian diners. And Ilios, at number 174, is an exceptional Greek restaurant.

Dial-a-Dino's Pizza has eight branches in Melbourne; check the *Yellow Pages*. For the very best pizzas, however, *Cheap Eats* recommends the takeaway-only Pizza Nova (111 Hoddle St, Richmond; 417 2791) and La Porchetta at 392 Rathdowne St, Carlton North (347 8906).

The up-and-coming area to eat is Fitzroy, notably the restaurants and cafés on Brunswick and Rathdowne Street (see below). Along nearby Gertrude St there are some interesting Yugoslav places, including the Jugoslavija (BYO) at 193 Gertrude St (417 4278) which has excellent *burek;* meat, cheeses and fruit wrapped in pastry.

One restaurant with a difference is the Old Vic BYO Theatre Restaurant at 1213 Glenhuntley Road (572 2033) which has a cabaret for you to eat by. The most unusual restaurant, however, is the Colonial Tramcar. Every evening except Mondays, this mobile tramcar-cum-restaurant makes a circuit of the city serving the diners on board with a five-course meal and excellent wines. The price (including drinks) is around $60, and you should make advance reservations through the office at 254 Bay St, Brighton (596 6500).

Cafés. Many people finish their meal by adjourning to one of Melbourne's excellent cafés for coffee and cakes. If you have eaten at one of the Fitzroy restaurants, a good place to finish up is at Mario's at 303 Brunswick St; this is also a fully-fledged restaurant with an all-day breakfast. There are several other good places on Brunswick St between Johnston St and Alexander Parade. They include 29 varieties of "the best ice-creams in the world" at Charmaine's boutique gelateria at 370 Brunswick St.

Cake-fetishists should head for Acland Street in St Kilda, which is lined with cake shops, most of which open daily.

DRINKING

Melbourne's licensing hours have recently been liberalized, and with a little application it is possible to drink around the clock. Pub hours are usually 10am-midnight except Sundays (noon-8pm), but some clubs and discos remain open until 7am daily, around the time when the market pubs open; for example the Central Club Hotel at the junction of Victoria and Queen Streets opposite the Queen Victoria market is open 6am-6pm. Apparently to reduce the level of drunkenness, it is illegal to drink at the bar of pubs after 10pm; you have to sit at a table. Most Melburnian males drink the local brew VB (Victoria Bitter). You can go on a tour to see how it is made at the new Carlton United brewery at Abbotsford (near Richmond), by calling 342 5511. Other local beers worth trying include Abbotsford Invalid Stout (5.9% alcohol, dark and sweet) and Old Ballarat Bitter (made by the Sovereign Brewery in Ballarat) which comes in at 4.9% but has far more taste and character than most bottled beers. For Bendigo lager, you need to go to the Rifle Brigade brewery-pub in Bendigo.

The range of pubs in Melbourne is nearly as diverse as the range of restaurants. Many have courtyards which are perfect for whiling away the hours on a sunny afternoon with a few glasses of wine. Others provide live rock or jazz music.

The answer to the old pub song "Does anyone know of a better old place — than Bourke St on a Saturday night?" is yes. Indisputably the best range of beers can be found at the Loaded Dog at 324 St Georges Road, North Fitzroy (489 8222). This is a roomy and friendly pub-brewery, making five different beers and selling around a hundred others. The name of the pub comes from a Henry Lawson short story, set in the mining days in Victoria. It concerns a retriever named Tommy who finds a stick of gunpowder, a yellow mongrel which steals it from him and a pub which subsequently explodes (together with the mongrel); the full story is related on the pub's menu and on the wall of the dining room, and there is a large sculpture of a beer-swilling dog. Beers available include Yellow Mongrel (light, cloudy and similar in taste to home-brewed beers), Cobrungra Bitter (golden, well-hopped), Ruby Bitter (like a stout) and Thunder Ale (9% alcohol, the same as light wines). The Loaded Dog also has imported beers, ranging from Samuel Adams' Boston Lager to Tennant's Milk Stout from Scotland. The menu (snacks, steaks, seafood) includes recommendations for suitable beer accompaniments; there is also a good wine list and live music every night, sometimes performed by string quartets rather than loud electric bands.

The Old Homestead Inn on Queen's Parade has a wide range of out-of-state and overseas beers but no real ales. It offers free games such as backgammon, darts and Trivial Pursuit for a returnable deposit of $5. The Flower in Bay Street, Port Melbourne is the current trendy place to spend a Sunday afternoon drinking and listening to a rock band. Its frontage is a complete glass wall which slides up to open out onto the street. The Red Edge in Albert Park is another trendy place to go during the evenings. The cosy Alexandra in Powell Street, South Yarra has a lovely courtyard where you can dine on good food. In winter, various roasts are served for Sunday lunch. The Lemon Tree at 10 Grattan Street, Carlton is a popular pub which specializes in Saturday afternoon "sessions" and which has an upstairs area whose roof is folded back in good weather so you can dine and drink in the sunshine. There is a shortage of pleasant, rather than merely functional, pubs in the city centre; one of the best is the Mitre on Bank Place off Collins St.

For civilized and not too expensive late-night drinking in the city centre, go to Mietta's on Alfred Place (a side street off the top end of Collins St). The main feature is a fancy restaurant upstairs, but there is also a lounge bar round to the right of the ground floor. Don't be put off by the rather grand facade and formality (they insist upon seating you, and serving you at your table). You can drink relatively cheaply (e.g. $3 for a bottle of beer) until 2 or 3am (midnight on Sundays) and study the fascinating clientele; sophisticates, illicit lovers and the solitary and sorrowful drinkers.

Victoria is not the greatest wine-producing state in Australia, but there are good local reds including some splendidly full-bodied Cabernet Sauvignons. The area around Rutherglen, in Northern Victoria near the Murray River, produces fine fortified wines such as Muscat, Tokay and vintage port. When buying wine to take to a BYO restaurant, you might want to try Dan Murphy's Cellar at 280 Chapel St in Prahran (51 1784) which reputedly has eight million bottles of wine and is the largest liquor store in Australia. Melbourne's few wine bars provide a pleasant alternative to pubs and restaurants. Try Churchers at 364 Church Street, Richmond and the Alphington House wine bar at 2 Grattan Street, Carlton. One cocktail you might wish to avoid is the Keating Sour named after the Australian Treasurer Paul Keating and served at the Last Aussie Fishcaf (256 Park St, South Melbourne; 699 1942). It consists of a glass of water with a twist of lemon. On the other hand, the fresh fish served here is highly recommended.

Entertainment

For a city of three million people, Melbourne has surprisingly few "sights", but in compensation there is a lively arts scene and splendid sport. Details of forthcoming cultural events can be found in the *EG* (entertainment guide) section of Friday's *Age*, while the monthly *What's On* magazine covers everything from Science Fiction Club meetings to riverside walks; it is published as part of the "Life — Be in it" campaign and costs $2 at newsstands or from PO Box 496, South Yarra, Victoria 3141.

For an overview of the city, the tallest building at present is Collins Tower, an office block at 33-45 Collins St. You're not officially supposed to go to the top, but some adventurous types have enjoyed the view before being turfed out by security guards. You can take a "lookout tour" of the AMP building at 535 Bourke St at 1.40pm, Monday-Friday; ask at the ground floor security desk. Melbourne is trying to outdo other Australian cities with the tallest building in the world, the proposed 150-storey South Pacific Centre, but the project is still firmly on the drawing board.

It should not take you too long to see the major points of interest in Melbourne. Edward "Ned" Kelly was hanged in Melbourne Gaol, aged 25, on 11 November, 1880. The last relics of his body were stolen from there in 1978.

The Gaol, at the top end of Russell St, is open daily (10am-5pm) but consists mainly of refurbished cells containing rather grisly death masks (plaster casts of heads) of former inmates. Admission costs $3.50. The Shrine of Remembrance on the King's Domain on St Kilda Road is a spectacular memorial to the Anzac troops who died during the two World Wars. It was constructed so that at the 11th hour of November 11th (Armistice Hour) a shaft of sunlight strikes the Remembrance Stone.

Captain Cook's Cottage, in Fitzroy Gardens on the eastern edge of the city centre, was the English childhood home of Australia's discoverer. It was dismantled in Great Ayton, Yorkshire and rebuilt in Australia in 1934. The cottage opens 10am-5pm daily, admission $1. In the centre of the gardens is a model Tudor village, presented to the people of Melbourne after World War II by Londoners in gratitude for food supplied to them. Also look out for the People's Art Path, a circular pathway made from over one thousand individually designed titles, and the fairies' tree carved for the children of Melbourne by Ola Cohn between 1931 and 1934.

"Fantastic Entertainment in Public Places" (FEIPP) is the city council's catchphrase for free entertainment. Venues include the City Square, the Sidney Myer Music Bowl and various parks and gardens. Events cover a wide range of music and street theatre. Programmes are available from the Town Hall or by calling 63 9283.

Festivals. Melbourne's rich ethnic mix means there are plenty of festivals during the year. The Lygon Street Fiesta is a weekend in early summer when the street is closed to traffic and becomes a mall. You can enjoy live entertainment, food from the many (mostly Italian) restaurants and street stalls, browse through craft displays and even take part in a spaghetti eating contest. Chapel St in South Yarra has a similar festival in early February each year.

Moomba is an annual festival running for ten days in late February/early March, with many activities in which most of Melbourne gets involved. Moomba is an Aboriginal word meaning roughly "let's get together and have fun". The beginning of Moomba is marked by a fireworks display which is visible all over Melbourne and is one of the best in the world. One very good unpublicized vantage point for the viewing of the fireworks is the 35th floor of the Regent Hotel; this floor is devoted to restaurants and a lounge area, and the best view is attainable from the large picture windows in the toilets, where you are high enough to be actually next to the exploding

THE BEST VIEW OF THE FIREWORKS IS FROM THE TOILETS ON THE 35TH FLOOR."

fireworks. Another highlight is the Moomba Masters Water Ski Championships on the Yarra River in the city, contested by the world's top water-skiers and well worth seeing. Other attractions include theatre and dance, exhibitions of art, photography, pottery, ceramics, and events like the Walk on Water Contest, for which young Melburnians invent some ingenious contraptions.

For the duration of the festival an amusement park takes over Alexandra Gardens. The focal point of the festivities is the Moomba Parade when many local organizations construct floats which participate in the procession down Swanston St. Despite the tacky aspects of this event (such as floats carrying bikini-clad aspirants to the crown of Queen of Moomba and, increasingly, many commercially sponsored floats), it is all part of the fun. The festival closes with another fireworks display.

For those interested in higher-brow culture, a less commercialized yet thoroughly enjoyable festival is Spoleto, held in the last three weeks of September. It is the third leg of the festival of the same name which takes place in Italy and the USA. Peformers from these festivals are joined by other artists from Australasia, Japan and Europe. There is a lively fringe and good writers' workshops. For enquiries in advance call 417 7872; during the festival itself there is a recorded information line on 650 9420.

Victorian Arts Centre. Compared with the setting of Sydney's Opera House, Melbourne's cultural centre has a second-rate site on the western side of St Kilda Road, just south of the Yarra River. Nonetheless the Victorian Arts Centre is a striking piece of architecture (particularly at night when its graceful 115m spire is illuminated), and its galleries and auditoria have sumptuous interiors. Performances are staged in the Concert Hall (2,600 seats), the State Theatre (2,000), the Playhouse (880) and the Studio (420). In addition there are often free foyer performances. You can take a guided tour from the tour desk on level 6 between 10.30am and 4pm daily, price $2.75.

A recorded message with details of exhibitions, concerts and plays can be heard by dialling 1 1681; dial 1 1566 for specific enquiries. Tickets for all events can be booked through BASS on 1 1500 (008-13 6036 from outside Melbourne for the price of a local call). Prices range from $10 to over $42, but concessions for students are usually available.

Museums and Galleries. Melbourne's major gallery is the National Gallery of Victoria, at 180 St Kilda Road (tel: 628 0222), adjacent to the Arts Centre. The gallery houses 75,000 items, including some excellent Aboriginal and early settlers' art, and is described as "Australia's richest and largest art resource". It opens daily except Monday from 10am to 5pm. Admission costs $1.20 (students 55¢) and this entitles you to a free guided tour (hourly Tuesday-Friday from 10.30am to 2.30pm, at weekends 2pm and 2.30pm).

Other galleries worth a visit include Ebes-Douwma (at the top of Bourke St) for antique prints and maps, and Heide Park and Gallery, home of several significant works of Australian art. The Performing Arts Museum (at the rear of the Melbourne Concert Hall at 100 St Kilda Rd; tel: 617 8211) is one of the most unusual museums in Australia. It has exhibitions featuring a wide range of arts and artists from Dame Nellie Melba to Dame Edna Everage. They are presented in theatre form, making it an easy museum to enjoy. Entrance is normally $2.20 but is higher for some exhibitions. It opens at 11am, Monday-Friday, noon at weekends and closes daily at 5pm.

The Museum of Victoria (tel: 669 9888) houses the Science Museum and

Children's Museum. The main entrance is at 328 Swanston Street (near the corner of La Trobe Street) and it opens 10am-5pm daily. The Museum has hi-tech features such as interactive video discs as well as ancient Aboriginal exhibits and numerous special exhibitions. The Australian Gallery of Sport is located at the Melbourne Cricket Ground (MCG) in Jolimont Terrace, Jolimont, and covers the whole range of sport in addition to cricket. It opens 10am-4pm Wednesday to Sunday, admission $3.

Theatre. Apart from the theatres at the Art Centre, Melbourne has a number of others offering a diverse range of entertainment. The major theatres are Her Majesty's at 219 Exhibition St, the Comedy Theatre at 240 Exhibition St, the Princess Theatre at 163 Spring St and the Athenaeum Theatre at 188 Collins St. Fringe theatres include the St Martin's in St Martin's Lane, South Yarra and the Union Theatre on the University campus (where Dame Edna began her career in the revue *Return Fare* in the mid 1950s). A listing of independent theatre productions appears in the *Live Theatre Directory* each day in the *Age*. For information on which theatres are offering cheap standby seats, dial 663 1171.

Opera. The Victoria State Opera season at the State Theatre runs through July and August plus November and December. Ticket prices start at $22 ($17 for students) but cheap student standbys at $14 are sometimes available on the day of performance.

Cinema. Melbourne has the usual chain cinemas such as Hoyts at 140 Bourke St (663 3303) and Greater Union at 131 Russell St (654 8133), but also has a lively independent circuit. These cinemas have their own listing in the *Age*. In particular, the Valhalla Cinema at 216 Victoria St in Richmond (428 6874) and the Trak at 445 Toorak Road in Toorak (241 9333) have good repertoires, and the Carlton Moviehouse at 235 Faraday St near the University campus (347 8909) specializes in late-night or all-night shows.

Music. Melbourne is always on the itinerary of visiting rock performers and most big concerts are held at the Sports and Entertainment Centre on the banks of the Yarra; others take place at the Festival Hall at 80 Collins St (654 5655). Concerts in summer are often held outdoor at the Sidney Myer Music Bowl in Alexandra Gardens, Olympic Park and Kooyong Stadium. In addition the Youth Affairs office of the Department of Labour sponsors some free outdoor concerts (no alcohol allowed). For rock music on a smaller scale go to one of the many pubs around Melbourne which feature live bands. The Albion Hotel at the corner of Lygon and Faraday Streets has free rock music every night to 1am (11pm on Sundays) and is popular among students. The Palace on Lower Esplanade in St Kilda (534 0655) is also a popular venue, as is The Venue over the road.

For a selective recorded gig guide to Melbourne dial the 3XY Gig Guide on 1 1688; more comprehensive listings can be found in the entertainment guide free with the *Age* on Fridays, or in the excellent music weekly *Beat* free from clubs, pubs and restaurants. The Melbourne-based rock magazine *Juke* is also a good source.

Jazz can be heard at the Tankerville Arms at 230 Nicholson St in Fitzroy, the Bridge Hotel at 1 Nepean Highway in Mordialloc and the Roxy at 172 York St, South Melbourne. The Melbourne Folk Club meets on the second and fourth Tuesday of every month at the Robert Burns Hotel, at the corner of Smith and

Easey Streets in the suburb of Collingwood; call 383 2706 for details.

The Melbourne Concert Hall is the home of the respected Melbourne Symphony Orchestra. A Summer Music Festival is held each January at the Concert Hall; contact BASS for details and bookings.

Nightlife. A Tuesday night Channel Ten programme — *The Club* — covers a wide selection of clubs, films, theatre and music. Most night clubs are open until at least 3am daily, some until 7am. King Street in the city is Melbourne's nightclub centre, and is very busy on Friday and Saturday nights. It has several very popular discos starting from the bottom end of the street with the Hippodrome (which has an "alternative night" on Wednesdays, intended mainly for students), the Underground, the Grainstore Tavern, the York Butter Factory, Inflation and Lazars. Don't try to get into any of these clubs while drunk, and make sure you are reasonably dressed.

Other popular nightclubs outside the city centre are the Chevron on the corner of St Kilda Road and Commercial Road, and Chasers in Chapel St, South Yarra.

Gambling. Apart from the usual TAB racing possibilities and the state lottery, there are few legal ways to fritter your money away. Poker machines, as mentioned earlier, are illegal in Victoria at present, and it is estimated that Victorians spend about $30 million annually gambling at the New South Wales border town of Albury. Victoria has no casino, but the state government plans to instal a 24-hour gambling palace at Melbourne's Menzies Rialto Hotel on Collins St. The Victorian TAB (which will run the new "Tabaret") promises to refurbish the building to its original Edwardian splendour and to offer betting on virtually any sport as well as the usual casino games.

SPORT

Melbourne is the home of Australian Rules Football, the Australian Open Tennis Championship, the Melbourne Cricket Ground, the Melbourne Cup horserace and many thousands of rabid sports fans. Tickets for most major events can be booked through BASS Sportscharge on 1 1522.

Most of the clubs in the Victorian Football League (VFL) are from around Melbourne. Throughout the winter you can see Sunday afternoon matches at various grounds, culminating with the Grand Final at the Melbourne Cricket Ground in late September.

The Australian Open Tennis Championship takes place each January at the new National Tennis Centre at Flinders Park. It is the first of the four international Grand Slam events each year and lasts for two weeks. Tickets are cheap (except for finals days, when the "scalpers" have field days); book from late September onward.

Australia's biggest horserace is the annual Melbourne Cup, held on the first Tuesday of November at Flemington racecourse. The 2.40pm race over 3,200 metres is considered so important that the day is declared a public holiday in Victoria, the federal parliament is suspended for the duration of the race and millions of dollars are staked on the outcome. While racing during the rest of the year does not achieve quite the same excitement, there are still some good events. As well as the Flemington track, there is racing at Caulfield and Moonee Valley (which also has harness-racing every Saturday evening). The dogs race at Olympic Park and Sandown.

While the Melbourne Cricket Ground (MCG) has no equivalent to Sydney's "Hill", the excitement generated by 100,000 cricket fans during Test matches or one-day games can be electric. You can take a tour of the ground each Wednesday at 10am; tel: 654 6066. For the latest cricket scores, dial 1188. The racing results are on 1185, and boating weather on 1 1541.

Not all of the city's inhabitants are purely armchair sports fans. Melbourne has plenty of places to keep fit, including the City Baths at the corner of Swanston and Franklin Streets (tel: 663 5888); north of the city centre try the Victorian Health and Fitness Centre at the corner of Johnston and Brunswick Steets (tel: 419 5000) or Hunt's Total Fitness Centre at the corner of Spring and Johnston Streets.

There are numerous public tennis courts, golf courses and public swimming pools in the city. In winter, the stage of the Sidney Myer Music Bowl is laid with ice and you can hire skates and spend the afternoon or evening ice skating.

Parks and Zoos. More than one-quarter of inner Melbourne is taken up by parkland. The biggest is Kings Domain which includes the Alexandra and Queen Victoria Gardens, stretching a long way along St Kilda Road into South Yarra. It is the home of the Floral Clock (opposite the National Gallery), the Women's Memorial Garden, the Sidney Myer Music Bowl and the Shrine of Remembrance. The Royal Botanic Gardens cover 40 hectares on the edge of Kings Domain and has 12,000 plant species from most countries of the world. It is also the home of the National Herbarium. You can take a free guided walk around the Gardens from Plant Croft Cottage on Tuesday and Thursday at 10 and 11am, and from gate F on Sundays at the same times. For details of Herbarium walks, call 63 9492.

Albert Park Lake (between the city centre and South Yarra) is very popular with joggers and cyclists, and also with picnickers who make good use of the gas barbecues at the lake's edge on summer nights. The lake is man-made and is surrounded by good roads which were originally designed as a motor racing circuit. At Studley Park (near Kew), you can hire a canoe from the boathouse.

The Royal Melbourne Zoological Gardens opened in 1857 and comprise Australia's oldest (and the world's third-oldest) zoo. It is north of the city centre on Elliott Avenue in Parkville (tel: 347 1522), on tram route 55 and 89, and opens daily from 9am to 5pm, admission $5. Animals are kept in an environment as close as possible to their natural habitat by the use of the open range system. The Zoo is also home to Mzuri, a baby lowland gorilla, the first surviving birth using artificial insemination. The kangaroo and wallaby section is a walk through area where the animals roam freely.

Beaches. Sydneysiders may tell you that Melbourne cannot hope to have a decent beach since its location on Port Phillip Bay is 60km from the open sea of the Bass Strait. Indeed, if you are after huge breakers for surfing, Melbourne will be a disappointment. There are, however, pleasant and safe swimming beaches west and southeast of the city. There is a windsurfing school on the beach at Beaconsfield Parade where you can hire windsurfers and/or have lessons.

The nearest ocean beaches are a long way from the city, at Torquay (96km southwest of Melbourne, beyond Geelong) and Portsea (96km south). The treacherous surf at Cheviot Beach, beyond Portsea at the mouth of Port Phillip Bay, has claimed the lives of many, including Prime Minister Harold Holt in 1967.

SHOPPING

Among foreign airline cabin crew, Melbourne is said to be the favourite destination in Australia since it has the best shopping. The time for bargains is during the January sales. Most shops in the city centre are open 9am-5.30pm Monday to Thursday, with late opening to 9pm on Fridays. On Saturdays shops open 9am-1pm. The major department stores are David Jones (Melbourne's most popular), Myers and (more upmarket) George's.

Chapel St in South Yarra and Toorak Road, Toorak have a huge selection of trendy boutiques and are wonderful for window shopping. For clothing bargains the "sample and seconds" shops run by mainstream clothing retailers and manufacturers can be good. There is a large selection of these shops in the area surrounding the junction of Church and Swan Streets in Richmond (mostly women's clothing) and more in Bridge Road, Richmond (with a few men's stores).

One of the several opal shops in the city centre is well worth visiting even if you have no wish to buy opals. The Lightning Ridge Store in the basement of 330 Little Collins St (at the corner of Elizabeth St; 63 7004) has a free display of lethal Australian wildlife. The owner, self-publicist Nick Le Souëf, will feed a stonefish, tickle a blue ringed octopus and waken a tiger snake.

You can buy all your camping gear from tin pans to tents, overcoats and sleeping bags from one of Melbourne's many disposal stores. These stores specialize in army surplus but also stock a wide variety of non-military gear. In the city Mitchell's Army and Navy Store at 134 Russell Street (just around the corner from the Backpackers City Inn and Carlton Hotel) is the best.

For cheap secondhand stuff, try the Salvation Army Thrift Shop at 144 Chapel St, South Yarra; further along at 350 is the Oriental Pearl pawnbroker (tel: 241 5179).

Books. The International Bookshop on the second floor at 17 Elizabeth St (614 2859), is hard to find but has an interesting selection of feminist, Marxist and gay literature. Readings, at 384 Lygon St (with branches in South Yarra and Hawthorn), is also radical, and was one of the first bookshops in Australia to stock Peter Wright's *Spycatcher*. Bonanza Books (at 191 Bourke Street) is open daily until 10pm and has some good bargains. The interesting Whole Earth Bookstore at 81-83 Bourke St opens until at least 10pm daily except Sundays (1-6pm). Paperback Warehouse at 54 Bourke St does even better, opening until 11.30pm every night except Sundays (noon-6pm). The widest selection of books is at the Technical Book & Magazine Co at 289-299 Swanston St. Don't be put off by the name: they sell books of all types and if you can't get it there it probably isn't available in Australia. Melbourne is one of the few places in Australia where you can buy a Filofax: try Normans at 109 Elizabeth St.

Records. Melbourne is saturated with record shops but the following are among the best in their field. For classical discs, Thomas's at the Southern Cross on the corner of Exhibition and Bourke Streets has long had the biggest selection. For pop/rock try the Mighty Music Machine in Chapel St, South Yarra. Hound Dog's Bop Shop at 313 Victoria St in West Melbourne specializes in re-issues and original 50s rock and roll, rockabilly and Country blues. Discurio at 20 McKillop Street in the city centre are stockists of obscure recordings, most notably of classical music but also of jazz, folk and pop. Readings (see *Books*, above) deal in secondhand discs.

Markets. The Queen Victoria covered market (near the corner of Elizabeth and Victoria Streets on the northwest edge of the city) is a wonderful place. As well as fresh produce it has a huge selection with stalls selling bargain priced clothing, household goods, and hardware items. It opens at 6am daily except Monday and Wednesday, and by 2pm most of the traders and shoppers have lost interest and gone home (except on Fridays when it opens until 6pm). On Sundays most of the food vendors are replaced by merchants selling souvenirs; the other days tend to be less touristy.

There are smaller but similar markets at Prahran and South Melbourne. The Prahran Market is open on Tuesdays and Thursday to Saturday, while the South Melbourne Market opens only at weekends. The Meat Market on Courtney St in North Melbourne may not sound promising unless you need a side of beef, but in fact it has been converted into a craft centre. For souvenirs try the makeshift market on the Esplanade in St Kilda each Sunday.

MEDIA

A recorded news summary can be heard by dialling 1197.

Newspapers. The Melbourne *Age* is both an excellent newspaper and a highly useful information source for visitors. As well as the Friday entertainment supplement *EG* mentioned above, Thursday's edition has a *Green Guide* to radio and television programmes. The *Herald* is Rupert Murdoch's representative in Melbourne, and is the city's only evening paper. It suffers by comparison with the *Age,* but is certainly more erudite than the tabloid *Sun.*

Radio. The best adult oriented rock is on Triple R (3RRR, 102.7FM) and Fox (101.9FM). Other stations include 3LO (Melbourne's ABC station), 3MP (easy listening in stereo on 1377AM), 3AK (mushy pop on 1503AM), and the outspoken "talkback" presenters on 3AW (1278AM). For good community radio and the best in Australian music, listen to 3CR (855AM). The AM station 3UZ is owned by Victoria's racing industry and hence features the sport rather heavily.

The city and most of Melbourne's suburbs are safe to walk around at night. Women on their own should avoid the darker streets behind Fitzroy St in St Kilda or risk being mistaken for a street-walker. Some of the parks and gardens around the city centre, which are beautiful by day, should be avoided by people of both sexes after dark, although it is safe to wander around the streets on the parks' peripheries. Melbourne has also suffered from the terror of random killings: despite Victoria having the strictest gun laws in Australia, the capital has been the scene of two recent massacres by psychopathic gunmen. One killed six passers-by in the suburb of Clifton Hill, while another went berserk in a Queen St office block, leaving eight dead. It may be some consolation to learn that semi-automatic weapons were banned after the second attack.

A great deal of marijuana is grown and smoked in Melbourne. Possession or use of even a small quantity is an indictable offence, and penalties for dealing are harsh. The Legal Aid Commission of Victoria is based at 179 Queen St, Melbourne.

The area code for Melbourne is 03. Call 000 for the emergency services.

The Victoria Government Travel Centre (known as Victour) has its main office at 230 Collins St (tel: 619 9444), plus offices in other state capitals:

Adelaide: 16 Grenfell St (51 4129)
Brisbane: 221 Queen St (221 4300)
Canberra: Jolimont Centre, corner Northbourne Avenue and Rudd St (47 6355)
Hobart: Sixth Floor, SBT Building, corner Murray and Collins Streets (31 0499)
Perth: Seventh Floor, St George's Court, 16 St George's Terrace (325 1243)
Sydney: 150 Pitt St (233 5499)

For specific information on Melbourne, it may also be worth contacting the Melbourne Tourist Authority on the 20th floor of Nauru House at 80 Collins St. There are various free tourist hand-outs, including *This Week in Melbourne* and *Australian Visitor News* (which, despite its title, is Melbourne-specific).

The Travellers Aid Society of Victoria is at 169 Swanston St (654 2600), with a branch at Spencer St station (67 2873). Like their counterparts in North America, they provide help and advice for travellers in difficulties.

British Consulate-General: CML Building, 330 Collins St (602 1877).
US Consulate-General: 24 Albert Road, South Melbourne (699 2425).
American Express: 105 Elizabeth St (699 2244); plus 18 branches in suburban Melbourne.
Thomas Cook: 159 Collins St (63 2442); plus ten branches in suburban Melbourne.
General Post Office: corner of Bourke and Elizabeth Streets (609 4265); open 8am-6pm, Monday to Friday.
Medical Treatment: Royal Melbourne Hospital, Parkville — 347 7111; Alfred Hospital, Prahran — 520 2811; Prince Henry's Hospital, St Kilda Road — 62 0621; St Vincent's Hospital, Fitzroy — 662 2000. AIDS hotline — 347 3000.
Dental Emergencies: 347 4222.
Women's Information and Referral Exchange (WIRE): Third Floor, 238 Flinders Lane (654 6844).

Helplines. Melbourne has a wide selection of useful numbers: Gayline 329 5555; Lifeline — 662 1000; Quitline (information for smokers) — 1 1531; Dial-a-prayer — 1 1611; Poison Information — 38 8485. To report a "national disaster" within Victoria you should dial 4688.

Although small in size, the state of Victoria has opportunities for the itinerant worker in most of the familiar categories such as fruit and tobacco picking, plus resort and city work. Furthermore its rate of unemployment (5.9%) is the lowest in the country. The *Age* has a massive employment section on Saturdays, though some visitors find it less stressful registering with one of the temporary work agencies. Drake has been particularly recommended and is accustomed to dealing with people on working holidays: Drake Overload is at 35 Collins St (654 4855) while Drake Industrial is at 9 Queen St (62 3575).

Another good place to hunt for work is at Melbourne University in Parkville north of the city centre. The noticeboards on the ground floor of the Union Building always have job advertisements, from babysitting to reading newspapers for a press cuttings agency. There is a Student Employment office nearby (784 Swanston St, at the corner of Faraday St) which may also be able to help. Student Services Australia in Melbourne (tel: 348 1930) run a Student Work Abroad Programme primarily for North American students, but they might be prepared to offer advice to any students on working holiday visas with specific queries about visa renewal, tax, etc. They have recently moved into the offices of STA, with whom they work very closely (224 Faraday St, Carlton).

The main Commonwealth Employment Service office is at 128 Bourke St (617 7166). It has a Templine section as well as a Hospitality Staffing section for those looking for casual work.

If your working holiday visa is in danger of expiring, you can apply for an extension at the Department of Immigration and Ethnic Affairs on Spring St (corner of Latrobe St; tel: 662 2011) bearing in mind that the Melbourne office is reputed to be less lackadaisical than others and generally insists on interviewing applicants.

Tourism. With so many restaurants, opportunities in Melbourne's hospitality industry are numerous. If you fail to find work through adverts in the newspaper or in restaurant windows, door-to-door visits often succeed, especially if you are neat, clean and eager.

If you happen to be in Melbourne in late October or early November for the Melbourne Cup, your chances of finding casual work escalate remarkably. It is not just hotels, restaurants and bars which become frantically busy in the period leading up to the Cup, but private catering firms are also often desperate for staff. An application to one of these in September or October is sure to turn up some casual work. Rowlands are the "society" caterers while O'Brien Catering (338 1600) do the catering at the Flemington racecourse and need people to make the millions of sandwiches, etc. that are sold at Cup time. In addition to caterers, an army of sweepers and cleaners is recruited to go through the whole course clearing the huge piles of debris left by the 15,000 odd spectators in time for the next day's races.

If you can get taken on by one of the luxury hotels (the Regent, Hyatt, Hilton, etc.) you will find wages and tips high, with subsidized meals and free laundering of uniforms provided. Experience is not essential since often they prefer young trainable staff, but they will expect you to stay longer than a few weeks.

Outside Melbourne, the highest concentration of tourist facilities may be found along the Victorian Riviera (see *Eastern Victoria,* below) and the resorts of the Great Dividing Range which are particularly active during the ski season. There is a strong demand for seasonal workers in the main ski resorts of Falls Creek, Hotham, Mount Buller and Baw Baw. Watch for adverts in the *Age* in April/May or ask at the CES in Wangaratta (at the corner of Ovens and Faithful Streets; tel: 057-21 5411).

Fruit Picking. More than New Jersey, Victoria deserves the designation Garden State. The fertile river valleys are prime fruit-growing regions. The Goulburn River has its source just north of Melbourne and flows north to join eventually the mighty Murray River near Echuca on the New South Wales border, irrigating the land along the way. Soft fruit is especially prolific around Shepparton and Cobram. Grapes are grown in most corners of the state though the harvest around Mildura in the northwest seems to attract the most itinerant pickers.

Grapes and other fruit are grown quite close to Melbourne. For example grapes are grown in Lilydale, cherries and berries are picked in the outer suburbs of Wonga Park, Silvan and Monbulk from November onwards while apples and pears are picked on the Mornington Peninsula from March to May. But for the mass harvesting of fruit you should travel to northern Victoria where the Northern Victorian Fruitgrowers Association in Shepparton (21 Nixon St; tel: 058-21 5844) and the Victorian Peach & Apricot Growers' Association in Cobram (21 Station St; tel: 058-72 1729) should be contacted before Christmas. These associations represent over 500 orchardists in the Goulburn/Murray Valley and will direct willing workers to farms where jobs are available between January and April. They are so eager to attract foreign fruitpickers that they have published a leaflet on working holidays for distribution abroad. The going rate for a half-ton bin of pears is $14 and of apples $14-$16.

The tobacco harvest is another possible source of employment. The area surrounding Myrtleford on the Ovens River and the Kiewa Valley further east are the places to head in early February.

If you would like to get to know Victoria better, you might volunteer to work on a farm or on a conservation project. See page 45 for details.

The main attraction of Melbourne's hinterland is its accessibility. The distance from Melbourne to the scenic mountains of the northeast or to the vineyards of the northwest can be covered in a day, though there are exceptional landscapes and attractions much nearer Melbourne, especially the coastal areas to the east and west of the capital. The density of roads in the state is high by Australian standards except in the large mountainous area east of Melbourne.

Victoria is more intensively agricultural than the other states, which accounts for the high number of dairy and wool museums, wheat research institutes and soup factories, all of which are open to the public. Of more interest to tourists is the fact that you are never too far from a winery. If you are exploring the state by car, get the Victour brochure *Vintage Victoria* which, in addition to details of vineyards, also includes reviews of restaurants (generally pricey ones) in the vicinity. The highest concentrations of wineries are along the Yarra and Goulburn Valleys not too far from Melbourne, around Avoca north of Ballarat, and in the northern corners of the state around Mildura in the west and Rutherglen in the east. Many of the wineries have colonial architecture and other features of interest such as the 130-year old champagne cellars at Chateau Tahbilk.

DAY TRIPS FROM MELBOURNE

Phillip Island. Within a day's drive or ferry ride from Melbourne is a substantial island (23km × 7km) named after the first governor of the colony. Although there is both a Dairy and Wool Centre on Phillip Island, most visitors come to see something quite different, a procession of penguins. A resident troupe of fairy penguins (so-called because of their relative daintiness though they still stand a foot high) regularly waddle up onto Summerlands Beach at dusk to their nests among the sand dunes. Special viewing stations have been set up, one newly restored for the Bicentenary, partly so that the rangers can keep an eye on the hundreds of tourists who might succumb to the temptation of using flash photography which is against the rules. Meanwhile the beach is floodlit, though the penguins remain happily oblivious to their role as circus performers. The advantage of visiting in summer is that the number of penguins swells; the disadvantage is that the number of tourists does likewise. Outside summer it can get surprisingly chilly at night so take a blanket.

Phillip Island is also worth visiting for its beaches — surfing on the south coast, sheltered swimming on the north — and for its other wildlife including koalas, water birds and seals; the latter are visible from Point Grant in the extreme west. There is a small Youth Hostel (tel: 059-52 2258) in the resort town of Cowes, as well as lots of holiday accommodation.

The island is accessible by road (135km via the Bass Highway and bridge to Newhaven), ferry ($5 between Stony Point on the Mornington Peninsula and Cowes) or air (well over $100 return on the daily Penguin Express out of Melbourne's Essendon Airport; ring Moloney Aviation on 379 2122 for details). If you are driving, get on to Dandenong Road (which is the Princes Highway) then turn onto the South Gippsland Highway at Dandenong.

Geelong and Environs. Although Geelong (pronounced Jer-*long*) is Victoria's second city it has little to recommend it. In addition to the National Wool Centre due to open in the Bicentennial year (tel: 052-26 4852), there are a couple of mid-19th century homes, both overlooking the Barwon River in the suburb of Newtown and both run by the National Trust. A worthwhile stopover may be made at Werribee Park, about half way between Melbourne and Geelong, which is an Italianate mansion built in the 1850s set in lovely grounds. It has a free range zoo, which is managed by the Zoological Board of Victoria, and other amenities for day-trippers. Polo is played here in season.

From Geelong, it is worth travelling 31 km to the end of the Bellarine Peninsula which encloses the western half of the enormous bay on which Melbourne is situated. Queenscliff, at the end of the highway, has some beautiful Victorian hotels which offer reasonably priced carvery lunches on Sundays. A more minor road follows the south coast of the peninsula past the lighthouse at Point Lonsdale (which guides ships through The Rip, one of the world's most treacherous stretches of water) and on to the beachside towns of Ocean Grove and Barwon Heads. The latter has a good pub popular at mealtimes, and both have good surf beaches.

The Dandenongs. The attractive hills called the Dandenongs 40km east of Melbourne are an ideal destination for a day's motoring or bushwalking. (Do not confuse the hills with the southeastern suburb of Dandenong, which is some distance away.) The main attraction is the rainforest ecology and slender pale gums which line most of the roads and tracks. There are several parks and forests, the best known of which are Ferntree Gully National Park and Sherbrooke Forest Park. The area is at its most beautiful in the autumn and should not be missed. The many galleries, nurseries and antique shops are open seven days a week, and so Sunday lunch in the Dandenongs is almost an institution. Another place of interest in the same direction is the William Ricketts Sanctuary at Mount Dandenong with a display of Aboriginal history.

About 25km further east along the Maroondah Highway is the world renowned Healesville Wildlife Sanctuary, a walk-through park with hundreds of wallabies, platypus, koalas, etc., many of which have been bred at Healesville. If you take a picnic, watch out for the emus and ibises which have been known to deprive incautious picnickers of their sandwiches.

Mornington Peninsula. The long Italy-shaped peninsula on the eastern side of Port Phillip Bay is a popular spot for holidaying Melburnians who flock down to the large developments of holiday homes; try to miss the weekend traffic jams.

In September 1987 a new passenger/vehicular ferry service began between Sorrento near the tip of the Mornington Peninsula across to Queenscliff which takes half an hour rather than the $3\frac{1}{2}$ hour trip by road. The ferry ride costs $25 per carload of passengers. You can also join a cruise of Port Phillip Bay from Station Pier at Port Melbourne on the *Spirit of Victoria* (tel: 62 6997) which makes several interesting stops and is a good way to spend $26 on a sunny day.

If you are not planning a winery tour elsewhere in Victoria, you might like to visit some vineyards along the Yarra River in Greater Melbourne or further out such as the Yarra Burn Vineyards near Yarra Junction where you can attend a spit roast and hear bush music on weekends, provided you book in advance (tel: 059-67 1428).

EASTERN VICTORIA

The Gippsland region of eastern Victoria is the home of Australia's largest inland waterway system and is heavily developed for tourism. Lakes Entrance, at the head of Ninety Mile Beach and bordering on an interesting coastal lagoon system, is part of an area dubbed the Victorian Riviera, though the national park status of much of the region saves it from being too spoiled by commerce. Lakes Entrance also serves as a port for one of the biggest fishing fleets in the country, keeping Melbourne's wholesale market well supplied with fresh fish and scallops. This area has long nautical associations as can be seen at St Peter's Church in the resort of Paynesville near Bairnsdale whose spire is in the shape of a lighthouse tower with a cross and a light to guide boats on the Gippsland lakes.

By driving further along the Princes Highway and turning south along unsealed roads, you can find unspoiled coastline at places like Bemm River and Mallacoota near the New South Wales border (where there is a Youth Hostel). East Gippsland boasts the best examples of rainforest in the state, particularly at Fairy Dell northeast of Bairnsdale. But closer to Melbourne in South Gippsland there is plenty of splendid rocky coastline and sand dunes, with some dilapidated resorts like Inverloch.

A few back roads head north from the Princes Highway towards the mountains, offering wonderful views (though mists are common in autumn and winter).

Wilsons Promontory. The "Prom" is a mountainous and thickly forested peninsula which has been made into a national park where wildlife and wildflowers abound. The park headquarters are at Tidal River, a small settlement at the end of the sealed road. In summer the rangers conduct wildlife-spotting tours at night and also give talks about the area. A dirt track continues to the granite headland at the end of the peninsula which is the southernmost point on the Australian mainland. A variety of walking tracks and nature trails invite further exploration.

WEST OF MELBOURNE

Great Ocean Road. There is a choice of route heading west from Geelong, the most scenic (though by no means the quickest) of which is the classic coastline drive along the Great Ocean Road. The 200km stretch of roads was built during the Depression in the 1930s as a job creation scheme and war memorial, and hugs the coastline for most of its distance between Torquay and Peterborough. After passing through the picturesque coastal town of Lorne and the seaside resort of Apollo Bay, both of which attract thousands of visitors in the summer, the road cuts inland through the lush forested hills of the Otway Ranges and Otway National Park.

Port Campbell National Park comprises the long strip of land between the road and the sea west of Cape Otway, so that the natural beauty of cliffs and beaches remains unspoiled. The most spectacular features are the Twelve Apostles (huge multicoloured sandstone sea stacks), The Arch, London Bridge (which you can walk on) and The Blowhole, all formed over thousands of years by wind and sea erosion.

Although the Great Ocean Road peters out at this point, it is worth continuing west to Warrnambool (another overly-popular resort in season), Tower Hill a dormant volcano, and Port Fairy, a harbour town of Irish origins which has changed little since the 1880s and is still an important crayfishing centre.

Ballarat. The most direct route west from Melbourne along the Western Highway takes you through Victoria's third largest city with a population of 75,000. Built on the riches of the 1850s gold rush, Ballarat continues to prosper as a bustling market town. The main attraction is Sovereign Hill, a recreated goldmining township complete with costumed staff carrying out the daily tasks of pioneer life such as baking bread, working in the post office, printing a newspaper, etc. Interestingly Sovereign Hill is a non-profitmaking enterprise. Hostellers staying at the Government Camp across the road from the tourist village are entitled to a discount on admission. For an easy introduction to the area you might want to board the so-called "talking bus" which meets the morning train from Melbourne and shuttles people the 3km distance to Sovereign Hill. Note the statue to honour the eight hour day, bearing the legend, "Eight hours labour; eight hours recreation; eight hours rest". The area was one of the first in the world to recognize the rights of workers, when resentment against the cost of mining licences led to the attack by British soldiers on the stockade at Eureka on December 3, 1854 in which 16 diggers and six soldiers died.

Lovers of history will also want to take in the historic town of Castlemaine 120km northwest of Melbourne with its grand market building and museum. About halfway between Ballarat and Castlemaine you might like to stop over in Hepburn Springs where you can help yourself to the natural mineral waters discovered by the early settlers. The springs are marked according to the predominant salt content, e.g. sulphate, bicarbonate etc., all with their various health-giving properties. The Hydro Therapy Centre offers a range of baths including herbal, valerian and Pela mud. The area is surprisingly uncommercialized.

NORTHERN VICTORIA

The Victorian Alps. The Great Dividing Range which starts near the Queensland border and runs parallel to the coast of New South Wales, reaches its highest elevations in the Australian Alps which straddle the New South Wales/Victoria border. The highest peak on the Victorian side is Mount Bogong with the memorable altitude of 1,988m. The Alps of Victoria are wonderfully scenic, and worth visiting even if you are not a skier or a bushwalker. Typical of the high country are lush alpine meadows and poor roads. On clear days you can sometimes see across to the Snowy Mountains of New South Wales, for example from the lookout near Omeo from which you can sometimes see Mount Kosciusko, Australia's highest peak. Facilities at the main resorts of Hotham, Falls Creek and Mount Buller are described in *Skiing* below.

The Great Dividing Range comes surprisingly close to Melbourne. The Calder Highway which runs north from the airport leads to Mount Macedon, a picturesque hill over 1,000 metres high which suffered devastation during the 1983 bush fires but which affords sweeping views over Melbourne.

Film buffs will want to make a pilgrimage to the ancient rock formation on which the book and film *Picnic at Hanging Rock* are based. Hanging Rock is about 75km north of Melbourne past Mount Macedon. Another remarkable place in this vicinity is Anti-Gravity Hill, where the lie of the land creates the illusion of going uphill when in fact you are rolling downhill.

The Gold Towns. When gold was discovered in the 1850s, many settlements sprang up and developed into flourishing towns, some of which like Bendigo have survived, while others like Walhalla are almost ghost towns. Many have superb railway stations, town halls and rambling old hotels, all lovingly restored with an eye to the tourist dollar. Bendigo's principal boast is that it has "talking trams", i.e. trams which have been rehabilitated and provided with a taped commentary on the points of interest in town. One of these places is the Joss House, a Chinese temple which served the large influx of Chinese miners in the 1800s. Beechworth and Yackandandah east of Wangaratta are in more scenic countryside and have a large number of National Trust listed buildings from the gold era. Beechworth has many well-preserved sites including the old powder magazine (where explosives were stored), the school and the cemetery. Even the Youth Hostel is in a 125-year old converted pub, with a new (and recommended) pub across the road.

From Beechworth it is advisable to turn south towards the mountains rather than north to the border town of Wodonga, immortalized in the opening lines of a song: "Who would linger longer in Wodonga?". It is a new planned city without a single gracious building to temper its ugliness. Another place you might choose to avoid is Glenrowan on the Hume Highway south of Wangaratta since it is stuffed full of Ned Kelly kitsch, which demonstrates the Australian penchant for turning criminals into heroes. To keep the commercialism at more than arm's length, take a scenic flight from Benalla airstrip which gives you a view of Kelly's chimney, the last vestige of the bushranger's hideaway.

The Murray River. The second longest river in Australia starts in the Snowy Mountains and forms Victoria's northern border, providing some opportunities for a spot of relaxing river cruising. Sleepily attractive river towns such as Kerang and Swan Hill are dotted along its banks. Echuca, at the confluence of the Goulburn and Murray Rivers, was once a very busy inland port and many reminders of the past have been preserved, amongst them paddlesteamers and gracious old hotels. The Port of Echuca Historic Area on Murray Esplanade offers a discount for youth hostellers. Similarly Mildura, several hundred kilometres downstream, has paddlesteamers offering two-hour cruises twice a day. The Murray River supports an enormous amount of agriculture, primarily vegetables, citrus and grapes; some wineries such as Mildara Wines near Mildura are accessible by riverboat. The river is particularly worth seeing when in flood July to September.

Bushwalking, ski-ing and water sports are especially accessible in Victoria. The tourist authority publishes a good survey of the possibilities in its *Victoria: State of Great Adventures* brochure, from five-day residential gliding courses (at Euroa) to cycle tours of wineries. An agency which specializes in wilderness trips whether on foot, skis, bicycles or balloons is the Outdoor Travel Centre at 377 Little Bourke St in Melbourne (tel: 67 7252). Gear can be hired from plenty of Melbourne outfitters, for example Outsports Wilderness Centre (340B Hawthorn Road, Caulfield South) which offers 10% rental discounts to YHA members. Further information about the national parks in the state, such as the Little Desert National Park in the west (where more than 200 species of birds have been sighted) and Wilsons Promontory National Park, can be obtained from the National Park Service, 240 Victoria Parade, East Melbourne.

The YHA of Victoria organize weekend outings which often incorporate an outdoor activity. Instead of staying at hostels, they set up mobile canvas camps and share the cooking. Ask at the YHA office (205 King St, Melbourne 3000; tel: 670 7991) about the forthcoming schedule of "portable hostel" excursions.

Bushwalking. If walking along the Yarra River in Melbourne's suburbs is a little tame, you only have to travel a short distance to the bushland with its lush ferns and lyrebirds. Mount Donna Buang (1,250m) is not much more than an hour's drive from Melbourne and can be easily climbed in a day. If you want to leave the big city behind, a tent is a valuable asset since there are excellent campsites near a host of tracks and nature trails from the "Prom" in the east to the Grampians National Park in the west. If you do not have your own tent and would like to join a weekend bush walk, contact Go Tramping and Camping (tel: 03-489 3482) who take groups to the southwest coast for camping weekends in Otway National Park. The cost is about $100 including transport from Melbourne.

Most of the bush near Melbourne, such as the fern gullies which are so popular among hikers, are lush and damp and so you should beware of leeches. Mosquitoes are also a nuisance in summer. If you want to evade all insect life (as well as plant life), it is possible to walk for several kilometres by torch-light through the Byaduck Caves near Hamilton (300km due west of Melbourne).

Cycling. Since Melbourne is so sprawling and is also surrounded by fairly daunting hills, it is a good idea to take a local train to places like Stawell, Geelong or Lilydale before setting off. It is usually possible to put your bicycle in the guard's van for a small extra charge. Otherwise you can wait until you are outside Melbourne before hiring a bicycle for example in Port Fairy Township, Geelong and Echuca. If you undertake any long trips you must consider your route carefully since many scenic back roads deteriorate into gravel or rutted mud, while traffic on the main arteries can be unpleasantly and dangerously heavy. Serious cyclists should contact Trochos, 16 Kellaway St, Maidstone,

Victoria 3012 which publishes very readable accounts of cycle tours varying from 40km to 500km. The State Bicycle Committee (see page 185) publishes a *Bike Tours Book* and a quarterly newspaper *Bike News*.

If you want to join an organized cycling holiday in Northwest Victoria contact Bogong Jack Adventures, PO Box 209, Wangaratta, 3677 Victoria (057-21 2564) which run rather exclusive tours of varying lengths between September and May. The cost is approximately $35 a day.

Water Sports. Downtown Melbourne is 60km from the open sea, so surfing is not as handy as it is in Sydney. Surf beaches are concentrated west of Melbourne for example Torquay, Bells Beach (where championships are often held), Anglesea, Lorne and so on. Swimming is safe for the most part, though be careful at Ninety Mile Beach in Gippsland where there are dangerous rips and sharks.

To be sure of avoiding the dangers of the ocean, you might prefer to enjoy your aquatic recreations at any of the many inland lakes, such as the enormous man-made Lake Eildon or the Crater Lakes around Camperdown. For white water rafting on the Snowy River go to the small town of Buchan, which is also well known for its caves. For details of rafting and other trips on the Mitta Mitta River in the Victorian Alps, contact Wildtrek, 343 Little Collins St, Melbourne (tel: 03-67 7196). For gentler river descents, you can hire canoes on the Upper Murray; contact Upper Murray Canoe Hire in Walwa. Naturally the Gippsland Lakes are a premier boating area; if you want to hire a leisure craft, head for Metung.

Skiing. The high plains of northeast Victoria become a skiers' playground from June onwards, and you may find yourself competing with many out-of-state visitors as well as Melburnians. The nearest snow recreation area to the state capital is Mount Donna Buang near Warburton, though it is not high enough to offer reliable snow cover. Similarly Mount Baw Baw, which is the nearest resort to the capital (170km due east), is subject to rain-bearing winds from the south. Yet it can provide some fine skiing, especially to novices and cross-country skiers, and is surprisingly uncrowded considering its proximity to a city of nearly three million.

The major ski resorts, however, are in the Victorian Alps and are outside the range of most daytrippers, although people do sometimes drive the 250km north to Mount Buller for a day's skiing. Mount Buller is Australia's largest and most popular resort with 80km of runs for both advanced skiers and beginners, and an extensive and ever-expanding system of ski lifts. Hotham and Falls Creek on the Bogong High Plains are a scenic five hour drive from Melbourne, though they still can be exceedingly crowded especially on the beginners' slopes. Both get plenty of snow because of their elevation (up to 1,828m at Mount Hotham), though hot shot skiers maintain that the runs are longer in the mountains of New South Wales. "Falls" is considered to be the most picturesque of the Victorian alpine villages, set in a natural bowl, while Mount Buffalo (about 70km away) is one of the oldest ski resorts in Australia.

All the resorts are well serviced with ski hire shops, restaurants, shops, public transport, post offices, etc. There is an abundance of commercial lodges, but by far the cheapest are those run by private ski clubs. For bookings and information ring the Victorian Ski Association (03-699 4655) and the Victorian Alpine Accommodation Centre (03-528 5588). As in Kosciusko across the state border, it is much cheaper to stay some distance from the slopes, for example in Harrietsville (31km from Mount Hotham) and Mount Beauty and Tawonga at the foot of Mount Bogong.

Much of Victoria's terrain is most suitable for cross-country skiing, which is always much less expensive than downhill. Marysville, an old-fashioned resort town not too far from Melbourne, has some excellent *langlauf* possibilities at Lake Mountain.

Helpful information on all ski resorts can be found in *Alpine News,* a free monthly newspaper available from all tourist offices and ski shops in the state. It includes the latest developments in the resorts, alpine and nordic trail maps, a ski event calendar and plenty of advertisements for accommodation. The national weather reports in the eastern states always include a snow report from the major resorts. Alternatively you can dial the "ski info line" for Mount Hotham (1 1578) or for Mount Buller (1 1579).

Calendar of Events

January	Australian Open Tennis Championships, Melbourne
January	Melbourne Summer Music Festival
February	St Kilda Festival
late February/early March	Moomba Festival
March (second Monday)	**Labour Day**
March/April	**Easter Tuesday**
March	Begonia Festival, Ballarat
mid-May	Australian Harness-racing Derby, Moonee
June (second Monday)	**Queen's Birthday**
late June	Melbourne Film Festival
September	Spoleto Festival
September (last Thursday)	**Royal Melbourne Show Day (public holiday in Melbourne)**
mid-October	Avoca Wool and Wine Festival
November (first Tuesday)	**Melbourne Cup Day**
November	Lygon St Festa, Melbourne

Public holidays are shown in **bold**

Note that Life Be In It (PO Box 496, South Yarra 3141; tel: 240 8222) sell computer lists of special weeks ($10.50) and festivals ($18) in Victoria.

Tasmania

Population: 450,000   **Capital: Hobart (population 180,000)**

The attractions of Tasmania are so plentiful that, were the island an independent nation rather than just a tiny part of Australia's massive whole, many more people might be tempted to go there. It has an area of 68,300km² (slightly smaller than Scotland) and is distinctly dissimilar to the rest of Australia, softer and damper than the dry environment of the mainland. Indeed, it is so different from mainland Australia that it has more in common — in terms of pace of life, people, terrain and climate — with the South Island of New Zealand than with Victoria or New South Wales. Other islands of about the same size, such as Sri Lanka and Ireland, at least have a national identity among discerning travellers, while Tasmania languishes as a low-profile state dangling from the coast of Victoria. But although the often dismal climate and cost of visiting the island (which, incidentally, can be cheaper by air than by sea) might deter you, few visitors are disappointed by Tasmania's charm.

The chief attractions are mostly outdoor ones, such as the wilderness of the southwest, the mountains of the north and the pretty east coast. The southeast has the historic capital of Hobart and some fascinating remnants of the island's past as an island of penal servitude. It is a relatively poor state, dependent largely on agriculture, forestry and hydro-electric power, which has brought confrontation between business and conservationists. It has been the scene of notable conservation battles about the commercial exploitation of the natural wilderness, but vast tracts remain untouched. Tasmania is strongly tourist-oriented, with numerous old buildings having been converted into showpieces and is popular among vacationing Australians, for whom the trip across the Bass Strait is something of an overseas adventure. And yet the island has not been despoiled by tourism.

As well as numerous scenic delights and some interesting towns, Tasmania boasts a rich modern history. In 1642 the Dutch explorer Abel Tasman first sighted the peninsula named after him. He called the whole island Van Diemen's Land after the then governor of the Dutch East Indies. The British subsequently settled at Sullivan's Cove (now part of Hobart) in 1804, and the island was subsumed into the colony of New South Wales. Because of its cooler climate and isolation, the island was considered good territory for establishing penal settlements. Tasmania, as it became, gained a separate identity in 1825 under the notorious Governor George Arthur. He was convinced that mankind was "born and saturated in wickedness", and treated his charges accordingly. The island had the smallest proportion of free settlers of any Australian colony, and for ten years was widely regarded as the worst spot in the English-speaking world. Governor Arthur gave free licence to his soldiers to kill the island's Aboriginals on sight, and two years later launched a military operation called the Black Line, intended to corner the Aboriginals on the Tasman Peninsula and eliminate them from settled areas.

Transportation ended in 1868 and freedom was eventually granted to those convicts who had survived the evils of hunger, disease and vicious treatment. The Aboriginals fared much worse: survivors of Governor Arthur's genocide were rounded up by a missionary and taken to remote Flinders Island off the northeastern coast. This misguided attempt to rehabilitate them failed and the last pure-blood Tasmanian Aboriginal died in misery in 1876.

During the next half century, Tasmania evolved into a harmonious state where man enjoyed a fairly peaceful co-existence with nature in what came to be regarded as Australia's backwater. Economic realism forced Tasmania to take the 20th century seriously. With barely adequate agriculture and no significant industry, Tasmania slipped well behind the other Australian states in terms of wealth. Local and national interests eyed the island's natural resources, particularly the opportunities for supplying timber and cheap hydro-electric power. Tasmania's extensive scope for water-driven energy was first harnessed over 70 years ago, and the construction of hydro-electric schemes continues. A few notorious ideas such as the proposed damming of the Franklin River have attracted considerable attention, with conservationists from around the world converging on Tasmania. The environmentalists eventually won that particular argument — without wholehearted support from the locals — but other large-scale projects are under way or proposed.

CLIMATE

Tasmania's climate is far removed from the normally warm and dry weather of Adelaide, Perth and Sydney. The island tends to be cold and showery for most of the year, and even in summer temperatures rarely rise above 21°C/70°F. Hobart has an average of 625mm of rain each year which compares favourably with Manchester or Maine. Even so, the weather in the west and south is very changeable, and summer blizzards in mountainous areas are not uncommon. Water temperatures are uniformly cold, so don't plan on too much sea bathing. The east coast is the warmest and sunniest part of the state; it is possible to enjoy idyllic winter days in Bicheno or St Helens. The Department of Tourism faces

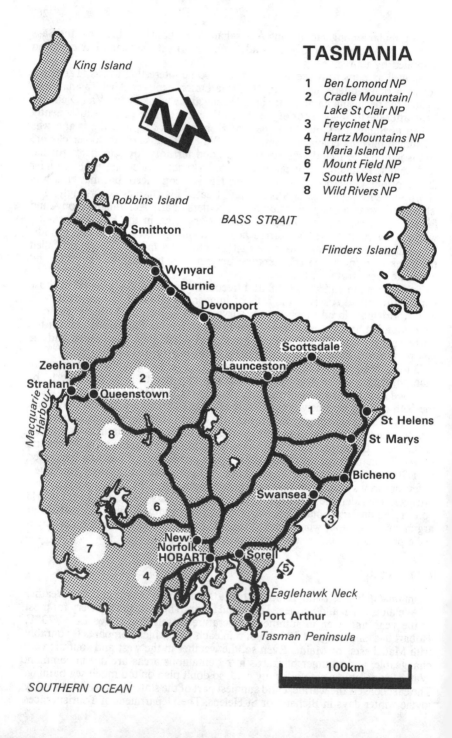

TASMANIA

1 *Ben Lomond NP*
2 *Cradle Mountain/ Lake St Clair NP*
3 *Freycinet NP*
4 *Hartz Mountains NP*
5 *Maria Island NP*
6 *Mount Field NP*
7 *South West NP*
8 *Wild Rivers NP*

King Island

Robbins Island

BASS STRAIT

Flinders Island

Smithton

Wynyard
Burnie

Devonport

Scottsdale

Launceston

Zeehan
Strahan

2

Queenstown

Macquarie Harbour

8

1

St Helens

St Marys

Bicheno

6

Swansea

7

3

New Norfolk
HOBART

Sorell

(5)

4

Eaglehawk Neck

Port Arthur
Tasman Peninsula

100km

SOUTHERN OCEAN

an uphill battle in convincing mainlanders that Tasmania is not always cold and wet. While it is quick to point out that the average winter minimum on the East Coast of the island is higher than several other places on the mainland (including Alice Springs, Kalgoorlie and Canberra), it has also recently requested that its climatic records are not published widely for fear of deterring tourists.

Cold, wet weather is not a permanent condition. Bush fires are a serious risk during hot, dry spells. The Tasmanian Fire Service declares "Fire Permit Periods" in summer during which picnic fires can be lit only in designated places, and dropping matches or cigarette ends is an offence. During total fire bans — announced by the media — lighting any fire out-of-doors is prohibited.

THE LOCALS

For about 40,000 years Tasmania was inhabited by Aboriginals. When ocean levels rose after the last ice age about 20,000 years ago, it became an island and the inhabitants grew racially distinct from mainland Aboriginals. They followed a semi-nomadic life, had very primitive tools and spoke more than one language. But as mentioned above, the destruction of the race began when the white colonists arrived. While there are still people claiming descendancy from Tasmanian Aboriginals, they face an uphill struggle not only for their rights but also for recognition of their very existence.

Modern Tasmanians (Tassies, or — if you wish to risk offending them — Taswegians) are almost a race apart from other Australians. The islanders tend to dissociate themselves from the mainland, and display an odd blend of Australian and New Zealand characteristics. If you arrive direct from Queensland or the Northern Territory, be prepared for a dose of culture shock. Most come from the same European stock that holds sway over the rest of Australia, but Tasmanians show a sensitivity that is less prevalent on the mainland. This quality of gentleness is often misinterpreted as a sign of dullness by other Australians, and jokes about Tasmanians roughly correspond to Irish jokes made in Britain or Polish jokes in the USA. There is a streak of puritanism, akin to the stoic Presbyterianism in the south of New Zealand.

Making Friends. You will find even more openness and hospitality than in other states, in both the towns and country. Indeed, Tasmanians who travel to other parts of Australia often remark that they realized how friendly their fellow-islanders are only after moving to the mainland. And a visit to Tasmania can be as much of an antidote to the sometimes strident mainlanders as the lush scenery can be to the parched terrain elsewhere. Tasmania has no large city where foreigners can meet each other and the natives, but makes up for this with its easy-going atmosphere and the camaraderie between travellers attracted to the great outdoors.

Meeting the locals is easy. Most are interested in you as a traveller and will bend over backwards to help you. Be discreet, however, in your conversation: while many Tasmanians are firmly committed to the preservation of their natural environment, others resent what they see as federal interference in the island's affairs (e.g. pro-conservation laws restricting logging and the woodchip industry). If you voice opinions agreeing with the government on preserving Tasmanian wilderness, or associate yourself with "those bloody greenie mongrels" you could be in for a lot of arguments. Taking the trouble to sound out the Tasmanian concerned — before you suggest, for example, that the halfwits logging the lemon thyme forest should be shot — will make your visit to Tasmania far more pleasant. If you do feel strongly about conservation and want to let off steam, go to one of the shops run by the Wilderness Society, where you're certain to find a receptive ear.

Your progress around Tasmania is likely to be slow unless you can afford the high fares on internal flights. There are no proper passenger trains, infrequent buses and no freeways. But journeys are enjoyable: the roads are uncluttered and meander through scenery varying from pleasant to spectacular. Up-to-date information on fares and schedules is available from Tasbureau offices, and is published in the free bi-monthly newspaper *Tasmanian Travelways*. A good booklet of maps of the island is the *Atlas of Tasmania,* price $3.50 from Tasbureau offices and bookshops.

ARRIVAL AND DEPARTURE

Air. The only international flights to Tasmania are from New Zealand to Hobart. Australian Airlines and Air New Zealand link Hobart with Christchurch, while Qantas serves the state capital from Auckland, calling at Melbourne. (If Hobart is "common-rated" with Melbourne and Sydney for international air tariffs, it will also mean you can reach Tasmania for the same price as the mainland cities, thus avoiding paying an additional fare for the journey across the Bass Strait).

The fares on Ansett and Australian Airlines are high, e.g. $157 single from Melbourne to Hobart, but there are several cheaper alternatives. East-West has services to the capital and Devonport from Melbourne and Sydney, and to Wynyard from Melbourne, saving around 15% on the fares of the two major carriers. If you are prepared to fly across the Bass Strait in a propeller aircraft (sometimes as small as an eight-seater), there are several smaller airlines offering lower prices still. For example Kendell Airlines (004-62 1322) have daily flights from Melbourne to King Island for $78, with a standby fare of $63 and a student ticket for only $58. Promair (056-88 1487) fly from Essendon airport in Melbourne to Flinders Island for $85. Aus-Air (004-52 1677) fly from Moorabin (near Melbourne) to Smithton for $90. Phillip Island Air Services have the cheapest fares to the Tasmanian mainland: $85 (standby $69) from Cowes on Phillip Island to Wynyard; call 059-56 7316 on the mainland, or 004-42 3838 in Tasmania.

Frequent internal services on Airlines of Tasmania, Ansett and Australian Airlines link Hobart with Launceston, the second largest city. Flights on Airlines of Tasmania (002-48 5030) from Launceston serve Flinders Island, King Island, Queenstown, Strahan and Wynyard. The same destinations — plus Devonport and Smithton — are available from Hobart. East-West links Devonport with Hobart and Wynyard. Sample fares from Hobart are Launceston $54.50, Devonport $69 and King Island $125.50.

In addition to these scheduled flights, there are numerous air charter companies offering sightseeing tours and one-way flights for bushwalkers. With two exceptions, they operate from the same airports as scheduled services. The exceptions are flights from Hobart (which use Cambridge Aerodrome, a mile or two from the international airport) and Wilderness Air seaplane services from the jetty at Strahan on the West Coast.

Because the travel market is much smaller than in other states, it is difficult to find cut-price international tickets out of Tasmania. If a search around the travel agents of Hobart, Launceston or Devonport fails to reveal any bargains, try Melbourne.

Sea. The only passenger ferry operating to Tasmania is the *Abel Tasman,* which is owned by the TT Line and sails three times weekly in each direction between Melbourne and Devonport on the north coast. Departures in each direction are at 6pm, with arrivals at 8.30pm the next morning. Services from Station Pier in Melbourne operate on Mondays, Wednesdays and Fridays, and from Devonport on Tuesdays, Thursdays and Sundays. Tickets can be booked through any travel agent or Tasbureau office, or direct with the TT Line on 008-03 0344 (toll-free from anywhere in Australia). Fares are calculated according to season and the quality of accommodation booked: paying for a berth is compulsory. The seasons are "bargain" (May to mid-September), "holiday" (before Christmas to March) and "shoulder" (the rest of the year). The cheapest one-way rate is for a berth in a cabin for two or three with shared facilities on C Deck, costing $74 during the bargain season, $92 in the shoulder and $114 for the holiday period. Student discounts are available. Vehicles are carried on the ferry, and a small car costs between $76 and $95 depending on season. Motorcycles are carried for $18-$26 and bicycles for $8-$10. Of the various distractions on board, the Roaring Forties Disco Bar is the most highly recommended.

If you wish to ship your car by sea from Melbourne or Sydney to Hobart, Union Bulkships offer rates of $255 return from Melbourne or $331 from Sydney. To qualify for these "tourist" prices, you must produce a confirmed return air ticket; passengers are not carried on these services and are expected to travel by air. Services are twice weekly in each direction from each city. The journey time is 30 hours to Melbourne, 40 hours to Sydney.

Bus. The leading operator is Tasmanian Redline Coaches (TRC); Greyhound bus passes are accepted on all their scheduled services. There are five or six journeys daily between Hobart and Launceston Monday-Friday, reducing to two at weekends. The journey takes 2½-3 hours and costs $12.60 each way. This main route along the Midland Highway is extended to Devonport (connecting with sailings of the *Abel Tasman* to Melbourne), Burnie, Wynyard and Smithton. Other sample fares are Hobart-Devonport $21.20, Launceston-Burnie $11.60, and Queenstown-Strahan $3.60. Some TRC services run only once daily, and there is no bus between Hobart and the west coast on Sundays. There are other bus companies (notably Coastliner Express, which charges $15.60 for the journey from Hobart to Launceston), including some which specialize in charter transport for bushwalkers.

The *Tassie Pass Open Ticket* costs $60 for seven days or $75 for 14 days unlimited travel on TRC. For comparison, a Hobart — Queenstown — Burnie — Launceston — Hobart circuit would ordinarily cost $65 and you should bear in mind before buying a pass that the TRC network is not comprehensive; for example the East Coast routes are covered by other operators who do not honour the TRC pass. Bus services in the east of Tasmania are generally slow, expensive and complicated (with different sectors run by different operators whose timetables do not connect). For example, to travel from Scottsdale to Bicheno (100km as the crow flies) requires three separate bus trips and an overnight stay in the "half-horse town" of Derby. Hitch-hiking is often much quicker.

Train. In the 19th century, Tasmania had a network of brilliantly engineered railways used mainly to support the mining industry. Sadly, the only remaining passenger lines in Tasmania are tourist runs, notably one from Ida Bay to Deep Hole in the far south, and another from Hobart to New Norfolk. The train from Ida Bay takes a pretty route along the banks of Line River and out to Deep Hole beach, but departure times seem to depend on the driver's mood. The New Norfolk run is on a historic steam train and costs $25.

Driving. Tasmania's roads suffer little from traffic. In the cities, a five-car queue is regarded as a jam, and the main highways are well-surfaced and almost empty. Beware, however, of dangers not normally experienced elsewhere in Australia: a sudden blizzard can make surfaces treacherous, many roads are icy in winter, and the massive slow-moving logging trucks can pose problems. The *Visitors Road Safety Guide* (free from Thrifty Rent-a-Car offices) warns that they are most common on the Tasman Highway in the east, in the Huon region (southwest of Hobart) and in the northeast. Bear in mind also that random breath tests are common: the blood/alcohol limit is 0.05%. The penalty for those over 0.15% is up to 18 months in prison plus a fine. The speed limit in towns is 60km/h, and 110km/h outside unless otherwise posted. Radar checks are used to catch offenders.

With distances of only 200km from Hobart to Launceston, and 100km from there to Devonport, most journey times are short. Road conditions, however, can vary alarmingly. While cross-country distances may look small on your trusty tourist map (and they are, particularly by Australian standards), many roads wind tortuously and must be driven carefully; take these factors into account when planning your 50km jaunt up the east coast. (The 50km between Bicheno and St Mary's often takes up to 90 minutes depending on the state of the Elephant Pass, a highly treacherous stretch of road which vertiginous visitors would rather crawl across than drive).

The road numbering system is better organized than elsewhere in Australia. National Highway 1 runs straight down the middle of the island, from Devonport to Hobart via Launceston. Other primary routes are prefixed *A*, secondary roads *B* and minor roads *C*. Unfortunately, everybody (except the mapmakers) uses the names of roads, rather than the logically assigned numbers, and there is no exact correlation between the names and numbers. Hence the A10 has three different names for separate sections, and the Bass Highway has two different numbers during its course. The main highways and their numbers are as follows:

Hobart — Launceston (direct)	Midlands Highway	Highway 1
Launceston — Burnie	Bass Highway	Highway 1
Burnie — Smithton (and beyond)	Bass Highway	A2
Hobart — Launceston (via East Coast)	Tasman Highway	A3
Melton Mowbray — Deloraine	Lake Highway	A5
Hobart — Southport	Huon Highway	A6
Sorell — Port Arthur	Arthur Highway	A9
Hobart — Queenstown	Lyell Highway	A10
Queenstown — Zeehan	Zeehan Highway	A10
Zeehan — Burnie	Murchison Highway	A10

Fuel prices are higher than in cities on the mainland due to extra transport costs and the lack of competition. Most filling stations open at 6.30am, Monday — Saturday, and close at 6.30pm (Monday — Thursday), 8.30pm (Friday) or noon (Saturday). A roster system operates in larger towns with stations open until 9.30 or 10pm daily including Sundays. On Christmas Day and Good Friday, everything closes. Emergency road services are provided by the Royal Automobile Club of Tasmania (RACT) whose head office is at the corner of Patrick and Murray Streets in the state capital. For road service in Hobart, call 34 5999; elsewhere, consult the telephone directory.

The major car hire companies, as ever, are represented, but there is a good range of low-cost alternatives. The lowest daily rate is $15, available from Hobart companies such as Lo Cost (002-31 0550), Mercury (002-72 1755), Rent-a-Bug (002-34 9435) and Rent-a-Rocket (002-34 4512) in Hobart. In the north of the island try Bargain (003-98 2140) in Perth, just south of Launceston or Alternative (004-27 9222) in East Devonport. Hiring a campervan is particularly popular in Tasmania; with the amount of spectacular scenery in national parks and the lack of cheap accommodation in out-of-the-way places, the advantages of having a home on wheels are considerable. One of the cheapest is Tourist Economy Rentals, 247 Elizabeth St, North Hobart (002-034 7089). Although the Auto Rent company is more expensive, they publish a useful booklet called *Everything you ever wanted to know about a Campervan Holiday in Tasmania,* which you can request by calling (toll-free) 008-03 0222.

Hitch-hiking. The short distances, friendly motorists and pleasing landscapes make hitching in Tasmania a more enjoyable experience than elsewhere in Australia. In summer you should have little trouble getting around. Winter hitching is less predictable: the second car will stop if the first one doesn't but you may have to wait hours for the first one, and it can get very cold by the roadside. Try to stick to "A" roads. Don't expect to be picked up by the innumerable logging trucks; not only do they run to very tight schedules but the drivers tend to see backpackers as "greenie ratbags", and prefer not to be accused of helping destroy Tasmania's wilderness in the course of their work. Some hitch-hikers have even been ejected from vehicles after expressing sympathy for the conservationist cause.

The only other warning concerns the hitchers' congestion in Devonport after the arrival of the *Abel Tasman.* To avoid this problem, try to fix up a lift over breakfast on board the ship, or invest $10 in the bus fare from the quayside to Launceston.

CITY TRANSPORT

The Metropolitan Transport Trust (MTT) provides cheap local bus services in Hobart, Launceston and Burnie. Weekday services are frequent, but on Sundays many routes stop altogether and others operate at two-hour intervals. The published timetables are often indecipherable to anyone lacking a close working knowledge of the area; ask a clued-up local to assist you. Elsewhere, such urban services as exist are operated privately and hence tend to be infrequent and expensive. This is not usually a problem, since almost every town is small enough to cover comfortably on foot.

Cycling. Riding around the towns of Tasmania is popular and much less hazardous than on the streets of overcrowded mainland cities. However, there are plenty of hills so be prepared for breathlessness (or walking up the slopes) if you're unused to cycling. Bikes can be hired in all the larger towns.

Away from the larger towns and developed resort areas, the problem with accommodation in Tasmania is the lack of choice. The range of options across the state — from campsites to colonial mansions — is wide, but in many "country centres" there is only one place to stay, often an expensive establishment. There are, however 22 Youth Hostels (see below), and a number of host farms (listed in the free magazine *Tasmanian Travelways*). If you wish to contain costs during your travels on the island, the HomeHost Tasmania scheme could be useful. Rates with host families start at $28 single, $44 double. The coordinating organization can be contacted at PO Box 550, Rosny Park, Tasmania 7018 (002-44 5442). Another scheme is the *Tassie Bed and Breakfast Pass* whereby you buy vouchers and a directory of 44 hotels around Tasmania, where you spend one voucher on each night's stay. Prices range from $65 per person for three nights sharing to $546 for 21 nights single accommodation. Call 002-34 7166 or 003-34 1787, or book through any Tasbureau office. The advantage is relatively low-cost accommodation; the drawbacks are the inaccessibility of some of the hostelries to those without transport, and the need to book ahead in busy seasons. A similar but more expensive option is available from *Tasmanian Colonial Accommodation* which offers 15 cottages and houses ranging from an old sea captain's cottage to country mansions. They are predominantly located in the south-east of Tasmania, with four in Hobart alone. Tasmania Bed & Breakfast (95 1582) have a more comprehensive coverage — their leaflet is available from Farm Holidays, PO Box 384, Woollahra, NSW 2025.

Hostels. The YHA of Tasmania is based at 28 Criterion St in Hobart (tel: 002-34 9617). Their hostels are extremely good value, with few charging more than $6 per night yet offering high standards of comfort. Many hostels provide additional services such as bicycle hire, canoeing trips and bushwalking tours. Demand in summer is high, so book in advance if you possibly can. Postal requests should be sent to YHA Tasmania, PO Box 174B, Hobart 7001 between three months and three weeks in advance.

Dining out in Tasmania holds few surprises. The usual range of European and Asian cuisines are represented in the cities, but — as with accommodation — choice in rural areas is limited. Often the best you can hope for is a pub serving decent-but-plain counter meals. A particular feature of eating in Tasmania is the number of "reef 'n' beef" establishments which serve seafood and steak. Americans will recognize this as the same idea as "surf 'n' turf". Generally speaking the steaks are fine, while much of the seafood is exceptional. In particular, you should try the Tasmanian delicacy of smoked trout.

There is normally no need to book ahead during the week, but on Friday and Saturday evenings the entire population of the island seems to go out to eat. Book ahead — if only by a few hours — to ensure you can eat at your chosen restaurant.

DRINKING

Licensing hours in Tasmania are liberal: although opening hours on Sundays are restricted to noon-8pm, during the rest of the week publicans can virtually choose their own hours. In practice, however, few hotels open beyond midnight.

One of the sources of Tasmania's native beer — Boag's in Launceston — claims to be the oldest brewery in Australia. Since it was established in 1881, it has failed to grab the world's attention as effectively as its mainland rivals. Yet it has more taste and character than some of its more celebrated competitors. Boag's is owned by the same company that runs the Cascade brewery in Hobart (which was damaged by bush fires in 1987). But there are fierce differences between the north and south of the island about which is best; you can usually tell where a beer-drinker comes from by the beer he or she drinks: Boag's in the north, Cascade in the south. Pub prices are noticeably lower than on the mainland; beer is some 10% cheaper than in most other states.

Winemakers have only recently started to take full advantage of the fact that the Tasmanian climate is the most typically European of anywhere in Australia, and thus ideal for growing premium cool-climate grapes such as the red Cabernet Sauvignon and white Chardonnay. Traditionally, most grapes have been sold to mainland winemakers, but the growing popularity of Tasmanian wines has led to the development of new wineries, particularly along the banks of the Tamar northwest of Launceston. The winery-visit industry is not nearly so developed as in, say, South Australia, but estates such as St Matthias (15km northwest of Launceston) welcome visitors. Tasmania is the first state in Australia to adopt a legally-enforceable wine appellation system.

Despite being the birthplace of artistes such as Errol Flynn, Tasmania remains well off the beaten track by leading theatre groups, rock bands and orchestras. Don't expect to catch too many big-name acts on the island: formal entertainment is distinctly low-brow, with farces being the theatrical staple and up-and-coming (or ageing-and-declining) musicians the best you can hope for. For details of forthcoming events, buy *Press Press,* the Tasmanian quarterly magazine on music, theatre and dance (price $2.50).

What it lacks in box-office attractions and sophistication, Tasmanian culture makes up for in charm. Folk music is particularly popular, although to the untrained ear a succession of songs about convict life can begin to sound dirge-like. There is an annual Folk Festival at Longford (south of Launceston), but recently its popularity has diminished as it has become strongly identified with "greenie" causes.

SPORT

The island has never figured highly on the sporting map of the world, although the occasional local boy makes it into the Australian national cricket or Rugby Union squad. Mainland teams are loathe to cross the Bass Strait, so Tasmanian sportsmen and women encounter little high-class competition. Cricket's Sheffield Shield, fortunately, requires that the other states' teams visit the island, so you can expect to see some good players. There is some trotting and horseracing, but with little of the fervour felt on the mainland. The main races are the Hobart Cup and the Launceston Cup, both held in February.

In terms of participation, it is difficult to define where travelling ends and sport begins. By hiking, cycling or canoeing around the island, you are doing what most Tasmanians regard as exercise enough. The larger towns have their share of gasping joggers, but there is little organized activity apart from Hobart's "Run For Fun" each May. Tennis and golf are well catered for, and the cool climate means that there are good facilities for indoor sports such as squash and badminton. For details of beaches, and the opportunities for skiing, see *The Great Outdoors.*

SHOPPING

There were proposals in 1987 to turn Tasmania into a free trade state, cutting excise taxes on liquor and tobacco. Until or unless that happens, Tasmania is hardly a shopper's paradise. Beyond the usual tourist trivia (notably the world's biggest eraser — "for really big mistakes") there is little that is not sold more cheaply on the mainland and hence little worth buying. Shops of the Wilderness Society can be found in all the main towns and offer the highest souvenir-credibility rating. In particular, their posters are excellent. You can also buy some good souvenirs made from Huon pine, but the bags of Huon pine wood shavings are perhaps a little tacky.

THE MEDIA

Newspapers. The Hobart *Mercury* and the Launceston *Examiner* are Tasmania's leading dailies. Both contain useful information for the traveller, such as air and bus departure times. The *Sunday Tasmanian* and *Sunday Examiner* are regarded as better newspapers. You can read the *Times* and *Guardian* of London and the *New York Times* at the State Library at 91 Murray St, Hobart.

A free weekly newspaper — the *Tasmania Mail* — is distributed each Tuesday; and *Treasure Islander* is a free monthly aimed, like the bi-monthly *Tasmanian Travelways,* at tourists.

Radio. The small audiences of Tasmania cannot support a very wide range of stations. ABC-FM is on 93.9MHz, easy listening on 92FM, sport and farming on 7NT (630 AM), and minority programmes on 7RPH (1620 AM). Some stations on the Australian mainland can be picked up, especially those broadcasting on the AM band.

Television. Options for the viewer are similarly limited. TasTV is the local commercial station, transmitting on channels 1, 6, 8, 9 and 10. ABC occupies channels 2 and 3, and SBS is available on UHF channel 28 in some parts of the island. As with radio, transmissions from some mainland stations reach Tasmania, particularly the north of the island.

Theft was rife during the early years of settlement: Ikey Solomon, upon whom Dickens based Fagin, picked plenty of pockets when he moved to Hobart from London. Nowadays, however, you would be most unlucky to be robbed, and violent crime is almost unknown.

Drugs. The average bluff Tasmanian has little to do with illicit drugs, preferring the legitimate attraction of beer. Tasmania is, however, a popular destination r people seeking an "alternative" way of life; some marijuana is cultivated, nd finds its way to the cities, but the penalties for possession are higher than more liberal states. If you are arrested for narcotic offences or any other crime, e subsequent interrogation is likely to be recorded on video.

The area code for Hobart and the south of Tasmania is 002; for Launceston and the Midlands, 003; and for Devonport and the north, 004.

asbureau's head office for enquiries by post is PO Box 1469, Launceston 7250. here is an office at 80 Elizabeth St, Hobart (30 0211) and in four other asmanian towns: Burnie (48 Catley St; 30 2224); Devonport (18 Rooke St; 4 1526), Launceston (corner of Patterson and St John Streets; 32 2488) and ueenstown (39 Orr St; 71 1099). Tasbureau also has representative offices in l the mainland capitals except Darwin:

Adelaide: 32 King William St (08-211 7411)
Brisbane: 217 Queen St (07-221 2744)
Canberra: 5 Canberra Savings Centre, City Walk (062-47 0070)
Melbourne: 256 Collins St (03-63 6351)
Perth: 55 William St (near Hay St) (09-321 2633)
Sydney: 129 King St (02-233 2500)

merican Express: c/- Webster Travel, whose offices are at 60 Liverpool St, Hobart (002-38 0200) and at the corner of Charles and Cimitiere Streets in Launceston (003-32 0555).

homas Cook: 40 Murray St, Hobart (34 2699).

Unemployment in Tasmania is the second highest in Australia (after Queensland), running at nearly 10%. Much of the available casual work is strictly seasonal, and most of it is taken up by the locals. Even o, there are casual jobs in agriculture, industry and tourism for those with the nergy to look for them.

Tasmania is not known as the "Apple Island" for its shape alone. The island roduces 70% of Australia's apples. Although picking apples is slow going for eginners (and badly paid compared to fruit-picking elsewhere in Australia), you nay be able to find work from late February until the snowfalls begin in earnest n mid-June. Head for the Huon Valley or the Tasman Peninsula, southwest and outheast of Hobart respectively. There is also some limited grape picking work n the Huon from March to May, with more along the Tamar north of _aunceston.

If you can bear the irritation of hop-itch, most of Australia's hops are picked n Tasmania from mid-March to the end of April. The main growing areas are round New Norfolk (inland from Hobart) and Scottsdale in the northeast, on he road from Launceston to St Helens. Men usually do the picking and tractor lriving, women work in the sheds on hop-stripping machines. Although the work s arduous, it is well-paid (you might earn $1,000 in three weeks) and some locals nanage to get by just working on the hops followed by the apples each year.

You may be able to find work in the fish-processing industry, although the raditional scallop-splitting season from August to beyond Christmas has been drastically curtailed recently by overfishing; casual workers who turned up at Bicheno in 1987 were lucky to find a week's work. In any event, the craft of splitting scallops is skilled and paid on a piece-rate basis. You may find yourself earning only $2 per hour until you acquire the knack, by which time the season might be over. The bad reports and poor forecasts for the next few years may drive most job-seekers away, so you might find other opportunities in the fish industry. Enquire at CES offices in the main ports — Hobart, Devonport, Bicheno and St Helens — if you have a working visa, otherwise approach the processing factories direct. To renew a working holiday visa, contact the Department of Immigration in Hobart (188 Collins St; tel: 20 5011).

Most vacancies in the "hospitality industry" are in the peak season from December to February. Non-specialists can find work most easily in the East Coast resorts and around the capital. There are also a few jobs in the skiing resorts of Mount Field and Ben Lomond from June to September, but not on the scale of resorts in the Snowy Mountains.

HOBART

Although Hobart is the state capital of Tasmania, its location tucked away in the southeastern corner of a wild and thinly populated land makes it difficult to exert much influence over the rest of the island. Its setting is more beautiful than any other state capital except Sydney, overlooking the broad Derwent Estuary and surrounded by rugged hills, dominated by 1,270-metre Mount Cook. The dignified Victorian architecture has been carefully preserved, and the overall impression is of a pretty provincial town in Britain. The city's proudest modern achievement is Wrest Point, the first casino/resort development in Australia. The rehabilitated waterfront warehouses, whose survival is also owed to tourism, have more charm and add to the considerable attractiveness of the city.

The city centre runs inland from Sullivan's Cove on the western shore of the Derwent Estuary. Most of Hobart's population lives on this side of the Derwent, and the suburbs extend southwest (to Sandy Bay, site of the Casino) and northwest through the pleasant New Town area and beyond. The eastern shore is less developed but no less charming.

ARRIVAL AND DEPARTURE

Air. Hobart's airport is 20km east of the city near Seven Mile Beach. The only bus service to the airport is operated by TRC; the fare for the 30-minute journey is $4. Buses leave the airport shortly after the arrival of flights, and most serve the Eastlands Shopping Centre (on the eastern shore) and the Wrest Point Casino as well as the bus company's city office at 96 Harrington St (tel: 34 4577). Services to the airport leave from this office about an hour before flight departures.

Bus. Long-distance services to and from Hobart are published daily in the *Mercury*. All TRC services — and several other companies — operate to and from the bus station at 96 Harrington St. The longest route on the island (to Smithton) leaves at 7am, Monday-Friday. Coastliner Express has services each weekday on this route, departing at 2.15pm, but fares are higher and the

Greyhound bus pass is not accepted. The Queenstown Service bus leaves Harrington St at 8.30am, Monday-Friday, and 9am on Saturdays, arriving at Queenstown at 2.30pm. For the East Coast, Glamorgan Line (tel: 20 4119) has services to Bicheno at 8am and 2.30pm, Monday-Friday. Tasmanian Motorways (tel: 23 8388) buses to Port Arthur depart from the Centreway Arcade on Collins St at 7.45am; the one-way fare is $8.

Hitch-hiking. It is easy to reach the best spot to hitch north on National Highway 1 (which also leads to the A5 northwest) or east on the A3: from the centre of town go northeast along Liverpool St to the roundabout at the junction of Brooker Avenue (Highway 1) and the Tasman Highway (A3). You should not have to wait too long, particularly if you carry a sign showing the next major town along your route (New Norfolk for the west, Melton Mowbray for the north or Sorell for the east). There is usually a high proportion of local traffic, especially in the evening rush hours, but don't be tempted to walk further out: there are no better hitching spots for miles along either route.

For the lightly-travelled A6 southwest, walk to the southwestern end of Davey St and catch the traffic as it starts along the Southern Outlet.

CITY TRANSPORT

Bus services operate 7am-11pm, Monday to Saturday and about 10am-6pm on Sundays. For a dollar you can buy the complex *Hobart Bus Timetables* booklet, full of mysterious footnotes such as "Departure times for Dynnyrne other than for route 51 are approximate only". Alternatively, call in at the MTT enquiry desk at the Tasbureau office (80 Elizabeth St) or dial 71 3232 for information. Most city services arrive and depart close to the Elizabeth St Mall; on some journeys to the northern suburbs, you have to take bus 100 or 101 (express) to the Springfield Interchange at Moonah and change to another bus there. Fares start at 50¢ with a maximum of $1. A Day Rover ticket costs $1.40 and allows unlimited travel on MTT services at off-peak times (not before 9am nor between 4.30pm and 6pm, Monday-Friday). You buy the ticket from the driver of the first bus you board.

There is a peak-hour-only ferry service between Brooke St Pier in Hobart and the Esplanade in Bellerive, across the Derwent Estuary; the fare is $1, and Day Rover tickets are not valid on this service. Call 23 5893 for schedules.

Bicycles can be hired from Graham McVilly Cycles at 65 King St, Sandy Bay (tel: 23 7284); YHA members get a 10% discount.

ACCOMMODATION

There is no really cheap accommodation in the city centre. The most central guest house is the Astor (Private) Hotel at 157 Macquarie St (at the corner of Victoria St; 34 6384), where bed and breakfast costs $25 single or $40 double. The Tasbureau office can provide a list of other options.

Hostels. Hobart has one Youth Hostel on each side of the Derwent, and both are attractive Victorian buildings. Especially in summer, you should call in at the YHA office at 28 Criterion St (34 9617) or phone the hostels ahead to check availability before heading out of the city centre to reach them. The closest and largest is "Woodlands" in New Town at 7 Woodlands Avenue (28 6720), on the western shore and reached by bus 100 to stop 13. The other, smaller but more pleasant, is across the river at 52 King St in Bellerive (44 2552), at stop 19 on bus routes 83 to 87 inclusive. You can also reach it during rush hours on the ferry from Hobart; walk 200 metres back along the Esplanade, and King St is on your left. Do not add to the misery caused to the unfortunate residents of King St, Sandy Bay (on the western shore): numerous travellers turn up there looking for the hostel, which is on the *eastern* shore.

Student Residences. During university vacations, comfortable rooms (with electric fires!) are let out to travellers on the campus at Sandy Bay. Students pay only $12 per night at Christ Church College (23 5190), and the price includes a hearty buffet breakfast.

Camping. The Sandy Bay Caravan Park (25 1264) on Peel St, 4km southwest of the city centre, charges $7 for a tent and two occupants.

EATING AND DRINKING

Hobart has plenty of top-notch restaurants where you pay dearly to eat well. Of the cheap-and-cheerful places, try the reliable Mexican fare at Taco Bill's (41 Hampden Road, Battery Point; 23 5297). It opens at 6pm from Tuesday to Saturday and you can bring your own alcohol. For pies and pasties, go to Banjo's opposite Tasbureau on Elizabeth St. The Centreway Café at 131 Collins St gives a 10% discount to YHA members, and if you want to prepare your own picnic you can get a similar discount at Eumarrah Wholefoods at 45 Goulburn St. The best pizzas in town are made at Saverio's Pizzeria, just up from Sandy Bay Road west of the city centre, which is also BYO. The new Mures Fish Centre — on the waterfront between Victoria and Constitution Docks — is expensive but very good, and has a fairly authentic sushi bar. The Drunken Admiral at 17 Hunter St has garlic prawns and Tasmanian oysters. If you feel hungry in the small hours, head for the 24-hour coffee shop at the Wrest Point Casino. The Casino also has a revolving restaurant — The Point — which charges high prices as you rotate 80 metres above the ground.

Drinking. Most of Hobart's pubs dwell upon their Victorian past. Although some on the waterfront have been tastelessly tarted-up, you can drink in a little history at the Ship, 73 Collins St (built in 1821); the Traveller's Rest at 394 Sandy Bay Road (1839); or the Custom House, 1 Murray St, at the corner of Waterman's Dock by Salamanca Place. The Dog House Hotel (at the corner of Barrack and Goulburn Streets) is highly recommended as a place to meet other travellers.

ENTERTAINMENT

A fine job has been made of restoring Hobart's Victorian buildings to their former stern elegance. Salamanca Place and the parallel Castray Esplanade (which run from Davey St to Princes Park) contain some splendid sandstone warehouses converted to a pleasant mixture of antique shops, galleries and restaurants. Most of the sights are within a 1km radius of the city centre, so within easy walking distance. The two main out-of-town attractions are Mount Wellington and the Cadbury chocolate factory. To reach the summit of the former, you will be encouraged to take an organized tour (bookable, like most things in the city, through Tasbureau). Be warned that tours run to the peak only in clear weather; at other times you may be taken instead to Mount Nelson but not be told until you are under way. The alternative is to take bus 45, 48 or 49 to stop 27 in the suburb of Fern Tree, at the foot of the mountain, and walk or hitch the remaining (badly signposted) 11km along Pinnacle Road to the summit.

The chocolate factory is in the northwestern suburb of Claremont. Coach trips and cruise boats up the Derwent from Hobart are organized by Tasbureau, or you can get out there under your own steam by taking bus 100 or or 101 to the Springfield Interchange then bus 38 or 41. Tours of the factory must, however, be booked ahead at Tasbureau and cost $5. The factory is closed on public holidays, for a week in September and for a month around Christmas.

Battery Point. This spur of land south of the city centre probably contains a finer collection of Victorian buildings than any other square kilometre in Australia. There are no signs of the battery of cannon which gave the Point its name, in 1818; the oldest structure is the signal station, dating from 1828, and most of the buildings were constructed in the mid-19th century. The leaflet *Let's Talk About Battery Point* (free from the Tasbureau office) guides you around the highlights, the most charming of which is the circle of 16 cottages that forms Arthurs Circus. Only occasional concrete monstrosities, such as the government's Marine Laboratory on the Waterfront, diminish the charm of the promontory. A walking tour is organized by the Battery Point Group of the National Trust each Saturday morning; just turn up at the Wishing Well in Franklin Square at 9.30, and pay $3 (which includes morning tea).

Museums. The Tasmanian museum and Art Gallery complex on Argyle St opens daily from 10am to 2pm, admission free. The most interesting features are the museum display on the now-extinct Tasmanian Aboriginals, the recently restored Commissariat Bond Store (the oldest building in Hobart, built in 1808) and the Gallery's display of works by early colonial artists.

Much of the rest of Hobart's historical artefacts are housed on Battery Point. The Tasmanian Maritime Museum at Secheron House traces the island's seafaring history, and opens from 1 to 4pm Sunday-Friday and 10am-4pm on Saturdays (admission 50¢). The Van Diemen's Land Memorial Folk Museum at 103 Hampden Road tells the story of the early European settlers, but with more emphasis on the governing classes than their convict charges. It opens 10am to 5pm except at weekends (2-5pm) and costs $2. The Postal and Telecommunications Museum is based in the former Ordnance Building at 21 Castray Esplanade. Admission — and the excellent booklet describing the building — is free. Hours are 8am to 5pm Monday-Friday and 9am to noon on Saturdays. Among the exhibits is a sheet recording "Mr and Mrs E. A. Stacey's Tour of the World 1929", with post office stamps from places such as Tahiti, Cairo and Basingstoke.

Theatre and Music. The major annual event since 1980 has been the Salamanca Arts Festival, held in late September/early October; call 23 7400 for details. Upcoming performances throughout the year are listed in *Press Press,* the *Mercury* and *Sunday Tasmanian,* and are publicized at the Tasbureau office. The Theatre Royal at 29 Campbell St opened in 1837 and has retained its ornate Georgian-style interior and near-perfect acoustics. Call 34 6266 to find out what's on, but don't be too fussy; the theatre is worth a visit for historic interest alone. More adventurous productions are staged at the smaller Backspace auditorium. Drama is performed also at the Peacock Theatre on Salamanca Place, the Tower Theatre Restaurant at 300 Park St, New Town (28 0166), and at the University Centre in Churchill Avenue on the Sandy Bay Campus (reached by bus 52 to stop 12); dial 64 1183 for forthcoming events.

Serious music can be heard at the University Centre, and the University also has a new Centre for the Arts in a renovated jam factory at Sullivan's Cove on the waterfront near Battery Point. The Centre includes galleries and workshops, as well as retaining some of the antiquated jam-making machinery as museum pieces.

The Dog House Hotel (see *Eating and Drinking,* above) has good jazz several nights a week. The Bothy Folk Club is at 304 Elizabeth St in North Hobart. Local rock bands can be seen at Ye Old Red Lion at 129 Macquarie St and Hadley's at 14 Murray St. Touring and country artists tend to appear at the Wrest Point Entertainment Centre, part of the casino complex at Sandy Beach. A new venue is being built at Glenorchy (8km northwest of Hobart) and should be open in 1989.

Nightlife. Much of the action takes place at Wrest Point Casino (25 0112), which opens from noon to the early hours. The complex has a cabaret room for those who prefer crooners to roulette, and the inevitable Regines disco. Mr Wooby's at the back of 65 Salamanca Place is more of a restaurant than a night club, but you can drink there until 2am.

Cinema. Film buffs from all over Australasia congregate in Hobart each September for the International Film Festival, an event which doesn't quite rival Cannes but which is nonetheless an interesting showcase, particularly of southern hemisphere movies. For the rest of the year, the choice is limited to three cinemas with a total of four screens: Hoyts Midcity at the T&G building, 115 Collins St (31 0300), the West End Twin at 181 Collins St (34 7288) and the State at 375 Elizabeth St (34 6318), which shows more arty films. To compensate for the shortage of venues, two or three separate feature films are shown on each screen through the day.

Sport. Yachting fans will wish to be in Hobart around New Year for the climax of the Sydney-Hobart Yacht Race, or in February for the Hobart Yacht Regatta. The finishing line is at Constitution Dock, and the race is followed by a carnival.

An Olympic-sized pool is located at the bottom of Aberdeen St (by the junction with the Tasman Highway. The Domain Tennis Centre is adjacent. You can go to the dogs at Hobart Greyhound Racing Club meetings at the Royal Hobart Showground. The Elwick Showground, in the suburb of Glenorchy, is the venue for horseracing and harness racing; check in the *Mercury* for details of meetings. Cricket is played at the Tasmanian Cricket Association ground in Queen's Domain.

Parks and Zoos. The Royal Tasmanian Botanical Gardens are refreshingly different from those in other state capitals, with excellent roses and herb gardens. They are just northeast of the city centre at Queen's Domain, and can be reached by bus 1 from the city (Monday-Friday, plus Sundays in summer). The gardens open 8am to 4.45pm daily.

There is no zoo in Hobart, so to see the island's wildlife (such as the Tasmanian Devil, a carnivorous marsupial the size of a small dog, with horn-like ears) you need to travel 60km to the Talune Wildlife Park in Gardners Bay

80km to the Tasmanian Devil Park on the Port Arthur Harbour in Taranna which gives a discount to YHA members).

hopping. Most shops open from 9am to 6pm, Monday-Friday. Some larger ores and shops in suburban malls stay open until 9pm on Fridays, and dditionally on Saturdays from 9am to noon. There is a late-night pharmacy t the corner of Macquarie and Harrington Streets which opens 9am-9pm daily. lizabeth St Mall is the main city-centre shopping street.

Greensleeves Bookshop, 247 Sandy Bay Road (between the city and the Iniversity) has the most interesting selection of books in town. The Wilderness hop is in the Galleria at 33 Salamanca Place (34 9370). The Saturday morning arket on Salamanca Place is lively, but don't expect to find too many bargains.

To buy the equipment you need to cope with the wilderness, try the Jolly wagman camping and hiking shop (opposite the tourist office on Elizabeth St) r the Scout Shop at 107 Murray St, which gives YHA members 10% off prices r camping gear.

Further Afield

THE SOUTH WEST

The first stretch of the journey south on the A6 from the capital reveals little of the desolation in store if you venture beyond the nd of the Huon Highway. The road splits at the small town of Kingston. About km south of Kingston on the Channel Highway are the headquarters of Australia's Antarctic Division, and you can visit their free exhibition between am and 4pm, Monday-Friday. If you head further south alongside the icturesque D'Entrecasteux Channel, your journey will be enlivened by ttractions such as the Model Train World near Margate and the Winterwood Winery (making wines from fruit and honey) between Woodbridge and Gardners Bay.

Halfway down the coast from Kingston is the small port of Kettering, where you can catch a ferry to Bruny Island. The ferry operates between 7am-6.30pm approximately; if you intend to catch the last boat of the day you should arrive a little early, since sailings can be erratic. The Kettering Hotel overlooking the harbour is a pleasant place to wait for the next ferry, and is warmed in winter and sometimes summer) by a log fire. The North and South parts of Bruny sland are linked by a thin strip of land; on a clear day, stop in the middle to admire the 360-degree views across Isthmus Bay to the west and Adventure Bay o the east. South Bruny Island claims to have the southernmost pub in Australia, as does Dover across on the mainland. To make sure you are able to boast about having drunk in the most southerly, have a drink in both.

The road southwest from Kingston first runs through the orchards of the Huon Valley; you can stop off to visit the Apple Museum in the village of Grove to learn about the history of the area and inspect hundreds of varieties of apple. The region's centre is Huonville. Although the town itself is unattractive, the Huon River has some of the best waterside scenery in Australia. If you follow the eastern bank south, you end up in the prettily situated town of Cygnet. The Youth Hostel (tel: 002-95 1551) functions also as a farm and teahouse, with the warden Tony Lewis reputedly making the best apple cake in Tasmania. The Hostel is linked with Tasmanian River Rafters and offers a selection of canoeing and rafting trips.

The highway along the western side of the Huon continues south to

Geeveston, Dover and Southport. From Geeveston you can make a detour to the Hartz Mountains National Park, 80km southwest of Hobart. The lakes and crags formed by glacial erosion are considerably more impressive than those of the Harz range in Germany, and have the added bonus of dramatic trails through the rainforest. Dover, overlooking Esperance Bay, is an appealing town and the last real settlement before the wilderness; stock up with petrol and provisions here unless you are prepared to risk the limited and expensive selection at Southport.

The highway proper ends at Southport, but most people who have come this far head west. There are thermal springs 8km along the unsealed B35. Although they tend to be tepid rather than hot, the short walk around them (with the possibility of spotting platypus) is worth the effort. The Hastings Caves, 3km along, have regular guided tours through the spectacular rock formations. The B36 road south leads to Lune River, site of the most southerly Youth Hostel in Australia. It is also one of the most active hostels in the nation: you can hire caving equipment (to explore the local glow-worm caves), borrow a kayak for canoeing on the River, or join a trek into the South West National Park. Just south of the Hostel is Ida Bay, which has a railway line running 5km east to Deep Hole. The line theoretically provides great possibilities for a day's bushwalking around the Southport Lagoon, but the train schedules are not renowned for their reliability: you could find you face a long hike back to Lune River if the last train fails to run. The remainder of route B36 south is suitable only for four-wheel drive vehicles, ending at Cockle Creek (unsurprisingly Australia's southernmost township). Should your vehicle break down, you might usefully spend your time sifting through the roadside earth while waiting for assistance; the Lune River area is famous for its gemstones.

The entrance to the South West Walking Track is close to Lune River. It takes bushwalkers through an uninhabited and inhospitable region that is one of the least-explored areas in Australia. The South West National Park is one of only three temperate areas on the UNESCO World Heritage List, and has so far remained virtually untainted by mankind. There are no real roads in the park, but those not confident enough to undergo the strenuous hike can fly into one of the few clearings suitable for light aircraft. One unforgettable feature of this wilderness is the "false floor" created in places by thick scrub; the closely-meshed greenery can be up to 10 metres above ground level. Attempting to walk on this treacherous surface is unwise, since anyone unfortunate enough to fall through has little chance of escape or rescue. Only the most experienced hikers should explore the Park without a guide, although plenty of tours are operated; see *Great Outdoors* for details.

THE SOUTH EAST

There are arguably more historical relics of early European settlements in this corner of Tasmania than anywhere else in Australia. Visiting the vestiges of a penal settlement is instructive rather than entertaining; but when you've seen enough of man's inhumanity to man, the views and fresh air provide a welcome relief.

Tasman Peninsula. The sea south and east of Hobart is filled with rugged yet beautiful peninsulas and islands, of which the Tasman Peninsula has most to offer in terms of scenery and interest. In addition to Port Arthur (see below), the Peninsula has a variety of natural and man-made attractions. The 90-minute journey along the Arthur Highway runs east from the state capital, then drops down through the Forestier Peninsula to reveal a spectacular view of Eaglehawk Neck, a natural causeway across to the Tasman Peninsula.

This narrow isthmus which formed an impediment to movement made the Peninsula a logical choice for the British authorities when setting up a penal settlement. A relatively small force equipped with vicious dogs was installed at the Neck, and — although a couple of diehards did get through — the guards successfully prevented any mass escape. The Neck was infamous in early Australia as "the isthmus between earth and hell". Nowadays the locals are far more hospitable, and Eaglehawk Neck is a pleasant little place. On the coastline just north of the Neck is a geological formation known as the Tessellated Pavement, vertical shafts of rock sheared off to give a surprisingly uniform geometric pattern, known as "nature's own footpath". A few kilometres south of the Neck there is a blowhole plus two other coastal phenomena known as the Tasman Arch and the Devil's Kitchen. You can hire a bicycle at Eaglehawk Neck and cycle along road C338 to take in these sights. Take time to enjoy the village of Doo, where every house has a name containing the name of the town, including a shack known as "Doo Nothing".

The road which leads you the long way around the Peninsula via Nubeena to Port Arthur is sealed; a detour via Premaydena to Saltwater River and Lime Bay is not, but is usually passable with care and is well worthwhile: the ruins of the early settlement at Saltwater River are fascinating, and the track down to Lime Bay leads to a pretty cove with clear green water. You can camp near the sea for free.

Port Arthur. The main town of the Peninsula lies on a pretty bay and, with well-manicured lawns, would be unrecognizable to those who knew it in darker days. From 1830 to 1876, it was the headquarters of Tasmania's main penal settlement with 25,000 prisoners. Many of the people sent to Port Arthur could be classed as "political prisoners", such as the Tolpuddle Martyr and early trade unionist George Lovelace. The penal settlement was designed to show the cruellest face of the British Empire. Most of the original buildings have been destroyed in a succession of bush fires, but a few Victorian remnants are still standing. The town has been somewhat overtaken by the tourist trade, but you can spend a pleasant couple of hours or days wandering among the ruins of the settlement. The visitors' centre is housed in the former Lunatic Asylum, and offers an audio-visual record of the most notorious penal regime in Australia. Among the other buildings you sense an altogether unhealthy interest in punishment. For example, the penitentiary was designed to compound the already miserable regime of servitude.

Free tours of the settlement — given by an enthusiastic and knowledgable guide — depart at regular intervals from the visitors' centre, ending at the Settlement Museum. Entrance costs $4, including a viewing of an unexceptional film about convict life. Far better value can be found every evening at the Broad Arrow Tea House, located within the "historic site" in Port Arthur: the original (1926) film of Marcus Clarke's story *For the Term of His Natural Life* is shown at 3pm and 8pm. This silent version is far more powerful than the tame television mini-series of the same name. The cost of $5 includes tea and scones or a light supper after the screening. The Broad Arrow also has a craft gallery; call 002-50 2242 for further information and bookings.

At the mouth of Port Arthur Bay lies the Isle of the Dead, where both convicts and free settlers are buried. While the officers and other free settlers were accorded the respect of a proper burial, convicts were interred seven or eight to a grave with no headstone to mark their existence. There are hourly cruises (price $5) of the harbour and its environs which pay particularly close attention to the Isle of the Dead.

Accommodation in the town is scarce but there are, at least, some alternatives to the "Old English Tudor Tavern and Motel Complex" as the Fox and Hounds on the Arthur Highway describes itself. The Youth Hostel at Port Arthur commands an exceptional view of the ruins and is good value at $6 per night. The Garden Point Caravan Park on Stewarts Bay, outside Port Arthur is a cheap ($4 per night) camping ground, but beware of the frequently bad weather.

South of Port Arthur the terrain becomes more rugged. The paved road ends at Remarkable Cave, so-called because of the fascinating formations you can view when the tide is out, and the impressive sight of the Tasman Sea rushing in and out at high tide. A few kilometres farther along a rough track is Cape Raoul, the Peninsula's own version of Land's End. Other, tamer attractions on the Peninsula include an animal park, marine park and the Bush Mill, a steam timber mill which boasts a half-scale steam train on a 2km track which runs back to the Fox and Hounds on Arthur Highway.

New Norfolk. While most visitors are tempted by the coastline or rugged mountain ranges of southern Tasmania, this town 30km inland has some interesting vestiges of colonialism and a predictable selection of tourist attractions. There is also a jet boat operating on the Derwent River which flows through the town: the "Devil Jet" runs half-hour trips along the river; dial 002-61 3460 for details.

The colonial buildings which remain include the Tynwald Mansion on the Willow Bend Estate (named after a twist on the Derwent River) which is now a hotel; the Oast House, now a museum of the Tasman hop industry; and the Old Colony Inn (21 Montague St) which doubles as a colonial museum and restaurant. It seems that the only two old buildings which have retained their original purposes are St Matthew's Church in Bathurst St, dating from 1823, and the Bush Inn on Montague St which, along with several pubs on the mainland, claims to be the oldest continuously licensed house in Australia. Undoubtedly the best place to eat in New Norfolk — and possibly Tasmania — is Cotswold Cuisine on Lachlan Road (tel: 002-61 2322). The owners cater only for groups of six to 14, and discuss personal preferences for food and wine in advance to produce a specially tailored meal. Before making a definite booking, you should also discuss the price.

A further 40km inland from Hobart is the Mount Field National Park, the first to be established in Tasmania. The Park is particularly popular because of its proximity to the state capital, and has some huge, ancient swamp gum trees. The Russell Falls are close to the entrance, falling over 40 metres with a midway ledge for close-up spectating. In winter, the downwardly-mobile head for the Park to enjoy the skiing.

THE EAST COAST

This part of Tasmania is often referred to as the "Holiday Coast" or the "Sun Coast". Fortunately, in spite of attempts by the tourist authority to attract tourists and develop resorts, large stretches of the coast are still unspoilt.

Starting from Hobart in the south, the first main settlement on the Tasman Highway is Buckland. This unprepossessing small town is most notable for St

John's Church, which has a 14th century stained-glass window painstakingly imported from Europe. Triabunna, the next settlement, has some excellent fish restaurants. You can go riding in the surrounding countryside on a horse from Woodstock Trail Riding (002-57 3186); there is a discount off-season for YHA members. The Louisville Resort, just north, is a good imitation of a slightly jaded British seaside resort; nearby Orford is livelier. To escape from these resorts, take the ferry from Louisville across to Maria Island, now a National Park but formerly a penal colony, the first to be established in Tasmania.

Further up the coast, Swansea is a "proper" town with easy access to beaches; Nine Mile Beach is the nearest, and, while not the island's best, has some beautiful shells and good views of the Freycinet Peninsula. The Freycinet National Park is very pleasant, with hills and cliffs falling into the ocean. Coles Bay, the only town on the peninsula and headquarters of the National Park, has a Youth Hostel close by and is ideal for a few days of peace and quiet. The walk out to Wine Glass Bay (so-called because of its shape) is recommended, but beware of the Bennet's wallabies which will go to extraordinary lengths to get any food you happen to have about your person. In fine weather, the beach at Wine Glass Bay is among the very best in Australia.

The midpoint on the coast is Bicheno, a former whaling port, which has attractions such as a wildlife park and marine life centre as well as some good foreshore walks. Easily the most attractive place to stay is the Youth Hostel, only 10 metres from a beach affording views of some spectacular sunrises and sunsets. At low tide you can wade out to the penguin colony on Diamond Island.

The road north then turns inland, twisting alarmingly through the Elephant Pass to St Marys, and returning to the coast near Scamander. There is a good stretch of beach from here up to St Helens, another "real" town and a useful centre to explore the area; the Youth Hostel is at 5 Cameron St (003-76 1661). The crayfish, scallop and abalone catches provide some casual employment, and after a hard day's work you can head for one of the excellent nearby beaches. The Tasman highway inland to Scottsdale and Launceston has some exceptionally good scenery; look out for the village of Wellborough, which looks as though it was shipped intact from Spain.

LAUNCESTON

Tasmania's second city has little in common with its craggy Cornish namesake. The Antipodean Launceston is a well-to-do market town which dominates north Central Tasmania and contains numerous colonial buildings, many converted to tourist-related functions. Also, the names are pronounced differently: while Cornwall's version is Laun'ston, in Tasmania the middle syllable is pronounced.

The city's chief visual attraction is the dramatic Cataract Gorge a mile outside the city, where the South Esk River cuts deep through the land. The view is especially worthwhile at night when the Gorge is floodlit. By day you can take the long and harrowing chairlift ride across the Gorge. Other attractions include the numerous pleasant parks and — for some people — the Casino at Launceston Country Club. Although many colonial buildings have been preserved, Yorktown Square is an unashamedly new (1984) construction of "cobblestone paths, story-book shop fronts and coach house lamps" housing a predictable collection of twee shops. The Penny Royal Mill (a renovation of old corn and gunpowder mills) is in a similar vein, but has the amusing bonus of a fleet of 10 gunpowder barges which transport visitors along the waterways around the complex.

For public transport information, dial 31 9911. A better way to see the city and its surroundings, however, is to hire a bike from Rent-A-Cycle Tasmania. This organization is part of the YHA-affiliated Launceston House Hostel at 36 Thistle St (tel: 003-44 9779). If you wish to cycle around the Central Highlands, they can provide you with special low-geared bicycles.

Launceston is large enough to support a reasonable variety of restaurants: the best alternatives to the steak/seafood/pizza staples are Shafi's Afghan Restaurant (150 George St; tel: 31 2679) and the Smiling Toad (91 George St; 34 0554) which offers an interesting vegetarian menu. Both are BYO.

In contrast to the mountains south and west, the Midlands around Launceston are scenically uninteresting, the recent drought having produced some very drab and un-Tasmanian landscapes, but nearby historic towns such as Oatlands are worth a visit.

THE NORTH WEST

If your time in Tasmania is limited, you can get a flavour of the island by sailing or flying to Devonport and heading northwest. The top left-hand corner of Tasmania has the same ingredients of dramatic coastline, rugged mountains, towering forests and undulating pasture (plus logging and hydro-electric projects) that the island possesses in such abundance.

Devonport, population 25,000, is a fairly lively and interesting port. It straddles the Mersey and, as in Liverpool, there is a ferry across the river: from close by the railway station to East Devonport (fare 50¢). A visit to the Showcase tourist information centre on the corner of Best and Formby Streets (004-24 1287) will equip you with the maps and information for a day's tour. You can rent a bicycle to explore the town from Hire A Bike (004-24 3889). As well as interesting historic buildings, there are some more unusual diversions: the Devonport Brickworks (opposite the Showcase in Best St) will sell you an unfired brick upon which you can inscribe your name. It is then fired and placed in the wall of the brickworks.

A short way west of Devonport is Ulverstone, a beach resort which is also a good base for exploring inland. You need not be an experienced walker to climb Black Bluff in Leven Canyon, just south of Ulverstone. In order to get there, however, you need to wade through the often icily-cold Leven River. The view from the top of Black Bluff on a clear day makes it worthwhile, across to Cradle Mountain and beyond almost to Lake St Clair.

Tasmania's third largest city is Burnie on the shore of Emu Bay, in an area of farmland. The main industry is paper production, and you can take tours of a papermaking factory. Other places of interest include the Pioneer Village Museum on High St (a re-creation of a turn-of-the-century commercial centre), Burnie Park Wildlife Sanctuary and the Art Gallery on Wilmot St. The area around Wynyard has some good beaches, the nearby Rocky Cape National Park, and good trout and sea fishing. Beyond Smithton, the road becomes little more than a track as it approaches Cape Grim, Tasmania's Land's End. The air here is reputed (at least locally) to be the cleanest in the world.

Cradle Mountain and Lake St Clair. This National Park is the most developed in Tasmania, and will become yet more popular when the new highway is built from Cradle Valley to the West Coast. Its highlights are the 1,545-metre Cradle

Mountain, plenty of leisurely strolls on well-marked tracks and good fishing for trout in mountain streams. The major trail is the north-south traverse from the Mountain to Lake St Clair, which should take five days and for which there is a $10 track user fee; it passes Tasmania's highest peak, 1,617-metre Mount Ossa. The Lake is 18km long and is the deepest freshwater lake in Australia. You can cruise the length of Lake St Clair on MV *Tequila;* the one-way fare is $13.90, and you should book in advance on 89 1137.

THE WEST COAST

There are strong similarities between the West Coasts of Tasmania and New Zealand's South Island. Both offer steep mountain ranges, fast-flowing rivers, precipitous gorges and inhospitable rain forest. They even have a town called Queenstown as a gateway to the wilderness. Although few would dispute New Zealand's claim to greater grandeur, a visit to the Tasmanian wild west is not without scenic — and human — interest.

Queenstown has depended for its livelihood upon mining copper from nearby Mount Lyell for over a century. The mine still functions, but is gradually being developed into a "living museum" of mining history. The new Mount Owen Track gives an interesting insight into the pioneering days, and provides some spectacular views. The reservoir which will result from a new hydro-electric scheme is to be developed into a resort area, in an unintentional imitation of the setting of Queenstown, New Zealand. In a major public relations exercise to promote the project, the Tasmanian Hydro-electric Commission (HEC) has converted the old Empire Hotel into an information centre. If you call in, don't expect to find out much about the consequent destruction of the environment; for that side, consult the Tasmanian Wildlife Commission. The Wildlife Commission will also tell you about the wrecking of the ecology of the King River by waste from the copper mine. You can see the spot where conservationist David Bellamy was arrested, a few kilometres east of Queenstown at the start of the road to Crotty. The road runs down to Wild Rivers National Park, but is accessible only by four-wheel drive vehicle.

Zeehan is a mining "ghost town" 60km northwest of Queenstown. In earlier days, it was a community of 10,000 living from a rich vein of silver, lead, and zinc. It reputedly possesses what was once the longest Main St in the southern hemisphere, and a theatre seating over 1,000 people which hosted world-famous performers. Close to Queenstown and Zeehan lies Strahan, an old port from where the ore was shipped. Its main purpose nowadays is as a base for tours across the 20km-long Macquarie Harbour to the Gordon River. There are half and full-day cruises up the river to Gordon Gorge, passing Sarah Island in Macquarie Harbour, a desolate former penal colony. The return journey takes in Hells Gates, the outlet to the ocean. YHA members can get a 10% discount on the normal prices of $28 for the half-day, $32 for a full day. Book through Tasbureau or direct with Gordon River Cruises on 004-71 7179. You can also fly by seaplane from the jetty at Strahan up the river for one or four days' canoeing. The day trip costs $88, and can be booked direct with Wilderness Adventure Camps on 004-71 7377.

BASS STRAIT ISLANDS

These offshore islands take isolation and wilderness a stage further. If the

Tasmanian bush does not feel remote enough for you, take a trip out to King Island or Flinders Island, off the northwestern and northeastern corners of the mainland respectively. The truly antisocial could visit some of the sparsely populated or uninhabited intervening islands — Robbins, Clarke or Cape Barren en route to Flinders Island, or Hunter or Three Hummock Islands between the coast and King Island.

King Island. The "Roaring Forties" dominate the Bass Strait, and these strong westerly winds (so named for the latitude) have driven over 150 ships on to the island. Only half the island has been cleared for farming, the rest being undisturbed native bush with a wide range of wildlife. There are good bushwalking tracks, especially along the unpopulated north coast, and excellent diving in the clear waters with plenty of wrecked ships to explore. In addition, the island has a penguin rookery, a calcified forest and the shimmering Lake Martha Lavinia. Currie, the main settlement, is a working port with an interesting museum tracing the history of seafaring in the Bass Strait, and a Youth Hostel in Charles St. King Island creams and cheeses are especially rich, and command high prices throughout Australia; look out particularly for King Island Brie.

Flinders Island. This is the largest of the Furneaux Group of islands, and measures about 60km by 30km. The main town on the island is Whitemark, and the airport is nearby. As on King Island, there is still some unspoilt scenery and interesting wildlife. The southernmost part of the island is occupied by Mount Strzelecki National Park, which has good bushwalking trails including a well-signposted track to the 756m summit; the walk should take 2½ hours and is well worthwhile. The Patriarch Wildlife Sanctuary is on the east coast, while on the west is the Wybalenna Historic Site near Emitta, which was the scene of the failed attempt to save the Tasmanian Aboriginals.

If the blowflies elsewhere in Australia have driven you mad, the next three years could see the entire blowfly population of Flinders Island eradicated. A federal government scheme plans to wipe them out by introducing flies bred deliberately with genetic defects.

The Great Outdoors

One-seventh of the land area of Tasmania is given over to National Parks. Such is the economic pressure to exploit these areas that the federal authorities police the territory by air, to detect and deter entrepreneurs. The visitors who get most out of Tasmania's wilderness are the sort of people who can cope cheerfully with cold weather laced with frequent downpours. The advice offered on safety in the section *New Zealand: Great Outdoors* holds good for Tasmania, but the island has characteristics which require special attention.

It is foolish to embark upon a visit to the wilderness without a good map. Tasmap produces an excellent range of accurate, large scale maps of the wilder areas of Tasmania. They have offices at 134 Macquarie St, Hobart (tel: 002-30 3382) and 1 Civic Square, Launceston (tel: 003-32 2339).

In the highlands it can snow at any time, so warm and waterproof clothing is essential. A pair of wellington boots can be useful for less ambitious hikes, particularly in the south of Tasmania, since you may find yourself ankle, knee or thigh-deep in mud or slush with depressing regularity. For more adventurous treks, you should use proper walking boots. Sufficient food supplies should be taken, although fresh water can usually be found (from melting snow if necessary). Before trying anything fancy in the wilderness, take advice from the locals and let someone know about your plans and intended time of return.

The real experts are the Tasmanian National Parks and Wildlife Service who, as well as issuing advice, maintain huts and shelters in isolated regions. Their headquarters are at 16 Magnet Court, Sandy Bay, Hobart (tel: 002-30 8011), and they have offices throughout the island. So if you wish to explore the island independently, take advantage of their considerable expertise.

Planning your own adventure in Tasmania is easy. Most of the established trails — and the biggest thrills — are to be found in the western half of the island. Hikers will be attracted particularly to the 200km stretch of National Park from Cradle Mountain through Wild Rivers to the desolate South West.

For the less ambitious, there are plenty of half- and full-day tours by four-wheel drive vehicles. Bookings can be made through Tasbureau offices. As a rough guide, a half-day tour might cost $20-$30 and a full day $40-$50 including lunch and "billy tea". Many operators who run tours by four-wheel drive vehicle, aircraft or raft belong to the Adventure Tours Association of Tasmania; this trade association seeks to ensure high standards of safety.

Fishing. Anglers travel to Tasmania from all over the world to take advantage of the excellent fishing on and around the island. There are game fishing clubs based in Hobart, Launceston and St Helens, and plenty of sea-angling charter boats in the south and east. Even with just a rod and line you will probably find it easy to catch Australian salmon, whiting and bream from the shore.

Since trout were introducd to Tasmania from England in 1864, they have spread to thousands of lakes and streams, making Tasmania prime territory for freshwater fishing. Licence regulations can be checked with the Inland Fisheries Commission at 127 Davey St, Hobart 7000 (tel: 002-26 6622).

Calendar of Events

January	"King of the Derwent" yacht race, Hobart
January	Burnie Day and Night Carnival
January	Folk Festival, Longford
February (first Wednesday)	**Hobart Cup horserace (public holiday only in Hobart)**
February (second Tuesday)	**Royal Hobart Regatta Day (public holiday only in Hobart)**
February	Launceston Cup horserace
March (first Monday)	**Eight Hour Day**
March	Fingal Valley Festival
March	Ross Highland Games
March/April	**Easter Tuesday**
April	Tasmanian Canoe Championships
August/September	Circular Head Arts Festival, Smithton
September	Hobart International Film Festival
September/October	Salamanca Arts Festival, Hobart
October	Royal Hobart Show
October	Launceston National Agricultural Show
November 2	**Recreation Day (holiday only in northern Tas.)**
November	Devonport Agricultural Show
December/January	Sydney — Hobart Yacht Race

Public holidays are shown in **bold**

Adelaide and South Australia

Population of Adelaide: 1,000,000   **Population of SA: 1,400,000**

Residents of the cosmopolitan cities of Melbourne and Sydney tend to regard Adelaide as a backwater, the unexciting capital of a bland, prosperous state, breathing conformity and complacency. Yet Adelaide is heartily recommended by almost everyone who has been there, and indeed it has a grace and charm lacking in the brasher eastern cities. Although it isn't the kind of city — like Sydney or San Francisco — with which visitors fall instantly in love, Adelaide is certainly a pleasant place to be.

A beautifully planned and sited city, with suburbs on the seashore and the Adelaide Hills rising up to the east, it has a centre which seems more European than others in Australia: the tall traditional lines of the railway station, the State Parliament and Town Hall would not be out of place in a middle European capital. Adelaide has the added bonus of being extremely easy to find your way around. As a model for city planners everywhere, the city centre is surrounded on all sides by green parkland. With its biennial arts festival, held in even-numbered years, and a burgeoning range of artistic events throughout the year, Adelaide has a reasonable claim to be the cultural centre of Australia. And the 983,000km² of South Australia (seven times larger than England) is a rich blend of varied coastline, fertile farmland (producing three-fifths of Australia's wine), rugged mountain ranges and seemingly endless stark desert.

The French landed in what is now South Australia in 1792, but found only the desolate Nullarbor Plain north of the Great Australian Bight. The British discovered more benevolent land in the south and plans were laid to settle there. Uniquely for Australia, the new colony was privatized. A South Australian Company was formed, and parcels of land were sold off to small investors — called "Capitalists" in the Company's charter — at £1 per acre. Assisted passages were available to those without the means of buying land, so that the new entrepreneurs could hire workers. The whole scheme was designed to be self-supporting and to attract solid, dependable citizens; convicts were specifically excluded. Alone of all the Australian colonies, South Australia was peopled entirely by free settlers.

The first settlers arrived aboard *HMS Buffalo* in 1836. Standing by a gum tree in what is now Glenelg, they proclaimed the area as a new colony and founded the city of Adelaide, named after the wife of William IV. (The gum tree still stands, at the corner of Bagshaw and McFarlane Streets.) They were led by Governor Hindmarsh, whose bickering with the Board of Commissioners who "owned" the colony led to the collapse of the South Australian Company four years later. Back in the hands of the British government the colony prospered, unfettered by the conflicts between convicts and their warders elsewhere in Australia. The capital benefitted from some remarkably forward-looking town planning. Its first Surveyor-General, Colonel William Light, claimed to have had a vision of how the city should be laid out. He put this into practice and, indeed, the streets of the central area still conform exactly to his plan.

The pattern of migration to South Australia continued to centre upon Adelaide, which today holds three-quarters of the state's population. Most of the rest are within easy reach of the capital, with only a very few venturing into the desert north and west of Port Augusta.

CLIMATE

The oft-quoted fact that South Australia is the driest state in the driest continent on Earth should not lead you to expect unmitigated harshness. Although the northern part of the state is largely inhospitable desert, the areas of interest to most visitors are comfortably benign. Adelaide averages ten hours a day of sunshine in January, and the low humidity makes the February mean high of 30°C/86°F quite bearable. And despite being 100km nearer the South Pole than Sydney is, Adelaide's geographic location gives it longer, drier summers and shorter, milder winters than the coast of New South Wales. The average winter minimum does not fall below 7°C/45°F, and the winter months of June and July average over four hours of sunshine a day. The average rainfall in Adelaide is a light 53cm annually, over half of which falls between May and August; at other times of the year you would be unlucky to come away without a suntan. For city weather (and fire ban information), dial 1196.

THE LOCALS

To this day, there is a chauvinistic tendency among the natives to regard themselves as a cut above residents of other states and their rather dubious extraction. In return, South Australians are known disparagingly as "crow-eaters" by those outside the state, a reference to the alleged dining habits of the early settlers.

The European roots of the settlers are more evident in South Australia than elsewhere in the continent. The state flag, for example, bears the colours of

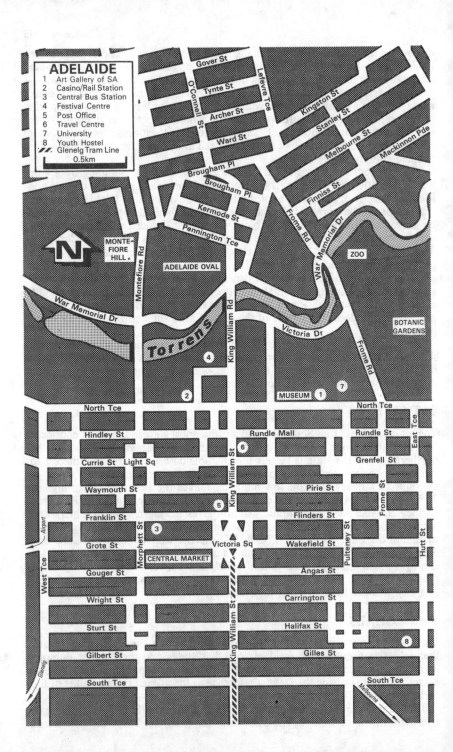

ADELAIDE

1 Art Gallery of SA
2 Casino/Rail Station
3 Central Bus Station
4 Festival Centre
5 Post Office
6 Travel Centre
7 University
8 Youth Hostel
⫽⫽ Glenelg Tram Line
0.5km

N

MONTEFIORE HILL

ADELAIDE OVAL

Torrens

War Memorial Dr

ZOO

BOTANIC GARDENS

Montefiore Rd

King William Rd

Victoria Dr

Frome Rd

War Memorial Dr

Gover St
O'Connell St
Tynte St
Archer St
Ward St
Lefevre Tce
Kingston St
Stanley St
Melbourne St
Mackinnon Pde
Brougham Pl
Brougham Pl
Kermode St
Pennington Tce
Finniss St
Frome Rd

4
2

MUSEUM 1   7

North Tce   North Tce

Hindley St   Rundle Mall   Rundle St

Currie St   Light Sq   6   Grenfell St

Waymouth St   Pirie St

Franklin St   Flinders St

5

Grote St   Victoria Sq   Wakefield St

3   CENTRAL MARKET

Gouger St   Angas St

Wright St   Carrington St

Sturt St   Halifax St

8

Gilbert St   Gilles St

South Tce   South Tce

West Tce
Morphett St
King William St
Pulteney St
Frome St
Hutt St
East Tce

Airport
Glenelg
Melbourne

Germany, and Teutonic names are common in the valleys around Adelaide. Immigrants from southeast Europe and the Middle East also assert their national identities. Recent migration has been mainly from Southeast Asia, giving Adelaide an even more cosmopolitan feel (and, incidentally, an excellent selection of restaurants).

Making Friends. In keeping with the relaxed lifestyle which they enjoy, natives of Adelaide and its environs are casual and friendly. If you set out on a specific mission to make friends, you could do worse than to try the pubs and clubs around Hindley St. This area, however, attracts a fair number of eccentrics and miscellaneous oddballs whom you may not care to befriend. It is safer to head across King William St to meet the cleaner-cut clientele at the pubs and restaurants of Rundle St (see *Eating and Drinking*) or to mix with the student fraternity at the University of Adelaide (conveniently located in the north of the city centre) or the would-be yuppies of North Adelaide in their trendy pubs around O'Connell St.

ARRIVAL AND DEPARTURE

Air. Adelaide airport is 6km southwest of the city centre, planted firmly in the suburbs, and pilots are adept at dodging the bungalows and shopping malls that clutter the approaches to the runway. The international and domestic terminals are five minutes' walk apart. The *Transit's* bus departs for the city centre from outside both terminals every half-hour from 7.30am to 9pm and takes about 20 minutes to reach the city centre. The fare is $2.40. Because the airport is so close to the centre, a taxi ride downtown costs only about $7.50 and if shared between two or three costs little more than the bus. There is a well sign-posted official taxi-share scheme for those travelling alone. The cheapest way to reach the centre is by catching a local bus (80¢-$1.20). You should walk along Sir Richard Williams Avenue to the airport gates (ten minutes from the domestic terminal, slightly less from the international terminal). Let yourself out of the gate beside the cattle grid, cross the main road and catch any bus from stop 15 into the city. Your ticket entitles you to free transfers to other buses, trains or trams within two hours.

"IF LEAVING THE AIRPORT BY PUBLIC BUS, USE THE GATE BESIDE THE CATTLE GRID".

Reaching the airport from the city is easy. The *Transit's* bus departs from a variety of lodgings (including the YMCA and Youth Hostel if you book in advance on 38 1531). Its main pickup point is the Gateway Hotel which is between the Ansett and Australian Airlines offices and opposite the Railway Station/Casino. As mentioned above, a taxi shared between two or three is almost as cheap, and it should not take long for a crowd of three to gather. If you're economizing, take bus 27b or 27c to stop 15, then walk to the terminal.

If you want a ticket out of Australia, Adelaide is a good place from which to depart. Although only three airlines (British Airways, Qantas and Singapore International) serve the city direct from abroad, there is a great deal of competition among other airlines. In order to get business in Adelaide, carriers such as JAT of Yugoslavia and UTA of France sometimes throw in free connecting flights to Melbourne, Sydney or Singapore. The best deal in 1987 for flights to London was by SIA to Singapore, thence on Aeroflot via Moscow or Royal Jordanian via Amman; the one-way fare was around $770. Staff at the Student Travel Australia (STA) office on Level Four of Union House at the University (tel: 223 5089) seem fully clued-up about the various options.

Coach. There are three separate long-distance terminals, but all are in the same northwestern quadrant of the city centre. The Central Bus Station (used by Bus Australia, Deluxe and several South Australia-only coach lines) is at 101 Franklin St (tel: 217 0777) between Morphett St and Victoria Square. Ansett and Greyhound are just along at 111 Franklin St. Aussie Express and Executive Express share a terminal at 230 Franklin St between West Terrace and Morphett St.

For information and bookings, call the following numbers:

Ansett Pioneer — 51 2075   Executive Express — 212 5200
Aussie Express — 231 1333   Greyhound — 212 1777
Bus Australia — 212 7999

One-way fares to Melbourne are $38 upwards, to Sydney from $75, to Brisbane around $100 and to Perth from $99 (on Bus Australia). Greyhound's *Statesman* service is the quickest overland link between Adelaide and Melbourne; the $9\frac{1}{4}$-hour journey costs $55 and includes a 30-minute stop for a meal provided by the company.

If you are staying in Melbourne but want to spend a couple of days in Adelaide, you could do worse than take one of the "gamblers' specials" offered by Executive Express. This bus company will take you overnight to Adelaide, give you a night in the Grosvenor Hotel at 125 North Terrace, and bring you back for $99. Visiting the casino (see *Gambling*) is not compulsory.

Train. Long distance trains serve the Adelaide Rail Passenger Terminal in Keswick, 2km southwest of the city centre (tel: 217 4444). There is a daily overnight service to Melbourne — the *Overland* — at 8pm, taking almost 13 hours and costing $53 in economy, with a bargain standby fare of $30. The corresponding daytime service, the *Daylink,* is a combined coach/train service, with the same fares, and takes 11 hours. It leaves Adelaide at 7.15am daily except Sundays. The *Ghan* departs for Alice Springs at 11am on Thursdays (with an additional winter service on Mondays), arriving 23 hours later for a fare of $141. There are five trains weekly to Perth (not Tuesdays or Thursdays), although only the Wednesday and Saturday services on the *Trans-Australian* are straight through; the ones on the *Indian Pacific* from Sydney involve a change at Port Pirie and take an hour longer, arriving in Perth after 35 hours. Whichever day you travel, the trip involves travelling for two nights and a day.

Adelaide has a small network of suburban trains which operate from the railway station on North Terrace, below — and concealed by — the casino. These trains are operated by the State Transport Authority (STA) and tickets are interchangeable with other modes of transport: see *City Transport* below. Note, however, that the *Austrailpass* is not valid on these suburban services.

Driving. Some locals claim that driving standards have deteriorated considerably since the Adelaide Grand Prix was inaugurated in 1985, by encouraging motorists to emulate their racing heroes. It is claimed that the low point is reached immediately after the race, with youths competing against one another on suburban streets. The roads of South Australia are more suited to those who prefer a gentle spin through the countryside, being adequate but by no means fast. The maximum speed limit in the state is 110km/h, reducing to 60km/h in towns. The minimum driving age is 16.

The blood/alcohol limit in South Australia is soon to be reduced from 0.08 to 0.05. Holders of learner or provisional licences may not drive with *any* alcohol in their bloodstream. Random checks are made at night. If convicted, you can expect a $300 fine and six months' disqualification from driving. Fines for most other motoring offences are levied on-the-spot. For speeding at 20km/h over the limit or jumping a red traffic light, you could be fined $80; this includes a $5 levy paid to the Criminal Injuries Compensation Fund.

The Royal Automobile Association of South Australia (RAA) is at 41 Hindmarsh Square (tel: 223 4555). Their free Tour Planning Map is adequate for most out-of-town trips, and incidentally contains reasonable maps of the eastern states. For the RAA breakdown service, dial 46 0321.

Hitch-hiking. Thumbing through the southern part of the state presents no great problems, with a reasonable amount of traffic and few intimidating superhighways. Sprawling Adelaide is sometimes difficult to get out of; the hills begin as the suburbs end. For Melbourne catch bus 100, 161, 164-166 or 830-851 inclusive to the junction of Cross Road, Portrush Road and Mount Barker Road (Highway 1). This is also the recommended route for Sydney. For Port Augusta and the north and west, take bus 501 to where it turns off Port Wakefield Road (Highway 1) into Salisbury Road. A local train to Cavan brings you out on the same road a little further south.

Don't be tempted to take the road across the Nullarbor nor the Stuart Highway to Alice Springs without ample supplies of water, food and fortitude. Be prepared for a long wait in Coober Pedy. Traffic is sparse and competition from other hitchers can be considerable. Arranging to share a lift (and expenses) is usually possible by consulting the notice boards at the Youth Hostel or the University Union House.

CITY TRANSPORT

City Layout. In accordance with Colonel Light's vision, the centre of Adelaide is elegantly contained by the four Terraces and measures precisely one square mile. Within this area the streets form a logical grid pattern. The heart of the city is the Hindley St/Rundle Mall area, with King William St — the main central artery — cutting between them.

Outside the centre, geography imposes restrictions on the grid scheme but with the aid of *Gregory's* street atlas or the RAA *Adelaide Tourist Guide* map (free from the Travel Centre) you can find most destinations. One "road" which follows no obvious pattern is Brougham Place (pronounced browem), just north of the city. It comprises three sides of an isoceles triangle plus an additional "dog-leg" from one corner, forming a curious geometric shape.

When asking for directions in the centre of town, note that Hindley St is pronounced to rhyme with kindly. Gouger St is pronounced "goojer" and Gilles St as "guiles".

Public Transport. Local buses and trains — and the single tram line to Glenelg — are operated by the State Transport Authority (STA), whose enquiry office is at the corner of Currie and King William Streets. There is another office at the railway station. Call 210 1000 for all local transport information. The Public Transport Map is good value at 50¢.

Adelaide's bus network has three noteworthy features. The first is the "Busway", a concrete track from the edge of the city centre to the northeastern suburbs on which specially adapted buses can run at speeds of up to 100km/h. The bus drives on ordinary roads to the start of the busway, but upon joining the track, small side-rollers grip the edges and steer the bus; when it leaves the busway, it reverts to normal running. The system is widely known as the *O-bahn*, after the original busway in Munich. In the few years it has operated, it has become quite a tourist attraction; a quick ride out to the inappropriately named Paradise Interchange and back can be exhilarating.

The second unusual characteristic is that bus numbers vary depending on whether the bus is running from or to the city. The bus which starts from the city centre and passes the airport, for example, is marked 27b on maps and on the bus itself. But when it turns round at the end of the route, it bears an entirely different number: the most usual is 1 (signifying a journey only as far as the city centre), but some buses may continue right through the city and become a wholly different route, in which case they bear the number of the new route. This system can be disconcerting at first but has a certain logic once you adapt. A further complication is that peak-hour services from the city bearing the suffix *X* for express do not set down passengers until they reach the suburbs. One exception to these rules is the Circle Line bus (route 100) which runs around the city about 5km out; it keeps the same number throughout and stops everywhere. This service operates from 7am to 6pm Monday-Friday, to noon on Saturdays. Most other buses and trams run from 6am to 11.30pm except on Sundays, when a limited timetable operates from 9am to 10.30pm with long intervals between services.

The third sophistication is the system for validating your ticket. When you board a bus or tram, you buy a ticket from the driver (or, for trams, the conductor). The ticket must then be validated in the machine provided (on buses, to the right of the driver). You insert your ticket (the diagram shows which way up), which the machine swallows. After clicking and beeping to itself, the machine expels the ticket, now printed with the price, date and time of expiry. This performance must be repeated if you use the same ticket subsequently when transferring from one vehicle to another.

Fares for all modes of transport are calculated on a system of "sections" and "zones". The city and many of the suburbs fall within zone 1, and virtually all other suburban destinations fall inside zone 2. Off-peak travel (from 9.01am to 3pm, Monday-Friday) costs $1 for one or two zones and $2 for all three. All but regular $1 tickets are valid for two hours of unlimited transfers within the appropriate zones. There is no obligation to continue in one direction, so round-trips on a single ticket are permitted within two hours. The $2.80 *Daytrip* pass allows unlimited travel after 9am, Monday to Friday, and all day at weekends; buy it on the bus or tram, or at the station. You can alternatively buy tickets for ten journeys at a discount of 30% from selected newsagents. If you are caught travelling without a valid ticket, you will be issued with a "Transit Infringement Notice"; this requires that you pay an "expiation fee" of $50 within three weeks or face a court hearing.

A sensible feature of the Adelaide transport system is that all bus stops are given a number (clearly shown on the stop itself) which is often quoted by people giving directions; so, for the airport, you should get off at stop 15. Alighting from STA buses is something of an acquired skill. After pushing the buzzer to persuade the driver to stop, stand at the centre door. When the green light illuminates, you need to push the handle; the door doesn't open automatically. Hold the door open for any passengers behind you, to avoid slamming the door in their faces, shopping, toddlers, etc.

Adelaide city centre has a free bus known as the BeeLine, number 99B. Every five minutes during shopping hours, it travels the 1km length of King William St between Victoria Square and the Railway Station/Casino on North Terrace.

The beautiful old wood-panelled tram linking Victoria Square in the city centre with Glenelg on the coast takes 30 minutes for the full journey. Some rush-hour services don't stop at all intermediate points. There has recently been a proposal to turn the line into another Busway, but this is most unlikely to be implemented given the outrage felt by the locals at the mere mention of the idea.

Taxis. There are ranks at strategic points in the city centre, or you can summon a cab by calling 223 3333 (Amalgamated), 211 8888 (Suburban) or 223 3111 (United Yellow).

Two-passenger pedicabs can be hired by calling 231 1686. They specialize in tours from the South Australia Government Travel Centre at 18 King William St ($11 per person for an hour), but are available also for private hire.

Car. Adelaide used to be known as the "15-minute city", on the basis that nowhere in the city was more than a quarter-hour's drive from anywhere else. As the suburbs have spread and traffic has increased, it is more like a 30-minute city, but driving in Adelaide is still quite painless. Most of the roads are wide and fast-moving. Only the annual Grand Prix in November brings chaos to the city, when traffic increases and some roads at the east of the city centre are blocked weeks in advance to become part of the circuit.

Many city-centre junctions have "no right-turn" signs which flash during business hours, but which are switched off to permit turns at less busy times. Particular hazards include extra-long "bendy-buses" used on the Busway, and the Glenelg Tram which won't hesitate to assert its priority. Parking during business hours within the city centre (enclosed by the four Terraces) is tricky. Either leave your car immediately outside this area, where you should be able to park free, or use the Park & Ride facility on the Busway at Klemzig Station or Paradise Interchange; the journey into town takes 15 minutes.

Most petrol stations open 7am-6pm Monday to Friday, 7am-2pm on Saturday. Outside these hours you can use the Shell garage at 111 West Terrace, or head out to Cavan, Darlington or Pooraha to find a 24-hour dispenser.

The cheapest alternatives to the major car rental companies are out in the suburbs, but the bus service is sufficiently good to make it easy to reach them.

Try Rent-a-Civic at 670 Port Road, Beverley (tel: 268 1879) who hire small Hondas from $20 per day, including 160 free kilometres. You can reach them by bus 30 or 31. Koala Car Rental at 39 Burbridge Road (tel: 352 7299) and Action Rent-a-Car, close to the airport at 280 Burbridge Road (tel: 352 7044) have similar rates. Moke Rent-a-Car at 37 Henley Beach Road (352 8033) have weekend specials offering a moke or Suzuki "Mighty Boy" (a laughably small utility vehicle) for about $90 including a full tank of fuel, and are on the route of the local bus in from the airport (get off at stop 1). Rentals from these and other cut-price operators are restricted to a radius of 160kms from Adelaide. No rental company allows its vehicles to be taken up the Stuart Highway to Alice Springs; to do so is to invalidate the rental agreement and insurance policy.

Cycling. Adelaide offers cyclists as good conditions as can be found in any city: few steep gradients, broad streets with plenty of room for bicycles and specially-designated routes through the parks. ts should beware, howemO
ram tracks on the road down to Glenelg. The Cycling for Pleasure Group (15 Donald St, Highbury; tel: 337 4214) has regular rural and urban rides for all grades of cyclists. You can take your bike on STA trains if you buy a separate ticket for it.

The best selection of bikes for sale is at the Adelaide Cyclery, 188 Main North Road. Considering what a good cycling city Adelaide is, there are few rental shops. Recycle, outside the city at 150 Fullarton Road (tel: 31 3255), have a fleet of ten 10-speed mountain bikes for $15 per day or $45 for a week. Three-and ten-speed machines can be hired in the city centre from Action Moped and Bike Hire at 269 Morphett St (tel: 211 7060), for $1.25 per hour or $10 per day. Mopeds, for which a car licence will suffice, cost $6 per hour or $25 per day. You can also hire a tandem here for $20 per day, but bicycles made for two are rented out for less ($15 per day) from Bike Moves in Unley; tel: 271 1854.

Adelaide suffers from a lack of cheap accommodation. If you arrive late at night in summer without having booked, you can resign yourself to touring the town before eventually paying a fortune somewhere or sleeping out in one of the many open spaces. The Accommodation Central agency (tel: 274 1222) offers a free reservations service, but specializes in more expensive hotels and motels. In the week building up to the Australian Grand Prix in early November, rooms of any description are hard to come by. A special Accommodation Unit (based at the tourist office at 18 King William St) finds "home hosts" for visitors for upwards of $25 per night.

Hostels. Adelaide's Youth Hostel is in the south of the city centre at 290 Gilles St (tel: 223 6007); it's a 15-minute walk, or you can take bus 16, 17 or 18 along Pulteney or Hutt Streets. The hostel is always busy so advance booking is a good idea. They accept telephone bookings only if you quote your credit card number (so you are charged if you don't turn up). If you're unable to book and find it full, consult the list of alternative accommodation posted outside. Across the street at 263 is Backpackers' Adelaide (tel: 223 5680) with dormitory beds for $7.50, and at 257 the International Student Hostel. Backpackers also has an inn at 112 Carrington St, originally a pub built in 1846. The YMCA, more central at 76 Flinders St (tel: 223 1611), is also often full. It accepts both men and women at $6.50 for a dorm, $10 per person for a twin and $13 for a single. Their breakfasts are good and cheap.

Hotels and Motels. There are many expensive up-market hotels in the city centre with depressingly few low-cost alternatives. The King's Head Hotel at 353 King William St (212 6657) charges $15 per person for singles or doubles. The City Central Motel at 23 Hindley St (51 4049) is very convenient but more expensive at $39 single, $45 double. You could also try the Afton Private Hotel at 260 South Terrace (223 5649), but it is often full. Other possibilities include the Austral at 205 Rundle St (223 4660), which costs $20 single, $36 double and often has good local bands playing in the bar; the Centralia at 65 North Terrace (51 4536); and the Criterion at 137 King William St (51 4302).

The cheapest seaside hotel is Schicks Lodge (49 5373), 14km northwest of the centre at 128 Esplanade, Semaphore, charging $10 per person for a room with breakfast.

Student Residences. The University of Adelaide has plenty of college residences which are empty during vacations. The direct approach is best: ring Aquinas (267 1226), Kathleen Lumley (267 3270), Lincoln (267 2276), St Ann's (267 1478) or St Mark's (227 2211) to check availability.

Holiday Flats. Outside school holidays, you can find fairly cheap rented flats along the coastline west of Adelaide. Seaside Holiday Apartments (71 Esplanade, Henley Beach South; 353 4217) and South Pacific (16 Colley Terrace, Glenelg; 294 1352) charge around $25 per day for two people. For a week's stay, Allawah Flats at 8 Renwick St, West Beach (356 5397) costs $105.

Camping. The closest caravan sites to the city centre are the Adelaide Caravan Park on Bruton St in Hackney (42 1563), reached by bus 301, 302, 530 or 531, and the Kensington and Norwood Caravan Park, at 290 Portrush Road, Kensington (31 5289). On-site vans are available from $24 per night. You can pitch a tent for $8 per night at the Marion Caravan Park, 323 Sturt Road, Bedford Park (12km south; tel: 276 6695); or, for $7, a little further out at the Recreation Caravan Park by Belair National Park (278 3540). There are other sites dotted along the seafront. Pitching a tent in one of Adelaide's many parks will attract unwelcome attention from the authorities, but sleeping out behind a bush has been safely achieved by many travellers.

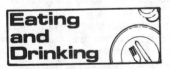

Eating and Drinking

Adelaide's chief contribution to the world of cuisine is the infamous "pie floater", a nondescript meat pie swimming in a bowl of pea soup. Diners should not despair, however: Adelaide does not have quite the range of eating places found in Melbourne and Sydney, but relative to its population the city has more restaurants than any other state capital. What Adelaide lacks in cheap accommodation is made up for by the wide choice of inexpensive eateries. Sundays, however, tend to be a problem; before resorting to the nearest fast-food chain takeaway, check out the list of restaurants open on Sundays which appears in the free magazine *This Week in Adelaide*.

Adelaide has relatively few purely BYO restaurants, but many of the licensed places allow you to bring in wine for a couple of dollars corkage. Many good, cheap places can be found around the Rundle St/Rundle Mall/Hindley St axis;

the following is a small selection of the available options, going along the thoroughfare from east to west:

Rundle St. For lunch, try the Greek specialities at Meze's Continental Café (number 287) and finish up at the Al Fresco Gelateria at 260 for a good selection of coffees, ice creams and sandwiches, which as the name suggests can be consumed outside on pavement tables. A few doors down at 230 Rundle St, Tingle Tangle sells its "fine food and cakes" at a 10% discount to students — not only those from the nearby University; it is especially good at lunchtimes. Don Giovanni at number 201 (tel: 223 2125) has excellent pizzas. The Bangkok (at the corner of Frome St; tel: 223 5406) is licensed and has fine Thai food.

Rundle Mall. Most of the restaurants are tucked away in arcades leading off the Mall. They include the Angkor Wat (BYO; tel: 224 0186), a contender for the most authentic Cambodian cuisine in Australia, at 28 Regent Arcade. Choy Sin on James Place (opposite Myer's store; tel: 223 4388) has a good choice of perfectly acceptable Cantonese dishes. For other options, investigate some of the other arcades.

Hindley St. Between the pubs, coffee shops and "adult" bookshops are some splendid restaurants. At number 21 is the English Roast and Pasta Café (tel: 211 8595); Noah's Ark at 116 is an extremely cheap Lebanese takeaway place with good *falafel* and doner kebab. The Quiet Waters Restaurant and Coffee Lounge (75 Hindley St; tel: 51 3637) is run by brothers Abdul and Aziz, and opens every night until late for excellent *mezes*. A belly dancer performs on Friday and Saturday evenings. If you're prepared to splash out, Le Jardin Parisien at number 34 (tel: 51 6016) is worth trying; their motto is "step in and put a toe in France." To keep the bill within reasonable bounds, take your own (Australian) wine. There are numerous cheap Italian restaurants, and the Pancake Kitchen (at 13 Gilbert Place, near the King William St intersection) is open 24 hours. So too is the café at the Rio Club at 111 Hindley St.

Rigoni's Bistro at 27 Leigh St is just off Hindley St; it has a good spread of pastas at lunchtime. To complete your meal, try the wonderful *gelati* at Flash Coffee Gelateria at 87 Hindley St.

For the most wide-ranging and tasty menu in Adelaide (from Moroccan-style quail to Thai seafood curry) go to Mona Lisa's Bistro at the corner of Hutt and Carrington Streets in the southeast corner of the city centre (tel: 223 3733); food prices are reasonable (under $10 for some excellent main courses) but the house wine will set you back $8 per bottle.

North Adelaide has several interesting places to eat, particularly on O'Connell St. Rakuba at number 35 (BYO) is the only African restaurant in town; it opens from 5pm to 11.30pm Tuesday-Saturday and shares its premises with an African craft shop. Slightly upmarket Bolognese cuisine is served at Balanzone, 143 O'Connell St (tel: 267 3820). For splashing out and putting on weight, try Mistress Augustine at 145: the "Stupendo Chocolate Torte" is highly recommended. La Piazza at 10 O'Connell St is a good place to read the weekend newspapers on Sunday mornings while enjoying coffee and *gelati*. Across at Melbourne St, the Café Istanbul at 87a has a Turkish Meze lunch for $10 (Wednesday-Friday) and dinner for $15 (Monday-Saturday).

There are plenty more restaurants out of the city centre, with Greek cuisine predominating among the southern beach suburbs. In addition, there are numerous good seafood restaurants; try King George whiting, the local speciality, at one of the cheap cafés near the fish market on Gouger St.

Each autumn the "Clare Adventure" provides the chance to sample the culinary skills of leading Adelaide chefs away from their home territory; see *Further Afield* for details.

DRINKING

Pubs in Adelaide are obliged by law to open from 11am to 8pm daily, and are allowed to open at any time between 5am and midnight. Typically they open 10am to midnight Monday-Saturday. Sunday hours are shorter, generally 11am-8pm. If you're desperate for a late-night or early-morning drink, some pubs around the Central Markets (such as the Woodman's Inn, 235 Grenfell St) open at 5am from Monday to Friday. During the week leading up to the Australian Grand Prix in November, many pubs open around the clock.

Cooper's, the local brewery, takes justifiable pride in its real bottled beer and stout. It is the only established brewery in Australia to stick to traditional brewing methods, including wooden barrels and bottle conditioning. "Cooper's Sparkling Ale" is stronger than average (5.75%) and requires careful pouring (like bottled Guinness) to leave the sediment undisturbed at the bottom of the bottle; don't take it back if it's cloudy. Also try the excellent Extra Stout. The South Australian Brewing Co produces less distinguished beers (including West End Bitter, the local fizzy lager), though their Old Southwark Stout is worth sampling.

The Port Dock Brewery Hotel out at Port Adelaide (10 Todd St, off St Vincent St; tel: 240 0187) has a prize-winning brewery on the premises. Beer is pumped to the bar using English brewing machinery. Notable brews include Collector's Pale Ale, Black Diamond Best Bitter and Old Preacher. Closer to town, try the Old Lion at 163 Melbourne St, northeast of the city centre. As well as a selection of beers brewed on the premises (including Lion Stout, which the management describe as the "Grange Hermitage" of beers), there are imported bottled brews from around the world. Between 5 and 7pm, Monday-Saturday, there is a "Social Club Special", allowing you a selection of beer, wine and food for only $7. North Adelaide is a good venue for a pub-crawl, with hotels such as the British (58 Finniss St), the Kentish Arms (23 Stanley St) and the Queen's Head (117 Kermode St). The Dover Castle (47 Archer St) has English-style "snugs" and plush upholstery, together with incongruous overhead fans.

Elsewhere there are plenty of pleasant hotels with few of the down-and-out-dives found in Melbourne and Sydney. In particular, pubs in the southeast corner of the city centre are rapidly acquiring cult status among drinkers. Try the General Havelock at 162 Hutt St or the Earl of Aberdeen at 316 Pulteney St. The Griffin's Head, on Hindmarsh Square at the corner of Grenfell St (tel: 223 7954) has live bands on Sundays in summer, and serves an all-day brunch for $5. For cheap city-centre drinks, hit the happy hour at the Marrakesh Bar (above Southern Cross Cellars in James Place, just off Rundle Mall) which runs each Wednesday from 5 to 7pm; schooners of most beers cost 60¢. A happy hour in more salubrious surroundings takes place every Friday (4.30-6pm) at the Festival Centre Piano Bar. Free beer tastings are held daily at the Kent Town Hotel at 72 Rundle St in the suburb of Kent Town.

Considering the amount of excellent wine produced in South Australia, there is a surprising absence of wine bars serving the local vintages. The biggest selection (over 300 wines) can be found at the casino wine bar. Otherwise, buy from one of the many well-stocked liquor stores (and drink at a BYO restaurant), or head out to the wine producing areas.

For a city of one million, there is far more going on in Adelaide than you might expect. The city sustains two high-quality monthly magazines: the *Adelaide Review* (for theatre, cinema, serious music, etc.), and *Network,* with excellent coverage of Adelaide's lively rock music scene. So while the verdant city of Adelaide has no great "must see" landmarks, there is plenty of culture of every description to enjoy.

During the day, you can breeze along Rundle Mall with the bustle and the buskers, up to the Torrens (really only a creek dammed to make an artificial lake) with the joggers, or out to Glenelg on the tram (which reveals a rather genteel English-style resort). Sensibly, planning regulations mean that there are no outstandingly tall buildings in Adelaide, although the price of a cup of coffee on the seventh floor of Myer's department store on Rundle Mall will be repaid on fine days with a clear view of the eastern hills. For a grand prospect of the city and its spectacularly extensive suburbs, head for the hills. Even the modest elevation of Colonel Light's lookout on Montefiore Hill in North Adelaide — where he had his "vision" about the city plan — offers a splendid view across the centre to the south. But those with a vehicle should try Mount Lofty Summit, most easily reached by following Greenhill Road up into the hills, where the road to Mount Lofty (and its disused lighthouse) is signposted. Windy Point (near Belair on tourist drive 57) is another good venue for viewing the sprawling city.

The South Australian Government Travel Centre at 18 King William St issues a brochure for a two-hour walking tour around the city. As well as the predictable historic sights, the centre has some interesting urban embellishments, for example the Flugelman's Balls sculpture in the middle of Rundle Mall: two huge steel spheres which were donated to the city by a local building society. And to celebrate the state's first 150 years, the pavement on the northern side of North Terrace bears the names of 150 famous South Australians.

There is a move afoot among tourism officials to lose Adelaide's reputation as the "city of churches." This arose as a result of the many fine places of worship built a century ago — such as the cathedral of St Xavier in Wakefield St, St Peter's Cathedral on Pennington Terrace and the Pilgrim Church at 12 Flinders St — but is now felt to project an image of "pious apathy". There is nothing to suggest apathy in the range of organized entertainments available to residents and visitors. For details of events, consult the *Adelaide Review* and *Network,* mentioned above (which are available from bookshops, record shops, restaurants, etc.) or the Entertainment section of the *Advertiser* which appears in the Thursday edition.

Museums. Adelaide has a dozen museums, several operated by the History Trust of South Australia. The Migration and Settlement Museum at 82 Kintore Avenue (behind the State Library on North Terrace; tel: 223 8940) claims to be the first and only museum to tell the story of migration to Australia. It is housed in a former asylum for impoverished women and children. Despite being slanted towards the history of free settlers of South Australia — rather than the convicts who populated other states — the museum is fascinating. You can glimpse life in a migrant hostel and watch audio-visual programmes about the lives of the early settlers. It opens at 10am from Monday to Friday and at 1pm on weekends and public holidays, and closes at 5pm daily. Admission is free.

The History Trust is also responsible for the Old Parliament House, on North Terrace between the new State Parliament and the casino/railway station. Hours are the same as for the Migration and Settlement Museum. The South Australian Postal Museum (next to the GPO at 2 Franklin St) is a pleasant reconstruction of a turn-of-the-century post office. It opens 11am-2pm, Monday to Friday, and admission is free.

The South Australia Maritime Museum is out at Lipson St in Port Adelaide (tel: 240 0200), and comprises a 120-year old lighthouse, several old ships and the Bonded Stores. It opens 10am-5pm from Saturday to Wednesday. The *HMS Buffalo*, moored on the Torrens at Glenelg is a reproduction of the ship which brought out South Australia's first governor. The $2 entry is redeemed only by the other settlers' diaries, which reveal in detail what a ridiculous figure Governor Hindmarsh was.

The most interesting of all is arguably the South Australian Museum on North Terrace, an Antipodean cross between the Natural History and British Museums. There is an excellent collection of Australian and Pacific wildlife, plus displays of Egyptian culture. Aboriginal history is well represented, with a unique collection of *toas,* painted sticks used as totems to represent a place or story. The museum opens daily from 10am to 5pm.

Galleries. The Art Gallery of South Australia on North Terrace has a good collection of foreign and local works, with regular touring exhibitions; dial 223 7200 for details. The Festival Centre (see below) often has up to three separate exhibitions at once, some related to current performances at the Centre. To see the state of the art of the state's modern artists, visit the Contemporary Art Society of South Australia gallery at 41 Porter St in Parkside. There is a different exhibition each month; call 272 2682 for the latest.

Festival Centre. Although a more modest construction than the Sydney Opera House, Adelaide's Festival Centre serves its purpose well as the cultural heart of the city. It is set in parkland on King William Road above North Terrace, and is part of ASER, acronym for the inelegantly-titled "Adelaide Station Environs Redevelopment"; this $200 million project also includes the casino, the Convention Centre, and the Hyatt Regency Hotel. The Festival Centre has three auditoria (the Playhouse, the Space Theatre Cabaret Club and the Festival Theatre), an open-air amphitheatre, a piano bar, Lyrics restaurant and the Playhouse Bistro. You can take a tour of the complex every hour from 10am to 4pm, Monday-Friday, and at 10.30, 11.30 and 12.30 on Saturdays.

The best performances are by the State Theatre Company, whose interpretations of anything from Shakespeare to modern Australian drama are consistently good. Most other productions are mainstream touring shows (many of which originate in London's West End), but the Space Theatre, with cabaret seating and a licensed bar, has a more innovative drama programme. Ticket prices for most performances range from $12 to $30, with students qualifying for a discount of about 20%.

Festival Centre events are advertised in the monthly programme, or you can ring 211 8999 for recorded information. (If you prefer to speak to a human being, dial 216 8600.) The box office is open from 9.30am to 6pm except Sundays. For credit card bookings by telephone, call Dial'n'Charge BASS on 213 4777 between 9am and 6pm except Sundays. If you're elsewhere in South Australia, 008-18 8014 will get you through for the price of a local call. A service charge of $1.50 is added to the cost of tickets booked by credit card.

The prestigious Adelaide Festival takes place in February 1988, 1990, 1992, etc. Modelled loosely on the Edinburgh Festival, it attracts theatre, dance and music groups from the English-speaking world and beyond. Although its "Fringe" does not compare with its Scottish counterpart, the Festival offers about 300 events in its three-week run. Call 213 4788 for programmes and information.

Theatre. The Festival Centre has no monopoly on drama in Adelaide. Commercial theatres include the John Edmund (89 Halifax St; tel: 223 5651), the Opera (tel: 213 4777) and the Odeon on Queen St in Norwood (tel: 356 4975). Mainland Australia's oldest theatre — the Royal Victoria on Waymouth St — will soon re-open. Bookings can be made direct through these theatres or through Dial'n'Charge BASS. Drama of a more experimental nature can be seen at the La Mama (184 Port Road, Hindmarsh; tel: 46 4212); the Royalty (65 Angas St, at the southeast of the city centre; tel: 49 1128) and the Junction (1a Falcon Avenue, Mile End; tel: 43 6200).

Cinema. Free showings from the extensive collection of the State Film and Video Library take place every Wednesday between 1pm and 2pm (and on some Wednesday evenings at 8pm) at the State Library Theatre on Kintore Avenue. Call 268 7366 for details of forthcoming shows. Several cinemas in or near the centre of Adelaide have interesting repertory programmes: the Piccadilly, a beautiful 1930s structure at 181 O'Connell St; the Chelsea at 275 Kensington Road; the Capri at 141 Goodwood Road, which has an organist on Fridays and Saturdays; the Trak at 375 Greenhill Road, Toorak Gardens; and the Classic at 128 Hindley St. The main commercial cinemas in the city centre are Hoyts in Regents Arcade, off Rundle Mall (223 2233); the Hindley, at 88 Hindley St (51 5961); and the Academy in Hindmarsh Square (223 5000). There are many others out in the suburbs, with drive-ins at Gillies Plains, Elizabeth, West Beach, St Agnes and Marion Twin.

Music. The biggest indoor rock venues are the Apollo Entertainment Centre and the Thebarton Theatre, west of the city centre at 114 Henley Beach Road, Torrensville (tel: 43 5255). Some touring bands play at the open-air Thebarton Oval. Tickets can be bought from branches of The Box Office in many record shops. In addition, there is a surprisingly lively local "underground" rock scene. Groups such as the Dagoes, Exploding White Mice and the Spikes may not yet have grabbed the world's attention, but each has a cult following in Adelaide. The best city-centre places to see some of the excellent local bands are the Exeter Hotel (246 Rundle St; 223 2623); Le Rox (9 Light Square; 51 3234); the Tivoli (261 Pirie St; 223 2388); and the Austral Hotel (205 Rundle St; 222 4660). Out of the city, try the Ark at 150 Glen Osmond Road, Fullarton (79 3614). Try to see the innovative Aboriginal band No Fixed Address play in their home city.

Free rock concerts are held on summer Sundays (from 4-6pm) at the Festival Centre amphitheatre, and on Saturday afternoons there is free jazz on the Centre's Bistro Terrace from 2pm to 5pm. A reliable regular jazz venue is the Southern Jazz Club at the Tonsley Hotel on South Road in the suburb of St Mary's.

The best serious music is performed during the Festival, but at other times consult the *Adelaide Review* for upcoming concerts.

Nightlife. There are estimated to be 3,000 prostitutes working in Adelaide, and the profession may soon be legalized in the state. Many of them work along Hindley St, Adelaide's rather tame answer to Sydney's Kings Cross. As well as a tacky collection of strip joints and restaurants with topless waitresses, there are nightclubs of varying degrees of respectability. It is difficult to recommend any particular disco; most have predictable names (Regine's, Bogart's, Mr Bojangles, etc.), predictable music and attract a predictable clientele. You could try the Rio at 111 Hindley St (tel: 212 2744) or Gravity on Hindmarsh Square. If, on the other hand, your idea of a good night out is browsing in bookshops until late, Adelaide is the place to be; see *Shopping,* below.

Gambling. The Adelaide Casino was converted from the above-ground part of the railway station on North Terrace, and has a fine marble interior. It opens from 10am to 4am, Monday-Thursday and straight through from 10am on Friday to 4pm on Monday. The only days on which you are unable to gamble away your savings are Good Friday and Christmas Day. The conditions for admittance are that you should be over 18 and wearing at least "smart casual" dress. Entrance is free, as is the *Adelaide Casino Gaming Guide* booklet which is dispensed to the uninitiated. The Australian Poker Championships are held at the casino each October, but an entrance fee of $175 is required.

SPORT

Spectator Sports. The event of the year is the annual Australian Grand Prix in November, which is run on a circuit at the east of the city centre (much to the chagrin of local residents, who require passes to reach their homes). Drivers make 82 laps of the 3.78km circuit. The cheapest ticket for the main race day (Sunday) is about $30, which buys admission to the circuit only. Seats in prime positions cost over $200. Tickets are sold by mail from the Grand Prix Office, PO Box 1111, Norwood, SA 5067, and through BASS ticket agencies throughout Australia. The event as a whole lasts a week, with various subsidiary races including the Celebrity Challenge which in 1987 featured Clive James, Mark Knopfler, Joe Bugner and New Zealand's Prime Minister David Lange.

If you prefer to watch animals, you can go to the dogs every Monday and Thursday evening at the Adelaide Greyhound Racing Club on Days Road in Angle Park (tel: 268 1923). There are four suburban horseracing courses, so one is likely to be running while you're in town. Check the green NewsTab pull-out in the *News* for venues and form. Club, interstate and Test cricket is played at the delightful Adelaide Oval just north of the Torrens; call 1188 for the latest cricket scores. South Australia does not excel in any of the codes of football, but if you want to catch a game check the sports pages of the *Advertiser.* The South Australia National Football League (Australian Rules) grand final is held early in October at Football Park. The best teams are the Glenelg Tigers and North Adelaide, known as the Roosters.

Participation. Free maps for joggers can be obtained by calling 227 4057. Early risers might also wish to join the Sunday morning outings organized by the South Australian Road Runners Association (tel: 212 6115). They meet at the junction of Bundeys Road and Mackinnon Parade, and start the day with a breakfast of coffee and muesli for only 60¢. There is a fun run from the city to Port Adelaide in April, and to the Bay in September; the Festival City Marathon takes place in the cool of August.

Tennis and squash courts are dotted around the city and its suburbs: for city centre tennis dial 51 3596 or 51 4371, and for squash 223 1611. The parkland of Adelaide lends itself to golf, and there are a number of public courses. The nearest to the city is at North Adelaide (tel: 267 2171). Swimming pools might seem superfluous with the beaches so close to the city. But if the bus or tram ride out from the city is daunting on a hot day, try the pool in North Adelaide (tel: 269 5595). Windsurfers may be hired from various points on the beaches, but beginners will find calmer waters out at the West Lakes, just inland from the coast and south of Port Adelaide.

Parks and Zoos. It is difficult to continue in any one direction in Adelaide for long without encountering a park. Of the many alternatives, the most popular is Elder Park, around the Torrens Lake just up from North Terrace, separating the city centre from North Adelaide. The careful landscaping allows you to relax amid peace and quiet. You can paddle around the lake in a boat hired from the stall next to Jolley's Bistro, by the southeast side of King William Road as it crosses the Torrens. At the eastern end is the Adelaide Botanic Garden; there are guided tours each Friday at 10.30am. The highlight of the Garden is a vast new glass tropical conservatory, built as a project for the Bicentenary and intended to create the effect of a miniature rain forest.

Adelaide's zoo on Frome Road (north of the Botanic Garden) is most notable for its collection of bird life and a Nocturnal House where you can see animals which are active at night. It opens 9.30am to 5pm every day except Christmas. If you insist upon cuddling a koala, you must go out 10km (bus 820) to the Cleland Wildlife Reserve in the Mount Lofty Ranges.

Beaches. Adelaide is favoured with a continuous stretch of safe and accessible beach, safe from sharks and with few towering shoreline buildings. From anywhere in the city you need only head west to find somewhere to lay your towel on the 32km of gently sloping sandy beach. Don't expect the massive breakers of the Indian and Pacific Oceans; the placid waters of Gulf St Vincent are protected from the high seas by the Yorke Peninsula and Kangaroo Island. The same geographical features ensure that the warmth of the ocean is conserved well into autumn, and even a midwinter swim isn't out of the question.

Citizens of Adelaide spend less time discussing the best beaches than their counterparts in Sydney, perhaps because there is little to distinguish one from another. Glenelg is the largest and most interesting resort and has a delightful beach, plus the biggest waterslide in Australia. The only beach officially designated for nude bathing, Maslin's Beach, is a long way south. It can be reached by suburban train to Noarlunga then bus 741J.

IF YOU INSIST ON CUDDLING A KOALA...

SHOPPING

Rundle Mall is the main shopping street. Prices are lower, however, at the numerous shopping centres out in the suburbs. The most expensive boutiques are to be found along Melbourne St in North Adelaide. The normal opening time is 8.30 or 9am, with closing at 5.30 or 6pm from Monday to Friday and at noon on Saturdays. Many city-centre stores open late until 9pm on Fridays, and suburban malls to the same time on Thursdays.

Adelaide has plenty of shops selling equipment for camping and bushwalking expeditions. Two city-centre stockists give a 10% discount to Youth Hostellers: Flinders Camping Centre at 106 Pirie St, and the Scout Outdoor Centre at 192 Rundle St.

South Australia produces four-fifths of the world's opals (see *Further Afield: Coober Pedy*) and, in terms of choice, Adelaide is the best place to buy them. A large number of jewellers make a good living from selling opals to tourists, including one merchant (Olympic) which has a simulated underground mine at its premises on Rundle Mall. Foreign visitors are able to avoid the 30% sales tax on opals if they present a passport and valid air ticket. A shop worth visiting if only for its name is Faulty Towels on Burbridge Road, which specializes in sub-standard bathroom accessories.

Markets. The Central Markets (in the city between Grote and Gouger Streets) offer an excellent selection of all kinds of food, and open on Tuesdays, Thursdays, Fridays and Saturdays, with late opening on Fridays to 9pm. After an hour or two spent checking out the exotic produce and colourful stallholders, you can collapse for coffee and cakes at the Providore Delicatessen in the Markets. Other markets — such as the Brickworks on South Road at Thebarton, and the Antique Market at 32 Grote St — are more commercialized. The Brickworks is most interesting at weekends when street entertainers are out in force. It also boasts seven "colonial shops", a miniature golf course and a go-kart track.

Books. Bibliophiles are spoilt for choice in Adelaide. On North Terrace, for example, both the University and the State Library have excellent bookshops, the latter particularly good for Australiana. The Europa Bookshop at 16 Pulteney St (in the AGC building) has a fine selection of travel books and maps. Mary Martin's at 91 Gawler Place specializes in art and cinema titles. For food and wine books, try Food in Print at 140 Unley Road, Unley (tel: 272 8210). There are also a number of late-night bookshops: the Third World Bookshop at 103 Hindley St (open to 1 or 2am), has a good (if chaotically organized) selection of radical literature, and also deals in secondhand books, cassettes and records; Imprints, at 80 Hindley St, is open until 11.30pm on Fridays and Saturdays and is good for browsing; and the Liberty Bookshop (17 Twin St, between Rundle Mall and Grenfell St) has a stylish range and opens late every night except Sunday. A cheap "book-swap" stall operates in the Adelaide Arcade, off Rundle Mall.

THE MEDIA

Newspapers. The leading morning daily is the *Advertiser* (40¢), a broadsheet which (as mentioned above) features a pull-out entertainment section on Thursdays. On Fridays, the pink Guide section highlights television and cinema. The down-market tabloid *News* costs the same.

Radio. The headquarters of ABC radio is in Adelaide, and the local ABC AM station is 5AN (891kHz). SA-FM (107MHz) transmits a safe diet of Adult Oriented Rock, while 5MMM-FM reflects the local "underground" rock scene. Current chart music can be heard on 5KA, and golden oldies from the 60s and 70s on 5AD (1323kHz AM). The University station, 5UV (531kHz AM), has news and reviews of Adelaide's cultural highlights plus Aboriginal, student and BBC science programmes.

Television. The usual collection of national networks is on offer. ABC is on Channel 2, while Ten is the leading station for sports coverage. If you've acquired a taste for Australian soap operas, remember that the 30-minute time difference between South Australia and the eastern states means you may have to readjust your viewing patterns.

Adelaide could not be described as remotely dangerous. There have been some tales of gratuitous violence — particularly against homosexuals — but nothing on the scale of attacks in European and American cities. Single women might not care to walk alone through the Hindley St area after dark, not least because of the risk of being mistaken for a prostitute. The parks are potentially dangerous territory, so it's safest to avoid them late at night.

Drugs. The good soil and benevolent climate of South Australia makes it ideal for growing marijuana, both in city back yards and — on a much larger scale — out in the country. South Australia has a more liberal attitude towards use of the drug than the other states, treating it effectively as a parking offence; possession of a small quantity (up to 5g of resin or 25g of grass) makes you liable for a fine of $150, but is not recorded as a criminal conviction. You will be handed an "Expiation Notice for a Simple Cannabis Offence" which you must pay within 60 days. The offending substance will, of course, be confiscated.

Anyone caught dealing, or in possession of hard drugs, can expect to be treated considerably more harshly. If you get into serious trouble, consult the Legal Services Commission of South Australia at 82 Wakefield St (tel: 232 1232, or from outside Adelaide, 008-18 8126). The Law Society Advisory Service provides low-cost advice at 33 Gilbert Place from 5.30pm to 8pm, Monday to Friday.

Help and Information *i*

The dialling code for Adelaide is 08. For fire, police or ambulance dial 000.

The main tourist information office is the *South Australian Government Travel Centre,* at 18 King William St (between Rundle Mall and North Terrace; 212 1644). If you have any specific requests, whether for Greek Orthodox church services or accommodation in a particular vicinity, place yourself in the hands of the staff and their computer. They can provide you with a free print-out of the information you need. There are also offices at 25 Elizabeth St, Melbourne (03-614 6522) and 143 King St, Sydney (02-232 8388).

American Express: 13 Grenfell St (212 7099).
Thomas Cook: 45 Grenfell St (212 3354).

General Post Office: 141 King William St (216 2361). Open 9am to 5pm, Monday-Friday; a restricted service operates from 7.15am to 6.30pm Monday-Friday, 8.30-noon on Saturdays and 12.30 to 5pm on Sundays.

Medical Treatment: Royal Adelaide Hospital, North Terrace (223 0230).

Dental Treatment: Royal Dental Hospital on Frome Road (223 9211).

Disabled Travellers: The tourist office normally stocks a free guide called *Access Adelaide;* further advice is available from the Disability and Resource Centre at 215 Hutt St (223 7522).

Helplines: Life Line — 212 3444; Poison Information — 267 7000; Dial-a-horoscope 11635.

Unemployment in South Australia is just over 8%, slightly above the national average, but the turnover in casual staff is high and so there are usually a good number of jobs around. Much of the available non-agricultural casual work in South Australia is within the Adelaide city limits, reflecting the fact that this is where three-quarters of the state's population resides. The main Commonwealth Employment Service (CES) office in Adelaide is at 45 Grenfell St (tel: 224 6111). Reports of the treatment experienced there by foreigners are not altogether encouraging. You may receive a fairer hearing at CES offices in the suburbs, e.g. 50 Leadenhall St, Port Adelaide (tel: 47 9555) or 12 Durham St, Glenelg (tel: 295 0888), or in offices outside the capital, but the amount of work is correspondingly lower. Private agencies in Adelaide include Drake Overload (55 Gawler Place; tel: 212 4141), Manpower (186 Pulteney St; tel: 223 5999) and Extraman (86a South Terrace; tel: 212 3924). The first edition of the *Advertiser* hits the streets of Adelaide at about 10pm. Ignore the short and unhelpful *Casual Work Available* section in favour of ads for bar and restaurant staff, labourers and swimming pool cleaners. To try to get your working holiday visa renewed in Adelaide, go to the Department of Immigration at 150 North Terrace (tel: 216 7111).

As South Australia is by far the leading producer of wine in Australia, there is scope for grape-picking. The five major vine-growing areas are the Riverland (east of Adelaide), the Barossa and Clare Valleys (north), the Southern Vales (just south of the capital) and Coonawarra in the extreme southeast of the state. Much of the harvesting is mechanized, but the vogue for wines made from hand-picked grapes means that demand for pickers is once again increasing. The chances for pickers are reasonable in the Barossa Valley (call in at the CES office in Nuriootpa), but a larger proportion of grapes are grown in the Riverland east of Adelaide. Rather than trailing around from one vineyard to another, install yourself in a town and phone around. If you get really good at hand-picking, you can enter the biennial Grapepicking Championship at the Orlando vineyards near Lyndoch. This competition marks the beginning of the Barossa Vintage Festival; should you win, your future as a grape-picker seems assured.

Towns along the Murray River like Renmark, Loxton, Berri, Waikerie and Barmera are flourishing fruit-growing towns, and are now very dependent on itinerant workers, of whom there are not enough to keep up with the oranges, melons, etc. Just ask in the local hotel or caravan park in any of these towns; the "Snake Pit" bar of the hotel and the campsite in Waikerie are particularly recommended.

The best time to find work in tourism is during the South Australian Christmas school holidays, when the seaside resorts all around the coast are at their busiest. The holidays usually run from just before Christmas until the beginning of February.

WINE REGIONS

There are many interesting places accessible from Adelaide for a day trip, although spending a little longer in some of them can be considerably more rewarding. Much of the interest centres on wine, and you might want to equip yourself with the excellent *South Australian Vineyards Map* (on sale at many Adelaide bookshops) before you set off. There are also maps of the nearby wine areas in the free magazine *What's On in Adelaide*.

Adelaide Hills. This attractive range of minor mountains southeast of the capital provides an effective bar to the continued urbanization in that direction. The Adelaide Hills are also known widely as the Mount Lofty Ranges, after one of the most notable peaks. Mount Barker road winds up over the hills to reveal a peaceful, central European landscape beyond. The first part of the journey takes you through an area devastated by bushfires on Ash Wednesday 1983. Over the hills, the major settlement is Hahndorf, which likes to think of itself as an outpost of Bavaria. Indeed, there is a Bavarian Motel on the main road through the town, together with numerous gift shops selling souvenirs with German connotations. Hahndorf is not representative of the area: hamlets such as Stirling, Aldgate, Balhannah and Mount Barker itself are more pleasant, and have some surprisingly good pubs and restaurants catering mainly for city dwellers and well-to-do locals.

The Adelaide Hills are becoming renowned as a centre for excellent cool-climate wines. There are wineries at Bridgewater and Clarendon, and the latter settlement, largely devoted to tourism, marks the start of the Southern Vales.

Southern Vales. The more modest inclines to the south of Adelaide have not proved much of an impediment to sprawling suburbia. The tentacles of high-density housing now extend well into the northern edge of the Southern Vales, to the detriment of this breezy vine-growing region. Whatever the winemakers of Barossa and Clare might say, the Southern Vales produces a lot of good wine. Most of the wineries are conveniently grouped together, permitting easy touring by car, bicycle or even camel: from November to March, the Outback Camel Co. organizes camel treks around half-a-dozen wineries from their camel depot near McLaren Vale (tel: 08-383 0352). The cost of $40 includes camel hire and a chicken lunch.

The first Southern Vale winery heading south from Adelaide is Marienberg in Coromandel Valley, under 20km from the city centre. It is renowned for its female winemaker, Ursula Marie Pridham. Sadly its proximity to Adelaide has meant that the suburbs have encroached upon the winery to an almost ludicrous extent; all the vineyards have been swallowed up by housing, and all that remains is a small winery and tasting room marooned in suburbia.

The best centre for exploring the Southern Vales is McLaren Vale, the main town in the area. The headquarters of Hardy's is within the town, and there are plenty of other wineries nearby. The Barn bistro on Main Road (tel: 383 8618) doubles as a modest art gallery and excellent restaurant with an appropriately wide choice of wines. It has the added advantage of being next door to a motel and 500m from the McLaren Vale Hotel at 208 Main Road (tel: 08-383 8208). This cheap and cheerful hotel, next door to Hardy's winery, is renowned for the size of its breakfasts. Together with a bed, they cost $15 single or $20 double.

The McLaren Vale Wine Bushing Festival takes place in the last week of October and the first week of November. It includes tastings of the new wines, jazz concerts and craft fairs. Call 08-323 8999 for more information.

Barossa Valley. The 8-by-30 kilometre valley was originally settled by Prussians and Silesians escaping from religious persecution in Europe in 1838, and Germanic culture still dominates. The rolling countryside of the Barossa is punctuated by small settlements, each with a prim Lutheran church. The name was given by Colonel Light who misremembered the spelling of the Spanish region of Bares. He fought there during the Peninsular Wars, and the scenery in the Valley reminded him of it. Compared with the relaxed attitude of the Southern Vales and the gentility of Clare (described below), the commercialism of Barossa wineries may be a shock. A glimpse of *Explorer News* (the Barossa and Clare giveaway newspaper) reveals how dependent the area has become upon wine-related tourism. The larger wineries have built "Public Relations Centres" and charge a fee for tours. The Valley produces 100 million litres of wine each year, over half of South Australia's total, although most of the grapes used are grown outside the district. The Barossa has not always been devoted to wine; in the mid-19th century the world's richest copper mines were in the area, and relics of this era are scattered around.

Transport to the Valley from Adelaide is limited: three buses each way Monday-Friday, two on Saturdays, one on Sunday afternoon and none on public holidays. Call the Barossa-Adelaide Passenger Service on 085-65 6258. The fare from the Central Bus Station at 101 Franklin St in Adelaide is about $5. An alternative is to take one of the regular trains to Gawler (a dormitory town for Adelaide, and southern gateway to the Barossa) and hitch from there along the Barossa Valley Highway which connects the main settlements.

The main town in the Valley is Nuriootpa, 70km northeast of the state capital on the Sturt Highway; the name is an Aboriginal word for "meeting place". The tone for the town is set by garish modern establishments like the "Vine Inn Hotel/Motel". The Barossa Information Centre is at 66 Murray St (tel: 085-62 1866), opposite the police station. You can pick up a free map of the Valley and details of its many wineries. The best winery to visit in Nuriootpa is Elderton at 3 Tanunda Road (tel: 085-62 1058), on the banks of the North Para River. After the viticultural tour of the vineyard, you can visit the Elderton tasting room at Burgundy Cottage on Main St, where Wesley Bike Hire can rent you a cycle for further exploration. Other good wineries are Saltrams in Angaston, Orlando in Rowland Flat and — for the best scenery — Seppeltsfield. Orlando is the only winery to offer a balloon flight (price $160 for an hour) at dawn or dusk; call 085-24 4383.

Tanunda, 8km south of Nuriootpa, is the most central settlement from which to explore the Barossa. Railway buffs might be attracted to "Barossa Junction", a motel/restaurant on the road from Nuriootpa, constructed from 31 old railway carriages. Tanunda has the best cake shop — Ziffandels — in the Valley. It is opposite the old fire station at 58 Murray St and offers good sandwiches and German dishes in addition to home-made cakes containing copious amounts of cream. The Tanunda Hotel at 51 Murray St (tel: 085-63 2030) is a comfortable and fairly cheap place to stay: a double room with shared facilities costs $30. Another alternative is Barossa House (tel: 085-62 2716) next to Hardy's winery just north of Tanunda, where a room for two is $33 including breakfast. The smallest motel in Australia is in Bethany: they can accommodate two people at a time in a restored shepherd's cottage. Other hotels and motels in the Barossa are less inspiring and quite expensive, but there are caravan parks where you can pitch a tent in Lyndoch (tel: 085-24 4262), Tanunda (085-63 2784) and Kapunda (085-66 2255). The Bunkhaus (tel: 085-62 2260), 2km south of Tanunda, is an independent hostel charging $7 per night, and provides long-term accommodation for grape-pickers as well as casual beds. You can also rent a bicycle here.

The week-long Barossa Wine Festival takes place the week after Easter in odd-numbered years. It takes the form of "Town Days" — carnivals in each of the Barossa settlements — and culminates in the Festival Finale at Angaston Park. For full details, write to 83 Murray St, Tanunda 5352. Each August, the Barossa Classic Gourmet Weekend enables you to sample some of the state's best food, when the leading chefs of Adelaide are invited to the wineries to produce selections of their fare to accompany Barossa wines.

A non-alcoholic treat in the Valley is to visit the Whispering Wall near Lyndoch. The wall holds nearly five billion litres of water inside the Barossa Reservoir. Like similar acoustic phenomena at St Pauls in London and the Imperial Palace in Beijing, you can whisper into the wall of the dam at one side and be clearly heard at the far end 140 metres away.

Clare Valley. The Clare Valley wineries are set in more rugged terrain than the Southern Vales or the Barossa, and have more charm; at most places in the Clare, the person who serves you at a tasting is likely to be the winemaker. The wineries cluster around the road north from Adelaide between Auburn and Clare, 80-140km from Adelaide. For those without a vehicle, the towns of Watervale and Clare are the best centres since several wineries are within walking or cycling distance of each town.

The Clare Adventure takes place in May each year. This Gourmet Weekend is regarded as a cut above the Barossa's counterpart, and is operated by the Clare Valley Winemakers' Association. The "weekend of indulgence" commences on Saturday afternoon with a tasting of new vintages in the Clare Sports Complex (basically an indoor volleyball court with a sign reading "Winning Team Must Mop Up"). The $5 admission enables you to try over 140 wines, but be warned that by no means all the new product is ideal for drinking. Amateur wine experts will declaim the virtues of certain wines and insist that they will eventually attain high standards, but some new reds are barbarically acidic and some whites appear mucus-green. Sunday is gourmet day, when you tour the wineries to taste food as well as old and new vintages. The food costs $4-5 per serving.

Interest in the Clare is not confined entirely to food and wine. Mintaro, a few kilometres east of the main highway, has been listed as a "heritage town" by the state authorities. It became a ghost town after the reserves of slate were exhausted, and has recently been restored to become a full-blown tourist attraction with a collection of old fire engines, Reilly's Cottage (Art) Gallery and the Magpie & Stump Hotel, dating from 1851. The most impressive sight, however, is Martindale Hall, a traditional Georgian country house 2km southeast of Mintaro. The mansion was built in 1879 by Englishmen imported especially for the job. Its main claim to fame is as one setting for the film *Picnic at Hanging Rock*. It opens daily (except Christmas Day and Good Friday) from 2 to 4.30pm and costs $3 for admission. The Hall (tel: 088-43 9011) also doubles as an upmarket guest house, each room equipped with a picturesque four-poster bed and costing $80 per night; this rate includes free use of the Billiard Room.

The best value accommodation in the Clare Valley is the Watervale Hotel on the Main North Road in Watervale (tel: 088-43 0109). The hotel appears to be a former police station as the back yard sports a small gaol which is currently being turned into a garden bar. There are only two double rooms (both in the hotel proper), one with a four-poster and the other with a waterbed. The rate for two of $40 per night includes a splendid breakfast prepared by the gregarious publican and his wife. Just behind the hotel is the Watervale Cellars winery, run by Englishman Robert Crabtree. In the town of Clare, try the Clare Hotel/Motel at 244 Main North Road (tel: 088-42 2816). It costs $12 per person for bed only, or $18 with a large breakfast.

The Riverland. Residents of New South Wales will tell you that the northern bank of the mighty Murray is best; Victorians claim that they have the most pleasing side of the river; and by the time it reaches South Australia there are few superlatives left. The Riverland around the Murray east of Adelaide is a low-key area with no great thrills for those uninterested in wildlife, but is a good location for lazing or working as a fruit-picker. From the Victorian border the river passes through wine territory, where the grapes for much of Australia's cask wine and cheaper exports are grown. There are some interesting settlements, notably the historic village of Loxton — which has a Youth Hostel — and the town of Berri. Wine is a better reason to visit Berri than to view the World's Biggest Orange (on the road to Renmark), which claims to be "the biggest spherical fibreglass object in the Southern Hemisphere." Berri is also a good place to hire a houseboat (see below). After irrigating the vines which go to make half of South Australia's wines, the Murray strikes south, spilling into the lakes and the Coorong before meeting the Gulf at Goolwa. The setting is remarkably similar to the Deep South of the USA, although the climate is more temperate and bearable. Drivers planning to take ordinary vehicles onto the beaches at the mouth of the Murray should note that local owners of four-wheel drive vehicles make good pickings from winching out those stuck in the sand as the tide rolls in.

The most civilized way to mosey along the river is to rent a houseboat. These crafts are more mobile than their counterparts on the Norfolk Broads or in Kashmir, corresponding roughly to Thames barges in terms of their manoeuvrability. The South Australian Government Travel Centre publishes a list of houseboats for hire. Rentals are high — from $250 for a weekend in a 4/5 berth vessel — but save of course on the cost of alternative accommodation. For those who prefer someone else to navigate, there are a number of paddle steamers plying the river, based loosely on Mississippi riverboats.

Coonawarra and the Southeast. The region of South Australia close to the Victorian border produces the very best red wines in Australia. The "Terra Rosa" of Coonawarra is a slash of red earth with a limestone base which mimics the Médoc of Bordeaux and supports vines of similar class. There is a crystal clear volcanic lake near the town of Mount Gambier which undergoes a dramatic colour change from dull grey to deep blue every November. The towns of the area are unexceptional, but there is some attractive pine woodland inland and quiet coves along the shore. The fishing ports of Kingston, Robe and Beachport are pleasant places to stay, not least because of their excellent seafood restaurants.

FLEURIEU PENINSULA

The tourist authority's description of this area, about 100km south of the state capital, is "Adelaide's Playground", which should prepare you for the resorts of Goolwa, Victor Harbor and Waitpinga Beach. These places are ideal for a few days' rest by the sea, and are only a couple of hours' drive from Adelaide. A more interesting way to reach Victor Harbor is on the Steam Ranger tourist train, which leaves Keswick station in Adelaide at 9am and takes $3\frac{1}{2}$ hours. The return fare is $25; call 08-231 1707 for further details.

Victor Harbor was formerly a whaling station, and was once mooted as the state capital of South Australia. Outside January and February there are plenty of self-catering apartments to rent in and around the town, plus a private hostel called Warringa and an associated guest house at 16 Flinders Terrace (tel: 085-52 1028). Details of other accommodation and local attractions can be found in the *Visitors Guide* published by the Fleurieu Regional Tourist Association and available from South Australian Government Travel Centres. If you have enjoyed swimming near Adelaide in the warm waters of the sheltered Gulf of St Vincent, be warned that only the Great Southern Ocean lies between these resorts and Antarctica. Off-season bathing is regarded with some curiosity by the locals.

KANGAROO ISLAND

"Nature's pleasure island" is the soubriquet of the third largest island off the coast of Australia, which should discourage those who enjoy the big city life from coming. Kangaroo Island is 150km from end to end, so you should allow at least a couple of days to enjoy its unspoilt flora and fauna. Nevertheless, you can visit the island in only a day. Philanderer Ferries (PO Box 570, Penneshaw 5222; tel: 0848-3 1122 or toll-free 008-01 3111) run a one-day tour from Cape Jervis. You leave on the 10am sailing aboard *Philanderer III* to Penneshaw, then take a coach to the main settlement Kingscote for lunch, out to Seal Bay and back to Penneshaw in time for the 6pm boat back to the mainland. The inclusive cost is $60.

You can take a freelance trip on *Philanderer III* for $20 each way; there are sailings from Cape Jervis at 10am and 7pm, and from Penneshaw at 9am and 6pm. YHA members are eligible for a concession. Sailings dovetail with the Kangaroo Island Connections coach between Cape Jervis and the Central Bus Station at 101 Franklin St in Adelaide. This is the fastest surface journey, although on a fine day the $6\frac{1}{2}$ hour crossing on *MV Troubridge* from Port Adelaide to Kingscote can be more pleasant; call 08-47 5577 for fares (from $30 one way) and timings of the thrice-weekly sailings. Some services start from or continue to Port Lincoln. Cars and cycles are carried on both ships.

Four airlines fly from Adelaide to the island in half an hour. Albatross (0848-2 2296) and Lloyd (08-352 6944) serve Kingscote several times daily; State Air (08-212 3355) also fly to Penneshaw, and Airtransit (08-352 3128) can get you to American River and Parndana. One-way fares are about $50, a little less on Airtransit.

Getting around the island can be a problem. The only public transport runs between Kingscote (town and airport), American River and Penneshaw and advance booking on 0848-2 2640 is usually necessary. To make the most of your stay, hire a car, scooter, bike or campervan. The best sources are KI Rental Cars in Kingscote (0848-2 2390) for cars; the private Youth Hostel in

Penneshaw (0848-3 1173) for motor scooters; the Sorrento Motel in Penneshaw (0848-2 2100) for bicycles; and Touralong in Broadview (0848-2 2225) for campervans. Hitch-hikers are solemnly warned in the tourist literature that, out-of-season, "there is very little traffic on most roads and they may find that they cannot easily obtain a lift". Although you shouldn't have to wait long for a lift in the eastern part of the island prospects diminish in the more beautiful western half.

Just as the isolation of the Australian continent has enabled many unique species to evolve, so Kangaroo Island is one stage further removed and has an even broader natural selection. The best site is Flinders Chase National Park, which occupies the western end of the island. It has a great deal of wildlife, including the unique Kangaroo Island kangaroo which is squatter and darker than its relations on the mainland (and also has a propensity to steal food from visitors). There is also some wild pigs, supposedly placed there by French explorers to enable shipwreck victims to survive. It is not known if any survivors from the 40 wrecks (so far) have tucked in.

Seal Bay, halfway along the south coast, is much easier to reach, being only 70km by road from the main sea and airports. The world's only permanent sea lion colony, it claims to be home to one-tenth of the Australian sea lion species. There are plenty of organized tours to this and other parks, by bus, four-wheel drive vehicle or camel; Transcontinental Safaris (tel: 0848-9 3256) has camel treks from October to April, plus boat charters and wild pig shooting expeditions. Other operators can be contacted through the Kangaroo Island Tourist Association, PO Box 244, Kingscote 5223 (tel: 0848-2 2540).

Apart from the Penneshaw hostel, which charges $5, the cheapest accommodation is available at Eleanor River Holiday Cabins in Vivonne Bay on the south coast (tel: 0848-92 4250) where the rate for two is $20; the self-catering cottages on Frenchman's Terrace in Penneshaw (tel: 08-332 1083 for bookings) which cost $25 per night, single or double; or the Cranmare holiday flats on Ryberg Road in American River (tel: 08-3 3020), charging $27 per night for two. A cabin in the Ravine Wildlife Park at Flinders Chase is worth trying at only $20 a night; book in advance through the South Australian Government Travel Centre in Adelaide. You can also camp in the National Park, but beware of marauding kangaroos. There are caravan parks at Kingscote and Penneshaw.

"PIGS WERE LEFT ON THE ISLAND TO FEED SHIPWRECKED SAILORS"

There is no shortage of beaches on the island, though the ones on the battered south coast are more suited to experienced surfers than sea-bathers. Inshore fishing is excellent all around the coast, whether from beaches, rocks or boats. The towns on Kangaroo Island could hardly be described as exciting: number six on the list of nine *Things To Do In Penneshaw* (in the free tourist guide) is "Visit Condon's Take-Away Food".

Some local traders would like you to believe that the self-styled "Ile de Kangouroo" is an independent nation; you can get a passport from 9 Osmond St, Kingscote, but don't expect it to confer residence status on you.

EYRE PENINSULA

Port Augusta, at the head of the Spencer Gulf, is an industrial town enduring decline but also a busy hub for travellers crossing Australia. Few stay for long (although the new Outback Centre is worth a visit) before heading west or north to Perth or Alice Springs. Those who take the Lincoln Highway southwest along the coast of the Eyre Peninsula discover first a steel town, then a series of sparsely populated beach settlements.

The steel town is Whyalla, South Australia's second city but 30 times smaller than Adelaide. The beaches begin here, and continue sporadically for nearly 300km to Port Lincoln. This city is sandwiched uncomfortably between Coffin Bay and Cape Catastrophe. Having travelled about 700km overland from the capital, you are now only 300km by air from Adelaide; not surprisingly, flights on Commodore between Port Lincoln and Adelaide are only slightly more expensive than the bus. Port Lincoln's seafaring activities are increasingly devoted to shark fishing; white pointer sharks breed prolifically around the offshore Dangerous Reef, and there are numerous deep-sea trips for anglers.

After Port Lincoln, the highway turns sharp right and becomes the Flinders Highway. The pattern of beach resorts continues as far as Ceduna, where you rejoin the Eyre Highway to cross the Nullarbor.

FLINDERS RANGES

Those who choose instead to turn northeast just before Port Augusta find themselves in rough, rugged terrain which will be familiar to anyone who has travelled through Arizona. The desert gradually rises up to the Flinders Ranges, which continue almost to the Queensland border. Stop off at the township of Quorn if the idea of a train ride on the Pichi Richi steam railway appeals.

Although the mountains of the Flinders are small by global standards, the gorges, canyons and other natural phenomena are highly spectacular and well worth visiting. The highlight, and one of the most accessible areas, is the Wilpena Pound — a massive horseshoe of sheer cliffs — reached by one bus each week from Adelaide. A Stateliner bus departs on Fridays, taking about six hours to reach the Pound, and returns the following Sunday; the cost is around $35 one way, and Greyhound bus passes are valid. A double room at the Wilpena Pound Resort (tel: 086-48 0004) costs $54 per night, but the campground outside the Pound charges only $2.50 per person. Alternatively you can camp at specific sites within the Pound with a permit from the Ranger.

A good map of the Pound and its surroundings is published by the Flinders Ranges Regional Tourist Association (PO Box 41, Port Augusta, SA 5700) and is available free from South Australia Government Travel Centres. The walk through the Pound and up to St Mary's Peak gives spectacular views of the Elder Range, the (normally dry) Lake Torrens and the rest of the Flinders. There are also a couple of hikes to waterfalls and gorges that are most attractive after some rain. An early morning start into the Pound enables you to appreciate fully the wildlife — kangaroos, emus and all manner of multi-coloured birds — before other people frighten them away from the trails.

COOBER PEDY

For years this unique settlement on the Stuart Highway was merely a tourist stop along the otherwise featureless journey between Adelaide and Alice Springs. The name is Aboriginal for "White Man's Burrow", which accurately describes the dwellings of the opal hunters who live here. The only sign that Coober Pedy is a town is the motley collection of shops and motels and a school which peer out above the ground. The inhabitants escape from the unremitting summer heat by residing underground in homes hewn out of the rock. These burrows began when miners arrived to seek their fortunes at the end of World War One, after opals were first discovered in 1915, and have since spread to include such embellishments as an underground church.

For a time, the business of mining opals was superseded by catering for tourists: visitors could step out of an air-conditioned tour bus into an opal mine or dwelling, then re-emerge straight into an air-conditioned motel. Although they were regaled with tales of lucky tourists finding priceless gems, the clear lack of wealth among Aboriginal "noodlers" (who sift through waste from the mines looking for opals) told another story. Then, in the winter of 1987, more desert was opened up for exploitation; a new seam was discovered and an opal rush began. The settlement is currently heaving with prospectors, tearing off for the surrounding desert in all directions and stirring up clouds of dust which choke the visiting masses. Since the new discoveries, Coober Pedy has become still more popular among visitors, and there are plenty of old-timers who find catering to tourists more profitable than prospecting.

This bizarre environment has bred a number of unusual local characters. Many of the organized tours take in the residence of "Crocodile" Harry; his underground house is unfortunately most memorable for the names of his "conquests" painted on the roof. A tour which involves a visit to Harry invariably requires you to donate a dollar to him. Mines also feature on the tours, but don't pin your hopes on finding a precious stone on the tourist trail. Most have long since been worked out.

Such social life as there is reinforces the frontier town image, consisting mainly of frequent drunkenness and fighting. Most low-budget travellers stay in the (underground) hostel/motel called the Radeka Dugout (tel: 086-72 5223), a smelly hole in the ground where dormitory beds cost $7.50. Your sleep is guaranteed to be disturbed by fellow guests rising to catch the early morning Greyhound bus. A quieter alternative is the Coober Pedy Budget Motel (tel: 086-72 5163), where a double room costs $22. Remember that water, like shade, is in short supply in Coober Pedy, so don't squander it.

THE OUTBACK

The relatively verdant and populated southeast corner of South Australia does not prepare you for the desolation found in much of the rest of the state. As you travel north or west, the roads become emptier, the landscape more unchanging and the heat haze more hypnotic. Even the most enthusiastic traveller can find that the appeal of arid plain or dry salt lake begins to wane after a few hundred kilometres. You might strike lucky and travel immediately after a rainstorm, which can almost miraculously draw out a sea of green plant life. But otherwise you should be prepared for mile after mile of bleak, dusty earth, punctuated by sleeping homesteads and sleazy roadhouses.

A number of operators run four-wheel drive tours in the state's Outback, particularly in the Flinders Ranges. G'Day South Australian Adventure Tours (PO Box 222, Nairne 5252; tel 08-388 6000) have been particularly recommended, and their trips can be booked direct or through South Australian Government Travel Centres. For other recommendations, talk to travellers returning from such adventures.

Bushwalking. More than half of the ambitious Heysen Trail through South Australia has been completed. This 1,800km trail will run from Cape Border on Kangaroo Island to the unfortunately-named Mount Hopeless near the Northern Territory frontier. The longest section completed so far is a 350km stretch from Cape Jervis on the Fleurieu Peninsula, bypassing Adelaide through the Mount Lofty Ranges to Lyndoch in the Barossa Valley. Another fair hike is through the Flinders Ranges from Parchina to Hawken — 180km. There are plenty of less ambitious sections of the Heysen Trail, but because of the wide range of conditions it is essential to obtain the official map from the Department of Recreation and Sport in Adelaide; their Publications Office is at 25 Grenfell St, tel: 08-227 1902.

Calendar of Events

January	*Schützenfest* beer festival, Hahndorf
January	International Bavarian Festival, Mount Gambier
February	Kangaroo Island Racing Carnival
March	*Glendi* (festival of Greek culture and food), Adelaide
March	Adelaide Festival of Arts (even-numbered years)
March/April (week following Easter)	Barossa Valley Vintage Festival (odd-numbered years)
April	Clare Valley Easter Festival
May (third Monday)	**Adelaide Cup** (horserace), Morphetville
May	Cornish Festival, Yorke Peninsula
June (second Monday)	**Queen's Birthday**
July	Coober Pedy *Glendi* Festival
August	Barossa Classic Gourmet Weekend
August	Festival City Marathon, Adelaide
October	*Oktoberfest,* Tanunda
October (second Monday)	**Labour Day**
October	National Camel Cup, Bordertown
early November	Australian Grand Prix, Adelaide
November	Christmas Pageant, Adelaide

Public holidays are shown in **bold**

Perth and Western Australia

Population of Perth: 1,000,000   **Population of WA: 1,410,000**

Western Australia is a vast and vibrant state with immense variety: the clean and cosmopolitan city of Perth and its pretty port of Fremantle, the fertile southwest and the vast wild northern regions with their rugged mountains and deserts. More than any other state, WA (as it is invariably known) brings home the immense scale of the Australian continent. It covers 2,525,000km^2, making it 20 times bigger than England and six times as large as California. But Western Australia is undeniably isolated: Perth is 2,000km and a time zone or two away from the other state capitals. By virtue of its geographical location, you can feel almost as if you are in another country.

Western Australia was claimed for Britain in May 1829, when Sir Charles Howe Fremantle landed at Murray Head (where the High St in Fremantle now ends). In the same year Perth was founded by Captain James Stirling, who modestly named the settlement after a different Scottish city from the one which bears his surname. Perth was an obvious place to settle — sheltered from the Indian Ocean by the Swan River estuary, and surrounded by flat and friendly terrain — but its detachment from the rest of the new continent made early development slow. When gold was discovered a few hundred miles inland around Kalgoorlie late in the 19th century, Perth prospered on the basis that one makes far more selling shovels to prospectors than looking for gold oneself.

The state is still one of the world's largest producers of gold, and the future glitters for Western Australia. Only a tiny part of the mineral and agricultural wealth of the state has so far been realized, and the current oil and mineral rush is creating new prosperity. Local people are fond of comparing Western Australia to California, and there are certainly strong similarities in climate, lifestyle and wealth. "Metro Perth", which takes in Perth, Fremantle and everything in between and around, likes to think of itself as a pulsating metropolis, straddling the Swan River and stretching out to the coast. Downstream at the mouth of the Swan, the rejuvenated port of Fremantle is, however, a much smaller and more picturesque neighbour to the big city of Perth.

That Perth and Fremantle are at last on the world map is due partly to the America's Cup. When Alan Bond's yacht *Australia II* took the trophy away from the USA for the first time in 137 years, the real prize — as far as Western Australia was concerned — was the chance to stage the competition at Fremantle in 1986-87 and the consequent priceless publicity for the state. Visitors to the yacht races were not disappointed by the style of the capital (although there were many complaints about the high price of everything from beer to beds). They found a city that is spacious and well planned, with sweeping freeways, striking modern architecture, sparkling white beaches and splendid parkland.

CLIMATE

Summer visitors are virtually guaranteed fine weather, and even midwinter can be pleasantly warm in Perth. The sun shines for an average 7.8 hours per day around the year. Summer is normally characterized by clear skies and an average high of 30°C/85°F from December to February (which can be uncomfortably hot if, as sometimes happens, the air does not cool significantly at night). Occasional heatwaves can bring temperatures of 40°C or more. On most summer days a climatic peculiarity brings welcome (but sometimes quite chilly) relief from the heat: the "Fremantle Doctor" is a breeze which blows in from the Indian Ocean between noon and 4pm.

The winter months of June to August manage a balmy mean high of 20°C/ 70°F, but this is often accompanied by plenty of rain; average rainfall in the wettest month of July is 17cm (more than twice as much as July in London and New York), and there are an average of 18 wet days. Over a year, mean rainfall is 87cm, falling on an average of 119 days. For weather reports in the Perth metropolitan area, dial 1196.

The state south of Perth becomes marginally cooler, while much of the rest of the state is desert. The northern extremes have a tropical climate with distinct wet (November-April) and dry (May-October) seasons.

THE LOCALS

Some say that the existing populace of Perth displays an uneasy mix between an expatriate way of thinking – as though their residence in this isolated city is only a temporary aberration – and a frontier mentality, that they are somehow involved in pioneering the unknown terrain beyond the city limits. The new prosperity and high profile of Perth and Fremantle have generated a stronger belief in the area: anyone who shows you around takes pains to point out the advertising signs painted by Alan Bond before he became a brewing/media/ yachting magnate. Another favourite "sight" is the exclusive suburb of Dalkeith, where many of the city's millionaires live in flashy houses overlooking the Swan

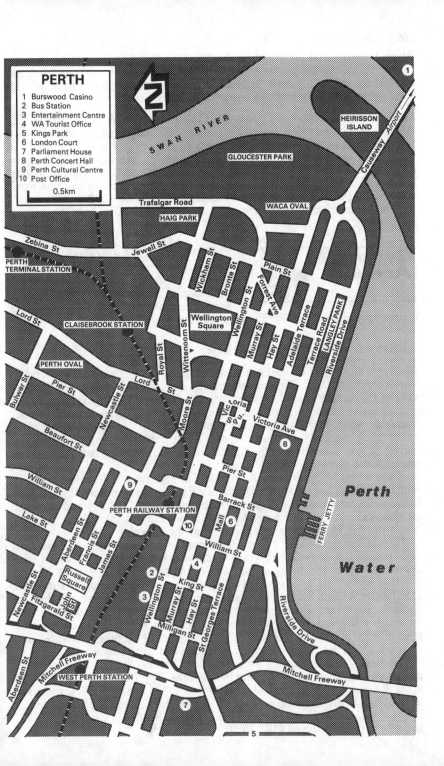

River. It seems that entrepreneurial attributes are still highly prized amongst "sandgropers", as the people of Western Australia are known. Hard work has resulted for many in a high degree of affluence, but the play is equally hard: leisure time is usually spent in energetic pursuits.

Making Friends. Perth has a young and lively population, dedicated to enjoying themselves. The best way to meet the people of the state capital is to join in with their leisure activities, whether on the beach, jogging in a park or drinking in the current most trendy pub. Sunday afternoon pub sessions in summer are perhaps the best, where you can laze in the garden or courtyard listening to local bands and drinking Swan beer (although Western Australians say you won't make many friends if you stick to Swan Light, only 0.9% alcohol). Or you can join in some of the many organized sporting activities, from walking to windsurfing.

The Western Australian Tourist Commission produces an excellent free map called the *Traveller's Guide*. It comprises a good map of the whole state, town maps of Perth, Fremantle and seven other towns, and a strip map of the Eyre Peninsula across the Nullarbor.

ARRIVAL AND DEPARTURE

Air. Perth airport, 11km east of the city centre is a major gateway for services from Europe and Asia. The international and domestic terminals are on opposite sides of the runway and 10km apart by road, making changing flights a tedious and expensive business. In addition, many international flights arrive at or after midnight, when there are no connecting flights. To compensate, however, immigration controls are usually speedy. You can also complete formalities quickly if you take the weekly flight from Bali to Western Australia's other international gateway, Port Hedland.

If you arrive at Perth from Abroad late at night, you will almost certainly miss the last Skybus into town. During the day this runs approximately hourly between the city centre and the international terminal ($4.50) and domestic terminal ($3.50). At other times you will have to take a taxi (about $12), for which there is an official sharing scheme at the airport.

There is a cheaper ($1.10) alternative from the domestic terminal: if you turn right out of the arrivals hall you'll find the stand for bus 338 which runs approximately hourly between 7am and 11pm on weekdays, 9am to 7pm on Sundays and public holidays. Travelling out to the airport, bus 338 starts at Stand 37 on William St in the city centre. You can also pick it up at the suburban station of Rivervale, which has frequent train services from Central Station and for which a single ticket allows a free transfer. The Skybus picks up from the main offices of Ansett (corner of Irwin St and St George's Terrace) and Australian Airlines (55 St George's Terrace), and from major hotels.

The market in international air tickets from Perth is lively, with lower fares to Europe than from anywhere else in Australia. Try Travelabout at Shop 52 at the St George's Terrace end of London Court (325 8888), or STA, who have three offices in the Perth area: Hackett Hall on the University of WA campus in Crawley (380 2302), the Student Guild at South Bentley in Curtin (458 6470) and 424 Hay St, Subiaco (382 3977).

Coach. The main operators and their terminals in Perth are as follows:

Bus Australia: 30 Pier St (325 5488).
Deluxe: corner of Hay and William Streets (322 5577).
Greyhound: 26 St George's Terrace (478 1122).
South West Coach Lines: Wellington St Bus Station (322 5173).

The railway authority Westrail also runs some buses in connection with its rail services (see below).

There are daily services from Perth to Adelaide (journey time about 32 hours) and the east. First out is Deluxe at 8am; Bus Australia sets off at 9am. If you are trying to save money on overnight accommodation, it makes sense to catch one of the evening departures which give you two nights on the bus: Greyhound at 9pm and Deluxe at 9.45pm. Ansett Pioneer are cutting routes in Western Australia, and most of the services in their timetable are run "in association with" (i.e. by) Greyhound. The cheapest fares at the time of writing were on Bus Australia: Adelaide for $99, Brisbane $187, Melbourne $129, Sydney and Canberra for $160, with 10% discounts for students and YHA members.

Buses to Darwin are less frequent: Greyhound and Deluxe have four services weekly, Bus Australia two. The fare is around $210. At the time of going to press, the status of the scheduled bus trip across the Outback from Perth to Ayers Rock was uncertain, although it was believed that Shoreline Coach Tours would continue to run the 32-hour trip (fare $160) in association with Greyhound: for the latest details, call Shoreline on 008-01 1435 (toll-free from anywhere in Western Australia).

Train. Passenger rail services are sparse in Western Australia. There are three suburban lines around Perth (see *City Transport,* below), plus the trans-Nullarbor route to the east and a line from Perth south to Bunbury. The main services east from Perth are the *Trans-Australian* as far as Adelaide and the *Indian Pacific* via Adelaide to Sydney. The Sydney train leaves Perth at 9pm on Sundays, Mondays and Thursdays, and takes 64 hours; the cheapest economy fare is $162.50. The *Trans-Australian* departs at 9pm on Wednesdays and Saturdays, arriving in Adelaide 38 hours later. The cheapest regular fare is $125, but booking seven days in advance qualifies you for a CAPER fare of $100. The trans-Nullarbor journey is an experience, but whether a fascinating or tedious one depends upon your attitude to train travel. These services, plus the prestige *Prospector* as far as Kalgoorlie, operate from Perth Terminal Station, a clean and modern building 3km southeast of the city and accessible by suburban train from Central Station in a few minutes.

The *Prospector* to Kalgoorlie is reputed to be the fastest train in Australia, taking $7\frac{1}{2}$ hours for the 650km journey. Unfortunately for the budget traveller, it has only first-class air-conditioned accommodation: the one-way fare of around $50 includes a meal. You can get there more cheaply in economy class on the *Indian Pacific* train, or on one of the trans-Nullarbor buses from Perth.

A new train between Perth and Bunbury was introduced in 1987 at a cost of $7 million to replace the previous forty-year-old *Australind.* It leaves Central Station on Wellington St and takes just over two hours to Bunbury for a fare of around $10. The return journey departs from Bunbury at 3pm. Country trains – i.e. to Bunbury and Kalgoorlie – are run by Westrail (tel: 326 2222); bookings are normally compulsory, and cease at 4pm the day before travel. Westrail also sell tickets for the interstate services.

Driving. The maximum speed limit in Western Australia is 110km/h, and the minimum speed on freeways is 60km/h. The blood/alcohol limit is 0.08%.

Before attempting to drive to Perth from any other state, ensure your vehicle is in good condition and that you have ample supplies of fuel and water: although the roads through from Adelaide and Darwin are sealed, it is still a very long journey. Most of the other roads in the Outback of Western Australia are dirt tracks, but some mining companies have built their own roads which are often much better than the public highways. Ask locally whether motorists other than employees can use them; some companies issue permits to visitors. In the north of the state, roads are sometimes flooded and impassable for weeks during the wet season.

Members of foreign motoring associations may use the services of the Royal Automobile Club of Western Australia (RAC) whose headquarters are at 228 Adelaide Terrace, Perth (tel: 421 4444). Their 24-hour emergency breakdown service can be summoned by calling 325 0333. The RAC publishes a good selection of maps of Western Australia.

Most service stations open 7am-6pm, Monday to Friday, and 7am-1pm at weekends. Each area of Perth usually has a station rostered to open later; dial 1 1573 for recorded information.

Hitch-hiking. Avoid the temptation to start hitching on one of the short stretches of freeway out of Perth; hitch-hikers are not popular with the local police, who can issue $20 tickets if you stand on the freeway or an approach road. For Kalgoorlie and the east, take the train out to the suburb of Armadale and walk out on the Albany Highway to the edge of town. To reach destinations south of Perth, get the train to Armadale then bus 220, 230 or 235 a little further out to Byford on Highway 1. For the road north to Geraldton, Broome and Darwin, take a suburban train to Midland and walk out to the Great Northern Highway. Given that long-distance journeys from Perth are daunting enough without the added unpredictability of hitch-hiking, you may prefer to arrange a lift in advance through the notice boards at Youth Hostel headquarters, the Youth Hostel itself or Travelmates hostel; see *Accommodation* for addresses.

CITY TRANSPORT

City Layout. Straddling the Swan River and bounded to the west by the Indian Ocean, Perth is a sprawling city with an extensive road network. The city centre is compact and lies just north of the River. Most commercial offices are on St George's Terrace (usually known simply as "the Terrace"). The main shopping street, Hay St, is one block north, and has its central section laid out as a pedestrian Mall, Perth Central station and most bus terminals are a further two blocks along Wellington St; the station is adjacent to the new Forrest Place development, Perth's closest approximation to a city square. Across the railway tracks is Northbridge, Perth's cultural heart, with the arts complex and many good restaurants. Subiaco, northwest of the city centre, is a rich and refined area; the name is often abbreviated to "Subi" (pronounced "soobee"). The suburbs of Perth expand north, south and inland as far as Midland, and form a continuous conurbation as far as Fremantle ("Freo") on the coast. The port of Fremantle is 20km from the centre of Perth and is small enough to be covered easily on foot. Note that the strange-looking street name of Mouat is not a spelling error.

Despite the good roads, distances in the metropolitan area can be long and outlying suburbs can be an hour away from the centre during rush hours. To find your way around the sprawl, the free Tourist Office map *Perth — Fremantle Visitor's Guide* is good but you may wish to buy a street atlas: either the ubiquitous *Gregory's* or the *MSD* (Metro Street Directory).

Public Transport. All bus, suburban train and ferry services in the Perth area are operated by Transperth. They have information offices at 125 St George's Terrace and the Central Bus Station (adjacent to the Railway Station on Wellington St). The offices open from 7am to 6pm Monday-Friday, 7.30 to 3pm on Saturdays and can provide free timetables for all services as well as the very useful *Transperth Route Map*. For transport information by phone, dial 221 1211 any day from 6am to 9pm. Not all buses from the city centre arrive at or leave from the Central Bus Station; many serve St George's Terrace, Barrack St or William St, but departure points are clearly indicated on bus schedules. Most bus stops in the suburbs comprise an inconspicuous metre-high orange post. A better clue is the yellow Bus Stop markings on the road itself.

Perth has the best system of free buses in Australia. Four *City Clipper* routes cover the city centre, as far east as Barrack St and west to Milligan St. A map of the services appears in the free *Visitor's Guide*.

Other buses cost from 50¢ to $2, depending on the number of zone boundaries you cross. For all but the cheapest tickets, you are entitled to free transfers to buses or trains within two hours, with no need to continue in the same direction (so round trips are permitted). This transfer facility is so flexible, and the free buses so useful, that the *Sightseer* unlimited-travel ticket costing $4 (or $17 for five consecutive days) may not be worthwhile unless you plan to travel extensively all day. The *Sightseer* does, however, have the advantage of giving discounts on a range of attractions and even accommodation. These tickets can be bought from Transperth offices or from Western Australia Tourist Offices. For longer stays, you can buy monthly tickets or "Multi Riders", giving a 10% discount on the normal price of ten tickets.

Fremantle can be reached by numerous buses from St George's Terrace, but the suburban trains from Central Station are faster. Trains run every 20 minutes during the day with a journey time of 35 minutes. The first train is at 6am (Monday-Saturday) or 8am (Sunday), with the last at 11.30pm except on Sundays (7.30pm). Suburban trains also run to the suburbs of Armadale and Midland from Central Station. Fares and transfer arrangements are identical to bus services. If you join the train at an unmanned station, you should buy your ticket from the conductor/guard; the fine for attempting to avoid payment is $100.

A pleasant, if slower, way to reach Fremantle is aboard one of the Transperth ferries from the Barrack St Jetty at the south of the city centre. There are also services to South Perth. You should try to take a ride on at least one ferry, if only for the striking aspect of Perth from the water.

Tram. Both Perth and Fremantle have motor vehicles dressed up to resemble trams, but they run on ordinary streets rather than tracks. The Perth Shuttle is a tourist bus which runs around the city (and out to the Burswood Island Casino) and allows you to get on and off at any point on its route for an all-day fare of $6.50. The Fremantle Tram provides sightseeing tours of the port.

Bicycle. Perth is something of a mecca for cyclists. Cycleways abound, and you can ride for long stretches without encountering motorized traffic. The cycleways along the River are particularly attractive, but watch out for pedestrians. Fremantle has a pleasant Foreshore cycleway running along the oceanside.

Among the hire outfits in Perth are Ride Away (275 2320) at the No. 4 Car Park on Riverside Drive (near the Causeway); Mike's Bike Hire on the Broadway in Nedlands (386 4703) and East Perth Bicycle Hire (325 6095), who promise to deliver a bicycle to your hotel or hostel within an hour of your call. In Fremantle, try Bridge Cycle Hire on Marine Terrace (364 6077).

There are guided bicycle tours in summer around Fremantle and Perth, taking in various local attractions, although you need to bring your own bicycle. Prices range from $6 for an hour to $24 for a three-hour ride including lunch; call 293 2445 for information and bookings. Make sure any bike you ride is fitted with a bell, since this is a legal requirement in Western Australia.

Taxis. In 1987, readers of *Executive Travel* magazine voted London cabbies as the world's friendliest. Few of those polled can have visited Perth, whose taxi drivers have long been renowned among experienced travellers as the most honest and helpful anywhere; for example, it is common for a driver to switch off the meter when approaching an unfamiliar destination to save you paying while he traces the exact address. The standing charge is $1.80 plus 55¢ per kilometre, increased by 30% at night and weekends. If you want to travel outside the city limits (a highly expensive exercise given the extent of the suburbs) you must pay a higher "country rate" and a "befouling fee" of $15 if the cab gets dirty.

The wide streets and substantial traffic in Perth make it difficult to flag down taxis in the street, but the location of the 30 ranks in Perth (plus five in Fremantle) are given in the leaflet *How to hire a Taxi,* free from tourist offices. To call a cab in Perth by telephone, dial Swan on 322 0111, Black & White on 328 8288 or Green & Gold on 328 3455. In Fremantle, call Swan on 335 3944.

Car. If you have made the journey across the Nullarbor or along Highway 1 from Darwin, you may find the busy roads of Perth difficult to cope with. Freeways extend more deeply into Perth than most other cities, and the tangle of freeways and slip roads west of the city centre can be confusing. However, traffic in the metropolitan area flows fairly freely, and signposting is not at all bad. The roads along the Swan River gave breathtaking views.

On some freeways into Perth there is a contraflow lane for city-bound buses during the morning rush hour, so outbound drivers should beware. Within the city centre there is a rule forbidding reversing a car during business hours. Note that broad zig-zag white lines on the road indicate a pedestrian crossing ahead.

Perth's major drawback for the driver is parking. The City Council deliberately restricts parking space in the centre, to try to reduce the amount of traffic. On most days the city centre car parks are full, and illegal on-street parkers are towed away. The City Council runs a number of car parks (costing around 60¢ per hour), but for some you need to buy parking vouchers in advance which you validate in the machines provided upon arrival at the car park. These vouchers are obtainable from newsagents or direct from the Parking Department at 27 St George's Terrace (tel: 425 3333). The Parking Department publishes a map of parking locations. To avoid the high charges and problems in finding a space, you can head for one of the side streets off Newcastle St (north of Central Station) where there are few restrictions (but check the kerbside signs before leaving your vehicle). It is then a short and pleasant walk to the city centre.

To make the most of Perth's sunshine, you could hire a convertible VW Beetle from Topless Rentals, 171 Albany Highway, Victoria Park (470 1148). Two companies which rent out older vehicles are Al-Cheepo (12 Ruse St, Osborne Park; 444 8999) and Ezidrive (corner of Wellington and George Streets; 322 2592). Econo-Car, at 133 Pier St (328 6888) has cheap local rates ($20 per day inclusive) and a one-week "country rate" for longer trips of $180.

If you arrive at Perth airport without a room for the night, there is a *Westaccomm* desk which will book a bed for you. The amount of accommodation in Perth and Fremantle has certainly increased because of the America's Cup defence. The problem is that few travellers can afford to stay at the Merlin, the Sheraton or the ritzy new Observation City resort complex. There are, however, a number of reasonably priced hotels plus several good hostels.

Hostels. The best cheap place to stay is Travelmates, a pair of hostels exclusively for foreign travellers aged 18-35. They are a fair way from the centre at 496 Newcastle St (tel: 328 6685), opposite the City Motors garage and on bus route 15. The nightly rate is $7, and as with Youth Hostels you are expected to do your bit with the chores. Travelmates has a good atmosphere and you can expect to pick up a considerable amount of useful information from the many travellers passing through. In addition, there is a ride-sharing board (at the front of the main hostel) with better-than-usual opportunities. Office hours are sporadic; typically 9am-noon from Monday to Friday, 10am-noon on Saturday and 10-10.30am on Sunday, plus a half-hour in the late afternoon every day. If you arrive outside these hours and wish to put in a bid for a bed, you can deposit the $7 in the envelope provided and slip it through the door, returning when the office is open to take up your claim. Travellers planning to stay for at least a few days are preferred, although if there is sufficient room one-night guests will be accommodated.

The city's two Youth Hostels (both in Northbridge) are usually full, and if you make landfall in Perth you might well wish to book ahead for a bed; contact the YHA headquarters on the first floor of 257 Adelaide Terrace (325 5844). One hostel is at 60 Newcastle St (east of the junction with Pier St; phone as above), the other at 46 Francis St (between Lake and William Streets; 328 7794). Even if both are full, it is worth going along to the Newcastle St hostel to look at the notice board which carries advertisements for flat-sharing. Fremantle's Youth Hostel is "Bundi Kudja" at 96 Hampton Road (335 3467), a long way from the rail station but close to the beach. A new annexe has greatly increased the number of beds, so try Fremantle if the two Perth hostels are booked up.

The YMCA has a hostel and an hotel, both open to men and women. The hostel is at 119 Murray St (between Pier and Barrack Streets; 325 2744), with single rooms at $19, twin rooms for $25 per couple. Although the rooms are small and tatty, it has the advantage of being open around the clock (a valuable attribute bearing in mind the propensity of flights to arrive at Perth airport in the small hours) and an arrangement with a nearby cafe which provides guests with a cheap and filling breakfast for $5. The YMCA also runs the Jewell House Private Hotel at 180 Goderich St (325 8488), which is slightly more expensive.

Hotels and Motels. Most of the new hotels built to accommodate visitors to the America's Cup are most definitely upmarket. The Western Australian Tourist Office on Hay St can provide a list. Those at the cheaper end of the market include the New Britannia Private Hotel at 253 William St in Northbridge (between Francis and Aberdeen Streets; 328 6121) and the Imperial at 413 Wellington St (just west of the junction with Barrack St; 325 8877).

Student Residences. The University of Western Australia (tel: 380 3838) is located in the suburbs of Crawley and Nedlands along the Stirling Highway from Perth to Fremantle. There are plenty of rooms during the college vacations, and a central register is held by the Accommodation Office. Most rooms are supposed to be for students only, but in practice most young travellers are looked upon kindly whether or not they have a student card. The University is also good territory for longer stays, since there is a fluid market in flat-sharing. Expect to pay $40-$70 per week for a room in a reasonable place.

Homestays. The organization Homestay of WA (1 Kalamunda Road, Kalamunda; 293 4566) can fix you up with bed and breakfast for £20 per person.

Camping. If you are prepared to get up early to avoid the attention of the police, there are several areas of greenery outside the city centre where you could risk pitching a tent. To keep within the law, try the sites at Scarborough, Sorrento or the Fremantle Village and Chalet Centre.

Eating and Drinking

Bill Bailey, an English-born journalist, once said that Perth's cuisine consisted of "steak, eggs and salad or eggs, steak and salad". Things have changed since then and Perth now has a fine range of restaurants, and a choice of cuisines covering almost every nationality. If you intend to do much eating out in Perth and Fremantle, invest $4.95 in the annual *Cheap Eats in Perth*.

If you arrived in Perth in the early morning and fancy a substantial breakfast, the Railway Hotel in Barrack St (between Murray and Wellington Streets) opens at 6am and serves an excellent fry-up. One of the best steak houses in Perth is the Adelphi on Mill St (322 3622) with meals from about $15. If you like Australian burgers, visit Fast Eddy's on the corner of Hay and Milligan St (321 2552). This is probably the best-known burger place in Perth and is open 24 hours a day. On a Friday and Saturday night it can also be quite an experience for viewing "alternative" parking arrangements, as customers double- and triple-park their vehicles.

There are numerous Southeast Asian-style food centres in Perth. One of the most popular is the Sunmarket Centre, down an alley off the corner of Murray and Barrack St; meals normally range from $4-$7. These centres have a quick turnover of customers and are often rowdy, so are perhaps not ideal for a romantic evening meal. For very cheap and good Malaysian food, try Hawkers Hut at 150 Oxford St, Leederville (444 6662); this is particularly popular with Southeast Asian students.

Gopal's Vegetarian Restaurant, in the centre at 129 Barrack St (midway between Murray and Wellington Streets), offers as much as you can eat for $4.95. It opens from noon to 3pm Monday-Friday, and from 5 to 8pm on Thursday and Friday. Miss Maud (at the junction of Pier and Murray Streets) has a similar lunchtime deal for carnivores for $13.50 ($15.50 on Sundays). The Magic Wok (Cantonese/Malaysian) is in an unlikely part of town at the corner of Fitzgerald and Roe Streets (227 8037), but is BYO and good value. Perth city centre has many upmarket restaurants with panoramic views; some of the best if you want to splash out are the Room with a View, 18 Esplanade (325 2000), the Heidelberg (German) at 473 Hay St (325 2829), Hana of Perth (Japanese) on Mill St (322 7908), the Clinker Grill at 207 Adelaide Terrace (325 0501), and Hilite 33 (French) on Level 33 of the Martin Tower at 44 St George's Terrace (325 4844); like most revolving restaurants, Hilite offers better views than food.

Northbridge (which is located as the name suggests, just to the north of the horseshoe bridge over the railway at Perth Central station) contains one of the highest concentrations of eating houses anywhere. There are popular and inexpensive restaurants serving Spanish, Chinese, Indian, French, Lebanese, Italian, Yugoslavian, Greek, Macedonian, Vietnamese, Japanese and Mexican cuisine. Worth mentioning are the Fishy Affair (seafood), 121 James St (328 3939), Pasta Place (Italian), 74 Francis St (328 8815) and, a little off the beaten track, Quoc Nam (Vietnamese/Chinese), 318 William St (at the junction with Newcastle St). After dinner you can take advantage of the lively local nightlife.

Fremantle has numerous excellent restaurants, particularly for seafood. The most famous is Lombardo's, which has two branches both overlooking the Fishing Boat Harbour on Mews Road: Sea Shells (430 4346) and Harbour Lights (430 4344); Sea Shells is the more informal of the two. Kaili's Seafood Takeaway (also on Mews Road) is dramatically cheaper, and sells everything from squid'n'chips to pineapple fritters. Other areas with good restaurants are West Perth/Subiaco and the suburbs of Claremont, Nedlands and Cottesloe.

DRINKING

Basic licensing hours are 9am-11pm from Monday to Saturday, and any six hours on Sundays between 11am and 10pm. Many pubs have more liberal licences permitting later opening during the week. Bottle shops are allowed to open 8.30am-8.30pm daily except Sundays.

The Perth/Fremantle area is good territory for real ale drinkers. The most celebrated pub-brewery is the Sail and Anchor at 64 South Terrace, opposite the markets in Fremantle. It brews four real ales, the most powerful being Dogbolter; this has the same alcohol content (around 10%) as some wines, and is not dissimilar to the beer of the same name brewed by the Firkin pubs in the UK. The Sail and Anchor sells tamer, fizzier beer as well; it is the biggest outlet for Fosters in Western Australia. Also in Fremantle, His Lordship's Larder Pub and Brewery at the corner of Mouat and Phillimore Streets sells a variety of bitters plus Old Fremantle Stout. The lunch specials here are good value and include a half-pint of your chosen tipple. The Brewery at 149 Stirling Highway, Nedlands (halfway between Perth and Fremantle) produces some interesting beers: Traditional Bitter (viscous and very well-hopped), Matilda Bay Dark Lager (resembling a substantial brown ale), and Brass Monkey Stout (for those who consider Guinness too light a beer).

The leading large-scale brewery in Perth is the Swan Brewery owned by Alan Bond, and indeed you will find Bond's beers everywhere. Pub prices are higher than elsewhere in Australia, which the *Sydney Morning Herald* blames squarely on the America's Cup: "Before the Cup, Fremantle was more concerned with beer than boats. The tradition has survived, but a middy (10oz) now costs $1.50."

Visitors are often taken aback by the tendency of a large number of pubs to feature strip acts (particularly on Friday lunchtimes) to attract (male) custom despite the high price of beer. The pubs in Perth change name and character at a phenomenal rate as new proprietors try to make their watering-holes the trendy place to be seen. The young of Perth are remarkably fickle in their drinking habits and quite spoilt for choice. Two favourites which seem to be withstanding this pressure are the Ocean Beach Hotel ("OBH") in Cottesloe, and the Nedlands Park Hotel (better known as "Steve's") at 171 Broadway in Nedlands. This is the most popular University pub, with live bands and an excellent garden atmosphere with a do-it-yourself barbecue.

The reliably fine weather of Perth adds a certain sparkle to most activities, whether swimming, seeing an outdoor concert or simply strolling around town. Although the heat in summer can sometimes feel excessive, summer is certainly the best time to enjoy the performing arts, as the Festival of Perth takes place between January and March. While no match for the festivals of Adelaide or Sydney, the city puts on an extensive programme of music, theatre and exhibitions, often with outdoor performances (including Australia's only outdoor film festival held in an amphitheatre surrounded by trees on the UWA campus).

Tall buildings are sprouting up all the time in Perth city centre, so it is difficult to recommend the best candidate for an all-round view. The panorama from the revolving Hilite Restaurant mentioned above is breathtaking, but is strictly for diners: the lift doors open onto the dining area, so surreptitious view-stealing is not feasible. When the new Central Tower (at least 50 storeys) on St George's Terrace opens, it is likely to have an observation platform. In the meantime the Mount Eliza lookout in Kings Park is a solid metal tower with splendid views, but if you are at all afraid of heights the wide open spaces between the steps to the top could be a bit off-putting. There is also the Legacy Lookout (near Kings Park Road and Hancock St, West Perth) where you can take the lift to the top of Dumas House, any day except Saturday.

There are still many reminders of earlier days dotted around Perth, one of the best being the Old Mill just over the Narrows Bridge in South Perth. This flour mill built in 1835 has been restored to its former glory and contains interesting relics of the pioneer years. (Another notable flour mill is the Dingo Mill just outside Fremantle on the Stirling Highway, whose advertising sign was painted by Alan Bond on one of his first assignments after arriving from Britain; although the mill's name has changed to Great Southern, the sign remains as a stimulus to other would-be millionaires). St George's Cathedral stands appropriately enough on St George's Terrace; the foundation stone was laid in 1880. Also on the Terrace opposite Pier St is Government House, the official residence of the Governor of Western Australia, and the Cloister, an impressive old building which served as the state's first secondary school and was built in 1858.

Fremantle has numerous places of interest, notably the Round House at the west end of the High St. This 12-sided building was originally built in 1831 as a gaol, and later used as a staging post for holding Aboriginals on their involuntary journey to Rottnest Island. It now opens daily from 10am to 5pm to allow visitors to see the cells in which up to 15 prisoners at a time were consigned.

Museums and Galleries. Because Perth is such an active sporting city, its museums and galleries are often overlooked. Close to the centre is the Art Gallery of Western Australia (328 7233) in the Perth Cultural Centre on James St. The Western Australia Museum on Francis St (328 4411) has an Aboriginal gallery, veteran and vintage cars, meteorites, mammal and wildlife displays. It opens at 10.30am Monday-Thursday, and 1pm Friday-Sunday; closing time is 5pm daily.

Fremantle has its fair share of museums and galleries. Some of the best are the Fremantle Art Gallery at 43 High St; the Western Australia Maritime Museum in Cliff St; the Fremantle International Motor Museum, 6 Josephson St; and Rolly Tasker's America's Cup Museum, 43 Swan St, North Fremantle which has a collection of model yachts from the first America's Cup race in 1851 through to the present day.

Cinema. Drive-in cinemas are extremely popular in the suburbs of Perth, and there are over a dozen screens. As well as numerous suburban cinemas, the centre of Perth has the following:

Academy West End, Entertainment Centre, Wellington St (322 6774).
Capri, 21 Hay St Mall (322 4188).
Cinema City, corner of Hay and Barrack Streets (325 2377).
Cinecentre, 139 Murray St (325 2844).
Hoyts, St Martins Arcade, 635 Hay St Mall (325 4922).

In Fremantle, try the Film and Television Institute (FTI), housed in the old Fremantle Boys' School at 92 Adelaide St, Fremantle (335 1055), and the Port, also on Adelaide St (335 1839). The Windsor on 98 Stirling Highway in Nedlands has a more highbrow programme. Details of all films are shown in the *West Australian* and *Daily News*.

Music. The economics of major-league rock music seem to dictate that Perth often misses out on the world tours of top musicians, simply because it is so far from anywhere.

Perth's Entertainment Centre (322 4766) is on Wellington St, close to the city centre. It is a thoroughly modern multi-purpose auditorium and Perth's only real venue for big rock concerts. The relatively small seating capacity of 8,000 means that for popular acts it is quite often booked up very early. For information on upcoming performances, look in the *Reflex* section of the *West Australian* on Fridays. The best places to see local bands are the larger-venue pubs, such as those mentioned under *Drinking* plus others like the Maylands Hotel (211 Guildford Road) and the Silver Slipper (88 Broadway, Nedlands). Look out for local bands such as the Swamp Monsters (rhythm and blues), the Kryptonics, Greenhouse Effect and the Stems. Scrap Metal, an Aboriginal rock band from Broome, are also worth catching. You can hear Country music at the Manning Hotel, 27 Manning Road, and Irish folk bands at the Irish Club, 61 Townsend Road, Subiaco (381 5213). The Perth Jazz Society is based at the Hyde Park Hotel at the corner of Fitzgerald and Bulwer Streets (328 6166); for other events, call Jazzline on 221 1237.

Serious music is performed at the Concert Hall, 5 St George's Terrace (325 9944) and the WA Academy of Performing Arts auditorium at 2 Bradford St in Mount Lawley (272 0443). There are often free lunchtime concerts at the Callaway Music Auditorium on the University campus in Nedlands.

Theatre. The centre of Perth's theatrical world is Her Majesty's Theatre, a recently restored building on the corner of King and Hay Streets (322 2929). Ticket prices can be high, and the "society" audiences it attracts can be snooty. The Playhouse Theatre at 3 Pier St (325 3500) stages everything from experimental theatre to classical plays, and performances are usually very professional. The Patch Theatre at 161 Burswood Road in Victoria Park (361 8364) also has a very good repertory company. Another theatre worth a visit is the "Hole-in-the-Wall" Civic Centre at 180 Hamersley Rd in the suburb of Subiaco (381 3694), which tends to favour up and coming Australian authors. Also in Subiaco, the Regal Theatre at 474 Hay St (381 1557) was once a cinema but has been converted into a venue for live shows. It is unusual in having a "crying room" which enables mothers with fractious young children to watch the show through a window without disturbing the rest of the audience. On the University of WA campus, the New Fortune Theatre has been built as a replica of Shakespeare's Fortune Theatre in London.

Theatrical performances in Fremantle tend to be more diverse. There are productions by the Tosamist Theatre Circus, Deck Chair Theatre Company, Swy Theatre Company and Spare Parts Puppet Theatre. For details contact Fre-Info on 335 7652.

Nightlife. Perth has many nightclubs, but they tend to be less sophisticated than their London or Manhattan equivalents. If you fancy a bop, head for the Underground, 268 Newcastle St; Eagle One, 139 St James; or Hannibal's, 69 Lake St. Slightly more informal is the Red Parrot, just across the railway at 89 Milligan St.

Gambling. The Burswood Island Resort is situated in 275 acres of parkland by the Swan River, between the city and the airport. When completed, it will have a theatre/convention centre for 2,400, an exhibition and sporting centre with permanent seating for 14,000 people, and a hotel complex. In the meantime, the main attraction is the Casino. With 142 gambling tables it is one of the largest

"THE THEATRE HAS A CRYING ROOM FOR MOTHERS WITH FRACTIOUS CHILDREN".

in the world, and is open for 24 hours a day. The dress rules require you to be reasonably smart and you may well have to queue to get in, but you can still spend an interesting evening at the smaller stake tables, where the minimum bet is $2.

SPORT

Spectator Sports. Cricket and harness-racing can be seen close to the centre of Perth. The Western Australia Cricket Association ground (more commonly known as the WACA, pronounced "wacka") is just east of the city centre and is the venue for Test cricket, one-day internationals and Sheffield Shield matches. Just along from the WACA is Gloucester Park (325 8822), the home of the Western Australian Trotting Association. Race meetings are usually held in the evening, and the highlight of the season is the Benson and Hedges Cup each January. You can also see harness-racing at Richmond Raceway in East Fremantle (339 2535). Horseracing takes place at the Ascot course in summer (the highlight being the Perth Cup on New Year's Day) and Belmont Park in winter, and the greyhounds race at the Cannington Raceway on Albany Highway (458 4600).

Australian Rules Football is played at venues all over Perth every weekend in winter. The only Western Australian team in the premier VFL is the Eagles, who play at the WACA Oval and at Subiaco. If, however, you pick one of the less well-known clubs you will be able to sit on the grassy banks that often form the "grandstands", enjoy a beer and sunbathe.

Hockey is popular in Western Australia, and First Division games are played on Saturday and Sunday from April to September at the Commonwealth Hockey Stadium in Bentley (451 3688). Ice hockey can be seen at the Ice World Rink in Mirrabooka (344 4400).

Participation. Watersports abound in Perth. You can hire windsurfers, water-skis and so on, from various beachside dealers including Surfscene in North Cottesloe (381 2815) and Santosha in Scarborough Beach (341 6843). Surfcats are rented out on the river by several operators on Coode St, South Perth. The Cable Ski Park in Troode St, Spearwood is also good fun: water-skiers are transported around the Park's waterways by means of a cable tow rope. Skis, life jackets and wet suits are all available, as is instruction for beginners.

Elsewhere around Perth the climate makes outdoor sports fun, even for the most indolent of visitors. There are numerous tennis courts in the city; the University of WA has about a dozen, which are busy in term-time but are hired out to visitors during the vacation for $1.50 per hour. Perth has several golf courses, but for the less able there is a miniature 18-hole Botanic Golf Course at 25 Burns Beach Rd, Wanneroo (405 1475), reached by bus 348 from the Wellington St bus station. The small landscaped course includes waterfalls, ornamental pools and exotic gardens, and a round costs $5.

Beaches. The ocean beaches have white sand and clear blue water. Going north from Fremantle Harbour, the most popular are Port Beach (near North Fremantle), Cottesloe ("Cott", where an Australian woman stole a kiss from Prince Charles), the nude beach at Swanbourne, City Beach, Scarborough and Trigg. They are mostly safe, although the heavy breakers at Scarborough (which make surfing there excellent) can be dangerous to the inexperienced; and the rocks near Trigg have a permanent rip current. The ocean beaches can get very crowded, however, especially as many office workers like to come down to the beach after finishing work. For more details of the city's beaches, pick up the free *Guide to Perth's Beaches* from tourist offices.

On the river there are several small beaches which are very safe for swimming. Try Crawley, Nedlands or Peppermint Grove on the north bank, and South Perth, Canning Bridge, Como or Applecross on the South Shore. The river is usually a hive of activity: windsurfing, waterskiing and sailing are among the major participation sports.

Parks and Zoos. Kings Park is one of the finest in Australia, with panoramic views over the Swan River and city centre. Much of it is still in the native state, with wild flowers abounding in spring: orchids, freesias and "kangaroo paws", the state emblem. There are special display greenhouses for desert and tropical flora. You can get a free guided tour if you book in advance on 321 4801. Look out also for exotic birds such as flocks of black parrots and the colourful green parrot known as "twenty-eight".

Closer to the city centre there are some more formal parks: Hyde Park, Stirling Gardens and the Supreme Court Gardens. Down on the Esplanade the Alan Green Conservatory houses a wide variety of tropical and semi-tropical plants. Queens Park, on the corner of Plain and Hay Streets, has some beautiful lakes and is quite romantic. Lake Monger in Wembley is a lovely lake with wild ducks, black swans and other birdlife.

Animals can be seen in a less natural environment at the excellent Perth Zoo at 20 Labouchere Road, South Perth (367 7988). For something rather more participatory, the Adventure World amusement park at Bibra Lake features native animals, thrill rides, parklands, waterways and the biggest swimming pool in Australia.

SHOPPING

Normal hours are 8.30am-5pm from Monday to Friday (with late opening to 9pm on Thursdays), and 8.30am to noon or 1pm on Saturdays; in summer, however, many shops open until 6pm on Saturdays.

Hay St Mall is the heart of Perth's shopping centre which extends to include Murray St, Barrack St and William St. There are numerous arcades off the Mall. Tourists are steered towards "Perth's historic centre", a highly-commercialized arcade known as Ye Olde London Court with touristy shops selling souvenirs such as tins of "Fremantle Doctor", containing only air. The Aboriginal Arts Australia shop at 251 St George's Terrace contains many traditional Aboriginal crafts including boomerangs, carvings, necklaces and didjeridus, and opens on Sundays from 2.30 to 5pm. The National Trust shop, just along the Terrace at 139, is also interesting.

Many goods are cheaper at one of the out-of-town weekend markets. These take place in Fremantle (Henderson St), Midland (The Crescent), Wanneroo (Finlay Place) and Subiaco (Station St). Fremantle and Subiaco are the best and provide great entertainment as well as cheap souvenirs.

Secondhand. For all manner of used goods, the area to head for is the junction of Fitzgerald and Newcastle Streets in West Perth. Try Beehive (right on the corner) or Old Wares at 103 Fitzgerald St.

Books. The usual assortment of multiple retailers have stores in the city centre. The Magic Circle Bookshop at 409 Wellington St (opposite Forrest Place) is a good source of secondhand books. You could also try the Arcane Bookshop, 212 William St, Northbridge. For comic fans, the Comic Shop at 252 William St, Northbridge (227 8005) has a remarkably good selection of magazines.

THE MEDIA

Newspapers. The only morning daily is the *West Australian,* a bulky tabloid with an entertainment pull-out (*Reflex*) on Fridays. The evening paper is the grossly downmarket *Daily News,* while the weekend *Western Mail* is published each Saturday.

Radio. The ABC networks are 6WF (702 AM), 6WN (810 AM) and ABC-FM, the only 24-hour service in town. The most popular rock station is 96FM, and there are several AM music stations such as 6PM and 6IX. The Curtin University station is 6NR (927 AM) broadcasts ethnic programmes in the evening, predominantly in Scandinavian and Baltic languages. The University of Western Australia station 6UVS (92.1 FM) has a broad range of programming including music for ageing hippies.

Television. Perth has four TV stations at present, and a fifth is planned. Viewers in outlying areas of Western Australia can watch satellite transmissions on the Golden West network, providing they have the right receiving equipment; many roadhouses and hotels are suitably equipped.

As in most Australian cities, you may encounter the odd brawl usually due to excessive drinking, but it is normally easy to avoid getting involved. Perth is relatively free of crime and there are few areas where you will feel uncomfortable late at night. For non-urgent calls to the police, dial 222 1111 (Perth) or 335 4555 (Fremantle). Prostitution is about to be legalized in Western Australia, although brothels will not be permitted in residential areas.

To help you steer clear of the perils of sunburn, smoke-filled restaurants, sexually transmitted diseases, etc. the Western Australian government has produced a *Health Guide for Tourists* which is free from tourist offices. One risk it fails to mention is the habit of the native magpies to attack people, particularly picnickers, during the spring nesting season.

The area code for Perth and Fremantle is 09. In an emergency, dial 000.

The main tourist information bureau is the Western Australian Tourist Office at 772 Hay St (322 2999), with a branch in Fremantle at 41 High St (430 5555). There are also Western Australian Tourist Offices in the following state capitals:

Adelaide: 108 King William St (08-212 1344).
Brisbane: Level 2, 307 Queen St (07-229 5794).
Melbourne: 25 Elizabeth St (03-614 6522).
Sydney: 92 Pitt St (02-232 8388).

The name has recently changed from "Holiday WA", so you may find some branches still using the old title. Giveaway tourist magazines for Perth and

Fremantle include *This Week in . . ., What's On in . . .,* and *Your Guide to . . .* The area has a network of electronic information points known as Infowest. These computer terminals are dotted around tourist haunts within the city and out at the airport. At the press of several buttons, you can get a display and print-out of current events, restaurants, entertainment and so on. The drawback is that many machines appear to be permanently out of order, and those that work are often monopolized by addicts of varying degrees of computer literacy. Fremantle has its own telephone information service: Fre-Info, on 335 7652.

British Consulate-General: Prudential Building, 95 St George's Terrace (321 5611).

American Express: 51 William St (322 1177); 177 High St, Fremantle (335 7977).

Thomas Cook: Shop 16, Wesley Centre, 93 William St (321 2896); 119 High St, Fremantle (335 3111).

General Post Office: 3 Forrest Place (326 5211).

Disabled Travellers: ACROD Access Committee — 222 2961.

Medical Treatment: Royal Perth Hospital, Wellington St (325 0101); Fremantle Hospital, Alma St (335 0111).

Women's Information and Referral Exchange (WIRE): 32 St George's Terrace (222 0444).

Helplines: Poison Information — 381 1177; Sexual Assault Centre — 389 3333; State Emergency Service — 277 5333.

Many travellers have reported that it is more difficult to find work in Perth than in the large eastern cities, which is perhaps surprising since unemployment is slightly below the national average. However, if you are not over-fussy, you should be able to find some way to earn money within a few weeks of arriving. Unless you have a working holiday visa you should tread warily since at the time of the America's Cup, the Perth immigration authorities went on the warpath to discourage foreigners from working illegally. To renew your working holiday visa, phone the Immigration Department on 220 2311.

Sources of Work. The main Perth office of the CES (at City Centre Tower, 256 Adelaide Terrace) is probably not as useful as the Templine office on the ground floor of 218 St George's Terrace (tel: 322 7466) which handles catering jobs. It is worth having a look at the cards on display in both offices. Also the suburban branches of the CES are smaller and more relaxed, and usually have more time to be helpful. If you can establish a rapport with the staff, your chances of finding work are improved. One of the best centres for casual work in Perth is the Innaloo office at 384 Scarborough Beach Road (tel: 446 0333), which provides a 24-hour phone service for employers so that they can lodge requests for labour at any time. These jobs are offered on a first-come, first-served basis, so aim to get to the office at least an hour before it opens at 7am. If you are not immediately successful, it is worth hanging around until 11am or so, since some employers prefer to walk in and take a look at possible recruits. If you still have no luck, at least it's only a short walk to the beach for the afternoon.

An innovative scheme outside the CES net but funded by the state government s known as Youthlink (58 Tyrell St, Nedlands; tel: 389 1230), which matches up local unemployed young people aged 15 to 30 with people who need help with household jobs such as gardening, decorating and cleaning. The pay of $6-$9 per hour is strictly cash-in-hand. But Youthlink is intended primarily for local people and will only help foreigners if there is a shortage of workers.

The *West Australian* is also a good source of jobs, particularly on Wednesday mornings. It is possible to get a copy in the city centre on Tuesday evenings, which is recommended since jobs for building labourers, etc. often commence at 6am and you should call as early as possible. Few of Perth's pubs and restaurants advertise in the newspaper; the best opportunities for bar and waiting staff are in the city centre, Northbridge and Fremantle areas. Women should be aware that a surprisingly large number of bars hire topless staff.

Agriculture. Opportunities in agriculture are concentrated south and east of Perth. Many travellers have fared well in the apple harvest (March to May) centred on Donnybrook, Pemberton and Manjimup. The former two towns both have Youth Hostels which claim that there is casual fruit-picking work in the vicinity at most times of the year.

Oranges, lemons and grapefruit can be picked around Bindoon (about 80km north of Perth) from September to February. Soft fruit — apricots, peaches and plums — ripen from December to March at Kalamunda, where there is a Youth Hostel which might offer suggestions. Be warned, however, that temperatures above 35°C are common at this time of year. Grapes for Western Australia's excellent wines are picked from February to April in the main wine-producing areas of the Swan Valley near Perth and, further south, Margaret River and Mount Barker.

The busiest time for agricultural work in the Outback is April to June when the massive wheatfields which cover much of the southern state are seeded. For a job as "Sheila of all trades" (mainly keeping the male workers supplied with tucker), you might get paid $200 a week plus free board and lodging. There are several agencies in Perth which deal with jobs in outback areas of the state, primarily station and roadhouse work. Try Statewide Employment (172 St George's Terrace; tel: 322 4236) or Pollitt's Employment Agency (251 Adelaide Terrace; tel: 325 2544).

Mining. Many are tempted by the legendary high wages paid at the mines located in the inhospitable Pilbara region in northern Western Australia. But the employment situation is very tight, with union membership and some experience the usual prerequisites. If you do want to have a go, visit the offices of mining sub-contractors which are concentrated in or near Mount Newman House at 200 St George's Terrace in Perth. The highest wages of all can be found in the offshore oil and gas industry at Dampier and Karratha, but for this work, experience in oil is essential.

The gold mines around Kalgoorlie are still thriving and there are employment possibilities in survey and drilling crews (but not the mines themselves). The accepted way of finding work in Kalgoorlie is to go around or phone all the relevant companies listed in the *Yellow Pages* or on the CES list of mines, drilling, surveying and lab companies. In fact the Kalgoorlie CES is reputed to be quite helpful to people looking for casual work. Exploration companies hire unskilled assistants (known as "fieldies", "TAs" or "offsiders") who are sometimes sent into remote areas where pay is $500 per week in the hand plus free caravan or motel accommodation. Most people work nearer town and earn about $10 an hour, with weekend work being particularly lucrative.

If your attempts to find work in the field fail, you can usually find a job (at lower pay) in mineral processing plants in Perth such as the Western Mining Corporation (193 Great Eastern Highway, Belmont; tel: 478 0711) or Analabs (52 Murray Road, Welshpool; tel: 458 7999).

Tourism. Despite the efforts of the Western Australian Tourism Commission, tourism is not yet a major industry outside Perth and Fremantle. Although this is likely to change over the next few years, as non-stop flights from Europe entice more travellers to begin their vacation in Perth and the "New Gold Coast" around Broome, resort jobs are scarce at present. The height of the tourist season around Broome is May to September, while the converse is true around Perth and the south (November to February). The stretch of coast from Broome to Carnarvon has good prawn fishing opportunities from March to October.

Further Afield

Obviously in a limited time it is not possible to see much of a state which is as large in area as Western Europe. If you are flying in and out of Perth, you will likely confine your travels to the southwest corner which includes the lovely coast south of Perth plus historic sites and natural features of considerable interest. On the other hand if you are making the journey through the state by land, you must choose between one of the great trans-continental highways, either north towards Darwin or east towards Adelaide.

Until America's Cup fever struck, Western Australia was always best known as the wildflower state. Now that the Cup has reverted to San Diego this will again become the state's main selling point. In many areas, but especially in the South-West, the rains of winter encourage field upon field of wild flowers to bloom (see *Great Outdoors* below).

If you have no fixed flight ideas about where to go, you could take an Ansett WA "mystery flight"; for $69 you book a same-day return ticket to somewhere which is revealed the day before you travel. You might end up in Kalgoorlie, Broome or any one of 13 destinations. You may even decide to view your $69 investment (or gamble) as a cheap one-way flight and conveniently forget to return to Perth. Call Ansett on 323 1122 for more details. Skywest Airlines (tel: 478 9898) also offers day trips to several destinations (of your choice) but these are much more expensive, from $175 for a day in Geraldton to $226 in Esperance.

DAY TRIPS FROM PERTH

Travelling in any direction from Perth, including out to sea, brings you to places of interest, though the distances make some of the following day trips fairly strenuous.

Rottnest Island. There is nothing strenuous however about the two-hour ferry trip to Rotto as it is known. This small island about 20km offshore from Perth has successfully resisted the threat of large commercial developments including a large marina, and remains a peaceful and unpretentious retreat. Locals refer to the mainland as "overseas". Visitors go to enjoy the beaches and the wildlife, by foot or on bicycle, since there are virtually no motorized vehicles. Bicycles can be easily hired from near the ferry jetty, and the 11km-long island can be encircled in three to four hours. You should have no trouble spotting a quokka, a unique member of the wallaby family which an early Dutch explorer mistook for giant rats, hence the name he gave the island in 1696. The island was made a leisure reserve not long after the turn of the century, and so all wildlife and vegetation are protected. The presiding Rottnest Island Board (tel: 292 5044) enforces the rules, including no campfires on the beach, no spear-fishing and no alcohol on the campsites (this latter to prevent the Perth adolescents who flock here on summer weekends from getting out of hand).

There is plenty of accommodation in case you decide to extend your stay, including tents and cabins for hire at Tent-land (tel: 292 5033). The island specializes in self-catering flats and cottages which, like all the island's accommodation, are usually booked up in the school holidays. The day return ferry trip from Fremantle costs $12 with the trip from Barrack St in Perth costing a little more; both prices have dropped substantially since the America's Cup. Alternatively you can take the faster hydrofoil ferries which take just over an hour; telephone 325 6033 for details. There is also a possibility of accompanying the supply-carrying barge run by Elder Prince Marine Services which takes a few passengers at bargain rates (tel: 335 8444).

The Swan Valley. Just half an hour's drive from central Perth and a little past the airport are the 33 commercial wineries of the Swan Valley, many of them established in the mid-nineteenth century. The Swan River flows alongside the historic town of Guildford and Midland and on through the wineries with the Darling Range in the background to contribute to the picturesqueness. Tourist cruises from Perth include lunch and wine tastings.

Many Yugoslavs settled along the banks of the Swan, just as they did in the wine-making Henderson Valley near Auckland. Consult the WA Tourist Office pamphlet *The Swan Valley Guide* for a map of the region, opening times and descriptions of the wineries. The distances are very manageable by bicycle though one drawback is that the Great Northern Highway, which links many of the wineries, is uncomfortably busy for cyclists.

The Beaches. If you want to venture further afield than the city beaches, you can travel north or south and as far as you like to find seaside resorts of varying character. A half hour's drive or bus ride south of Perth, Rockingham has long since been overtaken by Fremantle as the main port and is now a popular resort. One of the attractions is the short ferry ride from Mersey Point where fairy penguins can be seen on the beaches of Penguin Island in April and September-November (the island is closed May to August).

About the same distance north of Perth is Yanchep National Park with glorious ocean beaches as well as a large lake improbably named Loch McNess (after one Charles McNess who financed its dredging). The limestone caves called Crystal and Yonderup provide further interest.

Inland from Perth. Historic towns such as Toodyay (even the accepted pronunciation Too-jay indicates its sleepiness), Northam and York do probably not offer enough rewards to justify a long day trip by motor car, but if you are heading away from Perth they are worth a detour. These towns are on the Avon River (a major tributary of the Swan) whose fast-flowing waters are the scene of the annual Avon Descent Canoe Race held on the last weekend of July. The Avon Valley is well provided with old restored buildings (including the three Youth Hostels), local museums and congenial picnic areas. Tours of York —

Western Australia's oldest inland settlement — to see the well-preserved colonial architecture along the main street, operate from Perth on Thursdays for about $40 which includes a visit to a working farm and barbecue lunch. Independent travellers usually prefer to indulge in one of the cream teas for which York is famed. There are also Youth Hostels in Kalamunda and Mundaring Weir in the Darling Range just inland from Perth. They are linked by a 15km bushwalk.

The *Watsonian Flyer* makes special Sunday excursions in winter to small towns on branch lines, often to coincide with their annual festival or country fair. Ring 364 7626 for details.

SOUTH OF PERTH

A relatively new high speed train replacing the old *Australind* takes just two hours to get from Perth to Bunbury, the second largest town in the state (with a population of just 23,000!). Alternatively South West Coach Lines (tel: 322 5173) departs Monday to Friday from the MTT Bus Station on Wellington St at 1.30pm for Bunbury, Busselton and Margaret River, plus a few inland towns like Donnybrook. The cost varies with the destination from $15 to $20 single.

The coast south of Perth is the most developed part of the state for holidaymakers, and there should be no difficulty finding accommodation in Youth Hostels (all but a handful of the state's 26 hostels are in the South-West), on campsites or in lodges. Campus Holidays (44 St George's Terrace, Perth; tel: 221 1569) hire out pre-erected tents in Dunsborough, Augusta, Denmark, Esperance and the Porongurup Range starting at $8 per person.

The YHA of Western Australia run two-week expeditions by four-wheel drive vehicle between September and March, which cover most of the highlights of the South-West. The inclusive cost works out at less than $40 a day.

The Coast. Mandurah, Busselton, Dunsborough and Augusta are all charming coastal resorts with plenty of amusements and amenities. The gateway town of Bunbury is a little too commercially prosperous to be an ideal resort whereas Busselton with its famous old two-kilometre wooden jetty and gentrified architecture is very pleasant. Do not drive straight down the coast road without stopping at places like Mandurah to try to catch a crab for dinner or in Yallingup to visit the caves or admire the fierceness of the surf which intimidates all but the most experienced of surfers. The gracious hotel in Yallingup is especially recommended if you want to splash out on a night's accommodation and like a game of Scrabble around an open fire in the evening. Alternatively there is a summer Youth Hostel here. Another beautiful Indian Ocean beach with a hostel is nearby Quindalup near Dunsborough. The beaches between Perth and Cape Naturaliste are safe for swimming; thereafter care should be taken, though some places like Yallingup have coastal lake and lagoons suitable for children. The whole coast is also lined with national parks.

Turning the corner of the coast at Augusta, you can continue east though the road does not begin to follow the coast until you come to Walpole and the picturesquely sited Denmark. The latter is remarkable because of Winniston Park, home of an English antique collector who jammed his house (an average-size bungalow) full of antiques including the bed given to Mary Queen of Scots in 1554. This chaotic treasure trove is open to the public. There are also superb beaches nearby at William Bay and Ocean Beach, as well as an animal sanctuary with a range of rare marsupials like the agile, the bettong and the darma (free admission).

Fifty kilometres further along the coastal road (and 400km along the direct route from Perth) is Albany which was established in 1826 and is the oldest settlement in the state (as opposed to York which is the oldest *inland* settlement). Like so many old coastal towns in the Antipodes, this was a whaling station, and there is an interesting whaling museum. The coastline around here is spectacular. The strange rock formations, eroded by the pounding seas include blowholes (usually tame), the Natural Bridge and the Dog Rock, so called because of its resemblance to a sniffing bloodhound (on the road to Middleton Beach). There is a willow tree at Strawberry Hill which was grown from a cutting taken from Napoleon's grave.

Once again the road parts company with the coast and it is necessary to drive 470km before you reach the next coastal resort of Esperance, growing at a surprising rate given its remoteness. In addition to its wonderful seascapes, there is an interesting display about the US Skylab (which burst into flames over Esperance on its descent from orbit). Only 3km from town is the Pink Lake, coloured by the high concentration of salt. In the summer, there are cruises out among the 100 or so islands of the romantically-named Archipelago of the Recherche with its colonies of penguins and seals.

Wineries. In contrast to the mass-production wineries of the Swan Valley, winemakers around Margaret River, a small dairy town 270km south of Perth, are making wines of distinguished quality at rather high prices (although Cape Mentelle's 1.5 litre red or white costing about $8 is worth trying). The excellent WA Tourist Office pamphlet called *Vineyards of the South* has detailed maps of the area, with opening times, tastings and other facilities at the 18 wineries open to the public clustered in two areas just off Highway 10. The most famous of the vineyards is Leeuwin Estate (tel: 097-57 6253) which makes wines that thrill the experts and mounts publicity stunts that thrill everyone such as importing the entire London Symphony Orchestra to perform on the sloping lawns of the winery (apparently not quite drowning out the kookaburras).

Wine lovers might also like to explore the Mount Barker area, where vineyards are more widely dispersed and the wineries very new. Mount Barker is a leisurely three-hour drive away from Margaret River through countryside which by Australian standards is rolling, green and reminiscent of England, especially the

"SYMPHONY ORCHESTRAS HAVE TO COMPETE WITH THE KOOKABURRAS."

apple orchards around Pemberton. But the forests of giant karri trees, from which kangaroos are liable to hop at dusk, leave you in no doubt as to what country you are in.

The Southwestern Interior. Several highways from Perth veer away from the coast and take you through forests of Western Australia's famous answer to the Californian redwood — the karri tree. Karris are a kind of blue gum, which grow tall and straight to magnificent heights. In the early days they were used for street paving and railway sleepers among other things (partly because white ants could make no inroads into the wood) but are now logged more discriminatingly. Karri is an Aboriginal word whose similarity to the Maori word kauri for the equally fine New Zealand conifer, also highly prized as a building hardwood, appears to be accidental.

Driving along the main roads allows you to see the trees, especially beautiful in spring when they appear to arise from a sea of colourful wildflowers. If you have a good head for heights, you can even climb the giant Gloucester Tree near Pemberton, thought to be about 300 years old. A platform 61m above the ground is used as a fire lookout but visitors are permitted to climb up for the view. Not far away near Manjimup are four trees of similar age which stand in perfect single file formation. These can be best seen from Graphite Road, about a mile past One-Tree-Bridge.

Some distance east (just north of Albany and Mount Barker) is the Stirling Range National Park with weathered hills rising out of the flat plains. Bluff Knoll and Toolbrunup at 1,000m are the only places in the state where snow falls. When the summer heat haze dispels, it is sometimes possible to see the ocean 70km away though you are more likely to see the interesting vegetation close at hand, including many of the primitive grass trees known as black boys (since they grow from what looks like fire-blackened stumps). The splendidly named Porongurup National Park nearby has stark granite domes, lush vegetation and more karri forests.

There are other wonders of nature in southern Western Australia. Pre-eminent among them is Wave Rock near Hyden (340km east of Perth) set among the sweeping wheat and barley "paddocks" of the central part of the state. Whereas it may have required a little imagination to see the dog in the rock at Albany, it requires no effort to visualize a breaking wave in this giant rock, which is estimated to be $2\frac{1}{2}$ billion years old. It is worth exploring the other strangely eroded and ancient rocks in the vicinity, such as the Hippo's Yawn.

Apart from some Aboriginal rock carvings, the man-made wonders of the area pale a little in comparison. But if you are passing through the town of Wagin, self-proclaimed sheep capital of Western Australia, you are obliged to admire the nine-metre tall Giant Merino ram about which the rather modest claim is made: "it would have to be at or near the top in the all-time world record book of giant rams" (no doubt a gripping publication if it existed).

EAST OF PERTH

The Nullarbor. The Nullarbor Plain is a remarkably desolate area of unrelievedly flat arid scrubland, the kind of landscape for which Australia is famed. The word is often misspelled, so try to remember that it derives from the Latin for no trees "nul(l) arbor" (and ignore the fact that it is sometimes "a bore"). Conservationists are trying to have the Nullarbor included on the World leritage List of unique and precious environments, partly because of the normous (and accessible) underground river. With luck some amazing sights night meet your eye if you brave the epic crossing by train or coach, such as eeing a dust storm out one side and a rare rainstorm out the other.

Although one might have expected the trans-Canada railway to hold the ubious honour of having the longest straight section of railway in the world, he Nullarbor takes the prize with its 480km stretch. Unlike the railway, the Eyre Highway (Highway 1) touches the coast of the Great Australian Bight at a few places on the South Australian side. It is not hard to recognize the kind of road t is, when the only items marked on a 200km stretch of a road map are 'telephone" (twice) and "scenic lookout" (five times). If you do undertake this rip by road, be sure to take seriously the advice provided in the tourist literature, or example carry about 25 litres of water in case the water tanks (marked on he map) are dry or contaminated; if you do use the water in them for drinking t might have to be boiled. The map and facilities guide also provides a complete ist of accommodation (and recommends pre-booking though this is unnecessary f you carry a tent), bars (with opening hours), food sources (minimal) and petrol tations (sufficient so that you needn't carry fuel). If driving at dawn or dusk keep a sharp lookout for wandering kangaroos, wombats, etc. But straying animals are not the only reason to refrain from speeding: there are police aircraft which patrol the highway to enforce the 110km/h speed limit. If crossing in winter be prepared for disconcerting jumps in temperature from 5°C to 40°C and winds of up to 100km/h which can cause choking dust clouds.

The Goldfields. One of the last of the great Australian gold rushes brought hundreds of impoverished families to Kalgoorlie and its surroundings in 1893 pushing wheelbarrows 500km from Perth only to die of thirst since there was no drinking water (a problem that was solved a decade later when a pipeline from the west was opened).

There are abandoned gold mines and gold rush towns throughout Australia and New Zealand. What distinguishes Kalgoorlie is that the gold boom continues or at least has been revived in the 1980s by the jump in the world price of gold. In contrast to the picturesque ghost town of Coolgardie 29km away (the similarity of names can be confusing), Kalgoorlie is surrounded by ugly pits and piles of ore waiting to be processed. The affluence of former times is reflected in the grand civic buildings which line the streets of both towns. The gambling and womanizing are also perpetuated in the two-up games which are so popular and in the brothels along Kalgoorlie's Hay St; both are included on bus tour routes and both are illegal. Drinking, however, is legal and also well catered for, though the narrowest pub in the country (the British Arms) has been turned into the Golden Mile Museum, having lost its liquor licence many years ago.

You can stick to admiring the relics and recreations of the gold boom days, for example at the Hainault Gold Mine in Kalgoorlie or the statue-cum-drinking fountain dedicated to Paddy Hannan who first struck gold here. Or you can become a latter-day prospector. You can obtain a Miner's Right for $10 from the Mines Department and either head out on your own or join a half-day fossicking tour with Kalgoorlie Goldrush Tours who supply metal detectors. (A more reliable way of making money is to get a job with a contractor or survey company as mentioned above in *Work*).

NORTH OF PERTH

As you travel north, Western Australia becomes progressively more rugged, with tin shacks replacing the fine architecture of Perth. The population thins dramatically, as does the number of tourists, and care must be taken to carry spare petrol and water. Several coach companies make the marathon journey to Darwin, taking two days of straight driving to get to the Northern Territory border and a further 15 hours to Darwin. If you are driving yourself, you will have to get used to dirt roads unless you never deviate from Highway 1. These can usually be travelled comfortably at 50km/h, which is much faster than is the case in the Northern Territory.

Because of the vast distances and the lack of competition (and custom), food and services are pricey, particularly accommodation. Towns are quite likely to have just one charmless motel charging $60 or $70 single, so camping is the only way to accomplish the journey on a budget. In such isolated circumstances, camaraderie quickly develops among travellers of all ages, and advice on pleasant free campsites is always shared. All national parks have campsites with basic well-maintained facilities which cost about $5, paid on an honour system to the ranger who comes to collect in the early evening.

The main consideration for such a trip is the time of year. Although the northern areas can be beautiful in the Wet (December to March), especially the stormy skies, temperatures are too high for most people's comfort, often over 40°C. Although roads follow the high ground, flooding is persistent and can prevent cars and buses proceeding for days at a time. This is also the cyclone season, so most travellers choose the months between May and September. The residents of course endure all the extremes and in recognition of their endurance, the government gives a tax break of 20% to everyone who lives above the 26th parallel which is about half way up the state.

The Coastal Route. The first few hundred kilometres are relatively gentle, though even the first famous sight you come to only 230km north of Perth has only recently been made accessible to conventional motor cars, since the road was surfaced. This is the Pinnacles, calcified humps of eroded limestone in Nambung National Park near Cervantes. If necessary you can join a tour from the Cervantes Caravan Park.

Geraldton is a thriving port and, by Western Australian standards, a major town. Its winters are noticeably warmer than those of Perth, so most people go for the weather. Gourmets on the other hand, go for the huge rock lobsters, prawns, and other fish which can be bought fresh from the fishermen. North of Geraldton is the Kalbarri holiday resort development which is a pretty though touristy place. Geraldton and Kalbarri are part of the "Batavia Coast", so named after a Dutch shipwreck.

Another long day's drive along the West Coastal Highway brings you to Shark Bay and Monkey Mia where most people go, not to see the sharks (of which there are many) or the monkeys (of which there are none), but the dolphins. Monkey Mia is said to be the only place in the world at present where for nine months of the year wild dolphins come in to shore to frolic fearlessly among the legs of bathers. The owner of the caravan park is a dolphin devotee who does not want the place to become commercialized out of recognition, though pressures are being exerted on him to do so, and the bay is already on many tour itineraries. Fish with which to attract and feed the dolphins are sold at the caravan park.

Carnarvon is described in the tourist brochures as the tropical gateway to the north, though it is little more than a wide and dusty main street flanked by several shacks. However if you have journeyed this far, you will have come not for the architecture but for the natural landscapes, and near Coral Bay 238km north is the breathtaking Ningaloo Marine Park, a 260km stretch of coral that is closer to the coast than any such reef in the world.

Many miles further north is the semi-Asian sleepy hollow of Broome with the best beach in North West Australia, stretching 22km. This is a developing tourist resort, and is also known as the Costa-del-Dole because of the number of layabouts it has attracted. The oriental influence of the Japanese and Malay pearl divers who began arriving in the 1880s persists along Carnarvon St which, despite its modest size, is the second largest Chinatown in Australia after Sydney's.

For ten days in late August/early September, the colourful Shinju Matsuri Festival or Festival of the Pearl is held to commemorate the valuable gem pearl which brought wealth to this coast. Broome's population of 5,000 swells five or six times for the Festival, so this is probably not the best time to appreciate Broome at its lazy best.

From Broome the Great Northern Highway heads inland, away from the northern peninsulas which are mostly Aboriginal reserves.

The Inland Route. Beginning again in Perth, there is an alternative route which passes through large pastoral properties, fields of wild flowers (spring only), gold ghost towns and rugged mining country. One of the most unexpected sights is a fine collection of art, books and artefacts and an extraordinarily grand looking hotel in the country town of New Norcia, 135km north of Perth, which has had a Benedictine foundation since 1846. The museum is open seven days a week. Of all the anonymous farms you pass, one has turned itself into a bizarre tourist attraction by declaring itself a separate country. The Hutt River Principality northeast of Carnarvon has its own passports, currency, stamps, etc. which the farmer-turned-Prince Leonard claims are recognized worldwide. The shop which sells Hutt River memorabilia does a roaring trade, as does the caravan park, encouraging Prince Leonard to dream of building a huge casino and turning his principality into Australia's foremost tourist attraction.

Much further north is another of Australia's massive monoliths, in fact Mount Augustus is the largest rock in the world. But you will find very few Japanese tourists photographing sunsets here, mainly due to its inaccessibility even compared to Ayers Rock. It is on a track about 300km from either

"KUNUNURRA IS A GOOD JUMPING-OFF POINT"

the coastal or the inland highways. Furthermore its immense size is not apparent because of its gentle slopes and scrubby covering. Only those keen on climbing giant monoclines (folded strata of rock) will consider the detour worthwhile. Mid West Tours (274 Seventh St, Wonthella, WA 6430) conduct "safaris" of Mount Augustus and other sights which cost about $900 for 12 days.

The mining region of Western Australia is the Pilbara centred on the oddly-named town of Tom Price. The iron ore is transported mostly by rail to Port Hedland where it is shipped off to Japan. If you are in this area, it is worth taking one of the free tours of the mines put on by the public relations departments of the mining companies; the scale of the machinery used to dismantle entire mountains is a startling sight. As mentioned earlier, noting that the mining companies sometimes build their own access roads alongside the railway tracks, which are faster, straighter and better graded than the state highway. The public is allowed to use these roads, as long as permission is obtained from the Hamersley Iron Ore Company in Karratha or at the Tom Price mine site. A permit lasts for up to a week. Although four-wheel drive vehicles (which can be hired in Port Hedland on the coast) are preferable for exploring the dirt roads of the Hamersley Range National Park, it is possible to visit some of the high points, such as the spectacular gorge and giant ant hills at Wittenoon, in an ordinary vehicle. The geological formations of the Hamersley Range are remarkable for their mineral content and shifting colours. Try to see the Pilbara paintings of Fred Williams.

The inland highway joins the coast at Port Hedland, since it is impossible to cross the totally uninhabited and barely mapped Great Sandy Desert and Gibson Desert. Maps show a dotted route labelled the Canning Stock Route which was surveyed in 1906 but was never successfully established. It did however bring many Aboriginal people in contact with Europeans for the first time, and the history of the Western Desert Puntukunuparna people is being prepared for the Bicentenary. The Gunbarrel Highway further south is an actual road, though it is only open to expert four-wheel drivers who have obtained entry permits for the Aboriginal reserves through which it passes.

Broome marks the beginning of the most rugged and remote region of Western Australia, seldom travelled by individuals. This area, the Kimberley Plateau, is subject to extremes of rainfall and tropical humidity, so that at least for some of the time the landscapes are not as dry and dusty as they are further south. Massive dams and irrigation projects control the water and are heavily promoted by the tourist authorities. (In fact dams and reservoirs receive enthusiastic billing in many places in Australia, probably as a result of past water shortages). Most visitors prefer to visit the crystal clear waters of the mighty Fitzroy River which flows through Geikie Gorge. Remember that these waters are full of crocodiles. Kununurra in the top corner of the state is like an oasis on the Ord River and a pleasant jumping-off point for exploring the area, which includes some Aboriginal art. This is still 1,000km from Darwin.

Flora and Fauna. There are about 8,000 species of flowering plants in Western Australia plus a host of unique ferns, carnivorous plants, grasses and trees from the wonderful eucalypts of the south to the gnarled baobab trees which flourish in the tropical north (among them a hollowed-out specimen which served as a prison cell in Derby north of Broome).

The transformation which a day or two of rain can make to a barren-looking field is astonishing especially in the drier areas north of Perth where Sturt's desert pea carpets the land with red and black.

In addition to an unusual range of marsupials, Western Australia also has some very interesting birds in such habitats as the salt lakes of Clifton and Preston (20km south of Mandurah), the Archipelago of the Recherche (with seals and penguins as well as sea birds) and the Dryandra Forest near Williams. The Nullarbor is not a place where one would expect to find many birds, however there is a bird observatory 42km south of Cocklebiddy very near the Great Australian Bight. The Eyre Bird Observatory (Cocklebiddy via Norseman, WA 6443; tel: 090-39 3450) is accessible only by four-wheel drive, so it is necessary to make a booking in advance, either directly or through the YHA, so that the Warden can collect you. You can stay only on a full board basis which costs $40 for the first night and $25 thereafter.

In the north of the state, you should watch out for poisonous snakes such as the yellow whip snake. In the Kimberley region you are almost certain to see crocodiles, deadly sea snakes or water monitors (giant lizards).

Activities. Bushwalking can be enjoyed in many of the national parks from the Porongurups in the extreme south to the more forbidding Hamersley Range which contains the state's highest peaks (up to 1,245m). The usual caution with regard to heat exhaustion and dehydration must be exercised. If you are going to walk in scrub, wear sturdy long trousers to fend off attack by the spikes of spinifex which are coated with a natural chemical irritant. A company called Bushwalking Tours (57 Vickery Crescent, Bunbury, WA 6230 (tel: 097-21 4248) conducts gentle one day hikes near Perth for $33, while Action Tours (PO Box 279, Kalamunda, WA 6076; tel: 09-293 2344) charge a little less.

Yanchep National Park one hour north of Perth has an outdoor adventure centre which hires out rowing boats for Loch McNess, bushwalking trails, a wildlife sanctuary, a marina and limestone caves.

Most youth hostels hire out five-speed bicycles for about $6 a day plus deposit. The use of a horse will cost considerably more: contact Avon Valley Western Horse Trails (Harddrill Road, Millendon, WA 6056; tel: 09-296 1432) if interested.

Restricted Areas. If you wish to enter one of the many Aboriginal Lands in Western Australia, you should obtain prior permission from the Permits Officer at the Aboriginal Affairs Planning Authority in Perth (tel: 32 3744).

Calendar of Events

January 1	**Perth Cup, Ascot racecourse**
January/February *or* February/March	Festival of Perth
March (first Monday)	**Labour Day**
March (first weekend)	Dairy Festival, Harvey
March (last weekend)	Log Chop and Community Fair, Dwellingup
June (first Monday)	**Foundation Day**
August	Sunshine Festival, Geraldton
late August/early September	Festival of the Pearl, Broome
September/October	Perth Royal Show
October (first Monday)	**Queen's Birthday**
November (first Saturday)	Boddington Rodeo

Public holidays are shown in **bold**

The
Northern Territory

Population: 140,000   **Capital: Darwin (population 66,100)**

To foreigners and Australians alike, the Northern Territory is essentially Ayers
Rock: the red rock rising from the red centre of Australia, symbolizing the
uniqueness of this country. There is, of course, much more to the Territory: its
total area is 1,347,000 km², over ten times larger than England and twice the
size of Texas, yet with a population equal to a medium-sized town in Europe
or North America. Nowhere can you experience more sense of space or eerie
silence. Although the Territory has no monopoly on featureless landscapes nor
lush jungle, its Outback seems more primeval than that of the other states. Read
Capricorn by Xavier Herbert, or try to see paintings by Australian artist Brett
Bailey, to get a feel of the sheer, continuous emptiness.

Close to Ayers Rock are the Olgas, a range emerging from the stark desert
which many find more stunning than the Rock itself. Nearby — always a relative
term in the Territory — is the town of Alice Springs. In the middle of Australia's
"Red Centre", with its extremes of temperature and arid terrain, Alice Springs
once epitomized the pioneering spirit of a nation. Now, however, it provides the
security of safe suburbia and has what seems to be the highest density of
shopping malls in all of Australia.

The northern part of the Territory (known to Australians as the "Top End")
bears little relation to the dry south. Darwin, the capital of the Territory, has
more in common with Singapore than Sydney, and is surrounded by swamps,
gorges and more than a few crocodiles. The Top End and the Centre are linked

by the Stuart Highway, widely referred to as "The Track", the central spine and overland artery which is an essential part of the Territorian consciousness. The regions have very different climates, described below under *Darwin* and *Alice Springs* respectively. In short, the north is tropical — hot throughout the year with a pronounced wet season ("Wet") from November to April — while the south is semi-desert.

Between the extremes of north and south is the Never Never (immortalized by Jeanine Gunn in her book *We of the Never Never*). Although the term "Never Never" is sometimes used to describe any outback location, its narrower definition is the region around the town of Katherine. The Barkly Tableland is more strictly defined as the eastern centre of the Northern Territory, and is famed as the scene of Australia's last great gold rush. At present the main functions of the largest town, Tennant Creek, is to serve travellers on The Track, but recent gold discoveries may trigger another rush.

"Towards Statehood" is the motto of the Northern Territory Government, reflecting the growing self-confidence and desire for greater autonomy (although some Territorians do not have a high regard for their local politicians and are worried by the prospect of being governed by them). The Northern Territory fell under the jurisdiction of South Australia until 1911, when administration was taken over by the federal authorities; the Territory achieved a measure of self-government only on July 1, 1978. About one-third is Aboriginal land, and the vestiges of native Australian culture are better preserved in the Territory than elsewhere. This is partly because white settlers were markedly less successful in colonizing the Territory than other parts of Australia: only in the mid-19th century did the first Europeans travel across the continent from south to north.

The Northern Territory was eventually opened up because of the desire to establish a direct telegraph link between Australia and Europe, and indeed most of the names of towns and rivers in the Territory are those of the telegraph line's constructors and their friends. The region's great mineral wealth and agricultural potential were first identified around the turn of the century. Trade routes were initiated between central Australia and the south, with the help of camels and their drivers imported from Afghanistan. The discovery of gold in the Never Never added impetus to the development of the Territory, although the rush itself — like the later one in the Tablelands — was short-lived.

At the same time as the town now known as Alice Springs was in its pioneering days, fishermen and traders were becoming established at the coastal port of Darwin. Today these same towns have all the trappings of Australian urban life, but just beyond them much of the wilderness is untarnished. One practical aspect of the Territory's remoteness which is of direct concern to travellers is that prices for most things are noticeably higher. Because virtually everything has to be brought in from thousands of kilometres away, you will find that goods and services from accommodation in Alice to dinner in Darwin cost more. And the low density of population means that many settlements have only one combined hotel/petrol station/restaurant/general store/post office, which will usually take advantage of its local monopoly. When planning your spending, be on the safe side and assume that your cost of living will be at least 25% higher than in the southern states. If you want to save money, visit the Territory during the wet season between November and March/April when visitors are few and prices on many tourist-related services such as car hire and accommodation fall substantially.

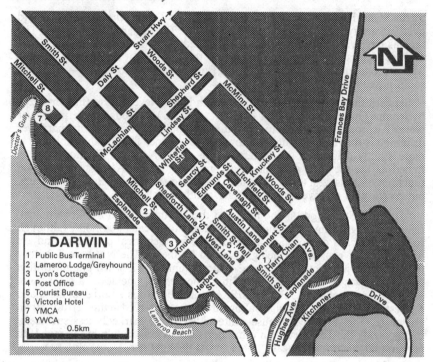

DARWIN
1 Public Bus Terminal
2 Lameroo Lodge/Greyhound
3 Lyon's Cottage
4 Post Office
5 Tourist Bureau
6 Victoria Hotel
7 YMCA
8 YWCA
0.5km

THE LOCALS

One in four Territorians is Aboriginal. Many of the native Australians living in the Northern Territory have successfully come to terms with the 20th century without compromising their cultural heritage, although the highly visible alcoholics on the streets of Darwin and Alice Springs show there are many victims of European settlement. Adding to the ethnic mix, there are strong Chinese and southeast Asian communities living in the Top End (the present mayor of Darwin is Chinese) and a number of Italians around Alice. The European inhabitants fall into two groups: confirmed Territorians who believe fiercely in their home territory, and a large transient population who come to work for a while in mining, industry or tourism before returning to the more comfortable life of the southern states.

It is said that you need to survive a few "Wets" before being accepted as a true Territorian. There is noticeable tension between these established residents and the hard-drinking and rootless bunch of (mainly) male Australians who come to the Territory to try to earn some quick cash.

Making Friends. Since visitors to the Northern Territory easily outnumber the locals, you will hardly be a novelty and should not anticipate receiving much more than basic courtesy from the locals. But conversely there are plenty of fellow travellers in the main centres and it takes little effort to make acquaintances.

GETTING AROUND

In winter, the Northern Territory is half an hour behind the eastern states and 90 minutes ahead of Western Australia. Like Queensland and Western Australia, the Territory does not implement daylight saving time in summer. Check your watch when you arrive in the Territory before catching an aircraft, bus or train.

Air. Three airports in the Territory can be reached from other states: Alice Springs, Darwin and Yulara (the airport serving Ayers Rock). Only Darwin has services from overseas. The local airline is Ansett NT, which links the three main airports with each other and with smaller settlements. Regular Ansett and Australian Airlines flights from Adelaide, Brisbane, Cairns, Perth and Sydney serve Alice Springs and Darwin; some flights also go direct to Yulara, including those on East-West from Perth and Sydney, and Air NSW from Broken Hill.

Bus. The major coach companies run regular services from the mainland states to Alice Springs and Darwin, although you should not expect the frequency of services found in southeastern Australia. Some services linking Darwin with north Queensland and Western Australia are interrupted during the wet season from November to May by flooding, sometimes for weeks at a time. Unless you can afford to fly across or are prepared to take the extremely long southerly route via South Australia, you will have to sit it out. Should the long bus journey to the coast of Queensland seem too daunting, you need only take the bus as far as Mount Isa to connect with the twice weekly *Inlander* rail service to Townsville. One service worthy of note links Perth with Yulara (for Ayers Rock) via the little-travelled Gunbarrel Highway. While this is an arduous journey over the rough tracks, it allows bus travellers to experience a real outback adventure and furthermore saves considerable time over the normal route. The service ran for most of 1987 but at the time of going to press it was unclear if it was continuing; call Shoreline Coach Tours on 095-27 9271 for confirmation.

Anyone coming into the Territory by bus (or indeed car) should consider bringing their own food for the trip. There are roadhouses every 200km or so, but they are notoriously overpriced: $6 for eggs on toast is typical.

Train. The idea of a railway line linking the south and north coasts from Adelaide to Darwin has been under discussion for over a century. The compilers of the Thomas Cook timetable have not yet despaired since they include an optimistic footnote on Darwin that "a line may be constructed at a future date". Unless and until it happens, the line north from Adelaide in South Australia terminates at Alice Springs: see page 312 for details. Connections to Melbourne can be made at Adelaide, to Brisbane at Sydney and to Perth at the small junction of Tarcoola where the line from Alice Springs meets the transcontinental railway.

Driving. There are three sealed roads leading to the Northern Territory. The busiest is the Stuart Highway ("The Track"), named after the early explorer John McDouall Stuart who successfully crossed from south to north in 1861/2. It runs 3000km up from Adelaide through Coober Pedy, entering the Territory 250km south of Alice Springs and continuing via the towns of Tennant Creek and Katherine to Darwin. A free strip map — *Drive The Stuart* — is available from Northern Territory Government Travel Centres. It covers the whole journey from Adelaide to Darwin, plus spurs to Ayers Rock and Kakadu National Park east of Darwin. If you plan to do much driving away from The

Track, invest $1 in the excellent *Touring Map* of the Territory.

The Stuart Highway is joined at Three Ways by the Barkly Highway from Mount Isa in north Queensland. The Victoria Highway (part of National Highway 1) crosses from northern Western Australia near Kununurra and joins the Stuart at Katherine.

In addition, the ironically named Plenty Highway is a shorter route from Queensland to Alice Springs, an unsealed route which is passable with care except during the "Wet". The shortest journey from Perth to Alice Springs is via the rough Gunbarrel Highway (mentioned above). Although specially built buses can cross it, it is hazardous for inexperienced drivers and most visitors take the long route via Port Augusta.

Before attempting any unsealed and lightly travelled route, you should follow the advice given in the introduction about driving in the Outback. In particular, your vehicle should be fit for the task ahead and in good working order; you should take copious supplies of fuel, food and water; and you should consult local people about your plans. At night, beware of the many animals from kangaroos to wild buffaloes which stray onto the roads.

The Automobile Association of the Northern Territory (AANT) is based in the MLC Building at 81 Smith St, Darwin (tel: 81 3838). You can obtain a free leaflet *Driving in the Territory* from them or Government Tourist Bureaux, providing a guide to the special requirements for driving in the Northern Territory. The more detailed *Traffic Code Book* is available free from Motor Vehicle Registries or police stations. One additional hazard is the massive articulated truck known as "road train". They haul up to three long trailers with a total length of 50 metres and a combined weight of 115 tonnes. On narrow stretches of road you should pull over to the shoulder to let them pass since their bulk is such that their drivers are unwilling to pull off the main strip. Before attempting to overtake one, make sure you can see clear road for at least one kilometre ahead, as it can take an interminable time to get past.

A more mundane warning concerns the local driving style. Territorian drivers do not rank among the world's best, and most are unused to traffic. Matters are made worse by the propensity of the locals to drink and drive. The local anti-drink/drive slogan is "It's too late when you're .08", and indeed if you are caught driving with a blood/alcohol level of 0.08 or over you face automatic disqualification. This is not yet enough to deter some. Speeding offenders are apprehended using mobile radar units.

In the wet season, news of road conditions can be obtained from the Northern Territory Emergency Service on 84 4455 in Darwin or 52 3833 in Alice Springs. During the rest of the year, dial 84 3585 (Darwin) or 52 7111 (Alice Springs).

Hitch-hiking. The need for careful preparation, and warnings about local drivers, are equally applicable to hitchers. You should take plenty of supplies (not least in case the vehicle breaks down, and the driver has not made provision for an extra passenger), and try to ensure always that you are dropped off near some form of civilization (usually a roadhouse) where if thumbing proves hopeless you can at least ask for lifts or jump on a bus. Don't expect to have the road to yourself: in high season almost every roadhouse has a hitcher or two, and the notorious settlement of Three Ways is often thick with rival hitch-hikers. One reason why they are such a common roadside sight is the long time it usually takes to get a lift. There is little vehicular traffic at the best of times, and much of what there is has no room for extra passengers. When you do get a lift, however, it should be going a fair way.

COMMUNICATIONS

Telephone. The Northern Territory has one single area code — 089 — but this does not mean that all calls are charged at local rates. For example, calls between Alice Springs and Darwin cost almost as much as those to other states.

Media. If you've enjoyed the variety of television, radio and press elsewhere in Australia, you should narrow your sights in the Northern Territory. Such newspapers and transmissions that exist are surprisingly good considering their limited market. Main stream television in Darwin is limited to ABC (channel 6) and the commercial channel 8 while Alice Springs has only ABC; however, a satellite system called *NT-Net* is likely to begin broadcasts to all parts of the Territory soon. The Aboriginal community operates a television station called Imparja, which broadcasts from a mission station in the MacDonnell Ranges west of Alice Springs. Unfortunately, it can't be picked up in Darwin. Darwin is best endowed with radio stations (it has four); in outlying areas you'll be lucky to pick up more than the ABC national programme.

The Territory's main newspapers are the *Northern Territory News* (published daily in Darwin), the four-times-weekly *Centralian Advocate* of Alice Springs and the *Sunday Territorian.*

CRIME AND SAFETY

Most people feel quite safe walking around the towns of the Northern Territory at night. If you are at all anxious you could hire a bike (a good way to get around Alice Springs and Darwin anyway), or take a taxi. You might prefer to avoid hanging around pubs at closing time when alone, as some of the worst-behaved hard-drinking Australian males seem to live in the Territory. You need have little fear, however, of the habitual drunks (both white and Aboriginal) so prevalent in Darwin, who are pathetic rather than malevolent. In an effort to reduce the level of drunkenness on the city streets, it is an offence to drink liquor out-of-doors within 2km of licensed premises.

Stories of people losing possessions from hostel or hotel rooms are rare, but with so many travellers passing through it is best to be cautious.

" *IT IS ILLEGAL TO DRINK WITHIN 2 KM OF LICENSED PREMISES* "

HELP AND INFORMATION

The Northern Territory is better at promoting itself than any other state with the possible exception of Queensland. It produces glossy, informative and up-to-date brochures on a wide range of subjects, from a directory of all accommodation in the Territory to an account of Aboriginal life entitled *People of Two Times*. These are available from the Government Tourist Bureaux in Alice Springs and Darwin, and from nine out-of-state offices:

Adelaide: 9 Hindley St (212 1133).
Brisbane: 48 Queen St (229 5799).
Canberra: 35 Ainslie Avenue (57 1177).
Hobart: 93 Liverpool St (34 4199).
Melbourne: 415 Bourke St (67 6948); plus a branch in the suburb of Dandenong.
Perth: 62 St George's Terrace (322 4255).
Sydney: 89 King St (235 2822); plus a branch in the suburb of Parramatta.

WORK

The good news is that rates of pay in the Northern Territory are higher even than in the big cities of Sydney and Melbourne, and that the federal government gives tax concessions to people prepared to work in the Territory. The bad news is that employers are few and far between, and when you eventually succeed in finding a job your living costs will be high. Don't place much hope in finding work through the Territory's newspapers, since there are few jobs in the "Positions Vacant" columns.

To minimize the time it takes to find work you should concentrate on the tourist trade. So long as you search in the winter high season (May to October), you should be able to find something. An advantage of the hospitality industry is that employees are often provided with food and accommodation, alleviating the high cost of living. The Yulara resort (which serves Ayers Rock) is reported to be a good place to look for a job. Although the resort has a long waiting list of job-seekers, many people who register move on before reaching the top of the list. The resort employs (and houses) about 500 people and the average turnover rate for catering and cleaning staff is about six weeks.

It used to be said that the labour shortage in Darwin was so acute that travellers were approached in the street and asked if they could work. This is no longer the case, but there is still a fair amount of casual employment available in the city during the dry season. The CES office in Darwin (at the corner of Woods and Knuckey Streets; tel: 81 4822) is a lively sort of place, catering for many transient jobseekers and especially busy at the beginning of the dry season. Some people sleep outside the building to be the first in the queue when it opens. Although you should get there early and be prepared to remain in the waiting area for hours, there seems to be plenty of temporary jobs around. Don't be deterred by the hordes of sunbeaten Australians; they may be after the same jobs as you, but you'll still stand a chance if you look "reliable". Much of the work revolves around the port (particularly unloading prawn trawlers), so you might decide to bypass the bureaucracy and look around at the quayside for employment. The *Northern Territory News* gives details of ships in port or expected, which could provide clues. You could always go one better and find work on a prawn trawler. Voyages usually last around three weeks and payment is made according to the size of the catch. Women are particularly sought after o act as cooks, although you should establish before leaving port the precise nature of your duties.

Women might find the more predictable setting of a shop or an office (if they can type) more relaxing. The current economic boom in Alice Springs means that shops and offices are quite often willing to employ transients, especially over the summer; for example the local K-Mart regularly hires travellers at casual rates (higher than normal wages) and you can easily find out when the weekly hiring takes place. The Alice Springs CES is at the corner of Bath and Gregory Streets (tel: 52 7122). Katherine, the largest town between Darwin and Alice Springs, is reputed to have good job prospects. The CES is in the Randazzo Building on Katherine Terrace; tel: 71 1655. And if the gold boom in Tennant Creek further south takes off, there will undoubtedly be work in the resulting side industries.

The Northern Territory is the place to experience real outback station life. The cattle farms of Central Australia are almost unimaginably large, and inexperienced jackaroos and jillaroos are occasionally needed. If you ensure the station is reasonably close at least to a roadhouse, you will at least be able to let off steam once in a while.

Extending visas is said to be easier in the Northern Territory than in some of the other states. Contact the Department of Immigration in Arkaba House on the Esplanade in Darwin (tel: 81 4566).

DARWIN

For some travellers driving north across the desert, Darwin assumes almost mystic proportions — the pot of gold at the end of The Track. The city certainly has more to offer than any of the other settlements north of Alice Springs. But due to the time and expense involved in getting to Darwin, it is hard to recommend a visit to the city for its own sake. If you decide to travel to the top of the Territory, do so for the experience of the journey and the natural wonders en route rather than simply to see Darwin; this will lessen the chance that you'll be thoroughly disappointed. As you approach Darwin and the end of the 2500km-long Stuart Highway, the road suddenly blossoms into an eight-lane racetrack. But then the Highway reaches an ignominious conclusion at a set of traffic lights just outside the city, and the last couple of kilometres into the centre can be deeply anticlimactic. The small downtown is a piece of typical urban Australia transplanted to the tropics. Darwin has something of the feel (yet little of the style) of Key West at the southern tip of Florida, a warm and relaxed but inescapably isolated city.

Darwin's natural harbour was first discovered by Europeans on a visit to the coast by *HMS Beagle* in 1839, and the port was named after Charles Darwin, the naturalist who had previously sailed on the ship. The Territory's capital was founded in 1869, after four unsuccessful attempts to build settlements at other sites in the area. The first settlements were a response to fears of other European powers creating a foothold in Australia, but after the Northern Territory was annexed to South Australia in 1863 a more serious attempt was made to colonize the area; the Surveyor-General of South Australia and a party of 135 arrived on February 5, 1869. Darwin has had a very rough-and-ready history since then, including one episode (in 1919) where the guns of the Australian Navy were turned on the town to restore order! During the Second World War Darwin was shaken out of its seclusion as it became Australia's frontline against the Japanese, who bombed the city on 59 occasions in the biggest air strike after Pearl Harbour. It is now a cosmopolitan and racially mixed city, with much evidence of new building as a result of Cyclone Tracy which devastated the area on Christmas Eve 1974, killing 66 people in Australia's worst recorded natural disaster.

Climate. Cyclone Tracy was particularly vicious and has been matched only a couple of times in Darwin's history (1897 and 1937), but less destructive cyclones are not uncommon. The threat of summer cyclones (known locally as "blows") is present from November to April, and you can call a special number (1 1542) for warnings about them. If you are unfortunate enough to get caught in one, head for the nearest new building; all those constructed since the 1974 cyclone are extremely tough and are required by law to have a cyclone shelter.

The months of November to April also constitute the wet season, known in tourist literature as the "green" season. Darwin is very much a tropical city and visitors should be aware of the debilitating effect the heat and humidity can have, especially when arriving from the drier central areas of Alice Springs and Ayers Rock. Darwin is closer — both geographically and climatically — to Southeast Asia than to other Australian cities; Melbourne is further away than Manila. The city reputedly suffers the highest suicide rate in the world in the month before the onset of the wet season, when humidity is typically 90-95%.

Getting Around

ARRIVAL AND DEPARTURE

Air. When the maximum range of aircraft was less than it is nowadays, Darwin was the first point of entry for most travellers to Australia. Now the only international flights are on Qantas to Singapore, Garuda to Bali, another Indonesian airline Merpati Nusantara to Kupang on the island of Timor, and Royal Brunei to Borneo. Domestic destinations include Adelaide, Brisbane, Canberra, Perth and Sydney, but most are served only once a day or less.

The airport (8km by road from the city centre) is shared with the Royal Australian Air Force, and has one passenger terminal for both international and domestic flights. You can take a shower in the washrooms upstairs, adjacent to what is rather optimistically described as a "cocktail lounge". There are several competing minibus services from the airport into the city, serving most lodgings. To save the several dollars demanded by the private operators, you can ignore them all and walk for five minutes to the Stuart Highway, cross the road and take a local bus (number 5 or 8) into the town for 60¢. The journey time is about 15 minutes, and the bus runs the length of Mitchell Street where most of the cheap hostels are located. A taxi to town costs about $7 on weekdays, $9 at night and weekends.

The market for onward international flights is quiet. There are plenty of regular travel agents but few discount specialists. Top Flight in Central Arcade (between Smith St and Shadforth Lane, behind the post office; tel: 81 5473) is probably the best bet.

Signs on the approach road to the airport urge "Don't Take Palm Leaf Beetle With You", but no checks are made upon departure to ensure you comply.

Coach. The Greyhound terminal is at Lameroo Lodge (69 Mitchell St; 81 8510). Almost opposite, at 50 Mitchell St, is the Deluxe terminal (81 8788). Bus Australia (81 1122) serves the Darwin Motor Lodge, also on Mitchell St but further from the city centre. Ansett Pioneer's local office is at 63 Smith St (81 6433). Fares are typically $100 to Alice Springs, $185 to Cairns, $200 to Brisbane and $210 to Adelaide or Perth; to reach other cities you must catch a connecting service at one of these destinations.

Train. With no rail services at all, Darwin is hardly a trainspotter's paradise (although there is an old locomotive on display in the city). The city's one railway line to Pine Creek no longer has passenger trains running on it.

Boat. Darwin is a major port of arrival and departure for yachtsmen sailing between Australia and Southeast Asia. Most of the hostels have notices advertising (working) passages to Bali or Singapore, or you can check the noticeboard behind Darwin Ship Stores at the harbourside. It is, however, a captain's market and you will have to pay dearly for the privilege. Prices quoted in 1987 included $250 to Bali and $750 to Singapore, both more expensive than flying. More locally, there are regular cross-harbour sailings between Darwin and Mandorah across on the Cox Peninsula. The MV *Darwin Duchess* makes three return journeys daily during the week, and one on Saturdays and Sundays; call 81 3894 for times. Ferries leave from the Stokes Hill Wharf at the foot of Kitchener Drive, and the return fare is $12.

Driving. Standards reach an all-time low in Darwin. In the suburbs, for example, drivers like to keep their options open about which side of the road to drive on, and the squeal of tyres is a familiar sound on the city streets.

It is often suggested that vehicles fetch a higher price on the secondhand market in Darwin than in other less remote cities. There is no solid evidence for this, and since the overall market is much smaller than elsewhere you could be forced to cut your asking price drastically if you need to sell quickly. If you're desperate, take the vehicle to Darwin Motor Auctions at the corner of Cavenagh and Daly Streets, near the beginning of the Stuart Highway.

Car hire is more expensive than elsewhere in Australia. Most rental companies impose a maximum distance from Darwin intended to prevent their cars being driven into Kakadu National Park; many hirers ignore this, but if you break down or have an accident in the Park it will cost you a great deal of money. For cheap car hire, try Marrara Motor Hire at 231 McMillans Road (beyond the airport in the northern suburb of Jingili; 85 2886), who advertise cars from $15 per day with no distance charge, or Rent-a-Dent who are centrally located at 90 Mitchell St (81 1411). Rent-a-Rocket are at 9 Daly St (between Smith and Mitchell Streets). Thrifty, at 131 Stuart Highway (north of the city centre), have a good range of vehicles from campervans to four-wheel drive Landcruisers. Cheapa Rent-a-Car (149 Stuart Highway; 81 8400) hires vehicles complete with a full camping kit, starting at $379 for three days for a four-wheel drive Holden Drover. They also have special weekend rates on ordinary cars.

Hitch-hiking. The only road out of Darwin is the Stuart Highway to Three Ways and Alice Springs. The first sensible place to start hitching is at the junction of Daly and Cavenagh Streets, beside Darwin Motor Auctions. For a 60¢ investment you can take bus 5 or 8 out to the major junction by the airport which will cut down the amount of local traffic.

CITY TRANSPORT

City Layout. The main city centre is on a small peninsula of land southwest of the rest of the city. The suburbs sprawl out to the north and east, bounded by the coast and the airport. Smith St and Mitchell St both run through the middle of downtown, with the Smith St Mall being the heart of the city centre. An excellent map of the city and surroundings is published by the Darwin Tourist Promotion Association and can be picked up free from many places. It can be confusing to realize that the Stuart Highway (the road to the south) is actually *north* of the city centre. The road curves around to go south a short way out of Darwin.

Bus. Public transport is run by Darwin Bus Services, and comprises about 20 routes. A complicated zone system is used to calculate fares, but the upshot is that most fares cost 60¢ for up to 8km, 90¢ thereafter. The main bus terminus for Darwin is on Harry Chan Avenue between Smith and Cavenagh Streets (tel: 89 7513). The other major interchange is at the Casuarina Shopping Centre (tel: 27 9446). A list of routes is published in the free magazine *Darwin — Top of Australia.* This publication suggests a cheap ($1.80) do-it-yourself sightseeing tour: take bus 4 from Darwin to Casuarina, and bus 10 back.

Taxis. Dial 81 7777 to summon a Darwin Radio Taxi. Like most things in the Northern Territory, taxis are expensive. On weekdays, rates are 57¢ per km on top of a $1.50 standing charge; at night (midnight-6am), weekends and for journeys outside the city limits the cost is 70¢ per km plus $2. This company also operates "multi-ride taxis" (12-seater minibuses) which operate as shared taxis, picking up additional passengers en route and charging less than the regular taxi fare.

Cycling. If you can dodge the dangerous drivers, cycling is a good way to get around Darwin. The best selection of bicycles for hire is at Darwin Bike Rentals, 57 Mitchell St (tel: 41 0070), but most hostels also rent them out and Pedlar's Pushbike Hire operates on Vesty's Beach at weekends. You can hire a tricycle from Tri-Hire (tel: 41 0257).

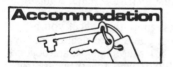

Darwin Youth Hostel is unfortunately a long way out of town, 12km from the city beyond the airport on Beaton Road, Berrimah (84 3107) and reached by hitch-hiking along the Stuart Highway or on bus number 8. It costs $6, and has a maximum stay of five days. There is talk of building a city-centre hostel; check with the Tourist Bureau or the Youth Hostel headquarters (84 3902). In the meantime, the hostel is highly recommended despite its distance from the city. It is smaller, friendlier and cheaper than places in the centre, and the staff sometimes organize informal excursions to nearby attractions for which you pay only for the petrol used.

The biggest and cheapest place to stay in the city is Lameroo Lodge (81 9733), a large ex-military camp at 69 Mitchell St; a bed in a dormitory costs $8, and a single room — fan-cooled but with no fridge — is $13. (Cooling devices become very important to the hotel-hunter in Darwin.) There are many permanent or long-stay residents and some find the atmosphere less pleasant than in most other hostels. The YMCA (81 8377) is 1km from the centre at the end of the Esplanade near Doctor's Gully. Beds in fan-cooled dormitories are

$11, single rooms $16 (plus $1 if you want a fridge). The standard is higher than the Lameroo, but could still be better. The YWCA is a similar distance out of town at 119 Mitchell St (81 8644). It offers dormitory accommodation at $15 (with a limit of three nights), single rooms at $19, twin rooms for $25 and bedsitters at $35 per couple. Weekly rates are five times the daily rate. The Larrakeyah Lodge, also on Mitchell St (at number 50; 81 7550), starts from $15 a night. Nick Pasterikos' Guest House at 33 Woods St (81 4842) is central and fairly cheap. The two nearest camp sites are a long way out of town: the Shady Glen and Overlanders are both on the Stuart Highway, 9km and 13km from the centre respectively.

There is a number you can call for emergency accommodation — 81 8874 — but this is intended for homeless Australian youths rather than travellers.

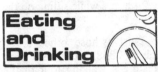

Eating and Drinking

Although food options are more limited, and prices generally higher, than in Australia's other capitals, you can still eat well and inexpensively in Darwin. Undoubtedly the best value for money is at the canteen of the Lameroo Lodge where $3.80 will get you a plate heaped with tasty Chinese or western food. Dinner is served *at* (not from) 5.30pm daily. Lunchtime snacks are available from numerous kiosks in the Smith St Mall: an excellent lunch can be had from the collection of Thai, Lebanese, vegetarian and Mexican counters in an arcade off the Knuckey St end of Smith St. The ritzy Diamond Beach casino on Gilruth Avenue should not be overlooked: from Tuesday to Friday you can have a three-course lunch in the Lorikeet Lounge for $9.75.

The Jade Garden in Smith St does a nine-course Chinese meal for $10. For a combination of Vietnamese and Chinese, try the Noodle House (BYO) at 33 Knuckey St (between Smith and Cavenagh Streets; tel: 41 1742). From Monday to Friday there's a hot buffet lunch from 11.30am to 2pm; dinner is served on weekdays from 6.30pm. For vegetarian food, try Simply Foods at the corner of West Lane and the Smith St Mall (tel: 81 9292). Late-night food is available to 2am at Gabby's bistro in the Hot Gossip Entertainment Centre at 21 Cavenagh St, and at Reflections (a café in Parap District Centre, between Darwin and Casuarina) where YHA members get a 10% discount on all food and drink.

Pizza addicts can satisfy their craving at Super Pizza (BYO) at the junction of Searcy and Cavenagh Streets in Darwin city centre, or Parap Pizza on Vickers St in the Parap District Centre (tel: 81 4580); if the heat has made you too exhausted to move, call Dial-a-Dino's Pizza on 85 6533 for free delivery within 4km of Darwin. You can sample local delicacies at the Victoria Hotel's Colonial Bar and Grill; prices for barramundi or buffalo steak start around $10, and are much higher for crocodile. "Buff and bar" is a Darwin speciality, rather like the American "surf 'n' turf".

Drinking. The bar upstairs at the Vic (as the Victoria Hotel is known) is a good place to go when the heat and humidity get too much; you can sit on a flower-lined balcony drinking beer and watching Darwin's uneventful world go by beneath you. Like most of the city's other pubs, it is not a good place to go if you just feel like a quiet drink: it caters for the people who have made Darwin reputedly the home of the most prolific beer-drinkers in the world (nearly 250 litres every year for each man, woman and child in the city). Darwin has its own version of a "stubby", containing a massive 2.25 litres. In a vain attempt by the authorities to diminish this thirst, it is illegal to buy alcohol before noon each day. When ordering, it is usual to specify the beer you want by the colour of its label; thus "Green" is Victoria Bitter, "White" is Carlton Draught and "Yellow" is Castlemaine XXXX. In addition, the local NT Draught is on tap at most hotels.

Other pubs in Darwin worth experiencing include the Top End (at the corner of Daly and Mitchell Streets) and Squires Tavern at 3 Edmunds St. If you prefer to drink *al fresco,* you might prefer to become a temporary member of the Rocksitters Club, which meets every Saturday to sit on a rock in the sea at Fannie Bay and drink beer. (By being offshore they appear to circumvent the law against outdoor drinking near licensed premises). Some members are in training for the annual competition in which male contestants are required to drink 18 cans and females nine cans of beer every 24 hours while sitting on the rock. The present endurance record is 12 days.

The National Trust (whose office is on Knuckey St; tel: 81 2848) produces a good brochure suggesting a walking tour of the few historical buildings which survived Cyclone Tracy. The Museum of Arts and Sciences has an interesting Aboriginal section as well as a fascinating exhibit of various Northern Territory nasties such as crocodiles, snakes and sea snakes. The museum is just out of town on Conacher St at Fannie Bay, reached by bus number 4, and entrance is free. Further north along Gilruth Avenue is the Fannie Bay Gaol with an exhibit on Cyclone Tracy. The Indo-Pacific Maritime Museum is nearer the centre (at the junction of Lambell Terrace and Kahlin Avenue) and claims to contain one of only four living reef ecologies on land. However, those travelling on to the Queensland coast or who have already seen the real thing there might be better off saving the stiff $5 entrance fee.

Darwin's past is reflected in Lyons Cottage, formerly the British Australian Telegraph Company residence and now a museum displaying the heroic feats of those responsible for the first telephone link between Europe and Australia. The museum is at the corner of Knuckey St and the Esplanade, and opens daily from 10am to noon and 12.30pm to 5pm.

Aquascene is a tourist attraction which sounds tacky but is in fact fascinating. Twenty years ago a resident started throwing scraps to the fishes in Doctor's Gully, down the hill behind the YMCA at the north end of the Esplanade. Now thousands of fish come in each day at high tide for a free meal. Some of the fish are over a metre long and many will take bread from your hand. Unlimited stale bread is included in the admission charge of $2. Feeding times are variable depending on the tide, and are shown in *This Week in Darwin and the Top End* or you can call 81 7837. There is $1,000 fine for fishing in the surrounding water, so don't get any ideas about catching an easy dinner.

The Bougainvillea Festival and the Beercan Regatta are both held in June. The Beercan Regatta is a natural consequence of the beerdrinking reputation which Darwin has; rafts made entirely of empty beercans race around the harbour. From the amount of beer-drinking which surrounds the Regatta, it appears that the participants are keen to obtain the raw materials for the following year's competition. Darwin Show is in July and the city's Rodeo in August.

Nightlife. "Unsophisticated" best describes Darwin after dark. It is tempting to suggest that the drinking habits of Darwinians are due to the fact that there's relatively little else to do. Cinema Darwin on Mitchell St (tel: 81 5999) is the city's only commercial cinema, although the Darwin Film Society screens predominantly arty films every fortnight on Tuesday evenings at the Museum Theatrette in Fannie Bay. There is a theatre in both Darwin and Casuarina, adjacent to the bus station in each case. Call 81 8424 for forthcoming shows at the small and charming Brown's Mart Theatre in Darwin, or 81 8211 for details of performances at the Casuarina Foundation Theatre. The Darwin Performing Arts Centre is at 93 Mitchell St (tel: 81 1222). It manages a respectable range of concerts (considering the size of Darwin audiences), mostly on Friday and Saturday evenings.

The Victoria Hotel in the Smith St Mall functions as the social centre of Darwin and has three distinctive features: it's the liveliest place in town, it has a motorized awning that swings to and fro over the upstairs bar to keep drinkers cool, and its juke box is so loud that you'll hear the pub several blocks before you see it. Every night except Sundays, the Vic offers live music and late opening (until 2am). A visit is worthwhile if only for the spectacle of Australian manhood drinking itself into a stupor.

The Hot Gossip Entertainment Complex at 21 Cavenagh St is the most notable of the city's clubs and discos, with regular live bands. From May to October there are regular Corroborees at the Darwin Travelodge (122 the Esplanade; tel: 81 5388) costing $5, or $20 including a barbecue.

Music. A problem afflicting live music in Darwin is the humidity. This is not so much because the audience and artists feel uncomfortably hot after a few numbers, but because it is difficult to keep instruments correctly tuned. Listening to a barely-competent band struggling vainly to stay in tune is not a pleasant aural experience. Nevertheless, some top-flight performers play at the outdoor Darwin Amphitheatre in the Botanic Gardens. Recent sell-outs include concerts by Dire Straits and Cliff Richard, and prices are around $25. A popular pastime at the end of these events is the esky-lid race; ice from the cold boxes is poured onto the slopes, and participants slide down while squatting on the lid of their esky. Alcohol is usually banned, so many of the locals buy a bottle of Coke, drain some off and top it up with rum.

Less well-known performers play at Hot Gossip and the Victoria Hotel, as mentioned above. Quieter entertainment can be heard at the Top End Folk Club on Sunday evenings at the East Point Gun Turret.

Casino. Many Darwinians strongly recommend a visit to the Diamond Beach Hotel Casino on Gilruth Avenue, overlooking Mindil Beach (on bus routes 4 and 6 from the city); indeed its cool, glamorous interior is a welcome contrast to some of the city's other nightspots. The casino recently changed hands, and the new owners plan to make it the gambling capital of Australia, attracting high-rollers from Southeast Asia. Make sure you are reasonably dressed (no shorts, denims or flip-flops and, to clinch admittance for men, a tie).

Sport. Horseracing takes place during the dry season at Fannie Bay Racecourse on Playford St (tel: 81 2328); there is little other organized sport in Darwin. Parap Pool on Ross Smith Avenue (near the Stuart Highway) has a waterslide; call 81 4842 or 81 1762 for opening times. There are other pools including one in the city (tel: 81 2662) and two others at Casuarina and Nightcliff.

Darwin has beaches (at times little more than mud-flats) running from

Lameroo Beach (along the Esplanade) to the "free" (i.e. nudist) beach at Casuarina. Only Nightcliff Beach (on bus route 4) is safe during the wet season since it has a net to keep out marine stingers. There are notices posted in Darwin city centre with pictures of scarred victims of attacks by marine stingers to emphasize the dangers. Even outside the wet season, be on your guard for the occasional crocodile; a couple of swimmers reported recently that they were chased by one while bathing off Casuarina beach.

Shopping. Darwin City Centre Traders proudly call their patch "your room-to-move shopping city", as indeed it is. What distinguishes the Smith St Mall from hundreds of similar malls elsewhere in Australia is the lack of crowds. Shopping hours in Darwin city centre are standard: stores open at 9am and close at 5.30pm except on Fridays (9pm) and Saturdays (1pm). There is free musical entertainment for shoppers in the Smith St Mall on most Friday evenings. The Shopping Centre in the suburb of Casuarina, has more liberal hours: 9am to 5.30pm daily (including Sundays) with late opening on Thursdays and Fridays.

Darwin has three weekend markets. The Smith St Mall has a flea market every Sunday from 9am to 3pm. Parap, 3km north of the city, has an open air market at Parap Place from 8am to 1pm on Saturdays. At the northern suburb of Rapid Creek there is a Sunday market from 8am to 3pm with a good selection of tropical fruit and vegetables.

Many souvenir shops will try to sell you Aboriginal crafts, but the Crafts Council of the Northern Territory Gallery (adjacent to the Darwin Museum and Gallery on Conacher St in Fannie Bay) is best for authentic, high-quality artefacts.

Bookworld is at 30 Smith St Mall, with a branch on the Darwin Institute of Technology campus at Casuarina. The District Centre in Parap is not the sort of place you might expect to find an enlightened bookshop, but Educational and Technical Books (7 Parap Place; tel: 81 3922) is — despite its name — a wide-ranging and well-stocked shop. The Jingili Book Exchange in Central Arcade (behind the post office and between Smith St and Shadforth Lane) deals in secondhand books and "nearly new" clothes.

Help and Information

The Northern Territory Government Tourist Bureau is halfway along Smith St Mall (tel: 81 6611). The "Tourist Information Centre" at 109 Smith St West is mainly an agency for the tours of certain operators. As mentioned earlier, there are two monthly giveaway magazines: the inaccurately titled *This Week in Darwin and the Top End* and the glossier *Darwin — Top of Australia*. You can pick up copies from the Tourist Bureau and most hotel receptions.

American Express: c/o Travellers World, 18 Knuckey St (81 4699).
Thomas Cook: Shop 1a, Star Village, Smith St Mall (81 4088).
Medical Treatment: Royal Darwin Hospital, Rocklands Drive, Tiwi, 12km north of the city (20 8410).
Dental Emergencies: Department of Health Dental Clinic — (81 9688).
Disabled Persons Bureau: Shop 8, Ground Floor, Casuarina Plaza (20 3213).
Helplines: Alcoholics Anonymous — (85 4479); Crisis Line (7pm to 7am daily) — (81 2040; Poison Information — (27 4777).
Women's Information Centre: Casuarina Plaza (27 7166).

Further Afield

You could easily blow a thousand dollars doing all the tours and places of interest around Darwin, and indeed you should try to set aside some money for this purpose since there is so much that is worthwhile. Virtually every operator has brochures at the Northern Territory Government Tourist Bureau in the Smith St Mall. There are tours to Wangi (the Litchfield Wilderness Park), to the Aboriginal land of Arnhem Land, crocodile-spotting tours, flights out to Kakadu National Park, day trips to swimming holes at Berry Springs and Howard Springs; the list is endless. The trouble is that they are quite expensive, understandably since many of them involve flying or four-wheel drive travel. One particularly interesting trip is the Mystery Tour run by Terra Safari Tours (1585 Strath Road, near the Youth Hostel in Berrimah; tel: 84 3470); they take you out to Wangi and the Tabletop Range, but on a route guaranteed to provide as much adventure as possible, e.g. crossing creeks, winching yourself out of mudholes, etc.

Dangerous Creatures. The local wildlife is worthy of respect, especially crocodiles. Signs in Kakadu National Park warn that "swimming is for sharks, barramundi, crocodiles and idiots". You should *never* swim in an area that you're not sure about. Even if there are no notices warning against bathing, check with locals; a lot of the signs are vandalized or taken home as souvenirs. In an attempt to reduce the frequency of thefts, the authorities have taken to erecting signs measuring 20 metres square. Never camp next to an outback river bank, and don't leave remains around from your fishing expedition. Freshwater crocodiles are smaller and, as one Darwin brochure puts it "in general terms they are not known to attack man". Even so, nesting females are definitely a menace. The Conservation Commission of the Northern Territory, PO Box 1460, Alice Springs, NT 5750 (tel: 50 8211) has produced a free pamphlet called *Crocodiles — A Few Simple Facts.*

To learn a number of more obscure facts, visit the Crocodile Farm 40km south from Darwin on the Stuart Highway; it is Australia's oldest, and opens daily from 9am to 5pm. Its inhabitants include Bert, the largest crocodile in captivity, and a recently acquired 40-year-old albino. The most interesting times to visit are at public feeding times: call 88 1450 for details.

Among the other local species, you should be warned that 14 varieties of Northern Territory snake are regarded as "dangerous", i.e. potentially lethal. Even so, Graeme Gow, the owner of Reptile World at Humpty Doo (50km southwest of Darwin) has survived being bitten 84 times in the last 35 years; his charges include 52 different kinds of snake and a score of species of lizard. In outback areas, water buffaloes should not be approached too closely, nor should wild pigs or dingoes. And the wetlands in the Top End attract hordes of mosquitoes, so take plenty of insect repellant.

BATHURST AND MELVILLE ISLANDS

Melville Island is about 80km due north of Darwin, and is the second largest Australian island after Tasmania. Bathurst is immediately to its west and almost touches it at several places. The islands are home to the Tiwi people, an Aboriginal race who have been able to preserve their homeland more successfully than other native Australians. Judging by the cultural dissimilarities between the islanders and mainland Aboriginals, there appears to have been little contact between the two groups. A Catholic Mission was established on Bathurst Island in 1911, and many Aboriginals have been converted to the religion. The islands, though fascinating from an anthropological point of view, are not exceptionally beautiful, and inland the terrain of forest and waterfalls is very similar to that around Darwin.

The most common way to reach the islands is by organized tour, normally by air from Darwin to the airport at Pularumpi, the main town on Melville Island. Contact Tiwi Tours at 27 Temira Crescent, Larrakeyah, Darwin (tel: 81 5115) or Australian Kakadu Tours, PO Box 1397, Darwin for details of their trips. Although the Tiwi people are not keen for their tranquility to be disturbed they allow paying tourists to accompany them tracking. For permission to visit independently, you should apply four weeks in advance to the Permits Office, Tiwi Land Council, PO Box 340, Darwin 5794 (tel: 81 4111).

ARNHEM LAND

In contrast to the well-travelled wilderness south of Darwin, the land to the east (named after the Dutch town of Arnhem) is mostly still in its virgin state. The Aboriginals who have exclusive rights to much of the area are expert in moving around these apparently impenetrable rain forests, which are mostly out-of-bounds to outsiders. Most visitors to the Gove Peninsula, at the northeastern tip of Arnhem Land, fly into the airport at Nhulunbuy. The town is an important centre for bauxite mining and a favourite holiday territory for the rich, perhaps because of its exclusivity: there is just one hotel, and a single room there costs $90. There are good sporting facilities, particularly for golf and fishing, but not a great deal else.

KAKADU NATIONAL PARK

Kakadu National Park lies about 200km east of Darwin on the Arnhem Highway, bordering Arnhem Land. The Park hosts three different habitats: the wetlands and estuaries, home to an astonishing variety of birdlife and wildlife; the ridgetop area, forested hills rising from the swamps; and the escarpments where much Aboriginal art can be found. Kakadu has several notable features, primarily Obiri Rock and Nourlangie Rock, which have fine examples of Aboriginal rock art; Yellow Waters and the South Alligator River, where cruises depart for crocodile and birdspotting; and Jim Jim Falls and Twin Falls, spectacular waterfalls reached by four-wheel drive vehicles. There are other attractive creeks, billabongs and camping areas all over the Park. Note that Jim Jim and Twin Falls are often inaccessible in the Wet, and that in the midst of the Dry, there is no water.

The first part of the Park to be opened is on the World Heritage List. A second part has recently been nominated for the List despite the lobbying of mining companies attracted by the uranium deposits. Uranium mining in Kakadu is a matter of much controversy in Australia at the moment; some of the mineral leases in the Northern Territory are only a couple of kilometres from outstanding examples of Aboriginal art. Australian conservationists argue the folly of allowing mining companies to despoil a beautiful area and export the uranium to France, only to see it come back to the South Pacific in the form of nuclear testing. There is only one operational mine in the park at present, near the town of Jabiru which is suitably distant from the more attractive areas.

Kakudu is a place you have to have time for, and indeed it's the kind of place you should make time for on a trip round Australia. Unfortunately it's also a place which takes money to see properly. A little time and effort spent investigating the various possibilities is worthwhile. The main topic of conversation among travellers in Darwin seems to be the best way to visit Kakadu.

Hitch-hiking is possible as far as Cooinda, an excellent hotel/bar/campsite on the edge of the Park. Once inside, hitching is difficult at times: there is little traffic and many of the cars passing through are full. To get a lift at all you may well have to ask drivers and be prepared to pay something for the journey. A tent is a must, although it is illegal and impractical (because of the thick vegetation and difficult terrain) to camp outside designated areas without a permit. Food and water also have to be carried. Another disadvantage is the unlikelihood of getting a ride to some of the most interesting spots: the chances of hitching down the 63 km dirt road to Jim Jim Falls are poor. You could instead try to fix up a ride before leaving Darwin. Putting a notice up on a hostel board and offering to share expenses can work, although demand is much greater than supply; it helps if you're young, blonde, Swedish and female.

Apart from hitch-hiking, the cheapest way to do it is to use a Greyhound bus pass which is valid for their scheduled services to Kakadu. A tour of Nourlangie Rock is included in the journey and the only additional cost is $15 for the cruise at Yellow Waters. Even for those without a bus pass the trip costs only $60 return from Darwin. You can also camp overnight at one of the areas in the park and pick up the next bus. Greyhound has a twice-weekly round trip from Darwin to Yellow Waters and on two other days runs Darwin-Yellow Waters-Katherine. Note that this is a regular bus service — not a tour — although the driver does give you a rundown on Kakadu and the sights. The disadvantage of doing it this way is the short time allowed for looking around e.g. only 30 minutes at Nourlangie Rock. An overnight stay is preferable.

Some reasonable car-hire deals aimed specifically at visitors to Kakadu are available. Rent-a-Dent in Darwin charge $190 for two days' hire of a car with 700 free kilometres. Four-wheel drive vehicles are considerably more expensive.

Most people settle for the easy but expensive option of taking a tour. A two-day tour with Terra Safari booked through the Darwin Youth Hostel costs $115, although you have to be staying there to qualify for this lower rate. One-day tours start from around $90 with the major tour companies, and longer ones are also available. All the companies have brochures at the Tourist Office in Darwin. Mostly these will take you to one of the rock art sites and on one cruise. Two-day tours, despite the extra cost, are worthwhile since you get substantially more time to relax and enjoy what you're seeing.

THE NEVER NEVER

The town of Katherine is the main settlement between Alice Springs and Darwin, and is the gateway to the Never Never, an area made doubly famous by Crocodile Dundee's ficticious company "Never Never Tours" (motto: you'll never survive, and if you do you'll never come back). The town is situated on the Katherine River, the first permanent river you encounter on the journey north from Alice Springs, and is where the Victoria Highway from Western Australia meets the Stuart Highway. The river and town are named after one of the daughters of a sponsor of explorer John McDouall Stuart (he of the Stuart Highway). Katherine is growing fast as a result of the tourist sights in the area and a number of industrial projects nearby.

The main attraction is the Gorge, 32km from town. The Katherine Gorge National Park contains a magnificent series of steep-sided gorges separated by rapids, many kilometres of walking trails and a number of examples of Aboriginal rock painting. The Cutta Cutta Caves are also close to town.

The Youth Hostel (72 2942) is about 2km out of town on the Victoria Highway. The nightly rate is $5, and there are thermal springs 100 metres from the hostel. The Riverview Motel and Caravan Park (72 1011) is a bit further on, and 8km down the road on the banks of the Katherine River is the Springvale Homestead (72 1159), with campsites for $3.75 and bunkhouse accommodation for $18. There is an Aboriginal corroboree held here three nights a week, but the ill-effects of packaged tourism is at times glaringly obvious. Despite its distance from Katherine, the Springvale Homestead may be the most convenient place to stay. The reason is that it is run by the Travel North/Katherine Gorge Tourist Agency (based at the BP Roadhouse at 6 Katherine Terrace in Katherine; tel: 72 1044), which seems to have a near-monopoly of tourism in the area. The same company runs the campground at the Gorge ($3.75 a night), the local tourist office and the tour buses, which theoretically stop only at Travel North-operated places.

The tours include trips up the Gorge by boat (ranging from $10 to $55), tours of the Cutta Cutta Caves ($20), tours to Edith Falls ($30) and a night-time crocodile-spotting tour from the Springvale Homestead ($23). The highlights of the Gorge, however, can be enjoyed without help from Travel North. There are ten walks in the park, taking you through various kinds of habitat from swamp and rainforest to plateau, and last from two hours to five days. But the best way to appreciate the Gorge is to hire a canoe and take off yourself. Canoes can be hired in town (you must provide your own transport) but are also available at the Gorge from Greg and Sandra Woods of Kookaburra Canoe Hire. They charge $5 an hour, or $20 a day for one-man kayaks and $25 per day for two- or three-man canoes. Renting a canoe for a full day will enable you to see much more of the Gorge than the boat tours, and you are provided with all the information that the boat trippers get. Kookaburra began operations only in 1987, yet already their "Survivors Book" is filled with raves. They operate all year except at the height of the wet season.

The Barunga Sports and Cultural Festival is a big event at Easter on Aboriginal land 80km southeast of Katherine. Music, art and workshops of Aboriginal culture are on display. Entry permits are not required during the Festival, but are necessary during the rest of the year. See *Great Outdoors: Restricted Areas* for details of how to apply.

A little further southeast (100km from Katherine) is Mataranka, with a pleasant campsite ($3.75 a night) and a Youth Hostel ($8). Just north of the settlement are thermal springs, with a pool so clear that at night you can lie on its bottom two metres underwater, look up and see the stars shining above the palms that surround the pool. During the day you can hike alongside the Waterhouse River or canoe down to the Roper River. The film version of the novel *We of the Never Never* was made around Mataranka, and an exact replica of the Homestead at Elsey Station (where the story is set) has been built at Mataranka as a tourist attraction/museum. Tours go from Mataranka out to Elsey Station itself, visiting places mentioned in the book such as "Red Lily Lagoon", "Elsey Falls" and "Flying Fox Creek", and some include a boat trip along the Roper River fishing for barramundi. Another tour is the Evening Safari, comprising a shortish walk and a camp fire in the bush with "billy tea" and damper (bush bread) for sustenance.

The Roper Highway east from Mataranka is surprisingly well-surfaced considering it is a road to almost nowhere, eventually petering out into a track to the Collera Mountains. There is hardly ever any traffic on it, and so it is ideal to travel along just to experience the seemingly endless space and understand the isolation of the tiny missions and stations which you pass.

TENNANT CREEK

Until gold was discovered in the 1930s, the Barkly Tablelands were less populated even than other areas of the Northern Territory. But in the few years of Australia's last gold rush the town of Tennant Creek was created almost literally overnight. The stories of the town's origins are confused, but one version has it that a wagon loaded with building materials and beer for a new hotel broke down miles short of its intended destination, and that rather than transport the contents a hotel was created on the spot. The old mines — with colourful names such as Eldorado and Noble's Nob — are now almost all exhausted, but a new gold rush may be on the cards since a retired meat worker living south of Tennant Creek struck gold a metre underground at the back of his shed. First reports in November 1987 suggested the rich vein may be worth up to a billion dollars, which will doubtless change the town's fortunes. At present, Tennant Creek functions largely to service travellers in the Track. It is halfway between Katherine and Alice Springs, and close to the important road junction at Three Ways (where the Barkly Highway from Queensland joins the Stuart Highway). The prospect of tourism has not been overlooked, and you can fossick for gold or watch demonstrations of gold refining at the Government Battery on Peko Road. The Tourist Information Centre on Patterson St (tel: 62 2401) can provide full details.

The best known geographic feature of the region is the Devil's Marbles, a series of granite outcrops on the Stuart Highway 114km south of Tennant Creek. Strangely, the smaller weathered outcrops known as the Devil's Pebbles (20km northwest) look much more like marbles than do the rocks to the south.

ALICE SPRINGS

The town now called Alice was founded in 1888 as a station on the route of a proposed railway through the centre of Australia. There was already a telegraph station there, built in 1871 as part of the trans-continental line to Darwin that put Australia in direct contact with Europe for the first time. But four years after the railway finally arrived in 1929, the name changed to that of a nearby natural spring; this had earlier been named in honour of Lady Alice Todd, wife of Charles Todd (Postmaster-General of Adelaide at the time), whose name was given to the town's river.

Alice has experienced a boom in the 80s fuelled by its role as a tourist centre for Ayers Rock and the MacDonnell Ranges, and also as a support centre for the controversial US intelligence facility at nearby Pine Gap (the biggest American military installation outside the USA). In October 1987 the Pine Gap agreement came up for renewal and Alice was the centre for rallies and protests by groups from all over the world, trying to close the base temporarily. Another technological intrusion is the planned dump for nuclear waste near the town, which is being strongly opposed by the locals.

Those who have read Nevil Shute's book *A Town Like Alice* might expect a rough-and-ready frontier town atmosphere. In fact it is a prosperous town of 25,000, until recently resembling a suburban building site much more than a pioneering place. Hence "the Alice" is a disappointment to many travellers, perhaps because many of them arrive from the spectacle of Ayers Rock, the cultural delights of Adelaide, or the beaches and islands of northern Queensland. But Alice is certainly a good place to meet fellow travellers as it is a jumping off point for travel to most other parts of Australia.

Climate. Over a year, Alice averages $9\frac{1}{2}$ hours of sunshine daily. Summer is hot and dusty — temperatures in the 40s are quite typical for February — but the dryness of the air makes it bearable. A real problem is the contrast between outside and air-conditioned buildings. Take a sweater if you intend to spend much time indoors. Winter days are warm, but cool off rapidly towards nightfall. The July average minimum is only a few degrees above zero and temperatures often fall below freezing. If you've spent the rest of your stay in the tropics or by the coast, you may be unprepared for the cold.

ARRIVAL AND DEPARTURE

Air. Alice Springs' airport is 7km south of the town, off the Stuart Highway. The main connections are with Adelaide and Darwin, as well as several daily flights to Yulara (for Ayers Rock) taking only 45 minutes. The Alice Springs Airport Shuttle Service minibus connects with arriving and departing flights and serves all city centres hotels, motels and hostels; fares are $3.50 one-way, $5 return. To arrange a pick-up, dial 52 7867.

Bus. The Greyhound (52 7888) and Ansett (52 2422) bus terminals are in the same building (and room) on Todd St just down from Parsons St junction; Ansett are shortly to move to a new terminal in Ford Plaza on Hartley St, already occupied by Deluxe (52 4444). The Bus Australia terminal is at Melanka Lodge on Todd St. There are four services each day to and from Ayers Rock, and the standard one-way fare is $54. Prices to Adelaide and Darwin are around $100, to Melbourne $140, Sydney $175, Brisbane $160 and Perth $200. If your destination is Western Australia, ask about the possibility of transferring at Ayers Rock to the Shoreline Coach Tour bus for the short-cut through the desert to Perth; this takes 36 hours from Yulara to Perth, about 14 hours less than the conventional route via Port Augusta and costs $160.

Train. The *Ghan* departs from Adelaide at 11am on Thursday and arrives nearly 23 hours later (9.50am on Friday) in Alice. After a short rest, the return journey leaves Alice at 5.10pm on Friday and takes a speedier $21\frac{1}{2}$ hours, getting in at 1.40pm on Saturday. You may sometimes hear it described as the *New Ghan*, since the route was changed several years ago. Previously it ran along the route taken by the Afghan camel drivers who opened up central Australia, and the train was named after the Australian abbreviation for "Afghan". The one-way fare is $141. The *Alice* links the town with Sydney, but carries only first class passengers between Port Pirie and Alice Springs. It leaves Sydney at 1.40pm on Monday, arriving at 12.30pm on Wednesday; the return journey leaves Alice

prings at 6pm on Wednesday, reaching Sydney at 3.25pm on Saturday.
ravelling first class all the way would cost you $295. All these are winter times;
heck locally for the effect of daylight saving time on schedules, and to find out
f extra trains are being operated to keep up with demand.

The railway station is a 15-minute walk from the western edge of the city.
f your luggage is heavy you may prefer to take one of the cabs which meet
rriving trains, or take the Alice Springs Railway Shuttle Service (tel: 52 7867)
o your lodgings for $2 one-way or $3 return.

Driving. Members of Australian or foreign motoring organizations can get
oadside assistance from the AANT's local contractor, Russ Driver & Co at
8 Sargent St (tel: 52 1087). The Shell service station at the northern end of
odd St is open 24 hours for petrol. The cheapest car hire firms are Centre Car
Rentals (specializing in Mokes) in the Ford Plaza on Todd St (52 1405), Cheapa
Rent-a-Car (52 9999) and E-cono Rent (52 3798).

Hitch-hiking. The first possible spot hitching north along the Stuart Highway
s at the junction with Wills Terrace. If you're heading south, go to the junction
with Stuart Terrace at the foot of Billygoat Hill. If you can get further south
o the junction with Ross Highway by Blatherskite Park, your chances are
etter.

Town Layout. The town centre is in the shape of a rectangle, bounded to the
west by the Stuart Highway and to the east by the Todd River. Don't expect
oo much from the designation "river"; it fills with water only once every few
ears, and a favourite saying is "you have to see the Todd flow three times before
you're a local". A good free map of the town (published by the Regional Tourist
Association) is widely available. The new Todd St Mall project is almost
complete, and so the town centre is beginning to look a little less like a building
ite. With Stuart Terrace, Stott Terrace and Sturt Terrace all in the centre of
own, it is easy to get confused when asking directions.

There are no local bus services. Many travellers hire bicycles, or even a
ricycle (tel: 52 9644) complete with sunshade. For a taxi, call Alice Radio Cabs
on 52 3700 or Alice Springs Taxis on 52 1877. There is a taxi rank on Gregory
Terrace opposite the Council Lawns.

At first glance Alice Springs seems to be well
served with cheap places to stay. But
although the average stay is only a night or
two, such is the number of backpackers
travelling through that many of the best
places are often full. You should have few problems finding a room from
November to April, and may well get a discount on the prices mentioned below.

The Youth Hostel, crowded and overstretched, is at the corner of Todd St
nd Stott Terrace and should certainly be booked in advance (52 5016). The
ightly rate is $5, with a maximum stay of five days. When the Youth Hostel
s full, travellers are often referred to the Melanka Lodge at 94 Todd St (52 2233)
which has a variety of rooms, with dormitory beds at $6 or doubles from $35.
This is centrally situated, and is particularly convenient for the Bus Australia
nd Deluxe bus terminals. It has good facilities including a fridge in every room,
ar and restaurant and a small swimming pool. However, the atmosphere is quite

impersonal, the room partitions are thin, and the dormitories can be crowded The place has been summed up as "scruffy and noisy".

The Sandrifter Safari Lodge (52 8686) across the river at 6 Khalick St, i popular. It has twin-share rooms for $7 per person. The Lodge is a bit of a hik from the centre, but nevertheless recommended. To get there, you should cros the Todd River in Stott Terrace and turn left at the Ford Resort Caravan Park The accommodation is simple: prefabricated cabins, each with two beds (whicl could benefit from a little cleaning). There are laundry facilities, a small kitche and a garden ideal for an evening drink. The warden, Gerry Gerrard, is friendl and helpful and owns a cheeky parrot. You can book a good variety of trip (including to Ayers Rock) with him since he also runs the Sandrifter Safari tou company. There are bikes for hire.

The Arura Safari Lodge is further out of town, also on the far side of the rive from the centre, at 18 Warburton St (on the corner of Lindsay Avenue; 52 3843) Winter rates are $5 for a dormitory bed ($2.50 extra if you need linen), $15 eacl in a twin and $20 for a single. These are reduced by 20% from November to March, giving a bargain $4 per night in dormitories. There is a swimming pool and bicycle for hire. The Stuart Lodge, run by the YWCA but open to both sexes is on Stuart Terrace (52 1894), and runs from $16.50 upwards.

If all the less expensive lodgings are full then there are more upmarket place: which have cheaper sections for backpackers. Since these don't cater specifically for budget travellers, conditions can leave a little bit to be desired. Toddy's (41 Gap Road; 52 1322) has dormitory beds for $8. Larapinta Lodge (3 Larapinta Drive; 52 7255) with singles at $35 and doubles for $45 is much more expensive but has the advantage of a toll-free number — 008 89 6118 — which enable: you to book ahead easily from out-of-town.

The long-distance buses coming into town will often drop people off at their accommodation.

Camping. The only site in the city centre is the Ford Resort (a combined motel/ camp site; 52 6699), on Stott Terrace across the river. Prices are high: $8 per person per night. The Wintersun Caravan Park (52 4080), 2km north on the Stuart Highway, is cheaper and more popular.

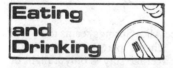

The Eranova Caffetteria (*sic*) at 72 Todd St (tel: 52 6094) has fairly expensive breakfasts, excellent coffee and good sandwiches and lunches. It closes, however, at 4pm (2pm on Saturdays). Grandads is on an arcade off Todd St Mall and does a variety of cheap hot sandwiches, special fried rice for $2.40 and a daily lunch special. It also specializes in ice-cream and milkshakes. Wild Waters Café is at the corner of Parsons St and Leichhardt Terrace, near Pioneer Market Place. Delicious vegetarian dishes such as quiche, salads and special dishes of the day are served in a relaxed atmosphere. There are numerous hanging plants and "alternative" magazines to read while waiting for your meal, which has probably been cooked by the two women who run the place. Julie's Coffee Pot (on Todd Plaza opposite the John Flynn Church) claims to be the only non-smoking establishment in Alice Springs. It opens for coffee, cakes and ice cream during normal shopping hours.

Ready Pizza is a BYO place in Hartley St which serves good-sized, tasty pizzas which are cooked while you wait. It is a popular, quite lively restaurant.

ou can eat in (and watch *EastEnders* on the television set) or take the food
way. La Casalinga, at 105 Gregory Terrace (tel: 52 4508), has unexceptional
ut inexpensive pizzas starting at around $6, is licenced and opens from 5pm
 1am every night. A less appealing late-night venue is Kentucky Fried Chicken
t the junction of Todd St and Stott Terrace (across from the Youth Hostel).
here are a number of excellent ice-cream parlours in Alice, a welcome relief
n long, hot summers' days.

Drinking. The landlords of Alice Springs seem to revel in running outback-style
ubs for hard drinkers, and most are rather noisy and rough with linoleum floor
nd plastic chairs. You can guarantee that you will sample a taste of lowlife by
pending a few evenings in pubs and bars in Alice. Some of the pubs — such
s the Old Riverside Hotel — have a bouncer on the door to turn away
nsuitably dressed (or looking) men, but plenty of other pubs don't.

Anzac Hill, above Wills Terrace at the north
end of the town centre, provides a good view
of the town and the MacDonnell Ranges. In
town, there are several interesting places to
visit in between the piles of brick, rubble
nd cement. One of the best is the old Telegraph Station, incorporating a small
nuseum, restored by the Conservation Commission. It is 2km north of the town
nd can be reached by walking north for about 30 minutes beside (or along the
ry bed of) the Todd River. The trail almost immediately takes you out of the
oise and bustle of the centre and winds past hills until you reach the station
nd the springs which give the town its name. The Conservation Commission
as produced an excellent guide to the buildings and there are Rangers on hand
o answer your questions. Admission is free.

Another interesting glimpse into outback life can be had at the Royal Flying
Doctor Service base near the Stuart Memorial on Stuart Terrace. The $1.50
ntrance fee gets you a short film on the activities of the service, a quick tour
around the radio room and a visit to the museum next to the souvenir shop. Alice
Springs also has an Aviation Museum (in the Connelan Hangar of the former
airport on Memorial Drive), with the stories of a couple of outback tragedies,
and an Oldtimers' Museum. The School of the Air (in the broadcasting rather
han aeronautical sense) is also worth visiting, since the teaching of children in
far-flung settlements by radio is a classic Australian institution. In the same vein,
the Magic Spark Radio Museum on Emily Gap Road has a good collection of
early wireless equipment. A walking tour booklet on the town issued by the
National Trust (available from the Tourist Office) will take you around most
of the remaining old buildings such as the Residency and the Town Gaol.

For a town in the middle of the bedrock conservatism of the outback Northern
Territory, Alice Springs has a surprising number of "alternative" events and
venues. Reading the posters in shops will tell you what is on, whether a radical
folk band, a yoga course, or a political demonstration. For anyone interested
in alternative culture, Australian group Redgum's song "The Last Frontier" is
a different view of the Adelaide-Alice Springs trip from that put out by the glossy
tourist brochures.

The Alice Springs Regional Tourist Association publishes the booklet *This
Month in Alice* which gives a good rundown on coming events. On the first
Monday in May there is a cattle-branding competition followed by the Bangtail
Muster, celebrating the traditional end of the cattle-mustering season. There is

a collection of satirical floats and a parade, and men on horseback rid
symbolically off into the sunset. In late May the annual Camel Cup races take
place on the track in Blatherskite Park, commemorating the races held by the
Afghan drivers who led the original camel trains in the late 19th century. Many
people dress in Arab clothing for the occasion. The event is followed by a big
folk concert and campfire in the evening, and a Beerfest starts the next morning.

Early October is the time to experience Northern Territory foolishness at its
best. As mentioned, the Todd River through the centre of town very rarely has
any water in it. That hasn't stopped local residents from having a regatta for
all classes of boat, just like England's Henley-on-Thames event. The Henley-
on-Todd version, which began in 1961 and is held each October, differs only
in that the boats have no bottoms and so contestant run down the course holding
the sides of the boat. A spotter aircraft patrols the racecourse searching for
sharks, and notices are posted which prohibit swimming and diving. There is
a surf rescue display and a sea battle in which two warships fight using flour
bombs and water cannon. Although the event is becoming increasingly
commercialized (most of the "boats" seem to be sponsored by banks), it is still
great fun, and needless to say a huge amount of beer gets drunk.

As an antidote to such zany antics, you can catch a highbrow concert, film
or play at the Araluen Arts Centre (tel: 52 5022). Arty films are also shown
at the Totem Theatre.

Nightlife. Despite recently expressed fears that Alice Springs is becoming the
King's Cross of central Australia, there is little outrageous nightlife. Lasseters
Casino on Barrett Drive (tel: 52 5066) has cocktail bars and a disco in addition
to the gambling facilities which are available from 1pm to 3 or 4am daily. Only
respectably dressed people are admitted, with particular attention paid after
7pm. The Todd Tavern (a large red-roofed building at the top of Todd Mall;
tel: 52 1255) is a little less fussy about its dress rules. There is live entertainment
in the piano bar from 8pm, Thursday-Saturday, Bobby McGee's folk club on
Sundays at 8pm, and Alice's Disco open every night (sometimes with live bands).
The folk music scene is highly developed, and the town hosted the Australian
National Folk Club at various hotels. The best known local band is Bloodwood,
who play electric outback folk music and are well worth catching on their home
territory. Try also to hear some traditional "gumleaf" music.

Bojangles Bar & Grill at 80 Todd St (tel: 52 2873) is a restaurant by day
(opening at 11am except Sundays) and a nightclub later on, with live
entertainment and dancing until 2am (Monday-Wednesday) and 6am
(Thursday-Saturday nights).

Sport. Horseracing takes place every Saturday at the Central Australia Racing
Club course on South Stuart Highway. In winter there are picnic race meetings
in the surrounding townships, culminating in the Alice Springs August races,
an event which lasts a week. Australian Rules football is played on winter
weekends in Traeger Park, and Rugby League each winter Sunday afternoon
at the Anzac Oval. Tennis can be played in Traeger Park; you should book a
court in advance at the Council Offices in Todd St. There are organized fun-
runs each Monday at 6pm; call 52 6967 for the current location. The large public
open-air swimming pool on Speed St (tel: 52 3757) is a pleasant place to relax
in the heat of the day, but the pool opens only from September to April.

Shopping. Most shops open 9am-5.30pm on weekdays with late opening to 9pm
on Fridays, and 8.30am-noon on Saturdays; many also open on Sundays.

Besides the endless souvenirs (such as T-shirts bearing the name "Alice Springs" pelt out in flies), there is a good centre for Aboriginal Artists and Craftsmen at 86-88 Todd St where you can see bark paintings, carvings and musical instruments. Prices are quite high, but you are welcome to browse. The Alice Springs Peace Group has a shop in Colocag Plaza off Todd St. Bookworm, a buy-sell-or-swap bookshop is also in the Plaza.

Help and Information

The Northern Territory Government Tourist Bureau is on Ford Plaza in Todd Mall (52 1299). The Alice Springs Regional Tourist Association in the old Hartley St School (52 5199) is more of a trade association, but produces some useful literature (most of which is available from the Tourist Bureau anyway).

Post Office: Hartley St (52 1020); opening hours are 9am-5pm, Monday to Friday.
American Express and *Thomas Cook:* The nearest offices are at Adelaide and Darwin.
Medical Treatment: Alice Springs Hospital, corner of Stuart Terrace and Gap Road (50 2211).
Dental Emergencies: Department of Health Dental Clinic (52 4766).
Disabled Persons' Bureau: (52 6499).
Helpline: Crisis Line (7pm to 7am, Thursday-Sunday) (50 2266).

Further Afield

Many people come to Alice Springs to visit attractions out-of-town, and the Tourist Bureau has plenty of information on tours. Chateau Hornsby, central Australia's only winery, is 12km from the town. Since it welcomes visitors, cycling out to the chateau is a most enjoyable day trip. You can also take a camel ride out there at sundown on Thursdays, Fridays and Sundays, which costs about $50 including a large meal. Either way, you should sample the various wines which are remarkably good considering the climate in which they are grown.

The main physical attractions are either east or west of the town and consist of gorges or "gaps" in the MacDonnell Ranges, Standlay Chasm being perhaps the most impressive. It is also possible to take (expensive) tours out to homesteads to "experience" outback life for a night. The Henbury Meteorite Craters — for those interested in holes in the ground — are just off the Stuart Highway south of town. Just south of the Larapinta Drive, 100km west from Alice Springs, is the Finke Gorge National Park and Palm Valley. While there are bus tours here, some allow you barely an hour to spend in the Valley. You need much longer to appreciate fully the natural delights of the area, so instead try to get together with two or three others to hire a four-wheel drive vehicle. Kings Canyon, Australia's modest version of the Grand Canyon 323km southwest of Alice, can be visited on its own or in combination with a trip to Ayers Rock. A new luxury lodge at the Canyon has increased visitor numbers, and it seems only a matter of time before a Yulara-style resort is built there.

AYERS ROCK AND THE OLGAS

The world's greatest monolith is almost in the centre of Australia, about 500km southwest of Alice Springs. Ayers Rock is a place of pilgrimage to the 200,000 visitors each year, most of whom travel vast distances to see one of the world's natural wonders. A few are disappointed and conclude that the pressures to which they succumbed are an elaborate con trick on the part of the tourist authorities. But the majority decide otherwise after coming upon the stunning sight of the Rock rising proud from the empty desert. And if this isn't enough on its own, just 25km to the west are the equally impressive Olgas.

Both fall within the Uluru National Park, to which the entrance fee is $1.50. Despite strenuous objections from the Northern Territory government, the federal government insisted that the freehold of the Park was transferred to the traditional Aboriginal owners in 1985. Since then it has been leased back to the National Parks and Wildlife Service. Most of the surrounding land is Aboriginal and a permit is required to enter it. In addition there are four sacred sites within the Park which are clearly marked and which you should not attempt to enter. Throughout the Park there is a policy of no photography of Aboriginals.

Don't imagine that a bus or aircraft scheduled to go to Ayers Rock will drop you at the foot of the Rock. Previously there were tourist facilities around the Rock itself; these were removed when the lodgings and shops were judged to be causing too much ecological and visual damage, which showed remarkable long-sightedness by the authorities. The nearest facilities are now in the resort village of Yulara, just north of the Park and 20km by road from the Rock. The area is so popular that Yulara is now the Territory's fourth-largest settlement after Alice Springs, Darwin and Katherine. However much you regret the despoiling of the area by any form of construction, you will be impressed by the amount of thought which has gone into the new resort. The colours blend in with the landscape as effectively as any hotel/campsite/entertainment complex placed in the middle of a desert could hope to, and there are some interesting technological innovations: solar sails which deflect the intense sun and create an artificial breeze around the buildings, and solar panels which heat most of Yulara's water.

Arrival and Departure. Yulara is most easily accessible from Alice Springs, with at least three flights daily (costing around $100) and three or four scheduled bus services costing $54 and taking about six hours. Connelan airport is just north of Yulara, with connecting bus services into "town". The Lasseter Highway, the road in from the Stuart Highway at Erldunda, is a fairly easy drive, but you should take care not to be mesmerized by the long stretches of unchanging desert. Beyond Ayers Rock the road to the Olgas is unsealed and, as it was built on shifting sand, is sometimes closed for repair. Although the Australian Tourism Minister proposed in 1987 that a monorail link should be constructed between Ayers Rock and the Olgas, it seems highly unlikely that it will every be built.

Hitching is difficult on the Stuart Highway north from Adelaide or south from Alice Springs, although possible with persistence. Once on the Erldunda-Yulara road it becomes easier since nearly everybody is going to Yulara. Hitching is feasible from Yulara to the Rock but trickier from Yulara to the Olgas. Commonsense is needed on the trip to the Olgas: despite the relatively short distance, people have been known to die of heat exhaustion and dehydration. If you haven't got a ride by the end of the day, be sure to catch the last bus which leaves about 30 minutes before sunset.

Accommodation. The options for budget travellers in Yulara are the Ayers Rock Lodge (tel: 56 2170), with dormitory-style accommodation for $12 a night, or the campground (tel: 56 2055) at $6 per person per night; there are also on-site caravans for hire. The Lodge is often full with people coming on the tours from Alice Springs and independent travellers should book ahead (which you can do through any Northern Territory Government Tourist Bureau at no extra cost) or come prepared with a tent. Although Yulara is easily small enough to walk around, a free shuttle bus runs around the complex every hour until midnight, and there is a free bus from the Tavern in the shopping centre to the Ayers Rock Lodge and campground late at night (for which passengers are requested to make a "silver coin donation" to the Royal Flying Doctor Service).

Eating and Drinking. Considering the potential for exploitation of hungry and thirsty travellers, food and drink are not as expensive as they might be. Breakfasts and dinners are served at the Lodge: the dinners are around $7. There is a fast-food shop at the shopping centre with burgers for $4 and small pizzas for $7. The Ernest Giles Tavern (named after the first European to see the Rock, in 1872) offers good-sized meals at around $10. Don't give a thought to the restaurant at the Sheraton or Four Seasons Hotels if you're on a tight budget. The best bet is to buy food from the supermarket (more expensive than normal) and cook it on the coin-operated electric barbecues at the Lodge and campground.

The Ernest Giles Tavern is a lively pub, and opens daily at 10.30am. It closes at 12.30am except on Mondays and Thursdays when it stays open until 2am. The bottle shop is open daily until 10pm. There is a disco in the Tavern (starting at 10.30pm on Saturday, Monday and Thursday) which is popular with off-duty staff. If you're blasé about the sunsets at the Rock, spend the time at the Mulgara bar at the Yulara Sheraton which has a happy hour every evening when most visitors are watching the Rock; you can still see the sun setting over the Rock in the distance.

Ayers Rock. The raw statistics of this lump of rock are that it is 340m high with a circumference of 9km. It is not the world's largest monolith (the title is held by Mount Augustus, 1,500km due west in Western Australia, whose visible mass is double that of Ayers Rock), but its appearance rising suddenly from the stark desert is magical. The Rock is also of great interest to geologists: whereas most "Bornhardts" (isolated, exposed rock features in otherwise flat plains) are composed of granite, Ayers Rock is composed of an ancient sedimentary mixture of sand and gravel. Experts believe that only a small proportion of the rock is actually above ground.

It is difficult to get a true picture of the scale of the Rock from a distance as there is nothing to compare it with. Only when you get close to it does the massive size become overwhelming. The most spectacular aspect is the change of colour which sometimes takes place at sunset and sunrise. When this happens, it last for only a few minutes but is captured by a thousand cameras. The scenes on the "sunset strip" west of the rock can be almost comical, with visitors clamouring for the best photographic vantage point, as if waiting for the arrival of an extra-terrestrial being. The colour changes are at their most spectacular after the rare summer thunderstorms; in winter you are most unlikely to see an amazing sunset as the skies are almost always clear.

Most people who go to Ayers Rock feel obliged to climb it, though the views of the surrounding desert from the Rock are considerably less rewarding than the views of the Rock from the desert. The prescribed route for the climb to the top is 1.6km long and takes about two hours return. It is steep and strenuous for those unused to climbing, and not recommended if you suffer from vertigo. Drivers of the tour buses claim that 33 people have died on the climb, two-thirds of them people under 42 who had heart attacks, so it's best not to rush. Be sure to wear a hat to keep the sun off, preferably one which you can attach firmly to your head since it can also become windy as you approach the top. Wear sturdy shoes and carry plenty of water. There is a rope most of the way up, which has a gap of about six metres on the lower part, left there deliberately by the Rangers on the principle that anyone who can't climb without the rope for this short distance has no business going up the whole way. If and when you reach the top, you can sign the inevitable visitors' book.

In some ways the walk around the Rock is more interesting. There are Aboriginal cave paintings (not as spectacular as the ones further north in the Territory) and waterholes. Some areas at the base of the Rock are restricted areas reserved for the Aboriginal community and warning signs should always be respected.

The Olgas. This is a series of dome-shaped sedimentary rocks 20km to the west of Ayers Rock. The Aboriginal name — Katatjuta — means "many heads". Mount Olga (named by Ernest Giles in honour of the Grand Duchess of Russia) towers above them at a height of 547m, and is considerably taller than the Rock. It is easy to spend a whole day here walking among the domes and through the gorges and many people consider the Olgas a more spectacular experience than Ayers Rock. The tour offered takes you around the outside and then up into Mount Olga Gorge. Alternatively, you can take a shuttle bus there early in the morning and return on it about 30 minutes before sunset.

There is an unmarked route which can be covered by foot in a full day between the car park on the southeastern side through the central Valley of the Winds and Mount Olga Gorge to the car park on the western side. Before you attempt to walk through, ask Rangers or other people who have done it for advice and route information. Sufficient food and water should be carried in this area, as it is inhospitable country and there are no facilities. Extreme care should be taken if attempting to climb any of the smaller domes as there is much loose rock; even experienced rockclimbers have scared themselves badly.

Tours. Those arriving on one of the many tours from Alice Springs will have no problem since everything is taken care of. Those arriving on scheduled buses have a couple of options. On Greyhound, for example, it is possible to buy tour tickets ($29) at the last stop before Yulara. Once in Yulara, Greyhound are not allowed to sell tickets as they are not a licensed tour operator there. These tickets include a tour of the Olgas the afternoon you arrive, a trip to the sunset strip, and a visit to the Rock in the morning for a tour and the climb. For anyone planning to spend just one night there these are good value.

The other option is to leave everything until you get to Yulara. The monopoly on tours there is held by the Ayers Rock Touring Company, which runs both tours and shuttle buses to the Rock. There are advantages and disadvantages to each, so you will have to decide which is best for you. On the tours, for example, you get information about the area you are visiting, explanations of Aboriginal legends and paintings, etc. But they last only about two hours, so some people find them too rushed. On the shuttle buses you just get dropped off and are left to find your own way around. Prices for tours and shuttles are quite similar; $18 for the tour to the Olgas and $15 for the shuttle; and $8 for the trip out and back to the sunset strip. Note the afternoon tours and the last shuttles to the Olgas and Ayers Rock both include a visit to sunset strip. There is a three day *Rockpass* available for $39 which gives unlimited use of the bus service. The Ayers Rock Touring Company also operates a trip called Evening in the Outback, which is the only opportunity to see sunset on the Olgas close up. It is followed by a campfire dinner, and a lecture on the stars of the southern hemisphere and the folklore and habits of nocturnal animals. This costs $39 and is not included in the Rockpass. Light aircraft flights lasting half an hour over the Rock and the Olgas are available for $35 from Ayers Rock Air Services, who sometimes allow their clients to steer the plane in flight.

Rangers. The Yulara Centre run by the Park Rangers is a very helpful and informative start to a visit to the Uluru National Park. There is a slide show about the Park daily at 2pm, and each evening there is another show about the Northern Territory's other attractions. Two tours are offered on alternate mornings, each lasting about two hours and highly recommended. One is on desert ecology and the other on "bush tucker" i.e. what Aboriginals use as food, how they find it, etc. Both cost $5. The Rangers also run a free stargazing tour every night; book for all three tours at the Ranger Station (tel: 56 2988).

Wildlife. There is much wildlife in the Park and around Yulara; plenty of lizards, the infamous baby-snatching dingoes, emus and euros (a kind of small kangaroo); there is said to be a pack of euros which actually live on top of the Rock. The Uluru area has many scorpions and snakes. Of the 27 varieties of snake around Ayers Rock, all but four are poisonous.

An excellent leaflet called *National Parks and Reserves — a Guide for Visitors* is available free from Northern Territory Government Tourist Bureaux. It gives a good summary of the many National and Nature Parks, and Conservation and Historical Reserves, with information on access and facilities. Free campsites are provided in many parks, although the facilities are primitive or non-existent; water may be provided, but it won't necessarily be wholesome. It is illegal to camp outside designated areas in the National Parks; in other areas, take care not to camp in a dry river bed (because of the danger from flash floods) or on the bank of a running river (because of the possibility of crocodiles). Before embarking on any adventurous activities, you should consult the Australian National Park and Wildlife Service whose headquarters in the Territory are at PO Box 1260, Darwin (tel: 81 5299).

If you prefer to join a tour, get hold of the free annual *Tours and Services Guide* from a Tourist Bureau. It lists nearly 100 operators and details the durations and prices of the many tours, from the brief scenic helicopter flight around Ayers Rock to a 25-day bushwalk using camels as pack animals and which costs $1,000. Such is the number of competing companies that prices for popular tours are low, some with discounts for students, and others with standby prices (where you can save 20% if you sign up on the morning of departure). YHA members can get a discount of 10% on tours operated by Breakwater Canoe Tours (PO Box 641, Darwin; tel: 27 2532), Mulga Track Tours of Tennant Creek and the Mataranka Homestead Resort, among others.

One of the more unusual options is to join the "Outback Mailman" for a day, flying to a succession of remote cattle stations and Aboriginal communities, delivering mail and freight. Chartair, the airline which runs the service, takes passengers on one of three mail runs which last up to seven hours and cost $145; dial 52 6666 for further details.

Camels. Central Australia is as much camel country as Egypt or Arabia, and indeed Australia claims to have the only wild camels in the world. The beasts were brought in from west Asia in the 19th century to assist in the development of the inhospitable Centre. While that role has been superseded by motor transport, many camels remain and some are used for treks into the wilderness. Call Central Australian Camel Treks (at Ross River Homestead near Alice Springs) on 52 7611. Be warned that while no great skill is called for in riding a camel, it can be most uncomfortable until you get used to it; before committing yourself to a potentially painful week on the back of one, you might wish to sample a one-hour camel ride along the Todd River in Alice, run by Frontier Tours (52 3448).

Restricted Areas. One-third of the Territory is Aboriginal land, and only a few areas (such as around Yulara) may be entered without prior permission. For entrance to other areas you should apply for a permit (which is normally granted if you apply at least a month in advance) to the Permits Officer at the appropriate address: Top End and Barkly Tablelands, Northern Land Council, PO Box 3046, Darwin 5794 (tel: 81 9744); and Central Australia, Central Land Council, PO Box 332, Alice Springs 5750 (tel: 52 3800).

Calendar of Events

March/April	Barunga Sport and Cultural Festival, near Katherine
May (first Monday)	**Labour Day**
May	Cattle-branding competition and Bangtail Muster, Alice Springs
May	Camel Cup races and Beerfest, Alice Springs
May	Gold Rush Festival, Tennant Creek
May	On the Beach Carnival, Darwin
June	Bougainvillea Festival, Darwin
June	Beercan Regatta, Darwin
June	Taps, Tubs and Tiles Desert Race from Alice Springs to Finke and back
July (first Friday)	**Alice Springs Show Day**
July (second Friday)	**Tennant Creek Show Day**
July (third Friday)	**Katherine Show Day**
late July	Darwin Show
July/August	Barefoot Mud Crab Tying Championships, Darwin
August (first Monday)	**Picnic Day**
August	Darwin Rodeo
October	Henley-on-Todd Regatta, Alice Springs
October	Food and Wine Festival, Alice Springs
December 29	**Public Holiday**

Public Holidays are shown in **bold**.

Brisbane and Queensland

Population of Brisbane: 1,160,000   **Population of Queensland: 2,550,000**

Queensland's coast fulfils most people's notion of paradise. Variations on the theme include the many offshore islands turned holiday playgrounds, the sleepy sugar plantation towns, the travellers' haven of Cairns and the wilderness beyond. What makes the coastline exceptional is the immense and fascinating Great Barrier Reef lying off most of the eastern shoreline. Perhaps less paradisical — except in name — but still extremely popular, are the unabashedly commercialized resorts around Surfers Paradise on the Gold Coast.

There is much more to Queensland than the coast and its reef: its area of 1,725,000 km² is thirteen times larger than England. Much of the state is uninhabited desert, but there are also excellent farming plains and mountain ranges rich in minerals. Unlike the other states which tend to be dominated by their capitals, Queensland has a number of important cities in addition to Brisbane. But it is the charms of the coast which attract most visitors, and tourism continues to be the boom industry of Queensland. The state has particular appeal to visitors from the crowded islands of Japan, and indeed many parts of the coastal area have been bought up by investors from Tokyo and Osaka.

The capital is anchored firmly near the foot of the state. The first attempt at colonization began in 1824 when a convict settlement was established near the mouth of the river, for the "worst class of offenders". Its swampy, humid location made it ideal for sheer punishment but untenable for any civilized existence. So a year after the first convicts arrived, the site was shifted upstream to the city's present site; it was named after Sir Thomas Brisbane, Governor of New South Wales which at that time included what is now Queensland. The penal settlement closed in 1839 and the area was thrown open to "free settlers" three years later. In 1859, the colony of Queensland was separated from New South Wales, and Brisbane established as its capital.

For the next century, the state was regarded by the British and most other Australians as an irrelevant backwater. Although Queenslanders were never ones to apologize for themselves or their state, it took some time for their self-esteem and indeed chauvinism to gather momentum, until today when some would say that pride in the state has got out of hand. As visitors from the southern states began to discover the hedonistic delights of the Gold Coast and the Sunshine State, Brisbane — the sleepy state capital which lies between these two touristic gems — began to take itself seriously. Like other Australian cities, it has made a determined effort to project a go-ahead image, hosting the Commonwealth Games in 1984 and the World Expo in 1988. Brisbane is now a curious mix of the crumblingly tropical, the handsomely colonial and the gleamingly modern, embroidered by pleasant parks and the slow, murky Brisbane River. But the condition of the capital is of little concern to the wide spectrum of visitors to Queensland who, for a variety of reasons, regard the state as a good approximation to a utopia.

CLIMATE

One essential reason for the popularity of Queensland is the relative benevolence of the climate. Queensland's weather is sub-tropical in the south of the state and becomes more tropical the further north you go. As with all tropical climates, there is a wet season in summer (October or November to March), much more pronounced in the north than the south. In the north the onset of the wet season is marked by violent thunderstorms, while around Brisbane January is the wettest month and also the cyclone season. In recent years the climatic cycle has been somewhat disrupted (attributed by some to *El Niño,* a warm air current from South America), and parts of the coast such as Bowen have suffered droughts.

Although Darwin is much nearer to the equator, Brisbane is the sunniest capital in Australia: it has an average of over seven and a half hours of sunshine a day. The coastal climate is on the pleasant side of hot for most of the year, except during the summer when the high humidity can be uncomfortable. The closeness is assuaged by sea-breezes, including the "Barcoo buster" (a westerly wind which cools the southern half of the state). While you're packing the T-shirts and shorts, don't omit to include waterproofs. Tully, halfway up the coast, is the wettest town in Australia with over four metres of rain each year (four times as much as Brisbane and eight times more than London).

For weather forecasts in Brisbane dial 1196; for marine conditions, 1182; and for cyclone warnings 1190.

THE LOCALS

It has long been fashionable for sophisticates elsewhere in Australia to ridicule the natives of Queensland, describing them as "banana benders". They are derided as uncivilized and aggressive "Ockers", with regressive politics to match.

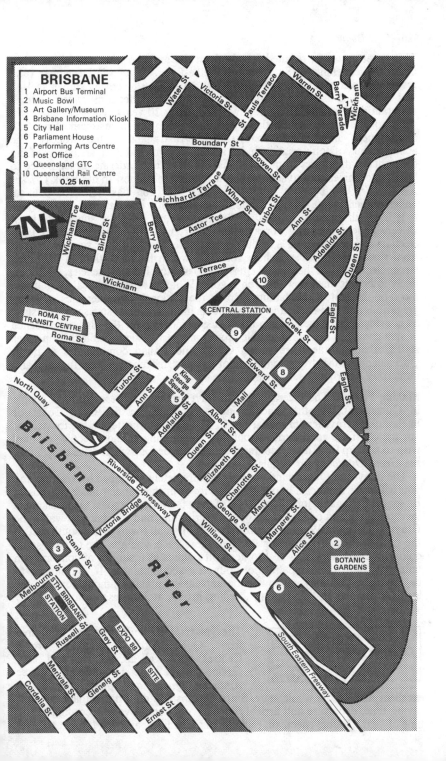

BRISBANE
1 Airport Bus Terminal
2 Music Bowl
3 Art Gallery/Museum
4 Brisbane Information Kiosk
5 City Hall
6 Parliament House
7 Performing Arts Centre
8 Post Office
9 Queensland GTC
10 Queensland Rail Centre
0.25 km

This latter assertion resulted largely from the antics of the state government under the leadership of Sir Johannes Bjelke-Peterson, who in December 1987 resigned to a collective sigh of relief. He and his wife (universally known as "Joh and Flo") had used the considerable electoral imperfections of the state to maintain the National Party in power for nearly 20 years. Their extreme right wing policies steered Queensland well away from the mainstream of political development and enraged many liberal Australians in the process. The achievements of Joh's reign included selling off National Park areas, repressing the rights of minorities from Aboriginals to gays, and ordering armed police to break into universities to seize condom vending machines. In her book *Cricket XXXX Cricket,* Frances Edmonds writes "Sir Joh has done for political enlightenment what Colonel Gaddafi has done for international air safety".

It is worth emphasizing that their party did not have the support of most Queenslanders; the party won a parliamentary majority in the November 1986 election with less than 40% of the popular vote. Much of their support derived from rural constituencies, where votes are worth far more than in the much larger electorates of the coastal cities due to electoral inconsistencies, which are likely to be reformed now that Joh is gone. Whatever their political allegiances, most of the state's inhabitants display the national characteristics of being gregarious and laid-back; and many lead an indulgent life of sun, sea and leisure, as is evident from the statistic that Queenslanders have the highest incidence of skin cancer in the world. Ethnic groups are perhaps less visible than in other states, although there are strong Greek and Italian communities in north Queensland, a 300-strong contingent of Basques in Trebonne (near Ingham) and numerous Aboriginal settlements.

Making Friends. The sheer number of travellers makes it easy to meet people in Queensland, whether vacationing Australians on the Gold Coast or backpacking travellers in the far north. The bars and hostels in the towns that line the coast are good territory, but for really getting to know people you may wish to sign up for a diving course, yacht cruise or four-wheel drive expedition; see *Great Outdoors* for details.

The natives of Queensland are not yet completely swamped by visitors, and you will meet the locals in one-hotel towns or in the trendier inner suburbs of Brisbane. Better still, join them in one of their favourite pursuits: Queenslanders love gambling and oddball races of all descriptions, and whether you watch the Crayfish Derby in Winton, the lizard races in small towns in the southwest of the state or the heavy-drinking Birdsville horserace, you are sure to meet some colourful characters. It is best to keep off politics as a subject of conversation until you know the sympathies of your new acquaintants. If you happen to be Japanese, you may encounter the unpleasant practice among some of the locals to indulge in "nip-baiting", yelling insults at Japanese visitors.

Getting Around

The *Queensland Public Transport Map* (free from Queensland Government Travel Centres) shows all air, rail, bus and ferry services in the state. In addition, the free *Amazing Queensland* publication is an excellent map of the whole state. Since Queensland does not employ daylight saving time, departure and arrival times to other states vary according to the time of year. Double-check air, rail and bus schedules, and don't forget to reset your watch (some unkind Australians from other states would suggest "back by twenty years") when you arrive in Queensland.

ARRIVAL AND DEPARTURE

Air. Brisbane airport has the most modern facilities in Australia, but both international and domestic terminals are inconveniently situated in relation to the city and to each other and even to the runway (some international flights must taxi for nearly 7km before being able to take off).

The new terminals are beyond reach of the city bus and rail services, so the only regular link is provided by Skennar's *Airporter* coaches (tel: 838 1148) from their depot on Wickham St, northeast of the city centre, and the Roma Street Transit Centre. Services run approximately half-hourly from 7am to 8pm. Skennar's also has direct buses between Brisbane airport and the Gold Coast; there are four services daily, except Sunday when only one operates in each direction.

Brisbane is well-connected by international flights: you can travel direct to New Zealand, Europe, North America, Japan, Singapore and Papua New Guinea. Queensland has two other international airports, Cairns and Townsville, but the best bargains in foreign air travel originate in the state capital. The local branch of STA is at Shop 2, Societe Generale House, 40 Creek St (tel: 870 8056).

A busy network of internal flights connect Brisbane, Townsville and Cairns with many other settlements in the state, although the independent airline Air Queensland has now ceased operation, after having been taken over by Australian Airlines.

Coach. Most long-distance coach companies operate from the Roma St Transit Centre, a combined bus/rail terminal on the northwestern edge of the city centre. Telephone numbers for information and reservations are as follows:

Ansett Pioneer — 846 3633	McCafferty's — 846 3263
Deluxe — 844 2466	Skennar's — 832 1148
Greyhound — 240 9300	Sunliner — 229 6155

Competition is fierce to most destinations from Brisbane, so it is well worth shopping around. There are numerous daily departures north and south, with fares to Cairns and Sydney typically $75 and $40 respectively. Deluxe has an interesting deal known as the *Reef Pass,* which for $109 permits travel from Brisbane to Cairns or vice-versa with unlimited stopovers within 30 days. On the long route up the coast to Cairns, bear in mind that arrival and departure times at intermediate points can be at unsocial hours in the early mornings. If you plan to stop off en route, check the schedules before you book.

Brisbane is linked by bus with all the other mainland capitals. Sample prices are Melbourne – $80; Adelaide – $110; Darwin – $185; and Perth – $187. Travellers with bus passes may find that the passes are not valid on some local services, and that a surcharge is payable on routes in remote areas (e.g. Cairns to Cooktown).

Smoking is banned on all buses in Queensland, a policy which seems at odds with the right-wing libertarian stance of the state government, but nonetheless one which is strictly enforced.

Train. Services are operated by Queensland Railways, whose central booking office is at 208 Adelaide St, Brisbane (tel: 225 0211). Queensland has a more extensive rail network than any other state. Over 10,000km of lines run along the coast and inland, all on narrow-gauge tracks (just over one metre wide) which were laid to cut costs; nowadays the effect is to keep trains' speeds down. There is a network of electric suburban trains around Brisbane, and electrification of long-distance routes is beginning which should speed up services.

Seat or sleeper reservations are compulsory on all long-distance trains; it is much easier to book at the hi-tech booking office in Ann St than at any of Brisbane's stations. It is worth noting that a second-class berth costs only $15 per night in Queensland, considerably less than in other states. This may be partly explained by the fact that no bed linen is provided in second class. Compartments can get chilly between May and October, so it's wise to bring extra clothes or a sleeping bag.

The only link from outside the state is the line from New South Wales. Services leave Sydney at 6pm daily, arriving at the Roma St Transit Centre at 10am the following day, except during daylight saving time in New South Wales when it arrives at 8.45am. The return trip departs from Brisbane at 1.45pm (winter) or 2.45pm (summer), arriving in Sydney throughout the year at 7am next morning. There are connections in Sydney to other destinations.

The main long-distance services from Brisbane to other parts of Queensland are the twice-weekly *Westlander* to Cunnamulla and Quilpie (1,000km and 28 hours) and the "Sunshine Route" up the coast. Three trains serve the coastal line, each with sleeping accommodation. The overnight *Capricornian* from Brisbane goes only as far as Rockhampton, leaving at 6.20 every evening except Sundays and arriving at 8.15 next morning. The *Sunlander* leaves Roma St at 7.15am daily except Fridays and Sundays for the $36\frac{1}{2}$-hour, 1,680km trek all the way to Cairns. Liquor is available on the train from 10.30am to 1.30pm and 4pm to 7pm; food at reasonable prices is served from 6am to 9.30pm. On Sundays the service is by the faster *Queenslander* train which has wagons for motor vehicles attached. The train departs for Cairns at 8.15am, arriving at 5.55pm next day. First class passengers can buy drinks in the Lounge Car (which also has video showings) from 10am to 10pm, while economy travellers are restricted to the same hours as the *Sunlander*. The one-way economy fare from Brisbane to Cairns using any of these trains is $95.

Other long-distance trains in the state include the *Midlander* from Rockhampton east to Winton (20 hours, 860km), the *Gulflander* which links the isolated settlements of Croydon and Normanton near the Gulf of Carpentaria, and the *Islander* from Townsville across to Mount Isa. A "Sunshine Rail Pass" gives unlimited economy class travel on all these routes — plus the extensive suburban network around Brisbane — and costs $145 for seven days, $175 for 14 or $220 for a month. The Rail Pass also entitles you to a 40% discount for sleeping berths on overnight services.

Ordinary one-way tickets allow unlimited stopovers within five days for distances up to 500km, ten days up to 1,000km and two weeks for longer trips. Breaking the long journey from Brisbane to Cairns is highly recommended and there are several obvious stops: Rockhampton for Yeppoon and Great Keppel Island, Proserpine for the Whitsunday Islands, and Townsville for Magnetic Island. There are also some places which you might prefer to travel straight through, such as Gladstone whose claim to fame is the largest aluminium smelting plant in the southern hemisphere.

When you book your ticket you will need to say where you wish to stop off and for how long, so that the appropriate reservations can be made for you. If you change your mind you can re-book the itinerary free of charge, but this can be a slow process at country stations.

Driving. Road surfaces on and near Highway 1 along the coastal strip of Queensland are good, but if you venture very far north or west you run into unsealed (and, during the wet season, frequently impassable) roads. The Queensland Government Travel Centre publishes a useful free guide — *Queensland Road Conditions* — which gives detailed information on road surfaces and work-in-progress, and which is updated every six months. The state's motoring organization is the Royal Automobile Club of Queensland (RACQ), whose head office is at 190 Edward St, Brisbane (tel: 253 2444).

The blanket speed limit in Queensland is 100km/h, reducing to 60km/h inside built-up areas. Drivers under 18, or those holding a provisional licence, can be penalized if their blood/alcohol level is 0.02 or above. For other drivers the limit is 0.05. Queensland motoring law has some unusual features. For example, in an effort to reduce car thefts, it is illegal to leave ignition keys in a vehicle in a public place; when a bus indicates it intends to pull out, you are legally obliged to slow down and give way; making a U-turn at any junction controlled by traffic lights is prohibited unless signs specify otherwise. On-the-spot fines of $60 or $100 are levied for minor offences. One to four "demerit points" are assigned for various offences, with disqualification likely when you reach nine points. When parking, you are legally required to leave at least one metre between you car and vehicles in front and behind.

Note that the rental agreements for most vehicles hired in Queensland specifically exclude the use of unsealed roads. A number of hire companies based at towns near the fringes of the wilderness rent out four-wheel drive vehicles which are not subject to these restrictions.

Hitch-hiking. Queensland comes closer than any other state to outlawing hitch-hiking. The state traffic code makes it an offence to "stand on any portion of the road while awaiting a vehicle" or "inconvenience, obstruct or hinder the free passage of any other pedestrian or vehicle". This legislation is frequently used as an excuse to hassle hitch-hikers. To keep on the right side of the law, therefore, you should pay particular attention to picking a hitching spot off the main

"IF YOU SPOT THE POLICE, SIT ON YOUR LUGGAGE AND TRY TO BLEND IN WITH THE SCENERY."

roadway, and keep an eye out for the police. This is not quite so simple as it sounds, since they use a variety of vehicles of which some are identifiable as police cars only when they pull up next to you. If you manage to spot the police before they see you, move away from the roadside, sit on your luggage and try to blend in with the scenery. If they stop, you can expect to be searched for drugs, since "hitch-hiker", "hippie" and "hashish" seem to be synonymous to some Queensland police.

Women who have happily hitched in the southern states of Australia should think twice before trying in Queensland. Some male drivers have misplaced ideas about lone women hitchers, and there have been numerous attacks: not just in isolated areas, but also around the Gold Coast and on the well-used Bruce Highway between Brisbane and Cairns. One stretch of this road — from Rockhampton to Mackay — has been the scene of several grisly murders, and there are signs warning "do not stop". Hitchers may feel safer approaching lorry drivers at one of the truckers' depots on Highway 1.

Leaving Brisbane can pose problems for hitchers. Heading south towards the New South Wales border, don't bother to try the South Eastern Freeway from the city centre; instead catch bus 191, 199, 501 or 509 to MacGregor or, better still, take a suburban train 35km out to Beenleigh where the Pacific Highway begins in earnest. For the Warrego Highway to Toowoomba and the west, take a train 20km out to Goodna and use a sign to ensure you get a ride beyond Ipswich. The Bruce Highway north is often crowded with competing hitchers: the most sensible place outside the city is 20km north of Brisbane at the start of the Highway proper at Bald Hills, which can be reached by suburban train. Nevertheless, some success has been reported hitching on the main road outside the Youth Hostel in Kedron.

Outside the capital, hitching on main routes near the coast is straightforward and — in places — positively easy. However, the harsh interior of Queensland and the treacherous roads north of Mossman are not conducive to hitching. Some people have successfully hitched rides on yachts along the coast: see *Great Outdoors — Yachting* for suggestions.

CITY TRANSPORT

City Layout. The centre of the capital lies in a fold of the Brisbane River, and streets within this area follow the usual grid pattern. A unique feature of the city's street names is that the female gender is used for main streets which run southwest to northeast (Ann, Adelaide, Queen, etc.), while those running perpendicular have male names (Edward, Albert, George, etc.). The heart of the city is the Queen St Mall. The location of King George Square can be confusing since it is in the middle of Albert St, one block northeast of George St.

The waterside is largely given over to swirling freeways, notably the Riverside Expressway running southeast. Across the river is South Brisbane, location of the Queensland Cultural Centre and Expo 88. The inner-city suburbs ringing the centre include Fortitude Valley (usually known simply as "the Valley", and a rough sort of area), Paddington, New Farm and Woolloongabba (called "Gabba").

Public Transport. Bus, suburban train and ferry services are operated by Brisbane City Council. The central information office is on the ground floor of the Brisbane Administration Centre at 69 Ann St, near George St. A free *Public Transport Pocket Map* is available from this office. For public transport information call 225 4444.

There are no less than five classes of bus, of which "City buses" are the ordinary stop-everywhere variety. "Cityxpress" (sic) services pick up only at certain suburban bus stops, then run non-stop to the city centre. "Rocket" buses operate during rush hours and serve only stops marked with a blue/orange missile symbol. "Citylimited" is yet another type of limited-stop service, distinguishable by being articulated and air-conditioned. Finally, the Great Circle Line (which has a separate fare structure) serves yellow stops at 800 metre intervals about 7km out from the city centre.

For trips around the city centre (shown by "City Heart" signs on bus stops) you pay only 30¢ a ride. Fares for longer journeys are calculated on the basis of three concentric zones: travel within one costs 60¢, across two $1 and over all three $1.40. Children and senior citizens pay half fare. Transfers are more restricted than in other cities. They can be made only by holders of two- or three-zone tickets, and then only at five specified interchanges to buses travelling in the same direction.

Single journey tickets can be bought from the driver, or from conductors who loiter around bus stops in the city centre with ticket machines; this is to save time in boarding at busy stops. Cheap deals are available from BCC Sales Bureaux and ticket agents, which are newsagents and corner shops showing a blue and yellow "Fare Deal" sign. Books of ten tickets save 25% on regular prices, and a monthly single-zone pass costs $18. An unlimited day rover can be bought from bus drivers for $4, but costs only $3 if you buy it in advance from ticket agents.

Brisbane City Council operates two ferry services across the Brisbane River to Kangaroo Point: one is the launch between the Customs House (on Queen St at the northeast of the city centre) to Holman St on Kangaroo Point, the other from the foot of Edward St to Thornton St. They operate from 6.30am to 11pm Monday-Saturday and cost 50¢ each way (20¢ for senior citizens, children and bicycles). There are also riverboat commuter services from Riverside in the city centre to outlying suburbs, which provide a good way of taking a budget-price cruise.

Taxis. Cabs in Queensland are distinguishable both by the sign on the roof and by their number plates, which have white figures on a green background (the reverse of plates on other vehicles). Fares are low: $1 standing charge ($1.80 after 8pm and at weekends) plus 52¢ per km. To request a taxi in Brisbane by telephone, dial Ascot on 831 3000, Yellow on 391 0191 or Black and White on 229 1000.

Car. For local traffic conditions, dial 1 1655. Parking in central Brisbane is a problem. Regulations within the Central Traffic Area are strictly enforced by the city authorities; the best plan if you insist upon driving into the centre is to find an off-street lot or a "parkatarea": this is a special meter where you are permitted to park all day, rather than for just an hour or two. Each meter has two slots; insert your coins in the side facing your vehicle. Alternatively, the City Council provides Park and Ride stations at Coronation Drive and in Ann St, Fortitude Valley. You can park all day and get a "free" ride into town and back for $1.60. Most suburban railway stations have free car parks, so you can invent your own Park and Ride scheme with ease.

City "transit lanes" can be used by buses, bicycles, taxis and cars carrying more than three people (driver included). They should not be confused with bus lanes, which are strictly for buses. The Gateway Bridge, crossing the river east of the city, is mostly of interest to those bypassing the city between the Gold and Sunshine Coasts. It opened in 1986 and has rapidly became the most popular suicide spot in Brisbane. Tolls will be charged on it until the year 2016.

Hire a Hack (tel: 52 3033) is located in Newstead, a few kilometres northeast of the city centre at 108 Breakfast Creek Road (at the corner of Jordan Terrace), and offers heavily-used vehicles from $15 per day unlimited distance. You might also try Cut Rate Rental at 43 Ainsdale St out in West Chermside (tel: 350 2081). Their rates start at $27 for a small hatchback (e.g. a Holden Gemini) with a 15% discount on weekly rentals. Rates include insurance, stamp duty and 250km per day. Rentals of three days or more qualify for free delivery and pick up at the airport or your hotel. Most convenient for those arriving by bus or train at the Roma St Transit Centre is Half Price Rent-a-Car, located at the Centre (tel: 229 3544). They have the added advantage of renting to people aged 19 and above rather than the usual age of 21. To hire a campervan, contact Budget at 21 Sandgate Road, Breakfast Creek (tel: 262 8833); YHA members can get a 10% discount on campervans rented by Apollo Motorhome Holidays, 22 Fir St, Victoria Point, 25km southeast of Brisbane city centre.

Cycling. The volume of traffic and complexity of one-way streets in the city centre, not to mention Brisbane's hilly terrain, makes cycling arduous, but there are havens such as the City Botanic Gardens where special bicycle tracks have been laid out. The most central rental point is Brisbane Bicycle Hire at 214 Margaret St (tel: 221 4528). Bicycles are not permitted on suburban trains, and the only city bridge that cyclists can use is the Story Bridge on Highway 1. You can, however, take your bike on the ferries across the river.

Australia's hospitality industry is at its most developed in Queensland. Much of the state's economic growth has been generated by tourism, and consequently there are plenty of luxury hotels, motels, self-catering apartments and hostels on offer. Jason's *Queensland Accommodation Guide* is a comprehensive list, with over 1,300 establishments; it is available from the publishers at PO Box 9390, Newmarket, Auckland, New Zealand. But be warned that the influx of budget travellers is such that hostels in the more popular coastal areas are often fully booked; even Brisbane itself has failed to keep pace with the demand for cheap accommodation and advance booking is advisable.

All three of the city's Youth Hostels can be booked through the Queensland YHA office at 462 Queen St (831 2022). Easily the best bet is Brisbane City Youth Hostel (221 0961), at the top of the hill on Upper Roma St, 500m west of the Transit Centre. Each of the 64 beds costs $7 per night. The next nearest YHA Hostel is 8km north of the city centre at 15 Mitchell St in Kedron (857 1245). Its 80 beds cost $5.50 each per night. You can reach the hostel by taking bus 172 from the Town Hall side of Adelaide St as far as bus stop 27A; you then turn left along Broughton Rd and right into Mitchell St. The third hostel is smaller and harder to reach, but its low rates ($4.50 per night) and splendid setting on the foreshore overlooking Moreton Bay may make you feel the journey is worthwhile. The hostel is 30km north of Brisbane on Hornibrook Esplanade in Woody Point (284 6167), reached by a suburban train to Sandgate then a Hornibrook Bus Lines bus to Oxley Avenue or Scarborough. Due to the lack of alternative cheap accommodation in Brisbane, advance reservations for any of the hostels is a good idea.

There are three Backpackers hostels in Brisbane, all in the nearby suburb of New Farm. One is at 71 Kent St (358 4504), another at 365 Bowen Terrace (358 1488) and, most central, Backpackers Bridge Inn at 196 Bowen Terrace (358 5000). Rates are around $7 for a dormitory bed; singles and doubles are also available. The cheapest hotels close to the city centre are the Tourist Private Hotel/Motel, 1½km north at 555 Gregory Terrace (52 4171) which charges $16 single and $28 double including breakfast; and the Yale Budget Inn at 413 Upper Edward St (behind Central station; 832 1665) costing $20 single/$28 double including breakfast. You could also try Pacific Coast Budget Accommodation at 513 Queen St (832 2591), although it is more expensive than other PCBA hotels: $20 for a single and $40 for a double. Prices are lower in the nearby suburbs. In New Farm, for example, you pay $15 single/$25 double at the Elizabeth Private Hotel at 14 Harcourt St (358 1866); or $18 single/$22 double at the AMC Guest House at 99 Merthyr Road (358 5203). For other alternatives, ask at the Brisbane City Council information office in Queen St Mall for their list of hotels and motels. Emergency accommodation is available at the Salvation Army Hostel in Pindara (832 1491).

Camping. If you are planning to travel much in Queensland it is well worth taking a tent, both to save money (camping is free in many National Parks and State Forests with the prior permission of the local Ranger) and for occasions when all other accommodation is fully booked. Don't try to pitch a tent in Brisbane, however, since a local ordinance prohibits camping within a 22km radius of the city centre. The time and expense of commuting in from one of the sites outside this boundary renders the whole exercise of camping uneconomic if you wish to spend much time in the city.

The key to eating well in Brisbane — and the rest of Queensland — is to take advantage of the excellent local produce. Beef, fruit and seafood are the best bets: in particular, mud crabs ("muddies"), prawns and Moreton Bay bugs (a cross between a large prawn and a small lobster, caught near the mouth of the Brisbane River) are usually good value. When combined with ethnic Asian cuisines, the results can be delicious. Most establishments adhere to limited evening opening hours: 6pm to 10pm, Tuesday-Saturday is the norm. For food at any time of the day or night, seek sanctuary at the Pancake Manor; it is situated in a converted church at 18 Charlotte St and never closes. YHA members get a 5% discount.

Almost all the restaurants listed below are BYO; some surprisingly ritzy establishments encourage you to take your own liquor, which helps to keep the bill within reasonable bounds. The glossy brochure *Dining out: Brisbane* may catch your eye, but it consists mainly of advertisements for plush, expensive restaurants and is of little interest to those seeking cheap or unusual food.

Brisbane city centre and Fortitude Valley have a wide variety of perfectly adequate cafés and restaurants, but little that is exceptional. The luridly decorated Pasta-Joke at 100 Commercial Road in the Valley is easy to find (being painted bright mauve) and is always busy. Brisbane's diminutive Chinatown lies on the city side of the Valley, bordered by Brunswick, Ann, Gipps and Duncan Streets; there are numerous Oriental restaurants within and around this block. For a quick lunch in Brisbane, the City Plaza (below City Hall, between Ann and Adelaide Streets) has a good range of takeaway kiosks and outdoor seating. The Cubana, just off the Mall on Albert St is also recommended.

For dinner, it's worth heading out of the city centre to one of the near suburbs. Paddington (2km west of the city) is the trendiest area, though a pale imitation of the Sydney suburb of the same name. Given Terrace is the best street for food: try the Elephant Path Sri Lankan restaurant at number 183 (369 9052) which opens every evening from 6pm. Faces (number 267; 369 0039) is a more expensive venue, but very chic with an open courtyard. The Paddington Palate at 231 Given Terrace (369 4823) also has a garden, but is more of a snacky place. Further along, Michel's "Le Scoops" Sorbets, at 283 (858 2640) is a pavement café specializing in ices; there is live music at weekends.

The suburb of Red Hill, a little north of Paddington, has some less expensive but equally interesting places. The Nataraja Indian Restaurant at the Red Hill Centre on Musgrave Road has cheap lunch specials. Benjamin's at 195 Musgrave Road has good seafood and vegetarian dishes. Le Figaro at 5 Enoggera Terrace is more upmarket, with an imaginative menu that changes monthly to take account of seasonal availability of produce.

The New Farm area occupies the first loop in the river downstream from the city centre. Le Bronx at 722 Brunswick Street (358 2088) offers "cuisine moderne" dishes which change with the seasons. It opens for dinner at 6pm from Tuesday to Saturday. The Baan Thai at 630 Brunswick St (358 4346) is good value and keeps the same hours. And Possum's at 681 Brunswick St (358 1442) has an excellent selection of plain Australian fare and traditional rough "bushwhacker" music in the backyard.

South Brisbane should not be overlooked. Squirrels vegetarian restaurant at the corner of Melbourne and Edmonstone Streets (844 4603) is cheap (a buffet for $7), and handy for the Queensland Cultural Centre. Out at St Lucia (near the University), Pasta Pasta at 242 Hawken Drive (371 1403) has homemade pasta and ice cream and opens daily from 8am to midnight. On Sunday mornings there's a craft market in the car park at the front, and a special brunch is served.

Other suburban places worth trying include the Breakfast Creek Hotel (which has won awards for its steaks) at 2 Kingsford Smith Drive, Albion and, for good seafood, Breakfast Creek Wharf. The best Mexican food is at Chillies, 385 Gympie Road, Kedron, with Sombreros at 735 Sandgate Road in Clayfield a close second.

DRINKING

Licensing hours in Queensland are 10am to 10pm, except on Sundays (11am to 1pm and 5 to 7pm). You will not be able to escape the fact that Queensland is beer territory. It is the home of Castlemaine XXXX (pronounced four-ex), rated Australia's tastiest mass-market lager by writer Michael Jackson in his *Pocket Beer Book*. The local Carbine Stout is also worth trying. Unfortunately for Queenslanders, Castlemaine is now owned by the Perth-based entrepreneur Alan Bond. It is made at the Bond Brewing Qld brewery, 2km east of Brisbane city centre at 11 Finchley St in Milton. If you call in advance (tel: 369 3188) you can take a tour of the brewery and enjoy free samples at the end. In view of the liberal quantities provided to visitors, you should travel to and from the brewery by suburban train or bus.

Wine is slowly becoming more popular in Queensland, but if you ask for it in remote hotels you may well get either a blank look or plonk from a bottle first opened a year earlier. If you're buying from a liquor store, look out for Queensland wines such as Robinson's Family Chardonnay and Rumbalara Semillon.

An extraordinary law makes it an offence for licensees to serve drinks to "deviants", part of the National Party's campaign to make life for homosexuals a misery. You will probably see T-shirts reading "Please Serve Me — I'm Straight". The centre of Brisbane has no particularly exciting pubs, so — as with eating — you should look beyond the downtown area. The trendiest pubs are those with live bands, including the gay hangouts of the Terminus and the Hacienda on Brunswick St in Fortitude Valley, the Captain Cook Tavern on Anzac Avenue in Kippa-Ring and the Country Club Hotel on Gympie Road in Strathpine.

Entertainment

Some travellers form an immediate and adverse impression of Brisbane as nothing much more than an ungainly country town. Although Queensland writer Robyn Davidson's description of Brisbane in the 1950s as "a town of never-ending Sundays" is no longer accurate, the climate appears to make the citizens more lethargic than those of the other state capitals. Away from the Queen St Mall, downtown Brisbane can be more deserted than other state capitals outside business hours. But behind the unpromising exterior is a surprising amount of activity and energy, much of it manifested in the many entertainments provided free by the local authority. Sunday afternoons in the parks around the centre are as lively as any European or American city, a direct result of the free activities sponsored by the City Council. If you visit Brisbane in late September/early October, try to catch an event or two at the city's Warana Festival; call 221 0011 for details.

Three city-centre buildings exemplify the contrasting architectural styles of Brisbane's early planners. The City Hall is solid Victorian, following the same basic design as London's Royal Albert Hall albeit on a smaller scale. This circular, domed building no longer dominates the city as the highest structure,

"YOU SHOULD TRAVEL TO AND FROM THE BREWERY BY TRAIN OR BUS"

but still makes an impressive sight at the corner of Albert and Adelaide Streets. On weekdays from 9am to 5pm, you can take a lift to the top for 50¢, or just stroll around the sturdy portals. St John's Cathedral on Ann St, on the other hand, was mostly built around 1910 in Gothic Revival Style, but is still waiting forlornly to be completed. To add to this architectural melange, Parliament House at the corner of Alice and George Streets (overlooking the Botanic Gardens) is in the style of the French Renaissance. On days when the state legislature is sitting you may view the unusually abusive debating style of Queensland politicians from the public gallery; call 226 711 for further details. Genuine early Queensland architecture — villas on wooden stumps in order to maximize air flow rather than to avoid flooding — can be found scattered around the city, but particularly in Paddington. For more information about the many contrasting styles, ask at the National Trust of Queensland in the Old Government House in George St (tel: 229 1788) for their booklet of listed buildings, churches and landmarks.

From 1990, Brisbane should have the world's tallest building, the spaceship-like Central Place. It is planned for the block bounded by Ann, Edward and Turbot Streets, opposite Central Station. The 107-storey tower (which is nicknamed "Joh's Tower" and has generated a huge amount of antagonism) will be 445m high, two metres taller than the current record-holding Sears Tower in Chicago. The tower is being designed very much with the visitor in mind, and is expected to attract one million tourists each year. Until then, the best views of the city can be had from the top of the Gazebo Ramada Hotel at 345 Wickham Terrace (by Albert and Birley Streets). The view will cost you the price of a drink at the "Top of the G" cocktail bar, but is well worthwhile in clear weather. You might also head west to the Mount Coot-tha lookout, for a view of the city that is particularly impressive by night.

You can take in Brisbane from ground level on the Lookabout bus tour. This three-hour trip is run by the City Council and is good value at $10. You will see, for example, the William Jolly Bridge ("one of the longest single through-arch bridges in the world"), and learn that until 1930 Brisbane residents could set their watches by the copper ball which was dropped from the top of the Old Windmill on Wickham Terrace each working day at 1pm. Departures are daily at 9.30am and 1.30pm from the Brisbane Administration Centre at 69 Ann St. You should book in advance on 225 5555. An unusual feature is that if you decide one attraction on the 55km route is too good to pass by, you can get out and catch an ordinary bus back to the city at any time using the same ticket. If you have a spare $150 you could spend it on a one-hour balloon flight over the city, or a "Biggles over Brisbane" trip in an open Tiger Moth biplane; call 844 6671.

Expo 88. The planning for this event kept the city busy for years, and the organizers ran into considerable artistic, financial and political difficulties (such as the unwillingness of more liberal Australian states to support an event instigated by Sir Joh Bjelke Petersen). Nevertheless 31 countries accepted Queensland's invitation to establish a pavilion at the Exposition from 30 April to 30 October 1988. The site has been developed by the river in South Brisbane, close to the Queensland Cultural Centre.

Bearing in mind the high status accorded to tourism in Queensland, the theme "Leisure in the Age of Technology" was predictable. The cost of admission was expected to be $25 for a day ticket for an adult and $15 for a child, with cut-price admission after 5pm. The price includes use of the monorail around the ite and performances at the amphitheatre, but rides at the space-age amusement park cost extra. The most terrifying rides are those on the Centrifuge, Titan and Supernova rollercoasters. After Expo 88, these facilities will remain open.

Queensland Cultural Centre. The State's artistic hub is on the south bank of the river (adjacent to the Expo site and South Brisbane railway station) and indeed has a great deal in common with London's South Bank centre both architecturally and artistically.

As you cross Victoria Bridge from the city centre, the Museum, Art Gallery and State Library are on your right and the Performing Arts Complex to your left. This angular monolith houses two 2,000-seat auditoria — the Lyric Theatre and the Concert Hall — plus the small Cremorne theatre for experimental drama. You can take a tour of the Complex on the hour from 10am to 4pm except Sundays (price $2.50, $1.50 for students), or a more extensive tour including backstage areas for $5. For the latter you should book in advance by calling 240 7483. There is a variety of places to eat, from the lavish and expensive Fountain Room Restaurant to a couple of cheap cafeterias. Ticket prices for most shows are in the $15-$30 range (sometimes with discounts for students). For recorded details of upcoming performances, call 1 1632. For bookings, dial 844 0201. If you are calling from out-of-town you can make a credit card booking by dialling 008-17 7341 for the price of a local call. Just as at the Sydney Opera House, there are free outdoor performances on Sundays in the plazas and walkways of the Centre; dial 240 7229 for details. In addition, there are always free exhibitions in the foyer of the Performing Arts Complex.

Theatre. Apart from the lavish productions at the Performing Arts Complex, there are three mainstream theatres: the SGIO in Turbot St (at the foot of the building of the same name; 221 3861); the Twelfth Night at 4 Cintra Road, Bowen Hills (52 7622) and the Brisbane Arts Theatre at 210 Petrie Terrace (369 2344). In addition, Henry Africa's Theatre Restaurant in the Melbourne Hotel on Browning St in South Brisbane (44 1571) has a three-course dinner followed by a show from Wednesday to Saturday for around $30. One local ensemble worth looking out for is the Grin and Tonic Theatre Troupe.

Cinema. Unlike its London counterpart, the Cultural Centre lacks a film theatre. The main city-centre venues are the Albert (183 Albert St, 221 5777), the Forum (160 Albert St, 221 3255), the George (346 George St, 221 7866) and Hoyt's Entertainment Centre on Queen St (1 1680). Cinemas are cheaper on Tuesday nights when a flat rate of $4 or $5 is charged.

Music. While Brisbane's local rock scene is less lively than that of the southern capitals, it is firmly on the map of world tours by megastars. These major league performers play at the Brisbane Entertainment Centre on Stanworth Road in the far northern suburb of Boondall (229 9077), reached by suburban train. Details of future events at the Centre can be heard on 1 1611. *Ticketworld* in Queen St Mall sells tickets for most concerts. Dial 1 1644 for recorded information on the events available. The best source of listings for gigs by local bands is the excellent free weekly *Time Off,* not to be confused with the less informative hand-outs such as *This Week in Brisbane* and *Discover Brisbane.* The *Blitz* pull-out section of Thursday's *Courier-Mail* is also useful. Good venues include the Roxy on Brunswick St in Fortitude Valley, the Mansfield Tavern and the Callemvale Hotel. Further out, try the Aspley Hotel on Gympie Road in Aspley (263 1570) and the Homestead Hotel at 114 Zillmere Road in

Boondall (265 1555) as well as the pubs mentioned above under *Drinking*.

You can listen to jazz while you dine at New Orleans on the Queen St Mall, although prices are high. Jazz can also be heard at the Caxton Hotel (38 Petrie Terrace; 369 5971); the Port Office Hotel (38 Edward St; 221 0767); and the Sweet Patootie at 480 St Pauls Terrace, Fortitude Valley (52 9606).

Serious music — particularly the accomplished Queensland Symphony Orchestra — is best enjoyed in the Concert Hall of the Performing Arts Complex. There are often concerts held at the Queensland Conservatorium of Music at the southeastern end of George St (by the City Botanic Gardens). Free chamber music can be heard each Thursday at 12.30pm in the Ithaca Auditorium on the second floor of the City Hall.

Nightlife. There is a sprinkling of night clubs and discos in the centre and the Valley, such as Tracks (in the City Plaza Tavern bordered by Ann, George and Adelaide Streets), Court Jester opposite and Sybil's at 383 Adelaide St. At the Fortitude Valley end of Queen St, try Yesterdays or Lulu's for 60s music. If you want to sample a "disco boat", Queensland style, the Rock'n'River boat sails every Friday night (from North Quay at 7.15pm, from Riverside at 8pm) and charges $15 including a chicken supper; call 229 7055 for further details.

Museums and Galleries. The Queensland Museum (240 7555) is part of the Cultural Centre on the south bank of the Brisbane River. Its collection is extremely eclectic — from geology through anthropology to technology — and appears to be designed to appeal to those who have no great interest in conventional museums. The more interesting amusements among the two million exhibits include the aircraft *Avian Cirrus* (in which Bert Hinkler made the first solo flight from England to Australia in 1928) and the almost Disney-style dinosaur garden which is popular for picnics. Admission to the Museum is free, although a charge is made for special exhibitions. It opens at 9am every day of the year, and closes at 5pm except on Wednesdays (8pm). The adjacent Queensland Art Gallery opens from 10am to 5pm daily, also with late opening on Wednesdays; there are free guided tours at 11am, 1pm and 2pm on weekdays, 2 and 3pm at weekends. Entrance is free, except for special exhibitions.

The Brisbane Civic Art Gallery and Museum is on the ground floor of Brisbane City Hall (tel: 225 4355) and opens from 10am to 4pm, Monday-Friday. The exhibits are (understandably) rather parochial, with artefacts and works of art from early colonial days.

There are plenty of specialist museums and galleries in Brisbane, such as Australia's largest toy and doll museum (Pandora's Playthings, 401 Lutwyche Road, Windsor) and the Antiquarian Print Gallery in the Mansions on George St (tel: 221 7178).

Gambling. Fruit machines ("pokies") are banned in Queensland, and many visitors cross into New South Wales at Tweed Heads at the foot of the Gold Coast to play the machines at the many clubs established for the purpose there. The Jupiter Casino at Surfers Paradise is the nearest gambling den to Brisbane, 80km away on the Gold Coast.

Beaches. Brisbane's city centre is 18km inland, so some ground must be covered before arriving at a beach. The nearest good beach is at Redcliffe, 25km north over the Hornibrook Highway Viaduct.

Parks and Zoos. The City Botanic Gardens are arguably central Brisbane's finest asset and among the best-kept gardens in Australia. You can get in at one of the three gates on Alice St (which face Albert, George and Edward Streets) from 8am to dusk daily. Part of the appeal lies in the coolness and freshness which contrast with the stifling atmosphere of the Brisbane streets in summer. These gardens are tiny, however, in comparison with the Mount Coot-tha Botanic Gardens west of the suburb of Toowong, 12km from the city. The Gardens open 7am-5pm throughout the year, and you can reach them by bus 39 from the city. The usual features of botanic gardens are supplemented by the Sir Thomas Brisbane Planetarium (the largest in Australia), kookaburra and duck feeding and picnic areas at the nearby J C Slaughter Falls. Nearer to the centre, New Farm Park on Brunswick St has 12,000 rose bushes and — in summer — blooming jacarandas and flamboyant poinciana trees.

Free fun is provided on Sundays, as the City Council runs a programme called FREEPS (Free Recreation and Entertainment for Everyone in Parks). Check the local press or call 832 5552 for details of the various bands, dancers, magicians and exhibitions. The major venues are New Farm Park, the City Botanic Gardens and the Albert Park Amphitheatre.

The nearest zoo is a long way north in the distant suburb of Kallangur. Much closer is the Lone Pine Koala Sanctuary at Jesmond Road in Fig Tree Pocket, 10km southwest and on bus route 84 from the city. Alternatively you can take a "Koala Cruise" from North Quay to the Sanctuary; dial 229 7055 for details. Visitors are guaranteed the chance to cuddle a koala, and can view a platypus during its feeding times from 11.30am to noon and 3pm to 4pm. The Sanctuary opens daily (except Christmas Day) from 9.30pm to 5pm. You can also see koalas in the city centre, at the Koala House "Wilderness Walk" at the junction of Adelaide and Creek Streets. This rather tacky indoor park opens 9.30am-5pm from Monday to Friday.

SPORT

The jogging track at the Queen Elizabeth II Sports Complex on Kessels Road in the suburb of Nathan opens from 7.30am to dusk, and costs 75¢ for admission. The Valley Pool, at the junction of East and Wickham Streets in Fortitude Valley northeast of the city centre, is a pleasant pool which is heated in "winter".

The biggest draw for sports fans in Brisbane is the chance to see Ian Botham of England in action for Queensland at the Brisbane Cricket Ground (on Stanley St south of the city in Woolloongabba; the ground, like the suburb is known as the "Gabba"). The all-rounder has signed up to play for Queensland until 1990. For the latest cricket scores, dial 1188. The full range of other ball games can be seen in the city. Both codes of rugby are followed (with the Redcliffe Dolphins the best for Rugby Union), and the Brisbane Bears represent the state in the Victorian Football League.

Greyhound racing takes place most nights at one of the circuits at Capalaba, the Brisbane Cricket Ground, Ipswich or Lawton. Horses race at Bundamba and Doomben tracks, and you can see trotting on Saturdays at Albion Park in Breakfast Creek (tel: 262 2577).

SHOPPING

There are moves afoot to allow shops in Queensland to open on Saturday afternoons. At present, however, most stores open at 8.15am except Sundays and close at 5pm during the week and at noon on Saturdays. Shops in central Brisbane and the Valley stays open until 9pm on Fridays, and suburban stores have late-night shopping on Thursdays. Shops in the Redcliffe area (a fair way northeast of the city) are open all day Saturday, but close on Wednesday afternoons.

Prices for many items, especially dutiable goods, are lower on Queensland. For example cigarettes cost only about $1.75 for a pack of 25 or 30. Brisbane is a good place to buy gear for trips to the Outback, and three equipment shops gives 10% discounts to YHA members: The Camping Centre, 25 Ipswich Road, Woolloongabba; Aladdin's Camping Service, 1974 Logan Rd, Upper Mount Gravatt; and, more centrally, Robinson's Sports Stores, 300 Queen St.

The Queensland Book Depot on Adelaide St is most notable for its range of postcards at only 10¢ each — possibly the cheapest in Australia. For books try the Awakening Mind Bookshop, 182 Ann St and the American Book Store at 197 Elizabeth St. Further along Elizabeth St at number 83 (between Albert and George Streets) is Folio Books, with the Circle Bookshop in the same arcade. The Women's Book, Gift and Music Centre is at the corner of Gladstone Road and Dorchester Streets in the suburb of Highgate Hill.

MEDIA

For up-to-the-minute news, dial 1197 in Brisbane.

Newspapers. Brisbane's quality daily is the *Courier-Mail* (40¢). The *Daily Sun* is a tabloid costing 40¢ from street vendors but available free from the dispensers provided in TAB betting shops in Brisbane. The sale of soft-porn magazines is restricted, although the Queensland Literature Board of Review recently lifted its ban on *Playboy* magazine.

Radio. The local ABC AM station is 4QR on 612kHz. The leading stereo AM station is 4BK on 1296kHz. For better quality sound, tune to Brisbane's answer to BBC Radio 3 (4MBS-FM on 103MHz), ABC-FM on 106MHz or FM 104 (104MHz) for rock. The local community station — 4ZZZ on 102MHz — broadcasts a wide range of material, including programmes produced by the women's radio collective MEGAHERS at 5pm on Tuesdays.

The rapid development of Brisbane has attracted a number of petty criminals, but the city is still by no means dangerous. There are some areas where you might not feel comfortable after dark, such as the less affluent parts of South Brisbane, but in general there is no cause for paranoia about attacks by criminals. If you are worried, you can actually hire a police officer for "special duties": the cost is $18 per hour (extra on Sundays). Some visitors, however, may well feel threatened by the illiberal laws of Queensland such as Australia's only statute prohibiting homosexuality among men (an attempt in 1987 to outlaw lesbianism was abandoned after a storm of protest) and a prohibition on walking more than four-abreast (aimed at preventing demonstrations). In addition, Queensland's laws governing Aboriginals break 11 articles of the United Nations Declaration on Human Rights.

Drugs. While most Australian states move towards more lenient treatment of drug offenders, Queensland's Drug Misuse Act provides severe penalties. The maximum for possession of more than half a kilogram of marijuana is life imprisonment, and this sentence is mandatory for carrying two grams or more of heroin or cocaine. A number of travellers report that their vehicles have been stopped by police and searched for drugs. A certain amount of illicit drug-taking does, of course, take place, and a large amount of marijuana is grown in the Atherton Tablelands inland from Cairns; but Queensland is one state where the uncommitted should choose to stick to legitimate pleasures.

The area code for Brisbane is 07. Dial 000 for the emergency services.

The main Queensland Government Tourist Centre is at 196 Adelaide St, Brisbane (tel: 31 2211). There is a Brisbane City Information Kiosk open daily except Sundays in the middle of the Queen St Mall, near the David Jones Store. There are branches of the QGTC in Alexander Headland (on the Sunshine Coast), Cairns, Mackay, Rockhampton, Toowoomba and Surfers Paradise, and in six Australian cities outside Queensland:

Adelaide: 10 Grenfell St (08-212 2399).
Canberra: 25 Garema Place (062-48 8411).
Melbourne: 257 Collins St (03-654 3886).
Newcastle (New South Wales): 516 Hunter St (049-26 2800).
Perth: 55 St George's Terrace (09-325 1600).
Sydney: 149 King St (02-232 1788).

British Consulate-General: 193 North Quay (221 4933).
American Express: 68 Queen St (229 2022).
Thomas Cook: 168 Edward St (221 9749).
Medical Treatment: Royal Brisbane Hospital, Herston Road (253 8111).
Dental Emergencies: Dentist Emergency Service, 131 Elizabeth St (221 8957).
Helplines: Alcoholics Anonymous 229 6566; Dial-a-Horoscope 1 1635; Dial-a-Prayer 229 8966; Life Line 52 7527.

Queensland has the highest unemployment rate in Australia, but at present its economy is growing faster than that of any other state. The hospitality industry is expanding in line with the increase in visitors, and while primary industry has encountered problems recently, Queensland is still a leading producer of raw materials: all Australian sugar, and many minerals, originate in the state. Unfortunately reports about the Commonwealth Employment Service (CES) offices in the state vary from "barely adequate" to "totally useless"; you are likely to do much better on your own initiative. Applications for renewal of your working holiday visa should be lodged at the Department of Immigration at 167 Eagle St, Brisbane (tel: 229 9144).

Brisbane is as good a place as any in the state to find work. The main CES office is at Block B, 232 Adelaide St; more promising, however, is the CES casual job centre at the corner of William and Gotha Streets in Fortitude Valley. Better still, get hold of an early edition of Wednesday's *Courier-Mail* and be first in the morning queue for jobs. You can, of course, approach employers direct for work. There have been reports of good opportunities at the Golden Circle Cannery in the northern Brisbane suburb of Bindha, and the Campbell Brothers' soap factory on Campbell St in Bowen Hills (tel: 52 3331); wages here are $9 per hour for those over 21, $6.75 for younger people.

Crops ripen earlier in Queensland than elsewhere, and the range of fruit and vegetables is extensive and exotic. Such is the diversity of produce that you could, with luck, find agricultural work throughout the year in the state. A good clue to the available work can be deduced from the ten-metre high models of fruits placed by the roadside. For example, the Big Pineapple near Nambour is an indication that the surrounding area (i.e. the Sunshine Coast) is prime territory for work during the pineapple harvest (from January to April), although pineapple picking is arduous work and poorly paid. You could move north for the winter to the citrus fruit region around Mundubbera and Gayndah (inland from Maryborough) from May to September. The apple, peach and plum crops in the "Granite Belt" around Stanthorpe near the New South Wales border may see you through the summer and autumn; this is also where most of Queensland's few vineyards are found. The Lockyer Valley in the Darling Downs near the town of Gatton has harvests of onions and potatoes lasting from September through to December, although problems caused by the increasing saltiness of the soil have cut yields recently. You may do better to head southeast from Brisbane towards the coast, since tomatoes and other vegetables are grown in the Redlands Bay area.

Other worthwhile prospects include strawberry-picking near the New South Wales border (probably the longest strawberry season anywhere: July-November); tomatoes around Bowen (between Mackay and Townsville) from May to December, with a particular labour shortage in September; mangoes in the same area in December; and tobacco-picking in the Atherton Tablelands inland from Cairns. The latter season lasts from late September almost until Christmas, but only the biggest farms can support pickers for the full ten or eleven weeks. It is worth noting that most of the plantations are owned by families of Italian immigrants who have not yet shaken off outdated attitudes to work; women therefore may find themselves confined to inferior work and lower wages. The sugar plantations along the coast, which previously employed many thousands, are now largely mechanized, but you may be able to find unskilled work at one of the many processing plants.

If you feel you could cope with the difficult (and often lonely) life on an outback sheep farm, work is easiest to find in February or March when station managers hire their seasonal helpers. Station work can be found through the Mount Isa CES or the magazine *Queensland Country Life*. Mount Isa is also a good place to find work in mining, although most employers will insist that you sign a minimum six-month contract. Life aboard the prawn trawlers sailing out of Cairns and Townsville is probably less arduous, whether as a male deckhand or female cook. Try the big companies such as Toros or Raptis, or ask individual boat owners at the quayside. A fair amount of shore-based work is generated by Queensland's fishermen, such as the three fish processing plants in the port of Bundaberg.

Australians visit the Gold and Sunshine Coasts around Brisbane in great numbers, while further north the coast and offshore islands are being developed at a fearsome rate. Since many of these islands lack a local population from which labour might otherwise be drawn, you should have little difficulty finding work in the hospitality industry particularly in the May/June to October/November dry season.

Further Afield

While Sydney is undeniably the jewel of New South Wales, Brisbane has no pretensions to be more than the administrative centre of a stunningly varied state. The coast of Queensland has charms unimaginable from the sturdy downtown of Brisbane. Before setting off on the well-trodden path to north Queensland, however, you might wish to relax for a few days or find work for a few weeks in the pleasant countryside inland from the capital.

Darling Downs and the Golden West. The region that Queenslanders describe as the Golden West is actually well inside the eastern half of the state. Toowoomba, the centre for the Darling Downs, is only 130km west of Brisbane. Its numerous parks and gardens and relatively high elevation makes it a pleasant place to stay. The Downs are rich agricultural land with fertile black, volcanic soil, and good territory for finding casual farming work. There is also some spectacular scenery in the Golden West, especially along the Great Dividing Range.

THE COAST

Queensland's reef and islands are what distinguishes the coastline from ordinary ocean coasts. The Great Barrier Reef marks the outer boundary of the continental shelf, a living organism that is undeniably one of the natural wonders of the world. It is a ridge of coral running north-south for 1,800km, at a distance of between 15 and 150km from the coast of Queensland, and consists of billions of living creatures existing on top of the corpses of their forebears. While coral is found in many other parts of the world, only Quensland's coast has sufficient of the right conditions of warm water and gently shelving ocean floor to permit such an extensive reef. The reef has been in existence for at least 10,000 years and, despite increasing threats from man and a plague of crown-of-thorns starfish, is still growing. You can get a close-up view by joining one of the many tours offered from the mainland, including snorkelling, scuba-diving or riding in a semi-submersible "submarine".

In a few places the reef protrudes above sea level to create real coral islands, but most of Queensland's islands are formed from sand or rock and lie within the shelter of the reef. From South Stradbroke Island off the Gold Coast to Lizard Island north of Cooktown, the islands range from unspoilt coral outcrops to garish "resort islands" with new airports to welcome the masses. Most of the islands, unlike the mainland coast, have the added bonus that you can bathe in summer without fear of harm from marine stingers.

There are also many resorts strung along the coast of the mainland, representing — according to your point of view — either opportunities for tremendous fun or gross examples of unmitigated commercial excess. The coast south of the capital is the most obvious candidate for either title.

THE GOLD COAST

The Pacific Highway runs inland for 70km south from Brisbane. If you turn off from it towards the ocean you can find a delightful archipelago of islands, of which North Stradbroke (reached by ferry from Cleveland and Redland Bay) has the most to offer. At Helensvale, you can continue on the Pacific Highway straight to the New South Wales border or turn left for the Gold Coast Highway. Most visitors choose the latter, and the tourist attractions begin almost immediately.

Dreamworld, at Coomera on the highway just north of the Gold Coast, is the largest theme park in Australia with 27 different rides; like Disneyland, your one-price ticket (around $20) buys you unlimited rides. The town of Southport marks the top of a 32km stretch of beach where the official motto is "The Visitor is King". The Queensland ethos for enterprise encouraged by Sir Joh is evident everywhere, although he might not approve of some of the less salubrious activities (such as the growing "escort agency" industry) which enable the Gold Coast to claim to be the place "where the fun never sets". The various attractions are undeniably popular: visitors each year outnumber the local residents by ten to one.

Southport is the commercial capital of the Gold Coast: just offshore on the spit at Main Beach is Sea World, the biggest marine park in the southern hemisphere. The strip of beach stretches south in an almost continuous resort development, the most notable being Surfers Paradise. Its Aboriginal name was Oomby Goomby, meaning "place next to the sea". Nowadays bikini-clad women representing the town's Progress Association top up visitors' parking meters. Further south is Mermaid Beach (setting for the new University of Technology established by entrepreneur Alan Bond), Palm Beach and the twin towns of Coolangatta and Tweed Heads. The Queensland/New South Wales border runs right through the centre of this last conurbation, bisecting Boundry (*sic*) St, and the runway of Coolangatta/Gold Coast airport straddles the state border. Just north of the airport is the Currumbin Bird Sanctuary, and facing that is Chocolate Expo, a museum/exhibition/tasting centre devoted to everybody's favourite weakness.

Although the Gold Coast is aimed primarily at big-spending tourists, the excellent Youth Hostel on the Gold Coast Highway at Bilinga Beach (tel: 075-36 7644) costs only $6.50 per night, has a swimming pool and a cheap restaurant, and is two minutes from the beach. A good alternative further south is the Backpackers Inn at Coolangatta (tel: 075-36 2422). And with a range of activities from go-karting to gambling, avocado plantations to zoos, you should never be without something to do if you encounter one of the 78 days in the year when the sun doesn't shine. With a large proportion of young people, you should not be stuck for company either. If the crass commercialism becomes too much, head inland for some good waterholes, waterfalls and views.

THE SUNSHINE COAST

This stretch of coastline has lost the battle with the Gold Coast to become the most popular resort area in Australia, and now seems content to be more refined and picturesque than its rival south of Brisbane. The Sunshine Coast runs from Bribie Island (50km north of the capital) for 80km up to Noosa Heads and has a much more intricate coastline than the Gold Coast, with the beaches indented by craggy headlands, spectacular cliffs and river outlets. Noosa Heads itself is a real beauty spot and is regarded by some as the most chic resort in Australia, with a good surfing beach and some sophisticated hotels and restaurants (but only one real pub). Out of season, however, it can be quiet and uninteresting.

The Youth Hostel 3km south of Noosa (at 35 Douglas St, Sunshine Beach; tel: 071-47 4739) is often full, although there is now a beautifully situated annexe overlooking the beach. Maroochydore, halfway down the coast, is an alternative; the Youth Hostel (tel: 071-43 3151) at 24 Schirrmann Drive costs $6 per night, and the town is a good base to explore the beaches, plantations and mountain hinterland of the Sunshine Coast.

The sugar plantations begin in earnest inland from the Sunshine Coast, and continue north all the way up to and beyond Cairns. Some of the carbohydrate is used to make Bundaberg rum at the town of the same name. You can take a tour of the distillery if you book in advance. Offshore lies the biggest sand island in the world, the 120km-by-15km Fraser Island. You can reach it by launch from Rainbow Beach or ferry from Hervey Bay, and an admission fee of a couple of dollars is levied by the National Parks and Wildlife Service. Four-wheel drive transport is necessary to see much of the island. The rewards include swimming in huge freshwater lakes, studying the fascinating wildlife and coloured sandcliffs and relaxing on the accurately named Seventy Five Mile Beach. Moreton Island, further south, is highly commercialized due to its proximity to Brisbane's airport 35km away. For the best beaches on Moreton Island, find a fishing boat prepared to take you to the leeward side of the north end (and arrange to be picked up later).

THE CAPRICORN COAST

If you follow the advice given earlier and break your journey north to Cairns at Rockhampton, you may be unnerved by the sheer quietness of the town. "Rocky" (or "Rockvegas" as it is known ironically by some locals) is not the most dynamic metropolis in Queensland, but serves as a good centre to explore the nearby Capricorn Coast (so called because of the Tropic which falls a few kilometres south of Rockhampton). The town itself has some quaint colonial buildings and pleasant riverside parks, but you get the feeling that the most exciting daily event is the train passing on the main Brisbane-Cairns line which runs along the middle of the main street. The Youth Hostel is northeast of the centre at 60 MacFarlane St (tel: 079-27 5288); the nightly rate is $6.

Infrequent buses link Rockhampton with the coastal resort of Yeppoon, but hitching out to the ocean is easy. Yeppoon is quiet and relaxed and ideal for a few days' rest. There is pleasant countryside around, plus a zoo (at Emu Park) which you should visit early or late to avoid coach parties.

Great Keppel Island lies offshore, linked to the mainland by a ferry and hydrofoil from Rosslyn Bay (just south of Yeppoon). With wide, sandy beaches and several riotous bars and discos, it is a favourite destination for young Australians and foreign travellers. There is a good Youth Hostel on the island ($6.50 per night), although advance booking is essential; this should be done through the hostel in Rockhampton. Otherwise you can stay at the adjacent Wapparraburra Haven camping ground; the name Wapparraburra means "final resting ground", and indeed Great Keppel Island was an Aboriginal burial ground.

THE WHITSUNDAY ISLANDS

This archipelago of 74 islands was actually discovered by Captain Cook on Whit Monday, 1770. Although none of the islands is on the reef proper, they form a delightful area to explore, with some coral formations visible to snorkellers

and divers. The existing dozen islands could soon be joined by more if a Brisban
developer has his way: he wants to build 500 acres of hotels, apartment, them
park and golf course on new islands built in the bay and linked by drawbridge

The jumping-off point for the Whitsundays from the Bruce Highway an
railway is the small, sleepy town of Proserpine. Regular buses serve the livel
resort of Airlie Beach (with a Backpackers' hostel on Heritage Drive; te
46 7267) and, a few kilometres further, Shute Harbour. If you arrive here b
9am, you will be confronted by a bewildering array of mariners hawking th
delights of their vessel and its voyages. You can visit virtually any of th
Whitsundays, including Long Island with its embarrassing Whitsunday 10
resort which specializes in "wet T-shirt" holidays for the 18-35s (a reference t
age, not IQ). The best trip is undoubtedly aboard the yacht *Nara,* which leave
daily at 9.15am. For about $30 you sail to an uninhabited island or two, lear
to snorkel and eat a hearty lunch, washed down with a bottle of sparkling wine
While participation in sailing the boat is not mandatory, most people join in witl
gusto. Such is the bonhomie of the crew that they may insist upon buying yo
a beer at the end of the voyage. To book in advance, call 079-46 6224. If yo
plan a scuba diving trip, you should ask about the 60-foot yawl *Rum Runner*

For longer stays, there are a number of resort islands such as Hayman
Daydream and Hamilton (where rock star George Harrison used to live unti
the crowds of gawking tourists turned the place into what he calls "Wally
World", and drove him away). If you want to be alone, it is possible to camp
on a deserted island for a night or two with a little advance planning. First yo
should contact the Ranger of Conway National Park, who is based in Shute
Harbour (tel: 079-46 9430). Then fix up with a boat operator to set you dowr
and pick you up at a pre-arranged time.

NORTH QUEENSLAND

Townsville. The largest coastal city (population 90,000) north of the state capita
lacks the amenities of Brisbane and the charm of Cairns. The suburban values
epitomized by the name "Townsville" are visible everywhere, down to the street
signs boasting "judged 'tidy street' in this suburb 1987". In fact the city's name
is not as tautological as it sounds, since it was founded by Robert Towns in the
mid-19th century as a port to service the region's agriculture.

Most of the city is flat and brown, although the 300m pink granite Castle Hill
provides some visual relief. With the multiplicity of attractions elsewhere on the
coast, there seems no good reason to remain in the town for long. But if you
are staying over in Townsville, you should find enough to keep you amused for
a day or two. In particular, the students of James Cook University sustain a
lively arts and social scene, and the gamblers at the Breakwater Casino provide
an interesting spectacle. For decorative buildings and interesting shops, go to
Flinders St East. And once the limited attractions of the city begin to wane, you
can take the boat across to Magnetic Island.

The North Queensland Visitors Bureau is at 303 Flinders Mall. The railway
station is close to the western end of the Flinders St Mall, and the boats for
Magnetic Island leave from near the other end. A new bus terminal is under
construction south of Ross Creek; until then, the Greyhound terminal is at the
corner of Flinders and King Streets on the north side of Ross Creek (71 2134);
Ansett Pioneer at the junction of Hanran and Stanley Streets (81 6611); and
Deluxe at 194 Flinders St East (72 6544). Buses to Townsville's international

irport are frequent, but as it is only 5km west of the city centre you can get
taxi without fear of bankruptcy, or even walk.

In order to become more firmly stamped upon the tourist map, Townsville
s bringing the reef closer in. "Reef Wonderland" near the city centre is a coral
eef aquarium, possibly to compensate for the Great Barrier being hard to reach
rom the city. Visitors can walk underwater through transparent tunnels.
Offshore, there is a seven-storey hotel/conference centre actually on the reef (not
lear any existing island) 70km from Townsville, linked to the mainland by
catamaran and helicopter. The Reef Link Resort was built in Singapore from
a 90-metre steel barge and a stack of shipping containers, and has 200 guest
ooms, a freshwater swimming pool and a tennis court. Low season prices start
at $124 per person per night. The Globetrotters hostel at 45 Palmer St has been
aighly recommended as a cheaper mainland alternative; it has a friendly
aroprietor who lets guests use his own swimming pool. The Backpackers' Inn
s at 262 Walker St (71 5381). Pacific Coast Budget Accomodation is at 287
Sturt St (71 6874), costing $16 single, $30 double.

Magnetic Island. Captain Cook was, it seems, never at a loss for names, however
nappropriate they later turn out to be. The island was so-called because of a
ault in *Endeavour's* compass which was wrongly attributed to a mysterious
nagnetic force on the island. It is one of the largest and most populated of the
slands off the coast of Queensland, and chiefly attractive for its fine variety of
aikes. These include the ascent of Mount Cook, but a number of less strenuous
oushwalks are clearly marked by wooden trail signs. You can pick up maps from
he Magnetic Island Visitors' Information office, an easy-to-find bright green and
orange building at the foot of the quay at Picnic Beach. They can give you details
of the man-made developments on the island, such as the Oasis Koala Park at
Horseshoe Bay and the Marine Gardens Shark World at Nelly Bay. The
cheapest place to stay is at the Youth Hostel at the Magnetic Island Recreation
Camp near Picnic Bay (tel: 077-78 5280), which costs only $5 per night; there
is a courtesy car service from the Picnic Bay Jetty. Wherever you are on the
island, beware of the local possums which take a lively interest in anything that
might contain food.

The passenger-only ferry from Townsville departs from the Hayles ferry office
at 168 Flinders St (on the north side of Ross Creek, 200m east from the end
of Flinders Mall); call 71 6927 for the latest schedules. There are about ten
services each day. Most serve only Picnic Bay (at the western corner of the
island; journey time 40 minutes) but some continue to Arcadia. The return fare
is $8, or you pay up to $25 for a day tour including a bus trip along the island's
coast and lunch at one of the resorts. Barges carrying vehicles across to the
Arcadia wharf on the island, so unless you rent one of the many Mokes for hire,
you will have to rely upon hitching, taxis or your legs.

The remaining 340km from Townsville to Cairns is not devoid of interest,
although as the wettest area of Australia its attraction may not be immediately
obvious during one of the frequent downpours. Inland there is a series of
National Parks — including the spectacular waterfalls of Jourama, Yamanie
and Herbert River — while offshore many of the islands are being developed
as resorts. Don't plan to stay the night at any of the new resorts unless you are
willing to pay at least $100 per person.

Halfway between Silkwood and Innisfail, on the road that runs between the
Bruce Highway and the sea, is Paranella Park. This is a fascinating folly in the

shape of a gaudily decorated Spanish castle. It has fallen into some disrepair, but you may find this enhances its appeal. The entrance fee is only $2.

CAIRNS

Cairns has all the elements of a traveller's utopia: sunny climate, relaxed tropical atmosphere, cheap places to stay and eat, and an endless variety of activities. Not surprisingly, there seems to be as many visitors on the street as locals (who at the last count numbered 70,000). And the expansion of Cairns as an arrival/departure point in Australia will ensure that the popularity of what was once a sleepy backwater keeps on increasing, although its charm is being noticeably diminished by mass tourism.

Cairns (prounounced as a cross between "cans" and "kens") is a long way from virtually everywhere. The nearest state or national capital is Port Moresby, 750km away in Papua New Guinea. Townsville, 600km south, is the only city of any size relatively nearby while Brisbane, Darwin, and Alice Springs are all close to the 2,000km mark. Although improvements to the roads, railway and airport have been made, the town retains its feeling of splendid isolation. Originally known as Trinity Bay, Cairns battled with the town of Port Douglas further north for supremacy in the far north of Queensland. The choice of Cairns as a railway junction ensured its success, although now the major source of revenue for the town is the tourist trade. What brings many of the visitors is, of course, the Great Barrier Reef; Cairns is one of the points along the coast where the reef is most accessible. But the town is also close to some of the best country in Australia, both inland on the Atherton Tablelands and north along the coast.

Climate. Being so far north the town has the typically tropical wet and dry seasons, the Wet (described euphemistically in tourist literature as the "rainbow season") lasting from around December until March. If you have planned a southern summer trip to Australia, however, don't be put off a visit to Cairns for fear of the weather. The rain is largely concentrated in sharp bursts, and Cairns itself enjoys enough sea breezes to keep the humidity down. But don't expect to get very far north from the city during the Wet since many roads are washed out.

ARRIVAL AND DEPARTURE

Air. The airport serving Cairns is just off the Cook Highway, 6km north of the city. In the last decade international services have expanded from one or two per week to a dozen or more, with flights to New Zealand, Singapore, Port Moresby, Tokyo and the west coast of North America. Domestic services are also numerous, including low-cost flights on East-West to Ayers Rock, Perth, Brisbane, Sydney and Melbourne. A minibus service links the airport with hotels in the city to connect with arriving and departing flights. The one-way fare is $3.50, and you should call 53 4722 to confirm a pick-up time.

There are several agencies specializing in low-cost international flights; STA Travel's local agent is YHA Travel at 67 Esplanade (tel: 51 9385).

Train. The station on McLeod St (tel: 51 1111) at the top of Shield St has services daily except Sundays to Brisbane, departing at 8.15am on Tuesdays and 7.15am on other days. There are additional services three times each week as far as Tully. Trains also run twice daily on the line up to the Tablelands. Most visitors take the special Kuranda Tourist Train, a collection of old-time carriages which stops halfway up at the Barron Falls for photography; see *Around Cairns* for more details. If you want to save money or avoid the tourist crowds, take one of the ordinary trains which leave at 9am daily and 3.40pm (except Sundays) and cost just $3 each way, saving $11 on the excursion fare.

Bus. There are plenty of competing companies on the Cairns-Brisbane run, and fares are correspondingly low. The Ansett Pioneer terminal is at 58 Shield St (51 2411), and Greyhound is at 78 Grafton St (51 3131). Other operators include Deluxe, Sunliner, and McCafferty's. Buses to the north and west are less frequent, although the service to Port Douglas and Mossman is adequate.

Hitch-hiking. There is a lot of competition hitching south from Cairns, so if you want to be sure of a ride check the lift-share notices at one of the hostels or ask around at the Backpackers' Restaurant (see *Eating and Drinking,* below), which is always full of people on the move. If you prefer (or are obliged through lack of funds) to hitch, you could try thumbing at the beginning of the Bruce Highway by Parramatta Park; get there by walking along Mulgrave Road and Florence St. For a faster start, book ahead for the morning train south from Cairns and invest $3 in the journey as far as Gordonvale. Hitching north is easier; for Port Douglas, Mossman and Kuranda, simply start walking out along Sheridan St which eventually becomes the Cook Highway. The road up to Kuranda branches off to the left a few kilometres out of town, so it's worth using a sign.

CITY TRANSPORT

City Layout. Cairns is a compact town. Although the suburbs sprawl a fair way out, all the major lodgings, attractions and places to eat are within easy walking distance. The centre spreads back from the Esplanade on the seashore to the railway station on McLeod St. The Shield St Mall is the heart of the city.

Public Transport. A fairly good local bus service links the centre with outlying suburbs. You can pick up maps and timetables from the Information Centre at the corner of Sheridan and Aplin Streets. For information by telephone, call the Transport Department on 51 5732.

Cycling. Cairns has the merits of being flat with wide roads and having little traffic. Bikes may be hired from several hostels or from a hire shop such as Cairns Cycle Centre, 15a Sheridan St (51 1545); Earlville Cycles, 503 Mulgrave Road (a little out of town at Earlville 54 3500); Sheridan St Bicycle Barn, 61 Sheridan St (51 7135) and the Trinity Cycle Works, 6 Aplin St (51 6380).

Car. The ideal transport if you want to drive is a Moke, which can be rented from Cairns Rent-A-Car (147c Lake St; 51 6077) or Peter's Rent-A-Car (276 Sheridan St; 51 4106). The RACQ emergency breakdown number is 51 6543.

ACCOMMODATION

Cairns is blessed with a large number of backpackers' hostels. You may find that when you step off the bus or train, you are surrounded by representatives of all the hostels, each trying to attract your custom. Such is the scale of the tourist invasion, however, that places are quite often full and it is worth booking ahead. Expect to pay around \$7-\$8 a night for a dormitory bed or bunk. A disadvantage with many of the places is their size and impersonality: Caravella, Jimmy's and the Youth Hostel — all on the Esplanade — suffer from this, as do the Parkview on Grafton St and the Backpackers Inn at 255 Lake St (51 9166). One excellent alternative is the Gone Walkabout Hostel at 27 Draper St behind the railway station (51 6160); a 28-bed house run by extremely friendly owners who live next door and operate (until now!) by word-of-mouth. They also run extremely cheap tours to the Tablelands. Prices are \$7 a night or \$45 a week. This place also doesn't suffer from the incidence of thefts from dormitories which afflict some of the larger places. The Pacific Coast Budget Accommodation chain has a typically old and rambling (but comfortable) hotel close to the station, at 100 Sheridan St (51 1264). A single room costs \$15, a double \$24; rates include a light breakfast. There are a number of campgrounds close to the city centre. If you wish to enjoy more comfort Cairns has a burgeoning number of deluxe hotels which sometimes offer special low rates during the wet season.

EATING AND DRINKING

Cairns has one of the best deals in Australia in the form of Backpackers' Restaurant in the mall. The price is \$4 for all you can pile onto a sizeable plate, and you can choose from four or five different main courses plus salad. Drinks are also cheap. With prices so low, the place is packed out every night. Slightly upmarket and certainly less crowded is Fresco's at 141 Grafton St, with the same deal as Backpackers' for \$4.50; this place is popular with the many visitors on diving courses. Cairns has numerous vegetarian, steak, Chinese and Italian restaurants, most of which are very good value. A stroll around the centre, particularly along Grafton St will turn up plenty, all of which are pleasant and reasonably priced. In particular, try Little Gringo's at 95, Ricardo's at 89, and Milliways at 142 (which calls itself "The Restaurant at the End of the Universe"). For drinking you have a choice between the bars of swanky hotels or some regular Queensland pubs.

ENTERTAINMENT

Despite its small population, there is a great deal to do in Cairns: from nightclubs to greyhound racing, and art galleries to zoos. Simply strolling around is also good entertainment. Little remains in Cairns of the early colonial days, but the lack of historic buildings is compensated for by the lively and picturesque waterfront. An evening walk to ogle at the marlin fishermen's gin palaces is recommended. The esplanade which runs north from the small yacht harbour is separated from the sea by a wide strip of parkland, with shaded areas ideal for picnicking.

While Cairns is too small and too isolated to attract top-notch performers, there is plenty of evening entertainment. A scan through the free *This Week in Cairns* will reveal which pubs and hotels are currently hosting live bands, and the longer residents at any of the hostels will know which clubs and discos are in vogue. There are four cinemas, including the Coral drive-in on the Bruce Highway, and a couple of small theatres.

HELP AND INFORMATION

The area code for Cairns and environs is 070. The main information office is the Far North Queensland Promotion Bureau at the corner of Sheridan and Aplin Streets (51 3588). The Queensland Government Travel Centre at 12 Shield St (51 4066) is more concerned with selling travel throughout the state than providing local information.

While Cairns could hardly be described as dangerous, an increasing amount of petty theft and clashes between drunken locals and (probably drunk) travellers have been reported. You should not allow the tropical tranquility to catch you completely off guard.

American Express: The local agent is the Northern Australian Travel Agency at 91 Grafton St (51 6472).
Medical Treatment: Cairns Base Hospital, Esplanade (50 6333).
Dental Emergencies: 51 6995.

AROUND CAIRNS

The Islands and Reef. Nowhere else on the coast is so highly organized for trips out to the nearby islands and the reef itself. There are a great number of options, sold direct by boat companies at the harbourside or through hostels and hotels. The main destination is Green Island, on the reef proper just over the horizon from Cairns. Its popularity as a day-trip destination means it possesses many man-made trappings, but the sheer fascination of the reef more than compensates for the crowds and production-line tourism. A standard day trip from Cairns is aboard a big, fast catamaran which stops off at both Heron Island (a small sand island with interesting bird life) and Green Island, then sails a little further out on the reef where it moors for the passengers to enjoy an hour or two of snorkelling. Use of snorkelling equipment is included in the tour price of around $50, and those with a diving qualification can hire scuba gear. Ropes are extended from the vessel and attached to buoys to give a hand-hold and thus provide reassurance to those unused to swimming so far from the shore.

There are many other variations on this theme, from a simple round trip to Green Island ($15) to expeditions involving a combination of boomnetting (being dragged along through the water in a net behind a speeding boat), glass-bottomed boat trips and the more exciting ride in a semi-submersible craft — the closest most people get to a real submarine. Some travellers strongly recommend a diving course (see below) as the best way to see the reef, and indeed since learning to dive costs as little as four times as much as a day trip to the reef they have a point.

Lizard Island is much further north and a far more exclusive destination, reputedly one of Prince Charles's favourite spots. Most visitors fly in (one hour and $120 from Cairns), and stay in luxurious and expensive accommodation while enjoying the beauty and relative solitude of this part of the reef.

The Atherton Tablelands. This plateau inland from Cairns is a lush dairy farming area, which British visitors often compare with the West Country of England. The most popular destination in the Tablelands is the small town of Kuranda, set in rainforest high above Cairns. Apart from the prettiness of the town and its setting, the main attractions are the Sunday markets and the faintly alternative communal-type atmosphere, although Kuranda is rapidly becoming a fully-fledged tourist trap. The Youth Hostel is at 6 Arara St, Kuranda (93 7355). There is an interesting museum of pioneer days whose location you can't fail to see: the entrance is overshadowed by an apparently crashed World War II aircraft (actually placed there strategically as a publicity stunt). The $5 admission charge is not unreasonable since it includes a cream tea at the end of your visit.

There are numerous bus tours to the area from Cairns, the cheapest being the $5 trip run by the Gone Walkabout Hostel. But whether you take the Tourist Train or travel on one of the regular services, rail is the best way to reach Kuranda. The journey ends at the beautiful fern-filled and much-photographed Railway Station. However, the return price on the Tourist Train (with commentary, photo-stop en route and a free booklet complete with an "Adventure Certificate") is $17, while the ordinary trains from Cairns cost only $6 return.

Other attractions on the Tablelands and the Cairns hinterland include Lake Eacham, a freshwater rain-filled lake surrounded by rainforest; the Curtain Fig Tree, a spectacular example of tree parasitism (a tree which becomes draped with, and is eventually killed by, a parasite vine); Josephine Falls; and the Babinda Boulders. Whitewater rafting trips are available on the Tully river, down the coast from Cairns.

North of Cairns. This area is one of beautiful beaches, rainforest stretching down to the sea and spots where Captain Cook had some of his unhappiest experiences (Cape Tribulation, Mount Sorrow, etc). The Cook Highway north to Port Douglas provides excellent coastal scenery, with several lookouts over the most dramatic stretches. After a hundred quiet years, Port Douglas is now experiencing a boom with the construction of a massive new resort. The township is the furthest north that many travellers venture, since the roads soon become impassable except by four-wheel drive vehicles. Despite the new buildings, the town has retained much of its quiet and elegant character. It has the flavour of an affluent village set in a well-kept park, surrounded by gentle hills offering pleasant coastal walks.

Assuming you are not rich enough to stay at the latest resort hotel, try the much-recommended Port Douglas Travellers Hostel (affiliated to the Backpackers' chain) at 111 Davidson St (tel: 070-98 5200). A dormitory bed costs $8 per night and allows you to use the swimming pool, barbecue facilities and common room building. Eating should not present much of a problem if you've come to terms with the Australian meat pie; Mocka's Pies on the main street is probably the most famous pie shop in the nation, and claims with some justification to offer the best.

There are tours out to the offshore Low Isles (a coral cay) on the catamaran *Quick Cat,* costing around $75 for the day with optional bus transport from Cairns. A marine biologist gives an illustrated talk before the boat departs. Call 070-98 5373 for more details.

Mossman, a sugar town near the end of the tarred road, has the beautiful Mossman Gorge to visit. Further north is Daintree and the Daintree Ferry, the barge which takes you across the river for the road to Cape Tribulation. A trip up to Cape Tribulation is one of the most worthwhile things to do in the far north, although you and all your gear will be covered in dirt by the time you get there. The Cape is accessible by Coral Coaches ($32 return from Cairns) or as a two-day tour which can be booked through the Cairns Youth Hostel for around $40 all-in. Over 40km of dirt road (which is little more than a muddy track in places) takes you through the national park up to the Cape itself. You will need a mountain bike if you wish to cycle there, and should be prepared for the constant stream of four-wheel drive trucks transporting less energetic visitors. Beware of the ford across the Bloomfield River, where the water often conceals dangerous boulders just below the surface. There is a campground on the Cape and also the Jungle Lodge, a hostel with attractive huts set in rainforest for $8.50 a night (but beware of the low-flying bats which sometimes intrude). Unless you go on an organized tour from Cairns, you need to book a bed well in advance. Horseriding and bushwalks are on offer, as well as tropical fruit-tasting and trips out to the reef. Walking through the lush rainforest (where creepers can grow a metre in a week) can be most rewarding.

The Daintree area has been a centre of environmental controversy: the Queensland government has been accused of exploiting the rainforest for commercial logging, damaging the natural environment by the construction of the Bloomfield Track linking the Cape to Bloomfield and causing erosion which threatens parts of the reef. The federal government has nominated the rainforest to the World Heritage List, restricting the commercial exploitation of Daintree and enraging the local timbermen who make a living from it. If the area is added to the List, some industry may continue but the new road will probably be closed down.

Cooktown. If you have a suitable vehicle, you can continue from Bloomfield up to the old gold-mining town of Cooktown (which can also be reached by bus from Cairns over a more circuitous route). In the Gold Rush of the 1880s, it had 41 hotels and 45,000 inhabitants; now it has less than a thousand people, but retains some lovely colonial facades.

CAPE YORK PENINSULA

The first area of Australia to be explored by Europeans is now the continent's last frontier. Virtually all of the massive finger pointing north towards Papua New Guinea has escaped the attention of white settlers. Its unspoilt beauty has been preserved by its extreme isolation. The inland scenery is an almost impenetrable jungle of thick scrub and rainforest, threaded with crocodile-infested creeks. The beaches on both sides of the peninsula are tropical gems and almost invariably deserted. To see these isolated places you will have to join a tour (see *Great Outdoors: Outback Adventures,* below).

Although much of Cape York is Aboriginal land — and thus likely to be preserved as it has been for centuries — the peninsula's isolation may soon be lessened by the construction of a satellite launch site on the western edge. At the time of writing, the government of Queensland has asked for tenders to build a spaceport at one of two locations near the Cape. Being just 12 degrees south of the equator and with predictable weather, launching space vehicles from this area would be cheaper than at most other sites, and it is claimed that American, Soviet and Chinese space organizations have expressed interest in using the site. If the project comes to fruition, a rapid development of support industries and tourism — and protest by conservationists — is inevitable.

The Cape itself is the most northerly point on the Australian mainland, but many of the islands in the Torres Strait between Queensland and Papua New Guinea are Australian territory. They are the homelands of the Torres Strait Islanders, a race distinct from the Aboriginal groups on the mainland and with their own unique culture. Turnagain Island is the northernmost Australian possession, just 35km from the mainland of Papua New Guinea.

THE GULF

The shoreline around the Gulf of Carpentaria is mostly saline swampland, changing further from the sea to savannah grassland laced with creeks and dotted with salt pans. Until the Gulf Development Road from the east coast is fully sealed, access is best by air to Karumba or Burketown; the alternative is a difficult road journey. The native fauna is even less hospitable than the terrain, with crocodiles a real threat to those venturing near the water, and poisonous spiders and snakes inland.

The first Europeans to arrive at the Gulf by land were the transcontinental explorers Robert Burke and William Wills, who reached the area (but, because of the swamps, not quite the sea) in 1861. Their journey is commemorated by place names such as Wills Creek, the "Burke and Wills Roadhouse" and Burketown. This latter settlement was Nevil Shute's model for the town of Willstown (a play on the names Burke and Wills) in his novel *A Town Like Alice*. It is a dry, dusty settlement which has never attained the dream of Shute's heroine, Jean Paget, of being "a town as good as Alice Springs". However, it is an excellent centre for studying the prolific wildlife in the area, and plenty of organised tours are available.

Karumba is a busy prawn-trawling port with job opportunities for those prepared to spend weeks aboard a trawler for uncertain reward. Inland along the wide Norman River, Normanton is at one end of the Gulflander railway line, a charming "line to nowhere" which was built to transport ore from the old gold-mining centre of Croydon, 150km east, to the port at Normanton. Nowadays there is one service each week in each direction, using a monstrously primitive engine hauling antiquated coaches.

INLAND QUEENSLAND

Mount Isa and Western Queensland. Most travellers visit this region of Queensland only through necessity, since it is en route from the coast to the Northern Territory. The long-distance buses funnel through Mount Isa and you may be tempted to disembark and take a break for a day or two. The attractions of this mining town (it has the world's largest silver-lead mine) and its surroundings would be unlikely to sustain a longer stay, although a visit to the Underground Museum or a tour around the Mount Isa mine can be fascinating. The most interesting attraction nearby is Sun Rock (about 40km north, close to the Barkly Highway) which has fine Aboriginal paintings in red ochre. Access is limited, and you should apply to the Ranger based at the Old Court House in Mount Isa for permission to visit. The Mount Isa Youth Hostel (tel: 077-43 5557) is on Wellington Park Road, opposite the Velodrome, and costs $7 per night.

Channel Country. Only intrepid travellers would wish to visit this desolate region in the south west of Queensland. It is so-called because of the many channels formed when normally dry creeks overflow after the rare rainfalls. Such is the paucity of precipitation that Lake Yamma Yamma (near Haddon Corner, where South Australia intrudes into Queensland) has been full only twice this century. Highways in the area have recently been improved with the construction of new "beef roads" for transporting cattle in the region, but are prone to be impassable in the unlikely event of a rainstorm. The region is most notable for relics of the pioneer past.

The state borders of Queensland, South Australia and New South Wales meet at Cameron Corner. About 100km north is the Dig Tree, where Burke and Wills died on their journey back from the Gulf of Carpentaria. The legend surrounding this sad event is gripping, if a little improbable. The Dig Tree is so-called because when the two explorers returned from their epic four-month expedition to the Gulf, they expected to find a relief party waiting, as arranged, at the solitary tree. But the party had moved off the day before, leaving a message pinned to the tree reading "dig 40 feet west". Burke and Wills did so and found some supplies, then carefully reburied the remainder so that Aboriginals would not find them. They then set off in search of the relief party, but headed in the wrong direction. Meanwhile the relief party decided to check one last time but, on finding the supplies apparently undisturbed, they abandoned Burke and Wills for good. The unfortunate explorers eventually returned to the Dig Tree, where they starved to death. A monument has been erected to their memory, and numerous four-wheel drive tourists visit the gnarled old tree.

Those properly equipped can cross the nearby border into South Australia and head north then west to Birdsville. Those less well prepared can fly there direct from Brisbane and several other points, as many do for the annual race meeting each September. The town (usual population 100) is at the top of the cattle track that bears its name, which runs 486km south to Marree in South Australia. For decades cattle were driven along the Birdsville Track to the former railhead at Marree, for onward transportation to the south and east. Birdsville is still an important cattle town (although new roads mean that the journey along the Track is no longer necessary) and lies on the edge of the bleak Simpson Desert. Its isolation does not deter the thousands of visitors to the Birdsville Races. Beer is imported by road train to the town's only pub, the Royal Hotel on Main St (tel: 011 and ask for Birdsville 15). Accommodation is in extremely short supply, so many racegoers sleep under trucks or beneath their light aircraft.

Beaches. Queensland's endless beaches are not only appealing to look at, they are almost unbearably tempting to swim from. Most slope gently down to the warm ocean, protected from the roughest seas by the reef. Despite the occasional shark, swimming is usually safe anywhere on the coast during the winter and spring months from June to November (although you should not bathe near river mouths in the north due to the risk of crocodile attacks). During the rest of the year, however, swimming from the northern part of the coast can be risky. Signs warning of danger from marine stingers are posted along the coast from Mackay northwards. Although they may overstate the period during which these creatures pose a threat, to be on the safe side the warnings should be heeded. It is frustrating to happen upon a deserted beach yet not be able to cool off in the sea, but save your swimming gear for the islands. Beaches on most of the offshore islands are free of marine stingers throughout the year, and you can swim, snorkel or dive quite safely. Note that a few of the islands close to the shore (such as Magnetic Island) are not free of the menace, although stinger nets are strung across some of the popular beaches. You should always take local advice before you take the plunge. For emergency treatment advice for sea wasps dial the toll-free Marine Stingers Line on 008-01 5160.

Diving. To select from the many competing schools, ask newly-qualified divers (of whom there are many) to assess which appears to be the best. Most courses last for five days, and the cheapest cost around $200. Normally three days are spent learning the technique in a swimming pool, followed by two days (or a day and a night) on the reef. Unless you are abjectly useless (i.e. afraid of the water), you will almost certainly earn a certificate as a qualified diver.

Sailing. Yachting enthusiasts from all over the world travel to Queensland to take advantage of the excellent sailing made possible by the many harbours dotted along the coast, the beautiful shore, and islands with safe anchorages and predictable weather. There are plenty of bareboat yachts available for charter. Bowen, Townsville, Cairns and the Whit Sunday Islands are popular bases. The largest operation is Whit Sunday Rent-a-Yacht, based at Shute Harbour. Costs are high: about $200 a day for a five berth vessel, or $550 for a luxury yacht sleeping eight. You can get cheaper rates through Checkmate (tel: 008-07 5067), who rent four-berth Hood 23 yachts for $500 per week off season. Instead of chartering a yacht, you could either sail as a paying passenger or try to charm a yachtsman and hitch a lift. The best places to try to get a free ride are Townsville, Shute Harbour and Bowen.

Cycling. The journey north from Brisbane along the Bruce Highway is not as enjoyable as it might appear from a glance at a map. The road is very busy and rarely runs right along the coast. You should look for interesting detours taking you further from the sea but using more pleasant roads; the inland route from Brisbane to Rockhampton via Gayndah and Biloela is quiet and scenic and, while not well-surfaced, is a pleasant ride. The next section north from Rockhampton to Mackay is desolate with only a couple of roadhouses and a few small townships on the 350km stretch of road. North of Mackay the traffic eases, but you may soon tire of rattling over the numerous railway crossings which link the sugar cane plantations. Going north in this way you will find a very helpful tailwind which will blow you all the way to Cairns, Mossman, Daintree and beyond. However, the tarmac stops at Daintree, and an all-terrain bike is essential for any further progress. The run up to the Tablelands west of Cairns can be an enjoyable ride, doubly so on the steep descent.

If you prefer not to battle against the headwinds all the way back to Brisbane, your bicycle can accompany you by bus or train. The cost of transporting a bike from Cairns to Brisbane is $12.60 by train, $10 by Greyhound (dismantled) or $20 by Greyhound (assembled). Dogs, a common hazard for cyclists everywhere in Australia, seem particularly vicious in Queensland; watch out for the one halfway between Mossman and Wonga Beach which is not averse to biting passing cyclists.

Outback Adventures. There are large tracts of Queensland where inexperienced travellers should not venture independently, but you may rest assured that there are plenty of tour operators willing to sell you a place on a package trip. Each company is licensed by the state government, but some expect more from their clients than others. While the established organization AAT/Kings (103 The Esplanade, Cairns; tel: 51 9299) may be too conventional for your tastes, you might prefer their well-planned tours to the one offered by one contractor who — after his expedition had to be rescued from Cape York — accused the participants of being a "bunch of wimps". As with diving schools, ask other travellers for their recommendations of the various tours on offer. Often the cheapest and most enjoyable tours are those organized by local hostels, but they also fill up the quickest. There are also numerous low-budget tours of Queensland organized from elsewhere in Australia and featuring a wide variety of activities; try Coast Rangers of Sydney (02-387 5995).

To sample the virgin territory north of Cairns you should go sooner rather than later, as increasing tourism and commercial development are rapidly encroaching upon the wilderness. You can choose between an expensive, comfortable tour by air or a slightly cheaper four-wheel drive overland expedition from Cairns. The minimum cost of a one-week land safari is around $1000. Tours using one of the four weekly flights between Cairns and Jackey Jackey airfield (just south of the Cape) with accommodation at the Cape York Wilderness Lodge start at about $1,200; bookings can be made through Queensland Government Travel Centres. You may, however, find a much cheaper day trip by air from Cairns as far north as Cooktown; you fly over the Atherton Tablelands, visit Cooktown then return flying low over the reef; prices are typically $100 including lunch.

Most overland tours north of Cairns take the coastal route to Cooktown, then strike inland skirting an Aboriginal Reserve to Lakefield National Park, the biggest in Queensland and with outstanding flora and fauna. The journey up to the Cape then becomes really rough, with narrow bush tracks and repeated difficult crossings of creeks.

Restricted Areas. There are two military reserves on the coast of Queensland — Wide Bay near Gympie, and Shoalwater Bay north of Rockhampton — where entry is prohibited. In addition, numerous areas in far north Queensland are Aboriginal Reserves, many of which require approval in writing from the Aboriginal Affairs Department.

Calendar of Events

January	World Series Cricket, Brisbane
February	Redcliffe Yacht Classic
March	Queensland Eisteddfod, Ipswich
March/April	Easter Cup, Brisbane
March/April	Brisbane to Gladstone Yacht Race
May (first Monday)	**Labour Day**
June	Mount Isa Show
June	Magnetic Island Rediscovery
August	Mount Isa Rodeo
August	Cooee-calling Championships, Cooee Bay
August	National Agricultural Show, Brisbane
August (third Wednesday)	**Brisbane Exhibition Day (public holiday in Brisbane)**
September	Birdsville Races
September	Redlands Strawberry Festival, Cleveland
September	Winfield Cup Grand Final (Rugby League), Brisbane
late Sept/early October	Warana Spring Festival, Brisbane

Public holidays are shown in **bold**

NEW ZEALAND

New Zealand is so far from everywhere else that it was one of the last places on earth to be settled by man. Despite the coming of the jet age, much of New Zealand remains isolated in ways that will strike the recent arrival from Europe, North America or even Australia immediately. The content of some New Zealanders' lives seems to have changed very little since their forebears arrived (mostly from Great Britain) in the 19th century. Farmers still muster their sheep with dogs and rural mailmen still know everyone on their routes by name. Admittedly this is gradually becoming a romantic fiction, since the fishermen of Stewart Island do now have access to television and most rural areas have had an automatic telephone exchange installed (though these "improvements" are very recent). The village atmosphere is perhaps less strong than it was 20 years ago but it still exists. Visitors will find themselves the object of much friendly interest and curiosity which they would be unlikely to find in Middlesex, Maryland or Munich.

This unfeigned interest and concern for visitors is what makes New Zealand society unique and uniquely attractive, and which causes writers to consider New Zealand as a candidate for the "last utopia", as a piece by that title in *National Geographic* magazine recently proved. This should be sufficient to attract large numbers of tourists. But New Zealand's remoteness is a serious impediment to potential visitors. Some recent figures indicated that the cost of getting to New Zealand accounted for an average of 70% of the total price of the holiday (which sounds horrendous until you consider that this is probably true of other destinations such as India for Britons or Venezuela for North Americans).

Fortunately New Zealand has its spectacular topography as a trump card. Volcanoes, glaciers, fiords and rivers have to be outstanding to justify an investment of hundreds or thousands of pounds or dollars, but no visitor could be disappointed with the natural wonders of New Zealand. One of the most fascinating aspects of its sharp and rugged contours is that many have been altered by volcanic activity in recent times and will be altered again. New Zealand's geology, like its history, is youthful, full of potential, and quite unlike anything in Europe.

So it is not too surprising to learn that New Zealand is a contender for the accolade of fastest growing tourist destination in the world. It is estimated that a million tourists will be arriving in this country of just over three million by 1991. This astonishing figure is due in large measure to the government's efforts to promote the country. Investment in tourism has been vigorous and on the whole beneficial. Facilities from luxury hotels to campsites, from public relations offices to local museums, from river-rafting specialists to ski resorts are expanding in number and improving their amenities. Like any country which is so heavily involved with tourism, there may come a time when New Zealand will be considered "spoiled" by crass developments and crowds. But that day is a long way off, and the visitor in the late 80s and early 90s will be amazed and delighted by just how little the pressures of modern society have impinged on the landscapes and psyche of New Zealand.

CLIMATE

New Zealand's climate may come as a shock, especially if you have been travelling in the hot dry areas of Australia and are expecting its neighbour's weather to be similar. Rainfall is terrifically high on the west coast of the South Island, which is where some of the country's foremost attractions are located. An entry in the visitor's book of a hut on the Routeburn Track reads, "In New Zealand you don't tan, you rust." The New Zealand Tourist & Publicity Department plays down the fact that visitors have to be lucky to see Mount Cook or Mount Taranaki out of cloud, or to see Milford Sound in the sunshine. Their evasive description of the weather, for example "the west-facing coasts are relatively exposed and therefore good for surfing" hardly does justice to the inconvenience to walkers and sight-seers caused by frequent torrential downpours. Many places receive over 500 centimetres of rainfall (nearly ten times more than London in a wet year) and locals delight in reminiscing about the time they received 24 inches in 24 hours.

Some heavy rains are not merely irritating, they are dangerous. It is not uncommon for bridges to be washed out on South Island roads, preventing traffic from getting through for anything from a day to a fortnight. The local airport might also be under a metre of water. Roads are frequently transformed into stream beds, and motorists must dodge uprooted trees and boulders while ploughing through a foot of water. After negotiating a major road like Arthur's Pass in such conditions, it is not unusual to emerge on the eastern side of the country to find hot dry weather. The eastern coastal areas of both islands are generally much drier, with some areas even suffering an occasional summer drought.

Fluctuations of temperature between areas are not as pronounced as differences in precipitation, though the mountainous interiors of both islands usually receive enough snow from June onwards to support a vigorous ski industry. Except in the mountains, temperatures throughout New Zealand are moderate, though obviously warmer in the Bay of Islands than in Dunedin which is 11 degrees further from the equator. When transferred to the northern hemisphere the corresponding latitudes would be Crete and Bordeaux or Los Angeles and Seattle. There are occasional heat waves in December/January, but air-conditioning is uncommon, unless you are using the term as New Zealanders do to refer to heating (as well as cooling). Generally summer temperatures, especially in the North Island are sufficiently balmy for men to don shorts and knee socks (known as "walk shorts" and "walk socks") before going off to work.

Another inescapable climatic feature is wind. Although windy Wellington takes the prize, Auckland and Christchurch often become blustery too. There can also be strong winds in the mountains. Calm conditions are rare and the air always has a fresh quality.

THE PEOPLE

It is (too) often said that New Zealanders are more English than the English. If this is true, why do they make a habit of inviting strangers into their homes and sharing the addresses of their friends and relations with mere acquaintances? Even people involved in the tourist industry seem to take a more personal than commercial interest in visitors' welfare; directories of accommodation will often include a line, "your hosts: Bob and Betty Tuckwell". Their refreshing generosity and hospitality no doubt derive from a not-too-distant time in the country's history when travel was extremely difficult and settlers would not hesitate to call on other farmers either from necessity (flooded rivers, blocked roads) or for company which has always been in short supply. Even now the population of New Zealand is just 3.2 million in a country whose area is greater than Britain's.

An overwhelming majority of the post-Maori settlers have come from the United Kingdom either in this generation or in the previous three or four. New Zealand was much more reluctant than Australia in the 1960s to accept waves of immigration from Southern Europe and more recently from Southeast Asia. This means that New Zealand lacks not only the Italian delicatessens of Melbourne and the Vietnamese restaurants of Sydney, but also the cosmopolitan character which a multi-ethnic society creates. The one exception is the relatively large population of Pacific Islanders, mainly people from Samoa, Tonga, the Cook Islands and other New Zealand protectorates. Although they represent only 2.7% of the total population of New Zealand, Auckland is the largest Polynesian city in the world.

MAKING FRIENDS

The New Zealand approach to foreign visitors is quite un-English in being less guarded and formal and more openly patriotic. They sometimes refer to their country as "Godzone" (God's Own) and assume that foreigners will agree with them that New Zealand combines most of the attributes of an ideal country. (Many nationalities are guilty of this but perhaps with less justification.) This chauvinism extends to male/female relationships. Although many New Zealand males like to think of themselves as less boorish than their Australian counterparts, many are unaware of their ingrained sexism. For example you may be hard pressed to find a New Zealand man in a pub able to accept graciously a drink from a woman.

They are soft-spoken (except in a pub near closing time), and so unhurried in their reactions that in conversation you sometimes wonder for a minute or two whether they have heard you. On a personal level the majority are unpretentious and modest, to the extent that one guide book warns the unsuspecting visitor not to give a New Zealander anything with a designer label visible.

There is a certain amount of parochialism at all levels of society and many New Zealanders exhibit a breathtakingly narrow range of interests. An intimate knowledge of sheep-rearing is almost universal. However the claim that, when they are not discussing the price of lamb, they are discussing the rugby results, is grossly unfair. You will meet plenty of New Zealanders who are informed on a wide range of topics from the impact of their country's anti-nuclear foreign policy to the ethics of planting pine trees instead of the slower-growing native trees like rimu and kauri. The high proportion of New Zealanders who have travelled extensively abroad further mitigates the rural insularity often encountered.

Though on the one hand many young New Zealanders consider an "Overseas Experience" to be obligatory, they (like Australians) also tend to be dismissive of England and English culture. There is a certain amount of inverse snobbery in the Antipodean habit of denigrating the old country for its supposed obsession with class backgrounds and for its lethargy. But generally speaking individual British travellers will be welcomed as warmly as the ubiquitous Canadians, Dutch, Germans and so on. New Zealanders cannot risk being too enthusiastic about Australians, since they feel almost as culturally threatened by them as Canadians do by Americans. Also Australians abroad do seem to assume some of the arrogance associated with travelling Americans (e.g. they can be overheard complaining in loud voices about New Zealand's backwardness) and so they may deserve some of the abuse heaped upon them by the locals.

Language. North Americans find New Zealanders quaintly English because of their terminology ("bangers" for sausages, "petrol" for gas, "knickers" for underpants, etc.) But there are also many colourful words and expressions unfamiliar to the British ear. For example a "dairy" (pronounced dearie) is a corner shop, a "bach" (pronounced batch) is a modest weekend cottage in the North Island, a "crib" is ditto in the South Island, "jandals" are flip-flops, "pikelets" are a kind of scone, and so on. Many expressions heard in New Zealand are also in common Australian usage, such as "chook" for chicken, "paddock" for field, "bludger" for sponger, "shout" for buying a round in a pub, etc. But don't assume that all Aussie expressions will be understood: if you ask a New Zealander what he has in his "Esky" he will probably return a blank stare. In New Zealand parlance that useful object, the insulated drinks cooler, is called a "chillybin".

A number of Maori words have entered the language of English-speaking New Zealanders such as *hangi* for earth-oven, *marae* for a Maori meetinghouse and enclosure, *pakeha* as a non-derogatory term for white person, etc. See below for more details about the Maori language.

The accent takes a little getting used to especially if you spend much time discussing the relative merits of different fush and chup shops. If you happen to overhear some locals talking about a "pine in the nick" do not assume that they are talking about a conifer in prison.

American readers will be especially interested in an amusing little book called *A Personal Kiwi-Yankee Dictionary* by Louis S. Leland Jr. on sale in airport bookshops and elsewhere.

THE MAORI PEOPLE

Seafaring Polynesians with a relatively advanced culture landed their giant canoes on the shores of New Zealand 700-1,000 years ago. Whereas Aboriginals represent a mere 1.5% of Australia's population, the Maori people comprise 9% of New Zealanders and are very much in evidence. Most of them — today it is 94% — remained on the North Island since in former times their limited food supplies would not permit them to survive the harsher South Island winter. You will soon notice that Maori place names — not too difficult to pronounce but hard to remember — are much more comon in the North than the South. If you walk into a North Island pub, chances are there will be a high proportion of Maori people who are quite likely to be evenly dispersed among the *Pakeha* (European) drinkers. The level of integration is a pleasant surprise after Australia. Mixed marriages are commonplace and most white New Zealanders whose families were among the early settlers have at least one Maori ancestor. This is cause for pride, since Maori culture has achieved a certain amount of respect both in New Zealand and internationally.

According to the official line as typified in the government tourist literature, integration of the Maori into New Zealand society is total: "today both Maori and Pakeha are a united population, sharing the same legal rights and enjoying a harmony experienced in few other countries." This version does not take into account the vociferous minority who maintain that the land deals between European settlers and the Maori people in the 19th century were unfair and should be renegotiated. The Treaty of Waitangi, which gives its name to New Zealand's national day (February 6), was signed in 1840 but has never been ratified by the British or New Zealand governments. If it were to be ratified (which, politically, is out of the question) the Maori would come into possession of a great deal more land than they hold at present. The sympathy of white New Zealanders with the Maori cause usually stops short of condoning the return of land which may have been farmed by Europeans for 100 years.

The government reserves certain places in government and the civil service for the Maori and has actively tried to foster the culture and language to the point where, according to a speech made by Prime Minister Lange in 1987, the Maori language will eventually have the same standing in New Zealand as English. In fact all Maori people speak English (usually with a particularly strong New Zealand accent) and many do not speak Maori at all. But with government assistance there is now a flourishing Maori-run network of kindergartens called *kohanga reo*, where pre-school children learn the Maori language, history and mythology.

Maori culture (known as Maoritanga) is more accessible to the visitor than Aboriginal culture. You might be honoured enough to be invited to a *hangi*, a Maori feast, after getting to know some of the locals. Maori legends are commonly quoted and usually involve mountains falling out with one another or making unsuitable marriages. Much of New Zealand's best literature such as Keri Hulme's *Bone People* and Maurice Shadbolt's books draw upon elements of Pacific mythology. This richly storied system of belief did not prevent the Maori from accepting the white man's religion (with certain adaptations) very quickly, and interesting architectural hybrids resulted.

The Maori Collection at the Auckland Museum provides a good introduction. Rotorua, about four hours south of Auckland, is the heavily promoted centre of Maori tourism and is discussed in detail below. Unless you are willing to put up with the artificial and commercial atmosphere of Rotorua and places like it, you are unlikely to see Maori dances, music or rituals. Many *maraes* do welcome visits from interested parties, though formal ceremonies (which entail the traditional *hongi* greeting of pressed noses) are rare. Maori handicrafts are easier to find since carvings from wood, bone, shell and jade are sold in souvenir shops throughout the country.

IMMIGRATION

Most nationalities, including British, Irish, Canadian and US, require only a passport to enter New Zealand. Some official sources maintain that it should be valid for at least six months, others for only three months, beyond your intended departure from New Zealand. Although the expiry date will be checked when you check in for your flight to New Zealand it is unlikely that the six month rule would be enforced. Until recently Australians required only proof of identity to enter New Zealand, but they now need passports. Arriving British tourists are usually granted a stay of six months, whereas Canadians and most Europeans are allowed three months, and Americans one month. To satisfy the immigration officers at arrival, you may be asked to show a return or onward ticket and enough money to fund your stay. In fact, if you look sufficiently well-heeled, they are unlikely to challenge you. The amount considered appropriate is NZ$1,000 for each month of your proposed stay or NZ$400 if you can show a letter from a New Zealand resident promising to provide accommodation and support. As in almost every country of the world, foreign nationals admitted as tourists are not allowed to work, though there are special provisions for working holidaymakers (see *Work* section).

It is not too difficult to obtain an extension of your stay from the Immigration section of the Department of Labour (addresses in local telephone directories) but only up to a further six months.

For more complete information on immigration requirements, contact the New Zealand High Commission, New Zealand House, 80 Haymarket, London SW1Y 4TQ (tel: 01-930 8422). Leaflet L75 is for those who intend to stay temporarily whereas L71 is for people who are considering emigrating. American citizens should contact the New Zealand Embassy at 37 Observatory Circle NW, Washington DC 20008.

CUSTOMS

You will be issued on the flight with "Passenger Arrival Papers", a combined immigration/quarantine/customs form. As in Australia, all incoming aircraft (except those arriving from directly across the Tasman) are sprayed on arrival by the Department of Agriculture. Upon landing there will be an announcement pleading with you to remain seated, since the fumigators will refuse to board the aircraft if people are standing.

New Zealand is very serious about protecting its agriculture from imported nasties. All arriving travellers must complete an Agriculture Quarantine form, declaring the potentially harmful contents of their luggage, including food of any kind, raw or processed. Many seemingly innocuous items such as tinned fish, shelled nuts, coffee beans and straw hats must be inspected for pests and diseases and treated if necessary. More exotic items such as bird's nest soup and dead bees are completely prohibited. In addition to all animal, plant and other food products, you are required to declare any "used tents, sporting equipment or other camping equipment" and also bicycles. If you confess that you have visited a farm or forest in the 30 days preceding your arrival in New Zealand, you may be asked to subject your footwear to disinfectant spray. Large "amnesty bins" are provided at international airports, urging you to dump your illegal imports before reaching Customs.

Goods and Currency. The standard duty-free allowances are 200 cigarettes or 250 grams of tobacco, 4.5 litres of wine or beer and 1.125 litres (40 fl oz) of spirits. Only passengers over the age of 17 are entitled to the allowance.

There is no limit on the amount of New Zealand or foreign currency allowed in or out. You are supposed to declare gifts if their combined value exceeds NZ$500.

The duty on luxury goods is very heavy, for example cassette players, clock radios and jewellery are charged at 59% of their value. Therefore some visitors try to make a profit by selling electronic goods and cameras in New Zealand which they have bought cheaply in Hong Kong or Singapore. Make sure that the equipment you are carrying looks convincingly like your "personal effects". And don't forget to surrender all your drugs, pornography and knuckledusters to the airport Customs official, since these are prohibited. For full details, request the leaflet *New Zealand Customs Guide for Travellers* from the Collector of Customs, Private Bag, Wellington.

Drugs. New Zealand Customs dogs must be among the fittest in the world since they do their sniffing while walking on-the-spot on baggage conveyor belts.

Travellers in the Antipodes who wish to earn some money have traditionally tended to work in Australia rather than New Zealand, partly because wages are higher in Australia, and because New Zealand does not offer a working holiday visa to British travellers. Australian citizens are free to take up employment at any time and US students can apply for a temporary work permit (see below).

In fact the minimum wage in New Zealand has just been raised from $4.25 to $5.25 — admittedly still less than in Australia — and unemployment is under 6% (considerably less than Australia's). Furthermore the visa regulations have recently been relaxed. If a traveller from the UK finds some seasonal work, he or she can take an offer of employment to the local Department of Labour and ask for a temporary work permit (maximum 12 months). Most people do not bother and encounter few difficulties, though in areas where there is high unemployment and a high concentration of foreign workers (such as Hawke's Bay), immigration swoops have been reported and visitor's visas have been revoked. If you can manage to regularize your status, you will be given an eight-digit International Revenue number and do not need to worry about the possibility of deportation.

Official Schemes. Undergraduates at British universities might be eligible for the vocational exchange scheme administered by the Careers Research and Advisory Council (Bateman Street, Cambridge CB2 1LZ) for the period July to September. Application should be made to June Motts in November for the following (northern) summer. GAP Activity Projects send several participants to New Zealand. American students are eligible to apply for a six-month work permit from CIEE (205 East 42nd St, New York, NY 10017) to work between May and October; the fee is $72. Also the Canadian Universities Travel Service (CUTS) administers a work abroad scheme for Canadian students in several countries including New Zealand. The registration fee is C$135. Most students experience little difficulty in finding jobs in catering, retailing, farming, etc. The point of allowing foreigners to work only during the New Zealand winter is in order to prevent competition with New Zealand students seeking holiday jobs during the summer.

FRUIT PICKING

The climate of New Zealand lends itself to fruit-growing of many kinds including citrus fruits and kiwifruit. You may find fruit-picking work by reading the notices in, for example, youth hostels or by approaching farmers directly, possibly after getting their names and addresses from the owners of small country stores. There is also a growing trade in fruits and vegetables from roadside stalls and direct from the farmers' properties, so you should keep your eyes open while travelling along country roads where you might even see signs posted "Pickers Wanted", and read the advertisements in local newspapers in order to get an idea of what is being picked where. Just turning up in town and asking around is a safe bet for work while the season is on. Below are some general guidelines as to what areas to head for in the appropriate seasons. Motueka, the Bay of Plenty and Kerikeri are favourites among travellers.

Most farmers are able to provide some kind of accommodation which is useful in a climate as rainy as New Zealand's. Farmers often provide fresh fruit and vegetables, milk and sometimes lamb. Some farmers are so keen to recruit pickers that they circulate notices around youth hostels, for example: "Orchard Work Available January to March; apply Alexandra Youth Hostel". Other farmers visit the local hostel early in the morning and round up their daily requirement of pickers. It is always worth asking the hostel warden if he or she knows of any possibilities, once you have distinguished yourself by carrying out your hostel duty with alacrity and cheerfulness.

The demand for workers is very great in the Nelson/Motueka area, for example the Motueka YMCA keeps a list of apple farmers looking for pickers. Many foreign travellers are hired for the apple harvest, and also the apple packing and processing works in Stoke, just outside Nelson. The union is strong here and they have succeeded in making it obligatory for farms to provide accommodation other than just a campsite. Orchard workers must join the union. The negotiated rate in 1987 was $18 per bin; the average picker fills three to four bins a day.

Another excellent area for finding work is the Bay of Plenty where the majority of New Zealand's kiwifruit is grown. The harvest traditionally commences on May 1, though it is wise to arrive a week or two earlier than this. The fruit must be picked carefully by hand and placed in a large canvas bag worn like an apron. An expert picker can pick up to 1300 kilograms in a day at the peak of the harvest which lasts for about six weeks altogether. Rates of pay (either by the bucket or by the hour — called "award rate") are said to be high for this crop. Students are not available at this time so there is less competition for jobs. Grave labour shortages have been reported, for example in Katikati north of Tauranga. The same is true of the apple and pear harvests on the North Island; for example the Apple and Pear Marketing Board in Napier recently suggested that university holidays should be rescheduled to solve labour shortages in boom harvests, though this is unlikely to change.

The far north of the country, which specializes in citrus growing since it is the hottest part of New Zealand, is another favourite. There are several major packing sheds which employ a large number of casual workers in November/December. Kiwifruit production is also on the increase here.

Finally the Christchurch area has opportunities. Berry picking allows you to earn no more than $10-$20 per day. Potato picking around Prebbleton and Lincoln, both just outside Christchurch, is better paid. The season starts at the end of January and lasts at least two months. Apples are also grown in this area and picked between January and May.

FARMS

The system of working on organic farms in exchange for board and lodging is well advanced in New Zealand. Anyone interested in working on the land should join WWOOF (Willing Workers on Organic Farms), c/- Tony West, 188 Collingwood Street, Nelson; tel: (054) 80-448. For a fee of £4 (if you apply from the UK) you will be sent a fix-it-yourself list of 120 or so farms and smallholdings which welcome volunteers.

Other work in farming generally requires some specialist skills such as milking cows or mustering sheep. Advertisements abound in regional newspapers such as the *Waikato Times* of Hamilton.

The tobacco harvest is another labour-intensive activity in the area which takes place in late summer (January to March). If you're willing to work hard you can earn a considerable sum, especially if you stay until the end of the season and get the farmer's generous bonus.

THE TOURIST INDUSTRY

The tourist industry employs large numbers of people, not all of whom can be supplied locally. This is perhaps most noticeable in the year-round resort of Queenstown. Many young people, from both New Zealand and overseas, congregate in this attractively situated town to find work in the many motels, restaurants, etc. Job notices can be seen on the notice board of the Youth Hostel or on the central town notice board in the pedestrian mall. A good place to get to know the transient working population is Eichardts pub. If you get a waiting or bartending job, remember that there will be virtually no tips to supplement your wage.

The New Zealand dollar, occasionally referred to as the "kiwi", has been on a steadily declining path since a sharp drop in early 1986, and the exchange rate has remained favourable to travellers:

£1 = NZ$2.80   NZ$1 = 36 pence
US$1 = NZ$1.55   NZ$1 = 64 cents (US)

Notes and Coins. The denominations of notes in circulation are $1, $2, $5, $10, $20, $50 and $100. The notes are easily distinguished from one another by their colours.

The following coins are in circulation: 1¢, 2¢, 5¢, 10¢, 20¢ and 50¢. Bronze coins (1¢ and 2¢) are seldom used except for awkwardly priced grocery or cosmetic items @ $2.98 or 69¢. The government's "coinage review consultant" is in favour of phasing out the small coins to create "more meaningful coins", namely $1, $2 and $5 coins to replace the notes. This is scheduled to take place by the end of 1988.

The NZ 10¢ and 20¢ coins appear identical in size to their Australian counterparts, however New Zealand machines such as telephones don't seem to like Australian coins. There shouldn't be much temptation to use them in any case since an Australian 10¢ is worth over 12 NZ cents.

Banks. The four major banks are the National Bank of New Zealand, Bank of New Zealand, ANZ and Westpac (formerly the Bank of New South Wales). The latter sponsors the Youth Hostels Association. Opening hours are from 9am to 4.30pm Monday to Friday except Tuesday when many open at 9.30am. The only one of the major trading banks to levy a charge for changing travellers' cheques is the National Bank which subtracts a flat fee of $2 per transaction. A modest stamp duty of 5¢ per cheque must be paid at all banks.

Until April 1987, every post office in the country offered banking facilities. However with the reorganization of the Post Office (see *Communications*) it is likely that many post offices will cease operating as banks. In any case, if you intend to stay in New Zealand for a while, you might find it convenient to open a post office savings account which entitles you to use the cash machines in many locations. If you are staying put and earning money, you can open a high interest term account (minimum four weeks) in a building society. The annual interest rate has recently dropped from 22% to around 16%.

Each international airport has a bank immediately outside the customs hall, which is open for passengers arriving on international flights.

If you need money urgently, see *Emergency Cash* on page 50.

Credit Cards. Plastic money has penetrated surprisingly far, and many little businesses in the "wop wops" (New Zealand expression for the back-of-beyond) accept Bankcard/Access/Master Charge and Visa. Take-away pizza joints as well as more established restaurants and stores often accept credit cards. You can draw cash up to your credit limit on Visa at branches of the National Bank and ANZ Bank, and on Access through Westpac.

Note that although the National Bank is associated with Lloyds Bank (even using the same black horse logo), Access cards are not accepted.

Tipping. There used to be signs posted in the arrivals hall of Auckland Airport exhorting foreigners not to tip. Although these have been removed, tipping is still virtually unknown in New Zealand. Service charges are not added to restaurant meals nor are credit card users given a chance to add a gratuity on the sales voucher.

Sales Tax. A goods and service tax of 10% is applied to almost every item and is going up to 12.5%, either from October 1988 or April 1989. As in Britain, it is incorporated into the advertised price of merchandise rather than added at the till. Some services are advertised minus GST however this fact is usually clearly signposted.

TELEPHONES

An early New Zealand telephone engineer must have suffered from either dyslexia or a sense of humour because the New Zealand telephone dial is numbered backwards. The dial face is the only one in the world to be numbered clockwise. Although the dialling motion remains the same (i.e. clockwise) it is disorienting to have the distance between 9 and the stop much shorter than the distance between 1 and the stop.

Public Telephones. All but the most modern pay telephones have a button on the front labelled A and another on the right hand side labelled B. For local calls the correct procedure is to insert two 10¢ coins, dial the number, wait for a reply and then push button A to connect the call. If no one answers, push button B, hang up and your money will be returned. As in North America, local calls within the "toll-free calling area," shown at the front of directories, are free of charge from private phones and cost a flat fee of 20¢ from "calling boxes" no matter how long your call lasts. In certain locations (such as the international terminal of Christchurch Airport) you may find free public telephones, and — a great rarity — international payphones. Extensive research in 1987 revealed only three international subscriber dialling (ISD) phones in the whole country. ISD phones take a maximum of six large coins (50¢ or 20¢) and nine small ones (5¢ or 10¢). The minimum time is one minute, which for a call to the UK costs $3.08. Instead of pressing button A to connect the call, you should press the # button.

Overseas Calls. It is much easier to phone Britain from a post office, and the price is the same ($3.08 per minute) though with a minimum of three minutes. The trickiest part is finding a suitable time to phone when your friends and family will be neither asleep nor out at work. The UK is 11 to 13 hours behind New Zealand (depending on daylight savings) and so mid-morning is often the best time to catch your nearest and dearest the previous evening. Morning is also suitable if you are dialling the US: when it is 11am in Auckland, it is about 3pm the previous day in Los Angeles and 6pm in New York.

Toll Calls. For long distance calls within New Zealand (called "tolls") you will need a mound of 10¢ coins which the operator will ask you to insert in batches of ten. The charges for long distance calls within New Zealand are clearly set out at the beginning of all New Zealand telephone directories. There are ten charging steps depending on distance, and four call rates depending on time. For example a three-minute call from Christchurch to Auckland costs $3.27 in the peak time (8am-noon Monday-Saturday), $2.85 in the early morning (6am-8am) and evening (6pm-10.30pm), and $1.02 in the cheap time (10.30pm-6am daily). Calls to certain rural areas must be placed through the operator, though these are gradually being replaced by automatic exchanges. Stories of operators telling callers that the person they want has just been seen walking towards the beach or the back paddock are common and reinforce the idea that New Zealand is one big village.

If calling from a private house and you want to pay for the call, simply ask the operator (010) for "price required service" before placing the call. The operator will then ring back a minute or so later with the cost. Alternatively you can dial a special code which will result in the call being specially featured on the next bill: dial 013 in place of 0 for an STD call (i.e. within New Zealand) or dial 016 instead of 00 for an ISD (i.e. international) call.

Directory Assistance. Local directory enquiries are available on 100, while long distance numbers are obtainable on 102. The area codes for the major centres are as follows: Auckland (09), Wellington (04), Rotorua (073), Picton (057), Nelson (054), Christchurch (03), Dunedin (024) and Queenstown (0294).

POST

The New Zealand Post Office has a storied past, originally using means as various as Maori runners, pigeongrammes and postmen-cum-mountaineers reputed to have carried items such as children's bicycles over mountain ranges at Christmas time. Apparently in 1842 it took mail 127 days to get from Auckland to Wellington and was frequently routed through Sydney to speed up delivery. Today the rural mailman maintains this colourful tradition by undertaking far more deliveries than just the mail, depending on his or her initiative. Rural mailmen are not employees of the post office but contracted freelancers, and so it is not uncommon for the mailman to deliver newspapers (without stopping his vehicle), milk, bread, library books, spare parts, bales of wool and anything else needed to be taken in or out of town. Many country addresses consist merely of a Rural Delivery number (e.g. R.D.6) which might include hundreds of farms. Unless the mailman knows everyone by name, the post cannot easily be delivered. A few mail runs to outlying areas accept paying passengers, and occasionally the mail truck doubles as a local bus (as is the case along the Wanganui River). Such trips are very worthwhile if you get the chance. Sorting is still done in the time-honoured way and there are virtually no post codes in New Zealand. Many government departments and other organizations collect their post daily from the post office so addresses often consist merely of the name of the body, "Private Bag", then the city. (Letters posted within New Zealand addressed to a government minister do not require a stamp.)

Post offices are normally open 8.30am-5pm Monday to Thursday, and 8.30am-8pm on Friday, though not all services are available on Friday evenings. An ordinary letter within New Zealand costs 40¢ standard or 60¢ air mail (recommended for urgent letters to all but the nearest destinations). Overseas air mail rates are as follows:

	Post cards/10 gram letters	Aerogrammes
Australia	80¢	70¢
North America	$1.05	80¢
Europe	$1.30	85¢

The standard price of a picture post card is 35¢. Unlike most other countries, post cards cost as much to send as letters. Air mail correspondence often arrives at its overseas destination in less than a week. Surface mail takes 6-10 weeks depending on the sailing dates, which are posted on post office doors.

The New Zealand Post Office was "corporatized" on April 1st 1987, which means that it is now forced to function at a profit independent of the banking and telecommunications divisions which used to be part of the Post Office. As a result, postal charges skyrocketed in 1987, and many village post offices are threatened with the closure of one or all of their functions, including the post office at Scott Base in Antarctica. One compromise is to transfer basic postal services from loss-making post offices to local shops which would become postal agencies (of which there are already 300 out of 1200 post offices in the country). It remains to be seen whether the quality of service will deteriorate as quickly as the incensed locals predict.

Telegrams. Telegrams are most easily sent from post offices, though this limits you to post office opening hours. Within New Zealand they are telephoned through to the recipient if possible or delivered by post the following morning. The first seven words of an overseas telegram cost $3.59 plus 27¢ per word thereafter. If you are sending a telegram from a private number dial 012.

THE MEDIA

Programme information for both television and radio is given in the daily press. The *TV Guide* (60¢) gives adequate details of the week's viewing, but the *Listener* (99¢, published by the Broadcasting Corporation of New Zealand) is more comprehensive and informative. It provides schedules and frequency information for all television and radio stations including the independents. In addition it has a useful *Arts Diary* covering the whole country.

Radio. The Broadcasting Corporation of New Zealand (BCNZ) operates most, but not all, of New Zealand's radio stations. The "National Programme" (news and commentary) and the "Concert Programme" are networked throughout the country. The Concert Programme is something of a misnomer, since classical music shares this frequency with Parliament (every minute of every debate is broadcast live), Sports Round-up, BBC World Service news and Access Radio, which consists of programmes made by ethnic and community groups. The National Programme is broadcast on AM (medium wave) and carries the suffix YA; in Auckland it is known as 1YA, in Wellington 2YA, in Christchurch 3YA and in Dunedin 4YA. The same identification procedure is used for the FM Concert Programme and for the limited network of "Stereo Hit Radio ZM FM". Commercial radio stations use the suffix ZB with the same numerical prefixes: 1 for Auckland, 2 for Wellington, etc. Local commercial stations of which there are 18 in total can be recognized by the number of the nearest big city and the first letter of their name in place of the B, so for example Wanganui's radio station becomes 2ZW.

The BBC World Service may be heard on the following short wave frequencies: 15.36, 9.915, 7.15 and 5.975MHz, corresponding to 19.53, 30.26, 41.96 and 50.21 metres.

Television. At present BCNZ has a monopoly, operating both national TV channels One and Two. Although their programming policies have been virtually indistinguishable, TV One aims to be a little more highbrow with more public service programmes, documentaries, British entertainment, etc. TV Two is reputed to be more populist, with the usual diet of sport, soap operas and American imports. Homesick visitors from Britain will be glad to hear that EastEnders is staggeringly popular and a new satellite now makes it possible for TVNZ to carry ITV's News at 10 and the BBC's Newsnight. Relatively few programmes are made in New Zealand, although TVNZ has a Maori programmes department; the Maori news, called *Te Karere*, can be seen on TV One daily at 5.45pm.

Both stations have a moderate amount of advertising, except on Sundays when commercials are banned. A new independent third channel, TV3, is due to start in early 1989, which may lead to an increase in domestic output.

Newspapers. The New Zealand press is more like that of Australia and the United States than Britain, with most people reading a local rather than a national paper. Each city has one or two dailies (mostly evening papers) which are read within the region. Reading one of the two Sunday papers — *The Dominion Sunday Times* from Wellington and the *Sunday Star* from Auckland — is not as entrenched an institution as it is in Britain but these come as close to national newspapers as any.

It is certainly worth buying a few of the papers during your stay to gain an insight into local concerns. The Friday or Saturday editions are useful for their entertainment sections. Saturday editions usually have the most pages, with supplements and long lists of classified advertisements. New Zealand newspapers are more independent than Australian ones (i.e. there are no Rupert Murdochs in New Zealand) and so some newspapers such as the *Christchurch Press* seem a little more sympathetic to the left than is usual in the Antipodes.

Newspapers cost 30¢ or 40¢ and are usually purchased from dispensing boxes on city street corners which operate on the honour system. It is customary for hotels and motels to deliver a complimentary newspaper, along with a pint of milk, to your room.

The Library of the British High Commission in Wellington has a good selection of British newspapers and periodicals. Because of the large number of British expatriates, the *Observer* and *Sunday Times* are sold in major city newsagents. The results of British football matches are published in most daily papers throughout New Zealand.

New Zealand has a well deserved reputation for its pristine water, clear air and absence of dangerous fauna. It promotes itself as safe, clean and benign. Certainly the mountain water is a delight — though caution should be exercised immediately downstream from a sheep station — and the air is like crystal. The freedom from poisonous insects and reptiles (with one minor exception) comes as a wonderful relief after the perils of the Australian outback or oceanside.

However dangers do lurk in New Zealand, especially if you intend to do any "tramping", i.e. hill-walking. The vagaries of the weather have already been noted in *Climate*. Rain, wind and cold can have dire consequences for trampers unless they are fully equipped. Details are provided in *Great Outdoors*, below.

Medical Treatment. New Zealand's social services are fairly progressive with free prescriptions and free treatment in public hospitals. As mentioned in the section *Before You Go: Insurance*, UK passport holders are entitled to these services free of charge, though they must pay for consultations with a doctor and for some medicines. If you do have to seek medical attention, ask if you should claim a refund from the doctor or from the local health office.

Furthermore, there is a unique and enlightened scheme whereby the government pays compensation for personal injuries sustained in any accident which takes place in New Zealand no matter who is to blame. If you would like full details request the leaflet "Visiting New Zealand" from the Accident Compensation Corporation, Private Bag, Wellington.

If your hotel or hostel cannot recommend a clinic or a doctor, then consult the list of doctors at the beginning of the local telephone directory. The emergency telephone number in large cities is 111.

Pharmaceutical products obtained without a prescription are pricey. Chemist shops are open 9am-5.30pm Monday to Friday with some staying open until 9pm on Fridays. Emergency contacts are posted on most chemists' doors at closing time.

Optical services are also expensive, with a decent pair of spectacles costing about $200. Dispensing opticians are called "optometrists".

HEALTH HAZARDS

Creatures. New Zealand is absurdly proud of its snake-free shores. Although many animals were brought to New Zealand by white settlers, for example the opossum which has done irreparable damage to the native forests, no one introduced snakes. There are also no venomous spiders or insects with the single exception of the katipo, a large spider which favours beach habitats. But it is not particularly common and in any case its bite is rarely fatal.

The wildlife, however, is not entirely benign. Swimmers should be aware that mako sharks (which are not especially dangerous) occasionally come in near the shore as recently happened at Taranaki. And jellyfish swarms very occasionally make swimming unpleasant (as opposed to dangerous). Sandflies proliferate in many areas and are a terrible nuisance, just as they are in coastal parts of Australia. The recommended repellent is called "Dimp" which is relatively effective if applied at frequent intervals.

Wasps have been a recurring problem on the west coast of the South Island, driving tourists out of their campsites and diminishing the food supply of native birds. Recently a wasp parasite has been introduced in the South Island to control the swarms of pests.

A less desirable parasite infests some of the lakes on the South Island. The rash which results from contact with the snail-borne parasite is known as "duck itch". Usually warning signs will be posted in affected swimming areas.

Acts of God. While getting off lightly on the flora and fauna front, New Zealand fares less well when it comes to natural disasters. Erupting volcanoes, avalanches, floods, tornadoes and earthquakes take a regular toll of life and property. Australian slang for their neighbour is "the quaky island" or the "shaky isles". Leaflets published by the New Zealand Ministry of Civil Defence on these dangers advise what action to take before and during times of emergency.

New Zealand is seismologically very active. The fault line running the entire length of both islands actually bisects Wellington, which makes the capital particularly subject to earth tremors. No part of New Zealand is considered free from earthquake danger, though the risk varies greatly. For example Nelson is liable to have a quake every 16 years, whereas Auckland can expect one every 260 years. All buildings in the country must be constructed so as to withstand disturbances of the earth. If you have the misfortune to be caught in an earthquake, resist the temptation to run outside. It is safer to stand in a doorway or shelter under a strong piece of furniture. The back page of all New Zealand telephone directories provides emergency advice.

Although the periodic flooding of cities like Invercargill is unlikely to cause anything more than inconvenience, flooding in the great outdoors can be more serious. It is not uncommon for river levels to rise dramatically making crossings which were previously quite safe impossible. Recently a small group of trampers was stranded in a cave south of Westport, South Island for many hours after the stream at the mouth of the cave rose six feet within half an hour.

The volcanoes of the North Island (Ruapehu, Tongariro, Ngauruhoe) are dormant and most unlikely to erupt in the forseeable future. However there is a great deal of thermal activity in the area which can be dangerous. Most people enjoy the sight of bubbling mud pools from the safety of boardwalks built in commercial thermal areas, however not all such areas are fenced off and charge admission. If you are planning to go hiking in Tongariro National Park, be careful of stepping through the crust into boiling mud as happened to an Australian tramper near Ketetahi Springs in early 1987, causing second degree burns.

New Zealand is also subject to occasional freak storms, cyclones and dangerous rip tides and undertows. See *Australia: Health* for advice on how to cope.

AIDS. Although the number of reported cases (i.e. 253) is low by American and European standards, alarm has been increasing (especially since a prominent New Zealand media personality died of the disease). The Lion Brewery recently began installing condom machines in men's and women's toilets in some of their hotels.

Offices of the New Zealand Tourist & Publicity (NZTP) department present a tempting prospect for the traveller, offering as they do instant bookings for most public transport services. Ask for their useful leaflet called *Summary of Main Coach, Rail and Ferry Services*. These and other services can be booked at NZTP offices. Whilst this is undeniably convenient, the diligent traveller can often find better deals by conducting some further research and by approaching the operators direct.

AIR

Although there is fierce competition between airlines on the main domestic routes, the competing companies maintain the same fare structures, though under different promotional names. The advantage of shopping around is that when one airline has sold all its bargain seats, another may have a few left.

The main operators are Air New Zealand, Mount Cook (an Air New Zealand associate which concentrates on tourist routes) and the newcomer Ansett NZ (which absorbed Newmans Air and was launched in July 1987). The establishment of competition on the major routes has also done wonders for the quantity and quality of in-flight cuisine; before the appearance of Ansett NZ, catering on domestic flights was decidedly austere, often consisting solely of a boiled sweet. Ansett NZ has also introduced special fares for overseas travellers, giving discounts of 20% on one-way trips and 30% on return fares. These can be bought before arrival in New Zealand (whereupon you save a further 10% on GST) or from any Ansett NZ office in New Zealand. With this "See New Zealand" discount, the one-way fare Auckland-Wellington is $104, Wellington-Christchurch $81, and Auckland-Christchurch $139.

Almost all destinations are served at least daily (with occasional Saturday exceptions). Peak-time services (especially on Monday mornings and Friday evenings), and flights to smaller centres like Hokitika and Taupo (served by small Fokker Friendships) quickly fill up in the busy season. Therefore, if you plan to fly to smaller centres, try to design your itinerary carefully and reserve seats as far in advance as possible; this can be done prior to your arrival through any airline office abroad, although you probably won't be offered the cheapest deals.

You can book most air services at any NZTP office. But since there are so many kinds of discounted fare — on return flights booked in advance, late-purchase one-way flights, student standbys, off-peak travel, and so on — it is worth trudging around to the various airline offices to compare prices. If you are able to book well in advance, you can take advantage of some excellent promotional offers; for example both Ansett NZ and Air New Zealand were recently offering a limited number of one-way flights from Christchurch to Auckland for $99 (normally $210). Air New Zealand's no-frills City Savers allow a 25% discount, whereas their cheap apex fares are called Thrifty and Super Thrifty. Student standbys (obtainable only at the airport on the day of flight) also represent excellent savings; the major three offer 50% discounts to

ISIC-card holders if there are empty seats 15 minutes before take-off. So with some planning you should be able to save between a third and a half of the regular fares. The freefone number for Mount Cook is (09) 395-395 and for Ansett NZ (03) 791-300 or (09) 376-950.

There is a "sky ferry" which shuttles between Wellington and Picton six times a day. The cost is $36, little more than the ferry. Telephone Wellington (04) 888-380 or Picton (057) 37-888 for further details. Meanwhile Pacifica Air run 18-seaters between Wellington and Nelson. There are also many small local airlines such as Sea Bee Air in the North Island and Motueka Air in the South. These may also offer student concessions, sometimes even on bookable seats, so it is worth getting the Student Travel Services' leaflet on discounts (see *New Zealand: Help & Information*).

Airports. Facilities range from a hut which is opened only once or twice a day to coincide with the arrival and departure of flights, to fully-fledged (if still somewhat inadequate) international airports in Auckland, Christchurch and Wellington. Air New Zealand and Anzett NZ each has its own domestic terminal at these airports, so you may find yourself having to change terminal if you change airline. Details of transport arrangements between the city and airport for Auckland, Christchurch and Wellington are given under the *Arrival and Departure* heading for each city.

Baggage. The weight limit is 20kg (44lb) for hold luggage and 5kg (11lb) for bags carried on to the aircraft. There are boxes at check-in to test the dimensions of cabin baggage, but these are not used as fastidiously as in Australia.

Air Passes. Air New Zealand operates two and three week air passes for overseas visitors. If you are considering spending $350 or $460, bear in mind that Air New Zealand's network does not include Queenstown or Milford Sound. Mount Cook Airline operate a separate air pass called the Kiwi Air Pass which allows you one return trip on all Mount Cook routes (which serve the Bay of Islands, Auckland, Rotorua, Taupo, Wellington, Christchurch, Nelson, Mount Cook, Queenstown and Te Anau). All travel must be completed within one month. The price is $649, which also includes discounts on Mount Cook's heavily promoted scenic flights. The Kiwi Air Pass must be purchased before arrival in New Zealand.

COACH

The three major coach lines are Mount Cook, Newmans and NZRRS (New Zealand Railways Road Services). A number of smaller companies operate along local or limited routes. Once again it is not wise to rely upon the NZTP office for the best deal; for example, if you want to go from Auckland to Rotorua, they will probably not tell you about an independent company called Mainline Coachways which may have seats when the large companies are fully booked. Many services are reduced or altered on Sundays. As in Australia, timetables use the 12-hour rather than 24-hour clock.

Although you should try to buy tickets in advance from bus depots or agencies, it is often possible to buy one from the driver; this can, however, be a clumsy and long-winded procedure (just as it is on National Express coaches in Britain). Bicycles are usually charged extra, usually about $10 on a long journey.

Coaches tend to be relatively antique but comfortable and reliable enough.

Some are divided into passenger and freight sections, with the front for around 25 passengers and the rear devoted to cargo. The front seats of many long-distance buses are fitted with safety belts, although few passengers use them. Some routes are patronized almost solely by tourists and on these routes coaches seem almost like tour buses, complete with sheepskin-covered seats. For example, on the trip along the west coast of the South Island, the driver will probably make several photo stops and may also provide a freelance commentary on the countryside. You therefore run the risk of catching a bus driven by someone much more interested in irrigation systems, power stations or birdlife than you are. But on the whole their local information is entertaining, and you are spared the catalogue of passenger rules which oppress the long distance coach traveller in Australia. Coach operators cannot legally ban smoking, but instead "strongly request" that smokers refrain.

Cheap Deals. The big three offer savings, usually about 25%, for mid-week travel. Day returns entitle you to a 30% discount. If you book your return journey with Mount Cook when you buy the outward ticket, you will benefit from a small discount. Newmans offer students a 50% discount on certain journeys.

Travel Passes. The Kiwipass is valid only on coach services run by the big three. It should be distinguished from the more expensive and more flexible Travelpass operated by NZRRS; see the *Train* section for more details. The Kiwipass must be purchased outside New Zealand and costs £62/US$100 for 7 days, £79/US$125 for 10 days, £103/US$165 for 15 days and £157/US$250 for 25 days; these are the equivalents of NZ$175, $219, $289 and $439. As a basis for comparison, the cost of buying tickets separately to cover the major centres (i.e. Auckland — Rotorua — Wellington — Picton — Christchurch — Franz Josef — Queenstown and back to Auckland) would cost about NZ$380; this excludes the ferry crossing which all bus passengers, including Kiwipass holders, must pay separately. Pass holders should reserve seats in advance, since they are not given priority when competing for space immediately before departure.

Newmans Coach Lines in co-operation with the Youth Hostels Association offers its own bus pass to YHA members for $245. This entitles you to travel on any ten days in a 30-day period. The advantage is that the days need not be consecutive. The disadvantages are that you are limited to the Newmans network, and that you cannot use the pass between mid-December and the end of January.

TRAIN

The New Zealand Railways *Timetable of Principal Services for Tourists and Holidaymakers* includes over twice as many pages of bus schedules as railway timetables, which demonstrates the secondary role played by the railways. Train services have been drastically reduced in the past few years, as have staff numbers which may account for the Railways' notorious reputation for incompetence.

There is only one class of travel. Rail journeys which take as long as the equivalent bus rides tend to cost about the same as the coach, but are a few dollars more if they are faster than the bus. Tickets may be bought in advance from stations, NZTP offices or other agencies. If you board a train without a valid ticket, you are liable for a "service charge" of a few dollars in addition to the cost of the ticket.

Few trains have buffet cars, but there is usually a half-hour refreshment stop at an intermediate station on long distance journeys. The two superior trains are the *Silver Fern* (daily Auckland to Wellington in 11 hours) and the *Southerner* between Christchurch and Invercargill (9 hours). Both services attempt to simulate air travel by providing steward service at your seat. Services to Wellington and Picton are scheduled to connect with ferry departures. There is also an overnight service to cover the 685km from Auckland to Wellington, the *Northerner,* on which there is neither a buffet nor sleeping accommodation.

Cheap Deals. As on buses, day returns cost 30% less than ordinary returns. Savers for longer trips are available on off-peak journeys and provide a 25% discount. To qualify you must cover a distance of more than 100km travel outside the holiday seasons, depart on Tuesday, Wednesday, Thursday or Saturday and pay seven days in advance. There are no student discounts.

Travelpass. The NZ Railways *Travelpass* is valid on all trains, the Cook Strait ferry, coaches and on a few additional bus routes. Unlike the Kiwipass, the Travelpass costs more during high season (15 December to 31 January) than during the rest of the year. The high season pass costs NZ $355 for 8 days, $540 for 15 days and $625 for 22 days. If you want to book it before leaving home (which is not essential), then ask your travel agent or contact Travelpass's UK agent, Compass Travel, 46 Albemarle St, London W1X 4EP (tel: 01-408 4141).

FERRY

Two vessels link Wellington in the North with Picton on the South Island, across the scenic Cook Strait. One is the new and luxurious *Arahura,* a Maori word meaning "Pathway to the Dawn". In fact dawn sailings are available only from the Picton end, and not on Mondays. With a few exceptions, there are four sailings daily in each direction. The journey time is 3 hours 20 minutes.

Wellington to Picton	*Picton to Wellington*
8.00am Wednesday-Sunday	5.40am daily except Monday
10.00am daily	12 noon Wednesday-Sunday
4.00pm daily	2.20pm daily
6.40pm daily except Sunday	7.45pm daily except Monday
	10.20pm Monday only

The cost of the crossing depends on season, falling substantially from $27.50 in the high season (between mid-December and early February) to $16.50 mid-September to mid-December except for the school holidays in late October when the fare reverts to the standard February-to-September fare of $24.20. There is no saving on return tickets unless you are buying a day return. If you want to try to make a small profit, you can buy a day ticket and sell the return half to a traveller at the other side.

A hovercraft service between Christchurch and Wellington for passengers, vehicles and freight is under discussion, and may be introduced by the end of 1989.

CITY TRANSPORT

There are few surprises, except that bus fares in some cities are reduced in off-peak hours from Monday to Friday, and many local buses have hooks on the front from which to hang (empty) push-chairs. Larger towns and cities have bus services run by the local authority; elsewhere, private operators run some urban routes.

Bicycles are fairly well provided for. There are sometimes specially assigned traffic signals for cyclists, some of which require you to push a button to persuade the lights to change in your favour. Pedestrians will find that most traffic signals provide a button to push; a "walk" sign and a loud buzz indicates when it is safe to cross, though often the traffic is so light that only the most cautious wait for the signal. The police are not interested in such minor infringements; the only penalty issued to pedestrians from time to time is the $25 litter infringement ticket.

DRIVING

Adequate as the bus and train services are, many people prefer to have the use of their own transport. Campsites, both official and *ad hoc,* are often difficult to reach by public transport, as are other inexpensive kinds of accommodation like motorcamps and lodges. If you shop around, renting a car can be one of New Zealand's bargains. Often travellers club together to hire a car or van, or else a car-owner will put up a notice in the local youth hostel offering a lift in exchange for petrol money, which makes the bargain even more attractive.

Be warned that New Zealand roads are even more dangerous than those in Australia. The 1987 toll was about 800, which for the small population is a frightening figure (50% higher per capita than Australia). It is easy to see how the still-uncluttered roads of New Zealand encourage speeding and carelessness among motorists.

Fuel. "Super" (96 octane, corresponding to 4-star) costs around $1 per litre ($4.50 per Imperial gallon, $3.50 per US gallon), with "regular" (91 octane, 2-star) a few cents cheaper. Diesel is about 25% cheaper. Because of the natural gas supplies in the North Island, New Zealand has been in the forefront of developing alternatives to petrol. When world oil prices peaked, an enormous artificial petrol plant was built at New Plymouth; it stands idle now that the price of oil has dropped. Many petrol stations advertise CNG (Compressed Natural Gas) or LPG (Liquid Petroleum Gas). These can only be used in engines which have been specially adapted, and although much cheaper than petrol they are also less efficient. CNG is not available on the South Island.

Filling stations can be surprisingly far apart, especially in the South Island, so before embarking upon a long journey (e.g. Picton to Christchurch, or Greymouth to Queenstown) make sure your tank is full. The same advice applies to weekend trips anywhere, although a rota for garages which open at weekends appears in the local press.

Road System. As in Australia most of the state highways have only two lanes, though there is sometimes one paved shoulder on to which slower vehicles move when they notice a vehicle coming up behind. Quite a few country roads are dirt or gravel (in New Zealand parlance, not "tar sealed").

The term "motorway" is applied very loosely in New Zealand. This results from a bureaucratic oddity whereby new motorways receive preference for funds from central government; so if a town needs a new bridge or bypass, the local council has a strong incentive to label the resulting two-lane road a motorway.

t is therefore unwise to assume that stretches of motorway marked on road maps will permit high speeds and safe overtaking.

Routes and Maps. A free map showing major roads is available from New Zealand tourist bureaux abroad, and from most NZTP offices. But if you plan to cover much of the country it is probably wise to invest in a road atlas such as the ones published by Shell or the AA; the latter costs $12.95 and is reasonably good though it has many annoying misprints. The AA of New Zealand has a reciprocal agreement with the British AA, RAC and the American AA, so if you are a member take your card to get a discount on books and maps, obtain free route information and use the ferry booking service (see *Before You Go*). The AA headquarters are at 342 Lambton Quay, PO Box 1794, Wellington (tel: 04 738-738). Even if you aren't a member in your home country, you can take out a special visitor's membership in New Zealand at a reduced rate.

Road Signs. National state highways are numbered 1 to 8 and are indicated on signs (and some maps) by white numbers inside a red shield. Secondary route numbers of provincial highways 10 to 199 will be marked in white on a blue shield. Signposting is generally less than adequate. The Automobile Association is responsible for destination signs, which are infrequent. If you do spot a small yellow sign in the distance, it is just as likely to be pointing you towards the local bowling green as to the next major town. Look out for such amusing signs as "Feed Moose" or "Peerless Sheep Nuts", both advertisements for animal feeds.

The New Zealand road authorities have no truck with fancy symbols; almost every instruction is clearly spelt out in English, both on signs and painted on the road, for example "Beware Wandering Stock". Few need any explanation, except perhaps "free turn" which appears at junctions controlled by lights and means you can turn left at any time with care. "No exit" is used in the sense of "no through road" (except at entrances to car parks, etc. when it means "no exit").

As in Britain, a white circle with a diagonal black bar across it means that the motorist can travel at the maximum permitted speed, however that speed is seldom signposted even on airport exit roads. A sign which might puzzle you is a red circle enclosing the letters LSZ for "Limited Speed Zone". This means that the motorist must be prepared to slow down to accommodate other traffic, animals, etc. Extra persuasion may be applied in the form of "judder bars", i.e. humps in the road designed to slow traffic.

The sequence of traffic signals is red-green-amber-red. Beware of jumping red lights, particularly if you see the sign "Red Light Camera Ahead"; this warns that an automatic photograph is taken of any car that jumps the lights. When a light changes to red as you approach it, don't assume you'll have time while stationary to consult a map, tune the radio or light a cigarette; the sequence is often fast.

Rules of the Road. Driving is on the left. The speed limit on the open road in good conditions is 100km/h, having been raised from 80km/h in July 1985. On city and town streets the limit is 50km/h.

Traffic officers, who function independently of the police and have limited powers, are a fairly serious menace to speeders, though if you are staying for any length of time in a small town it is remarkably easy to avoid trouble since everyone knows which day of the week to expect his visit. Ministry of Transport law enforcers drive black and white cars marked MOT. Don't be tempted to

drink and drive: you can be fined up to $1500 and lose your licence for driving
with more than 80 milligrams of blood alcohol (0.08%), which is the same legal
maximum as in Britain but a little less than in most of the USA.

Car Hire. You must be at least 21 to hire a car. Only Hertz and Avis are allowed
to operate desks at airports. This causes a great deal of jealousy among rivals
like Budget, which keeps lobbying the government in vain to break the
monopoly. Some agencies set up office in caravans just outside the airport doors.
If you have pre-booked a hire car through a smaller agency such as Thrifty,
Southern Cross or Dollar, a representative will meet you at the airport usually
free of charge. Competition among car hire firms is intense, and it is almost
always cheaper to find your own way into town and then shop around for a
discount rent-a-car outfit; you can usually pick up promotional leaflets in city
tourist offices. Offers such as "$32 a day unlimited distance" or "$18 a day plus
18¢ a kilometre" will catch your eye, but be sure to read the small print. Often
the unlimited rates apply only to rentals lasting three or more days, and collision
damage insurance (at least $5 a day) will be added, with GST of 10% applied
on the whole deal. Also many companies impose a surcharge on drivers under
25.

The major companies are based in Auckland, and their reservation addresses
are as follows:

Avis, 22 Wakefield Street; tel: (09) 792-545.
Hertz, 154 Victoria Street West; tel: (09) 799-888.
Budget, 83 Beach Road; toll free tel: (09) 396-737.
Godfrey Davis, PO Box 22413, Otahuhu; tel: (09) 572-046.
Thrifty, Auckland International Airport; tel: (09) 276-7161.

Four lesser known and cheaper companies are based in Christchurch:

Letz Rent-a-Car, 40 Oxford Terrace; tel: (03) 796-880.
Avon Rent-a-Car, 407 Ferry Road, PO Box 19778; tel: (03) 891-350.
Rhodes Rent-a-Car, 338 Riccarton Road, PO Box 6053; tel: (03) 488-219. This
company gives a discount to YHA members.
Percy Rent-a-Car, 154 Durham St; tel: (03) 793-466.

Campervans. Hiring a campervan is so popular in New Zealand that it may seem
on some roads that 90% of vehicles are Maui "Campas" or Daihatsu
"Travelhomes". The average size is considerably smaller than the average
American RV (recreational vehicle) though 6-berth deluxe vans are available.
Prices include unlimited mileage, and vary significantly depending on size and
season. A 2½ berth model in the off-season will cost about $50 a day, and $110
in the summer, whereas a 6-berth luxury vehicle will cost $90 a day in the winter
and $200 or thereabouts in the peak season. Campervans usually consume
about 10 litres of petrol or diesel per 100 kilometres (or 25mpg). As with hired
cars, mandatory insurance of about $5 a day is extra. Most companies impose
a minimum hire period of three days (but check for surcharges at weekends)
or, more commonly, one week. It is a good idea to compare various terms, since
some companies will allow you to pick up (or "uplift" in their jargon) in
Auckland and drop off the vehicle in Christchurch or vice versa for no extra
cost. Others throw in the ferry crossing free of charge. If you plan to take a
van across the Cook Strait in the summer months, you should book a ferry
crossing in advance.

Hertz and Avis (addresses above) rent out campervans; the other principal
companies are:

Maui, 100 New North Road, Auckland; tel: (09) 793-277. Their vehicles can also be booked through the New Zealand tourist office in London.

Mount Cook Line, 47 Riccarton Road, Private Bag, Christchurch; tel: (03) 482-099.

Budget Campervans, 5 Aintree Avenue, Mangere, Auckland; tel: (09) 396-737.

Newmans Rentals, Richard Pearce Drive, Mangere, Auckland; tel: (09) 275-0709. Their UK agents are Caravan Abroad, 56 Middle Street, Brockham, Surrey RH3 7HW, or Newmans Tours Ltd, 42 Harrow View Road, London W5 1LZ.

Car Delivery. If you happen to be looking for a vehicle at the beginning or end of the holiday period, you should enquire about cheap one-way rentals or deliveries. For example vehicles are often "abandoned" by holidaymakers in places like Queenstown or Picton and need to be returned to their Christchurch depots. A canny traveller disembarking from the Picton ferry in late January, for example, can negotiate a favourable rate for the trip to Christchurch (which rivals the train fare of $38) and then pick up a few hitch-hikers willing to share expenses.

Buying a Car. Because of extremely high import duties, cars are very expensive. This accounts for the high proportion of lovingly maintained old vehicles still on the road. (Seven out of ten cars are more than five years old.) Indeed, there are large profits to be made by any visitor to New Zealand who knows about veteran British cars and who can afford to buy and ship back to the UK some of the more pristine Morris Minors, Standard 10s or Rover 90s which are still in everyday use in New Zealand, and sell them to collectors. A typical advertisement in the provincial press (Saturdays are the best day to look) recently offered a 1947 Hillman in working order for only $250.

But travellers who merely want to buy a car to see them through a few months will have to invest substantially. The most basic new cars cost around $20,000, and most secondhand prices are high: a ten-year-old Mini can set you back $7,000, a 20-year-old Holden $1,500. Since cars have such a good resale value, you could reasonably expect to recoup a good proportion of your outlay at the end of your stay.

The documentation involved in buying or selling a car is similar to that required in Britain; road tax is known as "registration" (which together with licensing costs $100) and the MOT is a "warrant of fitness" or WOF renewable every six months at a cost of $6 (this is the seller's responsibility).

Insurance. Because of New Zealand's novel "no-fault" compensation scheme, whereby accident victims are recompensed by the government regardless of who caused the accident, motor insurance is not compulsory. But insuring your vehicle is recommended, even if comprehensive cover costs about $600 per annum. The AA of New Zealand recommends AA Mutual Insurance on the North Island and SIMU Mutual Insurance Association on the South Island.

HITCH-HIKING

It is difficult to imagine a country more favourable to the hitch-hiker. Most distances are manageable, large cities are few, crime is low and the locals are very hospitable. New Zealand must be one of the few places where it is common to be picked up by holiday-makers. Furthermore motorways are rare; they should be avoided since hitching on them is the one infringement for which the traffic police are liable to stop and lecture you. Since motorways are largely confined to the environs of the four major cities, start your hitching from a nearby small town if possible. You may run into some competition from other hitch-hikers, mainly German, Canadian, American and Australian, though surprisingly not much from New Zealanders or British travellers. (A middle-aged couple in Rotorua who have picked up 4,500 hitch-hikers in the past seven years report that only a few dozen have been Kiwis and Poms).

Competition is likely to be stiff leaving the ferry linking the North and South Islands. To avoid having to join the queue of hitch-hikers leaving Picton or Wellington Harbour, try advertising your desire for a lift during the ferry crossing by pinning a notice to the back of your seat or to your luggage, and by getting into conversation with motorists.

The road along the west coast of the South Island has the reputation among hitchers for being impossible. But if you do get a lift south from Fox Glacier or heading north from Wanaka, chances are the vehicle will be going the whole distance (265km) and so it is worth trying, especially if you make an early start. Some experienced hitchers recommend walking a few kilometres out of town to persuade drivers you have earned a lift.

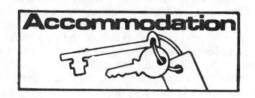

Comfort and congeniality at a reasonable price are easy to find, from the humblest youth hostel to the most genteel guest house. Even four- and five-star hotels cost less than their counterparts elsewhere. Campsites are also a popular option even for those who don't have a tent or caravan, and motels are ubiquitous. Often there is a small surcharge if you stay only one night. If you are staying in one place for more than four weeks, the rate of GST is lower. If you are travelling out-of-season, ask about reductions. In the high season (Christmas to early February), it can be difficult to find a vacancy, especially if you start looking in the evening. But the European experience, of trudging miserably between booked-up *pensions* and being greeted with indifferent shrugs, is very rare. It is far more probable that the staff will direct you to a more promising hostelry.

Youth Hostels. As elsewhere, you must be a member of a national Youth Hostels Association (and hence the International Youth Hostels Federation) to be eligible. Otherwise you must obtain an international guest card, valid for one year, at a cost of $25. Youth Hostels are located not only along the traveller's familiar circuit, but in some out-of-the-way locations like Okarito and Pigeon Bay on the South Island and Opoutere and Great Barrier Island in the North. The *NZ Hostelling Handbook*, which is available free of charge to IYHF members from New Zealand hostels or hostel offices, contains detailed entries for the 40 year-round hostels and 11 seasonal ones, and is far more informative than the New Zealand entries in the *International Youth Hostelling Handbook* readily available in Britain and North America. If you write to the National Office ahead of time (PO Box 436, Christchurch) their "mail-coordinator" will send you a list of hostels and overnight fees and other information condensed from the handbook. To obtain the handbook itself, you will have to send money to cover postage (about $2).

Prices range from $9 to $12 at most hostels. Some have a few twin or family rooms which cost the same per bed as dormitory accommodation. Since these are limited in number they often tend to be booked up in advance. Many hostels feature an impressive array of facilities from laundries to cycle rental. Quite a few operate shops which sell whatever the wardens (who prefer to be called "managers") have the energy to market, from post cards to individual cupsful of rice. Others act as agents for specialist local tours from white water rafting trips in Queenstown to glowworm-viewing expeditions in Franz Josef. The notice boards of Youth Hostels are always worth studying for offers of lifts, ideas for unusual excursions, equipment for sale, local or hostel events such as barbecues, etc.

As in Australia the main hostels are often full, especially from December to January, so if you know your dates in advance it is advisable to book. This can be done through the National Reservation Centre, YHANZ Headquarters, PO Box 436, Christchurch (tel: 03 799-970) by sending full payment, in the form of a bank draft, money order or fixed value international advance booking vouchers available from hostelling organizations abroad. The alternative is simply to risk leaving it until a day or two in advance. Hostel managers will ring their counterparts on your behalf to fix up a booking, collect the fee and issue a receipt to be presented at the relevant hostel. Occasionally you may be charged for the telephone call. Smoking is banned in every part of every hostel, except in a few which have a designated (and highly polluted) smokers' lounge.

Budget Accommodation. Surprisingly, other forms of accommodation cost little more than a youth hostel. For example many private hostels, tourist lodges and caravan parks known as motor camps offer beds at youth hostel prices without the panoply of youth hostel rules. If you intend to use this level of accommodation, take a sleeping bag or equivalent since bedding is not usually supplied, though sheets and blankets are sometimes available for hire. Cooking facilities by contrast are invariably supplied free of charge.

One useful source of addresses is a free leaflet called *Budget Accommodation in New Zealand: Where to Stay for $12 or Less*. There are 34 listings, from a new "no-smoking voyagers' venue" in Nelson to a cavers' hut at Waitomo. The kitchens in these lodges often become social centres in the evenings. The list is published by B J Thomas & Co, PO Box 2842, Auckland, but they cannot be relied upon to send the leaflet to enquirers, so you will have to wait until you arrive to get hold of a copy.

Motorcamps are of interest not only to campers; they also have a choice of cabins, flats, motel units or on-site caravans. Prices at the time of going to press were $20-$25 for a basic two-person cabin, $30-$35 for a well-equipped tourist cabin or for an on-site caravan, again for two people. You may stumble across even better bargains in your travels. Privately run lodges may offer bunkroom accommodation for even less than youth hostels, though facilities in such places will be primitive. Two useful sources of modestly-priced accommodation including motor camps are the *Camp, Cabin & Caravan Accommodation* brochure published by the Camp & Cabin Association of NZ, 41 Kanawa Street, Waikanae, and *Jason's Budget Accommodation* which costs $4.40 and is on sale in New Zealand bookshops.

Camping. Roadside campsites in New Zealand are excellent and numerous, and once again kitchens and hot showers are always provided. But prices are relatively high: tent pitches cost just a fraction less than caravan sites, about $7 per person. If you are planning to camp in New Zealand, be sure that your equipment can withstand torrential downpours. It is also common practice to camp anywhere along the road, though it is forbidden in rest areas. Even the glossy Maui campervan brochure advocates choosing your own sure-to-be-idyllic camping spot. From the Camp & Cabin Association's literature it would seem that camping in New Zealand is still a sexist activity where "Mother's list should include such items as bedding and towels, dishwashing gear, scissors, needle and cotton," while "Father will be responsible for the equipment, wheel chocks, hydraulic jack and emergency repair tools."

Each regional authority manages countryside parks in its area where camping is often allowed but sometimes only with pre-arranged permission (as in the case of parks run by the Auckland Regional Authority). This kind of camping is considerably less luxurious than the roadside variety. Although pit toilets are provided at all designated campsites, there may be no ready supply of drinking water, so always check before heading into the bush. There are usually restrictions on camping along the well-known walking tracks so a tent may become a liability. Huts are usually located at appropriate intervals along tracks, where bunks, gas rings and toilet facilities are provided for the hut fee of $7.

Hotels. When New Zealanders refer to "hotels" they normally mean bars. As in Australia, all premises which have a licence to sell alcohol must also provide accommodation as a condition of the licence. Many hotels fulfil the letter of the law by keeping one or two token unmaintained rooms, while others are attempting to rehabilitate the image of the country pub and are encouraging tourists to stay, with attractive offers, the use of bathrobes for those who object to shared bathrooms, etc. The cost of a double varies greatly but there are some real bargains, for example an old-fashioned wood-frame hotel in the centre of Christchurch was recently advertising beds for $10. The term for a private hotel without a bar is "private hotel."

Motels. Motels are nearly as prevalent in New Zealand as they are in the US, but without the neon signs. One of their most surprising features is that they are usually equipped with kitchens. While motels around the world are congratulating themselves for having just installed tea-making machines, New Zealand motel rooms come equipped with corkscrews and whisks as well as all the basic crockery and cooking utensils (though don't expect anything as exotic as a garlic press). These "motel flats" as they are known often have a separate bedroom and are designed for families, though they do very well for small groups of friends too. There are also serviced units in most motels which provide conventional non-catering motel accommodation. A comprehensive list of motels in NZ can be found in *Jason's Motels* which costs $8.80.

The charge for two people is usually between $55 and $65, with a surcharge of $12 to $15 for each extra person. Motel owners are knowledgeable about the local area and will be happy to share their information or gossip about their town.

Guest Houses. Most guest houses charge about the same as motels, but since they often have a more interesting atmosphere (e.g. colonial architecture, pleasant gardens) and the price includes breakfast, many travellers prefer them to motels. Surprisingly guest houses in Auckland are not noticeably more expensive than elsewhere. Ask for the leaflet published by the Travel Hotels Federation, which lists 26 bed and breakfasts well distributed over both islands, from a New Zealand Tourist Office or by writing direct to the Federation (PO Box 1023, Gisborne). The brochure is revised annually and published in October. Another bed and breakfast organization to contact is the Kiwi Tourist Group (Morihana Guest House, 20 Toko St, Rotorua) which comprises 24 homes averaging $25 single.

Farm Stays. No country could be better suited to the concept of farm holidays than New Zealand. While it is possible to attend a regulation sheep-shearing or demonstration of mustering at specially created tourist centres, it is more enjoyable to see, and even participate in, the genuine thing. Try any of the following organizations:

New Zealand Farm Holidays Ltd, PO Box 1436, Wellington.
Town & Country Home Hosting, 681 Victoria Street, Cambridge.
Homestay/Farmstay Ltd, PO Box 630, Rotorua.
New Zealand Travel Hosts, 279 Williams Street, Kaiapoi.
Farmhouse & Country Home Holidays, PO Box 31250, Auckland.
The Friendly Kiwi Home Hosting Service, PO Box 5049, Port Nelson.
New Zealand Host Homes Ltd, PO Box 60, Russell.
Hospitality Haere Mai, PO Box 56175, Auckland.

Most operate a voucher system aimed at affluent travellers and do not send out lists of farms to contact, but will be happy to fix up a farm stay at short notice once you are in New Zealand. The local public relations officer or New Zealand government tourist office should also be able to advise. Your stay is usually on a full board basis, though some listed above also arrange bed and breakfast only. The cost for full board is usually about $65-$75 per person per day, though Travel Hosts (run by an English expatriate) offers double bed and breakfast for $85-$100 for two. Many offer a highly personalized service and will try to accommodate your budget and your interests. It is not unusual for the hosts' hobbies to be listed in the agency literature, encompassing anything from spinning to antique guns.

If this seems too extravagant and you are willing to earn your keep, then contact Willing Workers on Organic Farms as described in *New Zealand: Work*. Alternatively you might like to consider joining an international home-hosting organization like Servas as mentioned on page 20. Not surprisingly the New Zealand host network is excellent.

It is only a slight exaggeration to suggest that the best New Zealand meal you may have is the one served on Air New Zealand international flights. This is both a tribute to the high catering standards of the national carrier and a condemnation of the cuisine on dry land. The tastes and eating habits of most Kiwis are infuriatingly conservative, with most menus at home and in restaurants based on "meat and two veg" plus perhaps a salad which features pickled beetroot. When asked for salad dressing, waitresses have been known to look quizzical and ask for elucidation of the concept. New Zealanders are the greatest consumers of meat in the world and it is difficult to avoid a surfeit of soggy meat pies and steak dinners while touring the country. Vegetarians will find it tough going. When a whole sheep can be bought for as little as $15 and retails in supermarkets for $2 a pound, there is not much demand for lentils.

The meat, seafood, fruit and vegetables are usually of the highest quality, which makes it all the more disappointing that cooking techniques are so antediluvian. Lamb is invariably roasted plain and long, while seafood, including beautiful clams fresh from the sea, is usually fried in batter and served with chips. As in Australia, hogget refers to one year old lamb. To sample typical home-cooking, watch for leaflets displayed in tourist offices offering lamb dinners in private homes for about $40. Apparently "home entertaining" appeals especially to American widows.

The dairy products are superb, and relatively inexpensive. New Zealand cheese — almost all of it cheddar — is excellent, though there is less variety than there once was due to the take-over of several small independent cheese-makers by large dairies (with names like Koromiko rather than Kraft).

There are some hopeful signs, particularly in the cities and tourist resorts where a more sophisticated clientele exists. One indication that there is a move in the direction of healthier eating is that the Health Department has finally got round to trying to amend the food legislation so that labels will have to show a breakdown of ingredients and additives. Also a few adventurous ethnic restaurants have opened from Afghani to Mexican, and home-delivery of pizzas has just started up in Auckland, Wellington and Christchurch. Furthermore an established cheese-making firm has branched out from plain old cheddar into making gourmet cheeses; look for Ferndale Abbey cheeses in delicatessens, assuming, that is, that you can find a delicatessen. 1988 has been designated Food Year in New Zealand, so things can only improve.

RESTAURANTS

Safe and dull family restaurants prevail in most towns, where the modest prices go some way to compensating for the predictable cuisine. A typical menu would be steak, chips and salad, possibly from a serve-yourself salad bar, for about $12-$15 including a beer. Many pubs sell food of this ilk, and quantities are so generous that no one could deny they are good value. In more upmarket resorts or city restaurants you might have to spend $25 for a steak dinner and $40 for a crayfish (compared to $15 for a whole crayfish from a roadside stall in crayfish areas).

One of the most frustrating features of dining out is the barbaric hours; even classy restaurants often close at 9pm. Outside the more sophisticated centres, you will be hard-pressed to find any restaurants at all, apart from fish and chip shops (where the locals go for their "greasies") and perhaps a fast food chain outlet like McDonald's or Pizza Hut. Tuesday evening in a typical town like Wanganui (which has a population about twice that of Stratford-upon-Avon) can be dire. You should be able to find a Chinese restaurant, though the brown sauce on the table will be of the HP variety rather than soy sauce.

When you can find them, imaginative restaurants also tend to be good value. Food in vegetarian cafés and ethnic restaurants is cheaper than it would be in its British counterpart, say $22 for three courses excluding wine. Do not be confused by the word "entree" which refers to the starter rather than the main course. In the main resorts more pretentious licenced restaurants have been accused of charging outrageous prices (i.e. $30 for a main course) on the assumption that Japanese tourists will pay whatever is asked. In some cases things haven't changed much over the past decade since J B Priestley described an upmarket and precious city restaurant as "making a half-hearted pretence not to be in New Zealand but in some more exotic place... with two or three solemn young men who looked as if an inspector from Michelin might arrive at any moment."

BYO Restaurants. A far better choice is a Bring-Your-Own liquor restaurant. Not only does taking your own "grog" keep the price relatively low but these establishments are often more fun and informal. BYO restaurants have proliferated in the decade since they were introduced and are now easy to find in the cities. There is a legal maximum corkage fee of 50¢, though about a third of BYOs charge nothing for corkage. A few licensed (i.e. non-BYO) restaurants have also begun to allow customers to bring their own beverages, however they may charge as much for corkage as they like, and have been known to charge according to the price of the wine. Always enquire beforehand.

Snacks. Pies are universally available and cost between $1 and $1.50. Normally you help yourself from a glass case after having chosen meat (mince) or bacon and egg. Dairies are found in all neighbourhoods and sell pies, filled rolls and other snack foods. They may be the only source of nourishment you will find open late at night or on Sundays. Another worthwhile snack food available at most dairies is ice cream. New Zealanders consume almost as much ice cream as the voracious Americans, and the quality and value is excellent. A single scoop costs about 70¢. Watch for roadside fruit stalls in country areas. Many operate on the honour system.

Fish and chip shops are also very numerous and the quality is reasonable. Shark is sometimes sold but euphemistically as "lemon fish" or "flake". Unfortunately you can't be sure that you are eating fish from New Zealand waters; because so much of the catch is exported they have recently had to start importing frozen fish from Argentina.

Tipping. The tradition of no-tipping in New Zealand is still going strong. There are no hidden extras on most restaurant bills; the price printed on the menu is what you pay. (A handful of restaurant menus show prices exclusive of GST but this is very rare.) Food service is prompt and courteous and, because there is nothing to be gained by favouring the wealthy-looking customers, completely egalitarian.

SPECIALITIES

The influence of Maori food can still be seen. Some fish shops, for example, sell "paua patties" which are green-coloured abalone burgers. Also watch out for *pipis* (similar to cockles) and the prized *toheroas* (like clams) which are made into soup, though the season is very short. Upmarket restaurants serve whitebait fritters, more like delicate omelettes, flavoured with the tiny transparent fish which go by the name whitebait. The striking green-lipped mussels can be bought fresh or pickled. Smoked eel is a treat for gourmets; confusingly, the Maori word for eel is "tuna". In the months of April and May you can find muttonbirds in some shops and restaurants. Muttonbird is a type of seagull with a high fat content which was a useful component in the early Maori diet before the introduction of mammals for food. By all accounts it is an acquired taste.

People from the far south maintain that Bluff oysters from Foveaux Strait are the best in the world, though the oysters have recently been hit by disease. If you notice some oyster shells while strolling along a beach, remember that it is against the law to prize any off for your dinner. A further regulation prohibits the selling of trout, even though the lakes and streams abound with the fish. So, unless you or a friend catches a trout, you will not have a chance to sample the national fish.

The traditional Maori method of cooking is in a *hangi* or ground pit. Vegetables, especially the Maori staple *kumara* (sweet potato), and fish are wrapped in flax leaves and lowered into a rock-lined pit, whereupon boiling water is poured over them and the earth replaced so that the food steams over a period of several hours. This is not often done these days except for special Maori feasts. There are commecial *hangi* evenings at a few hotels in Rotorua where the traditional fare is supplemented with European imports like lamb and venison. These evenings are pricey and appeal principally to tourists on coach tours.

DRINKING

Many of New Zealand's drinking habits are left over from an earlier time when all public drinking was crammed into the hour between 5pm and 6pm. The public bars in many hotels (i.e. pubs) are joyless establishments with virtually no seating; the practice of standing is a remnant of the time when pubs were so crowded for the 6 o'clock swill — which was in effect as recently as 1967 — that there was no room for chairs and tables. Even in hotels which claim on their signs to have incorporated "novel innovations, cultural amenities and modern facilities," there will probably be tacky plastic upholstery and a radio badly-tuned to the local country music station. As closing time approaches, pubs tend to become rowdy, often with one table of men engaged in juvenile drinking contests. There is often an irritating dichotomy between the public bar, where working men go to play pool or darts, and the lounge bar full of besuited businessmen where prices are often half as much again.

Despite all this, pubs are not usually hostile places, even to women travelling alone. You might attract some curious stares, but usually you will be served with courtesy. And some are not altogether gloomy. A few hotels in country areas have well-maintained gardens. Few things could be nicer than consuming a jug of draught beer and a crayfish in a hotel garden.

All hotels have a bottle sales counter where you can buy cans and bottles of beer as well as a depressingly limited selection of wines, at prices somewhat higher than in a city bottle shop.

Licensing Laws. The maze of legal restrictions on alcohol sales means that you will have to seek local advice if you want to maximize drinking time. Most pubs are open continuously from 11am to 10pm though some stay open an hour longer on Thursday, Friday and Saturday. Private clubs, mainly drinking clubs masquerading as sports clubs, can serve alcohol until 1am or even 3am to people who are also dining, though in fact most close well before midnight through lack of custom. The big cities all have a couple of cabarets which stay open until 3am. All pubs are closed on Sundays, though a few licensed restaurants serve alcohol with meals. Drinking up time is usually about half an hour, though most pubs display a sign "No jugs served after 9.45".

Other laws which might affect travellers are that the minimum drinking age is 20 unless accompanied by an adult relative in which case it is 18. (In fact few attempts are made to enforce this law.) In Auckland, Christchurch and Wellington, entire suburbs are dry, as a snobbish attempt to keep out unsavoury elements. Alcohol is not for sale in supermarkets. A strong lobby has been attempting to liberalize these and other laws, though a counter lobby supported by the surprisingly powerful Temperance Alliance wants to introduce afternoon closing to discourage day-long drinkers and it opposes all liberalization.

Beer. The differences among New Zealand beers are more marked than the differences among Australian lager-type beers, though their consumption is identical. Although lagers are certainly popular — Rheineck and the prize-winning Steinlager are the best known — many New Zealanders drink draught beer which approximates to British bitter.

There are two giant brewers which own almost all the pubs in New Zealand: Dominion Breweries and Lion. Dominion's DB (Draught Bitter) is a very ordinary but adequate beer containing 4% alcohol. They also promote a premium beer called Kiwi lager which is tasty, strong (8%) and costs over $2 for a third of a litre while a litre bottle of DB costs about the same. Also try their Kuhtze brew. Lion's Brown has the pale colour and inoffensive flavour of British keg beer; Lion Red is sweet and malty. Lion's premium bottled beer is McGavin's, a pleasant ale. Other names occasionally crop up on beertaps such as Leopard brewed in Hastings and Speights an old Dunedin brewery; both are now owned by the two giants.

The beers brewed by the few boutique breweries in New Zealand are worth searching out. Mac's began brewing at Stoke near Nelson in the early 1980s and produces an interesting range of bottled beers from Mac's Real Ale to Black Mac, a dark and delicious brew.

Measures. For a country so small New Zealand has a bewildering variety of beer measures. Just after you think you have mastered the sizes, you will find a completely different terminology being used in a different region. For example many South Island pubs continue to think of their beer glasses in the old sizes based on ounces: 3oz (rare and found only in a few pubs on the west coast), 5oz, 7oz, half pint or "handle" and 12oz. In fact the glasses are in metric units so what is called a "12" actually contains 360 millilitres which is closer to 13 ounces. The same range of metric glasses is available on the North Island but the metric numbers are used, so you ask for a "three-sixty" (which is one of the most common sizes), a "two-eighty" and so on. The terms "pint" and "half-pint" are still acceptable though the amounts they signify are not standard. A pint will get you anything from just under 500ml to just over 600ml for about $2.

Pairs or groups of friends often buy beer by the jug. The standard jug of beer contains one litre and costs over $3, though 2 litre jugs are also available. Usually you will be given 7oz glasses with a jug.

Cans of beer from off-licences are 440ml and start at $1. The price of a case of 24, known as "two dozen lots," starts at about $20. A flagon, formerly a half gallon or "half-g" and now 2.25 litres is what many drinkers take home with them from the bottle store.

Whisky and other spirits are sold in pubs, though are seldom drunk since hotels continue to act as beer emporia primarily. A nip will cost about $1.30. Gin and tonic drinkers will be interested to learn that gin is cheap; a bottle costs about $10.

Wine. After Australia, New Zealand wines are a disappointment, principally on account of their high prices. Although some excellent wines which win international awards are produced, there are also some that are downright filthy. (New Zealand may not have any poisonous snakes but it does have Corbans Velluto Rosso). Very few wines cost less than $7 a bottle and three-litre wine casks cost $14, well over twice the Australian price. One of the reasons for this sad state of affairs is the lack of enthusiasm from the home market. An average Kiwi drinks only 13 litres of wine a year compared to the Australian's galloping consumption of 22 litres. Another reason for the high prices is the hefty sales tax which the government imposes, about $1 a bottle and $4 on a three-litre cask. The duty on imported wines is even steeper and so the few Australian wines for sale are no cheaper than the home-produced ones.

The biggest wine-makers are Montana, Cooks, Corbans and McWilliams. Despite the Anglo-Saxon names, some of New Zealand's best winemakers are of Mediterranean extraction especially Yugoslav, such as Babich. But many of the smaller family-run wineries were bought out by the bigger ones during the crisis of 1985 when an enormous wine lake formed, prices were slashed and a quarter of New Zealand's vineyards were pulled up to prevent further gluts.

New Zealand's cool climate favours the production of white wines. Chablis-style wines, such as the one made by Montana, are especially recommended as are the chardonnays and sauvignons. Villa Maria Estate, which nearly went bankrupt in the price war, now produces a prize-winning chardonnay which is worth trying. Similarly Delegats makes good white wines.

Kiwifruit wine, a favourite with Japanese tourists, has a pleasant, not overly sweet fruit taste and makes a novel gift. It is slightly cheaper than grape wine, possibly because the locals tend to turn up their noses at it.

Unfortunately New Zealand has just jumped on the wine-cooler bandwagon and Corbans and Montana have started producing their own mixtures of wine (40%) and fruit juice. In fact New Zealand fruit juices are delicious even though most of them seem to be apple-based, and are best drunk neat. The small cartons cost 85¢.

It is easy to be rude about the nightlife and the artistic provincialism of New Zealand. But considering that its total population is only about twice that of the county of Hampshire or the city of Detroit, it is hardly surprising that it cannot offer a large choice of theatres, rock groups and so on. In fact for its size, the entertainment and artistic achievements it offers are remarkably varied and occasionally sophisticated.

The Arts. Despite its geographical isolation, New Zealand was for a long time culturally swamped by the mother country. Recently however it has produced a creditable number of indigenous artists and performers. Almost all have felt that it was necessary to spend time in Europe, particularly London, and much talent has inevitably been lost. The much larger potential audience of Australia is a constant temptation for creative New Zealanders. Some of the lost talent has been replaced by emigrés who value the chance to make their mark in a fledgling culture.

All the cities have established theatres which perform everything from Shakespeare to Alan Ayckbourn, with a preponderance of the latter. The National Orchestra and several ballet and opera companies tour the country during the season (mid-February to November).

Cinema. A few New Zealand-made films have made an international impact, and in fact the National Film Theatre in London mounted a season of Maori films in 1987. The industry has suffered a financial setback since the government cancelled tax incentives for film-makers in 1985. One rare box office success was the film *The Dog's (Tail) Tale* a cartoon film based on the popular Footrot Flats cartoon strip about a canny sheep dog. This is unlikely to win any prizes at the Cannes Film Festival but is very amusing all the same. There is usually a reasonable choice of films at city cinemas, all of which cost $5.50. Drive-in cinemas were prohibited for decades but in 1987 the government decided that they were not such a threat to community life and ordinary cinemas after all — yet another piece of evidence to support the claim that New Zealand is at least 20 years behind the rest of the world.

The censor's classification of films is a complicated business, ranging from G for General Admission to R18, approved for exhibition only to people 18 years or over. The censors are kind enough to spell out possible objections, such as "R16 — Content May Disturb" (e.g. *Night of the Creeps*) and "GY — Parental Guidance, Coarse Language" (e.g. *The Dog's (Tail) Tale*). "GY" films are considered suitable for young people over 13. The allocation of an "R" for Restricted can be enforced by law whereas "G" classifications are merely recommendations.

Popular Music. The only New Zealand band to have achieved international recognition is Split Enz which, like so many other groups, left New Zealand early in their career to make a name in Australia and subsequently Britain and the US. The Chills are New Zealand's most promising band at present.

A reasonable number of international stars tour New Zealand, from the Eurythmics to Lionel Richie, and people travel long distances and pay high prices to see them. The cities have their fair share of folk and jazz clubs, both with a decided tendency towards traditional music, plus a growing number of nightclubs. Some cosmopolitan visitors claim that advertisements for these clubs which read "Live and Raging" are a trifle optimistic.

Museums and Galleries. The standard of exhibits is normally very high, even in small local or regional museums, though you won't find many Old Masters on display. Many New Zealand artists, both Maori and Pakeha, exhibit their work at galleries throughout the country. Admission to museums is normally free.

SPORT

"Rugby, Racing and Beer" is a popular pub sing-along, praising the merits of New Zealand's purported favourite pursuits. Cricket and sailing are also capable of inciting a high level of national fervour. The cricket season runs from November to April, tennis from September to April, and soccer from May to September. Baseball is surprisingly popular, but more as a participation sport.

Rugby. The national sport of New Zealand has suffered a number of reverses due to the controversial links with South Africa which the national Rugby Union team (the All Blacks) maintains. Match attendance has declined noticeably since the Springbok tour in 1981 which divided the country and led to serious civil disturbances. The sport has tried to regain popularity by introducing cheerleaders, music and other American-style entertainments, much deplored by the purists. The season lasts from May or June until September and tickets range from $5 to $20. The premier Rugby League Club prize is the Tusk Cup.

Horse Racing. Racing takes place around the year and is a national obsession. All but the smallest towns have their own well-groomed floodlit race tracks which may host only one or two meetings a year, either trotting or flat racing. Successful horses, jockeys, trainers and breeders become household names in New Zealand for example Maree Linden who became the first female jockey to participate in the Melbourne Cup in 1987. There is also a large network of over 400 betting agencies licensed by the nationwide Totalisator Agency Board (TAB) which accept bets on Australian races as well as native ones.

Trotting or harness racing is nearly as popular as flat racing (or "the gallops") having grown, apparently, out of informal roadside contests among the settlers who brought horses with them. The foremost prize is the Lion Brown Interdominion Championship, in which Australian and New Zealand pacers and trotters compete, which is held during the first fortnight in March, and for which the stakes total more than a million dollars. To study form, consult *The Turf Digest* ($2). All racing and trotting radio broadcasts are on the Racing Network, which links the ZB stations and a number of others.

Dog Trials. Apparently the introduction of sheep dog trials in New Zealand predates those in Britain, having started in Wanaka in 1867 as compared to Bala, Wales in 1873. Rural competitions where farmers show off the sheep-mustering skills of their top animals are still popular and are worth seeing, especially if you happen to have missed seeing their Scottish and West Country counterparts on BBC-2's *One Man and his Dog*. Because of the enormous size and ruggedness of stations, New Zealand has bred a special tough dog called a "huntaway" whose loud bark shoos the sheep away and makes it possible for the heading dogs to take over. Demonstrations for tourists are given near Rotorua and Queenstown.

Tourists are also invited to sheep-shearing demonstrations. The annual championships take place in Masterton near Wellington every year in March and the whole nation follows the "Golden Shears" contest. It is not unusual for competitors to shear 20 in an hour.

If you are lucky, your visit will coincide with a rural show day, which are often the annual social highlight for country and small town locals. The Agricultural & Pastoral Society organizes many fairs around the country where prize stock and produce are displayed, handicrafts are exhibited and light-hearted entertainments are arranged.

GAMBLING

A nation of racing fans is a nation of gamblers, and off-track betting is universally enjoyed. Otherwise gambling is strictly controlled; for example slot machines (not including traditional one arm bandits) were only legalized in 1987, and only in approved premises. Football pools and casinos are still illegal, though this is bound to change as New Zealand clamours for the tourist dollar.

"Housie" or bingo is very popular. To confirm this just check under the heading "Housie" in any newspaper's classified section. Many pubs and clubs have a Housie night at least once a week, usually Wednesday or Thursday. A card costs from $4 to $5 and entitles you to play 40 games.

A national lottery, known as Lotto, has recently been introduced for those who prefer a wholly random form of gambling. Tickets may be purchased at participating dairies, shops and country post offices. A minimum four entries costs $2 while the maximum ten (per card) costs $5, and the winning numbers are read out on television on Saturday evening. With an investment of $5, the odds of winning the top prize of $350,000 are 383,000 to one. Proceeds go to a collection of charities including one to help compulsive gamblers.

If you enjoy shopping in Harrod's or Bloomingdales, you may find New Zealand's shopping facilities a little provincial (and a lot more friendly). Most shop fronts are functional at best and dowdy at worst, even in downtown Auckland. Shopping centres are depressingly similar and the range of products on sale very repetitive. The largest chain of department stores is called Farmers, whose unimaginative appearance some travellers have compared unfavourably with that of Eastern European shops. Trendy areas lined with boutiques and cafés are few and far between, though the main cities are slowly creating their own answers to Covent Garden. In cities there is less centralization than in other countries and many suburbanites are content to shop locally. Each residential areas has its own shops, its own butcher, baker, second-hand shop, etc. Look for Central Mission Goodwill Stores and Opportunity Shops for cheap second-hand goods. The large cities have second-hand bookshops which is lucky since new books from overseas are expensive. If you are shipping an expensive item out of the country, ask about GST exemptions; though many disclaim any knowledge of this, it does exist. Many shops geared to the tourist trade will arrange to ship goods; expect to pay about $10 for an item weighing one kilogram, and don't worry about its non-arrival until about three months after purchase. Duty-free shops are neither as numerous nor as cheap as they are in Australia.

Normal shopping hours are 9am (occasionally 9.30am) to 5.30pm Monday to Thursday and 9am to 9pm on Fridays. The expectation among shop employees of a 5-day week is prevalent but slowly weakening, since some downtown and suburban shops now open on Saturday mornings or occasionally until 4pm. Trading on Sundays and on statutory public holidays is largely prohibited. The corner dairy is the main exception and is a godsend with its long hours and range of essential foodstuffs.

A few items which you might want to buy but would have trouble specifying are "jandals" (the Kiwi word for flip-flops) and "Snowtex" (for tissues/Kleenex). Smoking is relatively cheap with a pack of cigarettes costing just under $3.

Imported rolling tobacco (e.g. Old Holborn) is a bargain at around $6 for 50 grams. The major brand of rolling papers (30¢) is Zig Zag; there are two varieties of which the blue packets are the lighter.

Souvenirs. The most common mementoes bought by tourists are greenstone or paua jewellery, sheepskin and woollen products or outdoor gear. Some of the signs and advertisements for retailers of such souvenirs are in Japanese, and their prices reflect this affluent big-spending market. Greenstone is a kind of jade peculiar to New Zealand, found only between two rivers on the South Island near Hokitika (where there is a greenstone factory open to the public). Although the supply of this semi-precious stone is dwindling, prices are not prohibitive. Many stones are fashioned into Maori "tiki", an ornate figure which is said to represent an embryo and hence the source of life. These carvings are understandably expensive so if you see a cheap one for sale it is undoubtedly a mass-produced imitation. The shells of paua (the Maori word for abalone) are vivid blue-green and are made into cheap jewellery; a pair of earrings, for example might cost $12. There is the predictable range of tacky souvenirs such as key rings and bottle openers adorned with greenstone or paua.

Woollen jumpers, socks and blankets are not remarkably cheap despite the overabundance of wool. Designer pullovers and hand-knits are popular and pricey. Knitting unusual jumpers is a thriving cottage industry. One material which you may come across is "slink", the very soft skin of newborn lambs.

New Zealand-made tramping boots, tents, sleeping bags, fishing rods, wetsuits, etc. are generally of very high quality, and the prices reflect this. Hallmark and Macpac Wilderness make good quality camping gear while Line Seven and Dorlon make sailing gear. One of the most famous names is Swanndri which makes woollen bush shirts and jackets ranging in price from $75 to $130. If you hear a New Zealander talk about his or her "Swanni", you will now know what they mean.

If you have some New Zealand currency left over when flying out of the country, you should not have too much trouble spending it at Auckland Airport. Especially recommended are tins of peeled lamb tongues, sure to impress and a bargain at $2.59. They also sell frozen packs of seafood, venison and lamb, though these are not permitted if your journey requires you to clear US customs.

If you want a preview of New Zealand specialities (including kiwifruit toothpaste), visit Kiwifruits Shop (25 Bedfordbury, Covent Garden, London WC2) or the Kiwi Ham & Jam Shop (47 Vanderbilt Road, Earlsfield, London SW18).

Photography. Top name film costs $5-$6.50 for a 24-exposure 135 or 110 cartridge. Developing costs $9-$12 in cities where there is competition.

Electrical Goods. New Zealand appliances operate on 230 volts and 50 Hertz which are compatible with the UK electrical supply but not with the American or Canadian one.

The Great Outdoors

Those who are prepared to throw themselves enthusiastically into the enjoyment of outdoor pursuits are those who find a trip to New Zealand most satisfying. The mountains and glaciers keep the skiers, climbers and hikers happy while the rivers and beaches provide entertainment for fishermen, divers and windsurfers. And between the mountains and the sea, people cycle, raft, watch birds, ride, explore caves, hunt and canoe — every adventure holiday in the book, it seems, with the possible exception of air sports.

Many New Zealanders consider their Great Outdoors as the country's greatest resource, as fish are to Iceland or coffee is to Brazil. Since they cannot export it (except in glossy calenders and *Beautiful New Zealand* magazines), they promote it heavily to foreign visitors, and the complete novice and anti-athlete are not neglected. Every local tourist office displays an impressive array of brochures to persuade you to don a wet suit, mount a bicycle or hire a mountain guide. The booklet *Outdoor Action Holidays* revised annually by the department of tourism is a valuable source of information; for each sport and activity a list of operators is given with an indication of prices.

National Parks. New Zealand has a long tradition of preserving its wilderness, partly in response to a Maori chief who gave three sacred peaks on the North Island to the nation in 1887 on the condition that they could not be settled and spoiled. They were then incorporated into Tongariro National Park, one of the four national parks in the North Island. The mountain range on the South Island is almost continuous national park, though divided into seven designated parks, from the mammoth Fiordland National Park in the south to the coastal Abel Tasman National Park in the north. They are vigorously maintained by the government and improvements for the benefit of visitors are constantly being carried out. For example, a 14th national park called Whanganui River was opened on Waitangi Day 1987, and a new walking track called the Kepler in Fiordland Park officially opens on February 20 1988 as a companion to the heavily used Milford and Routeburn tracks.

National parks are well provided with information centres which offer advice to people wanting to explore and often act also as miniature museums with interesting displays of anything from the geological history of the area to accounts of early hero-explorers and local characters. The staff seem uniformly knowledgeable and courteous and willingly try to answer questions ranging from "why is glacier ice coloured blue?" to "will I need my raingear today?" or "are there any places where camping is forbidden?"

Furthermore the parks run a semi-educational programme involving guided walks, films and demonstrations, all of which are free. Unfortunately it is only worth their while to provide this free entertainment in the busy season from Christmas to February. Parks will be especially active in the first half of 1988, since the festival celebrating a 100 years of national parks has taken for its theme "Parks for People". Without being as fearless or macho as, say, Crocodile Dundee, park rangers command a great deal of respect. If you are attempting anything out of the ordinary, always discuss your plans with a ranger and register your intentions in as much detail as possible.

In addition to the national parks, New Zealand also has three maritime parks (Bay of Islands, Hauraki Gulf around Auckland and Marlborough Sounds) and 21 forest parks, all of which are administered by the newly-formed Department of Conservation which swallowed the old Lands and Survey Department in 1987. One of the by-products of this change, much detested by many locals, was that rangers are now to be known as "Conservation Officers". There is also talk of bringing in an admission charge of $1 for New Zealanders and $5 for tourists.

Wildlife. Until the Maori arrived, New Zealand was completely devoid of mammals, with the exception of a rare breed of bat. Apparently moas, giant emu-like birds whose skeletons and fossilized eggs can be admired in many museums, served the purpose of cattle by grazing the land, until they were wiped out by the early moa-hunting Maori. A few unique species of bird have survived, though many were destroyed by settlers and by introduced animals which found these flightless birds easy prey. The most famous flightless bird has become New Zealand's national symbol (but not Air New Zealand's); the kiwi is difficult to spot in the bush since it is a nocturnal bird. But several zoos and "kiwi houses" scattered around the country make it easy to admire this surprisingly small creature.

Nowadays there are rigorously enforced laws protecting the native fauna (and also vegetation) and equally energetic attempts to keep the number of non-indigenous animals like deer, rabbits, wallabies and opossums under control. In fact a new company called the Kiwi Bear Company has begun farming and marketing possum fur and meat, the latter mainly intended for Hong Kong. Wallabies are such pests that they must be constantly culled. Some entrepreneurs have tried to pass this off as sport and have been charging bloodthirsty tourists $35 an hour to participate in wallaby-massacres from jeeps. Deer hunting is also encouraged and licences may be obtained from park rangers.

For those who simply want to observe the wildlife, there are many nature reserves and feeding grounds. Hector dolphins favour Akaroa Harbour. The prehistoric-looking lizard called tuatara is protected on a couple of offshore islands such as Poor Knights in the Hauraki Gulf or Stephens and Trio Islands in the Marlborough Sounds. But they are also on view to a wider public in Auckland Zoo and the Invercargill tuatarium. There are colonies of penguin and albatross on the Otago Peninsula near Dunedin. White heron gather on the west coast near Okarito and gannets breed at Cape Kidnappers, Hawke's Bay. One bird you will have no trouble seeing is the kea, a charmless dull-coloured parrot with red underwings and a discordant cry, an unlovable answer to Australia's kookaburra. The kea likes human habitations, especially rubbish bins, and will peck at almost anything from hiking boots left outside to sheep.

TRAMPING

Hiking, always known as tramping, is New Zealand's national pastime, and every visitor should make an effort to penetrate the country's bush on foot. If you are going to be based in one place for any length of time, you could join a local tramping club. Visitor information centres often distribute leaflets describing simple strolls and strenuous treks which can be made from the centre.

For example from the North Egmont Visitor Centre you can make a 20-minute circuit past some typical North Island vegetation or begin a four-day circuit of Mount Egmont, with of course several choices in between which are all well sign-posted.

Even Britons who have never tackled Mount Snowdon and Americans who have never strayed from the Midwestern prairies find themselves tempted by the idea of a relatively serious mountain walk while in New Zealand. For whatever reason, the Milford Track has become so famous, especially among American city-slickers, that many people book months in advance. But there are dozens of other tracks on both islands which may not be household names but are equally scenic.

The New Zealand Walkways Commission publishes an inviting little book describing over 100 walks ranging from one to 66 kilometres. The Commission, which is part of the Department of Conservation, has as its main object to develop walkways near urban areas. One of its long term projects, however, is to establish a network of interlinking tracks so it will be possible to walk from the North Cape to Bluff in the South. But it will take many years before unsympathetic landowners can be persuaded to allow the public access. Any office of the Department of Conservation should be able to give you a free copy of the Walkways booklet, or write in advance to the Department of Conservation, PO Box 10420, The Terrace, Wellington.

Tramps are designated according to difficulty: "walks" are simple enough for children and are usually maintained by the New Zealand Walkways Commission; "tracks" are easy-to-follow paths though they can be steep and strenuous; "routes" can be difficult to follow and therefore appeal to experienced hill walkers who can navigate by compass.

Many visitors of average fitness elect to do a two to four day tramp along a clearly marked track supplied with huts. The book *Tramping in New Zealand* (Lonely Planet, £3.95/NZ$8.95) describes in detail 20 tramps ranging from mild to strenuous and is useful for choosing a suitable trek. Access to the starting point of the walk is sometimes a little tricky, though enterprising locals usually operate a mini-bus or motor boat specifically for trekkers. It is also not uncommon to meet someone on the trail who has arranged for a car to be waiting for him or her at the other end and who will offer a lift.

Tramping huts are usually simple solidly-built structures, similar in atmosphere to youth hostels but without male-female segregation. Hut beds cannot be reserved beforehand, and so there is sometimes an undignified scramble for beds along the popular routes at the popular times. The tourist literature often advises trampers to carry a tent in case huts are full, but this is of little use when camping is prohibited. It is amazing how many bodies can be crammed into a hut after the bunks have been taken, and trampers will not be turned out into the cold unless there is a less crowded hut within easy range. On the main tracks resident wardens can help with any problems, though their main task is to maintain the hut and surrounding trails and collect the hut fee of $7. If there is no warden there may be an honesty box.

In all cases you must be self-sufficient in food, though gas rings and running water are normally provided. Unless you opt for one of the pampered escorted walks on the Routeburn or the Milford tracks (over $600 for the three-day walk) you will have to carry all your food as well as carrying out your rubbish so try to avoid an excess of tins. If you fancy the luxury of freeze-dried lamb dinners, you should purchase a camping saucepan before setting off. But it is perfectly feasible to dine on cold food for a couple of days such as muesli, dried milk, tinned fish, bread (preferably pumpernickel or rye if you can find them), cheese, dried fruit, "scroggin" (a New Zealand concoction of fruit, nuts and seeds specifically for tramping), etc. You can also take some packet soups which can be boiled up in a borrowed billy. It is a little trickier borrowing dishes and utensils, so you should carry your own.

Equipment and Safety. Despite the absence of dangerous creatures, much emphasis is placed on outdoor safety. Alarming posters published by the New Zealand Mountain Safety Council show innocent hikers wading waist-deep in freezing water a few hours after having enjoyed a picnic in the same place. In fact sudden changes of weather, very common in maritime climates, account for the bulk of the problems. Long dry spells are rare, but, if you are lucky enough to encounter one, keep your eye on the graphs which show risk of forest fire and be very careful with any flame.

In addition to your provisions — enough to last the walk plus emergency rations in case you become weather-bound — you must have a warm sleeping bag since bedding is not supplied and even summer nights can become extremely cold in the unheated huts. A worn-in pair of boots is a definite asset, though some people do attempt the simpler tracks in plimsolls, which soon become inadequate in bad weather.

Warm and waterproof gear is essential. Even if you feel like an idiot packing a woollen hat, gloves, long johns and rain gear in the middle of summer, you should not walk without these items. Snowfalls are not particularly rare on passes and saddles in summer, though you are more likely to be bombarded by torrential rainfall and piercing winds. The New Zealand Mountain Safety Council publishes a pamphlet on hypothermia, a condition which should be guarded against at all costs. Another of their useful leaflets is called "Heading for the Bush" which explains how to cope with wilderness dangers such as swollen river crossings and how to attract the attention of rescue parties. These are mainly relevant to the off-the-beaten-track routes which should not be attempted by the inexperienced. A large number of companies conduct escorted hikes in remote terrain which cost from $150 for two days to nearly $3,000 for three weeks.

WATER SPORTS

Jetboating. Most of the rivers of New Zealand are so fast and turbulent that a special boat had to be invented to cope with them. The jet boat, which was developed about 20 years ago, operates by sucking water in and jetting it out the back with such force that the craft is propelled forward. It can travel upstream, through rapids and in just a few inches of water. Although it is fast, the sensation is not much different from riding in an ordinary outboard motor powered boat. A typical trip would last half an hour and cost between $20 and $50. Often you will have to wait for a full complement of tourists to assemble before the trip can take place. In a few places it is possible to hire a jet boat and drive it yourself on lakes and gentle rivers.

Rafting. Adventurous travellers are more attracted to the idea of white water rafting. Rafting operators can be found in about ten towns on both islands, organizing trips lasting from a few hours to a week. Sometimes access to the starting point has to be by helicopter. Queenstown is the capital of rafting and few who visit can resist the temptations laid before them by the competing operators. Prices start at $60 for a morning on the Wairoa River (two hours drive from Auckland and therefore popular) to $675 for a five day camping expedition in the backcountry of the South Island. Rivers are graded internationally on a scale of one to six and several companies take novices through grade five rapids. Rafters are given a wetsuit, a paddle and half an hour of instruction, and usually a picnic or barbecue at the end of the run.

Fishing. New Zealand has a reputation for having some of the best fishing in the world, both for wealthy tourists in pursuit of big game like marlin or for more humble rod fishermen. The locals are so confident that their fishing is unsurpassable that recently some hotel proprietors on Lake Taupo (famed for its trout) were promising free accommodation to any fisherman who failed to catch a fish. But not all reports of fishing are as favourable, especially among game fishermen who are catching fewer and fewer marlin and shark in the once-fecund waters of the Bay of Islands, the Coromandel and the Bay of Plenty. Commercial Japanese fishing fleets are blamed for the depletion. Since big game charter boats costs between $400 and $600 a day, this will come as a disappointment to only a few.

There is no closed season for trout fishing. The sport is monitored by the many branches of the Acclimatization Society (headed at present by the aptly named Tony Drinkwater) which issue licences for trout and salmon fishing valid throughout New Zealand, though all government tourist offices can arrange a one-month permit for visitors. Special permits are needed for Rotorua and Taupo, while no permit is needed for game fishing. For a long list of fishing guides and outfitters, see the tourist brochure *Outdoor Action Holidays*.

Other Activities. Canoeing, windsurfing, surfing and scuba diving all flourish in various places. Since New Zealand lacks a reef, the bombed Greenpeace flagship *The Rainbow Warrior* was sunk off the North Island coast at Matauri Bay in December 1987, for the benefit of divers. The water is said to be clearest in April whereas in spring plankton obscures the fish. New Zealand is also a nation of yachtsmen, and sailboats may be chartered in resort areas such as the Bay of Islands. Cruising yachts should remember to fill in the Ministry of Transport's "ten-minute form" and hand it in at any police station, informing the authorities of your intentions; this is to help Search and Rescue in case of an emergency. Sometimes the best surfing beaches are accessible only by crossing private land; always ask the farmer's permission and be sure to close gates and refrain from littering.

SKIING

Skiing is centred on Queenstown, Wanaka, Mount Cook, Mount Hutt and Tekapo in the South Island and Mount Ruapehu and Mount Taranaki on the North Island. Most skiers prefer the drier conditions and more reliable snowfalls of South Island skiing, though the danger of avalanches is always present. Commercial ski fields equipped with a range of lifts, ski hire facilities, etc., are opening and expanding all the time, so that there are now 12 in total, in addition to five club fields. Because there are so few roads into the mountains, heli-skiing (where skiers are flown to mountain tops) is popular even though it costs from about $350 a day. The ski season lasts from June until October or even November in some places.

CYCLING

New Zealand, like the Netherlands, is considered an ideal cycling country, though the terrain could hardly be more different. The scarcity of traffic together with the magnificent scenery persuades many that cycle touring is an excellent way to travel around New Zealand, which is true, until it rains. Several holiday organizers provide everything short of good weather — a fully equipped bicycle, a guide, all meals and accommodation (either in hotels or camping) and a support van to carry luggage and help out with repairs. The best known is the Bicycle Touring Company (PO Box 23-215, Papatoetoe, Auckland) who charge about $1,200 for two week tours of the North Island. Several other companies arrange less expensive tours such as Bicycle Tour Services (PO Box 11-296, Auckland 5) and Pedaltours Bicycle Adventures (PO Box 49-039, Roskill South, Auckland 4). Independent cyclists should get hold of the relevant handbook from Southern Cyclist, PO Box 5890, Auckland: *Cycle Touring in the North Island* costs $9.95 and the companion volume to the South Island $5.

It is possible to hire cycles just for a day in many places such as Christchurch and Rotorua. You should expect to pay about $8 a day for an ordinary bicycle and $12 to $15 for a racing bicycle. If you are very keen and enjoy group events you can participate in the annual circumnavigation of Lake Taupo (about 160km) in November.

New Zealand enjoys a reputation for safety, both because of its distance from nuclear threats — applications to emigrate rose substantially following the Chernobyl disaster in 1986 — and for its sane, law-abiding populace. The country's wholesomeness and safety extend to its city streets where crime, by world standards, is very low. Many cyclists and car owners do not bother to lock their vehicles, in fact some older models of New Zealand-assembled cars are not even fitted with door locks. Police (who drive white cars with blue lights) are barely in evidence on town and city streets. Unless you are driving recklessly they will pay no attention, since there is a separate traffic department to cope with road offenders.

Crime does exist, however, and visitors are not exempt. Tourists are a favourite target of thieves throughout the world and New Zealand is no exception, even if it does happen infrequently enough to make headlines. Usually wealthy tourists are the main target of theft, however there have been several reported cases of theft from youth hostels, so be alert. You should exercise a reasonable amount of caution, especially in remote sightseeing spots where tourists park; for example there were 2663 thefts from cars in the Bay of Plenty region in 1986. In the busy tourist season of 1987, posters displayed in

Wellington and Picton warned of a worrying increase in disappearance of checked baggage including rucksacks on the ferry, so keep yours with you if possible. If you are unfortunate enough to lose one, pester the Railways Corporation for compensation, since they have been paying lump sums of $1000.

An even more alarming trend was reported in the South Island of travellers perpetrating crimes, such as one who stole a moneybelt from a fellow hosteller, another who stole the car of a local after accepting a lift and still another who mugged a native who had offered a bed for the night. This kind of thing soon sours relations between travellers and locals.

Gangs are common in New Zealand, especially the Mongrel Mob whose large gatherings (for conventions or heavy rock concerts) are well publicized.

Drugs. Cannabis thrives in the New Zealand climate and is very widely grown and consumed. The strain grown is said to be among the most potent in the world. The police periodically find large plantings in amongst maize crops or forests, though they are able to trace and destroy only a fraction of the total. The most recent discovey was on the roof of a University of Auckland building. The drug enforcement authorities concentrate on prosecuting pushers and growers, though ordinary possession incurs a minimum fine of $200 up to $1000 or a year's imprisonment. There is a fairly strong and respectable lobby for the legalization of cannabis, on the grounds that enforcement is a waste of taxpayers' money and police time, and also that the drug search warrant powers have eroded civil rights. Most hitch-hikers will be offered a joint at some stage. A peculiarly New Zealand term for marijuana is "electric puha".

Hard drugs are not as grave a problem as they are in Europe and North America, though there are growing indications that Mafia-led drug rings are infiltrating New Zealand.

Other Crimes. Motoring offences have already been discussed in *Getting Around: Driving*. One other minor infringement is topless bathing at public pools, which often earns a reprimand from the guard. If you want to strip on a beach, choose one which offers some protection by sand dunes to reduce the risk of causing offence.

The New Zealand government tourist organization is called the New Zealand Tourist and Publicity Department or NZTP and, true to its name, it energetically publicizes and promotes tourism. The figures are impressive: the number of overseas visitors has been increasing by over 15% annually over the past couple of years.

In addition to the annually revised *New Zealand Book* which provides a good introduction to sight-seeing possibilities, NZTP also publish a useful range of booklets on specific topics such as their *Outdoor Action Holidays* and *The New Zealand Motoring Book*. On the whole, NZTP literature contains a fairly high ratio of practical information to the rapturous twaddle so often favoured by tourism copy-writers. NZTP offices around the world efficiently distribute their printed information and are also happy to advise on specific questions. The British office is at New Zealand House, Haymarket, London SW1Y 4TQ (tel: 01-930 8422) and usually replies to enquiries within a week. North American office addresses are:

Citicorp Center, 1 Sansome Street, San Francisco, CA 94104.
Suite 1530, 10960 Wilshire Boulevard, Los Angeles, CA 90024.
Suite 530, 630 Fifth Avenue, New York, NY 10111.
Suite 1260, IBM Tower, 701 West Georgia Street, Vancouver, BC, Canada.

There are also NZTP offices in most Australian state capitals, since Australia sends more tourists to New Zealand than any other country.

In New Zealand there are NZTP offices in Auckland, Rotorua, Wellington, Christchurch, Dunedin and Queenstown, whose primary purpose is to help visitors to plan and book their itinerary for the country (addresses in relevant *Help & Information* sections). As well as disseminating information, they also act as booking agents for airlines, railways and many tour operators. This ambitious range of services means that their resources are sometimes stretched especially in the summer. When there is a long queue, you are expected to have a few specific requests, and you may not be told of the complete range of options.

If you want local information you should visit the town or city's Public Relations Office (PRO); these act as visitor information centres and may be found in the six cities listed above and in over 40 other towns. For these addresses, as well as those of the national and forest park information centres, ask an NZTP office for a useful map called *New Zealand Visitor Information Centres* with the North Island on one side and South Island on the reverse. This map also shows roads, railways, points of interest, etc. Another very useful source of information on local sights to see, special events and performances, etc. are the giveaway newspapers published in all the cities and distributed through tourist offices.

If you would like information about New Zealand before you go, you should look at a few copies of the free weekly newspaper *New Zealand News UK* aimed at New Zealanders living in Britain. It summarizes the political, sporting and local news from New Zealand as well as including travel features. If you are in London try to pick up a copy from its office at 25 Royal Opera Arcade, Haymarket, London SW1 (ajdacent to New Zealand House) or from distribution boxes scattered throughout London. The magazines *LAM, New Australasian Express* and *TNT* (free in London) are primarily intended for Australians, but contain a page or two of New Zealand news. Major New Zealand national newspapers are displayed at New Zealand House (address above).

The New Zealand Automobile Association has already been mentioned in the section *Getting Around: Driving* as a useful source of road maps, suggested itineraries and motoring information. They also publish their own accommodation guides. Local district maps are free of charge, however a small charge is made for country maps. They will also make travel bookings for members.

Mothers travelling with children may make use of "Plunket Rooms". The Plunket Society was formed at the beginning of the century to provide prenatal and postnatal advice and care. Their rooms are located centrally in most towns and have first class loos which women travellers may wish to visit.

Emergencies. To summon help by telephone, dial 111 in cities. Elsewhere call the operator (by dialling 010) or dial the toll-free emergency number posted in public call boxes.

If you are venturing into the wilderness, always register your route intentions with rangers or contacts who can alert Search and Rescue workers if you fail to return.

In the case of financial emergencies, see page 50 to find out about how to arrange for money to be transferred from home.

Consulates. The British High Commission is on the ninth and tenth floors of the Reserve Bank Building behind Parliament at the corner of The Terrace and Bowen Street in Wellington (tel: 726-049). There are also Consulates in Auckland (9th Floor, Norwich Union Building, 179 Queen Street) and in Christchurch (The Dome, Regent Theatre Building, Cathedral Square). The American Embassy is at 29 Fitzherbert Terrace, Thorndon, Wellington.

Students. The principal function of Student Travel Services (NZ) Ltd, which has branches and agents in all university towns, is to help New Zealand students. However visitors holding an international student card (ISIC) are eligible for the many discounts which STS has negotiated for students, and which are mentioned throughout the text. ISIC card holders should always ask at theatres, cinemas, etc. if there are discounts. In case students want to seek STS's advice on further travel arrangements, addresses are given in the city chapters.

PUBLIC HOLIDAYS

There are ten statutory holidays, five of which have fixed dates. These are Christmas, Boxing Day, New Year's Day, Waitangi Day on February 6th (to celebrate the signing of a treaty with the Maori people in 1840) and Anzac Day on April 25th (to commemorate the battle of Gallipoli where 88% of New Zealand troops died). Good Friday and Easter Monday of course change from year to year as do the Queen's Birthday (the first Monday in June) and Labour Day (the fourth Monday in October).

In addition each of the regions has an Anniversary Day which varies from place to place and is celebrated on the nearest Monday. Auckland's Anniversary is celebrated not only in the city but also in a region extending from the north of the country to Taupo. Here are the relevant moveable dates:

Anniversaries	*1988*	*1989*	*1990*
Auckland & Northland	Feb 1	Jan 30	Jan 29
Hawke's Bay	Oct 31	Oct 30	Oct 29
Taranaki	Mar 28	Apr 3	Apr 2
Wellington	Jan 25	Jan 23	Jan 22
Marlborough	Oct 31	Oct 30	Oct 29
Christchurch & Canterbury	Dec 19	Dec 18	Dec 17
Westland	Nov 28	Dec 4	Dec 3
Dunedin, Otago & Southland	Mar 21	Mar 20	Mar 26
Other Holidays			
Queen's Birthday	Jun 6	Jun 5	Jun 4
Labour Day	Oct 24	Oct 23	Oct 22

An unofficial holiday is the first Tuesday in November for the Melbourne Cup.

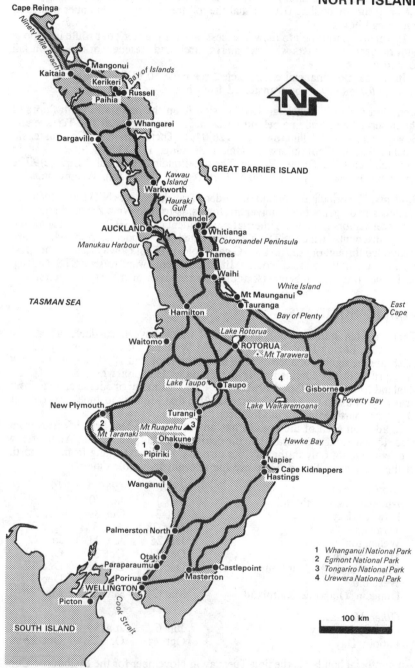

NORTH ISLAND

Cape Reinga
Ninety Mile Beach
Mangonui
Kaitaia
Kerikeri
Bay of Islands
Russell
Paihia
Whangarei
Dargaville

GREAT BARRIER ISLAND

Kawau Island
Warkworth
Hauraki Gulf
Coromandel
AUCKLAND
Whitianga
Coromandel Peninsula
Manukau Harbour
Thames
Waihi
White Island
Mt Maunganui
Tauranga
Bay of Plenty
East Cape
Hamilton
Lake Rotorua
Waitomo
ROTORUA
Mt Tarawera

TASMAN SEA

Lake Taupo
Taupo
Gisborne
Poverty Bay
New Plymouth
Lake Waikaremoana
Turangi
Mt Ruapehu
2
Mt Taranaki
3
1
Ohakune
Pipiriki
Hawke Bay
Napier
Cape Kidnappers
Wanganui
Hastings

Palmerston North

Otaki
Paraparaumu
Porirua
WELLINGTON
Masterton
Castlepoint
Picton
Cook Strait
SOUTH ISLAND

1 *Whanganui National Park*
2 *Egmont National Park*
3 *Tongariro National Park*
4 *Urewera National Park*

100 km

The North Island

Population of Auckland: 820,754　　　**Population of Wellington: 325,697**

The North Island is far more densely populated than the South, containing nearly three-quarters of the country's total population. In addition to the capital Wellington and the largest city Auckland, there are six other cities with populations in excess of 50,000 which by New Zealand standards is very populous indeed.

Whereas the geographic sensation of the South Island is its glaciers, the remarkable feature of the North is its volcanic history. The most impressive mountains of the North Island such as Mount Taranaki and Mount Ruapehu were formed as symmetrical cones by erupting volcanoes, and much of the surrounding land was enriched by the lava flows. Some volcanoes like Ngauruhoe are still active, though you are more likely to be swallowed up by an earthquake than buried in lava, since the possibility of full-scale eruptions is very remote.

Elsewhere in the North Island the scenery encompasses tame pastoral scenes, majestic tropical beaches and even a few barren near-deserts. Each of the two bulges of land halfway down the Island — the Taranaki Peninsula in the west and the East Coast Province — has its individual character and various attractions. There is a choice of routes from Auckland to Wellington but the boiling mud and geysers in the centre are not to be missed.

CLIMATE

Auckland's climate in summer is mostly genial, though you may be unlucky and visit during a rainy spell. Hot days in summer send everyone to the North Shore beaches. The blistering heat of an Australian summer's day is rare, partly due to the moderating influence of the water which virtually surrounds Auckland. There is quite often a stiff breeze which creates attractive shifting skies and keeps down the humidity, but can also chill the air. The winters are normally mild (around 13°C) but fairly rainy, with July as the wettest month with an average of 21 days of precipitation.

The rest of the island follows a similar pattern, with an average rainfall of 135cm a year, though the eastern areas are somewhat drier. The southern parts of the island are several degrees cooler than Auckland, while Northland, the narrow peninsula stretching north of Auckland to the same latitude as Sydney, is semi-tropical and winters remain pleasantly mild. Unfortunately, this is also the wettest part of the North Island.

"VISITORS MIGHT THINK THAT WELLINGTONIANS SUFFER FROM SOME EXOTIC DISEASE."

Wellington is notorious for being the windiest capital city in the world. A visitor might unwittingly come to the conclusion that the people of Wellington suffer from some dreadful genetic defect which causes them to walk at an incline. In fact, the winds that give Chicago the name "Windy City" are no more than breezes when compared to those into which you will find yourself leaning in Wellington. On some days the gales are so strong that only Captains (rather than First Officers) of Air New Zealand aircraft are permitted to land at the city's airport. To escape the wind, you will either have to cross over to the relatively sheltered South Island, or travel inland where the Tararua Ranges afford some protection. Wellington gets just as many hours of sunshine as the much balmier Bay of Islands.

AUCKLAND

Some say that Auckland is a Sydney for beginners. The harbourside location,

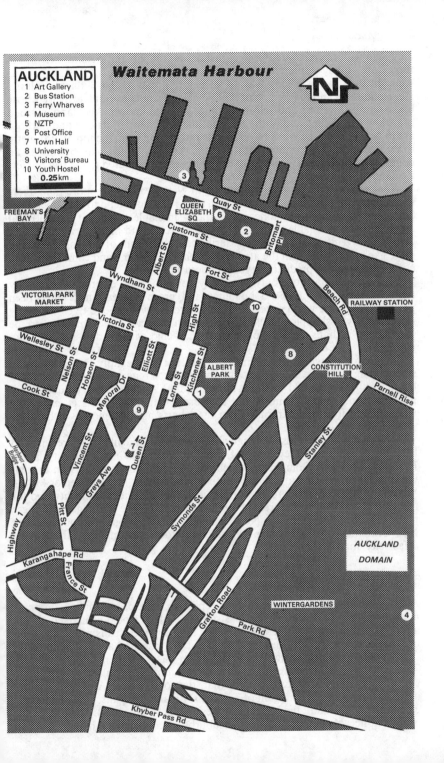

Waitemata Harbour

AUCKLAND
1 Art Gallery
2 Bus Station
3 Ferry Wharves
4 Museum
5 NZTP
6 Post Office
7 Town Hall
8 University
9 Visitors' Bureau
10 Youth Hostel
0.25 km

FREEMAN'S BAY

QUEEN ELIZABETH SQ

Quay St

Customs St

Britomart Pl

Albert St

Fort St

Wyndham St

VICTORIA PARK MARKET

High St

Beach Rd

RAILWAY STATION

Victoria St

Wellesley St

Nelson St

Hobson St

Elliott St

Mayoral Dr

Lorne St

Kitchener St

ALBERT PARK

CONSTITUTION HILL

Parnell Rise

Cook St

Vincent St

Queen St

Greys Ave

Stanley St

Harbour Bridge

Highway 1

Symonds St

Pitt St

Karangahape Rd

France St

Gratton Road

Park Rd

Khyber Pass Rd

AUCKLAND DOMAIN

WINTERGARDENS

complete with overcrowded bridge, justifies a comparison to some extent, but there are many differences. However much Auckland boasts of its sophistication, it has a long way to go before it can match Sydney's cultural life, restaurants and markets. Not that Auckland wants to emulate a city whose brash competitiveness and self-importance are well known. Auckland is proud of its low rise skyline and of the fact that the best views of its city and harbour are to be had from the grass-covered hills rather than from the top of 300-metre towers. Auckland is content with its achievements, which may be modest in comparison to those of Sydney but dramatic when compared to the rest of New Zealand.

What radical breakthroughs there are in New Zealand are more than likely to take place in Auckland. For example, shops and pubs tend to stay open later (Saturday shopping was pioneered in the fashionable suburb of Parnell) and night club acts are liable to be more risqué in Auckland than anywhere else in the country. This has the not necessarily desirable result of making Auckland more like other cities, with the attendant problems of crime and commercialism, not to mention the predictability of modern urban life.

Yet Auckland has gone only some way down the road of progress. The city centre boasts many fine old buildings and green spaces which have been preserved from the worst excesses of commercial development. Even the many American-style shopping arcades off Queen Street do not manage to be convincing, perhaps because of the less-than-chic window-dressing and sign writing.

Great efforts have also been made to preserve and beautify the harbour and surrounding buildings. The price to be paid for such renovations is that restored buildings such as the Old Customs House and the Auckland Ferry Building are now glorified shopping centres, but they are a definite visual asset, especially when viewed from the harbour. Even the wharfs and warehouses behind the station look quite spruce.

Auckland's setting is also distinguished by the volcanic hills scattered around the city. In fact there is evidence of about 60 volcanoes inside the city limits. Even the Auckland Domain on which the Museum now stands is an ancient volcano. The trip to the top of one of these hills, such as Mount Eden or Mount Victoria on the North Shore, is worthwhile for an overview of the city and for the sudden rural ambience created by the sheep and cattle which graze in these reserves (called "domains" in New Zealand). It is very odd — but typical of New Zealand — to see the sign "Wandering Stock" just minutes after leaving a fast city road.

THE LOCALS

Although the population of the city is creeping up towards one million, it retains many small town features. A shop assistant in Sydney would be unlikely to ask a foreign visitor about his or her proposed itinerary, yet this is not uncommon in Auckland where many residents have not yet lost the habits of hospitality.

A large proportion of Auckland's population was not born in the city. Greater Auckland has been growing at an alarming rate, both in population and in area, sprawling over an area even greater than that of London. Among the many newcomers is a large contingent of Samoans, Fijians, Tongans, Cook Islanders, etc., making Auckland the largest Polynesian city in the world. Their influence is most noticeable in those residential suburbs where there is a high proportion of rented accommodation. Although large numbers of Maori people live in the city, and the number is increasing, their profile is relatively low. In the downtown district, Karangahape Road (sometimes referred to simply as K Road) is the Polynesian area.

Getting Around

ARRIVAL AND DEPARTURE

Air. Auckland International Airport is 22km south of the city in the suburb of Mangere. If you arrive in daylight, you will have the sensation of landing on water as your aircraft banks over Manukau Harbour, on which the airport is situated. A shortage of space and of customs staff has been responsible for some long delays, especially in the mornings when several thousand overseas passengers arrive within a couple of hours. Partly because it is small, the airport is not in any way daunting, and has a couple of useful shops selling books, post cards and souvenirs in the arrivals-cum-transit lounge. Similarly, those departing from Auckland International Airport can spend their remaining dollars on Maori mementoes, kiwifruit wine, New Zealand cheddar, etc. in the departure lounge shops; remember to keep $2 aside for the departure tax which you must pay at check-in.

The journey into town takes about 50 minutes. Johnston's Blue Motors (tel: 275-9396) operates a half-hourly service between 7am and 10pm for $7 single, $12 return. Its final destination is the Downtown Airline Terminal on Quay Street, but it stops at several hotels (including one directly opposite the railway station) en route. The same bus departs for the airport from the Downtown Terminal every 30 minutes from 6am to 9pm. Tickets may be purchased from the driver if you have not been able to buy them from the relevant counter at either end in advance.

There are taxi ranks outside both international and domestic terminals, and the fare to the city centre is about $26, though with a surcharge after 10pm and at weekends. The two terminals are connected by a shuttle bus which charges $1.50; even with luggage you should manage the 800-metre walk in ten minutes.

Most airlines have their offices within a short distance of the Downtown Airline Terminal. Air New Zealand is at 1 Queen Street (tel: 797-515) and Ansett NZ is at 50 Grafton Road (freefone: 376-950).

If you are planning to fly in a small aircraft to more local destinations such as Great Barrier Island, there are a number of small charters such as Ardmore Air Charters (tel: 299-6692) and Sea Bee Air (tel: 774-406) which fly, for example, from Mechanics Bay to Waiheke Island three times a day for $44 return. For services to Great Barrier Island try Air North Shore (tel: 0942 64-273) and Great Barrier Airlines (tel: 275-9120).

Coach. The Downtown Airline Terminal also acts as a depot for several long distance coach companies such as Mount Cook, Clarks which serve Northland (tel: 796-056) and Mainline which serve Taupo (tel: 771-878). There is a coach office in the terminal which is open 6am to 9pm and can advise on schedules and prices. The Mount Cook travel office is at 105 Queen St (tel: 395-395) while Newmans at 205 Hobson St can be telephoned on 399-738. The government tourist office, NZTP, on Queen St can book coach journeys on the major operators. NZRRS (tel: 794-600) use the railway station as their depot and sell their tickets from an office inside the station as well as from NZTP.

Train. The railway station (tel: 792-500), is on Beach Road a street which, despite its name, does not run along the waterfront. Not many city buses pass the station, so you will have to walk the ten minutes from the city bus station or from the bottom of Symonds Street. Pedestrians (unlike cars which must make a detour) can reach the station by heading straight down Constitution Hill.

Like all railway stations in New Zealand, Auckland's rarely bustles, however its travel office is open from 7.30am to 7.30pm to advise; it is even open on Sundays though only from 8am. There are only two arrivals and two departures each day: the *Silver Fern* departs at 8.30am and the *Northerner* at 9.15pm, arriving in Wellington at 6.30pm and 8.30am respectively. There is a left luggage office which operates free of charge to NZR clients.

Driving. Comparison shopping among car hire firms is especially worthwhile. Here are a few of the cheaper local agencies:

Henderson Rental Cars, 9 Dora St, Henderson (836-8089).
North Harbour Rental Cars (444-4343/444-5404).
Pennywise Rent-a-Car, 110-116 Nelson St (394-757).
Percy Rent-a-Car, 219 Hobson St (31-129).
Southern Cross (276-3603).

Prices start at $20 a day plus 18¢ per kilometre. The cheapest unlimited mileage rate in 1987 (by North Harbour) was $38 plus insurance.

If you want to hire a campervan, try the major hire firms (whose telephone numbers are listed on page 381 in the Introduction) and the smaller companies such as Suntrek Campavans (tel: 501-404) who were advertising campers at $53 a day or Adventure Rental Vehicles Ltd (freefone: 642-905).

Prospective car buyers should attend the Saturday car market at Newmarket on the Khyber Pass Road (at Broadway) early in the morning (before 10am).

Hitch-hiking. Because of its massive sprawl, Auckland is more awkward than other cities to hitch out of. Invest in a bus to the end of the motorway, i.e. Albany if you are heading north and Otahuhu or Papakura if you are heading south.

CITY TRANSPORT

City Layout. Because Auckland incorporates a number of hills, streets do not keep to a grid pattern, and it is not always easy to get your bearings. Even locating the sea is not a safe means of navigating since the Manukau Harbour to the south-west and the Waitemata Harbour to the north are only a few kilometres apart could be confused by a newcomer gazing down from the top of Mount Eden. But it is usually possible to locate the cluster of downtown buildings since they are the only buildings more than a storey high.

Most tourist handout maps will cover only the downtown area, so if you want to visit the North Shore or the suburbs, you will have to purchase a detailed map with street index such as the one produced by Minimaps. The AA publish a useful map in colour of Downtown Auckland, which clearly shows the amount of green space, as well as many landmarks. Queen St running down from the Karangahape Road to Customs Street near the waterfront is Auckland's main shopping street.

Walking tours, along various routes such as the Domain and the waterfront, are organized by the Parks Department of the City Council free of charge; ring

792-020 for details. A private firm charges $15 for a 90-minute walking tour of the inner city; ring 790-031. The public library in Parnell (390 Parnell Road) occasionally organizes free walking tours of this historic part of Auckland.

Bus. The Auckland Regional Authority (ARA) operate all city and suburban buses which provide a fairly frequent and affordable service to most destinations. Unfortunately there is no central information kiosk downtown and not all buses originate at the bus terminal which is near the harbour, just off Customs Street East. But bus information is obtainable by phoning Buz-a-bus on 797-119 or from the Visitors Bureau in Aotea Square (tel: 31-889).

An inner city shuttle bus painted bright yellow with a red destination sign travels every ten minutes from the station, via Customs St and along Queen St. The flat fee for any distance on this downtown route is 30¢. Outside this area, prices vary according to distance; a typical suburban run will cost about $1.50. Exact change is not necessary.

Buses from outside the city centre will be marked either "Downtown" or "Midtown" depending on whether they terminate at the bus terminal near the harbour (i.e. Downtown) or at the corner of Victoria and Queen Streets (i.e. Midtown). This corner has a large number of bus stops where you are likely to find plenty of friendly Aucklanders willing to advise. A few of the buses you might need are: 635, 645 and 655 to Parnell, 005 to the Victoria Park Market, 302 to One Tree Hill (from Victoria St E.) and 274 to Mount Eden (from Customs St E.).

There are two free buses in Auckland. One is provided by Farmers department store (23 Hobson St) which shuttles between the corner of Queen and Wyndham Streets and also from the bottom of Pitt St near the Karangahape Road to the Hobson St store. A more interesting free bus is called the Questar Free Fun Bus which travels along scenic Tamaki Drive. This is a useful service if you want to visit the Kelly Tarlton Aquarium (described below) or if you just want to view the harbour from a double decker. Unfortunately it operates infrequently: every two hours at weekends and holidays only.

A monorail system to link Manukau with Auckland city centre is under consideration in honour of the 1990 Commonwealth Games.

Car. Parking restrictions normally operate between 8am and 6pm on weekdays except Fridays and late shopping nights when the restrictions are extended until 9pm. Car parks can be found at the following city locations (among others): Albert St near Victoria St W, Britomart Place beside the bus terminal, the Civic Centre on Mayoral Drive, and the corner of Customs St W and Hobson St. Charges in car park buildings and downtown meters start at 50¢ for half an hour.

Traffic does not usually get snarled up, except on the kilometre-long Harbour Bridge if there is an accident or repairs are being carried out. When the bridge was opened in 1959 it had only four lanes which soon proved inadequate. A Japanese engineering firm later attached four more lanes to the bridge which are universally known as the Nippon Clip-ons. But even eight lanes are not enough for the 90,000 vehicles which now cross daily and it is estimated that by 1995, motorists will face delays of up to four hours. In 1987 the Auckland Regional Authority approved the building of a tunnel (instead of a second bridge or a monorail suspended from the present bridge). This should be completed by 1991 and is likely to be a toll tunnel. Tolls may also be reinstated on the bridge to try to recoup some of the cost of the tunnel project.

Taxis. To phone for a taxi ring Eastern Taxis on 579-579 or Auckland Co-operative on 792-792. Do not try to hail a cab downtown. Ask to be directed to the nearest taxi rank.

Cycling. Although you would have to cycle a long way to get out of the city and into the countryside, a bicycle is a useful way of reaching points of interest within the city. Ring either 792-524 or 591-961 for information on hiring. You might be lucky and find that one of the three bicycles available for hire from the downtown Youth Hostel (address below) is available. One major disadvantage is that cycles are forbidden on the Harbour Bridge.

Ferries. A trip on the Waitemata Harbour by public transport should not be missed. The shortest trip is the one to Devonport on the North Shore, a service used by commuters who wish to avoid the bridge as well as by joy-riders. North Shore Ferries (tel: 33- 319) operate this 15-minute service every half hour during the rush hours Monday to Saturday (7-9am and 3-7pm) and once an hour otherwise: on the hour if departing from the Quay St terminal in the city and on the half hour returning from Devonport. Surprisingly the ferries are equipped with a bar and on weekend evenings, there is jazz entertainment. The price is $4 return, or you can pay $7 to cross back and forth without disembarking.

Ferries also serve the islands in the harbour. These trips are dealt with in the section *Further Afield*.

If you plan to arrive at Auckland airport, it might be worth booking your accommodation ahead, especially in the high season when many of the budget places are full.

Hostels and Budget Accommodation. There are two Youth Hostels, one downtown which is very often jam-packed, and one in the quiet residential location of Mount Eden, 4km from the city centre. The city hostel is called Percy Shieff and for the time being is located in a gracious building, formerly a Masonic Temple, at 7 Princes St (tel: 790-258). Before the lease on this prime location expires, a new building will have to be chosen, but this is so far unknown. The Percy Shieff is opposite the Hyatt Kingsgate Hotel, which is one of the stops made by the airport bus. Otherwise it is about a ten-minute walk from the bus and rail stations. If you haven't booked, your chances are better of getting into the slightly cheaper Mount Eden Hostel at 5A Oaklands Road (tel: 603-975). The airport bus passes within ten minutes' walk of this hostel; get off at the corner of Gillies Avenue and Queens Road. Or take bus 274 from Customs St E to Mount Eden.

Several private hostels rival the IYHF hostels for convenience and cost. Ivanhoe Lodge at 14 Shirley Road in the inner city suburb of Grey Lynn (tel: 862-800), which charges $11, is geared up for overseas visitors and will collect new arrivals from the Downtown Air Terminal on weekdays. Otherwise catch bus 045 from Customs St. It is also a good place to stay prior to departure from New Zealand since the hostel will drive travellers to the airport for a small fee.

Another hostel held in high regard is the Georgia Backpackers at the southwest corner of Auckland's Domain. Few buses pass nearby, so it is necessary to walk over the Grafton Bridge which soon turns into Park Road; the Georgia is at number 189 (tel: 39-560).

The final choices in this league are run by the International Travellers Network (whose headquarters are in San Francisco) and are open only to passport-carrying foreigners. They have a hostel in the upmarket area of Ponsonby; catch bus 015 or 016 and walk to the hostel at 2 Franklin Road (tel: 780-168). In addition there are two so-called "cotels" where dormitory beds cost $10 and a double room costs $25. One of these (tel: 34-768) is tucked away in the park on Constitution Hill downtown (up the hill from the railway station). The other is at 82 Jervois Road in Herne Bay near the beach (tel: 767-211) about 2½km from the corner of Queen and Victoria Streets.

The Metro YMCA on the corner of Pitt St and Greys Avenue charges $30 single, which includes all meals.

Guest Houses and Hotels. As usual there is a sizeable leap from the $10-a-bed hostel style accommodation to the $25-$30 single and $35-$50 double in bed and breakfasts or guest houses. Among the cheaper ones are Freeman's Bay Private Hotel at 65 Wellington St (tel: 765-046) near the Victoria Market, the Railton Hotel at 411 Queen St (tel: 796-487) which has the advantage of being very large, and the Grand Vue Tourist Hotel at 3 Princes St near the Youth Hostel (tel: 793-965). If you want to be near the airport for some reason, you may want to choose the Auckland Airport Skyway Lodge (30 Kirkbridge Road, Mangere; tel: 275-4443) which offers four-bedded rooms for $21 per person and operates a shuttle service to and from the airport.

If you want something more homely, try contacting Homestyle Bed & Breakfast (tel: 818-8615) whose advertised price of $25 sounds reasonable. Or you might prefer the often-recommended Aachen House at 39 Market Road in the attractive residential area of Remuera (tel: 502-329). It charges $38 single bed and breakfast, $52 double.

Camping. There are a number of motorcamps and caravan parks in and around Auckland. Meadowcourt Motel near the airport (630 Great South Road, Papatoetoe; tel: 278-5612) has plenty of space for tents. The North Shore Caravan Park, 5km north of the bridge has a large number of on-site caravans available for about $30 for two people. Finally the Tui Glen Motor Camp in the scenic wine-growing area of Henderson west of Auckland (3 Edmonton Road; tel: 836-8978) has budget units available for $22 double in addition to caravan and tent sites.

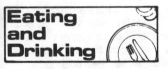

Eating and Drinking

Auckland is by far the most cosmopolitan city in New Zealand and therefore has the best range of restaurants and food shops. There are even some good delicatessens such as Escoffier's on 341 Remuera Road. As Aucklanders have gradually overcome their suspicion of foreign cuisine, ethnic restaurants representing a broad range of nationalities have sprung up, from Middle Eastern to Mexican. Some of these foods are served in rather anglified settings, for instance the Plaza Shopping Centre at 128 Queen St which has ten different ethnic food stalls serving only during shopping hours. But there are also some delightful and original restaurants scattered throughout the city. One of the most original rumoured to be starting up is one where you pay $75 for dinner plus having your fortune told and participating in a seance.

The highest concentration of good eating can be found in Parnell. Despite its elegant ambience, eating out here is not unduly overpriced, for example an Italian restaurant such as La Trattoria Café at 259 Parnell Road serves main courses from $10. Try also Mancini's at 311 Parnell Road. Many Parnell restaurants have courtyards or other outdoor eating areas to reinforce the European atmosphere.

A quite different atmosphere exists on the Karangahape Road, where the bars are rougher and the restaurants not quite so well-scrubbed. The El Inca restaurant can be found at number 335 (tel: 389-985) where South American food is served and live music is sometimes provided. Not far away and just off the Karangahape Road is a cheap Chinese BYO restaurant called Meido. Don's Wine Bar at 173 Karangahape Road serves café-style food and has jazz.

The Karangahape Road eventually runs into the Ponsonby Road which also has a good range of eating possibilities, including some high quality take-aways. If you are looking for fast food downtown after disembarking from a bus, look for Peppercorn's Deli in an arcade near the bus depot.

Chinese take-aways are generally of good quality, much better than their English counterparts. These are scattered liberally around the city and prices are low.

Throughout the city centre you will find other appealing possibilities, such as the Mexican Café (upstairs at 67 Victoria St W; tel: 732-311) which has music on Wednesdays to accompany your $11 main dish. Another choice for Mexican food fans is Panchos at 5 Elliott St (tel: 793-068). Further down Elliott St at number 39 is Epernay, which serves interesting lunches.

The Middle East Café at 23A Wellesley St serves convincing Lebanese food. Auckland has even graduated to Japanese food; try Michiko's Sushi Bar (tel: 398-151) near the main post office at the bottom of Queen St. Just a few minutes away is High St (running parallel to Queen St) where you might be tempted by Badgers' cheap vegetarian food or the more expensive Hard to Find Café. Continuing away from the waterfront, High St turns into Lorne St where another wholefood café called Domino's serves cheap food.

There are not many Indian restaurants but one you might like to try is the upmarket Maharajah appropriately located on Khyber Pass Road at number 19 (tel: 793-095). If for some reason you find yourself in or near the suburb of Balmoral, try the excellent and homely Italian restaurant La Fortuna on Dominion Road. Even further afield are the numerous restaurants in Mission Bay, a picturesque seaside community along Tamaki Drive. Remember that the majority of the restaurants mentioned above are BYO.

Many Auckland pubs serve food. Watch for special offers such as the $5 Sunday barbecues at Abby's Hotel (corner of Wellesley and Albert Streets). Further along Albert St at number 17 the Waitemata Tavern serves pub food.

If you want to visit a cheese factory there are conducted tours with tastings at one near the Mount Smart Stadium (5 Maurice Road, Penrose).

DRINKING

The standard closing time of 10pm is extended by a niggardly half hour (or sometimes an hour) on Thursdays or Fridays and Saturdays. So you might want to seek out the Entertainer's Club which is licensed until 4am on weekends. The only other official late night drinking spot is said to be the lobby bar of the

Sheraton Hotel on Symonds St. Nightclubs, of course, stay open late, but have expensive cover charges.

The Shakespeare Tavern on the corner of Albert and Wyndham Streets has the distinction of housing one of New Zealand few boutique breweries. A range of ales, stouts and lagers are brewed on the premises, of which some are available at the Shakespeare and others at pubs around town. For example Strand Stout is available at the Strand Hotel at the bottom of Parnell Rise and Thirsty Horse Ale is served at the two branches of the Hungry Horse, one at Royal Oak (756 Manukau Road) and the other at Browns Bay (526 East Coast Road). The most popular student haunt is the Kiwi, a basic pub on Symonds St which often gets packed. Two other independent breweries have started up very recently: Stockan Brewing Co in Henderson and Newbegin Brewery in Onehunga.

A great deal of New Zealand wine is grown not far from Auckland in the Henderson region. For information about vineyard tours, see *Further Afield*. If you are more interested in beer, ring Lion Breweries on 778-840 to see if a tour can be arranged.

Although Auckland lacks high skyscrapers — an 11-storey office building being built on the Karangahape Road caused an uproar — it is possible to get a good view of the city centre from the top of the Administration Building in the new Civic Centre on the corner of Greys Avenue and Queen Street. You might also want to visit the observation deck of the BNZ Tower at 125 Queen Street.

Auckland's downtown overlooks the picturesque Waitemata Harbour where yachts career over the surface and ferries wend their way to the offshore islands or to the North Shore where many fairly affluent Aucklanders choose to reside. The North Shore also has shops, museums and beaches of interest to visitors who can choose between the ferry or the Auckland Harbour Bridge to get there. Cruises on the harbour are a popular form of entertainment, and will become more so when the largest catamaran in the world, *Pride of Auckland II,* starts sailing.

The *New Zealand Herald* and the *Auckland Star* both carry extensive entertainment listings, with the *Star* devoting an entire section to what's on in its Friday edition. The Visitor Information booklet called *Great Time Guide* lists some (but not all) sports and cultural events, as well as including information on forthcoming exhibitions, as does the free weekly tourist newspaper *The Auckland Tourist Times.* Look out also for the *Metro Magazine.*

The Town Hall has a concert hall and a theatre, but it is hoped that the new Aotea Centre (which, like the Town Hall, is in Aotea Square) will become the arts centre of Auckland when it opens in 1988. Tickets to concerts of the Auckland Philharmonia or the New Zealand Symphony are in the $13-$25 range with good student discounts often available. The Town Hall box office can be contacted by ringing 586-094 or 687-073.

Tickets to most major entertainments can be bought through the BASS ticket agency in the St James Theatre in Queen St. To avoid queuing for half an hour, go in the morning or afternoon.

You will often stumble across free entertainment along Queen St, in Queen Elizabeth Square outside the Central Post Office and in Albert Park. In the summer check in the newspapers for information about special festivals, which are always an excellent way to observe a city at play. For example the multi-cultural festival sponsored by the Race Relations Conciliator featuring food, crafts, dance, etc. of many nationalities, may well be repeated in Grey Lynn Park just before Easter.

Museums and Galleries. Although the Auckland Museum is called the War Memorial Museum, military memorabilia comprise only a part of the collection. There are excellent Maori and Polynesian exhibits, including a meeting house and war canoe. Some of the Museum's holdings, such as burial chests, still hold spiritual significance for certain Maori tribes who are lobbying to have them returned, so the collection is unlikely to increase. There are free 45-minute guided tours around the Maoritanga hall at 10.30am and 12.45pm daily. The Pounamu Maori Cultural Group puts on performances of music and dance in the Museum auditorium at 11.30am and 1.45pm which last half an hour and cost $3.50 ($2 for students). Among the other exhibits is one devoted to paintings of early Auckland, while another shows Auckland from its geological beginnings to the present. The Museum is open from 10am to 5pm daily (tel: 390-443) and admission is free. Catch a Parnell bus (645/655) from the bus terminal.

The Auckland City Art Gallery is in the corner of Albert Park where Wellesley St intersects with Kitchener St (tel: 792-010, ext 661). Although it has some Old Masters, it specializes in New Zealand art both colonial and contemporary. One entire room is devoted to paintings in which the Maori people feature. The building itself is in an elaborate mock-French style favoured by the Victorians which was saved from demolition and recently extended. The gallery is open daily 10am-4.30pm and offers free guided tours at midday Monday to Friday and 2pm on Sundays.

There are of course many other specialist museums and art collections in Auckland. At any one time you should be able to choose from about 25 special exhibitions, ranging from a display of artists-against-mining of the Coromandel Peninsula to an exhibition of horseracing greats. Among the permanent museums in Auckland are the Museum of Transport and Technology which includes a sci-fi playground as well as old trains and trams (Great North Road, Western Springs; tel: 860-199), the Naval Museum on Spring St in Devonport (tel: 454-000, ext 623), the National Racing Museum at Ellerslie Racecourse (tel: 544-069) and Kinder House at the corner of Ayr St and Parnell Road. The latter contains photos and paintings of early Auckland and charges admission of $1; it is open 10.30-4pm and Devonshire teas are served for $1.

The New Zealand Historic Places Trust have opened several of their Victorian properties to the public, including one owned by an early clergyman with the glorious name of Vicesimus Lush. Locations and opening hours are readily available from the Visitor Bureau.

Music. As mentioned in the section on eating, a number of restaurants attract customers with live music. Similarly bars often put on evening entertainment both at the weekends and during the week when business is slower. Surprisingly, Saturday afternoons are a popular time for live entertainment, ever since the Alexandra Tavern in Parnell began this trend in the mid-1970s. The main venue for international name bands is the Western Springs Stadium with a capacity of 60,000. For the benefit of complaining locals, the City Council limits the number of summer rock concerts to six. The other main concert location is the Mount Smart Stadium.

The annual folk festival is usually held in late January at Oratia, outside the ity limits on the road to the Waitakere hills.

Live bands can often be heard at the Gluepot, a pub in Ponsonby (corner of ervois and Ponsonby Roads) including some good jazz sessions. Advance bookings can often be made through BASS; tickets vary in price but are usually n the region of $10.

If you want to hear some classical music without paying the $20 or $25 equired to see full orchestral concerts at the Town Hall, then try the School if Music's free lunchtime concerts given by students at the university; the theatre s at 6 Symonds St.

Theatre and Cinema. The theatrical life of Auckland is far from moribund. The stablished Mercury Theatre on France St (tel: 33-869) favours a safe programme (Gilbert & Sullivan, popular farces, etc.) but has a second stage upstairs called The Gods where more experimental plays can be seen (tickets about $12). The motorway bisects France St, so you should be aware that the Mercury is at the Karangahape Road end. Students can obtain substantial discounts for Mercury productions: standby tickets are often available for $5.

The Town Hall houses two theatres (tel: 586-094) where you might find a New Zealand play being performed. Tickets cost about $10. The large one hosts productions by the semi-professional Arena Theatre (who will be moving to a new theatre soon) and the small one upstairs, called the Town Hall Chamber, hosts music recitals and small scale theatre productions. His Majesty's Theatre tel: 735-100) is a pricey West End clone. In the summer it is far more enjoyable to attend an outdoor performance. Free performances of Shakespeare plays etc. are put on in the University grounds each January/February; remember to take a blanket or a cushion. Good plays are often mounted at the University of Auckland's Maidment Arts Centre during term, so make enquiries.

There is usually no shortage of films in Auckland, though many cinemas are located in distant suburban shopping centres. To find out what's showing at the Mid-City Cinema Centre, ring 397-445, though they don't take phone bookings. The Capitol Cinema in Balmoral is a lovely renovated old cinema, which often shows art films. You can also find interesting reruns at the Hollywood in Avondale (20 St Georges Road; tel: 888-393). It is the kind of cinema where you might expect to hear a Wurlitzer organ played to accompany a silent Charlie Chaplin film. If your interests lie more in continuous movies classified by the censor as having "explicit sexual content which may offend", then check out the Classic at 321 Queen St, ironically near the City Council Offices from which recently emanated a threat to close it.

Parks and Zoos. The largest park is the 200-acre Domain, whose volcanic hill is crowned by the War Memorial Museum. As you stroll up the hill from downtown, watch for confused-looking ducks trying to cross Domain Drive to the duck pond. The Wintergardens below the Museum contain some exotic plants; the greenhouses are open from 10am-4pm. If you continue past the Museum and down the other side you are on your way to Parnell.

The other big hills scattered around Greater Auckland are also domains (ie city parks). There are some remains of a Maori fort at the top of Mount Eden (bus 274 from Victoria St E) and an observatory at the summit of the instantly recognizable One Tree Hill (bus 302 from Victoria St E). On clear Tuesdays n summer, the telescope is opened to the public at night; ring 656-945 for confirmation.

The Botanical Gardens are located a long way from the city centre but migh be worth stopping to see if you are heading south on the motorway or killin time before catching a plane at the nearby airport. The Gardens are located i Totara Park in Manurewa (tel: 267-4726) and are open 9am-5pm (4.30 May October); free admission.

Auckland seems to have more than its fair share of theme parks, such as th Footrot Flats Fun Park (tel: 834-7015) just off the Northwestern Motorway Rainbow's End Adventure Park (tel: 277-9870) off the Southern Motorway, an the somewhat less frivolous Heritage Park in Mount Wellington (tel: 590-424 where Maori concerts, sheep-shearing demonstrations and other quintessentially New Zealand activities are featured.

WATCH OUT FOR FLOCKS OF DUCKS CROSSING DOMAIN DRIVE IN AUCKLAN

Auckland has a Lion Safari Park in the outer suburb of Massey (tel: 832-5319). If you prefer less ferocious beasts, visit the kiwis and sleepy tuatara lizards at the Auckland Zoo (tel: 761-415) among many other fauna. Take bus 043, 044 or 045 from Customs St to Western Springs. The zoo is connected to the nearby Museum of Transport and Technology by an electric tram.

Pursuing the wildlife theme, Auckland has an extraordinary aquarium which almost gives visitors the impression that they are under the sea. It is named after its late founder Kelly Tarlton who opened his underwater world in 1985. Despite the crowds and the steep admission charge of $6.50, it is fun to move alongside giant sharks, winged stingrays, etc. just on the other side of the acrylic tunnel. The moray eels, kingfish and a few other species are fed by divers at 2pm. The tourist literature makes it sound almost as big as Disneyworld, whereas the circular tunnel would in fact fit into an average school classroom. In case you feel you have not got your money's worth, there are films about Tarlton's wreck diving around New Zealand's shores. It is open 9am-9pm (tel: 580-602) and is accessible by any bus heading out along Tamaki Drive, e.g. numbers 736, 556, 766 or the Questar Free Fun Bus.

One final recommendation for those interested in wildlife: Microworld on the orner of Halsey and Madden Streets (tel: 370-227) enables you to inspect bee ives, ant hills, etc. through microscanners. It even has what it describes as a igh-tech café called Molecules. It is open 9am-11pm daily and costs $7.50.

PORT

he *Great Time Guide,* distributed free of charge through a number of owntown and airport outlets, carries a diary of forthcoming sports events, lmost all of which seem to be racing (either cars or horses). The two main tracks or flat racing are at Ellerslie and Avondale, whereas most trotting club meetings re at the Alexandra Park Raceway in Epsom, which has a happy hour from pm. Sample prices for admission to Ellerslie are $10 for the stands (where dress tandards are enforced), $4 on the lawn and free in the infield. It has pleasant ardens which are open 8am-7pm, as well as the museum of racing mentioned bove. Cricket and rugby are played at recently refurbished Eden Park.

Dedicated joggers will gravitate to the Domain (provided they are not iscouraged by the contours) whereas more leisurely perambulators might be nterested in doing the coast-to-coast walk through Auckland (see *Tramping* elow). Water sports lovers will take themselves off to one of Auckland's many eaches, such as Mission Bay, St. Heliers Bay and Judges Bay, all accessible rom Tamaki Drive, where you can swim or windsurf. Cheltenham Beach on he North Shore is within walking distance of the Devonport ferry wharf. You an hire a tennis court and equipment at the City Courts on Stanley St (tel: 33-623) or have a work-out at the YMCA on Pitt St (tel: 32-068). There is lso a 50km cycle track in and around Auckland, which leads from the Museum o the waterfront and follows the shoreline as far as the Savage Memorial, which ffords sweeping views of the harbour.

Unless you have a friend with a yacht moored in Westhaven Marina (just nder the Harbour Bridge) you will have to be content with watching the ailboats in Waitemata Harbour. If you happen to be around on Auckland's Anniversary Day in January, watch the races at what is billed as the largest one-lay regatta in the world.

SHOPPING

If the sheepskin and greenstone emporia along Queen St do not thrill you, the Victoria Park Market, a ten-minute walk away on Victoria St W, might hold more appeal. Craftspersons display their wares, farmers set up their fruit and vegetables and various traders try to entice you to buy from their $20 racks. Perhaps to prevent it turning into a flea market, second-hand goods may not be sold. You can also buy food and snacks (including good quality ice cream) and listen to musicians and buskers. It is open daily from 9am (10am on Sundays) and closes at 7pm (9pm on Fridays).

There are other markets in downtown Auckland such as the one on Albert St (open daytimes Wednesday through Sunday plus Friday evening), the Cook St Market off Aotea Square (Fridays and Saturdays only) and the recently opened Nelson St Market at weekends — a flower market during the week — in the warehouses at 78 Nelson St. It is primarily a craft and produce market but also has ethnic food stalls and second hand dealers.

Specialist craft shops abound both downtown and in Parnell, Remuera and

Ponsonby. On weekends you can visit some craft workshops on the North Shore, at The Works on King Edward Parade.

Department stores are the place to go for basic items. Try the six-storey Farmers Trading Company at 23 Hobson St or Smith & Caughy on Queen St. If you need something specific like a watch-repairer or stationery shop, you will either have to ask a local to steer you towards one, or traipse in and out of the numerous arcades off Queen St.

Most shops close at noon on Saturdays. The exceptions are Parnell (where shops stay open until 4pm on Saturdays) and the Customhouse, which is open seven days a week. The Customhouse is a renovated building from the 1880s, housing cafés and tourist shops, a kind of junior version of The Rocks in Sydney. There is an epidemic of such centres: the Queen's Arcade is just across the road and the restored Ferry Building has just opened as yet another upmarket shopping complex. Duty-free shopping is available nearby at the downtown terminal (Quay and Albert Streets).

The shop at the War Memorial Museum is worth a browse since it carries good quality artefacts, greeting cards, etc. Tisdalls at 176 Queen St specializes in tramping gear, though it isn't cheap. The Youth Hostels Association office and shop is at 36 Customs St at the corner of Gore St (tel: 794-224). There are plenty of bookshops in Auckland including Vintage Books at 39 Elliott St, the Book Cellar in the Customhouse and Wheeler's Bookshop near the Remuera post office which specializes in New Zealand books. The Broadsheet Bookshop at 485 Karangahape Rd carries feminist books.

Every suburb has its own shopping area and these are worth visiting if only for their evocation of neighbourhood shopping a couple of decades ago (though with some Polynesian adaptations). Beside a typical Antipodean bakery specializing in pink-iced buns, you will find a Polynesian greengrocer selling all manner of unrecognizable fruits and vegetables. Even the most staid-looking suburban shopping area probably has a Pacific Island emporium selling cheap and cheerful basketware, toys, housewares, etc. There is a good one in Three Kings.

THE MEDIA

Newspapers. The two stalwart Auckland papers have recently been joined by the new tabloid *The Auckland Sun*, which has an even greater emphasis on sport than the afternoon *Auckland Star* and the morning *New Zealand Herald*. The Saturday *Herald* has about 100 pages, most of which are solid advertising. Most newspapers are sold from honesty boxes.

A selection of overseas newspapers (including the British quality Sundays) is kept in the newspaper reading room in the basement of the Auckland Public Library on Lorne St.

Radio. Radio Pacific (1600AM), a 24-hour talk station, was named the Most Outstanding Station in Australia and New Zealand in 1987, and its main personality Chris Parkinson was voted the "Golden Voice of Australasia". If you want continuous rock music try 1ZM on 1250AM. The university radio station broadcasts on 91.8FM. The national programme is carried by 1YA on 756AM and the concert programme (1YC) is on 882AM. A new Maori station was scheduled to be set up in Auckland (to be transmitted nationwide) though at the time of writing its launch date had not yet been decided.

Because of a much publicized increase in crime in 1987 (sex assaults were up by nearly 12% and murders by 25%), a certain amount of paranoia has overtaken some Auckland residents who now consider their city to be a very dangerous place. South Auckland is regarded by middle class Pakeha residents as the most dangerous area, and some Aucklanders claim that they would not visit the southern districts of Mangani and Otara except in a car with locked doors. This is unnecessarily alarmist and Auckland is still a city in which the majority do not hesitate to walk alone at night and where there are still guest houses which have not bothered to instal locks on the doors.

A certain amount of red light activity can be seen on Karangahape Road and on Fort Street downtown.

The Central Police Station is on Vincent St (tel: 794-240). The Rape Crisis number is 764-404.

The STD code for Auckland is 09.
For fire, police or ambulance dial 111.

Auckland Visitors' Bureau: Aotea Square, 299 Queen St (31-889). Open weekdays 8.30am-5.30pm, and weekends 9am-3pm.
NZTP: 99 Queen St (798-180). Open Monday-Friday 8.30am-4.45pm and Saturday 9.30am-noon. There is also a travellers' information centre at the Airport which opens for all arriving aircraft.
British Consulate: 9th Floor, Norwich Union Building, 179 Queen St (32-973).
American Express: 95 Queen St (798-243).
Thomas Cook: 145 Queen St, near Custom St E (794-384). Open Monday to Friday 8.30am-5pm and Saturdays 9am-1pm.
Park Information Centre: Ferry Building, Quay St (799-972). Open 9am-3pm daily.
Automobile Association: 33 Wyndham St (774-660).
Student Travel Services: 64 High St (399-191).
Post Office: CPO, Queen Elizabeth Square (792-200). The newly formed New Zealand Post is threatening to sell off this prime downtown site so you may have to use another branch such as 127 Hobson St (30-845).
Medical Services: Auckland Hospital, Park Road, Grafton City (797-440).
Medical Emergencies: Epsom Medical Centre, 310 Manakau Road (794-540).
Emergency Chemist: 153 Newton Road, Newton (732-497).
Auckland City Creche: corner of High and Chancery Streets (735-251). Daytimes only. $3 an hour.

DAY TRIPS FROM AUCKLAND

From Auckland it is easy to explore a variety of interesting landscapes and attractions. For those who wish to join a small group tour, there are two good ones to choose from: Bush & Beach Ltd (PO Box 4,

Greenhithe, Auckland; tel: 779-029) whose imaginative full day tours cost about $80 and That Other Tour (306 Dominion Rd, Auckland; tel: 686-638) whose prices are similar. But it is also very easy to visit many of the places of interest under one's own steam.

Hauraki Gulf. Beyond the Waitemata Harbour, several islands of interest to day-trippers are dotted around the Hauraki Gulf. The most unusual is Rangitoto whose volcanic cone is clearly visible from downtown Auckland. Rangitoto last erupted in about 1750, the most recently active of Auckland's volcanoes. It is most remarkable to see vegetation struggling to survive, especially the unusual miniature kidney ferns, amidst the bizarre jumble of black lava rocks.

An easy track leads to the 259m summit, having been built by prisoners in the 1930s. Wear sturdy footwear since the crushed lava can be hard on the feet, not to mention unpleasantly hot on a sunny day. There are splendid views from the top, of Auckland on one side and the islands of the Gulf on the other. The island is well organized for visitors with all the points of interest well signposted, such as a gull breeding colony and lava caves.

Ferries leave several times a day from the ferry docks in Auckland and arrive at Rangitoto Wharf about 45 minutes later (cost $10.45 return). From the wharf you can walk to the summit (4km) and then down to the only other wharf at Islington Bay, or you can follow the edge of the island and avoid the central hill. Whichever you choose keep your eye on the time since you should not miss the last ferry back (about 5pm). The estimated timings on the signboards are unreliable, grossly generous for some stretches, and very tight on others.

Attached to Rangitoto by a causeway is the island of Motutapu whose verdant cover provides a complete contrast with the barren volcano. Motutapu is one large farm administered by the Department of Conservation; however visitors are welcome to walk across the paddocks, swim at the beaches and admire the harbour views. Unlike Rangitoto, Motutapu has a campsite. Prior arrangements should be made with the Ranger who is also in charge of Rangitoto (tel: 727-674).

The much larger island of Waiheke (93km²) has a permanent population of over 4,000, many of whom commute into Auckland on the Waiheke Shipping Company's one hour service (ring 790-092 for current timetable). Gulf Ferries (tel: 393-918) also serve Waiheke several times daily and charge about $20 return. All sailings are subject to weather. A bus meets each ferry arrival to take day-trippers to the sandy beaches on the northern side which are sheltered and safe: Oneroa has a choice of water sport facilities and Onetangi has a bird reserve and a Youth Hostel (tel: 728-971). The latter sometimes arranges special promotions to persuade hostellers to spend a couple of days on Waiheke; in 1987 transport from Auckland to the hostel plus two nights accommodation were costing $30, which included discount vouchers for cycle hire, bistro meals, etc. The hostel is within walking distance of lovely Palm Beach.

Great Barrier Island is 80km from Auckland and is therefore too far for just a day trip (see *Great Outdoors* below). Other islands in the Hauraki Gulf include Kawau Island (two ferries daily from Warkworth) famous for its governor's mansion overlooking the water; if you are around in January, telephone Kawau Island 882 or 867 for information about a programme of summer events. Tiritiri Matangi Island, has been made a reserve for endangered species, especially rare birds. Little Barrier Island has the largest remaining native forest in New Zealand and pristine wetlands which protect many unusual native animals. For permission to visit these zoological sanctuaries and information about access, contact the Hauraki Gulf Maritime Park Information Centre, Ferry Building, Quay St, Auckland (tel: 799-972).

Hibiscus Coast. The habit of tourism boards around the world is to assign glamorous names to sections of coast and the shoreline north of Auckland has not escaped the trend. The Hibiscus Coast stretches about 26km from Silverdale to Puhoi, an interesting little town — with a good and very crowded pub — originally settled by Bohemians (i.e. people from the Middle European province of Bohemia rather than people of unconventional morals). Orewa is quite a large seaside resort, complete with shopping centres, entertainment arcades and golf course. Waiwere, a few kilometres further north, is perhaps more interesting since it has hot springs and thermal pools, traditionally of therapeutic benefit. It is possible to bathe in the pools which are surrounded by the hibiscus bushes which provide the excuse for the coast's name. This area is billed as a winter resort though it is at its best in the summer. Not far away, the Wenderholm Park administered by the Auckland Regional Authority has lovely beaches and bush walks. To get to this coast by public transport catch bus number 895W which goes to Wenderholm between October and April, but only as far as Waiwere the rest of the year.

The Waitakere Ranges. This is a remarkably rugged area, whose highest peaks (up to 500m) are easily visible from the city and within an hour's drive of downtown. There are almost 200km of walking tracks, ranging from five-minute strolls suitable for grandmothers in high heels, to overnight expeditions for well-equipped hiking parties. There are many objects of interest from a kauri tree with a circumference of 7m to the unfortunately named Fairy Falls, a steep cascade of water which gathers in a pool surrounded by sheer semi-circular walls.

In addition to the pleasures of walking through virgin bush are added the pleasures of the ocean. You can get to the cliff-lined west coast via many walking tracks but by only four roads which branch off from Scenic Drive. The beaches at the end of these roads at Whatipu, Karekare, Piha and Anawhata are all very picturesque, particularly Piha guarded as it is by the 100-metre high Lion Rock just offshore which can be climbed in about half an hour. If you go swimming or surfing at any of these beaches, look for patrolled areas, since rips and currents can be dangerous.

The Park Information Centre (tel: 817-7134) is situated at Arataki and is open in the afternoons on weekdays, and from 10am-5pm on weekends and holidays. A short trail from the Centre leads you past many native trees and plants, all helpfully labelled. The Ranger can advise on suitable walks, issue permits for the primitive campsites and inform you of any special events such as guided "possum prowls". Anyone who plans to spend some time in the Waitakeres should purchase the Auckland Regional Authority's map *A Walking and Tramping Guide to the Waitakere Ranges*.

The Henderson Valley. Hedonists may prefer to tour picturesque valley vineyards rather than rugged hills. A large number of New Zealand's major vineyards are located within half an hour of downtown Auckland in the Henderson Valley, between the outer suburbs of the city and the foothills of the Waitakeres. The Winemakers of West Auckland publish a leaflet which describes the wineries, and gives instructions for finding them. Most are open

Monday through Saturday and offer tastings. For some reason the Yugoslav influence on wine-making in the district is enormous, and wineries are now or once were run by people with Serbo-Croat names. The names Corban, Babich and Delegats will be familiar to anyone who has browsed in a New Zealand wine shop, and these vineyards are all within about 5km of each other. Even without private transport you can visit a good number of them on foot after reaching the Valley by bus. Alternatively you can join a conducted tour, which costs $55 (ring AGM Promotions on 398-670 for details).

NORTHLAND

The 345km peninsula stretching north of Auckland is not much more than 100km at its broadest point, so beaches are never far away in Northland. Although the scale of Ninety Mile Beach (actually only 64 miles long) at the far north of the island is not quite typical, both shores of the peninsula have some wild and battered stretches of coast as well as sandy coves lined with semi-tropical trees and flowers. The main roads don't follow the coasts very closely so it is always worth venturing down a dirt track to see what you can discover. If only the latitude were closer to the equator, this could be a holiday destination to rival the Seychelles or Barbados, though with over 2,000 hours of sunshine each year and the highest average temperatures in New Zealand, the climate is at least as attractive as the Mediterranean or Florida. In any case this is an area superbly suited to a week or month of lounging and relaxation. Four of the six Youth Hostels do not impose the usual three-day limit, and there are many farms which will feed and house visitors. In 1987, one near Dargaville was advertising dinner, bed and breakfast for $35 (tel: Donnelly Crossing 744). If you drive north on Highway 1, be sure to take in the Waiomio Caves south of Kawakawa, which are far less touristy than the Waitomo Caves described below.

Bay of Islands. The most popular resort area of Northland is the Bay of Islands, 240km north of Auckland, which includes the adjacent towns of Paihia and Russell plus Kerikeri 23km further north. In addition to the glorious ocean scenery and opportunities to try water sports (especially game fishing), there are many places of historical interest including New Zealand's oldest stone building (the mission house in Kerikeri), the oldest wooden building (Kemp House in Kerikeri), the oldest church and the hotel with the oldest licence (both in Russell) and the Treaty House in Waitangi where Maori chiefs ceded their land to Queen Victoria in 1840. There is a recently constructed walkway through mangrove forest from Waitangi to Paihia which takes two hours and then Russell is only a short ferry ride away, so the attractions are not widely dispersed. The Bay of Islands is one of New Zealand's three maritime parks. The Park Visitor Centre is on the Strand in Russell (tel: 37-685).

Access to the Bay is easy, both for car-owning Aucklanders (which means that the resorts can be crowded at weekends) and for travellers who can take a bus run by Newmans, NZRRS, or Clarks Northliner Coachline. The latter specialize in serving Northland and charge $34 to the Bay of Islands, but unfortunately do not operate at weekends. NZRRS even runs day trips from Auckland on its "Bay Bullet" but this is too rushed to be of much enjoyment.

The obvious way to see the Bay of Islands is by boat. Try to befriend a local yachtsman (for example at the important yacht harbour at Opua) to take you for a sail. Otherwise you can cruise for a day on the yacht *Response* with Bay of Island Yacht Charters (tel: Okaihua 64-435) who also hire out a 26-foot bareboat. An alternative preferred by the more affluent is to join one of the several cruises organized by Fullers, whose so-called "cream trip" (because it was originally patronized by dairy farmers) is famous. It departs daily from Paihia at 10am and lasts a rather excessive seven hours. Many prefer the half-day Cape Brett trip ($28). The lovely Whangaroa Bay (40km north of Kerikeri) can be cruised for a more modest $15 or you can join a game fishing trip there for $50. Some say that nearby Tauranga Bay has the most beautiful beach in the country. Coopers Beach near Mangonui has a popular beach campsite, though if you are prepared to walk a few miles past the "Camping Prohibited" signs, it is possible to camp undisturbed. Some beaches which are owned by Maori councils charge admission at the access road.

This area is covered with orchards of kiwifruit and oranges. Travellers will soon notice signs, especially in the Kerikeri Youth Hostel (Main Road; tel: 79-391), advertising for fruit pickers at most times of the year. Citrus picking and packing takes place in October/November, the kiwifruit harvest starts in late April and other fruits like peaches and apricots are picked at the height of summer. You can easily earn $5 or $6 an hour.

Cape Reinga. Those who find the idea of visiting John O'Groats appealing will certainly want to visit the northernmost point in New Zealand, the lonely lighthouse on a storm-battered cape. (Just as Ninety Mile Beach is shorter than advertised, so Cape Reinga is not in fact the most northerly point; North Cape is a few kilometres closer to the equator, however it is inaccessible by road and so is ignored.)

The Maori name Reinga means "place of leaping", not because it was a favourite suicide spot but because it was believed to be the gateway through which spirits departed to their homeland. Anyone who has read of the similar belief held by Pacific Islanders as described by Arthur Grimble in *Pattern of Islands* will be relieved to hear that Cape Reinga and Spirits Bay are not nearly as spooky and dangerous. However in certain conditions swimming can be perilous, since the meeting of the Tasman Sea to the west and the Pacific Ocean can result in unpredictable currents and turbulence.

Although it is possible to drive to Cape Reinga from Kaitaia along the partially sealed road through the middle of the peninsula, many people prefer to join a half- or full-day tour by bus or four-wheel drive vehicle along Ninety Mile Beach, which is a very tricky drive in an ordinary vehicle (and the buses won't help private cars which are in trouble). There is even some quicksand on the Te Paki Stream flanked by giant yellow sand dunes which are fun to ski down barefoot.

Rather feebly, the tourist literature describes this as "one of the world's most exciting beach bus routes" (though it is not clear what competition they have in mind). Star Tours run trips in several different vehicles (including a six-wheel drive outsized dune buggy). One possibility is to camp overnight at the Cape and return on a later tour at no extra charge. Try Tapotupotu Bay about 3km before Cape Reinga where there is free camping with toilet facilities. Bookings for the trip can be made at the Kaitaia Youth Hostel at 160 Commerce St (tel: 1080). One indication of the growing popularity of the far north is that the number of people staying at Kaitaia Hostel doubled in 1987. Mount Cook Line (tel: Kaitaia 575) also offer tours, one including a barbecue.

The West Coast. The western side of the Northland peninsula is less developed than the east partly because of the notorious rip tides which make swimming dangerous. But the area is very beautiful. The special attraction north of Dargaville is the Waipoua Forest of kauri trees where many magnificent trees escaped the ravages of 19th century exploitation. Highway 12 (unsealed) passes through the forest for about 17km and many specimens can be seen right next to the road, such as the amazing one over 50m high, 13m in circumference and 1,200 years old. The Kauri and Pioneer Museum in the village of Matakohe (on the road back to Auckland) has exhibits of the colourful gum which was widely exported at the turn of the century to be used in varnishes and polished ornaments. The nearest Youth Hostel to the forest is Opononi, a tiny seaside holiday town overlooking Hokianga Harbour, where there are some strangely sculpted and always-changing sand dunes some of which are seven metres high. Look for blackberries to pick in February, and enquire at the hostel about local *hangis* (Maori feasts).

COROMANDEL PENINSULA

At first glance this rugged and mountainous peninsula, about an hour and a half's drive south and then east of Auckland, appears to be of interest only to holidaymakers eager to enjoy the beaches. But it has been heavily exploited by lumbermen, miners and fishermen ever since the first white entrepreneurs arrived. The great forests of kauri trees were ruthlessly logged for the ship-building industry though some regenerating kauri stands can now be seen among the dense forests. The peninsula is littered with abandoned mining relics, especially of the gold boom in the 1870s. Now that exploitation of the wilderness is no longer accepted as inevitable, recent attempts to revive the goldfields and prospect for other minerals have met with stiff opposition from environmentalists who lost their battle in 1987 when the Minister of Energy began granting licences both to multinational corporations and individuals to stake new claims.

The village of Coromandel with a population of less than 1,000 has many attractive colonial buildings left over from the prosperous times of the gold rush. Although its name (which derives from the first British ship to use the harbour in 1810) has lent itself to the peninsula, other larger towns like Whitianga and Thames are more popular centres of tourism.

The road which hugs the western side of the peninsula is unsealed beyond Coromandel, but it is possible to drive out to the tip at Cape Colville. Unfortunately there is no road right around the end so it is necessary to backtrack 30km before you can cross to the other side and down to Whitianga. The numerous beaches, many of them empty even in summer, are not only lovely for swimming, but are wonderful places to collect shells. The little seaside village of Hahei is famed for its pink-tinged beach, coloured by powdered shells. On some beaches you may also find fragments of gems such as agate and jasper. Horse trekking is available from Hahei.

Whitianga is a bustling tourist resort, especially popular with deep sea fishermen. The building of a controversial marina, large enough to accommodate 350 boats, has just been approved, so Whitianga will become even more crowded in future. It is already one of the more developed Coromandel towns with a large choice of motor camps and motels. Surprisingly there is no Youth Hostel on the peninsula, but there is plenty of affordable accommodation. Thames, at the base of the peninsula, is a good place to stay and has an interesting mineralogical museum (open afternoons most of the year). Try the Dickson Park Motor Camp in town (tel: 87-308) or the Sunkist Lodge (tel: 88-808). Another lovely resort is Pauanui, also on the ocean side of the peninsula.

Further information about the Coromandel can be obtained from the Information Office in Thames (Queen St; tel: 87-284).

CENTRAL NORTH ISLAND

If the North Island can be imagined as a giant sea creature swimming through the Tasman Sea — as indeed the Maoris did think of it — the two "flippers" on either side and everything in between constitute the central region. Maori legends give interesting accounts of the formation of the various mountains, valleys and lakes scattered around the centre of the island and are worth listening to. Falling within this region are the North Island's foremost tourist attractions of Rotorua with its thermal activity and Maori industry, and Waitomo with its glow-worms. Few visitors to New Zealand will miss either of these though there are many other places of interest. The original three national parks of the North Island are evenly spaced along a line bisecting the island horizontally. If you are travelling between Auckland and Wellington you will have to consider your route carefully, unless you are privileged to have enough time to explore both sides of the island.

THE EAST COAST

Much of the coastline south of the Coromandel Peninsula is equally rugged and beautiful, though the inland areas are more densely populated and agriculturally productive. Highway 2 follows the coast of the aptly named Bay of Plenty, continuing around the outstandingly scenic East Cape to the inaptly named Poverty Bay (things have changed since Captain Cook named it in 1769) and on to the resort town of Napier overlooking Hawke Bay, before turning inland towards Wellington. Although this area is popular with New Zealand tourists, it involves a sizeable detour for overseas visitors hurrying down to the South Island and so is often overlooked. Apart from its scenic attractions, the Maori influences are particularly strong and interesting in this part of New Zealand, especially in the relatively isolated East Cape where over a quarter of the land is owned by Maori councils.

Bay of Plenty. Although orchards and fields are not in themselves a prime tourist draw, they make a pleasant backdrop to the beaches and oceanscapes of the Bay of Plenty. In addition it is gratifying to indulge in freshly picked kiwifruit, and the occasionally delicious wines which are made from the excess crop can be sampled at wineries in Tauranga, the largest town on the bay, and also at nearby Te Puke. Te Puke (not pronounced as it looks but Poo-kee) is said to be the kiwifruit capital of the world and a new tourist complex called Kiwifruit Country has just opened nearby on the main road from Whakatane, which at least makes a change from sheep demonstrations. This area is also a good place to try unusual native fruits like tamarillos (which look like tomatoes) and feijoas. The National Citrus Festival is held in August each year. If you want to find casual fruit-picking work, head for this area, especially in May when the kiwifruit harvest takes place.

Tauranga's harbour is completely protected by Matakana Island, and has become one of the foremost shipping ports in the country mostly for pulp and paper. Despite recent industrial accretions, it remains a pleasant holiday resort. Even more pleasant is Mount Maunganui, situated at the harbour entrance, and accessible by an hourly ferry from Coronation Pier in Tauranga (Monday to Friday only). A full range of water sports is available on Ocean Beach which stretches for several miles along the coast. Alternatively it is possible to climb Mount Mauganui (232m) in an hour and a half. The summit affords fine views over the city, harbour and islands of the Bay. Many miles out to sea is White Island, a particularly active volcano which has foiled several attempts to mine it. You can see steam pouring from the craters from several coastal lookouts. This whole area is one of the most seismologically volatile; the town of Edgecumbe about 90km south of Tauranga suffered the worst damage in the 1987 earthquake.

A daily coach service between Auckland and Tauranga is operated by Mainline Coachways, a trip which takes about five hours; in Tauranga telephone 85-105 or in Auckland (09) 735-590. For further information on the Bay of Plenty area, contact the Tauranga Public Relations & Information Centre on the Strand (tel: 88-103). Pick up *The Authentic Visitors Information Guide* which, in contrast to so many of the genre, is stronger on items of historical interest than on advertising.

Hawke's Bay. The next large bay, past the lightly populated East Cape, is Hawke Bay (but note the province is called Hawke's Bay). Those without much time or without private transport will opt for the direct inland route along Highway 2 which bypasses the Cape, and thereby saves over 200km. However the long drive on Highway 35 around the coast of the Cape is spectacular. An NZRRS bus runs along the east side of the Cape to Hicks Bay but no further.

Whichever road you choose, you will arrive at Gisborne, a large and prosperous town on Poverty Bay, with pleasant beaches within walking distance of the town. Its claim to be the most easterly city in the world (i.e. closest to the international dateline which is about 900km away) will not necessarily enhance a visit, but will give you something unusual to put on your post cards.

It is a further 216km to Napier, a town which had to be completely rebuilt after an earthquake in 1931 which killed 256 people, the worst natural disaster in New Zealand's history. There is little evidence of the earthquake now, though much of the land on which modern Napier stands was under the sea before the earthquake. It is remarkable how many places around the North Island are of very recent creation, emphasizing how geologically young and capricious New Zealand is. The Napier Museum on Herschell St includes a fascinating exhibit and slide show reliving the disaster.

Napier is New Zealand's closest approximation to Blackpool or Coney Island, with many seaside attractions along the Marine Parade including Marineland and an aquarium, illuminated fountains, paddle boats, and so on — everything except donkey rides. It is therefore not surprising that a recent proposal to build a four-storey building in the shape of a sheep originated in Napier. To date New Zealand has not gone in for the absurd buildings-as-objects which Australia is so proud of, but that may be about to change.

At the bottom of the arc of Hawke Bay is Cape Kidnappers, famed for its colony of gannets, an attractive bird roughly the size of a goose which is virtually unafraid of humans, since it is related to the booby, so-called by sailors since it was absurdly easy to catch. Those interested in seeing the birds should go to the end of the road at Clifton Domain (no public transport covers this 21km distance from Napier) and then walk for a couple of hours along the sandy beaches to the cape. This walk can be undertaken only at low tide and is worthwhile only between October and April when the birds are in residence (the chicks are born in December). Tide times as well as all other travel information about the province of Hawke's Bay are available from the Napier Public Relations Office, Marine Parade (tel: 57-182).

ROTORUA

The town of Rotorua (population 52,000) attracts tourists on many counts. Best known for its hot springs, geysers and other volcanic features, it also has many aspects of Maori culture on show, a place for viewing kiwis, and a complex called the Agrodome which features a slick show about sheep farming. Its picturesque situation on Lake Rotorua clinches its irresistibility for the average visitor. With all this, it is inevitable that tour buses swamp the place, especially since Rotorua can be "done" on a day trip from Auckland.

Do not allow this apparently relentless onslaught of tourism put you off. Rotorua's attractions are so unusual that it is worth tolerating some commercialism. And the worst of it can be avoided; for example there is no obligation to attend one of the over-priced bad imitations of a Maori *hangi* (meal cooked in an earth oven) featured by several big hotels. Besides there are advantages to the commercial development: for example the range of restaurants is more interesting than it is in other New Zealand towns of comparable size.

Thermal Activity. A large area of the North Island from Mount Ruapehu to White Island in the Bay of Plenty, encompassing Rotorua and Taupo, is full of strange volcanic features. In many cases these have been fenced off so that admission can be charged and the dramatic features thoroughly tamed with pathways laid down between bubbling mud and boiling whirlpool, which have acquired cute names like Devil's Cauldron and Champagne Pool. But in many other cases steaming hot springs and mud pools can be seen in their natural state. The two problems with this are that a commitment to tramping is usually a prerequisite and that it can be dangerous. Every year there are numerous scaldings and an occasional death, one in 1987 of a boy who wandered off the path at the most heavily visited thermal site at Whakarewarewa. So it is best to heed all those signs, tiresome as they become, reminding visitors to the thermal centres not to stray from the pathways. Hot springs have proved dangerous throughout Rotorua's history. The Postmaster Baths, so named in 1892, were reputed to suppress the taste for alcohol. But as recently as 1950, the pool was bulldozed after a number of drunken bathers drowned in it. Recently a honeymooning couple died in a motel bed due to seepage of hydrogen sulphide.

There are five thermal areas in the vicinity of Rotorua. Whaka (as it is conveniently shortened) is under 4km from town, while Orakei Korakeo is 75km south. Waimangu boasts the world's largest boiling lake whereas Orakei features silica terraces. Read the tourist literature and decide which of the five appeal to you.

Whaka can be reached on foot or by the shuttle bus which operates from the tourist office at the corner of Fenton and Haupapa Streets (tel: 85-179) and charges $3 return. Its foremost attraction is the Pohutu Geyser which in the past regularly spouted over 30 metres. Unfortunately the pressure which causes it to shoot has been dissipated by the large number of Rotorua residents who tap the thermal source for their domestic heating systems. Recently the government ruled that all the private bores within a certain radius of Pohutu must be shut down. One of the town's most memorable aspects is the hissing and steaming of bores in most front yards, including that of hotels, not to mention the unmistakable sulphur stench. A further threat to Rotorua's unique resources is that there is apparently a market for Rotorua mud in exclusive beauty salons in Australia, though so far the depletion has not become noticeable.

The next nearest thermal area is Hell's Gate 15km around the east side of Lake Rotorua (admission $5). After visiting in the 1880s George Bernard Shaw claimed he would have gladly paid *not* to see the infernal sights at Hell's Gate. These thermal sites are most impressive in winter when steam rises everywhere.

Many Rotorua hotels and even hostels (including the Youth Hostel on the corner of Eruera and Hinemara Streets) have their own thermally-heated pools. For a fee you can also bathe in the mineral waters of the Polynesian Pools in the Government Gardens, open 8am to 10pm daily (tel: 81-328).

Maori Culture. Whaka also provides the focus for Maori traditions. Maori people live in the village though what tourists observe can hardly be considered typical. There is a reconstructed *pa* (fort) and a workshop where on weekdays carvers display and sell their skills.

The main Maori settlement was originally on the lake, a little west of the present town. Ohinemutu (which is poignantly translated "the girl cut off from the world") has an ornate neo-Tudor Maori church built in 1910. Wandering around the church's graveyard, it is interesting to see how many members of the Maori Expeditionary Battalion died in European wars. There is also a statue of Queen Victoria, incongruously under a Maori canopy, and also a magnificent meeting house where Maori concerts are held.

Performances of song and dance are also mounted in several of the main hotels (like the Travelodge in Eruera St or the Tudor Towers Restaurant in the Government Gardens) as well as in the Civic Theatre Building on Haupapa St. The latter costs $6 and includes a commentary between dances. One can't help but suspect that the traditional dances to celebrate marriages, battles, etc. have been somewhat diluted and tailored for the benefit of tourist audiences.

Scenic Attractions. One of the best ways to see the area is to hire a bicycle for a day or two. Cycles can be hired from several of the budget hostels such as Thermal Lodge at 60 Tarewa Road (tel: 70-931), Ivanhoe Lodge on Haupapa St (tel: 86-985) or the Youth Hostel (address above). The Thermal Lodge charges $12 for one day's hire of a ten-speed, and has excellent cheap accommodation as well.

With a copy of a sightseeing map (e.g. *Rotorua: Gateway to Geyserland* @ 55¢) you can plan your route. An obvious choice is to circumnavigate Lake Rotorua, about 45km. The minor road which hugs the northern edge of the lake is especially beautiful. There are plenty of attractions en route, though some of them, like the hedge maze at Fairbank or the peacocks at Hamurana Springs, are simply gimmicks to attract tourists into their souvenir shops and tea rooms.

The show at the Agrodome (on the west side of the lake) is worth seeing if you have not seen sheep dogs at work elsewhere and if you are at all interested in the many different breeds of sheep. There are shows at 9.15am, 11am and 2.30pm daily.

Tarawera. The Pink and White Terraces at Mount Tarawera were once considered among the world's most outstanding tourist attractions. Early descriptions of the terraces which stood about 20km south of Rotorua make them sound marvellous, and indeed photographs which survive in the Rotorua Museum corroborate this. But in 1886 the area suffered a volcanic eruption which was felt in Auckland and heard in Christchurch. Along with about 150 Maori who lived on the slopes of Tarawera, the famous terraces were engulfed forever.

There is not much to see today beyond the tranquil Lake Tarawera which filled in the giant crater. However the tourist authorities are looking into the possibility of recreating the terraces in a different place, at Wairakei (a geothermal power station just north of Taupo), after discovering in 1986 the chemical composition which turned the terraces pink.

AROUND TAUPO

Lake Taupo. An hour and a half south of Rotorua is yet another place of pilgrimage for tourists. Perhaps because of the proximity of the internationally famous Huka Lodge, Taupo has become a rather exclusive resort with expensive restaurants and accommodation (except for campsites and Rainbow Lodge at 99 Titiraupenga St). The town of Taupo is set on Lake Taupo famous for its oversized trout (average 2kg) and for its great depth, which has not yet been successfully measured. The lake is considerably larger than Rotorua, and a car rather than a bicycle is the preferred vehicle for covering the 105km distance of its circumference. There are campsites, boat jetties and swimming spots off Highway 1 heading south. The western side of the lake is less accessible but has some magnificent coloured cliffs called Karangahape and more hot pools at Tokaanu. Reasonably priced tours of local waterfalls, mud pools, etc. operate from the Youth Hostel (Taupo Nui-a Tia College, Spa Road; open December/ January only).

Tongariro. Tongariro National Park is roughly half way between Auckland and Wellington and incorporates the highest peaks of the North Island, all once volcanoes and all now pleasure grounds for sightseers as well as skiers and trampers (see *Great Outdoors* below). The park headquarters at the junction of Highways 4 and 47 (tel: Ruapehu 729) will guide you towards the most interesting geological formations such as lava monoliths and ash-covered deserts: look for the park publication *Volcanoes of the South Wind*.

Tongariro has been at the centre of national park centenary celebrations in 1987/8, since it was the first national park. A ceremony was held on 23rd September 1987, attended by the great grandson of the Maori chief who handed the land over to Queen Victoria in 1887, to honour the park's history and to open a new visitors' centre adorned with Maori carvings. Accommodation in the area may be found in Ohakune, Raetihi and Turangi.

WAITOMO

Prior to travelling around the North Island, many people have never thought of glow-worms as an obvious tourist attraction. But after ticking Rotorua off their list, most visitors head for the caves at Waitomo, renowned as a favourite habitat for glow-worms.

Waitomo is difficult to get to from Rotorua without transport although NZRRS run day trips from Rotorua and Hamilton. These allow a mere one hour stopover in Waitomo, which is a shame since the setting is pleasant enough to warrant a longer stay. On the other hand the return fare of $22 (from Hamilton) which includes admission to the caves is reasonable. Hitching is tricky though possible.

The caves are 8km west of Highway 3 and are not near any town amenities. In addition to the fancy Tourist Hotel Corporation hotel there is a very basic dormitory hostel a kilometre or so beyond the caves called the Topo Group Hut where a bunk costs $4 and you are bound to meet cavers who congregate in the area to explore the network of subterranean caverns. But non-cavers will have to pay the hefty $8.25 entrance fee to the tourist caves which have been specially adapted for mass tourism: spotlights show the insects and a short guided boat ride takes tourists into the blackness to see the glowing worms, which transform the roof of the cave into miniature heavens. Post cards can be purchased in the shop which describe the life cycle of the glow-worm, though for some reason they have not yet begun to market greenstone or paua shell worms. Tours of the Glow-worm Grotto depart every hour on the hour between 9am and 4pm with extra tours at 4.30 and 5.30pm in summer. Tours of the other tourist caves Ruakuri and Aranui (which feature odd limestone formations) are less popular, and somewhat cheaper. A minibus operated by the Perry Company leaves Waitomo in the early morning and goes as far as Te Kuiti on the main road (fare $3).

The little museum of caving in Waitomo (free admission) is excellent, providing a vividly illustrated history of the region's exploration. The Roadside Bar is pleasant enough and a good place to meet cavers, some of whom work as guides in the caves. This, together with a post office and shop, constitutes Waitomo, so it makes a pleasant contrast with the bustling commerce of Rotorua.

It is worth noting that Waitomo does not have a monopoly on all the glow-worms of New Zealand. They thrive wherever there are damp conditions with enough airborne insect life to feed on. Although they won't be as numerous in other places, it is fun to stumble across the pinpricks of light yourself. Locals can often direct you to a good viewing place.

THE TARANAKI

The capital of this western province is New Plymouth, once known for its parks but now associated with the offshore natural gas fields and for its synthetic petrol plant which has stood idle since the world price of oil dropped, making the process of deriving fuel from natural gas uneconomic.

Mount Egmont/Tarananki. The predominantly dairying province of Taranaki which occupies the western bulge of the North Island is dominated by a symmetrically formed volcanic peak. Until recently maps labelled this 2,517m mountain Egmont, but in deference to Maori protests, it is now officially also called Mount Taranaki, a compromise which many New Zealanders consider symptomatic of their government's indecisiveness.

Whichever name you choose to call it, it is a magnificent mountain. But like the mountains of the South Island which attract visitors from far and wide, you have to be lucky to see it on a clear day. Some maintain that the best chance of seeing the conical peak is from an aircraft, since it often pokes through the clouds which obscure it completely from landlubbers. The romantic Maori explanation for the persistent cloud and mists is that Taranaki is weeping for his lost love Pihanga (wife of Mount Tongariro); tacky post cards portraying the myth are widely available in the region, but provide little consolation for failing to see the mountain itself.

There are three approach roads from Highway 3, each ending at some visitor amenities. From the much less heavily used coastal road, a huge number of minor roads radiate in towards the mountain to serve the farms and Maori settlements in this area. The round trip from New Plymouth around the mountain via the coast is 180km, though there is a smaller circle which cuts a third off this distance. Unless it is a clear day, there is not much point in approaching the mountain at close range, though the displays at the North Egmont Visitor Centre about the geology and unique plant life are interesting. The park is known for its flag trees which have come to resemble pennants because of the constancy of the prevailing winds. From the North Egmont Centre there are walks of varying lengths (see *Great Outdoors*). There is no bus service to the mountain, so unless you have your own transport, you will have to rely on the good nature of motoring tourists.

WANGANUI RIVER

Although the genteel town of Wanganui (population 40,000) is unremarkable in most respects — though it does have an interesting museum with a good Maori and settlers' collection — it is the starting point of the trip up the lovely Wanganui River to the village of Pipiriki, now host to the headquarters of the new Whanganui National Park which opened in February 1987. (The "h" is a more authentic Maori spelling, and the "Wh" should be pronounced almost as an "f"). Even if you don't have your own car, you can join the rural mailman on his daily rounds along the 80km road. John Hammond (tel: 54-635) welcomes visitors on his mail bus. He will collect you from your lodging about 7am and bring you back in the mid-afternoon all for a modest $14. (For accommodation in Wanganui try the pleasant Riverside Inn at 2 Plymouth St which has budget cabins at the back as well as verandahed rooms, or the new Youth Hostel at 43 Campbell St.) The early morning start often means that you see the valley at its most beautiful with the mist clinging to the river. Frequent stops are made to visit old mills, fossilized walls, etc. plus the mailman is a fund of local legends and gossip. On the opposite (and roadless) side of the river you can see several farms which depend on private aerial pulleys to convey themselves and their produce across the river gorge to town.

River trips were once a very popular holiday for urban New Zealanders but these have now been reduced to day cruises in the summer. The preferred method nowadays of getting on to the river is in a jet boat, a method of propulsion invented in New Zealand (and, according to the Editor of the Oxford English Dictionary Supplement, himself a native of Wanganui, first used in 1964). While the road leaves the river at Pipiriki, jet boats penetrate further upriver. Trips will leave with a minimum of three people willing to pay $18 each. The main attraction is the "Drop Scene", where some people are able to persuade themselves that the river is flowing uphill. Unfortunately, the river has become increasingly polluted by a hydroelectric dam at the headwaters, though conservation officers are working hard to reverse this.

Anyone interested in the trip should obtain the leaflet about the river road published by the Department of Conservation from the Wanganui Visitor Information Centre at 100 Guyton St (tel: 53-286). A five day trip on the *MV Wakapai* is also available; contact Focus Travel, PO Box 448, Wanganui.

From Wanganui, it is a fast three-hour drive to Wellington. There is a frequent coach service run by both Newmans and NZRRS (cost $18).

WELLINGTON

The Wellington authorities have chosen to promote their city as one of the great harbourside cities of the world, comparable to San Francisco, Vancouver or Hong Kong. The setting is indeed magnificent, with steep hills descending to the spacious harbour, an ancient volcanic crater which the sea has appropriated. But Wellington is a tiny city by world standards (with a population of just 350,000, though there are over half a million in the region), and if it were not for the cluster of high rise buildings downtown, it would more closely resemble an English seaside town than a great modern capital city.

Some people maintain that of New Zealand's major cities, Wellington is the most genuinely New Zealand in character, having shaken off the colonial past. In the pursuit of progress, it has been more ruthless with its old buildings than elsewhere, and many charming old wooden buildings downtown have been replaced by concrete and glass. Even in the 1980s, when the obliteration of the past has become distinctly unfashionable, ornate turn-of-the-century hotels and theatres are under threat, though the New Zealand Historic Places Trust, the Save our City lobby and Wellington City Council are making vigorous protest.

Considering how susceptible Wellington is to earth tremors, it is surprising that there are any old buildings left at all. Before disembarking from your plane,

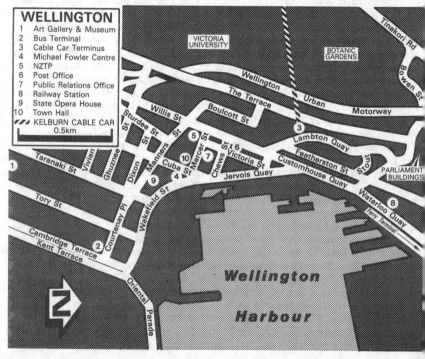

WELLINGTON
1   Art Gallery & Museum
2   Bus Terminal
3   Cable Car Terminus
4   Michael Fowler Centre
5   NZTP
6   Post Office
7   Public Relations Office
8   Railway Station
9   State Opera House
10 Town Hall
/// KELBURN CABLE CAR
0.5km

train, coach or ferry, read the introductory section on page 373 on what to do during an earthquake. In some parts of the city there are height restrictions of 30 metres (about six storeys) partly because of earthquake danger and also to avoid interrupting views of the harbour.

THE LOCALS

The rivalry between Auckland and Wellington is rather more subdued than that between Sydney and Melbourne, though it certainly exists. For example Wellington's recent campaign to attract tourists from Auckland met with mirth and scepticism. Wellington became the capital in 1865, after Auckland had been the seat of colonial government for 25 years. Nowadays Wellington is full of politicians, civil servants and a large professional class which is perhaps a little disapproving of the business ethics and commercial energy associated with Auckland. The difference can even be seen in the give-away newspapers which both cities publish. Whereas Auckland's *Tourist Times* carries pages of advertisements and accompanying editorial on souvenir shopping, the *Capital Times* of Wellington devotes the majority of its pages to reviews of art exhibitions and opera productions; Wellington fancies itself as a place of culture. There are no American-style amusement parks in the region, but rather restored colonial cottages and antique shops.

For such a small city it is surprisingly cosmopolitan, with a good range of ethnic restaurants. Like most white collar bureaucratic towns, it is also prosperous. Less affluent people tend to live in inland commuter towns like Lower and Upper Hutt, while the rich survey the city from houses on the hillside. Some houses are built on such steep hills that residents have installed private cable cars with which to winch themselves to their front doors.

Making Friends. The *Capital Times* carries a detailed list of club meetings, many of which welcome visitors, from the Backgammon Club to El Club Espanol y Latino Americano de Wellington.

ARRIVAL AND DEPARTURE

Air. Wellington International Airport is located in Rongotai on an exposed promontory just 8km south of the city centre. The domestic terminal is by far the busiest in the country, since many flights between towns on the two islands are routed through Wellington. Nevertheless it is the tattiest (even Prince Philip was goaded into being rude about it) and a massive revamping is planned. The international terminal — which has flights to Brisbane, Sydney and Melbourne — is situated between the Air New Zealand and Ansett NZ terminals. The bus service into town is privately run by Guthrey's Coachline (tel: 872-018). Services operate every 20 minutes from the airport and from Bunny St (near the railway station) between 6am and 9pm; the weekend service is reduced, running every half hour between 7am and 7.30pm. Guthrey's buses from downtown call at several stops on Lambton Quay, Willis St, etc. which are clearly marked with a red logo. In the reverse direction, buses will stop almost anywhere you request along its route. The one way fare is $3.50. For a cut price trip, you must walk one kilometre from the airport entrance along Calabar Rd, right on Broadway to Maramar Junction where you can catch city bus number 3, 25 or E24.

The Skyferry to Picton (the cheapest air link between the two islands) may be contacted at any time on 888-380. It is based in Air New Zealand's domestic terminal at Wellington Airport.

Flight information can be obtained by dialling 889-900. Ansett NZ's office is at the corner of Featherston St and Lambton Quay (tel: 711-050) while Air New Zealand is at 129-141 Vivian St (tel: 859-911) as well as several other locations.

Coach. NZRRS services stop on the Waterloo Quay side of the railway station (near platform 9). The booking office for coach and rail travel (tel: 725-399) is open from 7am to 7.30pm Monday to Saturday and 8.15am to 7.30pm on Sundays. The only other coach firm to offer express services to Auckland — the trip takes 11 hours — is Mount Cook, whose office is at 83-87 Courtenay Place (tel: 844-136). If you are planning to make this trip, try to reserve a seat in advance.

The Newmans Coachlines depot is quite a long way from the city centre past the Art Gallery at 260 Taranaki St (tel: 851-149) but they have a pick up point in town at the corner of Featherston and Stout Streets. They run daily services to Palmerston North and Napier, and also to New Plymouth.

Train. Wellington Railway Station is more bustling than those in Auckland and Christchurch since Wellington is served by fast commuter trains along the Hutt Valley (and beyond to Masterton) and along the Kapiti Coast to Paraparaumu. The station is at the top of Customhouse Quay, where tickets may be bought between 7am and 7.30pm (from 8.15am on Sundays); telephone 725-399 for information. NZR publish a leaflet describing the ten-hour Wellington to Gisborne run in glowing terms.

Driving. There is less choice of car hire firms in Wellington than in Auckland or Christchurch and so cheap deals are harder to come by. Try Thrifty at 47 Adelaide St (tel: 846-711), or other international firms such as Budget at 42 Waterloo Quay (tel: 726-336) or Avis at 25 Dixon St (tel: 850-266). The latter two have outlets at the airport and ferry terminals.

Hitch-hiking. Since there is only one corridor out of Wellington which serves the city's suburbs as well as further destinations, it is difficult to get a long distance lift from anywhere close to the city. For Highway 1 north to Auckland you should invest a few dollars in the train. The first good point is Porirua; when you leave the station, walk up to the right of the tracks to the traffic lights at the end of the motorway. A better point is a few stops further on at Paremata, where there is a roundabout on Highway 1 immediately outside the station. If this is crowded with other hitchers, take the train to its terminus at Paraparaumu which has a handy set of lights just across the road from the station.

You may find hitching advice posted on the notice board at the Wellington Youth Hostel or at private hostels.

Ferry. Information regarding the ferry service to the South Island may be found on page 377. For up-to-date times and prices, ring the railway station on 725-399. A shuttle bus runs between platform 9 of the railway station and the ferry terminal; it is a two kilometre walk if you are feeling energetic.

CITY TRANSPORT

City Layout. The geography of Wellington has forced the population to settle along the two narrow valleys which are traced by Highway 1 to the west coast and Highway 2 to Upper Hutt, and the downtown area is therefore rather elongated. It takes about 40 minutes to walk from the station to the art gallery for instance (longer into a headwind) and so it is worth mastering the public transport system.

If you are interested in taking a bus tour, enquire at the Public Relations Office about the daily tours run by the city transport company (cost $17) or by Hammond's Sightseeing Tours (tel: 720-869).

Bus. The two main city bus terminals are at the railway station and at Courtenay Place. You can obtain the free *Wellington City Bus Route Guide*, which carries detailed information about routes and times, from these and other outlets. Ring 856-579 for all city bus information.

Buses run from about 6am until 11.30pm during the week. Fares vary according to the distance travelled, ranging from 80¢ to $2.20. If you are planning to make a number of journeys, buy a ten-trip ticket from one of the city bus terminals, which will save you a fifth over the cash fare.

There are a number of worthwhile deals available. The Downtowner costs $2 and allows five trips within the central business district (between the station and Courtenay Place) including the cable car. It is aimed at shoppers and is valid from 9am-3pm Monday to Friday.

The Daytripper which costs $5 allows you unlimited travel on the Wellington bus network for one day as long as you begin your travel after 9am on weekdays. The *Bus Route Guide* sets out a suggested Daytripper itinerary which takes in the scenic waterfront drive along Oriental Parade, the drive up Mount Victoria, the Botanic Gardens by cable car and several other places of interest.

If you want to go further afield and make use of the suburban rail network, you will have to invest $12 in the Day Rover which seems not such a bargain as the Daytripper. It is not valid at commuter times (i.e. before 9am and from 4-6pm) but otherwise has no restrictions.

The frequency of many services is severely reduced at weekends, and some routes are discontinued completely, for instance the trip up Mount Victoria and the marine drive along Evans Bay Parade. So try to plan your itinerary for a weekday.

Cable Car. Like San Francisco, Wellington has a restored cable car (originally built in 1899) which runs from Lambton Quay opposite Grey St, up the Kelburn Hill to the eastern entrance of the Botanic Gardens. The trip lasts just four minutes and costs 70¢ but is included in the various special tickets described above. Most people turn north from the terminus and walk through the Gardens though the opposite direction brings you to the Victoria University of Wellington.

Car. The Wellington Urban Motorway takes traffic right into the city centre, keeping delays to a minimum. Also Wellington has a good record vis-à-vis drinking and driving; during a recent police campaign 10,752 drivers were tested and only 19 were over the limit (compared to 163 out of 9,000 in Auckland).

Parking, however, can pose problems. In order to cure the locals of their haphazard parking habits, the city council has taken steps to police Friday evening and Saturday parking, and fines have been doubled. There is a $10 fine for allowing your meter to expire and $40 for parking on double yellow lines. Car parks are located on Sturdee St, under the posh James Cook Hotel on The

Terrace and in the Williams Building at the corner of Boulcott St and Gilmer Terrace.

The Automobile Association of New Zealand office is on level seven of the shopping complex at 342 Lambton Quay (tel: 738-738).

Taxis. Taxi ranks are located outside the railway station, on Whitmore St (between Lambton Quay and Featherston St), outside Woolworths in Dixon St and at the corner of Willis and Aro Streets. To phone a cab, dial 859-888 for Wellington Co-op Taxis or 893-023 for Capital City Cabs.

Cycling. Between the strong winds and steep hills, Wellington is far from being a cyclist's paradise. If you are still keen, phone 873-036 for bicycle hire information.

Hotels and Budget Accommodation. There is enough choice of good budget accommodation and a fast enough turnover of visitors (most people tend not to linger in Wellington) that you do not usually need to worry about being roofless. Even if you arrive at the Youth Hostel at nightfall in the height of the season you are unlikely to be turned away. Not only does the IYHF hostel at 40 Tinakori Road willingly pull out mattresses for extra bodies, but it has an overflow hostel five minutes' walk away. The main hostel is very well placed for people arriving or departing by ferry or train, since it is about half way between the ferry terminal and the station, ten minutes in either direction. Tinakori Road branches directly from the motorway if you are driving or hitching in from the north. It is fine if you are self-catering but a long way from affordable restaurants otherwise.

The private chain of hostels run by Ivanhoe Inns is represented in Wellington at 52 Ellice St (tel: 842-264) which is just before the Mount Victoria tunnel begins. This is the way the airport bus approaches Wellington, so if you have your wits about you, you can ask to be put down near the Ivanhoe; ask to stop at the Basin Reserve. Otherwise take bus 1, 3, 4, 21 or 23 from the railway station. Dormitory beds cost $9, and singles are available for $11. They also offer some more expensive serviced rooms in all categories.

Just around the corner is the Beethoven House Hotel, an offbeat kind of place which will appeal more to classical music fans (since Beethoven is played continuously) than to smokers (since smoking is banned). It stays open around the clock, so that if you arrive at 10.45pm on the last ferry from Picton, you don't have to worry, though it is better if you can phone or write ahead to warn the manager. Take bus 2 or 5 to Brougham St and walk along to number 89 (tel: 482-226). If you enjoy being the centre of attention try to make your visit to the Beethoven coincide with your birthday, since the hostel makes a point of celebrating as many birthdays as possible.

The final possibility in the budget category is also on Brougham St. The Rowena Travel Hotel at number 115 (tel: 857-872) has an "international dormitory" with beds at $11, plus bed and breakfast for $25 single and $44 double. It has the unusual feature of a picnic and barbecue area complete with appropriate provisions if required.

The Emergency Night Shelter is at 204 Taranaki St (tel: 842-972).

Guest Houses and Hotels. In a more expensive bracket is the Terrace Travel

Hotel at 291 The Terrace (tel: 848-702) which charges from $23 single, $34 double, $38 triple, though it also has budget rooms for $14. The Balcairn Private Hotel (151-153 Ghuznee St; tel: 842-274) also has triples which cost $43, as well as standard priced singles and doubles. If you are looking for more luxury, try Tinakori Lodge, the restored home of an early New Zealand Prime Minister. It is at 182 Tinakori Rd (tel: 733-478) near the ferry terminal. Single bed and breakfast starts at $38, double at $54.

Camping. Although there are plenty of campsites along the Kapiti Coast north of Wellington, there are not many within easy reach of Wellington city. Hutt Park Motor Camp (95 Hutt Park Rd, Moera, Lower Hutt; tel: 685-913) claims to be the closest and it is 20 minutes' drive from the ferry port. It has 26 tourist cabins ($23 for two) as well as tent and caravan sites.

Eating and Drinking

Fortunately the distribution of restaurants around Courtenay Place is so dense that you can usually find a congenial spot simply by wandering around (unless it is Sunday). The southern part of the downtown area has better pickings than the northern part which is mainly given over to highrise government and commercial buildings (i.e. Lambton Quay, Customhouse Quay, Featherston St). Both Courtenay Place and Willis St are lined with restaurants, from businessmen's steak houses to a swish Japanese restaurant and a Texan café. One of the most interesting streets for restaurants is Cuba St incorporating the pedestrian Cuba Mall between Ghuznee and Dixon Streets. Although a high percentage of these restaurants are Chinese (you may prefer to avoid the Lotus where dining is accompanied by dancing), there is plenty of variety: from the Raging Apple at number 301 (a vegetarian whole food café), to Monsoon at number 124 in the Mall which is Burmese; and from Le Normandie, a licensed French restaurant at number 116 to Konditorei Aida, an Austrian cake shop at number 181.

If a stroll along the kilometre length of Cuba St has not succeeded, turn into Manners St where you will find the Ruby Chinese Restaurant at number 141 which advertises an 11-course set menu for $14, the BYO That's Natural at 88 Manners Mall which is mostly though not entirely vegetarian, and the Middle East upstairs in the Regent Centre where most main dishes cost about $8 (if you want to avoid a display of belly dancing, avoid Thursdays and Sundays).

Locals often recommend the popular Mexican Cantina at 19 Edward St (near the Manners Mall) though it closes early (9.30pm) and does not take reservations, so you may have to queue. Another good BYO restaurant is the Greek Restaurant upstairs on the harbour side of Lambton Quay where meals cost about $12.

Seafood restaurants tend to be located in fashionable harbourside locations and are therefore pricey. The Shorebird at 301 Evans Bay Parade and Otto's Hafen on Clyde Quay (near the Overseas Terminal) specialize in fish.

As throughout New Zealand, restaurants tend to close early. Even ones like Toko Baru, an Indonesian restaurant at 146 Featherston St which stays open until 1am, take last orders at 10.30pm. If you are having trouble finding anything open on a Sunday evening, head for one of the many Chinese restaurants most of which are open seven days a week. Or try Chevy's Licensed Café (97 Dixon St) which sells burgers and tacos from 11.30am-1am throughout the week.

If you're hungry but broke visit the Baptist-run Friendship Centre in Boulcott

St, where soup, muffins, etc. can be bought very cheaply. It is open for lunch every day except Saturday, plus Monday and Tuesday evenings from 5.15pm.

The Wakefield food market has recently opened at the corner of Jervois Quay and Taranaki St, open Friday 11am-8pm and weekends 11am-5pm. If you are self-catering and have your own transport, you should stop at some of the roadside stalls along the Kapiti Coast near Otaki (about an hour north of Wellington) where abundant fresh fruit, berries and vegetables are sold.

DRINKING

Wellington is not so well endowed with pubs as it is with restaurants; while there are over 300 restaurants, there are less than 50 licensed hotels. The restaurant district is also the best for pubs and discos. In addition, the 1860 Victualling Company on Lambton Quay is popular, though its complex of bars can seem a little soulless. The Cricketers Arms on Vivian St serves food in the Sticky Wicket bar and also has a music room (for which there is a cover charge). Try also the Romney Arms Tavern on Plimmers Lane for food and music, and Greta Point Tavern on Evans Bay Parade which closes at 9.30pm (9pm on Sundays).

Wine lovers may want to take a trip to Martinborough, 80km east of Wellington, where an increasing number of good wines are being produced.

There is no lack of theatre, music and art in Wellington, and the city has spent lavishly over the past decade on buildings to house the arts. The architecturally-striking Michael Fowler Centre (named after a dynamic mayor) is the venue for all kinds of musical performances, though it is often given over to business conferences. Even if you do not attend a concert, pop in to see the abstract wall hangings which represent Wellington in ten different aspects (including windy). Much of the interior is of rimu, a much-prized native timber, which gives the auditorium very live acoustics. The Centre is on Wakefield St at the top of Cuba St (tel: 723-088).

In addition to the weekend issues of the two Wellington dailies, the *Dominion* and the *Evening Post*, the free *Capital Times* has lots of detailed information on what's on. A Festival of the Arts has recently been inaugurated, to be held in even-numbered years.

But before deciding on what cultural offerings you intend to take in, you should admire Wellington's setting. The city is often compared to an amphitheatre, since it rises in a semi-circular bowl around the harbour. Some of the best views of the city can be had from the harbour itself, so if you take the Cook Strait ferry, be sure to admire the views of the approaching or receding city. Excellent panoramas may also be enjoyed from the top of Mount Victoria (bus number 20, Monday to Friday only), where the lookout is 200 metres above sea level. Ask for the special leaflet at the bus terminal about the Mount Victoria trip and the walks you can do from the summit.

Although the Botanic Gardens at the top of the cable are not so elevated, they are easier to get to than Mount Victoria and afford an impressive sweep. If you would like a drink to accompany your view, you will either have to pay a fortune for a cocktail at the top of the Williams Centre just off The Terrace or take a can of Steinlager into the Botanic Gardens.

Wellington has its fair share of outdoor entertainment. For details of summer events (December to March) ring the Parks and Recreation Department (tel: 724-599).

Museum and Galleries. The National Museum and Art Gallery are combined in one complex on Buckle St near the Basin Reserve. The National Museum houses a good collection of Maori and colonial artefacts, while the Art Gallery concentrates on the work of Antipodean painters, print-makers, etc. Free conducted tours of the Art Gallery are available on the first Wednesday of the month at 11am (tel: 859-703, ext 76). The National Museum, sometimes referred to as the Dominion Museum, is open from 10am to 4.45pm daily. Take any bus to the Basin Reserve or bus 11 to the corner of Taranaki and Buckle Streets.

Except for the Maritime Museum on Queen's Wharf (tel: 728-899) most of the museums are scattered around the Wellington region rather than in the city itself, for example the Settlers' Museum in Petone, the pioneer Cobblestone Museum in Greytown, the Tramway Museum in Paekakariki, and so on. In Wellington there is a private collection of musical instruments which can be inspected if you arrange an appointment with the Castle Collection, 27 Colombo St, Newtown (tel: 898-296). Bibliophiles will enjoy browsing in the superb collection of rare books and manuscripts including a copy of the Treaty of Waitangi and a log book of one of Captain Cook's voyages, now housed at the National Library in Molesworth St.

Buildings of note include the wooden church of Old St Paul's in Mulgrave St near the station (where concerts are sometimes put on), and a restored worker's cottage from 1858 called Nairn Cottage at 68 Nairn St (bus route 7) where volunteers bake and sell old-fashioned cakes. It is open 10am-4pm Wednesday to Friday and 1-4.30pm on weekends (tel: 849-122). The New Zealand Historic Places Trust is housed in Antrim House on Boulcott St (tel: 724-341).

Music. In addition to the classical concerts at the Michael Fowler Centre, there are operas at the State Opera House in Manners St (tel: 850-832). This booking office also handles tickets for performances at the nearby Town Hall and the Circa Theatre.

Quite a few pubs and restaurants have live entertainment. Also try the BYO As You Like It Café at 32/34 Riddiford St Newtown (tel: 893-983) where musicians perform at weekends. The Wellington Folk Club meets at 10 Holland St (near Tory St) on Sunday evenings.

Theatre. Wellington supports two professional theatre companies plus plenty of amateur ones. The Hannah Playhouse, home of the Downstage Theatre Company, at the corner of Courtenay Place and Kent Terrace, usually stage interesting productions (tel: 849-639). Student tickets booked in advance cost $14 for a downstairs seat and $10 in the gallery. The Circa Theatre on Jervois Quay (tel: 728-778) and the Stagecraft Theatre in Upper Cuba Mall are also worth checking; students are regularly given a $2 discount.

Parks and Zoos. The Botanic Gardens at the top of the cable car are pleasant without being thrilling. The Wellington Observatory is inside the Gardens and, as in Auckland, is open to the public on Tuesday evenings provided the night is clear.

You can go for a bush walk at the Otari Native Plant Reserve (take bus 14 to Wilton Road). To see native fauna instead of flora, visit the Wellington Zoo in Newtown, which has the regulation nocturnal house for kiwis. The zoo is open 8.30am-4pm daily; take bus 11 to Newtown.

Parliament Buildings. It is interesting to join one of the free tours of the Parliament Buildings which are at the north end of The Terrace. J. B. Priestley once compared the House of Representatives to a "cosy City Council chamber brought up to date with microphones," and the seat of New Zealand's government retains a small-town air of informality. The times of tours depend on when the House is sitting, but usually they take place every hour in the mid-morning plus a couple more after lunch; ring 749-199 for details. All tours include the Beehive, the easy-to-spot administrative building where the Prime Minister has his office. If Parliament is in session, try to turn up just before 2pm to see the opening ceremony. Watching a debate in Parliament House can be most entertaining, not least because of the colourful personal abuse exchanged between government and opposition. And when they are not insulting their opponents, New Zealand MPs seem to spend their time in Parliament reading newspapers or catching up on correspondence; each member has a generous supply of stationery. If you cannot get along in person, every debate is broadcast in full on the concert programme of BCNZ.

SPORT

The calendar in the *Capital Times* includes sporting events, not all of which are likely to interest the visitor, such as netball tournaments or under-15 water polo championships. Horseracing takes place regularly at Trentham in Upper Hutt and night trotting is at Hutt Park. Rugby Union football is played at Athletic Park (take the Island Bay route 1 bus) while cricket and soccer are played at Basin Reserve. Wellington City Transport puts on special buses when there are important matches. An international motor race is held on the last weekend of October.

The Public Relations Office can advise people in search of exercise, especially those who are content with walking. The Freyberg Swimming Pool (tel: 843-107) on the harbour is open daily from 6am-7.30pm (take bus 15). Those who prefer to brave the sea can travel further along the harbour to find beaches on Oriental Bay. The bays along this coast are full of yachts, especially at weekends. A new 400 berth marina is planned for Seaview.

Wellington is the perfect city to take up kite-flying. Check local papers for kite flying demonstrations staged by the recently formed New Zealand Kitefliers' Association.

SHOPPING

The main shopping stretch between the station and Courtenay Place along Lambton Quay and Willis St is styled (at least by the tourist office) the Golden Mile. The biggest downtown department store is Kirkcaldies. Cuba Mall, somewhat reminiscent of Camden Town in London, has some unusual shops including Cubacade Antiques and Curios. The Woman's Place, a feminist bookshop is at 59 Courtenay Place.

For pottery try Earthworks Pottery in the AA Centre at the end of Lambton Quay (which was voted Wellington's Top Shop in 1987) or the Potter's Shop run as a cooperative at 324 Tinakori Road. It is also interesting to browse in

Tala's South Pacific Centre at 60 Courtenay Place and Trade Aid Shops in the Manners Mall which sells third world handicrafts.

One of the best markets for finding non-tacky gifts (as well as food) is the Settlers Market in the suburb of Petone. It is open during the day on Saturdays and Sundays only.

THE MEDIA

Newspapers. The *Dominion* newspaper has established a reputation for even-handed and reliable coverage of political and business news, and is the closest New Zealand has to a national newspaper, closely rivalled by the *New Zealand Herald*. (It is the paper which took on the British Government by publishing excerpts from the banned book *Spycatcher*.) The *Evening Post* is more downmarket and has a considerably higher circulation.

Foreign newspapers may be read at the Public Library every day including Sunday afternoons; the entrance to the reading room is in Victoria St, though the Library itself is in Mercer St. Alternatively, you can read home newspapers at your embassy (see *Help and Information*).

Radio. On the AM dial, tune to 567kHz for 2YA, 657 for 2YC, 1035 for 2ZB and 783 for 2YB. FM radio stations ZM-91 (nicknamed Hitradio) and Concert may be listened to respectively on 90.9 and 92.5MHz. The commercial 24-hour radio station Radio Windy specializes in news and controversy, and broadcasts on 891kHz.

It is possible to tour the TV-NZ complex at Avalon in Lower Hutt at 2pm on weekdays. Ring 368-168 for details.

Wellington seems to have escaped the recent increase in crime which Auckland has been experiencing. The only crimes you are likely to see will be bureaucrats defying the parking regulations. The Central Police Station is off Lambton Quay between Johnston and Waring Taylor Streets (tel: 723-000).

Massage parlours and associated activities may be found in the Ghuznee and Vivian St area.

The STD code for Wellington is 04.
For fire, police or ambulance dial 111.

City Public Relations Office: 2 Mercer St, corner of Victoria St (735-063). Open seven days a week 9am-5pm.
NZTP: 25-27 Mercer St (739-269). Open 8.30am-5pm Monday to Thursday, 8.30am-8pm Friday, 9.30am-12.30pm Saturday.
British High Commission: 9th Floor, Reserve Bank Building, 2 The Terrace (726-049).
US Embassy: 29 Fitzherbert Terrace (722-068).
American Express: c/o Century 21 Travel, 276 Lambton Quay (731-221).
Thomas Cook Bureau de Change: 207 Lambton Quay (736-267).
Automobile Association: 342 Lambton Quay (738-738).

Student Travel Services: 1st Floor, Hope Gibbons Building, 11-15 Dixon St (850-561).
Post Office: Waterloo Quay (738-498). Post restante services.
Medical Services: Wellington Public Hospital (855-999); Iamat Centre, 189-191 Willis St (849-675).
Free Ambulance: 722-999.
Emergency Dentist: 727-072.
Emergency Chemist: 59 Cambridge Terrace (858-810).
Gay Switchboard: 728-609.

DAY TRIPS FROM WELLINGTON

The environs of Wellington are not as immediately appealing as those of Auckland, Christchurch or Dunedin, and are certainly less well known. However it is possible to spend an enjoyable few days exploring the region by car and on foot. There is a host of good beaches both on the relatively densely populated west coast and on the more distant and remote east coast. Freshwater swimming in rivers and lakes is popular and pleasant picnic spots can usually be found nearby. There are several ranges of hills for hiking (though the weather at altitude is often shockingly windy and wet). There are also several wildlife sanctuaries, historic buildings and the inevitable craft centres to visit. Some of these attractions are a little too far from Wellington to be visited comfortably on a day trip, however appropriate detours can be made when travelling to or from the city.

Several unsealed roads lead to bays at the southern tip of the North Island, for example popular Makara Beach, about half an hour's drive from the city. Although it can become crowded on fine days, the throngs are easily left behind by walking a short distance. Owhiro Bay is even nearer the city, at the end of bus route 1 or 4. A one-hour walk brings you to the volcanic feature known as Red Rocks and a few kilometres beyond is a seal colony which can be seen in winter only. Similarly on the eastern side of the harbour, scenic drives followed by stiff walks take you to a variety of headlands, all with vantage points for different views of the city.

The West Coast. Most weekending Wellingtonians head up Highway 1 to the so-called Kapiti Coast, a series of beaches which enjoy excellent weather and the shelter of Kapiti Island about 16km offshore. As is the case with so many small offshore islands in New Zealand, this one has also been made a bird sanctuary which can be visited, but only with a permit from the Department of Conservation (4th Floor, Borthwick House, The Terrace; tel: 725-821).

Further north on this coast is a very fine Maori church at Otaki (75km from Wellington). Many Maori adopted Christianity very soon after it was introduced to them, and Rangiatea church was completed in 1850. There are also old Maori mission buildings in Otaki as well as an interesting local museum and an 1830s whaler's cottage.

It is worth leaving the main coastal road to climb into the hills which afford excellent views. If you are fortunate enough to be in the area on a clear day, it is possible (or said to be possible) to see the South Island in one direction and Mount Egmont in the other. Advice on accommodation, special events etc. is available from the Kapiti Coast Promotion Council, c/o The Borough Council, Private Bag, Paraparaumu (tel: 058 88-993).

The Wairarapa Region. Since the average New Zealander's threshold of tolerance for crowds is lower than that of most nationalities, some Wellingtonians have forsaken busy Highway 1 and the popular coastal beaches for the more secluded hinterland. On the eastern side of the Tararua Range (hills rising to over 1,500m, locally famed for their almost unremitting rain and wind) is a sizeable region dubbed the Wairarapa. It is doing its best to promote itself as a tourist destination and in fact has a number of attractions such as the Mount Bruce National Wildlife Centre north of Masterton (closed during the bird breeding season October to December), the wineries around Martinborough (a town whose streets are in the pattern of a Union Jack) and some nearby glow-worm caves at Ruakokapatuna where there are no queues (enquire at Blue Creek Farm for details). Unfortunately accommodation is sparse outside Masterton, and even Masterton's lodgings fill up in the first week of March when the international sheep-shearing Golden Shears competition is held.

Although it is rather a long drive to the east coast it is worth following one of the unsealed roads down to the Pacific Ocean. Riversdale, where a number of holiday homes have been built, is the main centre. In an heroic attempt to entice visitors to this coast, the locals organize special events such as frog-races, sand-castle building competitions and obstacle races for tractors. A drive of 50km north brings you to Castlepoint which every March hosts a horse race on the beach. For further information contact the Wairarapa Information Centre, PO Box 814, Masterton (tel: 059 87-373).

The Great Outdoors

Anywhere on the North Island, whether near the cities or on farflung offshore islands, you will find enticements to swim, hike, fish and sail. The four national parks of Egmont, Whanganui, Tongariro and Urewera all offer tramps and climbs of varying difficulty, but many are well suited to the novice. For example, every summer thousands of day-trippers climb (weather permitting) to the summit of Mount Taranaki, the second highest peak after Ruapehu. There are also numerous state forests, some covering vast areas from one end of the island to the other. The Department of Conservation in Auckland is in the State Insurance Building on Wakefield St (tel: 771-899) and in Wellington it is on Stout St (tel: 725-808); they distribute much literature of interest to anyone wishing to explore the great outdoors.

The North Island also excels at water sports, with its hundreds of miles of ocean beach, some sheltered enough for safe bathing and snorkelling, others attractive to surfers.

TRAMPING

The long distance tracks of the North Island are not as well known as South Island tramps like the Milford and Routeburn Tracks, and therefore are often less densely populated. A further advantage of trekking in the North is that the season is longer, and most paths can be tackled in November and in April, months that are usually impossible in Fiordland.

Some might claim that the North Island treks are less spectacular, though this would be hotly disputed by many experienced locals and visitors. Certainly some of the best walking is not amidst high mountains but rather along coastal cliffs (for example near both Auckland and Wellington) or around lakes such as

Taupo and the exquisite Lake Waikaremoana. It takes about four days to encircle the latter, though this achievement is somewhat diminished by the knowledge that a road runs for a good distance. (Of course motorists are less likely to notice the orchids and kakabeak trees, some of which can be found only in the Urewera National Park since it has the largest area of untouched forest in the country.)

Near Auckland. The variety of walks in the Waitakere Ranges has already been mentioned. Several other regional parks within easy range of Auckland offer enjoyable tramping possibilities. Prolonged stays are possible at these provided you apply to the Regional Parks office at the corner of Nelson and Wellesley Streets (tel: 393-760) at least two days in advance. These very basic campsites are free unless you choose to drive to one which is accessible by road; vehicles are charged $5.50.

There is even an interesting walk within the city limits of Auckland, known as the coast-to-coast walk. Not many countries can be traversed in a few hours but New Zealand narrows to just a few kilometres at Auckland, and an official 13km walk has been designed which links the domains (parks) of Auckland and starts (or finishes) downtown. A leaflet and map describing the walk can be obtained from the Auckland Visitors' Bureau. Since you are never far from a city road, it is possible to curtail the walk at any point and catch a bus. If you would prefer a group outing, contact Quality Experiences (tel: 656-223) for details of their organized hikes around Auckland.

There are many miles of walking track on the Coromandel Peninsula, which are somewhat more challenging than a walk through Auckland but are nevertheless perfectly suitable for the amateur. The peninsula's state forest covers a large area of hills which rise to 835m. Although the area was heavily logged, many trees and flowers have regenerated. Some of the abandoned lumber operations and mines are sufficiently defunct to be almost picturesque. The walks in this forest can be a little daunting for the unfit, however they are well marked between huts and should not present difficulties.

Northland offers plenty of short and long walks, to which any youth hostel or public relations office will direct you. Although this part of New Zealand is not particularly mountainous, there are plenty of one day climbs which afford sweeping views. For example Mount Manaia just across the bay from Whangarei is a rigorous two hour climb. As is so often the case in New Zealand, artificial aids — in this case wire handrails — have been installed to make the climb possible for anyone. What is *not* usual for New Zealand is that the view from the top takes in an oil refinery. To find out about other little-publicized walks in this vicinity contact the Whangarei Tramping Club which have organized expeditions on Sundays and Mondays (tel: Whangarei 485-119).

Mount Taranaki. As well as a number of short colour-coded walks from the North Egmont Visitor Centre, it is possible either to circumnavigate the volcano or to climb it. Both are only of medium difficulty and are attempted by large numbers, though the one-day ascent of the 2,517m peak should be attempted by novices only if they are prepared to join one of the guided climbs organized by local alpine clubs. But the four-day hut-to-hut circuit can be done by the inexperienced.

Great Barrier Island. Being 5-8 hours away by sea (25 minutes by air) is indeed a great barrier to tourist overdevelopment. So despite its natural advantages, the Barrier (as it is known) is virtually unspoiled. Rugged bush covers most of the island, which houses several rare birds and a variety of native flora. There are enough residents (i.e. 960) to provide reasonable amenities.

There is a real pioneering atmosphere on the island. For example cooking at the Youth Hostel which is very near the beach in Tryphena (tel: Tryphena 20), is done on a wood-burning stove and power is supplied by a generator. But people do not go to Great Barrier for the night life or high culture; they go for the tramping, surfing, scuba diving, crayfishing and crayfish eating. Many of its little harbours, especially Whangaparapara, are favourite destinations for South Pacific yachtsmen. Since most of the island's residents — many of them having come to the island to lead an alternative lifestyle — appear to be dedicated sportsmen, it is not difficult to hire equipment and difficult not to get local advice on where the best places are to try out a sport. The east coast beaches are excellent for surfing whereas the west coast is tamer.

Getting to the island is one of the delights of a visit, assuming you do not opt to fly. From the Kings Wharf in Auckland the *MV Tasman* conveys passengers and vehicles (though there are no sealed roads once you get to the Barrier) every Friday and returns on Sunday. For sailing times and prices contact Gulf Trans (tel: 734-036). A more luxurious way to do the trip is on the antique schooner *Te Aroha* which visits Great Barrier as part of its four-day delivery-cum-tourist-cruise (cost approximately $275). From Tryphena (the largest settlement on Great Barrier) the *Te Aroha* visits tiny settlements along the coast. Fullers is now running a Supercat to the island once or twice a week, which takes from four to five hours.

SKIING

The main ski fields of the North Island are as far away from the centres of population as it is possible to be: Whakapapa Village, the centre for skiing on Mount Ruapehu is 350km from Auckland and 335km from Wellington. A more serious drawback is the unreliability of the weather, for example the season of 1987 was a disaster, with incessant rains washing away any snow which did fall. A much less likely disaster is that the ski mountains, which are active volcanoes, might erupt, though claims are made for a super-efficient early warning system.

When the conditions are right, the skiing on Ruapehu is excellent. Turoa together with the larger Whakapapa are the two commercial skifields, with all the appropriate amenities for both beginners and advanced skiers. Beyond the groomed trails there are usually empty and often exciting slopes. The nearest Youth Hostel is at Ohakune, on the south side of Mount Ruapehu and 18km from Turoa Ski Field. Turoa has seven ski lifts including the only lift in New Zealand which serves a glacier. Transport is available from the hostel on Clyde St (tel: 0658 58-724). During the season (July to October) Ohakune becomes a lively little town with about 15 restaurants and plenty of accommodation.

The second skiing area on the North Island is the southern slopes of another volcano, Mount Taranaki. Access to the Maunganui Ski Field is from Stratford where there is limited budget accommodation, except for the council-owned King Edward Motor Camp on Page Street.

SOUTH ISLAND

Farewell Spit
Golden Bay
Collingwood
Takaka
Tasman Bay
Motueka
Marlborough Sounds
WELLINGTON
Cook Strait
Picton
NELSON
Blenheim
St Arnaud
Westport
Murchison
Mt Fyffe
Kaikoura
Greymouth
Arthur's Pass
TASMAN SEA
Hokitika
Ross
Okarito
CHRISTCHURCH
Franz Josef
Methven
Lyttelton
Banks Peninsula
Fox
Akaroa
Mount Cook
Tekapo
Haast Pass
Lake Wanaka
Milford Sound
Wanaka
Cromwell
Queenstown
Clyde
Lake Wakatipu
Alexandra
Doubtful Sound
Otago Peninsula
Te Anau
Roxburgh
DUNEDIN
Lake Manapouri
Nightcaps
Invercargill
Riverton
Bluff
Foveaux Strait
Oban
Half Moon Bay
Mason Bay
STEWART ISLAND

1 Abel Tasman National Park
2 Nelson Lakes National Park
3 Arthur's Pass National Park
4 Mount Cook National Park
5 Westland National Park
6 Mt Aspiring National Park
7 Fiordland National Park

100 km

The South Island

Population of South Island: 862,000   Population of Christchurch: 322,700

Some say that the further south you travel from Auckland, the further you travel into the past, ending at a fisherman's house on Stewart Island with no electricity, motor car or telephone. South Islanders are frequently characterized as being sleepy and reluctant to accept change. While slightly resenting this reputation, they are at the same time proud of their unhurried, uncompetitive way of life and have no wish to emulate what they perceive to be the fast living of the North Island. They realize that the west coast of their island is geographically and scenically unique and they would not trade it for all the artificial petrol factories and "flash buildings" of the North Island, often referred to as the "Mainland". There is always strong opposition to proposals for hydroelectric developments since the South Island's environment suffers while the North Island's economy benefits. But there are also strong pressures to welcome investment which will create local employment and provide an economic boost.

Christchurch continues to promote itself as "the most English city outside England". But the colonial influences soon fade once you leave the big city, with the notable exception of the dignified city of Dunedin which betrays its strongly Scottish heritage. Much of the South Island is farming country, some of it rich and productive, much of it suitable only for running sheep. The society is fundamentally rural with all the advantages and disadvantages that entails. But of more immediate interest to the visitor is the wilderness, especially the Alps which extend for most of the island's length. Of the ten national parks, three have recently been added to the World Heritage List, in recognition of their unique international importance.

CLIMATE

Christchurch residents are contemptuous of the ignorance of North Islanders who assume that the South Island has a climate not unlike that of Antarctica. In fact, the east coast of the South Island is often hot and dry in the summer and droughts are not uncommon on the coastal plains and hill ranges north of Christchurch.

Between two and three inches of rain falls on Christchurch each month of the year, so there is no season when you can be sure of escaping one of the torrential downpours which periodically overtax the drainage system and render umbrellas useless. Still, the total precipitation is a fraction of what it is on the west coast since the Southern Alps force the clouds to drop most of their water in the west. The temperatures in Christchurch are moderate with very pleasant highs of around 25°C in the summer and crisp temperatures in the winter which usually stay above freezing but occasionally slip below and snow occasionally falls. If your luck fails you with Christchurch weather, the Golden Tan Solarium is located at 166 Gloucester Street.

Like the cities of the North Island, Christchurch is subject to strong winds at any season which the locals recognize for their various properties. For example the north-westerlies bring dry heat which can be extreme in summer, while the southerlies bring rain and cold. On the other hand, it can become so still, especially in winter, that the smoke from household fireplaces hangs in the air creating unacceptable levels of smog.

The northern part of the island has the best weather, with Blenheim and Nelson vying for the title of "Sunniest City in the South". Both have an average of about six and a half hours of sunshine a day year round. The west coast is mild but exceedingly wet; the quantity of rain which falls in some coastal and mountain areas, not to mention Stewart Island in the extreme south, is staggering. So don't plan to travel around the South Island without some superior rain gear. All the rain does of course account for the glorious lushness of the vegetation.

CHRISTCHURCH

Christchurch is the administrative and cultural capital with a population of about a third of a million. It is a civilized city, if a little dull, with a spacious centre, neo-Gothic stone buildings and an air of calm confidence which some would call smugness. They have a tradition of preserving their historic buildings and green spaces, though recently have embarked on large scale plans for redevelopment.

After a visit to Christchurch in the early 1970s, J. B. Priestley wrote that Christchurch looks "as if it might have been lent to New Zealand by the Anglican church — at its best". Most of the main streets are named after

Anglican diocese, both British (Durham, Hereford, Worcester, etc.) and colonial (Barbadoes, Montreal, Colombo). Punting has recently been introduced on the River Avon, uniformed school boys can be seen cycling home and the newest scheme to please tourists is to introduce a red double decker bus. Despite these eccentricities and anachronisms, however, Christchurch is unmistakably a New Zealand city where walking paths on the outskirts may be closed for several weeks in the spring for lambing and pubs are closed on Sundays, streets are called Papanui and shops which sell sheepskins seem to outnumber newsagents.

There has been a surprising amount of business development in the past couple of years, partly encouraged by the policies of the Labour government and partly to please the ever-increasing number of tourists, many of them on package tours which include a day or two in Christchurch. Many older buildings have been demolished by companies with names like Payeo Development and the Advantage Corporation, and five luxury hotels are under construction. The most recent plan is to build a 167m tower in Victoria Square, primarily as a tourist investment. Yet there are many excellent viewing places in the Port Hills nearby, and the proposed development has met with plenty of opposition from locals who don't want their city to lose its identity in a rush to imitate cities like Singapore, which are notorious for having modernized insensitively.

THE LOCALS

The people of Christchurch demonstrate few big city characteristics (and even fewer English city characteristics). They seem almost as friendly and generous

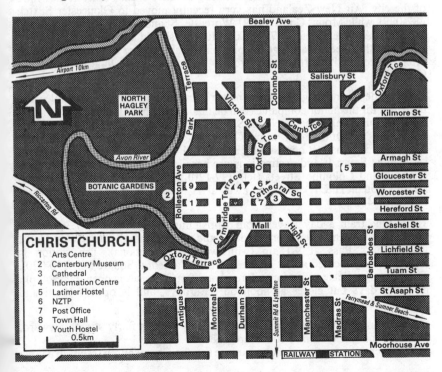

CHRISTCHURCH

1 Arts Centre
2 Canterbury Museum
3 Cathedral
4 Information Centre
5 Latimer Hostel
6 NZTP
7 Post Office
8 Town Hall
9 Youth Hostel
      0.5km

with their time as other South Islanders. They are also fairly conservative. A host of rules — for example jeans and running shoes are not permitted in a number of hotels and clubs — tends to inhibit and stultify social life to some degree. The people of Christchurch may strike you as more prim than spontaneous and fun-loving. But once you make their acquaintance, they are likely to devote themselves unstintingly to showing off their city.

ARRIVAL AND DEPARTURE

Air. Christchurch International Airport is 11km north-west of the city centre and easily accessible by public bus. The service leaves from the airport terminals about every half hour. Some buses will be marked with their final destination, e.g. Lyttelton, but they will all take you to the city centre. In the opposite direction catch bus 24L on Colombo Street just outside the Avon Theatre starting at 6.05am and finishing at 9.45pm. The journey takes about half an hour and costs $3 at peak times and $1.50 off-peak (i.e. Monday to Friday 9am-4pm). Services are seriously reduced on weekends so check the timetable. Taxis impose a surcharge after 10pm.

As the number of international flights coming into Christchurch has increased, the airport's facilities have been stretched beyond endurance. A new terminal was built (in 1987) for the new airline Ansett NZ, and this should relieve some of the congestion and delays.

The airline offices are within easy walking distance of each other in the centre of the city. Air New Zealand has very recently moved to Gloucester St (tel: 482-099), while Mount Cook is at 91 Worcester St and Ansett NZ is at 530-544 Memorial Avenue (freefone: 791-300). Students should check with STA at 223 High St if they need to arrange ongoing air travel. Another travel agency which offers discounted international fares is Travelseekers at 94a Worcester St (69-999).

Coach. There is no single coach depot in Christchurch, though timetables and bookings for the major companies can be made at the NZTP office in Cathedral Square. Surprisingly many NZRRS buses do not stop at the railway station, but rather on Durham St near Kilmore St (tel: 799-020). Meanwhile the Newmans depot is just opposite the station (tel: 795-641). H & H buses which serve most South Island destinations are based at 40 Lichfield Street between Durham and Colombo Streets (tel: 799-120), and Mount Cook Line (which recently bought H & H) is furthest away at 41 Riccarton Road just past Hagley Park (tel: 482-099).

Train. One train a day leaves from Christchurch for Picton at 7.30am, for Dunedin at 8.40am (but not on Sundays) and for Greymouth on the West Coast via Arthur's Pass at 9.15am (with weekend variations). The station is inconveniently located about a mile south of Cathedral Square (tel: 790-020). The passenger ticket office for rail, road and ferry services is open 7am to 7pm on week days but closes at noon on Saturdays, and is open 7-10am and 3.30-7pm on Sundays.

Driving. Entering and leaving Christchurch by road is fairly straightforward, although many city centre roads are one way.

The intense competition among car hire firms in Christchurch results in a large choice of reasonably priced hire deals. Here is a selection of the smaller firms:

Avon Rent-a-Car, 407 Ferry Road (891-350).
Johnston's Blue Motors Ltd, 132 Kilmore St (50-707). Also hires motor homes.
Percy Rent-a-Car, 154 Durham St (793-466).
Renny Rent-a-Car, 113 Tuam St (66-790).
Rhodes Rent-a-Car, 338 Riccarton Road (488-219). Offers a 10% discount to students and YHA members.
Roydvale Renta! Cars, 518 Wairakei Road (597-410).
Southern Cross Rental, 105 Victoria St (794-547).
Thrifty Car Rental, 136 St Asaph St (67-097).

Christchurch is reputed to be a good place to buy second hand cars, partly because the climate isn't conducive to rust, and also quite a few travellers decide to sell cars after touring the South Island; check on hostel notice boards.

Hitch-hiking. To hitch north towards Picton, catch bus 1 or 4 with the suffixes M, N, P, R or V. If you are heading towards Arthur's Pass, take bus 8G, and for Dunedin 8J. Ask the driver to recommend a good hitching place well away from the city centre.

CITY TRANSPORT

City Layout. Because the city of Christchurch is so flat, the Cathedral spire can be seen from most quarters and provides a useful landmark. The central streets are basically on a grid pattern with the exception of Oxford Terrace and Cambridge Terrace which flank the river. Colombo Street is the longest straight street in the country, if you don't count the short interruption made by Cathedral Square. In addition to the green strips alongside the two riverside terraces, there are many parks and gardens around the city. The Avon (which is named after a river in Scotland rather than the one running through Stratford) winds gently through the enormous Hagley Park and Botanic Gardens. If you are staying for only a day or two the tourist handout map should suffice. If you want more detail buy the official bus route map for $2 which includes a street index and extends to the suburbs.

In addition to the city centre, the other areas of Christchurch which reward exploration are Lyttelton Harbour, the beaches (such as Sumner and Brighton) and the Port Hills beyond the posh suburb of Cashmere. These are described in the section below on Day Trips.

The city's Transport Board runs daily sightseeing tours of these areas (details below). You may also wish to join one of the walking tours of central Christchurch run by Personal Guiding Services (68-243). These leave from Cathedral Square at 10am and 2pm daily and cost $7.

Do not be confused by numerous references on signs to Canterbury, the region of which Christchurch is the capital.

Bus. The Christchurch Transport Board (CTB) has an easy-to-find information kiosk in Cathedral Square, and all city buses pass through the square. Phone 794-600 for bus information. As mentioned above the CTB publish a map which is not really detailed enough to replace the individual advice available at the kiosk. Routes are designated by a number followed by a letter which indicates how far it is going, i.e. the closer to A, the nearer to the city centre the route ends. Fares are set in multiples of 50¢ (from 50¢ to $5) according to length of journey. All journeys are half price between 9am and 4pm Monday to Friday.

Frequent travellers can buy concession cards which allow a 25% discount. Officially you must pay an extra 25¢ for an item of luggage though this is seldom enforced.

Look for the excellent leaflet *Buses Can Take You Walking*. It briefly describes 32 walks which take from less than one hour to five hours to complete within easy reach of the city on public transport.

The sightseeing bus run by the CTB is called the Red Bus. A two hour tour of the city and suburbs costs about $10 while the three hour tour of Sumner beach, Lyttelton Harbour and back via the Summit Road costs $12. Ordinary buses also serve these destinations: take bus number 3 (J or K) to Sumner (a pleasant beach favoured by families) and bus number 28 (G, H, J or K) to Lyttelton.

Car. Parking problems are rare in Christchurch. There are several parking buildings in the centre of town, for example on the corner of Manchester and Gloucester Streets, on Lichfield St and on Oxford Terrace across from the Information Centre. There is metered street parking throughout the downtown area. The meters allow from half an hour to four hours, though you will require 10¢ or 20¢ coins no matter what the maximum permitted time is. Ten cents buys anything from 10 to 40 minutes, depending on how prime the location is. Meter regulations are in force from 9am to 5pm Monday to Thursday, 9am-8pm on Fridays and 9am-1pm on Saturdays.

Taxis. To phone for a taxi, call Gold Band on 795-795 or Blue Star on 799-799.

Cycling. Christchurch encourages cycling both with its untaxing terrain and its special traffic provisions for cyclists, including a pleasant cycle track through Hagley Park. Bicycles cannot be ridden nor parked in the pedestrian Mall, nor even wheeled through the Botanic Gardens.

Bicycles may be hired from Rent-a-Bike (139 Gloucester St), Discount Cycles (81a Riccarton Rd) or at Garden City Cycles based in a shed in the Arts Centre. Rent-a-Bike offers the best prices, e.g. $1 an hour for a basic bicycle to $10 a day for a 10-speed (compared to Discount's $16 a day hire charge). Garden City specialize in two-hour tours of the city which cost $12. You can also rent a scooter from 139 Gloucester St: the cost is $20 for a 24 hour period or $100 a week plus insurance of $5 a day.

Water Transport. Whereas in Oxford and Cambridge you can hire your own punt to pole yourself along the Rivers Cherwell or Cam, in Christchurch you must allow someone else to do the punting. The Christchurch Punting Co (PO Box 4188; tel: 794-834) began operating in 1987 and if you want to travel in style and luxury along the Avon, you can pay $5 for a 20-minute ride or $10 for 45 minutes. Punts leave from a landing on Cambridge Terrace near Manchester St. Progress south of Worcester St is impeded by the extreme shallowness of the river, though the punts are licensed to go anywhere between Montreal and Barbadoes Streets.

Canoes and paddle boats may be hired during the day from Antigua Boatsheds, 2 Cambridge Terrace (65-885); these do not come with a boatman.

Away from the city centre, there are ferries which leave from Lyttelton Wharf to Quail Island (a 30-minute trip) or across the harbour to Diamond Harbour (15 minutes). The one-way adult fare for the latter trip is $2.50. There are about eight sailings a day during the week, and four at weekends. Phone Lyttelton (28) 8368 for ferry times.

Jason's *Budget Accommodation Guide* lists about 40 guest houses, motels, lodges and hostels in Christchurch, ranging in price from $7 at a campsite to $30 at a relatively luxurious guest house. The average price is $25 for a single and $50 double, which often includes a cooked breakfast. Although many of the downtown hotels fall into the category of posh, others welcome travellers on a low budget by offering dormitory accommodation starting at $10 (the Hereford, 36 Hereford St; tel: 799-536) and $15 (at the Ambassadors, 19 Manchester St; tel: 67-808). The centrally-located bright yellow wood-framed Hereford Private Hotel is often full, so advance booking is advisable. Single rooms cost $16 and doubles $24. If you need a hotel near the railway station try Ogilvie's at 11 Manchester St (62-839) or the Ambassadors mentioned above.

Hostels. There are two IYHF hostels: one is in the city centre, the other about two miles north-east of Cathedral Square. The Rolleston House Youth Hostel opposite the Museum is housed in an old building, formerly a university residence, and charges $10 (tel: 66-564). The Youth Hostel headquarters are across the road in the Arts Centre and it is worth browsing in their book and equipment shop which opens 8.30am-4.30pm. The suburban hostel is called Cora Wilding after the founder of the New Zealand Youth Hostel movement, and is in a lovely setting. It often has beds when the downtown hostel is full. To get there take bus 10 D or H from the Square and after a ten-minute ride get off at Tweed Street. It is in a very pleasant neighbourhood for cyclists, and can also be reached on foot by walking alongside the River Avon past Swans Bridge and left into Evelyn Couzins St. The castle-like hostel is at number 9.

The YMCA at 12 Hereford St (60-689) charges $16.50 single ($20 with breakfast). A private hostel called the Latimer Hostel, housed in antique premises formerly occupied by the YWCA, is one of the most popular places to stay for low budget travellers. It is at the corner of Madras and Gloucester Streets, which is not too far from the city centre. Rates are $11 in a dormitory, $14.50 per person in a double and $20 single. Out of season, try asking to share a room since you may get a double to yourself at the lower rate. There is a courtesy coach, so if you want a lift from a train or bus depot, give the obliging management a ring (798-429). The hostel foyer has a free local telephone and a useful notice board.

Another very reasonable lodging is the non-smoking Avon View at 208 Kilmore St (69-720). Unfortunately they don't accept advance bookings.

Camping. Several motor camps are located in the vicinity of the Addington Racecourse about 3km from the centre; try Addington Motor Camp (Whiteleigh Avenue; tel: 389-770), Amber Park (308 Blenheim Road; tel: 483-327) or Riccarton Park Motor Camp (19 Main South Road; tel: 485-690). Another good one is Meadow Park Motor Camp at 39 Meadow St off Papanui Road (tel: 529-176). If you don't mind being further from central Christchurch try Pineacres Motor Park in Kaiapoi (0327 7421) or South Brighton Camping Ground (889-844) not far from the beach.

Eating and Drinking

There are nearly 100 Bring-Your-Own grog restaurants in Christchurch, compared to less than five in the late 1970s. There is now a broad range of ethnic cuisines from pizzas to Greek souvlaki to Cajun gumbo. Recommendations for cheap eateries often find their way onto hostel notice boards, so keep your eyes open. The giveaway monthly *Christchurch Tourist Times* includes several pages of restaurant reviews and recommendations (unfortunately not always impartial since the paper is funded by advertising). Also consult the free *South Island Restaurant Review* for ideas.

Try the Mykonos Taverna (112a Lichfield St; tel: 797-452) which serves Greek food from Tuesday to Sunday, along with Greek music Wednesday, Friday and Saturday; they offer a set menu costing $23.50. Spagalinis is a basic pizzeria on the corner of Colombo and Kilburn where a good one-person pizza can be bought for $7. A more expensive Italian restaurant which specializes in fresh pasta dishes is Il Felice at 150 Armagh St. Good cheap Chinese food is available at the Dragon Café at 165 High St (tel: 790-098) where you can fill up for $8. The Main Street Café at the corner of Colombo and Salisbury Streets serves good quality vegetarian food seven days a week in pleasant wood-panelled surroundings (tel: 50-421); main courses cost about $15. All of these restaurants are BYO. A take-away pizza service called Stallones operates only in the Riccarton Road area (tel: 599-647).

Dux de Lux is a pleasant licensed vegetarian restaurant, if a trifle earnest. It is situated in the Arts Centre with an outdoor dining area. Queues at the cafeteria-style counter can be long at lunchtimes and bookings for the dining room are often necessary in the evening, especially if you intend to go on a night when musical entertainment is being provided. There is also an outdoor café, a tavern, and a West Indian restaurant called Jambalaya (tel: 50-566) in the Arts Centre, all of which are on the pricey side.

While wandering around central Christchurch, you will have no trouble finding tasty snack food during the day. On a hot day, you might like to buy something from a Middle Eastern take-away to eat in the Square; falafels — spicy deep-fried chickpea rissoles served with salad and pitta bread — cost about $3. Then you could amble through the Chancery Arcade to buy a frozen yoghurt. The Saturday and Sunday market in the Arts Centre includes ethnic food stalls which will sell you a cheap and interesting plate of Brazilian bean stew or Ukrainian dumplings. The Boulevard Café at 124 Oxford Terrace has good home-cooked food, especially appetizing cakes and sweets and is open until 1.30am Wednesday to Sunday in a city where most restaurants close at an absurdly early hour. Another exception is the unpretentious Café Leo's at 750 Colombo St, a good place to go for a late-night coffee.

If you want an unpretentious pub meal, seek out the Star & Garter at the corner of Oxford Terrace and Barbadoes St. Here you can get a steak and vegetable dinner for $10. The Oxford Victualling Co by the river is open seven days a week for traditional roast meals at low prices. The upstairs Skiff Bar serves counter lunches (e.g. sandwiches) and is patronized mainly by shoppers.

There is no shortage of upmarket restaurants, best known of which is Fail's Café at the west end of the Cashel St Mall by the Bridge of Remembrance. It claims to be the oldest seafood restaurant in New Zealand, and offers main courses for about $18. Get hold of the free advertisers' broadsheet called *The Garden City Gourmet* which prints the menus of about 20 restaurants.

DRINKING

Licensed premises open at 11am from Monday to Saturday, closing at 10pm except on Friday and Saturday (11pm). One of the bars in the Coachman Inn at 144 Gloucester Street stays open till 1am Thursday to Saturday. The Metro Cinema in Worcester Street has opened a bar on its mezzanine, so there are some signs that more liberal drinking habits are creeping in.

The cheapest off-licence is the Imperial bottle store on the corner of Barbadoes and St Asaph Streets, followed by Wilson & Neil on Hereford St at Fitzgerald Avenue. If you are not committed to getting a bargain, the city centre grog shops are adequate, for example the "cut price liquor store" below Warners Hotel on the eastern side of Cathedral Square. All of these are good places to stock up on supplies for a BYO restaurant.

A few pubs to try are Nancy's (Riccarton Road and Deans Avenue), the Fitzgerald Arms (Fitzgerald Avenue and Hereford St) or Warners in the Square. You can go to Dux de Lux for drinks only, though they are expensive. Two pubs which are on the rough side and therefore untouristy are the Royal George (Fitzgerald Avenue near St Asaph St) and the New Zealander (St Asaph at Madras).

Although the bulk of New Zealand wine is made around Auckland, there are a few wineries around Christchurch. The oldest commercial vineyard in the area is St Helena Estate, a 20 minute drive north of the city. It is possible to taste and buy between 10am and 5pm Monday to Saturday (tel: 238-202 for directions).

The evening *Star* is the better of the two newspapers for entertainment information, especially the Friday edition. It gives a complete listing of plays, films and music both popular and serious.

The Arts Centre, housed in the gracious buildings of the original university, is the focus of the city's cultural life. The complex encompasses the two Court Theatres plus three others devoted to art films, dance and experimental theatre. Concerts and recitals are sometimes held in the Great Hall. There are other theatrical options in the city: try the Theatre Royal at 145 Gloucester St (tel: 795-147), the Elmwood Playhouse in Fendalton (tel: 559-875) or the Repertory Theatre at 146 Kilmore St (tel: 798-866). Tickets usually cost $16, though student stand-bys are sometimes available for $10. If you have a student card, it is always worth enquiring about discounts before buying a ticket. For example the following cinemas give students a 75¢ reduction on all tickets: the Avenue, Roxy, Northside, Academy, Midcity, Skyway and Hollywood/Stagedoor.

The main music venue both for the symphony orchestra and big name popular artists is the Town Hall on Kilmore St. The box office at the Town Hall (68-899) sells tickets to other concerts and productions as well. If in doubt ask at the Visitor Information Centre. Naturally there is nothing much going on between November and March at the University, now on a pleasant green campus in the suburb of Ilam. In term time the Canterbury Film Society (481-002) organizes weekly film showings at the campus, and in some cinemas on Sunday afternoons.

In the summer, Cathedral Square provides plenty of free entertainment. Jugglers, clowns and musicians find the square ideal for busking and many performers participate in the Summer Times Festival (early January to late February) when performances take place over the lunch hour. Festival events are also held in the Arts Centre Quadrangle and in North Hagley Park.

One of Christchurch's unique forms of entertainment has recently returned. The Wizard of Christchurch amuses a tolerant audience every day at 1pm outside the Cathedral with orations on topics as diverse as media bias and the inferiority of women. Despite his eccentricities he commands much local respect and finds his way into all the official promotional literature. Cathedral Square is the New Zealand equivalent of "Speaker's Corner" and the Wizard has to compete with Bible-bashers and many others.

Museums and Galleries. The Canterbury Museum is especially recommended for its reconstruction of a colonial street, including a pub, gun-maker and provision store. Those interested in the exploration of Antarctica will be interested to see the sledges, fur apparel and meagre entertainments which accompanied Scott, Shackleton, etc. on their expeditions. The natural history sections are also most interesting, especially if you have not seen a giant moa skeleton elsewhere in your travels. The Museum is located on the edge of the Botanic Gardens and is open every day of the year from 10am to 4.30pm. Admission is free.

The principal art museum is the Robert McDougall Art Gallery next door to the Museum, with the same opening hours except Sunday when it is open 2-4.30pm only. The Gallery has more Maori artefacts than the Museum whose collection is not on display for conservation reasons. You are more likely to find Maori art at a commercial gallery such as the CSA (Canterbury Society of Arts) at 66 Gloucester Street. Even better is the Nga-Hau-E-Wha National Marae (250 Pages Road; take bus 5N) where you can admire Maori carvings on the building itself as well as pieces carved by a resident craftsman.

The Cathedral was built in 1864 and is of limited architectural interest, though you can have a free guided tour if you like (daily except Sunday at 11am). On a clear day, it might be worth paying $1 to climb the 133 steps of the tower to try to glimpse the distant Alps.

The transport and technology museum at Ferrymead will interest even those who are not train-spotters. In addition to the vintage cars, steam locomotives and restored tram cars, there are displays on everything from old washing machines to mechanical musical instruments, with a reconstructed settler's sod (turf) cottage from 1863 thrown in for good measure. It is open 10am-4.30pm daily and admission is $6. Catch the Sumner bus numbered 3G-3K. In summer some of these call at the park entrance; otherwise there is a bit of a hike from the bus stop. A rail link to Ferrymead, using the Lyttelton rail line, has been proposed by a tourist promotion group but it is too early to know whether this will materialize.

Music. Check the newspapers for events. Pubs which often have music include Warners Tavern on Cathedral Square for Irish music, the Star & Garter on Oxford Terrace for various genres (but nothing very avant-garde), and Bush Inn Courts at 364 Riccarton Road. Also try Le Café Concert for live music (especially jazz) in the Arts Centre Thursday to Saturday. Cover charges are sometimes levied. Unfortunately music venues tend to be either rough or dressy with few adopting the casual approach familiar in Europe.

The nightlife lacks the sparkle of even Auckland and Wellington and you may find things pretty quiet after 10pm when the only sound to cut through the still of the evening is the occasional roar of a Honda 90 or souped-up Morris Minor as teenagers, (or "hoons" as they are known, just as in Australia), most of them sporting Rod Stewart hairstyles, vainly try to generate a little excitement. There are a few nightclubs, but they charge $10-$15 admission, unless you arrive early (between 7 and 8pm). Of course drinks are expensive, and dress standards are enforced. If interested try the Firehouse on Colombo St, the Palladium on Gloucester St opposite the Library or the Xanadu on Kilmore St near the Town Hall.

Parks and Zoos. One of Christchurch's nicknames is "Garden City of the Plains" so you will not be surprised to find plenty of green space in the city. The long-established Botanic Gardens behind the Museum provide a pleasant venue for strolling or reading on a sunny bench. British visitors will be less interested in the rose garden than in the display of New Zealand native plants. Greenhouses specialize variously in desert plants, ferns, orchids and tropical plants.

The old zoo and aquarium at 155 Beach Road (bus 19M; admission $2.50) has been somewhat eclipsed by the Orana Wildlife Park beyond the airport. Since the park operates like a safari park, you must have your own transport or join a Red Bus tour mentioned above. The South Island's first Kiwi House is open 10am-5pm and is included in the park entrance fee of $6 per adult.

A small area of native bush has been preserved close to the city. Dean's Bush is easily accessible by bicycle, bus 8, 21 or 24, or on foot through Hagley Park and along Kilmarnock St. It contains many fine rimu, white pine and tea trees, as well as one of Canterbury's oldest buildings (1843), originally a homestead now a museum.

SPORT

The *Visitor's Guide* distributed free of charge by the Information Centre gives a thorough rundown of two months' sporting events from race meetings at Riccarton or Addington Racecourses to cricket matches at Lancaster Park. During championship race meetings, special city buses take punters from the city to the racecourse. There is a TAB office on Gloucester Street just east of Cathedral Square.

If you would like to take some exercise yourself, Hagley Park is perfect for joggers, the River Avon good for rowing, the Estuary and Ellesmere Lake (a shallow body of water south of the city) suitable for windsurfing not to mention birdwatching, and to the east there are many beaches for swimming and surfing (see *Further Afield* for more details). The outdoor Centennial Pool (Oxford Terrace near Manchester St) is open weekdays 8am-2pm and 5-6pm, while the main indoor pool is at Queen Elizabeth II Park in Burwood.

SHOPPING

The central pedestrian mall has all the stores you would expect plus one or two unusual ones. More interesting shops are likely to appear in the redevelopment of Colombo Street north of Kilmore Street, where a ritzy shopping and restaurant area is planned. Ballantynes Department Store, accessible from the City Mall, is fairly expensive; DIC across the road and the Farmers Trading Company on Gloucester Street are both cheaper. Routine shopping is even cheaper outside the city centre, for example at the Riccarton Mall. The Central Mission Goodwill Store (Armagh and Manchester Streets) and the Save the Children Fund charity shop (Bells Arcade between Cashel and Lichfield Streets) sell secondhand clothes and other items. There are several Army Surplus stores; the best one is at 77 Manchester St.

There is a shortage of dairies and grocery shops in the central business district of Christchurch, so if you want to buy some provisions ask a local for directions.

The outdoor market held in the quad of the Arts Centre on summer weekends (10am-4pm) has many interesting stalls selling arts and crafts, including jewellery, pottery and many other portable and affordable items. In fact the Arts Centre provides permanent studio space for potters, sculptors, candle and toy makers, leather workers, etc. Craft shops remain open throughout the week. The Riki Rangi Maori Carving Centre in the Arts Centre complex sells distinctive and expensive wood and bone artefacts. A shop called Hands at 5 Normans Road (off the Papanui Road) carries all the materials and equipment for handicrafts.

Browsers in downtown Christchurch will be struck by the number of souvenir and sheepskin shops, whose names all seem to incorporate the word "Nature". The city centre is fairly deserted on Saturdays though a few shops (mainly catering for tourists) are open. Saturday shoppers should head for the beach suburb of Brighton where most shops stay open until 9pm on Saturdays.

Scorpio Books at 138 Oxford Terrace is the most interesting bookshop in town and a good source of information on "alternative" events. There is a good children's bookshop at 454 Colombo Street. New and secondhand sports goods can be found at Recycled Recreation, 81 Manchester St near St Asaph St.

Duty-free shopping is available at the corner of Colombo and Gloucester Streets to those flying out of New Zealand from Christchurch.

THE MEDIA

Newspapers. The *Press* is a respectable morning paper whose masthead bears a strong resemblance to that of the London *Times*. The evening rival is the *Star* available from 3pm onwards. Both cost 40¢. The *Press* is usually bulkier than the *Star* especially on Saturdays, and to a lesser extent Wednesdays, when it carries many pages of classified adverts for jobs, cars, etc.

Radio. The BC-NZ National Programme is carried by 3YA on 675AM while the Concert Programme (3YC) is on 963AM and 89.7FM. The local independent station is 3ZB (1098AM) and 3ZM (91.3FM) is the "stereo hit radio" station of Christchurch, often relaying the ZM network from Wellington. The university station broadcasts on 91.8FM, while the commercial Radio Avon is on 93FM.

Visitors to Christchurch are as safe as they could be anywhere in the world, and the worst that is likely to happen is that your pint of milk will be stolen from the hostel fridge. The few incidents affecting tourists which have been reported lately have been perpetrated by other travellers staying in cheap accommodation. It is probably unwise to wander around Hagley Park or the city centre alone at night, but nowhere else could be described as a no-go area. Avoid rough pubs like the King George (at the corner of Madras and St Asaph Streets) and Foresters Tavern (on Oxford Terrace near Manchester St) where gang fights are not unusual.

The police station is at the corner of Cambridge Terrace and Hereford St (793-999) and the free Legal Advice Centre is at 203 Gloucester St (66-490). The Community Law Centre at 84 Worcester St (tel: 66-870) is open evenings Monday to Friday.

The STD code for Christchurch is 03.
For fire, police or ambulance dial 111.

Visitors' Information Centre (Canterbury Promotion Council Inc): 75 Worcester St, at the corner of Oxford Terrace (799-629). Open Monday-Friday 8.30am-5pm, and weekends and holidays 9am-4pm.

NZTP: Government Life Building, 65 Cathedral Square (794-900).

Outdoor Recreation Centre: 28 Worcester St, Arts Centre (799-395).

Automobile Association (Canterbury) Inc: 210 Hereford St (791-280).

Post Office: Cathedral Square (531-899).

Medical Services: High Street Medical Centre (60-237). Drop-in surgeries held daily 9-10.45am. Also Papanui Medical Centre, 438 Papanui Road (529-053), and 24-hour service at Bealey Avenue clinic.

Medical Emergencies: Christchurch Public Hospital, Riccarton Road at Oxford Terrace (792-900).

Rape Crisis Line: 796-202.

Emergency Chemist: Bealey Avenue.

Babysitting Service: Plaza Corner, Cathedral Square (791-660). Daytimes only.

British High Commission: Christchurch Trade Office, The Dome, Regent Theatre Building, Cathedral Square (63-143).

Public Library: Gloucester St near Avon River (796-914).

American Express: Guthreys Travel Centre, 126 Cashel St (793-560).

Thomas Cook: Cnr Armagh & Colombo Streets (796-600).

DAY TRIPS FROM CHRISTCHURCH

Once the modest pleasures of the city have been exhausted, there are places outside Christchurch which deserve a visit. The Railway Corporation publish a brochure called *Day Trips from Christchurch by Train* which includes some ambitious destinations such as Kaikoura ($3\frac{1}{2}$ hours due north) or Greymouth (5 hours away on the opposite side of the island). But since the principal reward of so many journeys in New Zealand is the scenery en route and since there are bargain day return fares on the trains ($25 and $45 respectively) you may want to contemplate doing these as day trips. The Outdoor Recreation Information Centre in the Arts Centre of Christchurch also has a selection of leaflets on less well known forest reserves and other scenic areas within a few hours of the city.

Lyttelton. The port of Lyttelton, 11km east of the city centre is perhaps a little like Fremantle must have been a decade or so ago, before the Yuppies transformed it. To get there take a Lyttelton bus (28) which follows the road tunnel to the harbour. The alternative route available to those in cars is 8km longer but preferable since it winds its scenic way through the delightful Port Hills which divide the city from the harbour. It is worth stopping to go for a short walk for better views.

Lyttelton is unpretentious to the point of slumminess, yet it is an area full of character. The setting is picturesque with Victorian streets rising steeply from the water and old houses most of which have not been over-renovated. The pubs are typical seamen's pubs since Lyttelton is a major international harbour, and cafés like Chans Café serve steak and chips for $7.

Beaches. There are many lovely beaches within easy reach of Christchurch such as the charmingly-named Taylor's Mistake which is always a few degrees warmer than the city. Scarborough Beach at Sumner and New Brighton Beach are favourites among surfers, whereas the beach on Corsair Bay on the Lyttelton side is better for bathers. Although only 10km from Christchurch, Sumner has some interesting wilderness, and an away-from-it-all atmosphere as well as a good beach. In the early days a Christchurch tram served Sumner and Scarborough, but nowadays you'll have to get there by car or bus.

The Banks Peninsula. Despite its proximity to Christchurch the Banks Peninsula has a feeling of remoteness. Some of the roads over the 850m hills seem like goat tracks to the uninitiated and are signposted as unsuitable for caravans. The main town is Akaroa, about 80km from Christchurch. It is a pleasant town stretched along the waterfront, with a lighthouse (which was in active service for the guidance of shipping as recently as 1976), a herb farm (open daily) where a craft market is held on the first Saturday of the month, a charming museum with relics of the local Maori people, whalers, etc., and an old established newspaper called *The Akaroa Mail*. It also boasts one of the best restaurants on the South Island (the Old Shipping Office) not to mention a superb fish and chip shop where you can buy marinated green-lipped mussels and paua patties.

Akaroa is very proud of its French heritage since it was here that a shipful of French settlers landed in 1840 just days after Britain had laid claim to the area. In fact the French influence survives only in a few street names and in the imported vegetation such as fennel which now grows wild in the nearby valleys. For those who have more than a day to spend, there is plenty of accommodation in Akaroa which is a popular resort, though none of it is especially cheap. Some farms offer accommodation and there is an idyllic Youth Hostel in Pigeon Bay on the north side of the Peninsula which is just one of many picturesque villages along the eastern bays. NZRRS serves the Peninsula twice daily. The journey lasts just under two hours and costs $11 single. Return day excursions on NZRRS cost $15.50.

NORTH OF CHRISTCHURCH

State Highway 1 between Picton and Christchurch is especially scenic north of Kaikoura where it traces the magnificent coast, but with a range of hills always in sight. Although it is a good road with few hazards and not much traffic, don't drive too quickly around the mountainous bends or through the tunnels, one of which has such a sharp curve in it that articulated lorries cannot get through without reversing in the middle.

The resort town of Kaikoura, about halfway along this road, is famed (justly) for its surf and for its enormous crayfish which can be bought from roadside stalls for about $15; supplies have usually run out by mid-afternoon. Restaurant menus also include them in season. If you are driving from the north, perhaps you could buy a bottle of one of the excellent wines made in Marlborough to accompany your crayfish.

The beach has rock pools to explore, paua shells to collect and seals to watch. Surf freaks from Christchurch flock to Kaikoura especially on summer weekends. There are several hotels but the New Commercial Hotel on Brighton St is the only one to have a garden, complete with do-it-yourself barbecues. A couple of miles inland the Mount Fyffe State Forest has several signposted bush walks, including a fairly strenuous one to the 1,600m summit of Mount Fyffe.

Arthur's Pass. Highway 73 through Arthur's Pass is the most scenic way to cross the island, especially in summer when the flowering rata trees cover the hillsides around Otira with scarlet. The road can be a challenge in good conditions (caravans are not allowed over Otira Gorge), but downright frightening in heavy rains which cause trees and boulders to tumble down the vertical mountains onto the road. Occasionally, the Pass has to be closed to traffic, especially in the winter when snow and ice add to the difficulties. The rail journey is spectacular and more relaxing, taking over three hours to complete the 140km journey (cost is $20 single). New Zealand Railways publish a detailed leaflet of the journey called *Coast to Coast* which describes the trip so vividly that you may feel the trip itself would be superfluous.

The township of Arthur's Pass has some accommodation (including a Youth Hostel), the Visitor's Information Centre for the surrounding National Park (tel: 500), and ski equipment hire shops for the winter season June to September. It is an excellent starting point for tramps, including a six-day trip to Lewis Pass. There is a good choice of huts, so simply obtain a map of the area and plan a walk.

Nelson and the Northwest. The northwest corner of the South Island encompasses lakes and mountains but is particularly appreciated for its hot weather and its coastline dotted with lovely beaches and small resort towns. Access to Nelson is by Highway 6 from Blenheim on the east coast or Westport on the West Coast. These routes are covered by Newmans Coachlines (220 Hardy St, Nelson; tel: 88-369) and the Blenheim-based company Delta Coachlines (53 Grove Road, Blenheim; tel: 81-408) which offers a 20% student standby rate. There is no rail link, but two direct flights on Mount Cook link Christchurch daily with Nelson Airport.

Nelson is a laid-back town. It is well known for its high concentration of artists and craftsmen, so there are many studios of weavers, potters, jewellers, glass-blowers, etc. in the region open to the public.

The large sweeps of Tasman Bay, on which Nelson is situated, and Golden Bay, 100km to the west, have many safe sheltered beaches and accompanying campsites. Since it is not difficult to find isolated beaches, especially at the western end of highway 60 which ends in the fishing village of Collingwood, you may not be tempted by the "most complete holiday park in Australasia", Tahuna Beach Park near Nelson, which boasts one thousand caravan sites, a camp supermarket, skating rink and "baby's powder room". In some ways this coast is New Zealand's nearest equivalent to the Gold Coast of Queensland, since it has some large beach developments, as well as a large population of retired people and sun-loving holidaymakers. There is even an accidental echo in the name Golden Bay, which was chosen during the gold rush to replace the much less inviting name of Murderer's Bay assigned by Abel Tasman who lost a couple of his crew members to hostile Maori here in 1642. But it is on a considerably more restful scale than the Gold Coast, with beautiful unspoiled scenery predominating over tacky commercialism.

Nelson is at the heart of a prosperous agricultural region where hops, tobacco, apples and other fruits are grown. Travellers running short of money may want to investigate the possibility of participating in a harvest, especially between February and May (see introductory section on *Work* for further details).

The Nelson Lakes National Park is one of the several national parks on the South Island, and is often overlooked in favour of the more spectacular fiords, glaciers and high peaks further south. The township of St Arnaud, a few kilometres east of Highway 6 and 100km south of Nelson, is where the park's Visitor Information Centre is located (tel: 806), plus a petrol station, a shop and a private hostel called the Yellow House. St Arnaud is at the head of Lake Rotioto, which is one of the two main lakes (or "twin jewels" if you prefer) together with Lake Rotoroa meaning "large waters" (not to be confused with Rotorua which means "second lake"). Camping, swimming, boating, tramping and skiing (August/September) are the primary attractions. The tourist literature describes it as "a family man's park since he can enjoy it without special skill or equipment" (which makes it sound as though mountaineers and skiers never have kids).

The other national park in the region is Abel Tasman with headquarters at Takaka (tel: 58-026) and a seasonal information centre at the tiny coastal settlement of Totaranui. The Abel Tasman trek begins (or ends) in Totaranui (details in *Great Outdoors*). There are virtually no roads into the park, in fact it is something of a challenge just to reach the periphery. When strolling along the sandy beaches look for colourful shells and living shellfish which might supplement your camp dinner, though the famous Nelson scallops will have to be enjoyed in a restaurant. There is even a carnivorous snail which achieves the length of a light bulb. Unfortunately the species is sufficiently threatened that eating them or collecting their shells is prohibited. The bird and insect life of the region generally repays patient observation, though be careful picking up driftwood on beaches since this is where the poisonous katipo spider lives. If you fail to see any fat bush worms, short-eared bats or oystercatchers, then you may have to derive your wildlife thrills from visiting one of the several "tame eel" colonies in the area, namely at Moutere

TAHUNA BEACH PARK BOASTS A
"BABY'S POWDER ROOM"

halfway between Nelson and Motueka, and Kotinga near Takaka. (So far the locals have avoided the cuddle-a-koala syndrome and still refrain from urging visitors to embrace-an-eel.)

The free pamphlet *Nelson Provincial Visitor's Guide* published by the Public Relations Office in Nelson (at the corner of Halifax and Trafalgar Streets; tel: 82-303) provides a worthwhile introduction to local attractions and includes useful lists of emergency numbers, car hire firms, handicraft centres and accommodation suggestions. There is a year-round Youth Hostel in Nelson as well as some which are open for one month (from just before Christmas) in Takaka, Motueka and Picton. There is a relatively new private hostel (for non-smokers only) in Nelson called Tasman Towers (10 Weka St; tel: 87-950) which is recommended, as well as a large choice of motorcamps, park huts and motels throughout the area.

Willing Workers on Organic Farms is especially strong in this area with headquarters in Nelson (c/o Tony West, 188 Collingwood St), so if you want to experience farm life while saving money, get the list of farms looking for volunteers.

MOUNT COOK AND THE GLACIERS

Although on a map the townships of Fox Glacier and Mount Cook are separated by a mere 35km, the fastest land connection takes nearly nine hours, about twice the time it takes to drive the 330km from Christchurch to Mount Cook. So it is perhaps a little misleading to group these two tourist magnets together since many visitors cannot manage to see both. However they are all manifestations of the remarkable geology of the Southern Alps which have been described as an economic nuisance but a geographical masterpiece. In this region, the Alps, with Mount Cook surpassing the rest at 3,764m (12,431ft) are so high and so numerous that there is no possibility of crossing efficiently from the two famous glaciers of Fox and Franz Josef near the coast to Mount Cook village without resorting to an advanced mountaineering course or else to the air.

Mount Cook. As the Grand Canyon is to the States and Ayers Rock to Australia, so Mount Cook is to New Zealand, and is possibly its most heavily visited scenic wonder. Yet even here commercialism has been kept at bay, and it is easy to leave behind the coachloads of honeymooning Japanese — apparently Mount Cook is one of the most popular destinations for newly-weds whose overweening ambition is to take one of the aggressively marketed "flightseeing" trips. This type of visitor normally stays at the grand (and expensive) Hermitage Hotel which opened in 1884 and dominates the place. Budget travellers are more likely to stay at the new Youth Hostel (tel: 05 621 820), in a tent at the White Horse Hill Camping site or at the Glentanner Motorcamp, 15km from Mount Cook village.

With a little exertion, you can hike away from the village of Mount Cook and within an hour or two you will have certainly gained some solitude and possibly some superb views. The good views are irritatingly unpredictable and the weather cooperates no more than half the days in the year. Often a large measure of patience is required before the clouds finally permit an unimpeded view of the peaks and so it is fortunate for many of the Japanese newly-weds that they have each other to distract them from their disappointment. Surprisingly, the chances of having fine weather are better in the winter. So if you are determined to admire Aorangi the cloud piercer (the Maori name for the mountain whose ownership they now dispute), be prepared to spend a few days in the vicinity. The Tourist Corporation attempts to console disappointed visitors by reminding them that without the high precipitation the glaciers such as the 29km Tasman Glacier behind Mount Cook would soon disappear.

The same degree of chance affects scenic flights, which are able to take off only 50% of the time. Mount Cook Line offers the largest range from their 15-minute flight over the Hooker Glacier for $62 to the hour-long "Grand Circle" which includes a ski-plane landing on a glacier snowfield for $201. Many of the flights operate from Fox and Franz Josef as well as from Mount Cook. Helicopter rides are also available: 1987 advertised prices in Franz Josef were $45 for 10 minutes, $85 for 35 minutes plus an extra $15 for an eight-minute landing to allow photography of the glacier surface.

The Glaciers. Franz Josef and Fox Glaciers are the most easily reached and arguably the most spectacular glaciers, especially since they come so remarkably close to sea level; however there are 58 others in Westland National Park alone. If you have been disappointed by the grimy appearance of glaciers in other parts of the world (such as the Alps and the Rockies) the Franz Josef and Fox are delightfully pristine, almost as though they had been manufactured in Hollywood. Their most remarkable feature is the speed at which they travel — recently as much as one metre per day, i.e. one kilometre every $2\frac{1}{2}$ years — caused by the steepness of their long descents (11km and 13km respectively) and the mighty quantity of snow which falls at the top.

The two glaciers are 25km apart and each has sprouted a township complete with post office, shops, accommodation, pubs and tourist facilities. Both also have national park visitor centres where informative displays are mounted, questions answered and brochures describing local walks and activities distributed. Although it is possible in both cases to view the glacier from the car parks, it is more rewarding to approach or even climb onto the glacier on foot. Glacier walks should not be undertaken independently. Local guides will take you on half-day walks on the glacier for about $20 which includes the hire of crampons if necessary. The pace set on these walks is usually more suitable for a fit hiker than a day-tripper.

An alternative independent walk is to Robert's Point, which is situated beside the Franz Josef Glacier affording good views of the blue and deeply crevassed surface of the glacier. The three-hour walk through dripping temperate rainforest is not overly strenuous, though the slippery stream crossings can become a little tricky and, as throughout New Zealand, people who suffer from vertigo might not enjoy the swing bridges and rockface ladders. If you are lucky you may hear a booming crash as chunks of ice break off from the glacier. But over the past centuries, the glaciers have been generally receding and the approach road to the car park at Fox follows the gouged out valley, now littered with enormous boulders and mounds of rubble indiscriminately dumped by the glacier, which has retreated $3\frac{1}{2}$km since Captain Cook visited in 1770. Interesting geological formations abound, such as sculpted rocks known as *roches moutonnés*; but those who think they have seen enough sheep for a lifetime need not worry: *moutonnés* here does not mean "sheep-shaped" but rather "wig-like".

The West Coast. The natural attractions of the West Coast are not confined to geological ones (though don't miss the amazing blowholes at Punakaiki). The gold rush of the 1860s and 1870s has left some traces of historical interest. For example the Ross Historic Goldfields Walk near the coast north of the Glaciers follows the network of water races and abandoned tailings for 3km and provides an interesting introduction to the brief mining boom. A few places like Westport, Hokitika and Greymouth survived the depletion of gold supplies, but most faded away. A few kilometres south of Greymouth is Shantytown where you can try your luck at gold panning. It is also worth visiting one of these genuine ghost towns, such as Okarito, which now has a handful of tumble-down houses set along a windswept shore, a shop which opens for a few hours on Saturday, a Youth Hostel without electricity and an atmosphere of desolation. (Apparently this combination appeals to the Booker Prize-winning novelist Keri Hulme, who has chosen to live here.) As the tiny museum on the wharf indicates, there were once dozens of hotels to supply the hard-drinking miners.

Okarito Lagoon is a reserve for the white heron or *kotuku*. Although you need a permit to enter the sanctuary, you can sometimes see the birds from the road. Further south along the coast there is a seal colony at Gillespie Beach. As you go along the tiny road from the highway to the beach, keep checking over your shoulder for a view of Mount Cook and Mount Tasman. If you have time, stop at Lake Matheson on your right which is renowned for its capacity to mirror the high peaks. Even if the mountains are not visible, the one hour walk around the lake's reedy banks is very peaceful and pleasant.

The West Coast has an interesting mixture of people: some have their roots there, others are newcomers including alternative types. Some find the social life somewhat cliquey though the pubs are often classics of their kind (try the pub in Barrytown north of Greymouth which has music at weekends). Many pay scant attention to closing time.

QUEENSTOWN AND FIORDLAND

If you have seen just one glossy New Zealand magazine, chances are that the photos of mountains, lakes and fiords were taken in the south-west corner of the South Island. Even visitors who have begun to feel that they have had a surfeit of magnificent scenery, still make the trip to Queenstown and beyond. Only callous cynics remain indifferent to the sublime landscapes of Fiordland since, according to the *Oxford English Dictionary*, sublime things in nature inspire awe, deep reverence or lofty emotion by reason of their beauty, vastness and grandeur.

Fiordland National Park runs into Mount Aspiring National Park to cover a vast area of the country, pockets of which have yet to be explored. Roads are few and the ones that exist are often of relatively recent construction. Although motoring or flying allows the visitor to appreciate the scenic attractions to a certain extent, this is an area which should be enjoyed on foot or on water. For more details of the famous walking tracks in the area, and of rafting expeditions based on Queenstown, see *Great Outdoors* below.

Queenstown. The small town of Queenstown (permanent population 3,300) is New Zealand's boldest attempt at an international resort, and while some Kiwis consider it *the* place to go, many others consider it *the* place to avoid. From having been a sleepy picturesque lakeside village not so many years ago, its appetite for development nowadays seems rapacious. While a new and bigger airport site is being considered and hopeful bids lodged to host the Winter Olympics in 1996, hotels are being built even faster than they are in Portugal's Algarve, and mini-golf courses and alpine slides are frantically being built to amuse the ever-increasing numbers of easily-bored tourists. There is even some ghastly plan afoot to build a self-enclosed holiday camp for millionaires (mainly Americans) in the mountains near Queenstown. The downtown streets are lined with signs which clamour for the tourist dollar. Queenstown traders are alone in the country for being allowed to open seven days a week, 24 hours a day; the usual shopping hours are 9am-5.30pm and 7.30-9pm except on weekends when the shops close for the afternoon. An American developer plans to build a cable car across a stretch of water to the holiday peninsula of Frankton, and eventually hopes to build a monorail all the way from Queenstown to Milford Sound, though this is meeting with much local opposition.

Not many visitors can withstand completely the pressure to participate in at least one of Queenstown's attractions. One of the most obvious is to take the cable car up the hill ($5) to see the view and to watch other tourists eating overpriced food in the Skyline Restaurant. It is perfectly possible to walk up the 450-metre hill starting on Kent St and proceeding amidst exotic trees, though it is a steep two-hour climb on a hot day. (Tickets for the cable car trip down the hill are rarely checked.)

The *TSS Earnslaw* is a 75 year old working steamer which chugs out onto Lake Wakatipu several times a day. Obviously the tour organizers are not convinced that the scenery alone will entertain since there is a stop-over at the Mount Nicholas Sheep Station for the usual demonstration of sheep dogs and shearers at work, and then on the return journey there is a sing-along which seems to appeal greatly to the over-60s. This 2¾-hour afternoon excursion takes place daily and costs $18; there are other trips available in the mornings and evenings. The Maori legend attached to Lake Wakatipu is interesting: the wicked giant who abducted a beautiful princess was set alight by the the hero-rescuer. As his body melted a giant depression formed in the earth and soon filled with water (Wakatipu means "the hollow of the giant"). Only his thumping heart survives, said to account for the phenomenon of the level of the huge lake rising and falling 8cm every quarter of an hour.

On the basis that "a million people can't be wrong" you may want to visit another of Queenstown's top attractions: the "only live stage show in the world to portray the beef and dairy industry" held daily at the Cattledrome about six kilometres north of town, at 9.30am and 2.30pm. This is "your chance to see, smell and touch a live beast".

There are many other excursions to be made, one of the most interesting to Skipper's Canyon, where the road is so tortuous that rental car insurance becomes void and the elements so brutal that telephone wires are made of much thicker wire. This was a thriving community during the gold rush. Twenty minutes from Queenstown is the historic and popular village of

THE ONLY LIVE STAGE SHOW IN THE WORLD TO PORTRAY THE BEEF AND DAIRY INDUSTRY.

Arrowtown, a gold-mining town now restored to evoke the atmosphere of pioneering times in the South Island. But despite the inescapable commercialism and inflated prices, Queenstown is a pleasant town to spend a few days preparing for (or recovering from) a foray into the wilderness. The development has not been indiscriminate, for example the strip of park between the lake and the Esplanade has been preserved intact with trees carefully pruned so as not to impede the lovely view. One of the real advantages is the wide choice of eating and drinking establishments, which keep reasonably late hours. Highlights include the deservedly popular pizzeria "The Cow" in Cow Lane (about $12 a head), a congenial Italian restaurant called Avanti in the Mall (pasta for $8), a Mexican restaurant called Saguaro's and a coffee shop with tasty cheap food called Gourmet Express; all are BYO. Even the Youth Hostel kitchen functions partially as a restaurant and produces delicious curries and vegetarian dishes for $6. There are a number of pubs, the best known of which is Eichardt's Hotel around the corner from the steamer wharf, where it is not difficult to meet people. Many of these, on both sides of the bar, will be travellers who have decided to spend more than a few days in Queenstown. Watch for happy hours between 5 and 7pm especially in the winter ski season. Even though long-stay residents use the pejorative-sounding word "loopy" to refer to tourists, their hostility does not run deep and many will be only too glad to point you towards their favourite trip or drinking hole.

As always, the Youth Hostel is a good place to decide which tours or tramps to sign up for. The obliging management will store baggage and offer advice, though much can be learned simply by studying their notice board and chatting to people in your dormitory. It is essential to book a bed in the summer. Among the large choice of other budget accommodation, the Pinewood at 48 Hamilton Road and Wakatipu Lodge in Frankton (free shuttle bus into town) are most often recommended. The Queenstown Accommodation Agency at 39 Shotover St (tel: 0294 27-518) charges no commission for putting you in touch with one of the lodgings registered with them. The Queenstown Information Centre (tel: 27-933) is located at the corner of Stanley and Ballarat Streets, while the NZTP office is at 49 Shotover St (tel: 28-238).

Milford and the Fiords. The south-west coast of the island is among the most dramatic in the world. Even the names evince an atmosphere of daring exploration and brushes with death such as Resolution Island, Preservation Inlet or Doubtful Sound, or on a more mundane level, of foul weather, in names like Dark Cloud Range and Wet Jacket Arm. Although these deep inlets are called "sounds" a more exact description is fiord.

Milford Sound is the most northerly of these fiords, and its fame relative to the other 14 fiords probably has more to do with its accessibility than its intrinsic superiority. Unless you are a yachtsman, you will not be able to make a comparison since the area of Fiordland (4,725 square miles) has very few roads. Only one other fiord, Doubtful Sound, can be approached by road (which includes the steepest road in New Zealand), though to reach this road you must first cross Lake Manapouri by boat. Even Milford could not be reached by motor car until 1954 when the Homer Tunnel was completed.

But the drive from Queenstown still takes about five hours, since there is no direct road, but rather a 291km loop via Te Anau (pronounced Te-an-*ow*). Apparently hired cars are very often damaged on this road by drivers paying more attention to the scenery than the bends in the road; Avis is experimenting with providing free bus tickets to clients for the Te Anau to Milford jaunt. It is possible to travel from Queenstown to Milford in a relatively straight line, but for this trip you will need a stout pair of boots, a stock of provisions and a reasonable level of fitness (see description of the Routeburn Track below). Of course many visitors avail themselves of the countless scenic flights which converge on Milford at midday when the tranquil bay becomes like a wasp's nest which has been disturbed. At least the angry humming of those 65 to 70 small airplanes distracts you from the silent humming of the sandflies which are a torment here like everywhere else in Fiordland. (The $4 million which is planned to be spent on the monorail from Queenstown might be better invested in a sandfly eradication programme.)

Mount Cook Line runs flights from Queenstown varying from one hour at $109 (no landing) to three hours including a cruise on the sound ($181). There are also scenic flights from Wanaka (Mount Aspiring Air; tel: 02943 7493) and from Te Anau (Waterwings Airways; tel: 0229 7405). There are also short flights from Milford starting at $35 for 10 minutes. Seats on Mount Cook flights back to Queenstown are bookable only after arrival in Milford, and often the flights are full. Bear in mind that cancellations due to weather are commonplace. Even when the planes do take off, the turbulence can be alarming to all but fearless flyers. There are also lots of coach trips from Queenstown and Te Anau, for example NZRRS and H & H run trips which depart from Queenstown at 7.30am and return at 8pm, and cost about $85 including the cruise.

The boat cruises on the Sound are worthwhile not only because they whisk you out of the range of sandflies but because they take you amidst some of the most spectacular scenery anywhere. The boats, often accompanied by dolphins, take about an hour to reach the Tasman Sea at the mouth of the fiord before they turn back. Because the rock faces rise vertically from the 300-metre deep water, the launch can approach very close to the fiord walls, so that spectators are often drenched by the incessant run-off. It is usually possible to see seals (though not possible to photograph them successfully), and to see the improbable vegetation clinging to the sheer rock with clear evidence of past avalanches. So much rain falls on this coast (24 inches in 24 hours on one occasion as the commentary boasts, which turns out to be a slight exaggeration), that the cliffs are almost constantly dripping with water. Yet there are only two permanent waterfalls: Bowen Falls near the wharf and Stirling Falls which is the second highest in the world with a drop of 150 metres (equivalent to 50 storeys). The commentary is informative and lively even if the jokes can become a little forced ("Stirling Falls, so-called because it *pounds* down, to *coin* a phrase, which makes *cents*," etc.) and the assumption that everyone will recognize elephant and lion shapes in the rock formations is somewhat optimistic. The guides have worked so hard at inventing a spiel to cheer up those depressed by rainy weather that they seem positively disappointed on a sunny day.

There are two rival tours: the Red Boats run by the Tourist Hotel Corporation and the *Milford Haven* launch run by the Fiordland Travel Company. Both cost $20 for about two hours and leave several times a day. (Try to avoid the early afternoon sailing which is the one taken by all the day trippers arriving in Twin Otters.)

Considering that it is one of New Zealand's foremost attractions, there are precious few facilities. However there is Milford Lodge, set back a kilometre or so from the water, which offers mountain hut-style accommodation. It operates from November until April and costs $15 per person. Since many people make reservations through the Tourist Hotel Corporation (THC) hotel in Te Anau (PO

Box 185, tel: 0229 7411) there may be no space for casual visitors.

There are many other charming settlements in the region in which to base yourself for sport and relaxation. Te Anau is more convenient than Queenstown for access to Fiordland; the park headquarters are on the edge of the tame and pleasant Lake Te Anau near the road to Manapouri (tel: 0229 7521).

Wanaka is another very popular resort town, especially for people who want to break the journey between Fox Glacier and Fiordland. There are Youth Hostels in both Te Anau and Wanaka as well as a wide choice of other accommodation, restaurants and services. The Te Anau Youth Hostel (tel: 0229 7847) reports that it has recently been spider-proofed.

DUNEDIN AND THE SOUTH

Looking at a globe, the southern tip of the South Island looks as though it should have been one of the last places on earth to be settled, as if they are the Falklands of the South Pacific. In fact there were Maori moa-hunters in the region in the 13th century. European settlers arrived much later; the small town of Riverton, a few miles beyond Invercargill on the southern tip, is thought to be the oldest European settlement in New Zealand since it was an important sealing and whaling post in the late 18th century.

Unlike the wild frontier atmosphere of Fiordland, south-east New Zealand has a feeling of solidity and rootedness, just like the stone-built towns of Scotland on which it was modelled; since the word "stalwart" was originally a Scottish dialect word it is a particularly apt description for Dunedin and many other southern towns. It is not difficult to hear a Scottish intonation and slightly rolled r's in the local speech even now. Otago province has always regarded itself as fiercely independent.

Dunedin. For such a remote and small city (population 110,000), Dunedin has a distinguished history and vigorous civic life, principally because the oldest university in New Zealand, the University of Otago, has been located here since 1869. Early prosperity based on the discovery of gold in Otago meant that there was enough wealth to endow a university and build impressive buildings both public and private, most of which can be admired today. Notice especially the railway station, the university clock tower and various churches.

The heritage of the province is described vividly at the Early Settlers' Museum on Cumberland St, very near the railway station (open 8.30am-5.30pm with later opening hours at weekends; admission $3). Obviously the people of Dunedin are an energetic lot; when the first two settlers' ships landed at Dunedin, they tied up outside what is now the main post office on Princes St. The intervening land has all been reclaimed. The Otago Museum on Great King St near Union St is also interesting with a good Polynesian collection.

All of this may sound a little staid, which is only partially true. Any city in which a couple of eccentric locals have as their hobby filling up the parking meters of negligent parkers just before the traffic warden arrives can't be all bad. Also there are plenty of things to do which are not as culturally elevating as the architecture, for example tours of the Cadbury Chocolate Factory at 30 Castle St, and also of Speight's Brewery (tel: 779-480); the latter is even recommended by the alcohol-free YHA. Tours and tastings are free but are not available daily so ring for details and be sure to book in advance for the chocolate tour (closed December to February). Not surprisingly these factories do not feature on the route of the "Culture Shuttle" which departs regularly from the

Octagon and goes to the Otago Museum, the Art Gallery, the Hocken Library (which has a large collection of early maps, pictures and diaries relating to New Zealand's history), etc.

The Visitor Centre is part of the Municipal Chambers on the northeast side of the easy-to-recognize Octagon (tel: 774-176). The Centre has a computer "information station" which dispenses all kinds of information, but if you want a print-out of any specific page you have to pay 20¢. A range of walking tour brochures are also available for 45¢. The NZTP office at 131 Princes St (tel: 740-344) opens from 8am to 5pm weekdays only and Saturday morning. The student campus travel office (tel: 775-911) can issue a concession card valid for productions at the only professional theatre of the five in Dunedin, the Fortune Theatre in Stewart Place.

The local tour company (Newton's Tours) publish a brochure called *Dunedin Top 5 Attractions,* only one of which is in the city itself. The rest are on the Otago Peninsula described below. Olveston is a young colony's equivalent of Blenheim Palace, billed as a stately home and full of antiques imported from Europe. It is at 42 Royal Terrace (773-320); places on the tour should be booked in advance and the cost is $3.

There are several good look-outs for a panorama of the city. If you are restricted to foot or bicycle go no further than the Northern Cemetery near the pleasant botanical gardens and aviary. Those in vehicles can drive up to the Centennial Memorial on Signal Hill, but make sure the brakes are in good order since the descent is very steep.

Despite its Scottish Presbyterian heritage (the name Dunedin is a Gaelic form of Edinburgh) there are plenty of pubs and restaurants, though not very many non-Anglo Saxon ones. If you feel you need building up the Elim Church Hostel on Gladstone Road to the north of the city offers three meals a day in addition to a bed for $16 (tel: 730-260). The Youth Hostel is a little over a kilometre from the Octagon at 71 Stafford St (tel: 741-919). The YWCA in Kinnaird House (97 Moray Place; tel: 776-781) is expensive at $30 single bed and breakfast. You might do better in student accommodation out of term time. There is a large student contingent of 8,000 centred around the imposing Victorian university. During vacations, many rooms in colleges (i.e. halls of residence) are let out with visiting students getting priority and paying lower fees than non-students. If you don't mind being away from town, there are several motorcamps, particularly Tahuna Park Seaside Camp near St Kilda Beach (Victoria Road; tel: 54-690) which charges $9 per person in a cabin the first night and $5 thereafter. Bus 27 serves St Kilda.

All city buses depart from the Octagon, including the privately-run airport bus which takes about 40 minutes to cover the 29km (cost $7). Ritchies' airport buses leave the city about an hour before scheduled flight departures (tel: 779-238). For further information about other bus routes and about the $6 family day ticket ring 772-224.

The three main coach companies serve Dunedin from the north but only H & H (now owned by Mount Cook) and NZRRS continue south to Invercargill, as does the train which leaves Monday to Saturday at 1.27pm and arrives over three hours later ($28 single).

Otago Peninsula. Several of the top attractions which Dunedin claims as its own are in fact on the Otago Peninsula, a projection of land about 25km long on the south side of Dunedin harbour. The most unusual attraction is the colony of royal albatrosses at the end of the peninsula. Elsewhere in the world these impressive birds can be viewed only by dedicated ornithologists and sailors, but in this case there is a breeding colony just a few miles from a city. It is exciting to see these birds swooping overhead but you must be lucky to visit under the right conditions, i.e. a windy day. Visiting times are restricted (closed on Tuesdays and Sundays, and sometimes other days) so ring for information (740-344/775-010). Also you must buy a ticket in advance from the NZTP office in Dunedin.

Not too far away on McGrouther's Farm, which is well-signposted (tel: 780-286) there is a community of yellow-eyed penguins which usually make an appearance in the late afternoon/early evening. Seals also favour this headland and can be seen at any time.

The manmade attractions on the peninsula are perhaps less thrilling: the gardens and pottery at Glenfalloch and the Victorian castle at Larnach, built by an eccentric in 1871 and reputed to be the only castle in Australasia. But an excursion to the peninsula is recommended, and the drive along the harbour shore is very scenic. Dunedin City Transport buses do not serve the peninsula, but Ritchies buses go part way. Otherwise you will have to hire a car, try to hitch or join a tour. The established tour operator is Newton's at 105 Melbourne St (tel: 52-199) but a better choice is the nine or ten hour tour run by a local, recommended on various Youth Hostel notice boards around the South Island. His price of $19 includes all the attractions except the albatross reserve which can be visited by arrangement. Another way to see the peninsula is from the harbour. Harbour Cruises Dunedin (Kitchener St; tel: 740-924) use a 12-seater hovercraft to take visitors on demand out to Taiaroa Head, where the albatrosses can sometimes be seen from the water. If you want to spend more than a day on the peninsula, a good place to stay is the Larnach Castle Lodge (tel: 761-302) where there are affordable bunk rooms as well as singles and doubles.

Stewart Island. The third largest island in the unequal archipelago of New Zealand is Stewart Island, 65km long and about 40km wide at its extremities, which is almost the same size as Tenerife. But Stewart Island is not the Tenerife of the South Tasman Sea. With very high rainfall levels, a resident population of no more than 500, and a total of 20km of roads, it can hardly provide the facilities associated with tourist paradises. Furthermore there is no electrical supply (though one is going to be installed by 1990 to replace the household generators and wood-burning stoves used at present) and until very recently the telephone system was extremely antiquated, many numbers consisting of a single digit followed by a letter, coded for a party line.

Despite all these inconveniences, or perhaps because of them, many New Zealanders and foreigners make the long trek to this southern outpost, and it can't just be to get away from the sheep. The principal attraction is the wildlife. The island was declared a nature reserve in 1903 and, although some animals such as deer and possums were introduced, the damage they have done to the vegetation and native animal life has not been as extreme as it has been elsewhere in New Zealand. Kiwis are more numerous than anywhere else in the country (the birds, in contrast to the people) and it is said that Mason Bay, a 14km sweep of beach on the west side of the island, is one of the easiest places to spot a kiwi.

Mason Bay, however, like the rest of Stewart Island, is accessible only on foot or by water. It is almost comical that the AA's *Road Atlas* should devote most of its final page to Stewart Island, showing the four or five streets around Oban (the only settlement on the island) and the rest as red dotted lines to denote footpaths. Walking on Stewart Island is not to be undertaken lightly. Almost all of the tracks are rated "strenuous" since they climb and descend constantly, with slippery mud underfoot rain or shine (and it usually does both dozens of times in a day). The further you get away from Oban, the more confident you should be of your abilities in the bush. The Department of Conservation (formerly the New Zealand Forest Service; tel: 391-130) maintains the very simple huts (which are free) and the tracks, some of which have wooden walkways over the most boggy sections. But you will have to reconcile yourself to hours of squelching and frequent spills on the steep sections or on stretches with picturesque names like Chocolate Swamp. Check in with the ranger's office on Main St for maps and advice.

Launch trips are also available from several local characters to otherwise inaccessible beaches, small offshore islands and perfect fishing spots. One of these islands is called Mutton Bird Island, after the bird prized by the Maori and still hunted by descendants of the original inhabitants of the island. No one else is allowed to kill them.

There is very little accommodation on the island, though some locals take in young travellers; ask for information at the Invercargill Youth Hostel. The Horseshoe Haven Motor Camp has a budget lodge among its many facilities, though it may be necessary to reserve one of the 18 beds in the high season (Box 75, Half Moon Bay; tel: 391-466). Try also Stewart Island Lodge (tel: 391-085) and Ferndale Caravan Park (tel: 391-157). Dining facilities are extremely limited. Even milk and bread may be unavailable from the general store unless you have ordered in advance. The best bet is to try to buy some of the fish brought in daily by the local fishermen. (Apart from tourism, fishing is the only source of livelihood on the island.) If you are planning to do some tramping, try to bring supplies with you to the island.

You can reach Stewart Island by air or by sea. Southern Air flies daily (weather permitting) taking 18 minutes to travel from Invercargill to Oban. The standard return fare is $105, though there are ways of getting there for less. For example pairs travelling together are entitled to a $15 discount each. But best of all students and Youth Hostel members can travel standby for about half the full fare. Day returns are popular but there are no discounts. To make advance bookings contact Southern Air, PO Box 860, Invercargill (tel: 021 89-129 collect).

The ferry takes over two hours to cross Foveaux Strait, reputed to be one of the roughest stretches of water in the world. The ferry is operated by Stewart Island Charter Services Ltd (PO Box 24, Halfmoon Bay; tel: 391-134). Sailings from the fishing community of Bluff are at 9am and from Stewart Island at 2pm daily in January, Monday to Friday in February, and Monday, Wednesday and Friday the rest of the year. The fare is $30 single, $60 return. To confirm times and prices on the mainland, ring Invercargill (021) 77-031 or Bluff (021 37) 7006. Also local fishermen sometimes take passengers for less than the price of a ferry ticket; look for adverts in the Invercargill Youth Hostel. If you are a committed hitch-hiker, you can go down to the docks in Bluff and see if any of the fishing vessels is willing to give you a lift. Even if you don't succeed, perhaps you'll have the chance to sample a few of the famous Bluff oysters available between February and July (though their numbers have been severely reduced by a parasite over the past two seasons).

Invercargill. Stewart Island is billed as the place where you can get away from the hurly-burly of urban life. If you find yourself in Invercargill, you will soon plan a trip to Stewart Island, not so much to get away from the hurly-burly as the boredom. The Public Relations Office does its best to persuade you to admire the "fine old brick city water tower" and to tour the aluminium smelter at Tiwai Point, but really the only destination which holds much appeal (apart from the airport and even it is flood-prone) is the tuatarium, where you can see this prehistoric-looking reptile; tuatara is a Maori word meaning "spine on the back" and the creature is like a miniature dinosaur.

The only other remarkable feature of Invercargill is the number of street names which are Scottish monosyllables: Tay, Earn, Lowe, Bond, Don, Doon, Forth, Spey, and so on.

The Rest of Southland. The obvious prosperity of Invercargill derives from the rich agriculture of the region, acknowledged in one of the city's monuments, a revolving blade of grass. Sights to be seen in other towns in Otago and Southland include things like the memorial to the first refrigerated shipment of lamb to be sent to Britain in 1882. Some places achieve local fame because they host stud ram sales. None of this will be of much interest to non-locals.

Further inland, there is a rich fruit-growing belt where apricots, peaches, cherries and strawberries can be bought at wayside stalls, or blossoms admired, depending on the season. This area around Alexandra, Clyde and Roxburgh is a useful destination for people looking for casual fruit-picking work. One crossroads to head for is Fruitlands, much more plausibly named than another southern town called Nightcaps.

The Great Outdoors

Just as every Dutch town boasts of its nearby windmills and bulb fields, all South Island towns with unmemorable names like Omarama claim to be set in the midst of unsurpassed scenery and to be ideal bases for boating, fishing, tramping, skiing, etc. Just in case this isn't sufficient, they usually try to find something else with which to entice you, such as "farm safaris", horse and wagon rides, potters' studios and the inevitable sheep shearing. In most cases these little known townships are telling the truth: the opportunities for exploring the unspoiled natural world are remarkably various throughout most of the island.

TRAMPING

The majority of Kiwi visitors as well as those from overseas choose to do at least some bushwalking. In addition to the wonderful views, other incentives to bestir oneself are the exotic vegetation (giant tree ferns, the largest buttercup in the world known as the Mount Cook lily, etc.) and the birdlife (including the charming fantail which can frequently be seen fluttering in the branches of trees). Travellers who have planned to do some fairly serious walking from the outset will have brought their hiking boots, sleeping bags and heavy duty rain gear. It is possible to hire boots and packs in Te Anau, Queenstown, Mount Cook, etc. though relying on a pair of boots that you have not worn in yourself is risky. Those without equipment will probably content themselves with one of the less demanding tracks or with a day walk, wearing a comfortable pair of sturdy running shoes.

The national parks service publish leaflets which provide enough route and hut information for the average walker. Of course specialist guide books are likely to enhance your pleasure, like Jim Dufresne's *Tramping in New Zealand* (Lonely Planet, $8.95; last published 1982), *Moir's Guide Book* or the *AA Book of New Zealand Walkways*. Unless you are very confident and experienced, you should select your walk carefully; the relevant guides will rate them from mild to strenuous to help you choose accordingly. If you have a local friend prepared to escort you, you probably don't have to worry. Otherwise you might prefer to choose from among the more popular tracks, despite the crowds (most of them foreign tourists), since they are well provided with huts and sign posts to minimize dangers from erratic weather which causes flash floods, blizzards, etc. Most of the tracks are well maintained with wooden walkways placed over slippery sections, for example, and huts located in strategic locations. The more difficult the access to the starting and finishing points, the less crowded a track is likely to be. For example the Hollyford Track, which follows the longest valley (80km) in Fiordland National Park, is very difficult to reach without the help of the Hollyford Tourist & Travel Company (PO Box 216, Invercargill; tel: 021 44-300) who operate jet boats and air charters usually for a minimum of four hikers.

Milford Track. The most popular of all is the Milford Track, which is so famous that it seems to have become a household name with a great many slightly overweight Americans. Magnificent as the four-day walk from the end of Lake Te Anau to Milford Sound undoubtedly is, many prefer a less heavily used track. Until recently, you had to book as much as a year in advance to guarantee a place on a given departure date on the Milford Track. However the hut capacity was expanded recently so that it should be possible now simply to turn up and start walking. Further pressure will be relieved by the opening of the new Kepler Track in Fiordland on February 20th, 1988.

With the Milford (as with several other tracks) you must choose between a guided walk with a commercial company or a "freedom walk". The cost of joining a guided party on the Milford is over $600, which entitles you to stay in a more luxurious standard of hut and includes all meals. Some participants have commented that the atmosphere is a little reminiscent of summer camp, with evening singsongs and a great many rules (e.g. you must vacate the hut by 9am) but most are delighted with the experience.

Freedom walkers must also pay a fee and book ahead, since only 24 walkers are allowed to set off each day in the season (November to March). Bookings must be made with the Tourist Hotel Corporation, Box 185, Te Anau (tel: 0229 7411). You must pre-pay the three nights of hut fees at $8 a night, the launch from Te Anau

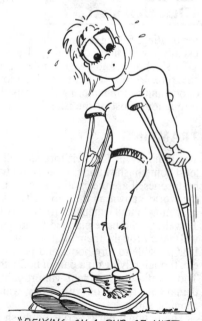

"RELYING ON A PAIR OF HIRED HIKING BOOTS CAN BE RISKY!"

Downs to Glade Wharf at the end of the lake ($28), a launch from Sandfly Point at the end of the walk to Milford and a booking fee of $4.40. If you pay for coach transport to and from Te Anau and have an overnight stay in Milford, the walk will cost an independent walker well over $100.

The Routeburn Track. The widely accepted runner-up to the Milford is the Routeburn Track which is unquestionably beautiful and un-pre-bookable (unless you choose to go on a guided trip with Routeburn Walk Ltd, PO Box 271, Queenstown). But there is really no reason why a person of average fitness and with the basic equipment should not do this walk independently. The three day walk (which can be completed in one day by supermen/women) can be done in either direction, though most people start out in Queenstown and end on the Milford Road about 30km from Milford. The total distance covered is 39km as compared to the Milford at 54km.

There are two ways of reaching the starting point. One is to catch the Magic Bus which leaves Queenstown at 8.30am and arrives at the start of the walk about 10.30am (tel: 20-308 for current prices). It is preferable to take the Glenorchy Holiday Park shared taxi from 56 Shotover St in Queenstown at 6pm, spend the night in the lodge or camping at Glenorchy which is 48km along the north shore of Lake Wakatipu, and then proceed to the walk the following morning at 8.30am (total price $26.40). The advantage of this plan is that the village of Glenorchy is in an extremely beautiful location (with a good pub), and also that you begin the walk earlier than the rest and therefore can lay claim to a bunk at the Routeburn Falls hut. The huts are often so crowded that people end up sleeping on the kitchen floor, but no one is turned away. When you emerge at the other end you can either hitch or wait for the daily NZRRS bus to Te Anau or Milford.

The Glenorchy taxi-cum-minibus also transports hikers to the beginning of the Rees-Dart walk (another magnificent though more strenuous walk north of Glenorchy) and the Greenstone-Caples walk which intersects the Routeburn so that the two can be done consecutively.

The Abel Tasman Track. If hiking up and down mountains and risking three solid days of rain does not appeal, an alternative is the Abel Tasman trek by the shores of Tasman Bay. The 27km walk is mostly along tidal beaches (so the tide times should be attended to), with a few steep trails that require cautious footing. Most people complete this walk comfortably in plimsolls, and so the $425 fee for having a guide and equipment seems excessive.

Since this is in the sunshine belt of the South Island you are much more likely to have hot weather here, and the walking season is longer than in Fiordland. A local called John Wilson operates a launch service along the coastal length of the walk (Kaiteriteri to Totaranui) which connects with a bus from Motueka (launch price $22, discounts for youth hostel members). Camping is permitted. Also in the north-west of the island, the Wangapeka Track (five days) and Heaphy Track (four to five days) are more strenuous and also trickier to get to. But they are well known and popular with Kiwis, especially the Heaphy, which was almost as hotly contested by conservationists and developers a few years ago as the Franklin River in Tasmania. If you are on the windswept Farewell Spit, contact Collingwood Safari Tours (PO Box 15, Collingwood; tel: 0524 48-257) who are permitted to drive out onto the spit to admire the Arctic waders, which migrate to Siberia in the autumn. Walkers are not allowed into the reserve and must stop 4km from the vehicle track.

Mountaineering. Anyone who has some mountaineering experience might be interested in undertaking the Copland Track which connects Mount Cook and Westland National Parks over a high pass at 2,150m. At this altitude crampons, ropes and ice axes are necessary. Alpine Guides Ltd (PO Box 20, Mount Cook; tel: 834) offer climbing courses and guided trips over the track. Another company of the same name in Fox Glacier (PO Box 38; tel: 825) can airlift you to a high mountain hut from which you descend the next day; the cost is $150. They also operate guided glacier walks and, in the winter season, glacier skiing.

SKIING

There are quite a few fully-serviced ski areas in the South Island, though wealthy skiers still rely to a large extent on helicopters to convey them to the tops of mountains. There are heli-skiing operators in Mount Cook, Tekapo, Wanaka, Queenstown, etc. Heli-skiing down virgin mountain sides is primarily of interest to strong experienced skiers who can afford to spend over $300 for a day's skiing. Novices will prefer the conventional facilities of a ski resort such as Coronet Peak, the family-oriented ski field at Tekapo or one of the club fields near Christchurch. Youth hostellers should obtain the YHA leaflet called *Ski New Zealand*.

The Queenstown Area. There are two ski fields near Queenstown: Coronet Peak (18km along the road to Arrowtown) and the Remarkables Ski Area which opened in 1985 in the jauntily-named mountain range (28km east of Queenstown). The Mount Cook Company has invested heavily in the Queenstown ski industry since the 1950s and now own and operate both ski areas. There is a single method of ticketing for the shuttle bus and lift passes are interchangeable. A full day pass costs $32, a half day $24 and the return trip on the shuttle bus is $15.

Although the Remarkables has a few routes for advanced skiers, it is best for beginners, with 75 instructors in the ski school. They even guarantee that any beginner will be able to ski after one day of lessons. Instruction costs about $20 for a half day and $30 for a full day. Both ski fields have several chair lifts, plus Coronet Peak has T-bars and other lifts. There are of course all the other facilities expected at ski resorts including lights at Coronet Peak to allow night skiing (Fridays and Saturdays only from 4.30-9pm for $30, when there is sufficient demand) and the only licensed restaurant in a New Zealand ski area.

Snow is moderately reliable between June and September, especially at the Remarkables, though the more distant ski areas at Cardrona (1½ hours north) and Treble Cone are almost never bare and can be used by Queenstown-based skiers if necessary. However bad weather closes down all skiing in the area from time to time. One feature of the Remarkables Ski Area is that there is a high level, cross-country ski trail and instruction is available if required. The day's expedition costs $30 with a guide, with extra charges for equipment.

Mount Cook Line organize week-long ski packages out of Christchurch starting at about $400 if you travel by coach and stay in the dormitory at the Mountaineer Establishment instead of at a motel or hotel. If you do not want a package, ski equipment hire will cost $20 a day and the coach trip from Christchurch to Queenstown (including the overnight service at the weekends in the ski season on Mount Cook Landline) costs $60 single. It is usually a little trickier booking accommodation on your own during the Queenstown Winter Carnival held during the last week of July. This annual event involves such unlikely diversions as dog races on the slopes at Coronet Peak as well as ordinary ski competitions. The Remarkables holds a less flamboyant, more family-oriented, festival during the first week of September (school holidays). Even outside the festival periods Queenstown has a lively atmosphere geared to skiers, with many bars showing videos of the day's skiing, before the disco music is struck up. A few nightspots such as the Penthouse (formerly Alberts, upstairs from Eichardts Hotel) stay open until 3am. Consult the local *Mountain Scene* paper for information about pub entertainments.

Mount Hutt. Mount Hutt (not to be confused with Lower Hutt near Wellington) is about an hour's drive west of Christchurch. Accommodation, restaurants and shops are all located in the nearest town of Methven which is a half-hour's drive from the lifts along a toll access road. There are several buses a day to the ski field all of which stop at the Youth Hostel (open early June to late October). The ski season is longer here than elsewhere in New Zealand. For information on transport from Christchurch, contact the Leopard Ski Coach (tel: 50-193).

Wanaka. Treble Cone and Cardrona ski fields are serviced by the resort town of Wanaka. Treble Cone is 29km from town around the southern end of Lake Wanaka and Cardrona is about the same distance due south. The Wanaka Information Centre is at 99 Ardmore St (tel: 7930).

Mount Cook. There are no ski lifts or other facilities at Mount Cook. Skiers with experience and $320 to spare may want to join an Alpine Guides Ltd ski-plane trip to the Tasman Glacier where it is possible to ski down 12 uninterrupted kilometres between June and November.

There are many other centres of alpine activities in the South Island such as Mount Robert in the Nelson Lakes National Park and the Temple Basin Skifield at Arthur's Pass which is run by the Christchurch Ski Club though you don't have to be a member to ski there. Porter Heights is the closest field to Christchurch (89km), but you might prefer to travel a little further to a club field (which are often friendlier than commercial fields) such as Mount Olympus, Mount Cheesman or Craigieburn all in the Arthur's Pass area.

RAFTING

Every article about rafting on the rivers of the South Island goes on about adrenalin rushes and heart-stopping moments of fear. Yet the New Zealand Professional Rafters Association claim that the most dangerous thing about rafting is the drive to the river. So anyone in search of thrills without danger may want to sign up with one of the many competing rafting companies.

As with skiing, Queenstown is the rafting capital of the South Island. The two main rivers are the Shotover (claimed to have once had the second highest concentration of gold of any river in the world) and the Kawarau. On the scale of one to six (with one representing a river fit for swans to glide on and six unraftable), the Shotover is graded 4+ to 5 and the Kawarau is grade 4.

The launching points are reached either by helicopter or minibus, the former costing about twice the latter. The Kawarau is an easier expedition (though with four separate sets of rapids) and is usually a little cheaper. For example a three-hour descent of the Kawarau costs $54 if the raft is launched from the road and about $100 if by helicopter. The cheapest trips on the Lower Canyon of the Shotover start at $60 for four hours. You can also do a full day's descent

through the scenic Upper Canyon of the Shotover River (grade 2+) for about $100. It is possible of course to raft on tamer stretches of these two rivers, where the duration and cost of the trip is considerably less, for example $35 for two hours from Tucker Beach on the Shotover.
Since wet suits are worn, rafting can take place around the year. The recommended age limits are 13 and 60, and on some a good level of fitness is expected of the participants. All the companies provide transport, wetsuits, foot gear, helmets and life jackets, plus usually some social event at the end such as a picnic, barbecue or sauna. Any travel agency in Queenstown will steer you towards a rafting company, for example the Challenge Rafting Centre at 39 Shotover St (tel: 27-920) will help you to choose from among the options, as will the NZTP office a few doors along (49 Shotover St; tel: 28-238) and the Whitewater Rafting Information Centre on the corner of Camp and Shotover Streets (tel: 27-318). The following is just a selection of Queenstown rafters:
Challenge Rafting, PO Box 133, Wakatipu; tel: 27-820.
Danes Back Country Experiences, PO Box 230; tel: 27-744.
Kawarau Raft Company, PO Box 266; tel: 29-792. (Their trips are sold through the Youth Hostel.)
Skippers Canyon River Expeditions, PO Box 405; tel: 14-805.
Value Tours Rafting, 37 Camp St; tel: 27-340. (True to their name, their trips seem to be the cheapest.)
Rafting takes place on many other South Island rivers from the Motueka River in the north to the Taieri River in Otago. Many involve an overnight stay and some are accessible only by helicopter. One of the most ambitious trips is offered by Sun City Raft Tours (PO Box 216, Motueka) which lets rafters control their own raft down the Clarence River, while the guides float along in separate rescue boats.
If you are in Christchurch and are considering a rafting trip, consult either Canterbury Rafting Tours (c/o 110 Cashel St, Christchurch; tel: 60-419) or Rakaia River Raft Company (PO Box 350, Christchurch; tel: 69-999). They offer expeditions on rivers ranging from grades two to five.

FISHING

The merest glance at a map of the South Island reveals the large extent to which the island is covered with a network of lakes, rivers and tributaries. Almost all claim to be prime venues for trout fishing, from Stewart Island (where the season is best in April) to the Motueka River in the north. Fishing lodges abound and often hotel proprietors will be glad to advise on local opportunities. Guiding services are available in all areas and start at $40 an hour/$200 a day. Some of the swankier operations fly their clients into remote wilderness areas and then transport them by jetboat. But it is perfectly feasible to catch a fish after renting tackle and a boat (motorized or dinghy) and spending a peaceful few hours trolling or stationary on Lake Wakatipu, Te Anau, Wanaka, Tekapo, etc.
Trout weighing 2kg are commonplace and some are as large as 5kg. Remember that you will have to obtain a tourist licence and obey the local regulations; enquire at any fishing equipment shop about catch and size restrictions, the dates of the season, etc. (The usual rule is that any fish less than 35cm must be thrown back.) As though to be consistent with their names, rainbow trout will bite gaudy lures whereas brown trout prefer more sober colours.